The
Making of
Sociology

A Study of Sociological Theory

VOLUME ONE

A

The
Making of
Sociology

A Study of Sociological Theory

Ronald Fletcher

VOLUME ONE

Beginnings and Foundations

NELSON

THOMAS NELSON AND SONS LTD
36 Park Street London WIY 4DE
PO Box 18123 Nairobi Kenya

Thomas Nelson (Australia) Ltd
597 Little Collins Street Melbourne 3000

Thomas Nelson and Sons (Canada) Ltd
81 Curlew Drive Don Mills Ontario

Thomas Nelson (Nigeria) Ltd
PO Box 336 Apapa Lagos

Thomas Nelson and Sons (South Africa) (Proprietary) Ltd
51 Commissioner Street Johannesburg

ISBN 0 17 712076 2
Printed in Great Britain by A.Wheaton and Co., Exeter

To Roma, Paul and Adrian
with love

No science can be really understood apart from its special history, which again cannot be separated from the general history of Humanity... A new science must be pursued historically, the only thing to be done being to study in chronological order the different works that have contributed to the progress of the science.

AUGUSTE COMTE (1853)

... I have come to the conclusion that the best way of finding out what sociology is, and what it is worth, is to approach it historically. . . .

ALBION W. SMALL (1923)

Do we wonder that modern sociology has ceased to have any vital relationship either to science or to man?

A sociology without any sense of its own history will also be a sociology without any knowledge of what its own illustrious scientists have already lived and thought through; it will be a sociology without any sense of its own achievement, a sociology of the 'utterly convinced' beliefs of each new generation of graduate students. Thus for all its methodological pretentions to 'hard' scientific standing, it will be unscientific.

ERNEST BECKER (1968)

Contents

(*a*) Practical Need

Moral feelings; moral feelings in themselves not enough; a science of society not in disagreement with our moral persuasions, but additional and of service to them; moral concern insists on scientific accuracy; knowledge enables us to act more effectively—'Causal determinacy' does not preclude purposive action; in society something more than the wills of individuals is involved; reflection on terms and concepts necessary.

(*a*) Order and regularity prevails in society as it does in nature.

FOUNDATIONS

(c) The illustration rather than the testing of hypotheses.
(d) Evolution and Progress: ethical ambiguities.

    Science provides knowledge of 'Nature'—experiential,
    testable, relative, never final—akin to Positivism;
    scientific knowledge is knowledge of 'Reality'—without
    philosophical limitation; scientific knowledge—a sheer
    empiricism; scientific knowledge—the rigidity of 'laws';
    scientific knowledge—the limited control provided
    by foresight; scientific knowledge—experiment and
    practice; scientific knowledge—classification; scientific
    knowledge—probes beyond surface appearance to
    'hidden laws'; scientific knowledge—the significant
    characteristics of nineteenth-century developments.

(*e*) Teleological explanation and the construction of 'Types' of 'Action'.

(*f*) Agreed *rejections* of method.

(*a*) Sociological knowledge never final: *Relative* but not *Arbitrary*.

(*b*) The most reliable basis for Prediction and Social Practice.

(*c*) The Sociological Perspective the Only Perspective for Social Study and Social Action.

Appendices

Bibliography

Indices

Diagrams

Acknowledgements

In working on this book I have been helped by many people, and would like to acknowledge my indebtedness to them.

First, my wife. Recently, I resigned the Chair I held at the University of York to devote myself wholly to study and writing. This was a decision which obviously had implications for others. If I say that my wife was completely behind me in it, and perfectly ready to meet any risks that might be entailed, my indebtedness to her will be readily understood. I owe much more to her than can be expressed, but it is at this juncture, with the appearance of this book which is among the first products of our decision, that I would like to say this.

Secondly, I owe a great deal to Mr Peter Hebdon, whose recent death was so untimely. Peter Hebdon was much more than a publisher. His generosity, good-nature, and humanity were a commonplace among those who knew him. This book was written with the benefit of his continual encouragement and understanding, and it is a matter of the deepest regret to me that he is not able to share the result of what we planned together.

I am grateful, too, to the Rockefeller Foundation for the award of a fellowship some years ago, which freed me from teaching for a year, and enabled me to devote much time to re-reading the theorists with whom I have tried to deal. Any thoroughness I have been able to achieve owes much to this assistance.

I would like, too, to acknowledge a personal debt to many who cannot be named. A book of this kind is not written 'from scratch'. I have taught sociology at various levels over many years, and it is the continuous discussion with students which I have found always such as to raise new dimensions of the subject, to stop one in one's tracks, and to persuade one to question, and to turn over again, many points. For me, a many-sided appreciation of any contribution to the making of sociology is something which has come very gradually out of the continuous argument of teaching. Many students will recognize in these pages arguments of the past, and I would like, here, to express my gratitude to them: for the pleasure, as well as the benefit, of it all.

This manuscript is a large one, and has involved a good deal of secretarial work. I am grateful especially to Jane Murray who helped me with some early drafts during my last year at York, and to Mrs Thelma Warden who typed the final manuscript.

My thanks are also due, finally, to the following publishers for permission to quote from works in which they hold the copyright: Lawrence & Wishart Ltd., London, for permission to use extracts from *Marx: Economic and Philosophical Manuscripts* translated by Martin Milligan; The Macmillan Company, New York, for permission to use extracts from *Elements of Sociology* by Franklin H. Giddings; The London School of Economics and the Athlone Press for permission to use material from my Auguste Comte Memorial Trust Lecture (No. 7, 1966); New Society and I.P.C. Magazines Ltd. for permission to use material from an article on *Frédéric le Play;* and Penguin Books for permission to use quotations from Goethe's *Faust* translated by Philip Wayne.

Preface

Sociology is at a strange, even a perilous, juncture. And curiously enough, this is directly attendant upon the fact that it has become 'accepted'. Since the last war especially it has not so much entered as flooded through the gates of the universities (having long existed outside them) and has come to be popular and in great demand. It is not only students who want it, but also many professional bodies—social workers, social administrators, town planners, architects, educationalists, and many more besides—who think it an essential analytical context for the several arts which they practice. Few other subjects have enjoyed such rapid vogue and expansion.

Yet never was any subject more prone to suspicion, superficial caricature, and sometimes outright enmity and derision. Many think its terminology either a grotesque inflation of the most simple common-sense notions, or such a pretentious inflation as to be completely and unintelligibly removed from all common experience. Many deny that it is a separate social science; that it has a clear outline distinguishing it from others. They (quite mistakenly) think of it as the newest of the social sciences—immature, undeveloped, inexact; little more than a loose assortment of little related contributions—and discount it as an academic discipline. For some it is even a subject of ill-repute, in that sociology departments—both staff and students—seem often conspicuously at the heart of student 'troubles': in demonstrations and disturbances both in the universities and in the streets and squares of cities.

On the one hand, sociology is popular and fashionable; has seized the interest and imagination of many; and is seen—for better, for worse—to be of central significance in and for our time. On the other hand, it is disliked, feared, denigrated and misunderstood. The situation is, indeed, so complicated, so vexed, that if I were to attempt, in this preface, to set out all the elements of error and misrepresentation to which the subject is exposed, my voice would seem too strident. It would be thought that I was 'protesting too much'. In this book I certainly want to argue strongly. I shall take issue with, and I hope defeat, many misconceptions. But I would not want it to be thought that I was taking my stand on an exaggerated or biased point of view. I shall be content, then, only to *indicate* the fevered atmosphere that surrounds the subject, and shall hope to lift our own discussion out of it.

It is worthwhile, however, to point out that this concern about the quality of the subject as it has to face and come to terms with the many factors in the context of its acceptance is far from being a personal view, and is not new.

Even at the beginning of the century, when sociology had already been introduced into colleges and universities in the United States, much disquiet was voiced about its problems. In a situation of rapid growth, it was found that the supply of qualified teachers could not meet the demand, and that the subject therefore came to be taught by many who did not themselves possess a sufficient grounding in it. Sociology was also introduced into the universities uneasily, with misgivings, and was deliberately tied to other departments in ways which were almost bound to circumscribe the development of the subject, and could not have been better calculated to create academic factions and discord. It was found, too, that any kind of literature whatever concerned with the 'social'—including popular journalism and descriptive 'reportage' of very variable quality—came to be called 'sociological', and that the reputation of the subject therefore suffered from those who themselves sought to gain reputation by the use of the adjective. Such opinions, expressed by an American professor when addressing the British Sociological Society in 1906, are quoted in the introduction to the second volume of this study. Similarly, no less a person than Radcliffe-Brown expressed his profound scepticism about the successful development of the subject in the universities. In a discussion in 1937, which has since become famous, he emphasized two factors in particular. The first was the trivializing effects—upon both teaching and research— of those who made demands upon sociology for quick practical returns (who wanted a kind of 'instant-sociology') and who had no knowledge of it, and no interest in it beyond its relevance to their own immediate social problems. The second was the entrenched interests of the existing social sciences, whose concern would be (in terms of money, staff, resources, power, as well as intellectual ideas) to keep their boundaries intact.

Such men were far-sighted, and their misgivings have proved well-founded and true. The problems which face the establishment of sociology as an academic discipline, which they foresaw, and which have increased in range and intensity as the scale of expansion has increased, now seem almost intractable. Whether they can be solved is doubtful. Those who know the situation well, know that the forces making for superficiality, trivialization, philistinism, to which sociology is exposed—both inside and outside its own camp— are legion. The situation is chronic: far worse in its complex actuality than can fittingly be said.

All this leads to my central point: that this study—in the context of this fever and confusion—is essentially an effort of simplification and clarification. The one thing most conspicuously lacking in the contemporary uproar is *knowledge* of what sociology is.

This is therefore an essay in constructive argument which seeks to assemble all the major contributions to the making of the subject in such a way as to *demonstrate* its continuity, its unity, its clearly defined shape and nature, and also to do justice to its many profound dimensions which are still not realized, and are not easy to grasp. It is a task of teaching: not in the sense of an exposition of what is generally accepted, but in the sense of an argumentative appraisal of what (I cannot help but believe) is *not* now commonly known, and is *not* now, any longer, even commonly *read*. It is an effort to lay bare—plainly, fully, demonstrably, and with a stark clarity— the basic elements and dimensions of the subject in such a way as to show their truth, their profundity, their strength, their permance, their acceptability—so that they may not be hidden, perhaps lost, behind the roundabout of variegated lights (whether of professional, ideological, or polemical trivia) which, for the time being, will continue to whirl flashily and noisily about them.

A great subject, with a literature of high quality, and perspectives of knowledge and understanding which are vital for our time, is in danger of faltering; of being diminished, impoverished, despoiled. This is a defence of it.

RONALD FLETCHER

Suffolk
July 1970

Introduction

1
Aim

In this essay, I have attempted a critical clarification of the more important contributions to the making of sociology in order to state clearly that system of analysis which they provide, about which we can now be agreed, and which we can employ effectively in the investigation of any problem.

Common and fashionable criticisms of sociology, coming frequently either from those who have not read any, or have read only a little, or from those who think that something is unintelligible because they themselves cannot understand it, are: that it suffers from vagueness, from a lack of definition or distinctiveness of subject-matter, from a lack of discipline, and, perhaps most of all, from a proliferation of unintelligible terms—many of which are unnecessary inflations of commonplace ideas. My main endeavour has therefore been to be perfectly clear always.

To this end I have dealt with the subject boldly. To have been comprehensive; to have attempted a detailed exposition of *all* contributions to the subject; would have been unnecessarily to blur its outline. The shape of the building would have been obscured by ornamentation. I have therefore been selective in order to give as definitive an outline as possible.

2
Preoccupations

Certain preoccupations lie at the heart of all that I have to say. I want to make these perfectly clear at the start: not as limits of what I intend, but because—as assumptions, motives, aims with which I begin—they will provide some understanding (though not necessarily a justification) of certain aspects, directions, and concerns of my thought.

Sociology as a humane subject: not as a narrow professional expertise

First of all: I wish to clarify the nature of sociology not only, not even chiefly, for the sake of possessing or promoting a reputable professional expertise, but because, as a person, my fundamental desire is to understand the nature of man and his place and predicament in the world—which means, crucially, his place and predicament in the world *now*. I am a person first, a sociologist second. I am a sociologist because I find the subject, among other subjects, necessary to me as a person. My concern about sociology is a necessary part of a much wider philosophical concern to understand man and the world in which he lives, and to know, as best as I can, how to improve man's situation. I am puzzled, and seek understanding; and I am a social idealist.

I make this point because I think it is of the greatest importance to emphasise that sociology need not, indeed *should* not, be falsely and narrowly regarded (whether by sociologists themselves or others) as a 'technical expertise' of interest only to professional social scientists. It is, on the contrary, a broad, humane subject—concerned with those personal problems and questions which are of the most fundamental importance to all men. Contrary to some expectations (for the word THEORY suggests, to some, a desert of arid abstractions), sociological theory is a subject of the greatest fascination—relevant to almost any question that can be raised about man and his concerns. What can be of greater interest, as well as importance, for the understanding of our nature and our situation in the world, than a study of all those theories which, in both the distant and the recent past, have been offered not as a matter of intellectual interest only, but also for the establishment and justification of those systems of

4

power and authority, whether orthodox or revolutionary, which, for both good and ill, have affected the lives of countless men and women in the most fundamental ways?

Though this is an 'academic' essay, it is not, therefore, by any means written only for 'academic' students. Indeed, I should like to think that *all* students (whether within or without the walls of academies) dislike the term 'academic' as much as I do. Though I hope it will prove useful for 'courses of study', it is written not with any kind of examination in mind—but primarily for those who are concerned with the perennial task of seeking to understand their own nature. In my opinion, there are far more people *outside* than *inside* educational institutions who are keenly interested in this subject, and it is for these people, too, (students in the best sense of the word) that this essay is written. I came to this subject as part of the task of working out my own perspectives, and this essay is written in the hope that it might be of aid to others in working out theirs.

It is written also not only out of a deep interest and pleasure in the subject, but out of a firm conviction of its importance for understanding the situation throughout the world which mankind now faces. Sociology—I hope to show—is *not* only one subject among others, but a subject which pervades, informs and transforms all others. It is a subject which stems from, and attempts to satisfy, the modern need to articulate all human knowledge into one large, ordered perspective both for the sake of *understanding*, in itself, and to provide a basis for sane and well-balanced social *reform*. It is the subject of central importance in and for our time.

The critics of sociology

The outline of this first preoccupation will seem grandiose to many critics, and will bring a smile to the lips of some. And this leads to my second preoccupation: that sociology is still far from being accepted as a distinctive academic discipline in Britain. Much of my argument will stem from a desire to combat these critics and to argue as strongly as I can in support of the subject.

However, my reactions to this critical opposition to sociology are not at all simple, and I would like to make my position clear.

In some ways, I believe it to be a good thing that sociology encounters strong criticism here in Britain. It is a sign of intellectual health, as well as of much stupid conservatism (and sheer ignorance) of the worst kind, that its acceptance in the universities is resisted. There are, without any question whatever, very real and very considerable difficulties in the attempt to study human individuals, human relationships, and human societies 'scientifically'. There are also real dangers. Not the least of these is that some scholars tend to forget 'the study of man' in their desperate desire (for there is nothing in sociology to warrant it, and it becomes a kind of blind religion) to be 'scientific' at all costs. Much that is bogus results. In their attempt to be 'scientific', they would rule out of consideration—indeed, out of existence—all those subtleties of human nature which cannot be nicely squeezed into their techniques of existing 'scientific methods'. They become, that is to say, empirically naive! Instead of bending their methods to the intractable subtlety of facts, they see facts only in terms of their available techniques of dealing with them.

Similarly, some insist that the *only* knowledge we can gain of human nature and human society is that of a 'scientific' nature. They do not consider art, for example, or critical philosophy as being productive of knowledge at all. This can lead to a philosophical naivety which is infinitely worse than the possession of philosophical competence without scientific sociology; though both are nowadays unwarranted. Views of this kind lead to a sharp differentiation between sociology and philosophy, sociology and literature, and the like, which is unjustified and harmful, and which can drive people into fields of uneducated, specialist ignorance.

There are also dangers in the field of practice. More knowledge about man and society makes it easier for some men to exercise power over others, whether it be for personal, governmental, religious, or other ends. 'Experts' in psychology and sociology (as in education, social administration, social work, etc.) can be a menace to society if given too much power and too much money, especially if their expertise is limited, superficial, or even spurious. As, for example, if a person who has reported on the interviewing of twenty-five families in a certain part of a certain city, comes to be considered an 'authority' on 'The Family in Britain'. The near-criminal—certainly amoral, and frequently immoral—activity of salesmen, whose techniques and acumen probably rest, nowadays, upon research which includes depth psychology and sociology, is sufficient to make anyone of good sense feel critical about accepting the use of the human sciences too unguardedly. The way, for example, in which some sales experts glibly advocate their techniques of advertising to secure certain ends in the spheres of morality, religion, government, are enough to demonstrate the extreme simple-mindedness and danger which can accompany 'scientism'.

There are, of course, many other points of criticism—academic and practical—which could be made, and I agree, then, with much of the scepticism of the critics. I think it better that, in Britain, the subject should only come into general acceptance after having proved its worth by meeting these (and any other) doubts and suspicions successfully. Better this, than that it should be accepted with glib, uncritical attitudes, thereby unleashing a horde of dangers. The human sciences, and the employment of the knowledge which they provide, must always bristle with dangers, and it should surely be a first principle of all social scientists that they themselves should always be far more soundly and thoroughly critical of their own subject than are any of their critics.*

Having said this, however, I am strongly, indeed militantly, opposed to the critics of sociology on many counts.

First: there is, amongst many of them, a deplorable ignorance of the subject. Most critics do no more than utter—parrot-like—fashionable clichés; being clearly totally unaware of the long, continuous, argumentative literature of sociology which has been produced during the last hundred and fifty years or so. They seem totally unaware also of the way in which their clichés immediately announce the profundity of their ignorance. Others, a little more knowledgeable (they at least know the *names* of some sociologists), will light-heartedly dismiss, frequently with a joke calculated to set audiences rolling in their seats, considerable and serious thinkers —Comte, Spencer, Marx, Hobhouse, Weber, Durkheim—at the same time showing quite clearly by their comments that they have never once thoroughly read, let alone studied, the works of such men, and are really, again, either mouthing clichés or referring to some secondary chapter or article they have read which is itself superficial and inadequate. People, for example, who say that Spencer's sociological theory was no more than a mistaken extrapolation of the biological theory of evolution; that Durkheim rejected psychology in sociological explanation; that Hobhouse was a philosophical humanist who, believing in progress, allowed his ethical persuasions to distort his sociological study of facts; that the 'social evolutionists' were 'grand manner sociologists', constructing large-scale theories without studying *facts*—that they were not 'empiricists' like, say, Booth or Rowntree, and had nothing to contribute to the understanding or solution of current social problems; that Max Weber failed to see the importance of a 'structural-functional' approach in advocating the 'subjective understanding' of social action . . . and so on, and on, and on . . . immediately betray the fact that they can never have studied with any care the theorists to whom they refer. There is, indeed, a good deal of ignorance among students and

---

* It will not escape notice though I have not mentioned it—not wishing to be too argumentative here—that, of course, all these criticisms apply to all the *other* social sciences: psychology, economics, political science, etc. They are not only relevant to sociology; and they must be faced equally by all the other social sciences.

teachers of sociology themselves, owing to the extent to which fashion has entered into teaching,* but the ignorance is far worse amongst its critics. This, clearly, is not an objection to well-informed and valid criticism, but this—alas—is rare. It is simply a denunciation of so much that goes by the name of 'criticism' of sociology which is, in fact, nothing more than the most uninformed trash.

There is, secondly, an understandable, but intellectually pusillanimous and indefensible, tendency on the part of some other social scientists—psychologists, economists, political scientists, lawyers, and others—to attack sociology because it challenges, invades, and disturbs the territories which their own 'disciplines' had long ago (so they think) marked off and cultivated. Sociology is looked upon as a kind of latter-day interloper. This again shows how completely at fault many people's perspectives are.

The virulence of this conflict should not, by any means, be understated or underestimated. The human sciences are all relatively young and vulnerable. All are hedged round with claims and qualifications, which are almost like fortifications of sensitive antennae. Having had to struggle to secure their own foothold, the practitioners of each are intensely sensitive to marauders on their boundaries, and their mode of defence is explosive attack at the slightest provocation. Touch one of their tentacles and you are at war. In this context, social scientists are both egotistically and occupationally wedded to their loves. In defence of them much vanity is involved and careers are at stake. It is, then, not only that social scientists disagree with each other; they are in a state of active *enmity* with each other. The atmosphere is at its best boldly militant, at its worst conspiratorial—and to a degree which would make Machiavelli turn pale. In earlier days they would have fought duels or slipped poison into each other's wine; now they are able only to slip it into the ears of their students, which they do, either boldly or with much innuendo and smoothness of academic tongue, or into the clique-ridden ears of the members of administrative boards in the ongoing engineering of resources and power.

I hasten to add that sociologists are no less adept at this art of throwing verbal vitriol, or behind-the-scenes manipulation of administrative affairs, than are their colleagues in other sciences. Also—without wishing to diminish in the slightest degree this picture of the real and intense conflict which exists—it must also be said that not all social scientists in different fields are sworn enemies, and that even those who are, once they have accommodated themselves to the situation, derive some pleasure and benefit from the

---

* This, again, is true of all other social sciences, and indeed of other subjects altogether—such as philosophy and history.

battle. Social scientists, like certain generals who recently trundled across the Western Desert, sometimes enjoy a good enemy.

Two other aspects of this attack on sociology from the so-called 'established' disciplines are particularly noteworthy and important.

One is the frequently reiterated claim that, unlike the other social sciences (each of which has its own distinctive form and definition), sociology is a kind of rag-bag of ill-assorted contributions which has no distinguishable shape at all. It seems simply to borrow bits and pieces from other subjects—history, politics, geography, statistics, law—and fits them together into some kind of amalgam. When it is not doing this (the argument goes), it is concerning itself with those residual topics—the family, sexual morals, crime, for example—with which no other discipline deals. But it possesses no clearly recognizable area of problems, or intellectual discipline, of its own. The most outstanding fact (say the critics) about all the major founders of the subject—Comte, Spencer, Marx, Durkheim, Weber, Pareto, etc.—is that they offered approaches which were totally *different* from each other. The subject has no kind of unity; it consists of a large number of disparate 'bits'. It cannot be said to constitute a definite or distinct 'academic discipline' at all.*

The second noticeable characteristic of these attacks (already slightly touched upon) can only be called, without more ado, a deplorable defect on the part of the critics. It is that, frequently, they show a marked ignorance not only of the history of thought in subjects closely allied to their own, but also even in their own subject. This leads to completely erroneous perspectives. Thus, some economists, political scientists, and the like, seem to believe that their disciplines were established *before* sociology, and that sociology is a newcomer to the ranks of the social sciences. This is, of course, quite untrue. Similarly, some do not appear to know or to remember that the development of their own subject was not an isolated matter, but that it developed, by and large, *simultaneously* with sociology, and often at the hands, or in the minds, of the self-same people. 'Les Économistes' were rooted in the ideas of Montesquieu, as was also Rousseau (in his political thought) as well as Comte and Durkheim (as sociologists). Adam Smith was not an economist of the contemporary kind, but a 'political economist': a social and economic historian, a moral philosopher, a psychologist, indeed—a shockingly broad non-specialist; a member of a school of thinkers in Scotland who were concerned with a theoretical study of society as a whole in the widest (sociological) sense. Consider Marx, too. Was he an economist? A philosopher of history? A political theorist?

* Other subjects—politics, history, literature, social work training even—are thought to *be* disciplines.

A sociologist? How should we refer to him? And Pareto? And Weber? What labels should we use for them?

Similarly, some historians—who still seem quite satisfied that their own subject has a distinct form, unity and discipline—seldom seem to be aware (when criticizing sociology) that the methodological preoccupations of sociology during the past 150 years have been, just about exactly, the preoccupations of theoretical history too. From Guizot and Buckle to Collingwood, Toynbee, and E. H. Carr (to mention but a few) historians have been concerned to ask the same kinds of questions as sociologists about the epistemological foundations of their subject. When, consequently an Oxford historian leans across the table at a London lunch-party to say with a kind of quizzical profundity: 'How can you possibly have a *science* of society? when you study society, surely you are studying individuals? And individuals have free wills? They can exercise *choice*! How, then, can you possibly make scientific predictions about them?'—one is not only so astonished as not to know whether he really wishes himself to be taken seriously; but also embarrassed in that he does not seem to realise how forcibly he is proclaiming his ignorance and incompetence as a historian. For this issue was dealt with very deliberately, indeed conclusively, by the middle of the nineteenth century. Indeed, a little time before that, Aristotle gave answers that were not at all bad. Yet this Oxford gentleman appears not to know it! All he is really doing is ostentatiously hanging a notice round his neck which says:—'I have never read John Stuart Mill's *Logic*, and have not even begun to understand its significance for the study of man and society, and the writing of history, and—what is more—I am proud of it!'

Now I am emphatically opposed to these kinds of criticisms of sociology.

It goes without saying, surely, that the first thing one should require of people in academic discourse is that they should at least have taken steps to *know* what the contributions of various scholars are before stating criticisms of them. By and large, the critics of sociology do not give much evidence of such preliminary industry. There is little one can do about this lack of knowledge of the history of thought which leads to such false perspectives, except both to note and to lament it; indeed to voice one's sheer disgust about it.

I believe, however, that these egotistically defended barriers between the social sciences must be broken down, and, in particular, that this perspective suggesting the supposed 'late emergence' of sociology should be shown to be the ridiculous point of view that it is. I do not mean at all that social sciences should no longer be significantly distinguished from each other; only that the act of defending one's supposed academic territory like a wild beast at the mouth of its lair, or like a stickleback at its invisible boundary, is no longer a tenable or sensible intellectual posture. It is only melodramatic. We should all be prepared to loosen ourselves from our ego-involvement in our chosen words—'Economics', 'Sociology', 'Psychology', 'History', and the like—and to consider open-mindedly and critically, the entire and common question of how the scientific approach to the study of man and society should most properly be arranged and conducted. We must, as Mannheim put it, do our best to break down the defence-mechanisms which each specialism has tended to set up against the others, and make an effort towards theoretical integration.

Consider one slight example of the kind of situation which nowadays actually occurs, and which, to a mind not already fitted with intellectual spectacles must surely seem absurd. There are some scholars who, having given their minds to the design of a joint degree in psychology and sociology, sit round a table in a university and actually decide, after many discussions, that it does not seem possible to combine the two disciplines. Now this, surely, must be an absurdly unreal problem. The disagreement is either artificial or it is contrived. It can only possibly arise because it is previously taken for granted that two separate disciplines, each adequate in its separateness, already exist. If the disagreement is approached, conversely, from the point of view of the *subject-matter being studied* its absurdity is evident at once. The study of man and his social relationships (*one* clearly cannot be satisfactorily studied without the *other*) must necessarily include a study of *both* psychological *and* sociological aspects (a study of the experience and behaviour of man in the context of social organization and social situations), as well as other aspects—such as the biological. Far from it being impossible to bring the two together—in any sensible and adequate approach to the study of the subject-matter, *it is impossible to keep them apart.* Indeed, keeping them apart must necessarily falsify one's conception of the subject-matter, and lead to a consolidation of the inadequacy of both so-called disciplines. If they continue to be considered apart from each other, it is only because either (*a*) people are too vain to relinquish their intellectual positions, or have ulterior motives for retaining them, or (*b*) that departments already established insist upon retaining their autonomy. It is not because any convincing intellectual grounds exist.

Also, it is simply not true that sociology is a 'rag-bag' of disconnected contributions; a heap of unrelated bits fitted haphazardly together. The main contributions of sociology have developed out of each other, in an ongoing process of criticism, amendment, and constructive development. Comte, Spencer, Durkheim, Weber, Pareto and others, did not maintain totally disparate and opposed points of view. All were concerned (as part of their criticism of others) to make a place for the study of some dimension of social reality which others had overlooked or neglected. And each concerned himself with the elaboration of concepts and methods appropriate to the study of this new dimension. In this way, the system of sociological analysis initially stated with great clarity by Comte, has been gradually filled out, supplemented, made more complete and more adequate. Furthermore, this literature of sociology stems from, and is a more sophisticated development of, the long line of thought concerning the nature and problems of man in society which has grown from the Greek thinkers onwards. Sociology is the relatively recent development of the speculation concerning the nature of man and society which has existed almost as long as man himself, but which has gradually become more systematic, more coherent, more reliably subjected to criteria of evidence and testability; hence providing a more reliable basis for practical social and political action.

Needless to say, in this essay, I wish to *prove* these critics wrong. I shall clarify the chief contributions to the subject; demonstrate the cumulative, critical, constructive growth to which I have referred; and make clear, by so doing, the nature and shape of sociology as it now exists—so arguing for its full recognition.

In all this I do not think it right to adopt a modest tone.* There have been some tendencies recently—in the face of criticisms from the specialist sciences—for sociologists to diminish the claim of their subject; to maintain that the 'founding fathers' of the subject were too 'grandiose' in their claims; that sociology is simply one new social science among many; or, indeed, that it is only a different 'approach,' a different 'method' which borrows from other sciences.

With this I cannot agree.

This, it seems to me, is solving a problem by default; assuming a problem is solved simply by abandoning it—in the same way that many people now say that the clash between the theory of evolution and Christianity has been solved, whereas, in fact, people have simply ceased to be bothered about it.

Modesty, here, I believe, would really be false modesty. Sociology cannot be modest in this if it is to be true to its nature. Sociology is a culmination of the earlier studies of man and society which profoundly alters the nature, perspective and frames of reference of all those approaches which preceded it. All this, of course, was said by

* i.e. 'modest' from the point of view of sociology, as a subject.

Comte with perfect clarity in his 'foundation-statement' of the subject. Unfortunately, men have ceased to see, if, indeed, most of them have ever seen, the truth of the matter as he saw it. I shall advocate a return to his position. In matters like this, however, to speak of 'modesty' or 'arrogance' of claims is clearly beside the point were it not for the disputes which continue. It should be not a question of what is modest or immodest, but a question of what is *true;* what is *intellectually correct.* But it is just because this is what is at stake that one has to adopt a militant approach. The struggle for ideas is, I am afraid, a war!

The necessary characteristics of this study

These first two preoccupations dictate a certain shape and character to this study, which it is worthwhile to point out.

(*a*) In the first place, I have implied that we need a study of sociology which, not too heavily loaded with detail, offers a critical assessment of important contributions in order to present, clearly and distinctly, the nature of the subject. The literature concerning itself with 'sociological theory' is, to put the matter very mildly, voluminous and variable indeed. It is therefore desirable to provide a clear framework about which this complicated literature can be arranged. It must be not only a *starting-point* for further study in the sense of an over-simplified first statement, an 'elementary introduction', but a clear and complete outline of the developed subject into which all details can be intelligibly fitted. This study therefore aims at this kind of treatment.

I am also concerned, however, and obviously, to criticize critics as thoroughly as I can. Therefore this essay cannot be concerned only with straightforward exposition. Throughout, I shall be arguing a case. But my endeavour will be to include all important points of criticism in the exposition, in the hope that they will be dealt with (as it were, incidentally) in the ongoing flow of the argument.

Since I wish to clarify the value and the distinctive point of each contribution, to demonstrate the inter-connected nature of them all, and to show that they have developed *out* of each other to provide an over-all system of sociological analysis which is richer than any one of them taken in isolation; my study must be not only a *list* of critical appraisals but also a constructive argument, aiming ultimately at the cumulative exposition (with all its dimensions made clear) of the entire system of analysis which, taken together, these contributions provide.

Though, therefore, the study aims at providing a kind of over-all text, its nature is still, more properly, that of an essay. Comprehensiveness is an ideal I bear in mind, but in this study my effort is, in so far as it seems necessary, to *pare away detail* for the sake of clear outline. But the outline itself must be as complete as possible, so that all details of the subject may be fitted into it. It is, then, an effort towards *constructive clarification*. It does not claim finality, but it does attempt to move *definitively* to a certain position of agreement—from which further considered growth, development, and elaboration can take place. At the same time, I do think it possible to settle *some* questions finally, so that ongoing disagreement about these, at least, can be dispensed with.

Essentially the essay (as a literary form) is an exercise—an effort—in articulation; a kind of exploration, seeking the most satisfactory statement one can achieve of something one deeply feels. I should like to think that I am doing no more than stating clearly and articulately what many of us in sociology have already come to feel—and I am sure that this is true of some. But I cannot feel too confident. There are some scholars I know who would still be impatient with some of the views I shall put forward. However, we can only argue—and let argument prevail. I can only state that the position I shall outline is not only the position to which I myself incline, but the position at which, to the best of my own understanding, sociology has in fact arrived.

One other characteristic of the essay that·follows from these initial preoccupations is that it must be *both* historical *and* analytical. That is to say, I must consider the contributions to the subject *more or less* in their chronological order, since I wish to demonstrate the cumulative development of the subject. But I do not want to offer *just* a chronological account, nor do I want to tie myself too meticulously to it. I wish to consider each of these thinkers in turn only in order to achieve a satisfactory analytical appraisal of the main strands of the argument as it proceeds, and in order that we may arrive, finally (with a full understanding of its several dimensions), at the system of sociological analysis which we now possess.

I want, that is, to explore and lay bare the main steps of argument that have gone into the making of a new science: a science which men envisaged dimly in their early myths, and which they have been struggling to clarify from the very beginnings of their critical thought.

Some very important points, of a preliminary but profound nature, are attendant upon this.

The first is that I disagree with those who think it sufficient to offer a straightforward exposition of the components of sociological analysis as they now exist, without a critical understanding of past arguments. Such a 'stream-lined' analytical statement would lack very important dimensions. I believe that the best way, if not the only way for us to come to the system of sociological analysis as we now conceive it, with a full comprehension of all the profound issues involved, is to *participate* in the difficulties and the involved arguments of those who struggled towards its making.

Indeed, were there more time, I would dearly like to make this essay a much more messy and leisurely matter. In other sciences, it is sometimes thought that once the contribution of a scientist has been built into the science, any further detailed study of him appears to be unnecessary. One *uses* Charles' Law, Boyle's Law, Ohm's Law, without needing to know the men themselves and their general ideas. One can outline the contemporary nature of any 'natural' science without delving too much into its history. Whether or not this is really true for the so-called 'natural' sciences, it is certainly far from being true in sociology*.

The work of the many thinkers who have devoted themselves to the study of man and his place in the world of nature and society is such that—even when one has abstracted its most useful contribution to the current nature of the science, one cannot simply throw away the rest; dropping it, and the man, as it were, into the wastepaper basket of history. No matter how much one agrees or disagrees with the work of such men, there is always something fundamental to be learned from it. Furthermore I believe it to be of the most vital importance at the present time—especially in the context of the present pace of so-called scholarship (when students are galloped like horses through a packed three-year course in which there is little time for grazing, and then immediately involved in jobs, or in highly specialized 'research')—that we should both realize and emphasize that one *cannot* simply read the work of these thinkers *once*, immediately sift the wheat from the chaff, and then put them aside as having been sufficiently dealt with. After many re-readings of the same author, one is continually coming across insights one had not properly appreciated; learning lessons one had not properly digested; noting the use—whether erroneous or otherwise—of methods one had not properly assessed. It is with a good author as with a person of ability and character—one encounter is not enough. And one learns so much more about an author's ideas as one deepens one's acquaintance with his character, his idiosyn-

---

* Actually, I believe this to be so only at the most elementary level of science. Scientists of any profundity are always keenly interested in knowing as much detail as possible about the methods of their fellows. *The Art of Scientific Investigation* by W. I. B. Beveridge gives very good examples of this, as does, also *The Art of the Soluble*, and other writings by Peter B. Medawar.

crasies, his circumstances. If communication with our most intimate colleagues—indeed, with our most intimate friends—is so extraordinarily difficult, how much more painstaking is the effort one should devote to a man's books in order to make sure that one has properly understood him.

In short, one should never allow the dust to settle for long on Plato, Aristotle, Lucretius, Hobbes, Hume, Mill, Comte, Spencer, Durkheim, Weber—to mention only a handful of names. If a student never really experiences the excitement which authors of this stature offer; if he follows only the fashionable trends of the moment and is persuaded by some brash lecturer that 'the philosophers'* are outmoded and that one must simply learn 'modern social science'; that the earlier sociologists were too 'historical' and 'speculative,' and that to be 'empirical' is to go with a notebook and pencil or a blocked out interview card through the backstreets of Birmingham, literally looking at what is under one's nose; then, indeed, he will be lost in the superficiality of what one can only call the parochial attachment to the present. He will join the army of investigators marching to and fro between the pavement and the hollerith machine; just one more 'technicist'.

Later, I shall return to this link between philosophy and sociology and the other connected questions raised here. Now, I wish only to say that the thinkers with whom we shall have to deal are, and remain, of perennial worth, even after we have ransacked their bags for our own particular purposes. As students, we shall be all the richer in our understanding of our present-day subject if, in addition to gleaning what is strictly and immediately useful, we are also more leisurely in our study, dwelling upon it with pleasure, achieving and indulging in the quiet mind—despite the universities; *thinking;* escaping the continual tyrannical pressure of the utilitarian present; acquainting ourselves with the detailed idiosyncrasies and circumstances of the men whose work we are studying. What is certain is that we shall be better equipped to participate in contemporary affairs and in contemporary social science if we have the perspectives that a study of these authors brings, than if, in the absence of such study, we know all there is to know about the techniques of, let us say, the social survey.

Another preliminary point to which I have come to attach very considerable importance is with reference to the so-called 'schools' of sociology.

I have said that it is part of my intention to demonstrate that what have come to be called the several main 'schools' of sociological

* i.e. all those who exercised their minds in all that period of man's history before Talcott Parsons gazed luminously across the Atlantic.

theory (the 'evolutionary school', the 'functionalist school', the 'Durkheimian school'—focusing upon the study of 'social facts', the 'Weberian school'—insisting upon the 'subjective understanding of social action', and others) are *not* isolated, different, unrelated, antagonistic contributions, each giving a totally different 'theory' of society, but that they are all contributions developed in critical awareness of each other; attempts on the part of their authors to extend the subject by emphasizing the importance of some particular aspect of society which others had neglected, and to work out a new and appropriate methodology which could be incorporated into the body of sociological analysis as it had so far been constructed.

Thus, to give one or two brief examples of the kind of mis-understanding that I wish to attack, it is frequently thought that Durkheim *rejected* 'evolutionary sociology', whereas he *was*, in fact, himself an evolutionary sociologist. It is often thought that 'func-tionalism' strongly differentiated some theorists from 'evolutionary' sociology, whereas all the evolutionary sociologists adopted 'func-tionalist' assumptions, and vice versa! It is sometimes thought that Weber rejected systematic 'functionalism', whereas in fact he stated quite definitely that functionalism was not only a useful but an *indispensable* preliminary basis for the additional kind of analysis he offered. All this, however, we shall come to in detail later.

The crucial point which I wish to emphasize here, however, is this:

I have come very definitely to believe: *that it is an error and a harmful distortion to divide the development of sociology into 'schools' at all.*

When the chief contributors to the subject are studied in relation to each other, and in detail, it can be seen that sociology had almost all its necessary components at the time of its earliest foundations; indeed, in a less reflective way, even before then; and that the sub-sequent contributions are all developments and refinements of the same system of analysis. I can only make this point with the weight it deserves when I come to it in the text, but, bearing it in mind, I shall not speak of 'schools' at all. The prevailing idea put forward in many present-day attempts to systematize the subject—that several 'schools' of sociology were independently and separately created in the past, but are now *converging* to form one central system of analysis, I believe to be wrong. It is the supposed initial *divergence* which has been peculiarly undemonstrated, and uncritically taken for granted. And therefore to claim and to trace this supposed 'convergence' is, frequently, to give the air of quite a false originality.* Again, to give

* I shall, in the final section, argue that Talcott Parsons had a quite wrong perspective at the very outset of his study 'The Structure of Social Action', and

a brief example, it is thought to be quite a recent innovation in the philosophy of science that—if it is true that every theory must be based upon observed facts, it is equally true that facts cannot be observed without the guidance of some theory. It might even be thought that this is a statement drawn from Talcott Parsons, or perhaps from Sir Karl Popper. It is, in fact, word for word from Comte. Much of this supposed convergence is no more than a recognition of, a coming to a realization of, or indeed, a sheer repetition in slightly different terms, of what was *originally* said at the very commencement of the subject. Much of the best contemporaneous sociology is, in fact, 150 years old in its originality. Those text-books (and there are many) which elaborate and, indeed, multiply such supposed 'schools' are, I believe, positively creating and continuing, rather than dissipating, the confusion that attends the subject.

My method, therefore, will simply be to give a critical exposition, both historical and analytical, of that constructive line of argumentative exploration which has constituted the making of sociology. At the end, we should have a clear statement of the science that has been made.

Other recent work aiming at a synthesis of sociological theory

Another preoccupation that underlies this study is my awareness of the considerable body of work which has been undertaken during the past thirty years or so towards the same end. In particular, many American scholars have applied themselves to the same task of theoretical clarification and integration. Many of them have a perspective similar to that which I wish to suggest. Most conspicuous amongst them, perhaps, is Talcott Parsons, but many others have made substantial contributions from different directions—Robert Merton, C. Wright Mills, and the like.

My reactions to these recent contributions of American sociology are also rather complex and ambivalent, and must be made clear.

First: I accept entirely the value of the concern and effort of these American scholars. I believe that the most serious and searching discussions of sociological theory during the past few decades have taken place in America, and we need to deplore the misplaced intellectual snobbery with which American scholarship has seemed,

that, to a large extent, a false perspective has thus been imposed upon several generations of students.

sometimes, to have been greeted by British scholars—though this, for a long time now, has very definitely been declining. Indeed, it might be said that the fault has been reversed, and that the readiness to accept American sociology is now too *un*qualified and *un*critical; sometimes appearing more like discipleship than a matter of intellectual agreement. The fact is that, for many reasons, the intellectual horizons and the adventurousness of British sociology have been curtailed until very recently. By contrast, American sociological theory during the past few decades has been decidedly positive, critical and challenging, cosmopolitan in its interests, and generous in its appraisal of the contributions of scholars of other countries. Furthermore, American sociologists have themselves been as ready as others to review their own positions critically, and to acknowledge the theoretical and methodological shortcomings of their earlier positions when these have been challenged and made clear. With characteristic frankness and energy, they have pre-occupied themselves with a critique of sociological theory and have made a very considerable contribution in this direction.

At the same time, it is clearly misleading to think of any such thing as 'American Sociology'—as something to be pitted against the sociology of other 'nations.' American sociologists are a very mixed bag. Amongst them are to be found 'evolutionists', 'be-haviourists', 'functionalists', 'operationalists', and sociologists of many other brands. Also, there are many cleavages between them. The arguments in theoretical sociology there have been extreme and intense. A Wright Mills can attack a Parsons with an intensity becoming a Roman Catholic priest attacking a Luther (or should it be the reverse?) Nonetheless, all these relatively recent theoretical discussions have been rooted in a painstaking attempt to assess critically the earlier contributions of both European and American thought; and here, the Americans have been more thoroughgoing in their searching; wider in the range of their enquiries; more con-cerned to appraise thoroughly the tradition from which they have sprung, than have sociologists in Britain. Indeed, the absorption of some American scholars in 'theory' has been so great as to have been criticized just as hotly as the enthusiastic absorption of some, a few decades ago, in 'bit-and-piece' or 'directionless' empirical investiga-tions. But there is much evidence that the pendulum which was thought to have swept so completely from directionless empiricism to 'grand theory empty of empirical content' is now beginning to swing more moderately to a mid-way position. Recent studies by Merton, Smelser, Harrison, and many others, show that theoretical analysis is being fruitfully employed in the detailed investigations of very real and concrete problems—both historical and contemporary. The best American sociology now shows a maturity that is to be readily acknowledged and admired. Indeed some recent books such as *Enter Plato* by Alvin Gouldner, *The Sociological Tradition* by Robert Nisbet, and *The Structure of Evil* by Ernest Becker are of the very highest standards of excellence and—quite apart from the impressive range of work which they embody—prove beyond doubt that these American scholars are deeply aware of the traditional roots of their subject, and are profoundly concerned to perpetuate these traditions in their own teaching.*

It will be clear, then, that I am very much in sympathy and to a considerable extent in agreement with many of these American efforts. At the same time, I have one or two intellectual differences with some prominent American viewpoints, and the nature of these I would like also to make clear, though a full account of them must wait until the final section of the book.

My first criticism is simply that, in all these attempts at synthesis, far too little emphasis has been placed upon the contributions of British sociology.

Now I want it clearly to be understood that this is not merely a patriotic protest on my part; it is not a kind of puling complaint— a cry for attention. It is something much more important than this. From its beginnings, British sociology (I am ignoring, for the moment, the 'fact-finders' like Booth, Rowntree, etc.) has had certain well-marked characteristics.

First, it has been very strongly rooted in philosophy. Indeed, it has been bedded in epistemology, in ethics, and in political philosophy. This is a much more deep-rooted and important matter than such a simple statement makes it appear. It is not simply the usual story: that sociology as a science grew out of the philosophical thought which preceded it—which is a commonplace. It is much more than that. For the moment, I will only say that many British scholars (and those who helped to create sociology—and were, and are, in sympathy with the subject—not by any means only its opponents) have been genuinely and deeply doubtful whether sociology can ever sever its ties with philosophy.† This scepticism springs from epistemological considerations; from ethical considerations in relation to the 'factual' study of values in society; and considerations of practical issues of policy-making and administration—i.e. from questions as to what is really involved in making

---

* Exactly the same qualities and concerns can be found in many of the editorial articles of *The American Sociologist* over the past five years.

† Fundamentally, indeed, many would maintain that the distinction between science and philosophy as it has been developed over the past few decades has itself become seriously misleading.

judgments about the so-called 'knowledge' of social facts in the formulation of policy. I strongly support this emphasis, and shall try later to demonstrate its worth. Indeed, I would go so far as to say that one of the greatest dangers to sociology and all other human sciences—such as psychology—is that they should lose touch with the philosophical problems which lie at their roots. And this can lead to the worst kind of superficiality and naivety.

Also, secondly, British sociology has always been strongly persuaded of the *historical* nature of both the subject and its subject-matter. The main emphasis in nineteenth and early twentieth century sociology, of course, was upon conceptions of 'social evolution', 'social development', and, indeed, of 'social progress'. Now much scepticism has been directed against such ideas, and a good deal (though not all) of American scholarship either rejects or ignores it. I believe (not only with some British thinkers, but with Comte, Durkheim and Weber) that the historical, developmental and evolutionary approach to sociology has not only much to commend it, but is absolutely essential to the satisfactory formulation of the subject. In all this, too, there are very interesting ways in which the British sociologists (from the 'Scottish School' right up to Hobhouse and Westermarck) have had insights which are of quite basic importance; but these can only properly be dealt with later. Consider a small example, however, by way of immediate illustration. One of the main strands of sociology in Britain during the past eighty years or so has been concerned with 'Comparative Morals' (as, for example, in the cumulative work of Hobhouse, Westermarck, and Ginsberg, and now recently and critically commented on by C. von Fürer-Haimendorf), and this is sometimes regarded by critics as a rather odd concentration of interest. Why morals? Why was this one set of social facts selected from society as a whole and dwelt upon to the exclusion of others? Well—there was, in fact, a very good reason for this concentration, and to say that 'morals' were dwelt upon to the exclusion of other social facts is plainly to show that these writers have not been properly read and understood. Far from being a *selection* of one *sector* of society isolated from others, their emphasis really rested upon a profound hypothetical insight of the very greatest importance, namely that 'morals' in society were exactly those fundamental values which interpenetrated the whole of society; which lay at the heart of all social institutions—marriage and the family, property, procedures of legal and industrial arbitration, education, government and the like. Furthermore, though far from maintaining that changes in 'morals' *caused* changes and developments in social institutions, their persuasion was that significant patterns of change and development would show themselves as conflicts and changes between old values and new, and thus the recorded development in the 'morals' of a society might well be an excellent central indicator of the development in all social institutions. When these men—from Adam Smith, Lord Kames, through John Stuart Mill, to Westermarck, Hobhouse and Ginsberg— thought of the human sciences as the 'Moral Sciences'—it was not by any means that they were guilty of a kind of intellectual 'myopia' of British philosophical moralists, but, on the contrary, that they possessed a clear insight and a clear hypothetical guide for empirical, historical, and comparative study as to what constituted the distinctive features of human social institutions and their interdependence in societies as total political communities.

In this essay, I shall argue strongly for the reinstatement, as it were, of much British sociology. I shall defend its philosophical basis, its concern for the study of morals and ethics, and its insistence upon a historical, developmental, even an evolutionary approach. In short, I shall argue as powerfully as I can for all those things which are at present outrightly unfashionable.

Also, however, I want to support this reinstatement by showing (what ought not to be necessary) that British sociology has been part and parcel of European sociology from its first foundation.

It is quite false and misleading to think of European sociology on the one hand—consisting of the 'great names': Comte, Durkheim, Weber, Pareto, etc.—and British sociology, quite distinct, consisting of a small group of 'evolutionists', on the other. On the contrary, there has been a continuous communication and debate between British and continental scholars. Their ideas took shape together: British thinkers, like their fellows in Europe, always contributing as much as they borrowed. Kant (and everybody else after him) drew from Hume. Comte drew from both Kant and Hume, and also from Adam Smith and Ferguson (amongst many others). Mill and a small group of friends in Britain were among the first to recognize and support (with money as well as with critical praise) the work of Comte. Spencer and Comte, as we know, were much of a muchness in many matters; between them exercising an enormous influence. Durkheim, too, simply cannot be understood except in terms of his development of the insights and leading ideas of Comte, and his critical development of Mill and Spencer in Britain (amongst others). Indeed, though I am far from wanting to belittle Durkheim to any degree, it is certainly true that much of his supposed originality would be a good deal dissipated if readers were as intimately aware of the work of Comte, Mill and Spencer as they are with the *Division of Labour in Society* or the *Rules of Sociological Method*. I need not point out that these scholars are not only 'British' and 'European' but are chief among those who have powerfully influenced and shaped sociology in America. Nor need I point out (though, since people's perspectives are so hazy once the word 'history' is used, perhaps it is necessary) that all this has taken place in the past 150 years or so; that is to say—only yesterday. All these thinkers are *modern thinkers*. They are writing for *us, now*. This whole debate—the process of creating sociology—is almost wholly a *contemporaneous* affair. However, this is a kind of emphasis to which I shall return.

Here it is sufficient to point out that British sociology is far from having been a poor relation, distinct from, separate from, and inferior to, the more prominent continental scholars. On the contrary it has participated in the cosmopolitan development of the subject from the time of its foundation. Indeed, as in more practical affairs of the moment, it is not that Britain needs to 'join Europe', or that both need to 'join America'. It is, more correctly, that we need clearly to recognize that, all the time, we have been members of one co-operatively created world. This point needs particular emphasis, curiously enough, in Britain itself at the moment. For there is a curious tendency at present to worship continentals and Americans and to deprecate compatriots; to roll the scientific-sounding names of Max Weber and 'verstehen', Emile Durkheim and his 'représentations collectives', Ferdinand Tönnies and his 'Gemeinschaft und Gesellschaft', Vilfredo Pareto and his 'residues and derivations', and Talcott Parsons and his 'Pattern Variables', round one's ingenuous Anglo-Saxon tongue, and to look upon Herbert Spencer (the chap from Derby) and Leonard Trelawney Hobhouse (an Oxford philosopher) as outmoded philosophical freaks. All of which, of course, is sheer rubbish.

Having said this, however, I must confess that, in seeking to effect this reinstatement and redress this balance, a certain edge of patriotic justice does intrude. I would like to see these British scholars receive their proper due. Their social thought has been and is second to none. They are good philosophers, down to earth in their thinking, clear in their analysis, never too far from common sense to be absurd, never too close to it to be thick-headed in their empiricism, never practising mock-profundity, and, above all, men of clear style. They say quite clearly what they think. And more British scholars fall within the range of sociological thought than is commonly supposed: Walter Bagehot, for example, in his *Physics and Politics*. Graham Wallas, too, wrote with much wisdom and judgment, and from a wide scholarship and practical experience. And a man like Henry Sidgwick was far more of a sociological thinker than many people who now bear the name. His book on the *Growth of the European Polity* is as good a book on the comparative social institutions of European societies as any, and yet I doubt whether anyone knows of it now, let alone reads it.

In these ways, at any rate, this must be a British book. But I hope this will not be thought to detract from its nature as an essay on theoretical sociology at large; and I hope that my arguments in support of much British sociology will be seen to rest not at all upon sentiment, but upon a warranted conviction of its essential intellectual worth.

A final, particular, preoccupation in connection with American sociology is this. The system of analysis outlined by Talcott Parsons has been the most prominent recent contribution from America, though not necessarily the most important, and it is notorious for its extremely elaborate terminology and its involved manner of expression. I do not think, myself, that this is a crucial criticism of Parsons, though, in the extent to which it is true of his work, it is certainly damaging. Reading Parsons is like chewing cardboard. It is neither appetizing nor rewarding beyond a certain limited point. However, any fair-minded student can see with perfect clarity that Parsons has struggled genuinely to develop sets of categories which he feels to be essential for a full analysis of all the dimensions of social reality. Consequently, his system of categories deserves careful study. He has not concerned himself with the elaboration of difficult terminology for its own sake, but for the sake of achieving a comprehensive 'general theory' from which specific theories can be deduced and in terms of which they can be clearly stated. Even so—I believe that, from the beginning, Parsons' perspectives have been wrong; that he has pedantically pressed rather specious points and considerations; that he has misconceived or misrepresented certain viewpoints and has falsely juxtaposed them (as, for example, 'positivism' and 'voluntarism'); that his analysis of social systems is gravely at fault and has a spuriously exact 'schema'; and that his theoretical work has advanced sociology very little, if at all.

What I am certain of is that the system of sociological analysis that we are trying to achieve both can and must be stated far more simply, far more economically, and in a way far more readily applicable to empirical investigations than that achieved by Parsons. We shall attempt, then, a much simpler statement of all this; to indicate and clarify the simpler statement that lies at the heart of all the major contributors to the making of the subject.

Sociology is sometimes criticized for its 'jargon' unjustly. Edward Shils once said at a conference that every German child of five years old knows what is meant by 'Gemeinschaft und Gesellschaft'. This aside, any subject which goes beyond common sense must invent terms which are not familiar to it. There is nothing wrong with this. However, because of this criticism, I shall try in this essay to achieve *simplicity of statement, in so far as this is commensurate with adequacy.* In many ways I think it is true that sociology is inflated. It seems to me a good thing not to forget that, like all other sciences, sociology stems from reflection upon common sense assumptions. If this is borne in mind, our abstractions, though they may be unfamiliar to common sense, need never become too remote from it, and they can at least, no matter how sophisticated they become, always be clearly related to it. And if we find that what we are trying to say can, after all, be stated quite simply, why should we be reluctant so to state it? Simplicity, surely, is an objective to achieve; something to be desired; not a naivety to be escaped. There is no virtue in trying to give an impression of wisdom or 'professional expertise' by wrapping ourselves in an outward garb of complexity. A pretence of profundity can help no one, but must only be misleading.

A British Text on the Making of Sociology

One final preoccupation of a 'British' nature must be stated.

A British textbook on sociological theory has not yet been written.* Individuals, of course (Spencer, Hobhouse, and others), have offered large-scale theories of their own, but there has been no attempt to assess, and to relate to each other, the many contributions to sociology (British, continental, American and others) for the purposes of clarifying the nature and advance of the subject as a whole. The attention paid to sociological theory, even by sociologists, until shortly after World War II, was curiously and very narrowly selective. To this day few people in Britain outside academic sociology know Max Weber, excepting, perhaps, for his *Protestant Ethic and the Rise of Capitalism.* Many have never even heard of Durkheim. Scarcely anyone has read Mill in relation to sociology, or has read Spencer, Westermarck, Hobhouse and other British contributions. One of my concerns, then, is to fill this gap and try to provide a British perspective on the making of the subject.

This concern is uppermost in my mind because of the position

---

* Professor Morris Ginsberg has written much of value on theory and method in sociology—but these are collected essays of a very wide and varied range. Professor John Rex has written on theory, but this is, quite literally, a concentration on what he takes to be 'key problems'. The nearest book to a text is *Modern Social Theory* by Percy Cohen, but this focuses attention upon modern theory only, drawing upon the leading ideas of a few writers—such as Simmel, Durkheim, Weber—and offering a critique of much modern American thinking. For details of these books: see bibliography.

25

of sociology in Britain today—which is vexed and problematical to say the very least. The sociological scene in Britain at present is characterised by a many-sided dissatisfaction and restlessness, and many real difficulties in the teaching situation. In a curious way this derives both from a sudden and enormous expansion in popular demand and from the constraints and frustrations connected with it. The situation has many aspects. Firstly, for example, it is commonly supposed that sociology is newly established in many departments in the universities, colleges of education, colleges of technology, and other institutions of higher education; and yet—the actuality is that more often than not, sociology is still constrained within the contexts of the departments and courses of other social sciences. Also, the demand for teachers is so great that many people are employed to teach it who have had no previous education and training in it. Also, so many other departments—of Education, Social Administration, and the like—have courses in 'sociology' which are not 'sociology' at all. Consequently there is a bewildering variety in the teaching of sociology, and the subject is, curious though it may sound, positively *endangered* by the very extent of its new popularity and vogue. It seems to me imperative, therefore, that some agreed statement of the nature of the subject should be achieved; and one which insists upon, preserves, and makes clear, all the many dimensions which its makers have succeeded in establishing. This need, too, I have centrally in mind, and in this sense also, therefore, this must be a 'British' book*. It cannot avoid bearing in mind the present state of the subject in this country.* Again, however, I hope that this will not detract from its clear concern with the clarification of sociological theory proper—going far beyond the bounds of any local, national problem or perspective.

These, then, are the conscious preoccupations which underlie my efforts in all that follows. They are not stated as limited objectives, only as guides to some of my stronger attitudes. I do not ask, or expect, that the reader should be sympathetic to them—only that they should be borne in mind so that some directions of the argument will be fully understood.

* Actually, I believe that these concerns for a clarification of the subject; these feelings that it is in the grip of a very profound 'malaise'—in its academic situation; in relation to the application of its knowledge and perspectives in all the tasks of politics and government and in many specific professions; in relation to its own professional development and its relations to other social sciences; in relation to these who supposedly want it—but have only the most superficial awareness (indeed downright misconception) of its nature—are far wider than any local 'British' situation. In facing up to our own dilemma, our thinking may therefore be found to have a far wider relevance. These problems are going to be experienced in education in all contemporary industrial societies. They are universal.

3
Plan

The study is divided into four distinct sections:

1 Beginnings

In an opening section, I want to make two things clear beyond doubt: first, that sociology is not remote from common sense or necessarily at war with it, but, on the contrary, is firmly rooted in our common-sense assumptions about our life in society; and second, that sociological theory is not something altogether new and strange, but has grown consistently out of earlier theories of philosophy and religion. It is a good thing to see that sociological theory is rooted in common sense and other social theories, and that it has been a *necessary* development: stemming from the insufficiencies of both.

2 Foundations

A clear understanding of these roots of sociology can then lead to a statement of the first foundation of the subject as a systematic attempt to employ science in establishing *knowledge*, rather than speculative opinion, about the nature of man and society. Here we shall see the first basic outlines of the subject laid down; the first systematic statement of its nature and elements; the first theories which it produced. At the hands of a relatively small number of thinkers—Auguste Comte, John Stuart Mill, Herbert Spencer, Karl Marx, and a few men in America who were strongly influenced by them (all working individually, it may be noted, and most of them outside the universities)—the subject was created. In this section we shall clarify the 'conspectus' that had been achieved by the end of the nineteenth century.

Let us just note that this was *only just over fifty years ago*. We are not speaking here of the 'history' of a subject in 'distant' terms, but of the arguments of very recent times. The brevity of this perspective might be emphasized more vividly by putting it in more-or-less personal terms. Herbert Spencer published his *Principles of Sociology* in the same year that my own grandfather began work as a boy of 9.

His (i.e. my grandfather's) grandfather was alive not long after the French Revolution when Auguste Comte was walking through the streets of Paris on a Sunday (in his typical black clothes, now still folded in a box in his bedroom) to deliver free lectures to working men, or working painstakingly in his small sitting room, sitting at the writing table with the mirror facing it, writing quickly in his small neat handwriting on the small pad of paper between the two tall candle-sticks . . . all still there to be seen in the rue Monsieur le Prince. All this took place only yesterday, and is very close indeed.

And in 1903, in the London School of Economics, meetings were attended by people like H. G. Wells, George Bernard Shaw, Beatrice Webb, Charles Booth, Rowntree, as well as the first 'official' academic sociologists in Britain whom we shall mention later, to discuss the establishment and furtherance of the subject and to form a Sociological Society following the death of Herbert Spencer. The firm foundations were laid.

3 Developments

Some of the men present at these meetings, and some who contributed by correspondence—Tönnies, Westermarck, Durkheim, Hobhouse—were agreed about the importance of the newly founded subject and about the basic outlines of its nature and scope which had been laid down. They then worked, each in his own way, to develop and improve it: to sharpen its methods; to fill out its scheme of comparative and historical analysis; to use its methods in studying those problems of society with which they were deeply concerned, and to test its worth by deepening the knowledge of society in specific fields of research and in demonstrable ways. In this third section, these new developments of the subject will be dealt with.

In various ways, the theories of social change, development, and evolution which had been stated by Comte, Spencer and Marx, were criticized, deepened, and corrected; and practically all the scholars of this generation—Tönnies, Durkheim, Hobhouse, Weber, and others—contributed to this. In addition, however, there were new developments of theory (and appropriate method) for the better exploration of certain dimensions of social reality. Emile Durkheim proposed methods for studying 'associational' facts of a certain kind. Max Weber insisted upon the importance for sociological explanation of the 'subjective understanding' of the sequences of social action which men pursue. Georg Simmel tried to elucidate certain 'forms' of human relationship which might prove to be common to all aspects of social organization—economic, governmental, religious, military—all of which might, at first glance, be thought to be distinctively different. All these secondary developments enriched, extended, and made more satisfactory, the nature of sociological analysis, and this third section will give a clear review and summary of them.

Book 4 Re-assessments: Consolidation and Advance?

Perhaps the chief thing to notice in this final title is the last word of it and the question mark which follows.

This last section will deal with the most recent discussions of the subject. The past thirty years or so, especially in America, have been largely devoted to a task of critical reappraisal. Talcott Parsons in particular has undertaken a critical stock-taking of the position at which, in his view, sociology has now arrived. He claims to have traced a certain 'convergence' among some of the theorists mentioned —Durkheim, Weber, and others, such as Marshall the economist, and Pareto—and has gone on to elaborate a synthesis which forms a unified 'general theory' in sociology. Such a movement from earlier 'theories' to 'general theory' he has thought to be essential for the subject. There have been many criticisms of this claim, and other points of view as to the best ways of 'improving' sociological analysis have been put forward. The title 'RETROSPECT AND PROSPECT' which has marked so many conferences, is indicative of much of the discussion that has taken place among sociologists during this period. And we are still, at the present time, in this position of seeking a fundamental clarification of the nature and achievements of sociology.

In this final section, we shall critically review the contributions of the recent Americans. Then, having formed our judgment as to how far they have provided a consolidation and advance in the subject, we shall move finally to as clear a statement as we can achieve of the nature of sociological analysis as it now exists.

By following this plan, our study will encompass all that has gone into 'The Making of Sociology'. It will give a clear story of the subject from its earliest roots, its first foundations, its chief developments, through its most recent debates, to a clear understanding of its present nature.

Beginnings

1
The Common-Sense Roots of Sociology

Science begins as critical reflection upon common sense. Common sense is not to be understood however as the lowest common denominator of simple-mindedness amongst all men. It is already a set of rudimentary theories about experience; a set of assumptions: of virile, shrewd, penetrating insights into the nature of things; but expressed only in the rough-and-ready words of everyday usage. Sometimes these words are more pungent and articulate than more sophisticated expressions might be (sophistication, too, has its dangers for accuracy!), but sometimes they are limited and insufficient. Already, in common sense, we know that all aspects of nature are intricately interconnected and interwoven with each other; and that some events, in particular, seem always to cause others—but it is when we need to know what *exactly* these interconnections are, what events *exactly* cause others, that our common-sense experience often fails us. Consequently, we are compelled to think more critically and analytically about our ideas and about the nature of the facts we experience, and we have to devise systematic methods whereby the various factors involved in the situation we seek to understand can be isolated, distinguished, and measured, and whereby our theories about their cause-and-effect relationships can be tested. These methods of critical analytical thought, careful observation, recording, and description, and this testing of theories against the facts, *are* science; and the pursuit of these methods leads to the elucidation of 'laws'—the discovery of regularities of interconnection between phenomena—which make the explanation of events possible.

Common sense is not, therefore, different from science, but is science in embryo. And our common sense and scientific interests in the facts of our experience, stem always from two characteristics of human nature: practical need, and curiosity. We are driven to seek exact explanations because, frequently, we *must:* as when we wish to quell an epidemic, ensure a clean water supply, grow enough food for survival, build enough houses for the shelter of our population. But also, we seek explanations because we are *inquisitive;* puzzled. We simply *want to know*. The excitement of curiosity, puzzling, searching and then discovering, is one of our most absorbing and rewarding experiences. Once a problem is there—we find it difficult to leave it alone until we have solved it. And since *all* aspects of the world in which we live excite us to inquiry, our common sense and scientific activity leads us to desire not only partial understanding, but also an entire knowledge of nature: of the universe as a whole and the place of man within it. The various sciences—astronomy, physics, physiology, biology—all provide us with a knowledge of particular aspects of the world, but they are all complementary contributions towards our desired entirety of knowledge.

Of course, the similarity of common sense to science does not mean at all that science is limited to, or circumscribed by, those aspects of common sense from which it arises. Clearly *in* its reflection and sophistication it goes far beyond the assumptions of common sense and frequently shows them to be provisional, limited, inadequate, false. But this does not mean that the two are essentially different; only that the *more* adequate stems from the *less* adequate and comes to replace it.

All this is simple, clear, undeniable.

A. N. Whitehead expresses this relation between science and common sense in a very simple and colourful way, showing how its most sophisticated abstractions stem from our most ordinary experiences.

'Consider', he says* 'how all events are interconnected. When we see the lightning, we listen for the thunder; when we hear the wind, we look for the waves on the sea; in the chill autumn, the leaves fall. Everywhere order reigns, so that when some circumstances have been noted we can foresee that others also will be present. The progress of science consists in observing these interconnections and in showing with a patient ingenuity that the events of this ever-shifting world are but examples of a few general connections or relations called laws. To see what is general in what is particular and what is permanent in what is transitory is the aim of scientific thought. In the eye of science, the fall of an apple, the motion of a planet round a sun, and the clinging of the atmosphere to the earth are all seen as examples of the law of gravity. This possibility of disentangling the most complex evanescent circumstances into various examples of permanent laws is the controlling idea of modern thought.'

No-one, I believe, could possibly fail to understand the characteristics of science in so far as it is concerned with our understanding

---

* A. N. Whitehead, *An Introduction to Mathematics*, Home University Library, Oxford University Press, 1911, pp. 3–4.

of the natural world. Nor would anyone deny its claims, or the validity of its endeavours.

Why, then, is there doubt, criticism, and even bitter denunciation when these careful methods of science are employed in seeking exact knowledge about the nature of man and society?

Sociology is the scientific study of human society, or—to be more modest and detailed—it is the attempt to study as scientifically as possible all the known forms of human association: their nature, functions, interconnections, and patterns of change in various types of society.

Why should this scientific endeavour raise so much argument and bitterness? Not, we shall find, from the antagonisms of common sense. If we consider our common sense assumptions about our life in society, we shall find that such criticisms of sociology are not rooted in any uneasiness or hostility of common sense at all, but from sophisticated scholars who have allowed their attachment to their own subjects, or their own interests and motives, to blur their clarity of mind and judgment. Common sense tells us quite distinctly and convincingly—and again from both practical need and curiosity —that the attempt to achieve a science of society is both necessary and important.

In order to see this clearly, let us set out, in an orderly way, what our common-sense assumptions are. Such a process of clarification is a first step of scientific inquiry, and we shall find that, already, in the requirements seen to be necessary by our common sense ideas, we have a fairly clear idea of what components a scientific study of society should consist. Our common-sense assumptions already tell us what sociology would have to be like in order to satisfy the kind of thing that we already know *roughly*—but would like to know more *exactly*.

The Necessity of a Scientific Study of Society

As soon as we stop to think about it, it is obvious that we possess common-sense views about our own nature, and about the historically changing society in which we live, as much as we do about the world of nature. And we also see quite clearly the necessity of going beyond our common-sense ideas to a more careful investigation, if we are to ensure that our supposed knowledge is going to be really reliable.

At least three things convince us of this.

(a) Practical need

As soon as we become involved in particular conflicts with other groups in society; as soon as we are brought face to face with particular social problems; we are at once made aware how little we really *know* about social reality, and at once realize that a more painstaking study of the facts is necessary.

Consider a few examples:

We would like to eliminate from society war, poverty, crime and delinquency. We are often hotly indignant when we encounter the intractable inequalities of opportunity in society for children who, no matter what their abilities and qualities might be, happen to be born into different social classes or different 'races'. We would like to improve matters; to remove these obstacles to social justice; and would therefore like to know the underlying *causes* of these social facts. Then, on the basis of this knowledge, if we could get it, we would like to formulate effective social policies and institute political reforms.

As soon as we embark upon this more careful investigation, however, and upon this well-intentioned activity of social reform, the more we are driven to see the great complexity of these social facts and the order of society in which they exist. In spite of all our efforts, both intellectual and practical, we find it extremely difficult, if not impossible, to alter the social facts which we thought were simply a product of individual intention, or evil, or misunderstanding. It turns out to be far more difficult to eliminate war, poverty, crime, and differences of class, status, and educational opportunity than we had imagined. Some of the characteristics of society turn out to be as intractable as the 'stubborn facts'* of nature.

What is certain is that we find it absolutely necessary to probe far beyond our common-sense ideas; to devise far more rigorous methods of thought and practical investigation; in the effort to establish *reliable* knowledge *on the basis of which to act*. For we quickly learn that we can only effectively *change* the nature of society to approximate as closely as possible to the ends we desire, *if we know what that nature is*.

Just as we can only convert water-power into electricity to improve the material well-being of a nation, when we know the 'laws'—the regularities of interconnections—of the physical factors involved; so we can only change social facts when we know the 'laws'—the regularities of interconnections—pertaining to them.

Several important points are to be noted here.

(I) MORAL FEELINGS

Much of our concern to think about society (i.e. many of our

* William James.

'needs') stems from our *moral* feelings; our feelings of moral indignation; our desires to eradicate injustice and to establish justice.

(II) MORAL FEELINGS IN THEMSELVES NOT ENOUGH

But we know that moral ideals and good intentions *are not in themselves enough*. Without knowledge and power we cannot make them effective. Also, we find that, without knowledge, they often pave the road to something other than a good society.

(III) A SCIENCE OF SOCIETY NOT IN DISAGREEMENT WITH OUR MORAL PERSUASIONS, BUT ADDITIONAL AND OF SERVICE TO THEM.

The development of a scientific study of society is not *in disagreement* with our moral persuasions, does not *contradict* them, is not *incompatible* with them; neither does it replace moral concern and clear ethical thinking, or render them unnecessary. It is something *additional* to them and clearly *of service* to them.

(IV) MORAL CONCERN INSISTS ON SCIENTIFIC ACCURACY

Moral persuasions and practical needs do not—as critics have often supposed—make it impossible for a scholar to be careful, honest, exact, impartial, 'objective', in his pursuit of scientific truth. On the contrary, *they insist upon it*. We can only hope to achieve our humane ends *if we rest our social policies upon the truth, and not upon any kind of distortion of it*. Subjective feelings, subjective passions do not necessarily make a scientific study of society impossible. It is just some of these feelings which *enjoin it*. Certainly some unconscious values and assumptions may lead us to bias in our theories—but (*a*) our efforts should always be towards the impartial self-criticism which would make such grounds of bias conscious and clear, and (*b*) such initial bias does not matter crucially *so long as our ways of testing our theories are reliable, clear, and always open to the scrutiny of other investigators*. Conscious distortion of scientific work—in human sciences and 'natural' sciences alike*—is likely to arise not so much from passionate feeling or ethical conviction, as from a lack of integrity, or a lack of rigour in one's methods of investigation.

(V) KNOWLEDGE ENABLES US TO ACT MORE EFFECTIVELY. 'CAUSAL DETERMINACY' DOES NOT PRECLUDE PURPOSIVE ACTION.

It is already clear, in our common sense, that there is no incon-

---

* Later, we shall quarrel with this distinction between 'human' and 'natural' sciences. It is used here only to indicate that this problem—of passion in investigation—is as much attendant upon the activity of the natural as the social scientist. Science positively *requires* passion and imagination.

sistency (as, again, some critics have supposed) in thinking (*a*) that there are definite 'laws' of social facts (i.e. regular interconnections between them) and (*b*) that, by knowing them, we can act in such a way as to *change their manifestations*. When we know the 'laws' of the tides, we can calculate the strength of sea-walls necessary to prevent the erosion of the coast. We do not *change the laws*; but, knowing them, we can act to prevent them having particular effects. Similarly, when we know the 'laws' pertaining to the formation of class and status in society, we can so organize our political constitution, our distribution of income and property, our educational system, as to prevent the occurrence of rigid class boundaries and intractable class conflicts. The 'laws' are not changed; but, knowing them, we can act to prevent the effects we think undesirable and to ensure as closely as possible the consequences we want.

(VI) IN SOCIETY SOMETHING MORE THAN THE WILLS OF INDIVIDUALS IS INVOLVED

It is also clear in our common sense that, in looking for the explanation of some social facts, conditions, and problems, we must look for *something more than individual wills and intentions*. This is not to say, by any means, that we believe that individuals cannot, and do not, make individual choices or have individual intentions, and that these can never be effective. It is not at all to say that men do not possess some measure of 'free will' in that they can exercise conscious choice and act deliberately and with clear purpose. It is only to say that in many human situations *something more than the wills and intentions of individuals is involved*.

If, then, we find that some sociologists (men who *have* reflected upon these common-sense concerns and problems, and who *have* tried to develop more precise methods to get at the truth about human nature and human society) are inclined to say that social explanations must go *beyond* propositions about the motives and wills of individuals, and that we can only act effectively to change human nature and society if we know the 'laws' of society and the nature of the group conditions within which men exercise their will, we shall not think them absurd, or 'metaphysical' in any derogatory sense. If people object to these ways of talking, it cannot be on the grounds of common sense. It can only be that they themselves have become confused by their own sophistications. There is nothing unclear about this way of thinking.

It is also quite a clear understanding in our common sense that the necessity for a scientific study of society has become more urgent as society has become larger and more complicated, and as the growth of knowledge in all spheres has given rise to a wider range of doubts and a more insistent questioning of traditional beliefs and assumptions. In our modern industrial society—which has grown so rapidly and spread so quickly to all parts of the world during the past two hundred years—our needs for a science of man and society (needs both practical and of curiosity*) have obviously become greater. Our problems have become more numerous and more pressing and, in the prevailing confusion about 'supernatural' and all types of 'traditional' authority, hitherto taken for granted, we are also driven to a clear awareness that the solution of our problems now depends upon us; upon our own responsibility. If we do not solve our problems in society, no-one else will!

We are quite clear that, during the past two hundred years, a more careful way of studying society has been made necessary by the facts of social change themselves. Sociology is the subject peculiar to the characteristics of the modern human situation, the modern predicament of man. And we feel, in terms of our common sense convictions, that it is essentially a *humanistic* subject: not only in that it is of broad human concern and interest, but, more fundamentally, because it is the subject necessarily connected with our growing awareness that, in this new situation, we ourselves are responsible for the making of our own destiny. In the past, men have believed they could rely with confidence upon an authority outside man—the power of providence, or God; but now, whether we like the situation or not, we are faced with a clear consciousness of responsibility for the direction of our own social and individual affairs.

Again, then, if we find some sociologists speaking as passionate humanists, speaking with zealous concern and anxious persuasion, inspired both by moral enthusiasm and by intellectual conviction of the great significance of their subject for contemporary human problems, we shall not find it surprising—for this is attendant upon the emergence of the subject itself, and our common sense clearly appreciates this. The fact that a subject is 'scientific' does not mean that it is not 'humanistic'. Indeed, the distinction between 'sciences' and 'humanities' seems an absurd distinction in some respects.

(VII) REFLECTION ON TERMS AND CONCEPTS NECESSARY

It is also clear, if we believe that scientific activity involves the devising of more precise methods of investigation and the testing of theories, that sociology must necessarily weigh its *terms* and *concepts*

---

* It can be seen that 'practical need' and 'curiosity' are not as sharply distinct from each other as we have been supposing. They are frequently simultaneous, springing from the same problems. One is often the cause of the other.

more carefully, more reflectively, than is usual in common sense, and that, when necessary, it may well be driven to the invention of *new* terms. It is clear to us, for example, as soon as we start arguing about a topic like 'Christianity', or even one division of the 'Christian Church' (the 'Roman Catholic Church', say, or the 'Baptists') that these simple terms become quite inadequate. For 'Christianity' is far from being the relatively simple unity that our initial common-sense notions sometimes suppose. The 'Baptists', for example, are very differently organized in Coleford in Gloucestershire than they are in the United States of America. 'Roman Catholicism' is not the same in the West Riding of Yorkshire as it is in Ireland or in Italy. Our words have therefore to be examined scrupulously, and no-one will object, therefore, if we begin to use words like 'founded religion' (as distinct from other 'traditional' kinds of religion), 'episcopalian organization' or 'sect', or 'denomination' (and many others) in our attempt to become clear in our grasp of the facts.

Our common sense would have no objection at all to a careful analysis of our language, or an invention of terms, if this were for the purpose of useful clarification. It would object to such an exercise of preoccupation only if it were seen to be *useless*, leading *not* to clarification but to *confusion*; to unwarranted and pointless obscurantism.

(b) Curiosity

Quite apart from the practical needs which prompt us to examine more deeply the nature of society we are also led to such inquiry by curiosity itself—or, to give the matter the degree of concern which we feel—by our need for personal understanding.

One immediate aspect of this point is the supposed distinction between 'natural' and 'human', or 'natural' and 'social' science. It is clear that common sense does not make this kind of distinction at all. It is made only by scholars of various kinds. In our own common-sense awareness of our predicaments in the world, we have a far more mixed up and bewildered experience, but, on the other hand, an experience which has a far greater unity than these distinctions would suggest.

We feel ourselves to be both of the world and not of it; in tune with it and in conflict with it; in harmony with it and hostile to it; members of it and strangers in it; and all this simultaneously. We feel sometimes with deep satisfaction that our own nature is deeply rooted in nature itself. The whole living universe of stars, earth, skies, trees, is in some curious but definite and tangible way linked with, indeed knitted into, our own nerves, veins and flesh. We are all creatures of nature. We are all of the one body of the universe. It cannot be otherwise! On the other hand, we so often and so obviously feel at odds with nature! The most urgent improvements of our condition (such as vaccination against fatal diseases), and the most sublime qualities of our artistic and social achievements (the novels and symphonies which move us, the forms of government or religion which have given us a basis for co-operative, peaceful and creative living), are certainly not simply given to us. They are not simply there, to be found by us, in nature. They are the outcome of thousands of years of cumulative effort and struggle. They have been won by unceasing battle with the elements of nature (storm, wind, flood, fire, plague) and with bewildering and sometimes distasteful elements of society (social distinctions, racial differences, wealth, privilege, power). We are at war with nature, just as we find our deepest peace in our communion with it. We are at war with society, just as we find our most satisfying purposes as members of it.

And we are different from all other creatures in nature in that we are members of a historically developing social heritage which transmits the cumulative achievements of our ancestors from one generation to another. And it is quite clear in our common-sense experience that our own individual nature is largely an outcome of the complex influences of this social tradition itself.

I speak English. I love the diatonic harmonies—in their simplicity and in their intricate developments—of Vaughan Williams, Stanford, Herbert Howells, Ivor Gurney, Peter Warlock. I find some of my deepest moral experience couched in the phrases of Shakespeare, Wordsworth, Emily Brontë, Blake and others. And I have these personal experiences *not* simply because I was created in this way as an individual soul, but because I was born in England. Had I been born in some other society and brought up within the many subtle influences of another social tradition—my individual nature would have been different. If I had been born in India, I would have spoken a different language with all its many different connotations of experience. I would have enjoyed quartertone harmonies in music; and found my moral experience couched in terms of, say, the Vedic hymns, or the requirements of a particular 'caste'.

It is perfectly clear, then, that if we are to understand our place in the world we must also understand our place in society, and the place of our own tradition within the wider context of history and of the natural world. To put this in another way, it is quite clear to us that a careful study of society is as necessary a part of our full understanding of the nature of the world and our place within it, as is any other science or any other branch of human thought.

Indeed, there is a second consideration of common sense which inclines us to think that a science of man and society is especially central and fundamental in its importance. This consideration is simply this:

All the knowledge of the world and man's place within it which we can establish is necessarily and unavoidably *human* knowledge, stemming, as we have seen, from the practical needs and the curiosity *of our own nature*. It cannot possibly be otherwise. Nothing is more obvious to our common sense than that the kinds of knowledge— ordinary, religious, scientific, philosophical—which exist at any time in any society are (*a*) themselves social facts of that period, and (*b*) inescapably characterized by the level of development of that society. In short: human knowledge and its growth necessarily form a part of the subject-matter of a science of society; and all the various kinds of knowledge should thus find a coherent statement of their nature, development, and interconnections (with each other and with other social circumstances) within the over-all account provided by a science of society. The science of society—providing within itself, as it does, a perspective of all the other sciences—is also *a study of the several ways in which man has conceived the entirety of nature*. All knowledge—of the world, of nature, of God—is human knowledge; it takes the form of systems of records, doctrines, theories, in societies. And therefore the science of man and society is of the most fundamental importance for understanding the development of man's many conceptions of nature: those sets of concepts, assumptions, ideas, theories, which—at any one time—actually *comprise* nature for him.

This is not to say, by any means, or in the slightest degree, that sociology is in any sense *superior* to other sciences. All sciences are equally necessary and important in providing knowledge about particular aspects of the world, and, taken together, in providing a full picture of our natural situation as we see it. It is only to say that sociology, because of its subject-matter, has a peculiar significance of quite a fundamental and central nature that other sciences do not possess: that of throwing a perspective of inter-connectedness over all human activities.

In order that our understanding of nature and man can be complete, therefore, a science of society—sociology—is obviously necessary to us.

Something else must be noted, finally, with regard to this distinction between 'nature' and 'society'. Many scholars have drawn this distinction between the 'natural' and the 'human' or 'social' sciences very strongly. Indeed, they have gone so far as to maintain that it is improper to use the word 'science' in connection with the study of man and society at all. Sometimes they have claimed this because of religious beliefs that man possesses spiritual qualities which are quite distinct from the other characteristics of the 'natural' world. Sometimes they have believed that individuals possess 'free will', and that this renders any attempt at generalization or prediction about human behaviour impossible. And sometimes they make this claim believing that the nature of man, both as an individual and as a member of society, is so complex that, as a subject of study, it defies all hope of manageable, measurable treatment, and so cannot be dealt with in terms of 'scientific method' at all.

Now, clearly, our common sense tells us that something is wrong with these distinctions, between 'natural' and 'human', or 'natural' and 'social', and that, in some way or other, these scholars must be muddled and mistaken. At the same time there seems to be something in what they say. The matter is not very clear.

Common-sense experience tells us without any doubt whatever that 'man' and 'human society' are just as much a part of 'nature' as, say, ants and ant-hills, or as bison and their herds. What is *un*-natural, or *non*-natural' about man and his relationships which should make it necessary to regard our study of them as being something other than a 'natural' science? There is, of course, *nothing*. These several objections rest upon simple confusion.

The religious objection is obviously, at bottom, purely a disagreement about words. Whatever one believes about God and man's relation to him, it is clearly arbitrary whether we use the word 'nature' to refer to everything that exists *including* God and the human spirit, or to everything that exists *apart* from God and the human spirit. If God is responsible for the nature of the created world and man within it, and is active in the world (even though he himself may transcend his own creation and possess qualities that go beyond it) it is difficult to see in what way a 'natural science' of man and society could be thought faulty or inadequate—whether we use the word 'natural' narrowly or all-embracingly. The strongest criticism that could be made on these grounds is that such a natural science of man could not explore *all* the dimensions of man's nature and of reality; but no-one would have any objection to this. At the same time this criticism could not possibly controvert, nor would it undermine or lead us to doubt, any knowledge about man and society in nature which such a science *did* demonstrate.

Presumably God, if he exists, is the ground of creation of all his creatures other than man, too—foxes, trees, woodlice, volcanoes, vermin, and viruses—and if a scientific study of these can be termed a 'natural science', why not a scientific study of man? Of course, theologians may well claim that this is naive (theologians always do claim that their critics are naive—it is one of the few kinds of criticism left to them), but this is not so. The fact is that even man's so-called 'knowledge' of God, or his knowledge of 'revealed truth' (i.e. of those 'non-natural' or 'spiritual' qualities which are supposed to be beyond the reach of a scientific study of man), are only experienced within the context of human feeling and human thought and can only be expressed in human terms of communication. *Nothing* can be known or experienced by man excepting through the medium of his own nature. Theological dimensions of knowledge, which claim to be additional to that of science, turn out, therefore, to be propositions about human experience—as all else. Furthermore, its purported 'knowledge' is in no sense superior to that of science. It cannot be held to be a ground of superiority that it does not possess the same grounds of demonstrability. The truth is that this particular objection is an outmoded theological quibble which is not now worth our consideration. Let us note very clearly, however, that this is not an 'anti-religious' position. If God does exist and has created the world, there is no reason at all why we should not use scientific methods in order to secure as full a knowledge as possible of man's nature and place within it.*

The objection resting upon the existence of 'free will' we shall return to, in more detail, later.† Here, we need only note our common sense conviction that man, differently from other animal species, is capable of establishing a knowledge of his nature and circumstances and, on this basis, of exercising personal choice and acting in a progressive way to achieve his ends. This capacity is part of man's nature. There is therefore no reason whatever why a study of man which takes this fact into account should not be called 'natural'; and, even if this fact should prove to make *exact* study difficult, our problem is only this: to make our scientific study *as exact as possible*, and only to claim that which we can demonstrate.

The third objection—concerning the great complexity of human society as a subject for science—clearly does make an appeal to our common sense. If we want to study what happens at the boiling points and freezing points of liquids, it is a relatively easy matter to set up tests in a laboratory and to alter the temperature of the liquids until our knowledge is established. If, however, we want to study the causes of 'crime', or the factors which give rise to 'feudal societies', clearly the facts are incredibly complicated and we cannot put them into a laboratory to observe them. Indeed, it is extremely difficult not only to examine the isolated factors involved, but even to be clear whether there *are* distinguishable *factors* to be *isolated* at all; or, even when there seem to be such factors, whether we can

---

* A scholar (theologian) like St Thomas Aquinas would be completely in agreement with this.
† See especially: John Stuart Mill, p. 201.

manage to isolate them sufficiently for anything approximating to a *testable* explanation. It is all very complicated, and, no matter how careful we are, it seems likely that our findings are likely to be much less precise than, say, our findings about the liquids. Our common sense feels very firm, indeed, adamant about this, and, of course, no social science worthy of the name would wish to deny it.

But the fault, here, lies again in a confusion.

Many people have come to *equate* the terms 'natural', and 'scientific', and 'exact'. 'Natural' sciences are those which can be exact, (which have, say, the exactitude of mathematical calculability.) 'Human' and 'social' studies are not 'natural' or 'scientific' because they are relatively inexact (they do not permit of mathematical calculability). And this, incidentally, has had the effect of firing some social scientists with the zeal to attain mathematical calculability in their subjects at all costs, simply so that they can claim to be 'scientific'. But this is to take part in a spurious competitive charade. And it rests upon quite erroneous reasoning. Indeed, it is not reasoning at all, but stems from a basic misconception.

Since varying aspects of the natural world have differing degrees of complexity, the scientific study of each of them will require different methods and will result in differing degrees of certainty, but—whatever their degrees of exactitude—they will all be different departments of 'natural science'. And whether the subjects are *scientific* or not has nothing whatever to do with *whether their results are equally precise*, but only upon their nature and the methods they employ. Even if a scientific study of some subject or problem yields no positive results at all, it will still have been the scientific method which resulted in these findings, and it will remain for critics to demonstrate what better and more fruitful methods could be pursued in their place; indeed, upon what criteria they themselves rest the supposedly better 'knowledge' that they may profess. But why the 'human' and 'social' sciences should be specially selected for this criticism is very difficult to understand. For all the so-called 'natural' sciences have very differing degrees of exactitude among themselves. Biology cannot achieve the exactitude of chemistry. Physiology cannot achieve the precision of physics. But no-one would argue that biology and physiology were not sciences. The subjects employ scientific methods to establish testable knowledge— and the results are *the most exact that the nature of their subject-matter permits*. Later, we shall see that philosophers and scientists have long been aware of this. It is nothing new.

There is one other point that common sense suggests, which might here be posed only as a question.

Is it really true that the phenomena of man and society are more

complicated and more difficult to study than those of other sciences?
In our common-sense experience there is at least a lot that inclines
us to think that the reverse might well be the case, and that the
study of man and society—though certainly complicated—might
well be simpler than the other sciences of nature. Might it not be that
too much fuss is being made about the difficulties involved?

It is clear to us that we cannot put people in laboratories with
either ease, moral conviction, or even prospects of success, in testing
theories about their behaviour. Social facts are certainly more
imponderable, more unwieldy to handle, than are some other facts of
nature. At the same time, some sciences seem simple to us now only
because they have been reduced to order after long ages of thought.
We are told, for example, that astronomy is a simple science. But
if we were to face the bewildering array of the heavens and the earth
without the accumulated observations, calculations and techniques
of the past (without telescopes, for example), would we find the task
of explaining the courses of the stars and planets simpler than
explaining the causes of social conflict in our locality, or even between
nations? At least the basic nature of social institutions—such as
property or marriage or education—can be found by examining legal
and other documents and by understanding their meaning for us.
And even when institutions are different in other societies, the people
there are men and women like ourselves, and, with study, it does not
seem difficult to understand the ways in which they act and feel.
Indeed, sometimes we are astonished at the similarities between them
and us despite institutional differences. Social rules and arrangements are at least evident to us, and many of the complexities are due
simply to the fact that there are a lot of people and documents
involved, and the 'testimony' we can get is of very variable reliability.
The understanding of the principles of genetics in heredity, however,
or the knowledge of the ways in which viruses cause disease, were
exceedingly difficult to explain because these facts were hidden
from us, unintelligible to us, unknown. The very existence of genes
or viruses was completely beyond our expectation. Similarly, if we
think of what is involved—let us say in neuro-physiology—in
attempting to unravel and track the many interconnections of the
brain cells and other nerves in the body, we are far from being fully
convinced that this is less difficult than tracing the interconnections
between social institutions.

We would not feel confident in *asserting* this on the basis of
common sense without further thought; but we would at least feel
it sufficiently a matter of doubt to raise *as a question*.

Might it not be that sociological analysis is a relatively simple
matter of clarifying—by means of careful thought, analysis, and

investigation—the networks of institutions in various societies and understanding the courses of action which men pursue within them? And might all this talk of complexity have arisen because sociologists had to sound more profound since they were doing what everyone else thought fairly self-evident? In common sense, we suspect that it might be so. We suspect that unnecessary mystification might have crept into the whole matter. And we suspect, after a little thought, that the difficulties of being clear about the nature of a science of society may possibly be because the subject has only been developed recently (historically speaking), whereas other subjects (like astronomy and physics) have been studied scientifically over a much longer period of time. This, at any rate, is a question which we would like to see considered.

Many and complex arguments have been conducted in the past about 'natural' as against 'human' and 'social' sciences. We can ignore most of them. A subject may be called 'scientific' when, reflecting upon common-sense assumptions, it then goes beyond them: carefully analysing experience; carefully clarifying its concepts and procedures of thought; carefully observing, recording and describing the facts about which it seeks to establish knowledge; clearly stating theories about them, and, at the same time, making clear and explicit the conditions whereby these theories can be subjected to test. Each science may be named according to the range of facts it studies. The words 'natural', 'human', 'social', need not enter into the matter at all. Sociology is a valid science of all forms of society, just as biology is a valid science of all forms of organic life.

There is, then, no problem here.

(c) Testing existing theories

There is a third important element of our common sense experience which obviously makes necessary a scientific study of society—and that is the existence of many theories about the nature and destiny of man and society, each of which not only claims to be true, but also continuously, and sometimes hotly, clamours for our attention and allegiance. Furthermore these theories challenge us with extremely important decisions, for, in supporting one or other of them, we are not only acknowledging the truth of one and the falsity of others, but are aiding or constraining some of the most important struggles for power in the world about us.

Sometimes these are total 'world-views': as ambitious, if not more ambitious, in their scope than even the most grandiose sociological theory ever presented, and asking for our commitment to them on far less adequate grounds.

There are, for example, the varieties of 'Christianity', which offer a total world-view of the author of the universe, the creation and destiny of the world, the sinfulness and salvation of man, and a detailed theory of civil society. Similarly, all the other religions of the world claim the truth and significance of their enormous theories of the universe and man and the nature of spiritual reality. In addition there are the total world-views of a pseudo-philosophical and pseudo-scientific nature like Communism—offering, in the same way, theories about the entire nature of reality, and, within this context, total theories about the origins, growth, and destiny of human society. And, far less imposing than such systems of thought, are what one might call (if it were not for their grave seriousness) the 'comic-opera' theories of society—such as Mussolini's directives for 'Fascism', or Hitler's struggle for 'National Socialism'. How, we now ask ourselves in amazement, could men ever have taken seriously a 'credo' containing such fantastic, reiterated phrases as 'Mussolini is always right'; 'The Duce is always right'? Surely, we now think, men must have been demented to accept such nonsense? Yet millions of men were, and are swayed in this manner.*

All these 'theories' are far more grandiose, and rest on far less reliable evidence than any theory proposed by sociology, yet the greater part of the human race accepts one or other of them. And here, it behoves the critics of sociology to examine self-critically those positions of thought and belief other than sociology which they themselves accept. Do they submit their 'Christian' or their 'Communist' theories to the same critical tests which they require of sociology? Many who reject a sociological theory—say that of Spencer—because of doubts concerning its validity or sufficiency of evidence, are ready to embrace a far more pretentious world-view on far less adequate foundations. Many who will not accept what Durkheim says about suicide are quite ready to accept what religious 'authorities' say about the 'Trinity', the 'Crucifixion', 'Reincarnation', 'Nirvana', and even ecclesiastical injunctions about the use of 'the pill'. Unless these questions of the 'criteria' of knowledge are examined carefully, this is, of course, sheer perversity.

Then there are the more limited creeds concerning specific social problems: like the belief of the Calvinistic church of South Africa that God created white and black men quite distinctly different from each other, and that the organization of society should reflect his will; or the theories of political parties about 'laissez faire' or 'collectivism', and the like.

As we well know, such theories—large or small, limited or all-

* viz. the waving of Chairman Mao's little red book. An excellent book on some of these political positions is: *The Social and Political Doctrines of Contemporary Europe* by Michael Oakeshott, London, Basic Books, 1940.

embracing; many of them ill-founded—are legion. They continually, in our day to day lives, seek our support, and they exercise a great deal of power in society.

The sole point upon which I wish to lay very great emphasis, and it is something which we encounter in all our common-sense bewilderments and deliberations, is this:

In the face of these competing theories—theories which are of vital importance in that human happiness or misery to some extent depends upon our acceptance or rejection of them—we are in need of some reliable basis of judgment. We need a body of well-founded knowledge which will, at least, give us the necessary basis for *testing* these theories, for *adjudicating between them*. Unless we pursue those methods which will establish the most reliable knowledge about human society it is possible to attain, we shall have no grounds whatever on which to exercise reliable judgment. And unless we achieve clear and reliable ideas about the validity and adequacy of methods of study themselves; about what constitutes good evidence and grounds of testability; we shall not even be in a position to know which, amongst all these theories, is at least the most responsible and reliable in the procedures it adopts, and the claims that it makes.

Two points are worth noting and realising very clearly here.

(i) The development, the clear statement, and the wide dissemination of a science of man and society is of the greatest urgency and importance not only from the *positive* point of view of giving us new knowledge and new theories; but also from the *negative* point of view of demolishing theories which are false; of giving us a *mode of critical analysis* which we can readily use to *test* any theory which people put before us, or seek to impose upon us. To my mind this *negative* contribution is of the greatest *positive* worth. It is a very considerable step—to know how to eliminate error; to be able to clear the ground of rubbish—whether old and hallowed or new and brash—even though we may not yet be in a position to replace it with a new building. At least we shall be able to see clearly within the range of our known uncertainties instead of continuing to be misguided by 'certain' attachments to what is obsolete and useless.

(ii) The second point of interest here is that, willy-nilly, these various religious and ideological theories, in their competition for people's allegiance, all drive men increasingly to the necessity of scientific investigation. Indeed, their moralizing zeal finds it difficult to deny its worth. If these theories claim to possess the *truth*, then they should not fear or disapprove of, but should only encourage, any scientific activities which aim at seeking and *demonstrating* the truth more clearly and more fully. One clear sign of the bogus nature of any such group or theory is that they discountenance, discourage, or forbid the pursuit of free inquiry. But since, fortunately, several such groups are *competing* with each other, perplexity increases and the need for extending careful scientific study becomes ever more apparent.

In facing the claims of *existing* theories, then, (quite apart from proposing theories of its own) social science has to clarify the criteria of validity and truth and the procedures for ensuring these in studying the nature of man and society, and this, too, is a *necessary* and extremely *useful* function of which our common sense misgivings and disturbances completely convince us.

Sociology, then, according to common sense, is a *necessary* science. For a wide range of purposes, we *need* it. But let us now analyse our common-sense assumptions still further, to see what they imply about the subject-matter of this science, and the kinds of method that it seems to dictate. Our common-sense assumptions may contain more than we suppose.

(2) Common-Sense Assumptions about the Nature of Man and Society

(a) Order and regularity prevail in society as they do in nature
Remembering the way in which Whitehead described the regularities of events which we perceive in nature; the constancy and order of the connections between them; our common-sense experience equally impresses upon us the fact that order, regularity, constancy of expectation, also prevail in society.

Sometimes, hearing critics attacking sociology on the grounds of the *unpredictability* of human behaviour, one would think that, from their point of view, human society was an ever-changing scene of completely spontaneous, arbitrary, and always varied individual behaviour. On the contrary, however, our common sense experience of social life is that it is characterized (sometimes depressingly*) by repetition, by a continual 'sameness', and, furthermore, a sameness that most people cannot avoid. Indeed, within this routine pattern of activities, we find that individual men and women, in their

---

*This was certainly the view of Oscar Wilde. For him it was the artist who conveyed truth in *style*, while—he wrote: 'Life—poor, probable, uninteresting human life—tired of repeating herself for the benefit of Mr Herbert Spencer, scientific historians, and the compilers of statistics in general, will follow meekly after him . . .'. See *The Decay of Lying*.

personalities and behaviour, come to be characterized by deep-rooted habits and almost unalterable ways of doing, saying, and even thinking things.

We do *not* find, in our everyday life, that everything in human nature and society is completely arbitrary and spontaneous, differing from day to day. We do *not* find Mr Smith going to work at 9.0 a.m. on one day, 10.0 a.m. the next, and 3.0 p.m. the next; or taking a holiday on Monday, or Wednesday, or Friday, or all three—quite arbitrarily during each following week, simply according to his whimsical feeling as to whether he wants to go fishing, or go to the cinema. People do not and cannot choose, solely according to a momentary personal whim, what time they will go to work. It is, in fact, just the reverse. People have, and for definite reasons, to start and finish work together; so that *every* morning we shall find millions of Mr Smiths standing on the platforms of their same local stations at exactly the same time, all contributing to the 'rush hour' in our towns and cities. Usually, too, Mr Smith will not only be *there* at the same time, he will be wearing the same kind of clothes, carrying the same kind of newspaper, in the same kind of way, saying the same kind of thing to the self-same companions—or, perhaps, being predictably the same as ever in that he does *not* speak to his travelling companions but blocks them from view by his open newspaper, and then, after having read the main articles, settles down to the crossword puzzle—in the same corner of the same page! Regularity is the rule. The man who has the 'Mail' on Monday, the 'Mirror' on Tuesday, the 'Times' on Wednesday, the 'Telegraph' on Thursday, and sits in his carriage on Friday with no newspaper at all—naked to every suspicious eye—is not only an exception: he simply does not exist! In the same way, we find that the way in which children are registered at birth; the way they are 'christened'; the ways in which they are educated; the ways in which people get married; the ways in which they vote, worship, bury their dead . . . are all characterized by a very marked order, regularity, repetition.

Now this does not mean at all that, in our common-sense experience, we believe that people *could not* behave differently *if they tried*. We do not think they are all 'determined', like parts of a machine. All we are saying, and all that we need to say, is that, almost invariably, they *do not* behave differently. On the basis of this regularity it is quite obvious (and it is *testable*) that we can both know and *predict* what people will do. This is nothing akin to fortune-telling. Neither does it make any metaphysical assumptions about human nature being 'determined' or 'free'. It means only that we can know so accurately the pattern of institutional rules, procedures, expectations and constraints in which individuals are involved that we can say that they will behave in certain predictable ways. Indeed, if they do *not*, we shall have to look for a special explanation.

Without wanting to press the matter too far at this stage, and without wishing to imply even the vaguest suggestion of 'determinism' (which, in fact, I would want emphatically to reject), it is surely true, in our common-sense experience, that we find individuals predictable even at a much more intimate level than the broad regularities of social behaviour which we have been considering. People *do* become habituated to certain modes of thought, feeling, speech and behaviour, and manifest these habits even in spite of themselves. A husband and wife come to know each other so closely that they can tell almost exactly what each of them is going to do, say, or even think, in response to particular situations. They can, and do, predict one another's reactions, and, indeed, even if they do this openly, whether jokingly or otherwise, and even if the other is fully aware that his or her response has been predicted, they will, nonetheless, still find themselves slipping into the predicted habits in spite of themselves. Indeed, it is when the *exceptional* reaction takes place which they did *not* predict, and did *not* expect, that close partners look up and 'take notice', wondering what is wrong.

People—though being able to exercise choice in their conduct, and to do much by way of self-discipline to shape and govern their own characters—are, nonetheless, not *super*human. They live within a social context and comply with its demands. In many ways they are quite predictable, and it is, if properly understood, a necessary corollary of character-formation that they should be so. Furthermore it is difficult to see why anybody should be distressed that this should be thought to be so. To hear the bitterness of some critics, one would think it was degrading or humiliating to human beings to maintain that they were predictable; instead of being, on the contrary, a simple recognition of their humanity, and an accommodation to the reciprocal requirements of human life. A humanity, we may note, that, curiously enough, critics admire when it is displayed in novels or plays. In a novel, we come to love a character because we come to *know* him: so intimately that we know exactly what he will do if such and such a thing happens. We know that, in 'War and Peace', Pierre will be forever wandering round Russia through some vague feeling of wanting to see what is going on. And when that event *does* happen, and when the character *does* react as we had expected of him, we have a warm sense of affection for him. We love him because we know him so well; and consequently we understand and forgive, with humorous affection, all his little foibles. When Charles Dickens has Ebenezer Scrooge snarling at the world in general in every third paragraph, or has Uriah Heep squirming his way repulsively through every third line, we think, with admiration and affection, what a fine portrayer of human character he is; but if a sociologist assumes that we can arrive at clear, testable descriptions about the regularities of human society, he is thought to be guilty of dehumanizing the race. Again, there is some kind of perversity among critics here.

At any rate, our common sense has no difficulty whatever either in recognizing or in admitting these matters.

There is a further fact that common sense knows very well.

Though it is true that all people *could* behave differently *if they set themselves out to do so* (that is to say, if they chose to be as unduly perverse as the critics) it is clear (*a*) that social chaos would ensue if they did, and consequently this spontaneous variety could not continue for long,* and (*b*) that, in fact, the nature of social necessity is such† that they would have either to submit to a certain modicum of conformity with the accepted regularities of community life, or be put into prison or otherwise constrained. And even the ways of being constrained and put into prison in any society are predictable and regular.

If, for example, Mr Smith stopped away from work whenever he felt the slightest inclination to do so—his inclination being the only excuse he offered to his employer when questioned about his behaviour—we all know that Mr Smith would not keep his job for long. This, again, is a prediction that can be readily tested by anyone. If, in Britain, given the nature of British institutions, a man openly married three women at the same time, or decided not to bother registering the deaths of his relatives but simply disposed of them under the rubbish heap at the bottom of the garden, or undertook some similarly unusual forms of behaviour; we all know that he would soon find himself in either a penal, or a mental institution. And that, with little doubt, is where he ought to be.

Indeed, the constraints of society are such that we can even predict, with reasonable nicety, which kind of individual eccentricity and deviance will be permitted, and which kinds will be forbidden and prevented, either by social disapproval or by the very heavy hand of authority.

* We might note that this is a ground for a testable prediction that people who are in any way bound in close proximity to each other in shared social life *cannot* be irregular and completely ungoverned in their behaviour for long. They *must* abide by certain regular rules, obligations, and constraints. They *must* settle upon some *order* of behaviour. It is then up to the critics to find a human group of which this is not true!

† This is not to *justify* all forms of social constraint, only to claim that they exist.

(b) Society is something more than a collection of individuals
The experience which we all have of the rules, obligations and constraints in social life makes another important fact quite clear: *social institutions are something more than the individuals who are constrained by them.*

This, again, is not to belittle individuals at all. It is simply to recognize that the rules and the social organizations which constrain our behaviour are, in a very real sense, *there*; independent of our-selves and of any other individual. Their existence is not just a matter of our feelings about them, or of any other individual's feelings about them. They exist in the general organization and the collective conditions of society. And they exert definite constraints upon us; playing an extensive and important part in influencing our behaviour and, more deeply, in shaping the innermost nature of our personalities.

For the moment, we need not ask how or why these institutions came into being; how they have come to be what they are. What is certain is that, in our common experience, they are *there:* in legal and constitutional rules and precedents, in established governmental procedures, in the ritual of religious worship and the organized hierarchy of the clergy, in the routine administrative rules and practices of civil service departments and local government author-ities, and the like, together with all the symbols which clothe them: the Crown of the Realm; the Wigs and Robes of Judges and the Court Procedures themselves; the Cross of Christ, the magnificence of Cathedrals; the music and the liturgy of services, and so on. And they must be investigated, known, and taken into account as the definite institutional fabric of society in any explanation of the approved regularities, or the 'frowned upon' irregularities, of human behaviour.

It seems clear to us, then, even at the level of common sense, that we cannot understand and explain the many institutional regularities of a society simply in terms of the personalities of the individuals who happen now to be living within it. The social heritage has a definite, historical nature. On the contrary, it seems true that we can only fully understand the lives, personalities and characters of the individuals now living within it by taking into account the many-sided influences upon them of this social setting of their birth, upbringing, and pattern of adult obligation.

This also makes it plain to us that Psychology—'the scientific study of experience and behaviour', and Sociology—'the scientific study of human society' are essentially linked in some way. Perhaps, even, they should not be separate studies at all.

It also makes it abundantly clear that any *full* explanation of social *change* must be very difficult indeed to achieve. It is clear, at least, that both social institutions *and* individuals have to be taken into account. Obviously, to some extent, social institutions have themselves, *in the past*, been shaped by individuals in their relations with each other, and by their joint, group activities. But these individuals, too, in their own time, must have been influenced by the social and cultural setting of their own lives. It is obviously difficult to disentangle 'psychological' and 'social' factors. Certainly, no *simple* conceptions of social 'causation' could possibly seem to be adequate. A very careful and detailed analysis is clearly necessary.

One point we might make especially clear in concluding is that—of course we are not saying that something called 'SOCIETY' exists like the material structure of some building in total independence of the people who live within it. The regularities of social rules and organizational procedure which are laid down in law, government, religion, and the like, persist because they are practised and carried on by generation after generation of people who become, as it were, living bearers of their social heritage. The institutional regularities which are something *more* than individuals thus come to be embodied in the collective life of individuals in their associations with each other. The two are very closely knit together, though they are not to be equated with each other. Clearly, if we use the word '*structure*' of social institutions within which, or in terms of which, individuals live their social life, we are referring to something definite—though *not* entirely independent of individuals. If, therefore—when we make this point—someone were to charge us with the error of thinking of 'Society' as being something of a metaphysical nature, totally 'over and above' individuals, and actually existing in some form totally separate from all of them—they would be making a false caricature of our position.

At the same time, it is interesting and chastening to think that, frequently, in the ruins of times past, in the records of civilizations gone to their destruction, it is the evidence of the *institutions* of a people which remains. The individuals are the dust and air that blow about the walls which they built. In the structure of these derelict buildings, in the artefacts, the documents, the legal codes, the records of contracts made according to fixed procedures, lies a knowledge of the institutions within the framework of which a community of people lived their social life. And it is within the context of this knowledge (when it is at last elaborated) that we are then able to begin to conjecture as to what sort of ideas, emotional attachments, aesthetic experiences, these individuals may have had. Thus, an Egyptologist like, say, Sir Flinders Petrie, does not write initially about particular persons who were fan-bearers or mat-spreaders or clerks to the Pharaoh; he writes a book (based on the study of scripts, ornaments, buildings and paintings) on *The Social Life of Ancient Egypt*, and the book gives an account of the framework of institutions of that ancient civilization. Only within this reconstruction of a *society* do we begin to catch the flavour of the feelings, ideas, actions of the individuals who lived there.

> 'My name is Ozymandias, king of kings:
> Look on my works, ye Mighty, and despair.
> ...... Round the decay
> Of that colossal wreck, boundless and bare,
> The lone and level sands stretch far away.'

So wrote Shelley. Ozymandias is gone, as are all those who once gathered in multitudes beneath his sway. But some ornament, some piece of wrinkled parchment, some weapon, some stone or clay tablet of a legal transaction, has outlived them; and it is from these that a reconstruction of the 'society' may be possible; by means of which we may then come close to the feelings and thoughts of the actual individuals who experienced them.

In some curious way which we cannot readily understand or express, a 'society', an interconnected network of social institutions, is the shared creation of many generations of individuals, which has come to have an existence, a power, both massive and subtle, with even something of sanctity about it, which then cumulatively goes into the shaping of the nature of subsequent individuals. What, for example, is patriotism, if it is not a love for our social heritage—something more than and greater than ourselves as individuals—which made us, in large part, what we are.*

In some way, society helps actually to create and enrich, as well as to confine and constrain, our innermost individuality. Society, somehow, is a *creative* reality. It is a distinct creative process in nature. It is a cumulative historical creative process without which the nature of humanity cannot be understood.

(c) But society is rooted in basic aspects of our human nature.
Having said that social institutions are certainly something more than individuals, we do nonetheless feel very strongly, in our common-sense awareness, that many human associations are *natural:* both in the sense that they spring from those inclinations, impulses, emotions, needs, with which we are by nature endowed; and in the

---

* An excellent example of this blend of the recognized dependence of the fineness of individual character upon the accumulated qualities of a social tradition is to be found in Pericles' funeral speech. (Thucydides: *History of the Peloponnesian War*. Book 2. Chapter 4).

sense that our own individual nature seems to need them for its own fulfilment. We feel that we could not fully *be* individuals excepting in the context of continuous social commitments. To some extent to be natural *is* to be social. For us, at any rate, whatever may be the case for other creatures, to speak of the *individual* as something separate and distinct from the *social* seems itself to be false. It seems, somehow, to violate the actuality of our experience. The two terms—natural and social—somehow embrace each other. *To be human means both.*

For example, from the beginning we have parents, brothers, sisters with whom we develop a deep and abiding bond (though by no means only harmonious). Later, we ourselves desire, and get involved in, sexual mating, and—having children—feel love and feelings of protection for them, and a sense of identity and intimate responsibility which is difficult to describe, but which gives us a concern for the continued security and stability of the basis of social life which we hope they will enjoy. And we are not members only of one or two families—but of a much wider community of families with whom we have to co-operate in the economic tasks of earning our living, in the governmental and legal tasks of deciding and upholding rules and judging the people who break them. We also experience a moral need. We feel duties towards our own kin, and a powerful sense of justice or injustice with regard to the ways in which they are treated by others or by the community in general; we naturally need rules of reciprocal conduct whereby mutual right-dealing may be assured and disputes resolved.

According to our common-sense experience, then, *society is natural.* All these elements of social organization are necessary aspects of our natural life. We have no difficulty in understanding or explaining this. It is obvious to us. Indeed, if anyone maintained that society was *not* naturally attendant upon the satisfaction of our many needs, we should require an explanation of this point of view from them, and we think they would be hard pressed to find one. Society may have become so complicated as to perplex us in many ways; some groups may have become more privileged and powerful than we think warranted in terms of social justice, so that we may feel opposed to society as it is; but whatever disagreements, problems and conflicts we experience within it at present, we know, fundamentally, that co-operative activity in society is natural and right for us, and that total isolation is unnatural, intolerable, and, indeed, inhuman. No individual could possibly fulfil his natural impulses and propensities without associating with others.

It follows, then, from our common-sense experience, that some of our associations and institutions can be readily understood, and explained to a degree, in terms of our natural, instinctual and emotional needs, the interests, purposes, and ideals related to them, and the kinds of social regulations and more general interests and purposes which they entail and which go beyond them. If any sociologist therefore speaks of the 'functions' of social institutions in terms of the needs or purposes they serve, or the ways in which they are linked together in their working, we shall find no difficulty whatever in understanding this. If, for example, it is said that one 'function' of judicial institutions is to resolve disputes, or that one 'function' of governmental institutions is, in a formally agreed way, to take decisions centrally which are to be binding upon all, we shall find this a perfectly straightforward and sensible way of speaking. It is a perfectly clear idea. Indeed, if anyone maintained that institutions could *not* be understood, in part, in terms of their 'functions', the needs and purposes they served and the ways in which they worked interdependently, and that this was being 'teleological' and 'unscientific' because it was an *error* to think that institutions and individuals sought to fulfil certain 'purposes', we would not be puzzled—we would be flabbergasted. Whether it was described by the word 'teleological' or by any other confusing word, we would be unable to see anything wrong with it. Men *are* prompted to communal action by needs; they *do* act in accordance with purposes; they *do* participate in, and, indeed, create institutions and associations which further their purposes. This is a plain fact that we cannot and will not relinquish. And we shall expect any scientific sociological analysis to take it adequately into account. If it does not—we shall think there is something wrong with it.

(d) Society is essentially a historical process

Society, as we have said, is in many ways *natural* to us, but is something *more* than ourselves as individuals. It is something which has a 'traditional power' of its own and which *constrains* us in our behaviour and character—not only in the sense of forcing certain rules upon us, but also by persuading us of the worthwhileness and rightness of certain values and obligations. But in common sense we have no difficulty in explaining or understanding this. It is quite obvious that as a community, over many generations, encounters problems, challenges, difficulties, both among groups within it and with other communities outside it, its social institutions come to possess definite characteristics which are upheld by each generation as being matters of proud achievement. Whether *all* aspects of the social tradition are pleasing to *all* its members is another matter; indeed, this would be very unlikely. Some may be a matter for pride among certain social classes and for disgust among others; but still—the historical continuity of the institutions of the community as a whole is not in any sense difficult to understand.

The essential point here, then, is that—in our common sense—we know, without doubt, that *human society is essentially a historical process* and can only be understood as such. If someone tried to explain social regularities without taking past history into consideration, we would immediately think that there was something very odd, something lacking—indeed, something perverse—in his position. We would think that such a person could not properly have understood the nature of the facts he was studying. Our methods of studying society, then, must be in some way historical. They must enable us to investigate society as a set of changing, growing, developing social institutions and social traditions.

Our common-sense convictions about this point are so powerful and immediate as to entertain no denial. When we see, for example, the ceremonial attaching to the British Monarchy, or the ritual procedures in the election campaign for the President of the United States—we know completely that these traditions cannot possibly be explained without a knowledge of their nature and changes in the past. Similarly, when we see the conflicts between Trade Unions and Employers in relation to a 'Prices and Incomes Policy' of the Government; or the revolutionary conflicts that have burst upon institutions of higher education in France; we know that these cannot be explained unless we have a knowledge of how and why these institutions came into existence, and how they have changed in changing circumstances to become what they are now.

This fact of historical development also gives us a clear ground for understanding the obvious *differences* that exist in social traditions throughout the world. Our common-sense awareness of the fact that the family, the religion, the form of government of, let us say, China, are different from ours, is readily understood in that we know that the people of China have had a set of geographical conditions and historical circumstances very different from our own. Different social traditions are bound to develop when communities confront different kinds of situations. Though we cannot possibly claim to *know* the details of the historical causes of these differences, there is no obscurity, no insurmountable difficulty in our minds concerning this point. We know very well that our own society has changed even in our own brief lifetime, and that it is impossible to understand the nature of our society *now* without knowing of the problems, conflicts, and disturbances which we ourselves have experienced, which our parents experienced twenty years or so before we were born, and which have brought about these changes. For example, many present characteristics of our society are an outcome

59

of the last war; the problems of the war itself and the post-war period; and any explanation of the nature of society *now* must take these historical facts into account. And if this is true of our own period, it is very likely to be true of any other period, and of any other society.

Again, then, if anyone tries to explain social institutions *without* taking history into account, we shall want him to explain how he can manage to do so, and on what grounds he should want to try.

(e) We expect societies, nonetheless, to be basically similar to each other

The fact that, in common sense, we feel it necessary to understand the *differences* in societies, is one aspect of another of our deep-rooted assumptions, namely: that all human societies must be basically alike. They must have something in common with each other. They must have some basic similarities in their forms of association as well as differences of detail. They must encounter the same basic problems—even though these may well have been experienced in the context of different circumstances and have developed differently. This common sense assumption is rooted in the very simple fact that, despite historical differences, we are all human beings; members of one biological species. Consequently, we expect our own natural needs, problems, concerns, and ways of dealing with them to be shared by men and women everywhere.

For example, we expect all communities to regulate sexual behaviour; to protect young children; to care for old people; to have some form of 'marriage' for the foundation of the family groups in society. We expect all peoples to instruct their children in the skills and knowledge they themselves possess, and to educate them in their values and beliefs. We expect all peoples to establish some form of government and some procedures of law for taking central decisions about matters of common concern and for interpreting and applying these decisions with regard to particular disputes between individuals and groups. We expect all peoples to divide the many jobs of the community amongst themselves in some systematic way; to allocate different jobs to different people in accordance with some notion of their general fittedness for the work. We expect all peoples to devise rules of property—making clear the rights and responsibilities of legitimate control over the material things of society, and guaranteeing a security of possessions to all.

Different societies, with different historical traditions, will have different ways of dealing with these problems; their institutions are likely to have *forms* which are different from our own; but the needs and the problems underlying the institutions are the same everywhere, and because they are the outcome of our universal human nature.

We expect *universal similarities* in human societies, then, despite some differences; and it is a simple common sense matter to see how this assumption can be tested by comparing societies (both of the past and of the present) the world over, and by gradually achieving a more detailed and precise analysis of what human needs are, and what institutional provisions are made for them. *Analysis* and *comparison* are therefore essential procedures in any reflective and careful method. There is nothing difficult or un-clear about this.

With reference to this assumption, too, we often feel—in terms of our common sense—very suspicious of some of the claims which seem to be made by some modern social anthropologists that human nature, human experience and behaviour, is not only widely *different* among societies, but is *infinitely variable*. When some statements *seem* to say that in some societies sexual behaviour is not regulated at all; that there are no rules of private ownership whatsoever; that children are not loved and cared for but often killed without concern; that no forms of central government and law exists whatsoever; and so on . . . we feel, even though the anthropologist has the evidence, and we have not, that they must be somehow mistaken. We are perfectly ready to agree that human beings may differ to some extent, even to a great extent, in their modes of behaviour and their varieties of social feeling and regulation, but—and about this we feel convinced—not *so* much. We cannot believe that human nature is *infinitely malleable*. We cannot believe that the variations of society can be such as to eradicate basic elements of our human nature, and the common kinds of need for social regulation to which they give rise. The varieties are at least, we think, bound to be variations upon certain very fundamental and common themes.

(f) Societies do exist as distinguishable wholes

So far, we have been considering the various associations and institutions of men and communities in the widest and most general way, but this question of similarities and differences between distinct historical societies leads us to another common-sense assumption which, with unmistakable clarity, we possess. It is very simple, but it is also very important, and must be noted.

It is: that *societies*, as *total systems of interconnected institutions, do exist;* that they are *entities* which can be clearly distinguished from each other, even though some of them may well share, and have shared in the past, common cultural features and influences. We do not have the slightest difficulty in thinking that France, Germany, Great Britain, Italy, are separate *societies*, having systems of social institutions with distinguishable characteristics, in spite of the fact that they have all been shaped in important ways by the same elements of culture, thought, beliefs, and even by common institutional developments such as the Christian Church and earlier common institutions of 'feudalism'. If we were pressed on this, we would probably say that the chief factor leading us to distinguish one *society* (as a whole) from another is the fact that it is a separate independent *political community*. Its members acknowledge a common allegiance to the one central political authority and not to other authorities outside. They abide by the laws which apply to them all, and consider themselves citizens of this one society, accepting the rights and duties which these laws entail. And this, of course, does not prevent us from being able to distinguish differing 'cultural groups' or 'regions' or 'local traditions' *within* the same single society. Wales, Scotland, and Northern Ireland have certain distinct differences from England, but all constitute, in a very firm allegiance, the single society of Great Britain, which is an entirely distinguishable from other nations, and has a system of institutions which the people of all these 'regions' share. In the same way, we would recognize 'culture areas' going *beyond* the political community.

A few important points are well worth disentangling here.

The first (of the very greatest importance) is that we recognize clearly, in our common sense, not only that the many associations of men are characterized by order and regularity; but also that this order is one simple aspect of the fact that all the parts (the particular institutions) of a society are intimately interconnected with each other; mutually influencing each other in the ongoing process of social life; and coming to be pervaded with the same general character. We see quite clearly that the many associations of a community form an *interconnected pattern*; a *system*; and the total system is what we call the *society*.

Thus, in Great Britain, the form of central and local government administration, of the law, of property and economic organization, of education, of communications, of the Churches, of marriage and the family, and all other associations besides, are inextricably interwoven. So much is this so, that we know quite well that it is impossible to understand any one of these excepting in the context of the others. We cannot understand the law, or, let us say, the institution of marriage, excepting in relation to government, religion and morals. We cannot understand the educational system excepting with reference to social classes, private and public sources of wealth, religion and the welfare policies of government. The same is true of all other institutions without exception. Again, too, history reinforces this point, for this *is* a *system* of institutions because they have all developed together in the closest relationship with each other throughout the experience of many generations. It is clear, because of this close interconnection, that if change occurs in any one of these institutions it is likely to bring about some sort of change in the rest.

On the basis of our common sense, then, we clearly expect that a full understanding of any one social institution must involve the understanding of the whole society of which it is a part. *Sociological* analysis must be an analysis of *systems of social regularities*; and no account of a separate institution or a particular social change can possibly be adequate unless it has been investigated within the context of such analysis. What we are really saying here, in short, is that *it is our awareness of the existence of total systems of social regularities which makes sociology necessary as a science.* The existence of *societies*, of *social systems*, and what this implies for seeking knowledge of any aspect of them, is the crucial fact, the distinctive point of departure, the distinctive orientation of sociology as a subject.

If, then, sociologists, in pursuit of clear analysis, liken a society to an 'organism', and speak of the 'functional interconnection of institutions in the social system as a whole', it will be perfectly clear to us what they mean. There is nothing obscure about it. We actually find it in our experience. Our common sense tells us that this way of thinking about the nature of society is necessary.

A further important point is that it is quite clear to us that if we are to compare examples of social institutions carefully, in order to understand their nature—we can only do this reliably by taking into account the total societies of which they form a part. Since we cannot understand a *single* institution in *one* society without considering its characteristics and place within the whole *system* of which it is a part; so we cannot compare the same institution in *different* societies without taking the differences of these total social systems into account. This clearly presents a very great problem indeed: how are we to manage comparative studies of this kind? And it leads us to a further consideration.

(g) In common sense, we distinguish 'types' of society
As soon as we stop to think about the matter, we find that it is, in fact, common-sense practice to compare and contrast social institutions within the context of total societies, and we try to manage this, in our rough and ready way, by *dividing societies into types*.

For example, if it is discovered that the Soviet Union has put a space capsule into orbit successfully, but that this had received no mention in the press *before* the event, we say:—'Ah, yes. That is typical of communist countries (societies). The government will only release news which is beneficial for its own purposes. If the launching had been a failure, we would have heard nothing about it.' 'In democratic countries (societies)', we might continue, 'the failures are as widely publicised as the successes. It is thought that the people should know the truth of what is going on and so the government is continually bombarded by alert criticism from the press.'

We obviously believe that different 'kinds' of society have 'typically' different institutions, and that the entire network of institutions in the one type has an over-all character which is qualitatively different from that of the other. We speak of 'totalitarian societies', for example, to include Fascist as well as Communist societies, and to distinguish them from 'liberal' societies. We also speak—when we are comparing different ways of life—of 'capitalist' societies, 'feudal' societies, 'primitive' societies, and so on.

It is quite clear from this that we believe that societies can be *classified into types* according to certain very well marked characteristics; and also that illuminating comparisons of them can be made, giving a sharper understanding of their distinctive institutions, and providing us with a certain basis of judgment. In our heated day-to-day arguments, for example, we compare the educational system, the families, the religions, of these different types of society. If sociologists pursue this same method, then, trying to do more carefully and methodically what we already see the necessity of doing approximately or roughly in our everyday arguments, we shall readily see both the point and the good sense of their efforts.

It is worthwhile to draw attention to a further point here.

Often, we find that we do not compare societies only as 'total' types, which differ *altogether* in *all* their institutions. Sometimes, we compare them because of the *dominance* of one or two *specific* characteristics which *seem* to us very important. For example, we may compare societies which are chiefly 'Roman Catholic' societies with societies which are chiefly 'Muslim'. These societies may, in other respects, be similar to each other. They may, for example, all be peasant societies in which sudden wealth has been produced for small minorities by the discovery of oil, and in which vast industrial changes are just beginning. But we may select the one dominant characteristic, the religion of the societies, because we feel it to be relevant to the particular problem which we have in mind; in this case, perhaps, the different attitudes of the people to social and economic change. Similarly, sometimes we may compare 'capitalist' or 'socialist' societies for some purpose (for example, the development of technology, or bureaucracy, or 'managerial élites') and may ignore the fact that some are Roman Catholic, some Muslim, some Jewish, and the like.

The point which is worth very considerable emphasis here is that, even in our common sense, we do not think it always necessary to think of our 'types' of society in terms of an *exhaustive* description of *all* institutions. We think it useful, sometimes, to distinguish 'types' in terms of one selected feature which, we have a strong suspicion, is the most significant feature for the kind of understanding we are seeking. This means, too, that we do not suppose, in thinking about the problems of human societies, that we must set up a rigid set of 'Types of Society' which—for ever after—will be the only basis, the true basis, of comparative analysis. On the contrary, we think that the distinguishing of 'types' of society should be left fairly flexible, since it will depend a lot on the problem we are concerned about. A social scientist can be left free to clarify his own particular 'types' for his specific purposes of explanation at the time. The test of whether the 'types' he constructed were worthwhile would simply be the degree to which they proved useful in leading to more satisfactory explanations.

(*h*) *Existing societies and social institutions have developed from a simpler, primitive condition*
It also seems obvious to us (whether or not it may be proved by more sophisticated study) that all the complex civilizations of man, all the highly complicated modern societies which employ such sophisticated levels of knowledge and skill, must have *developed* through some long historical process of struggle, conflict, and effort, from earlier, smaller and simpler groups which were very primitive in their conditions. By primitive, we are perfectly clear what we mean. We do not mean anything derogatory or blameworthy: we mean 'simple', 'rudimentary', 'undeveloped', not possessing the cumulative achievements of civilization. For example, a mud hut in some ancient encampment, the summer tent of an Eskimo tribe, or a rural labour-er's cottage in eighteenth-century Britain, are thought of as 'primitive' dwellings when compared with well-designed and well-built houses of today incorporating modern technical skills. But this applies, we feel, not only to material things, like houses, but also to social arrangements and forms of social organization. For example, we think that economic organization, the division of labour and rules of property, must have been very simple in the earliest human groups of hunters and food gatherers; and that their language, their education, their communications must all have been a matter of direct face-to-face contact. Their government, their laws, their ways of resolving disputes, indeed, even their very conceptions of justice, must, we suppose, have been very simple compared with those of later, larger, settled civilizations and modern industrial societies.

This, at least, is what we are strongly disposed to think. And there is plenty of evidence in ordinary (non-sociological) writings to show that, in general, people *do* think that not only material things, like tools, weapons, and vehicles, but also social institutions, have *developed* to meet new contingencies. A good example can be seen in a small, straightforward history of Methodism, written in 1903. The author, W. B. Fitzgerald, writes as follows:

'The circuit,* like every other part of our organization, has had a gradual development. And just as in the Northrop loom, with its electric motor, its delicate adjustment, its lightning speed, and its shuttle changing automatically when the thread is spent, you can still see the old hand-loom of a hundred years ago; so in the modern compact circuit, with its up-to-date methods and economy of power, you can see a distinct relationship to the simple arrangements necessitated by the spread of Methodism in the middle years of the eighteenth century.'

The writer's meaning in this paragraph is perfectly clear and sensible. Again, then, if we find sociologists attempting to uncover, describe, and make clear, the nature and the *developments* of social institutions (and even of total societies) which have taken place, we shall find nothing questionable in this. It will not puzzle or confuse us, but will be seen at once to be necessary.

Two other matters are also clear in connection with this.

Firstly, we are all persuaded in common sense (just as Fitzgerald assumed that he could give us an understanding of the present organization of the Methodist Church by making clear the nature, and reasons for, its past developments) that we cannot possibly have a full and correct understanding of *the institutions of the present*, unless we know the ways in which they have *developed from the past*. We feel that we understand the nature of the Trade Unions as they are *now* much better (including the attitudes of individuals within them) when we know how and why and in connection with what struggles they originated, and how they have developed in the growing complexities of industrialization. We feel we understand the nature of the political parties *now* much better if we have a knowledge of their historical development. And the same is true for any social institution. Furthermore, we know that we can take far more effective action now in seeking to change these social institutions (if we do wish to change them), if we have this full knowledge of their past development as well as a knowledge of their nature in the immediate present. We have already noted this point in insisting earlier upon a *historical* account of social institutions, but here there is

* W. B. Fitzgerald, *The Roots of Methodism*, London: Charles H. Kelly, 1903. p. 144. 'The Circuit', he says, 'is the Methodist parish.'

the additional consideration that we need not only an account in simple terms of chronological sequence, but also an analysis of the cumulative *developments* as institutions come to deal with different and more complex problems. This notion is not easy to distinguish from the idea of 'progress', and we must come back to it later.

We believe, then, on the basis of common sense, that we can only fully understand the present nature of society, in order to act reliably and effectively in relation to it, if we have an understanding of the social developments of the past. *With* this knowledge, we have a perspective within which we can make reliable judgments; *without* it, we are looking only at a final picture, without any understanding of how it came to be what it is and what its many dimensions are.

But secondly, we find that we are interested in how things began and how they developed *simply because we would like to know*. A knowledge of this kind enables us to have a perspective, a clear conception of our own place in the ongoing process of nature and civilization. It gives us a direction and a set of purposes in the context of past human effort*. To state this as simply as possible for the moment, there are at least some of us who like to have a 'world view' within which we have some understanding of our nature and our destiny. As full a knowledge as possible of the development of human society from its origins up to the present time gives us a necessary part of such a 'world view'. This is a highly unfashionable point to which we shall return later; but, for many of us at any rate, it is important.

We might note, however, before leaving these considerations, that in connection with them, any science of society is immediately faced with a very serious criticism. If so much knowledge of a historical and comparative nature is needed to understand our present-day institutions, our knowledge must always be incomplete. It will always be impossible for individuals or groups to know so much.

Common sense has only one view about this criticism. It must concede it. It is true. Our knowledge must always fall far short of completeness. Even so, we shall see that even this obvious and very clearly known inadequacy of our limitations can be turned to very great advantage in laying down certain rules of method. It has long been said that a knowledge of our ignorance is the beginning of wisdom. And it has not been commonly understood that when Socrates made this the centre of his teaching, he was not speaking simply of his own limitations—he was making clear the perennial

---

* This does not mean that we will blindly follow the directions of change which we discover have taken place. We may wish to oppose them. But, whether we support them or try to alter them, the perspective of knowledge gives us a meaningful basis for our judgment and action.

condition of man. Putting the matter very minimally, we can be liberated from making great mistakes in attempting the impossible— if we know it *is* impossible. Knowing what is, and is not, feasible, we can provide ourselves with rules of procedure which will delimit and sharpen our knowledge accurately. Furthermore—knowing the limitations of our *knowledge*—we are able to formulate sound criteria of *judgment*.

(i) In common sense, we believe in progress
Just as we believe that social institutions have *developed*, so, at least in many cases, we believe they have *improved*. And therefore just as we find it necessary to think of human society in terms of development, so we also find it sensible to think of it in terms of *progress*. We are, of course, not so foolish as to think that things *inevitably* get better. We know only too well that quite unforeseen problems can arise: as, for example, unemployment as a result of technical progress. Neither do we think that *everything* improves simultaneously, in a single ongoing sequence. Frequently, as in the example just given, we know that an improvement in one aspect of social life may give rise to what seems to be retrogression in another. There seem always to be losses as well as gains. But, on the whole, we are inclined to believe that our own society is in many ways *better* than that of our parents' or grandparents' day, and certainly much better than the simpler societies with their very limited resources and knowledge. It is better to have our teeth out *with* rather than *without* a pain-killing injection. It is better that *all* children, rather than only a small privileged minority, should be educated. It is better to drink *clean* rather than *contaminated* water. It is better to work eight hours a day for five days a week in safe and pleasant conditions with regulated meal-times, than to work eighteen hours a day for six days in harsh, dismal, insanitary and unsafe conditions with no regulated break-times at all. It is better to be healthy during a long life than unhealthy during a short one. It is better to have some democratic representation in government and to be protected from arbitrary power than to suffer tyranny—whether from kings, nobles, bishops, or employers. The list could be endless!

It seems a feasible question, then, to discover what improvements in their various modes of social life men have achieved, and what can be done to consolidate these gains for everyone and to make matters even better still. Clearly the increase of knowledge about nature and society has given man a greater degree of control over his environment and his affairs; over his own destiny. It is instructive to know in what ways he has used this knowledge for good or ill, and what kinds of improvement it at least makes possible. If it could give us a balanced picture of this kind, sociology would clearly perform a great service in enabling us to direct our efforts to worthwhile objectives. Sociology could be one useful subject among others which could enable us to 'learn how to learn from our experience'.

What is certain is that the question of social progress or social deterioration is always a matter of controversy, and has especially been so during the past two hundred years, during which industrialization has disrupted the long established traditional societies of the past. Since consciously directed progress has become a *possibility* there have always been those reformers who thought they could improve things, and those conservatively inclined traditionalists who were convinced that the golden age was being ever more rapidly torn asunder and destroyed. This controversy is with us, now, in every generation. At the very least, then, it would be a good thing to have the issue clarified; to provide ourselves with a body of knowledge which would give us a basis for careful discussion and reliable judgment. It would be a great gain if sociology could only provide us with a sound *perspective for judgment.*

(j) *Common sense needs science. Scientific method is the only way to answer the questions to which common sense gives rise.*
     There is one final assumption of common sense which is quite a decisive matter.
     Once questions have been raised by a disturbed awareness of the insufficiencies of common sense (i.e. about our knowledge of social institutions, social development, types of society, social progress, and the like), it is clear to common sense that *there is no other way of resolving them excepting by careful reflection, careful observation, the careful statement of theories, and the testing of such theories against the facts we are trying to explain.* In short, common sense knows perfectly well, and is perfectly ready to admit, that *science is the only way of exploring and answering its doubts.*
     Once this matter is put, it becomes perfectly clear that the attempt to establish rigorous scientific methods of investigation is absolutely unavoidable for both the proponents and the opponents of sociology alike. The assertions made by critics against sociology require (if they are to be preferred to the generalizations of sociology) the same kinds of supporting evidence, the same methods of testing, as do those generalizations themselves. For example, if some critic argues with us that there are *no* regularities of institutional behaviour in human society; that human behaviour in society is completely unpredictable; that it is impossible to classify 'types' of society in order to compare social institutions for a better understanding of

their nature, and so on; this critic must not only *assert* these things, he must *demonstrate* that his generalizations are valid and true.* And he must do this by showing us that the facts give better support to his propositions than they do to those of the sociologist.

If it does not sound too dialectical, what this amounts to is that once the common-sense assumptions about man and society are questioned, sociological theory has *necessarily* to be employed even in order sufficiently to criticize (and perhaps deny) sociological findings. The simple truth is that once the issues have been raised, the subject can not only *not* be rejected, it cannot be *avoided*.

The only thing to do, whatever our dispositions towards the subject might be, is to develop it as honestly, clearly, carefully, and rigorously as we can—and see where it gets us. If its methods and findings are proved to be valid, true, and useful in answering the questions we pose, then they must be accepted by both practitioners and critics alike—just as they must be rejected by both if they are invalid, useless and false.

Summary of common-sense assumptions about the nature of man and society

In our common-sense assumptions, then, the following persuasions are clear:

(1) That it is sensible to reflect critically upon our common sense ideas about society and social problems, and develop scientific methods of study (careful analysis, careful observation, the careful statement and testing of theories) in order to establish more precise and reliable knowledge than common sense itself can provide.

(2) That, once this has begun, even critics must adopt it, since the only kind of knowledge about society which can rightly be preferred to that of sociological science will be that which, itself, rests upon more reliable grounds.

(3) That sociology is necessary from the point of view of:

(*a*) practical need,

(*b*) curiosity and the desire for understanding,

(*c*) the testing of those important and influential theories about man and society which already exist.

(4) That sociology, in its development as a science, can rest firmly on the facts:

(*a*) that there is order and regularity in social life, the nature of which can be increasingly clarified by careful study,

(*b*) that this order entails definite rules, procedures, and forms of

---

* It is not seen by some of these critics that the statement: 'You cannot generalize about human behaviour' is itself a vast generalization, which requires support, and *evidence*, not just a loud tone of voice.

social organization which are other than and more than the nature of individuals, and which are known to exert considerable influence upon the behaviour and personalities of individuals,

(c) that these associations are rooted in human needs and purposes of various kinds, and are interdependent in their operation in society as a whole, and that these functions could be further clarified by careful analysis and comparison,

(d) that society is essentially a historical process, that different historical circumstances give rise to different social traditions, and that the science of society must therefore incorporate appropriate historical methods,

(e) that societies must be basically similar to each other despite some historical differences because of the universal features of human nature, and that this gives a firm ground for expecting that significant and useful comparisons between societies can be made, and that universal generalizations are possible.

(f) that societies exist as distinct entities, as entire systems of inter-connected institutions, and that particular institutions can only be properly understood in the context of such systems,

(g) that societies do not seem *infinite* in their variety, but can be divided into '*types*' so that they can be *classified* and *compared* in order to seek general truths about the nature and functions of their institutions,

(h) that society and its many institutions have developed from simpler forms, and that sociology should study this process of development in order fully to understand the present, and in order to act effectively in relation to it,

(i) that it seems very probable that human society has progressed in certain ways, and that it will be useful for the direction of our efforts if we can be clear what the grounds of these improvements are, what improvements have in fact been achieved, and what others might still be made.

Finally:

(5) Scientific sociology need suffer no anxiety as far as critics are concerned, for these critics themselves can only be considered seriously if the methods they employ can be shown to be *more* reliable than those employed by sociology—in which case, of course, sociology would itself accept them since it seeks, in fact, the most reliable methods possible. Sociology can therefore only welcome serious criticism; indeed it should look for it.

As far as criticism of an ill-informed kind, which is what most criticism of sociology is: this may well be irritating, but it can be safely ignored, excepting when it has such telling influence as to misrepresent and despoil the development of the subject (which, unfortunately, is frequently the case in educational circles), in which case it must be attacked—root and branch,

Sociology, then, is the scientific study of all forms of human association: their nature, functions, interconnections, and patterns of change, in various types of society. Beginning with reflection upon common-sense assumptions, and thereafter employing analytical, observational, classificatory, historical and comparative methods, it seeks to establish testable knowledge, testable theories, about these associations.

In what follows, we shall find that all the major contributors to the making of sociology have concentrated upon a refinement upon these initial reflections upon common sense. All have contributed to the clarification of one or other aspect of them, and therefore, taken together, they have created a more exact, satisfactory, and useful system of analysis than common sense itself possesses. But this still remains a system of analysis which, when carefully stated, common-sense can readily understand and approve, because it remains firmly rooted in its own assumptions.

Some Reservations of Common Sense

In concluding this survey of our common sense assumptions, and in order to be completely fair in our presentation of them, we should note a few misgivings about sociology which we also feel. Some of our common-sense assumptions are critical of sociology, as well as being in support of it.

Though all we have said so far seems plausible, there are two or three reasons why we have some initial and serious doubts about the possibilities of creating a satisfactory science of society.

(a) Is the subject-matter of a science of society manageable?
The first of these stems from our rough-and-ready awareness of the difficulties involved. To speak of 'all forms of human association known to us', in the same way as in biology, we speak of 'all known forms of living organism' is, without doubt, perfectly clear, but, when one stops to think of what this involves, one is staggered and overwhelmed by its extent and its detail. It seems in fact, to involve the entirety of human history: the nature of human groups and communities, their manifold rules and social arrangements, from the simplest and earliest hunting and food-gathering societies throughout the whole detailed and diverse development of all the historical civilizations . . . Egypt, Babylon, India, China, Greece, Rome . . . up to and including all the societies of our modern industrial age. Now it

is very clear to us that, for any one of us to know in any detail, even *one* society, even our *own* society, is a job which outwits and defeats us. We do not know completely all the details of even the county, the town, the village, indeed even the street or the family in which we live, and we are doubtful whether we ever could. Surely, then, to speak of a science of *all* human associations is being over-ambitious almost to the point of megalomania?

There are one or two ways of meeting this objection, but, at this point, it will be wise to let it have full weight, for there is no point whatever in denying the extraordinary difficulties experienced by the subject in dealing satisfactorily with its subject-matter. Indeed, it is best to realise these difficulties to the full and never to lose sight of them. In *this* sense, modesty is *always* the only correct attitude. However, two points may be made which are themselves of a common sense nature and which serve at least to allay our first fears arising from what seems a very real and fundamental misgiving.

The first point is very simple and clear. The definition of the 'universe of discourse', the 'range of subject-matter', dealt with by a science does not rest upon the question as to whether *one individual* is capable of comprehending it *all*. The definition is that of the total distinctive area of the subject covered. Within this area of course, and of necessity, individuals will have to specialize. All sociologists can agree about the entire theoretical scope of their subject though each of them will be satisfied to devote his attention and efforts to that particular set of problems which interests him.

The statement that biology is a science of 'all forms of organic life' does not fill us with an immediate sense of the impossibility of comprehending all the many living species in nature, for we know well enough that, though all biologists have a commonly shared outline of the nature, boundaries, and methods of the whole subject, they each of them concentrate upon those problems which interest them. All of them may share the general classification of species, but within that classification they will concentrate upon, let us say, the 'arthropods', or, like Fabre, on the detailed study of insects, or even upon very specific responses which one species may have to a very specific aspect of its 'habitat'. In exactly the same way, sociologists may share a general classificatory schema of the societies which have existed and now exist, but, within this context, they will each concentrate upon that society, that kind of society, or that aspect of society which interests them. Some may be interested in the development of various political constitutions in the Greek City States; some in the relation between morality and law, or religion and education, in an early period of Egyptian society; some in the relationship between myth and social and ecological control in an early period of

Babylon; some in the changing nature of the institution of 'property' in twentieth century Britain; and so on. There is clearly, then, no problem here in terms of the sheer size and complexity of the subject-matter: for no-one would expect any one person to have a know-ledgeable grasp of the whole. The definition of a subject does not depend upon that.

The second point need be reiterated only briefly here, though it will be seen to be of considerable importance later. It is simply that a clear recognition of our limitations may be the very firmest foundation for attaining clearly such a degree of certainty in our knowledge as is possible. Knowledge of our shortcomings is of positive value. It can be liberating in our studies, and can secure accuracy by ruling out those efforts which are shown to be *beyond* the bounds of possibility and leading us to concentrate upon sharpen-ing, as clearly as we can, our methods of studying that which lies *within* them.

(b) Confusion about the relations between sociology and the other social sciences

A second source of misgiving in our common sense (whether justified or not) is that, though all that has been said concerning the necessity of sociology seems plausible, we are still doubtful about its claims for one particular reason. The impression we are given is that there are already many social sciences which study just the sort of questions which we have raised. Political science studies forms of government and other political associations. Economics studies the market-relationships of men in the production and dis-tribution of wealth. Criminology studies the 'deviant' behaviour of men in society and those institutions which detect, and punish, or treat it. Jurisprudence studies the systems of law in human societies. History studies the ongoing nature of social change and development in the way we have been speaking of it. What, then, remains for sociology to do? Is it not the case that *all* social institutions and *all* social problems are already studied by special sciences and that therefore sociology, as a *new* science of society seems not only unnecessary, but also unnecessarily confusing?

Here, again, we will leave this impression and misgiving of com-mon sense to have its full weight, until we come to deal with it later. It is obviously a question to which we must give a careful and satisfactory answer.

Meanwhile, having made clear those assumptions and questions of common sense which are at the root of sociology as a science, we can now clarify the science which has developed from them.

Sociology, however, has its roots not only in common sense, but also in those subjects which, before its own foundation, had speculated about the nature and problems of man and society. In order to be aware of the distinctive nature and contribution of sociology itself, it is obviously necessary to have a perspective and estimation of those kinds of theories which had been elaborated and adopted by men before sociology arose.

2
Early Social Theories

If sociology is so strongly rooted in our common-sense assumptions and in the practical needs and inquisitiveness of our nature, it would be very surprising, indeed inexplicable, if we were to find that theories of a sociological nature had emerged only in the modern world. In fact, there have been 'theories' of man and society almost as long as man has existed, though some of these, in the form of early, simple myths, must have been very rudimentary indeed, differing in character very considerably from what we would now call a 'scientific' theory. Even so, in the simplest myths that we know, some of the same ingredients are there: the effort to achieve a total picture of man's situation in the world, in the context of which both 'society' and 'individual' possess meaning and significance.

It is obviously impossible to give an account of all of the kinds of social theories which preceded scientific sociology, but it is worthwhile to attempt a brief assessment of their nature and the achievements which they embody, and to see them in some perspective, for several reasons which are very important.

The first is, that it is only if we have some such perspective on the nature and development of human thought and speculation on social matters in other times, and in other social conditions, that we shall be able to appreciate the significance of the emergence of sociology proper—as a *science* of society, in the modern *industrial* world. For though sociology did not spring to birth by some isolated process of special creation, but was rooted in these earlier traditions of thought and feeling, it is different from them in very important ways—which we must understand as clearly as possible.

Secondly, it is wise to remember continually that sociology is not just a modern innovation, a twentieth century expertise, but the culmination of a broad, perennial concern with fundamental questions concerning the nature and destiny of man. Sociology severs its connections with these earlier roots only at its peril: at the risk of dehumanizing itself and becoming nothing more than a set of professional techniques (of investigation and action) which many people are already beginning to fear; a set of techniques for salesmen, market researchers, social workers, and the like, whose intellectual horizons are parochially confined to a specific utilitarian end.*

* See C. Wright Mills: *The Sociological Imagination*. New York, Oxford University Press, 1959; especially ch's 4, 5 and 6.

Thirdly, bearing in mind that many early social theories were *philosophical speculations* as distinct from *scientific theories*, it is worthwhile to remind ourselves that these are not as clearly and distinctly separable as we are nowadays inclined to suppose. 'Philosophy' was a love of *knowledge*, just as 'science' is now thought to be. The early Greek philosophers laid great stress on the fact that their subject sought to distinguish '*knowledge*' from mere '*opinion*' or '*belief*'. It was certainly not only knowledge of material matters of *fact* which they sought, but of other questions and other dimensions of human experience also, such as the nature of mathematical 'forms' or of moral 'ideals', and this raises important questions for us.

Clearly, on the one hand, *knowledge* entails more than the particular kind of knowledge which *science* itself attains. In this sense science is simply *one* kind of knowledge: that which permits of empirical testing. It is the most simple category of knowledge within the wider subject of philosophy. And it may well be that, in our own time, we are in danger of interpreting 'science' itself too narrowly, in such a way as to impoverish both it and ourselves by losing sight of its place within the wider context of philosophy, or indeed even denying that there is such a wider context. It may be that, in general, we are tending to lose sight of the imaginative range of 'science' and coming to think of it—falsely—in narrow terms of utilitarian technology.

There is an important sense in which the very nature and limits of 'science' depend, themselves, upon philosophical clarification, and that, without this, there is a real danger that 'science' might be misunderstood and impoverished, even among practising scientists themselves. There is a danger that science might even come to be taught as a practical technology only. In short, science rests, essentially, within a context of philosophy, and to pluck it from this context and to consider and practise it independently of it, is highly questionable. This is true of all sciences—including sociology.

But also, philosophy aside, even religious myth and the works of art and literature have their own oblique ways of evoking our appreciation of *truths* of the human situation which are additional to, and which are not quite like, the more mensurable propositions of science. It may be that it is we (i.e. scientists) who are in danger of becoming the philistines in this quest for 'truth'. It may be that *we* are blinding ourselves to the wider exploration of truth by wearing *only* special spectacles of science, which, of course, have their own uses for enhancing our vision in certain directions, but which should, perhaps, be taken off, or replaced by others, for different kinds of view.

It must be remembered, too, that many of these earlier theories were concerned to make as clear as possible not only the *facts* of human nature and society, but also the *ethical* basis of what human conduct *ought* to be. They were, that is, theories including ethical and 'normative' considerations.* This also raises questions, some very profound indeed, which make it always important to see modern sociology in the context of its intellectual forebears.

A first question is whether there really *is* the clear distinction between the study of ethical principles and the study of matters of fact that many modern scholars now assume. Is there really a fundamental cleavage between studying what *is*, and what *ought* to be? It is common practice to insist that this is so. But *is* it? Might not our enquiry into the implications of our compelling experiences of moral obligation lead us to uncover moral ideals which, in fact, exist? Are not ethical principles a species of '*fact*'? Do moral ideals not *exist*? Many would dismiss this question as trivial—but this may simply be a matter of their unreflective dogmatism concerning what we may accept as 'categories' of 'existence'. They may simply be a lot of Dr Johnsons kicking posts in the street, and deluding themselves that this is an argument.

It may be, for example, that, in witnessing the factual struggle for the equal rights of negroes in the United States; the factual struggle against what is considered to be *injustice;* we can discover, by careful, analytical thought that certain principles of equality in political citizenship, and of impartiality in the making and treatment of claims in society, are essential ingredients in the idea of justice. Now this may well be a *fact* which must be taken into account in exploring certain kinds of social conflict. And I am not saying only that this may be an *operative ideal* which is at work (as a 'norm' or 'convention') in a particular society, but that, *in fact* it may be a *universal feature of the ideal of justice* and, therefore, that none of the struggles of men against arbitrary power *in any society* may permit of explanation or understanding without taking it into account. It may be impossible to explain the *facts* of social conflict, without a clear knowledge of the facts of the ethical entailments of the feelings of '*injustice*' among subjected groups, but the uncovering of these facts is a matter of reflective philosophy rather than of empirical science.

* It is worthwhile to note that these theories were not *only* normative. There is a tendency in modern thinking sharply to distinguish between 'normative' (i.e. concerned with what *ought* to be) and 'positive' (i.e. concerned with what, in fact, *is*) theories. Most early social *theories* were concerned with *both*. Confucianism, for example, seeks to know the actual nature of the world in order to see man's proper place within it, which will be a guide as to how he ought to behave. Plato, too, examined the actual nature of the 'soul' and 'society' in trying to clarify the '*ideal* constitution' for both.

The philosophical understanding of 'what ought to be' is a necessary element in the scientific explanation of 'what is'.* It is therefore at least possible that early philosophers were right in thinking that ethical concepts were a necessary part of social explanation and, if this is true, then philosophy continues to be a necessary part of the social scientist's equipment.

Furthermore, it may also be, as early philosophers thought, that *knowledge* is not only a matter of intellectual apprehension, but carries with it certain kinds of commitment and obligation: of maintaining qualities of integrity; of seeking and sustaining truth; of insisting upon the freedom and the procedures of enquiry necessary for this; even, perhaps, of denying the rightness of certain kinds of action because they rest upon falsehood.† It may be, then, that sociological theory, and any other scientific theory, may carry with it more connotations of an ethical kind than we are ready to admit, and than appears to be the case on its 'scientific' surface.

Whatever we may think about these matters, it is certain that we should be wise to understand as fully as we can what the philosophers and other early social theorists actually said before shrugging off their systems of thought, and a fashionable stereotype of the nature of their activity, too easily.

If this is thought to be outlandishly unorthodox in the present-day context of thought in social science, it might be well to bear two points in mind.

Firstly *all* sociologists until the last few decades (and I believe the same could be said of the greater number of sociologists today) have been concerned with sociology because of their ethical concerns. They have been humanists first, and sociologists second. Or, to put it minimally, their sociology has been one part of a much wider concern to understand the human situation and to act in relation to it.

Secondly we might stop to ask ourselves *why*, nowadays, we are sceptical about ethical principles as such, but why, as scholars, we insist upon a commitment to *truth* in scientific inquiry before everything. There is nothing in science itself to oblige us to do so, unless we regard the pursuit of truth in science itself as an *ethical* matter. And this, in fact, is what we do.

Why do we take the ideal of scientific integrity itself for granted, as being something beyond question, whilst thinking of all other moral ideals as being 'relative' in some sense, and always a potential source of 'bias' in our scientific activity? Without wishing to be too dialectical, might it not be possible that the scientific insistence upon

---

* This kind of consideration lies right at the heart of Plato's philosophy.
† In short, a commitment to the quest for scientific truth might have very definite political entailments.

the pursuit of truth by certain procedures alone, is itself a 'bias' in intellectual matters?

It seems to me, at any rate, that we are in great danger of rushing into a very glib and superficial conception of what sociology is aiming at, and what its nature is, if we do not have a good under-standing of the insights of earlier systems of myth, religion, and philosophy. Later, I hope to show that sociology is, quite fundamen-tally, a humanistic and ethical activity, and must falsify its nature and be a social danger in consequence if it tries to avoid or deny such a role.

I think this consideration so important as to be stated very strongly indeed. I believe it to be true that many modern approaches to social science, because they do not properly appreciate this necessary and continuing philosophical context, are much more superficial than the philosophers whom they have supposedly superseded. There is more knowledge of human nature and human society in a few pages of Plato, or Hobbes, or Spinoza, or Hume or even of Montaigne, than in whole volumes of modern social science. And frequently it is those who pride themselves on their 'scientific advancement' who are least informed about these theories of the past. In my view 'scientism', and a glib assumption of its 'modernity' and 'superiority', is one of the very greatest dangers facing our subject; one of which we have continually to be aware.

A further point of great importance is that a study of these earlier theories of society shows—whether they were myths, religions, political theories, or philosophies of history—that they were not only theories intellectually held by scholars or priests, but were also important ideologies of the societies in which they existed; focusing the feelings and commitments of entire communities upon certain values and certain ends. The point here is this: though sociological theory now strives towards the achievement of a scientific basis, *it cannot, even if successful in this, avoid this same kind of ideological role in our own time.* Modern sociological theory has emerged partly because these earlier theories of society have been seen to fail. Its own birth, its own nature, are rooted in criticisms of them. It therefore becomes an important basis, or at least a necessary part of whatever ideology modern man adopts. Modern man may, as Jung put it, be 'in search of a soul', but he is also 'in search of a sociological theory' appropriate to his own time and conditions, and perhaps the two are more closely linked than appears at first sight.

Sociological theory provides a picture of man's place in the world as much as any other theory in the world ever did. This is its absorb-ing interest; this is its humane value; quite apart from its scientific pretensions—necessary and of fundamental importance though these are. In sociological theory all earlier ways of thinking about man's history, moral and political philosophy, biology, psychology, religion, come to be critically assessed and fused. Sociology is the new focal subject, the new 'orientating' subject of human enquiry in the twentieth century. And this is not the grandiose claim that it must appear, but is no more than a working out of what was already foreshadowed by earlier theorists and clearly envisaged, for example, by David Hume and John Stuart Mill.*

In order to provide, though briefly, a perspective of the subjects within which, and out of which, sociology took shape, I propose to discuss them under four headings: (1) Religion, (2) Moral and Political Philosophy, (3) Philosophy of History, (4) Natural Science and Epistemology. In a final section (5) we can then outline the particular needs which led to the emergence of sociology proper—which drew critically from all these subjects and then created something going beyond them.

* See for example, David Hume in his introduction to the *Treatise of Human Nature:*
'It is evident that all the sciences have a relation, greater or less, to Human Nature . . . Here then is the only expedient, from which we can hope for success in our philosophical researches, to leave the tedious lingering method which we have hitherto followed, and, instead of taking now and then a castle or village on the frontier, to march up directly to the capital or centre of these sciences, to Human Nature itself; which being once masters of, we may everywhere else hope for an easy victory . . . There is no question of importance whose decision is not comprised in the Science of Man; and there is none which can be decided with any certainty, before we become acquainted with that Science. In pretending, therefore, to explain the principles of Human Nature, we in effect propose a complete system of the Sciences, built on a foundation almost entirely new, and the only one upon which they can stand with any security.'
See also John Stuart Mill p. 198 in the present volume.

A   RELIGIOUS THEORIES

The myths and religious systems which preceded scientific sociology, and which continue to exist side by side with it, are not only theories concerning man's spiritual relationship with God or with some kind of supreme spiritual reality. They are also theories about the nature of man and society in the context of the natural (as well as the 'supernatural') world. No matter how 'transcendental' some of these theories become with regard to their ideas of 'God' or the divine ground of reality, they always contain theories about the actual nature of man, and his place in both the natural world and in society. And they frequently lay down, in addition, rules of a social and moral, as well as of a spiritual kind, which man ought to observe. It is not too much to say that mythical and religious systems of doctrine, feeling, and ritual, were man's earliest ways of achieving a systematic picture of the nature of things, including himself, and that critical theology, philosophy and science have grown out of these roots.

Sociology has a clear line of descent from them, and is clearly relevant to them. In some ways it remains like them—though it has considerably refined the nature of its theories and its methods. It tends to replace them—since it emerges because of their inadequacy, and, in developing, increasingly demonstrates their inadequacy. And it continually encounters resistance from them since *its own way* of establishing knowledge, as well as the substantive knowledge it produces, is frequently in sharp conflict with those which they employ and insist upon.

The Simpler Societies

The simpler (non-literate) societies always have systems of myths built about those aspects of their environmental setting which are of supreme importance to them. Most myths, indeed, deal with both the ecological and the social problems which a society experiences.

One good example is sufficient for our purpose.*

The Ihalmiut, a group of Eskimoes living in the Canadian Barrens, were almost entirely dependent for their survival upon the seasonal

* Other myths of the simple peoples, colourfully presented, can be found in: Lewis Spence, *An Outline of Mythology*. This is a *Thinker's Library* book (Watts, 1944) and has a useful bibliography. A book which vividly shows the social functions of myth in relation to ritual is *The Elementary Form of the Religious Life* by Emile Durkheim.

migration of the deer. All the things of importance in their life—their dwellings, clothes, tools, weapons, food—were derived in some way or other from the deer. And we find that their 'theory' of creation centred about the deer. The myth, in very simple form, was this.

Kaila—'He who is Thunder in grey skies'—prepared the land, created hare and ptarmigan, and then made man and woman. Everything was very still in darkness. The hunters could not see and were hungry, so the woman cried to Kaila for help. Kaila then created fire and it was the woman's task to keep the fire alive. But soon the hare and ptarmigan grew wary of man and his torch of fire, and he again suffered hunger. Again the woman cried to Kaila for help, and he told her to dig a great hole in the ground. Then he told her to make a rope of the sinews of the hare, a hook from the wing bones of the ptarmigan, and see what she could draw from the hole. In succession she gradually caught all the beasts of the earth—but she was not satisfied with them and freed them to multiply over the land. 'She had still', says the story, 'not caught the one thing which she sought.'

'We do not know how long she lingered by the hole, for then there was no winter and no summer, no day or night. But in the end there came a great jerk on the line so that it was almost torn from the woman's hands. The man sprang to help her and together they pulled the sinew rope out of the pit. It was a mighty struggle, and yet man and his woman triumphed and so at last beheld the antlered crown of Tuktu—first of all the deer!

The woman cried out with joy and flung her hook away, and the deep hole closed up and vanished. Then the woman spoke to the first deer, saying:

'Go out over the land and become as many as all other things which live in water, land or air—for it is you and your kind who will feed me and my children and my children's children for all time that there is yet to come.'

The first deer heard, and heeded what the woman said, and so it came about that there were many deer. . . .'

It is a very simple 'theory' which gave meaning to the entire social and individual mode of life of this people struggling in their exceptionally harsh environment and being entirely dependent upon a few natural resources. There were, of course, many other attendant theories in their entire system of myths, but it can be seen, from this central example, how the 'story' links all the main social problems (darkness; cold—and fire; hunger—and food) with a clear picture of man's place in the world of nature as he experienced it.

These elements of myth seem quite unbelievable, simple-minded, even bizarre to our (supposedly) more sophisticated minds. But, as the man who recorded these myths put it:

'It must be remembered that the People of the Deer are of *their* world and know nothing of us and ours, and so what seems like gross unreality to us can remain unassailably real to them. Their beliefs are a product of centuries, and they fit the needs of their life and the shape of the land they live in. *They believe*! That is the point.'*

The myths and doctrines of more complex literate societies were not greatly different in their main components (they still dealt with social functions and ecological problems) though more elaborate in their details.

Ancient Egypt

In ancient Egypt for example, the Isis and Osiris myth reflected the physical characteristics of the Nile Valley, and signified the ultimate political union of Upper Egypt and Lower (Delta) Egypt as well as the attendant fusion of all the thousands of lesser deities of Egypt into one pantheon of gods at the head of which was Pharaoh—the one, living, visible, divine authority of the unified society, indeed of the 'world'—in whom ecclesiastical, military, political and legal authority were all fused.

Within this pantheon most gods were responsible for some social function. SAFEKHT, for example was the goddess of writing; ANUBIS—the guardian of the cemetery; NEIT—the goddess of hunting, always depicted holding bows and arrows. The over-all myth therefore vested all the aspects of social organization with a divine meaning and sanction, indeed a divine supervision.

The idea which had emerged of the judgment of men at death, and of a life after death, also entailed a theory about the nature of the human soul. A man was thought to consist of three elements: his physical body; 'Ba'—depicted as a human-headed bird whose seat was the 'heart' or abdomen, which could fly from the body, but returned to it for its pleasures; and 'Ka'—the mental aspects of personality, the identifiable intelligent consciousness of the personality itself (a 'double' of the personality), which was something of a spectator or onlooker in its appreciation of the pleasure of life. And the tomb arrangements in ancient Egypt were such as to take account

* Farley Mowat, *The People of the Deer*, Michael Joseph, 1952. I say *supposedly* more sophisticated minds, because Farley Mowat has much to say in this book about the very considerable sensitivity and subtlety of the minds of the Eskimo people. Among themselves, for example, they worked out a very much simplified version of their own language, which all of them took care to use when they were within earshot of Mowat. Only when he was familiar with this did they acquaint him with the details of their language, and only then did he learn their 'strategy' of simplification!

of all these features. Passages were provided so that 'Ba' could revisit the body. A life-like statue was placed in the tomb so that 'Ka' could take up its residence there and see the things which had given it pleasure in life. And, of course, all this necessitated the preservation of the body itself; and even this emphasis upon the physical preservation of the body seems to have been an outcome of 'ecological factors', namely the preservative qualities of the sand of Egypt.

Breasted, for example, wrote:

'Experience in the land of Egypt has led me to believe that the insistent faith in the hereafter was greatly favoured and influenced by the fact that the conditions of soil and climate resulted in such a remarkable preservation of the human body as may be found under natural conditions nowhere else in the world. In going up to the daily task on some neighbouring temple in Nubia, I was not infrequently obliged to pass through the corner of a cemetery, where the feet of a dead man, buried in a shallow grave, were not covered and extended directly across my path. They were precisely like the rough and calloused feet of the workmen of our excavations. How old the grave was I do not know, but anyone familiar with the cemeteries of Egypt, ancient and modern, has found numerous bodies or portions of bodies indefinitely old which seemed about as well preserved as those of the living. . . . The surprisingly perfect state of preservation in which the Egyptian found his ancestors whenever the digging of a new grave disclosed them, must have greatly stimulated his belief in their continued existence, and often aroused his imagination to more detailed pictures of the realm and the life of the mysteriously departed.'*

The myths of Egypt, therefore, reflected the physical conditions of the life of the people and provided theories about the unity of society, the importance of many social functions, and the nature of the individual soul in life and in death. They included also a system of laws, and certain moral directives, which defined the nature and requirements of social institutions and laid down rules for the regulation of social behaviour.

As a matter of interest a brief example of such moral rules might be given from the Egyptian 'Book of the Dead' which contains sets of 'negative confessions' by which the individual declared his innocence. According to Sir Flinders Petrie, these were arranged in sets of five, to facilitate learning by finger-counting. The rules are amusing in that they indicate what people might be prone to do in certain areas of social life and conduct, and I have selected illustrations of two or three of them.

---

* Examples of such bodies can, of course, now be seen in many museums.

85

Religious Obligations

(1) I have not lessened the bread offerings in the temples.
(2) I have not ravaged the cakes of the Gods.
(3) I have not carried off the bread of the glorious dead.
(4) I have not cohabited in the temenos of the God of my city.
(5) I have not defiled myself in the temenos of the God of my city.

Commercial Honesty

(1) I have not lessened the corn measure.
(2) I have not lessened the palm.
(3) I have not deceived in the fields.
(4) I have not added to the weight of the balance.
(5) I have not made poorer by means of the plummet of the balance.

Other rules which indicate the importance of social and ecological factors were:

I have not turned back water in its season, nor divided by a dam at running water.*
I have not driven away cattle which were on their pasture.
I have not netted birds of the records of the Gods.

Social and moral regulations obviously found a clear place in these religious 'theories'.

Ancient Babylon

The same was true of ancient Babylon. Amongst a people whose chief ecological problem was that of extending the boundaries of fertile land, developing and maintaining a reliable system of irrigation, keeping control over the artificially canalized waters, and whose chief disaster was that of flood, their myth of creation was very appropriate.

It was APSU—the god of fresh water, and TIAMAT—the dragon of unbounded salt-water (chaos), the earliest divine forces of the world, who first created a number of lesser gods. These lesser gods, however, began trying to bring *order* into things. They tried to canalise the fresh water and to drive back the salt-water by extending the land. This interference irritated and then angered APSU and TIAMAT, and they therefore decided to destroy them in order to restore their earlier and untrammelled peace. But the lesser gods rebelled, and engaged in battle with them. One among them—Marduk —was elected chief, and he fought TIAMAT in battle and defeated

* Irrigation, of course, was of vital importance in this society.

her. He then 'split her like a flat fish into two halves'. Of one half he made the canopy which holds back the water above the heavens. With the other he covered the waters which lie under the earth. Then, within this firmament, he fixed the stars, and then created plant life, animals, and, finally, man.

'My blood will I take', said Marduk, 'and bone will I fashion. I shall create man who shall inherit the earth.'

It will be seen that in this story of creation—which was achieved in an orderly sequence of six days followed by rest on the seventh—Marduk, the God of creation, was on the side of man. It was he who had defeated the forces making for chaos, and had created an order of the elements of the world within which man could live in security and peace.

In this society, too, we find the myth of the Flood—clearly stemming from the Babylonian experiences of the flooded river deltas. It was not, in this case, however, Noah who built his ark of so many cubits high, so many cubits wide, so many cubits long, but the Babylonian figure—UTNAPISHTIM.

The myth is almost exactly the same as the Judaistic myth of Noah with which we are familiar, and not surprisingly, since the latter seems to be a later version of it.

Again remembering the relation of the Isis and Osiris myth to the political union of Upper and Lower Egypt, it is interesting to notice that this unification of myths occurred at a time when Hammurabi was succeeding in consolidating the earlier Sumerian cities into the unified civilization of Babylon which then endured for some twenty centuries. And, again, we find that lesser deities were now absorbed or combined into an all-embracing pantheon of the gods.

The Greek City States

The ancient Greeks had their pantheon of gods, too, and their many and beautiful myths. But the Greeks of course, were invading conquerors, and when the Olympian pantheon came to be consolidated, the gods, though certainly possessing social functions, were by no means altogether suited to the settled life of the City State which ensued.

As Gilbert Murray put it:

'It is a canon of religious study that all gods reflect the social state, past or present, of their worshippers. From this point of view what appearance do the Olympians of Homer make? What are they there for? What do they do, and what are their relations to one another?

The gods of most nations claim to have created the world. The Olympians make no such claim. The most they ever did was to conquer it. . . . And when they have conquered their kingdoms, what do they do? Do they attend to the government? Do they promote agriculture? Do they practise trades and industries? Not a bit of it. Why should they do any honest work? They find it easier to live on the revenue and blast with thunderbolts the people who do not pay. They are conquering chieftains, royal buccaneers. They fight, and feast, and play, and make music; they drink deep, and roar with laugher at the lame smith who waits on them. They are never afraid, except of their own king. They never tell lies except in love and war.'*

It was because of this mythical presentation of the gods as super-human beings whose vices were as strongly exaggerated as their virtues that philosophers like Xenophanes and Plato began to criticise such 'religious and mythical theories' and to offer what they thought were better theories in terms of qualities of human excellence and reason. Hitherto, theories of God, nature and man had 'reflected' and fitted society, but from this point of reflection onwards, men began, at least to some degree, to 'reconstruct' the gods they believed in, in the image of their own moral, intellectual and aesthetic aspirations. They could not accept that what was divine was of a lower standard of excellence than that of which man himself was aware. They made the Gods in their own image. And as their knowledge improved, so the picture of the Gods improved. It was, in part, in terms of this dissatisfaction with myth and religion that critical philosophy began. Firmer foundations were now sought for theories of man and society.

Examples of these same kinds of mythical and religious theories could be drawn from the history of every society.†

Japan

In Japan, the creation myth began with the two fundamental principles in Nature: Male and Female; IZANAGI and IZANAMI respectively. It was they who created the Japanese Islands and their people. The eight chief islands stemmed from IZANAMI's womb. When IZANAMI died and went to the underworld, IZANAGI followed her. But she was in a state of decomposition and warned him against seeing her. But he broke in, saw her, and was polluted. He then rushed back to the earth to cleanse and purify himself. In doing

* *Five Stages of Greek Religion.*
† There is an excellent *Larousse Encyclopaedia of Mythology* (paperback) which contains good and interesting accounts of myths in many societies.

so, he created other gods. The filth cast from one eye became AMATERASU—goddess of the sun. That from the other eye became TSUKI-YOMI—the moon god. That from his nostrils became the storm god, and so on. In this way all the Japanese deities were brought into relationship with each other in, again, one pantheon.

Men, as usual, however were unruly. Because of their disorder, AMATERASU sent her grandson, NI-NI-GI, to establish a firm government of the islands. The offspring of NI-NI-GI were the Japanese Emperors. All the leading families of Japan traced their descent from some deity or other, and every aspect of nature came to be represented as a deity. The system of myth, once again, served to unify nature and society.

But what is of greater interest is that this mythical unification seems to rest, again, upon a necessary historical imposition of unity. The Japanese people are not the native inhabitants of their islands, but initially came from the Asiatic mainland and from some Pacific islands. Early Japanese society appears to have been a loose association of tribes, having three chief centres with three chief gods: the Gods of the Sea, the Gods of the Stars, and the Sun Goddess. The myth we have briefly described represents the conquest of one of these tribes—the YAMATO—over the others, and the fusion of all the gods into one unified myth with the Sun Goddess as the supreme deity.

China

The religion of China is, similarly, most impressive in the entire interrelated order of nature, society, and the propriety of individual life and conduct, which it presents.

China has, for millennia, been an agrarian civilization. Its traditional religion—in both doctrine and ritual—rested upon a conception of the Order of Nature. The entire universe, the heavens, and the dependent nature of the world, were characterized by order, regularity, harmony, majesty. All was governed by a *law* of order in nature. Two conflicting but co-operative principles were fundamentally at work: the male and female principles; but a certain pre-ordained *way* of creative development was entailed in these forces of nature, which led to harmony, propriety and beauty in its pattern. Man and his society were part of the whole order of nature, and the major institutions of society were there to make the full harmony of human relationships possible.

The Emperor was the father and representative of the people who carried out ceremonials on their behalf and achieved order in relation to Heaven. The continued order of society depended upon his diligence and devotion. From the Emperor down to the lowliest peasant, the family was the important group within which good human relationships were realized and sustained, and the family included not only the living family group, but also the continuous line of ancestors. There was a living interdependence in the family and society between the dead and the living. The whole of existing society, and the whole of its history, was thus permeated by filial piety, and in Confucianism, which is a reflective systematization of traditional beliefs, this family regulation became the means of achieving and sustaining several specific sets of relationships, with their attendant qualities, which were thought to be of fundamental importance for the natural harmonious fulfilment of both social and individual life.

There were five such relationships and sets of qualities:

(1) Between Ruler and Subject. (The Ruler should possess the qualities of benevolence, care and responsibility, and the subjects that of loyalty.)
(2) Between Father and Son. (The Father should possess kindness and care, and the son filial piety.)
(3) Between Husband and Wife. (The Husband should observe righteous behaviour and the Wife obedience.)
(4) Between the Oldest and the Younger Brothers. (The Oldest brother should possess gentility, the younger brothers humility and respect), and
(5) Between the Elders and the Young in general. (The aged should have a humane and tolerant consideration for the young, and the young should show deference to the old.)

In this system of doctrine and morality there was clearly a theory of nature, society and man, and a theory about those social institutions which were considered essential for achieving the natural order and fulfilment of individual life in society, and for the engendering and development in individuals of those qualities of character which were necessary in order continuously to achieve these ends. *Character* was seen as the chief aim of government and education, and Confucius was very meticulous and subtle in working this out; showing how the quality of order of the state and the quality of order of the individual soul were inextricably linked with each other. In this he was remarkably similar to Plato. Here, for example, is what he said about the necessity for *clarity of language* and the importance of *knowledge*.

When asked what his first task would be in undertaking the control of a prince's administration, he replied: 'The one thing needed is the rectification of names.' For, he argued, without care over words and names, education and ritual would be disordered, laws would not be just, and people would not know what to expect in relation to each other. Clarity and truth were a basic necessity for the right ordering of society.

'The rectification of names,' one of his followers elaborated, 'consists in making real relationships and duties and institutions conform as far as possible to their *ideal* meanings. . . When this intellectual reorganization is at last effected, the ideal social order will come as night follows day—a social order where, just as a circle is a circle and a square a square, so every prince is princely, every official is faithful, every father is fatherly, and every child is filially pious.'*

And in the 'Great Learning' it was put like this:

'The ancients (i.e. the ancient kings) who wished to cause their virtue to shine forth first ordered well their own states. Wishing to order well their states, they first regulated their families. Wishing to regulate their families, they first cultivated their persons. Wishing to cultivate their persons, they first rectified their hearts. Wishing to rectify their hearts, they first sought to be sincere in their thoughts. Wishing to be sincere in their thoughts, they first extended to the utmost their knowledge. Such extension of knowledge lay in the investigation of things. Things being investigated, their knowledge became complete. Their knowledge being complete, their thoughts were sincere. Their thoughts being sincere, their hearts were then rectified. Their hearts being rectified, their persons were cultivated. Their persons being cultivated, their families were regulated. Their families being regulated, their states were rightly governed. Their states being rightly governed, the whole kingdom was made tranquil and happy.'

Clearly, the teaching of Confucius was not only a theory of nature, society and the individual; it contained also an appropriate theory of education.

Summary: The Nature and Elements of Religious Theories

Many other examples of mythical and religious theories could be given, but we have seen enough for our own particular purposes. Though we have been able to describe them only briefly, it is quite clear that all these 'theories' possessed certain definite characteristics.

(1) They were appropriate to the conditions and problems experienced in the societies in which they existed.

* The great similarity to the ideas of Plato can be seen in this.

91

(2) They were *pragmatically based*. They were shaped to deal with concrete problems.

(3) They were *empirically based* in the sense that they rested upon the facts—both evident and underlying—of the world and society as far as they were known.

(4) They included a justification, almost a sanctification, of the order of society as it existed.

(5) They included an analysis of the nature of social institutions and their functions.

(6) In their proposals for conduct they offered an analysis of the psychology of the individual in relation to the institutions of society. They saw the one and the other as being, at least to some extent, interdependent. In short, these theories all presented a rudimentary analysis of:

   (*a*) the institutional framework of society,
   (*b*) the psychology of the individual, and
   (*c*) 'social' psychology—the influence of institutions upon individuals, and vice versa.

But two quite clear and considerable points must be made before leaving these kinds of theories.

The first is—that though we may readily concede that some of these myths contain valuable insights into human nature, and have much continuing interest and value—in our modern society, characterized not by a simple natural setting or a stable tradition resting upon rural and agrarian conditions, but by a complexity of industrial technology resting upon rigorous scientific methods for the establishment of knowledge, they cannot be retained. They are no longer adequate. Their basic assumptions concerning nature, and the origins of man and society are almost entirely without foundation. But again, to put the matter only minimally, they are couched in terms which no longer have significant meaning for us. The analysis of society and of human nature which they offer are of little value in relation to our own complexities. Their propositions do not approach the most elementary requirements of scientific exactitude. They cannot be accepted. We may like them—as we like fairy stories, or allegories, or any symbolic presentation of stories and ideas which illuminates some aspects of our nature; but we must reject them in the same way. They cannot help us in our own task of dealing with our own situation within the context of our own required standards of knowledge. And when I say *we*—I mean mankind throughout the world *in* the modern world; all who have confronted and experienced the new conditions of scientific, technological and industrial change during the past three human life-times or so.*

No doubt this will be fairly generally agreed, since I have purposely selected religions which people commonly attribute to the 'pre-historic' or the 'ancient' world.

But the second point of the very greatest importance is this. The world is still, in the second half of the twentieth century, influenced very considerably by inadequate 'theories' of this kind; indeed some parts of the world are dominated by them. All the religions of the world—Hinduism, Islam, Buddhism, Christianity—offer a set of myths of this kind. In a world in which the requirements of scientific knowledge form the basis of their every practical and social activity, the minds of millions of men and women are still in great part immersed in 'theories' of this kind.

Clearly, then, in describing these kinds of 'early social theories' we are not dealing, by any means, with something remote from, and irrelevant to, our own time. These 'early theories' are still with us. They remain very powerful. We have still not struggled out of the trappings of these intellectual infancies. But in struggling to replace these 'outworn dreams of a time outworn' with more accurate and satisfactory theories of man and society, sociology must inevitably lead to some new ideological position for mankind—even if this is only the recognition, from now onwards, of the *impossibility* of a unified, collective ideology. *Some* ideological position must, necessarily, follow in its train. In these struggles between 'old' theories and 'new', and in our confused considerations of the nature, the place, the worth, and the importance to be attached to each, lie many of our present-day dilemmas. And, indeed, we cannot assume that, having found certain 'theories' insufficient, we can succeed in putting something better in their place. We face very great and grave problems here.

---

* I do not say this either totally or brashly, or cynically. All such myths and doctrines contain insights into human nature and include perennial truths about man's situation. My sole point is that—as *theories*—they cannot stand as being possible within the modern criteria or perspective of scientific knowledge.

B MORAL AND POLITICAL PHILOSOPHY

We have seen that among the early Greeks most conspicuously, a criticism of the 'theories' of myth and religion took place at a certain point in their history. The same thing happened in other societies, too. Confucianism was an outcome of critical reflection upon the earlier traditional elements of Chinese religion. Brahminic Hinduism (let alone later philosophical schools) was an outcome of long reflection upon the earlier Vedic Hinduism. Similarly, the founded religions of Buddhism and Jainism were the outcome of criticisms of Brahminic Hinduism. Zoroastrianism arose from a criticism of the traditional religion of Persia. And many other examples could be given. Religion changed by reflection. Myth gave way to philosophy. Theories of nature, society and man, both of a factual and normative kind, came to be worked out in terms of reflection and a critical analysis of experience. Some mode of explanation other and more reliable than that of religious doctrine came to be required.

The richest source of such speculative theories is undoubtedly the long argument of moral and political philosophy which developed throughout the history of Western Europe, stemming roughly from the time and the personality of Socrates, and the important philosophers—such as Plato and Aristotle—who immediately followed him. The thought and observation, the critical analysis of experience, and the systematic deduction embodied in the elaboration of these theories are such as to compel the utmost admiration. In some respects it is doubtful, even now, whether we have advanced beyond them. What is certain is that one of the best corrections to any naive 'scientism' is a thorough study of these early philosophers.

Theories of the Greek City State

The first theories of man in society stated in *general* terms (i.e. in terms of analytical and critical philosophy) appeared in the context of the Greek City States. It is worthwhile to ask why this was, and what factors might have been involved, because an awareness of these factors throws much light upon the relationship between the actual experience of the Greeks and the theories themselves. Some factors, at least, are quite definite and clear.

The Greek City States consisted of populations which were, relatively speaking, so small and self-sufficient that their members had little difficulty in knowing each other, in being familiar with each other in reasonably personal terms. As in an English village or a moderately sized city, many people would know each other as persons, or, even failing this, they would know each other as members of certain families. There was a 'familial' sense of belonging to the community. Also, each city state was politically independent. It could support itself economically and defend itself from outside attack, and in large part this was due to the facts of local geography. The territory of each community was usually bounded by mountain ranges on two sides and the sea on the third. This made for ease of military protection. But there were also very considerable differences of altitude in each of these small territories and therefore very differing degrees of climate and kinds of soil. Conditions varied from sub-tropical to alpine, and from pastoral to forested kinds of vegetation. This made possible a wide range of products. Such a circumscribed territory with such a small population living within it, made for a centrally organized communal life in which all the people shared, and in which all participated as individuals.

The central ordering of communal affairs took place about the 'polis'—literally, the most convenient central point of the whole area, and usually an up-raised place from which the entire area of the state could actually be *seen*. Professor Kitto translates the term 'polis' as *'central rock'* or *'stronghold'*, and upon this centre was focused the military, commercial, religious, 'political' life of the community, so that it sometimes developed into a town. Kitto says that because of this the term 'city state' is not a particularly good translation of 'polis'. A better conception is simply that of a community living in its own limited territory and coming to the central stronghold to discuss and manage its affairs; though it should be emphasized, however, that these 'City States' were deliberately and ceremonially founded and therefore had, from the beginning, a strongly symbolized central unity. This intimacy of involvement of the Greeks as individuals and families in their social life accounts for many things, as for example the extreme extent of their democratic citizenship under some circumstances. Not *all* political constitutions, by any means, were democratic, but, when they were so, *all* citizens had the same equal status, and *all* participated in legislative and judicial duties. Indeed, sometimes the representatives of tribes to the central councils or to the courts were arrived at by *'lottery'*; so that it was quite possible for a poor man of lowly origins to sit in judgment upon the rich. The Greek citizens, very positively therefore, came to look upon the central political business of their community quite literally as 'their *own*' business.

Another important fact was that the 'polis' was founded upon *blood*-relations. It was a formally founded extension of earlier clans and tribes. Membership was a matter of being *born* into it. There was consequently, in this most profound sense of being a group of *kinsfolk*, an extended 'family' feeling about communal life. The Greeks never liked their 'own' business, their own personal and family concerns, to be taken out of their hands—even by benevolent tyrants from among their own number. They realized very well that the power of a second generation of tyrants was not necessarily as benevolent as the promises and good intentions of a first.

Greek life was therefore characterized by an intense, stubborn individuality among a number of people who were all fully and sensitively aware of their own desires and demands upon society, and their reciprocal tasks and duties in the community. They made continuous demands upon each other in a concrete, responsible way, as members of a family do, and one important outcome of this was that the Greek notion of 'goodness' or 'virtue' was therefore, also, always a very concrete thing; something definite and perfectly clear. A good man was reliable in his group, capable of good advice, courageous, intelligent, temperate, capable of sound judgment, impartial, honest, helpful to others, generous, and able to manage his affairs effectively and successfully. The Greeks' idea of virtue had nothing vague about it. They had a clear conception of personal goodness, of qualities of human excellence, which was clearly related to the achievement of a good and just society.

One other important and obvious aspect of this was that *ethics* was considered the same thing as *politics*. The life of the polis was the necessary context for the enjoyment of the good life on the part of each individual citizen. The polis gave him the necessary basis for, and the opportunity of achieving, a full, rich and responsible life. The serious debates, religious festivals, dramatic performances, were not highbrow entertainments but 'popular' activities; activities of the people. The Greeks were clear, concrete, mature in their personal and communal life and in their artistic and athletic activities, and were continuously accustomed in all their concerns to serious personal responsibilities. The city was a clear framework for the individual citizen's entire life. His moral conceptions, personal and social, were perfectly clear. He knew exactly where he stood in society, what values to approve and what objectives to aim for.

The Greeks were also, because of this, quite accustomed to what we would now call a *planned* society. That the members of a community should deliberate upon, and then plan, their social activities seemed to them a perfectly natural and correct thing to do. In politics, law, defence, in all public affairs, everyone played a responsible part, fulfilling his appropriate and clearly seen functions in society, and all these facts tend to suggest that the theories of the first critical philosophers—Socrates, Plato, Aristotle etc.—were not so much their own unique speculations as reflections upon the actual social practices of the Greek community. Before considering these ideas, however, one or two other matters should briefly be mentioned.

The Greek cities were, of course, not isolated, but in touch with each other. More important, however, they were also involved in communications—especially in trading relations—with the larger civilizations that existed round about them in the Mediterranean. This led to complexities of commercial, political, and military contacts with many different peoples and to a changing economic structure at home. In particular it led the Greeks to make quite detailed comparative observations of the customs of other peoples —Egyptians, Persians, and others—as in the accounts of Herodotus. But it also led to the growth of internal conflicts within the city states themselves: conflicts between the new commercial classes and the established agricultural aristocracies. Each city came to contain within itself 'a city of the rich and a city of the poor.'

Finally, a certain development of the political and philosophical life of these communities must be mentioned. With the growing complexity of public life and the diversity of social interests stemming from it, the struggle for power and influence among demagogues, and the pressures for social, economic and political reform, increased. In this context a new kind of tutor came into prominence, the *Sophists*. These men sceptically criticized all moral rules, all principles of justice and righteousness—discounting them as superficial *conventions* to be calculatedly complied with, rather than being *natural* in the sense of being deeply rooted in human nature and its needs in society, and requiring, therefore, full commitment and obligation. They taught, in short, how a person could become a successful man of the world. Their teaching was one of expediency and self-interest: how to understand affairs of the world in such a way as to manipulate people in society successfully, in order to get your own ends. And in this teaching they drew the distinction between *nature* and *convention;* insisting that the latter (morality) was only man-made, and therefore 'relative' to those who possessed power, and therefore alterable. It was in direct opposition to this superficial doctrine of the Sophists, as they so thought it, that Greek moral and political philosophers developed their own theories.

In connection with this new centrality of the philosophical investigation of human nature and morality, two or three things seem to have been of great importance.

Firstly, the mere existence of Socrates, as a person, seems to have had tremendous and vital influence upon the nature of this early philosophy. His character, his scepticism, his argumentativeness, seem to have stimulated not only enthusiasm, but also both affection and irritation, love and antagonism. Above all, his moral integrity and his intellectual tenacity in pursuing the peculiarly insistent demands of his conscience had a profound influence upon his contemporaries even though he seems to have done little but profess his ignorance about most matters, and—in arguing to demonstrate this—to have shown that most other people were a good deal more ignorant than he. In fact, of course, Socrates, as we have noted, was stating the perennial human predicament—of having to exercise sound judgment whilst clearly recognizing the horizons of our ignorance—and insisting that the recognition of ignorance was the beginning of wisdom.

Secondly, through Socrates and his arguments against the Sophists, the philosophical enquiries of the Greeks into the nature of the physical world were somehow orientated about the central importance of the study of human nature and moral ideals; an emphasis that was to continue throughout the history of Western philosopy. And thirdly, it is important to note again that the work of the philosophers who followed Socrates was directly concerned to show that morality in society was rooted in *the individual and social nature of man*, and was not, in any specious sense, a matter only of *convention*.

In short, this led moral and political philosophy to become, at once, a theory of the *facts* of human nature and human society, as well as a theory about the *ideals* in terms of which one could clarify what man and society *ought* to be.

One final point is worth making. Because of the smallness of scale of the city states and the intensity of their political life, personal ambition became a factor of tremendous importance. Tyrants could spring up quickly and dominate the entire community by their influence. A command of the art of rhetoric on the part of a demagogue could influence the minds of citizens to a marked and crucial degree. This therefore became an important social matter, and a supremely dangerous one. This point is of importance in indicating the *urgency* to the Greeks of the political and moral questions into which the philosophers looked. Again it is clear that the 'theories' of philosophy were not a matter only of intellectual interest, but also of compelling *need*.

The Theory of Plato (427 BC – 347 BC)

The danger of tyranny was, to a considerable extent, the starting point for Plato's own theory.* He was devastated by the execution of Socrates (the man he most loved and admired) at the hands of the court of Athens (the city he most loved and admired) and his immediate objective in his moral and political philosophy was to attack the decadence of his time, to discountenance the superficiality of the Sophists' teaching and to demonstrate that morality was as much rooted in the nature of things as any other attribute of human nature and that its presuppositions could be elucidated by reason and clearly known. He attempted an account of the qualities of excellence and righteousness in individual and social life at the level of *demonstrable knowledge*, and sought to lift it from the easy-going and false level of expediency and whimsical opinion. His analysis was *both* factual ('positive' as we now say) *and* normative; for Plato believed that to *know* was a part of striving to *become*, that no moral endeavour towards excellence could be based on anything less than a *knowledge* of the *truths* concerning the nature of society and the individual soul, and concerning the *ideals* that the facts of our nature and our social commitments were seen to entail.

Using the methods of critical reflection; undertaking a careful analysis of his common-sense assumptions about the psychological and social aspects of human nature; and drawing upon such comparative knowledge about other societies as he possessed; he offered a general theory of man and society in terms of *functional excellence*. In order to make clear the nature of justice and righteousness he thought it necessary to consider first the factual nature of man and society.

The basic reason for the existence of human society, Plato claimed, is the simple fact that men have many needs, but, as individuals, cannot satisfy them. We are insufficient, as individuals, for the individual fulfilment that we need and desire. Men must therefore live in communities in which different tasks are allocated to those who are best fitted to undertake them, for the purpose of satisfying, in the best possible way, the needs of all. Society is a necessary mutual interdependence of men which achieves a satisfactory division of functions among them.

The origin of a community, he wrote, '. . . is due to the fact that no one of us is sufficient for himself, but each is in need of many things. . . . Men, being in want of many things, gather into one settlement many partners and helpers to satisfy their diverse needs, and to this common settlement we give the name of city.'

Plato then enumerated certain basic needs—for food, clothing, dwelling places, and the like—and made clear the division of labour which they required. Obviously, the community must have farmers,

* See chiefly *The Republic* and *The Laws*.

builders, weavers, shoe makers, and others who make necessary commodities. But since the most excellent performance of any job, for the benefit of all concerned, is achieved when men can concentrate upon it *entirely*, a more extensive division of labour is necessary so that these essential workmen do not have to concern themselves with jobs not strictly their own. Other craftsmen are necessary in addition to the first group of workers. Specialists such as carpenters, smiths, herdsmen, shepherds, are necessary to support them with particular materials and special skills.

Plato also thought it extremely unlikely that any community could be so completely self-sufficient as not to benefit to some extent from external trade. Trading required a further group of people: the merchants. Also, 'markets' are necessary even within the community itself. Some intermediaries anticipate the needs of consumers and buy from producers accordingly. These, Plato called the 'shopkeepers'. In addition to all these there are those possessing no special skills, but who are useful for carrying out simple and routine kinds of work, and who hire themselves out as unskilled labourers for wages. A community, on the basis of a simple division of labour of this kind, can live a secure, peaceful, happy life.

'Let us consider', Plato argued, 'what will be the manner of life of men so equipped. Will they not spend their time in the production of corn and wine and clothing and shoes? And they will build themselves houses; in summer they will generally work without their coats and shoes, but in winter they will be well clothed and shod. For food they will make meal from their barley and flour from their wheat, and kneading and baking them they will heap their noble scones and loaves on reeds or fresh leaves, and lying on couches of bryony and myrtle boughs will feast with their children, drink wine after their repast, crown their heads with garlands, and sing hymns to the gods. So they will live with one another in happiness, not begetting children above their means, and guarding against the danger of poverty or war.'

Plato conceded, however, when others argued with him, that many people would not be contented with such a simple way of living. Many desire a more luxurious manner of life with more sophisticated commodities and pleasures. Plato then went on to consider the more elaborate division of labour which is necessary if this greater complexity of desires is to be satisfied. Before he agreed to move on to this more elaborate analysis, however, it is worth noting that Plato went out of his way to make it clear that it is in these desires for greater complexity and luxury, and all that they entail, that the seeds of war, social differentiation, and social division lie. It is not, in short, Plato's view that war and extreme social distinctions are *necessary* accompaniments of human society; only that they are brought into being by what he calls 'the inflamed society'.

'I, for my part,' he wrote, 'think that the city I have described is the true one, what we may call the city of health. But if you wish, let us also inspect a city which is suffering from inflammation . . . We need one swollen in size, and full of a multitude of things which necessity would not introduce into cities . . . But,' he continued, 'let us only notice that we have found the origin of war in those passions which are most responsible for all the evils that come upon cities and the men that dwell in them.'

Having made this warning clear, he then proceeded to analyse the more complex kind of society which men, with their 'inflamed desires', bring into being.

His account of the ideal constitution of society and the individual was still based upon the division of functions, and the qualities of excellence required for their fulfilment, and he considered society (rather than the individual) first of all, because he felt that the nature and importance of functional excellence would be likely to be so much more clearly apparent there. He began his analysis with the simple question: whom would we approach if we wanted a good pair of shoes, a good saddle, an efficient navigator for a ship, or the performance of any job of that kind? In all cases, he argued, it is obvious that we would go to the man who had the talent and the appropriate training to make shoes, to make saddles, to navigate ships, and so on. These men and only these men could be relied upon to perform that particular function most satisfactorily. People without talent and people without training would lack the requisite skill. Those who perform special skills to satisfy specific needs of this kind Plato called 'the Artisans', and these constitute the first large 'class' of people in his society. Plato also argued that such people will be very *preoccupied* with performing the skill for which they are best equipped and trained, and to which they have devoted so much of their lives. Their trade will be the basis of the immediate welfare of their families. There is bound to be in short, a certain propriety of *self-interest* amongst the artisans; a limited focus of attention and effort, if their function in society is going to be fulfilled with the highest standard of excellence, and if it is going to form a satisfactory basis for their lives.

However, an additional class of people in society is also required which must *not* be motivated by self-interest or by any single-minded devotion to a specific utilitarian skill. The members of a complex society will unavoidably make claims and counter-claims upon each other; they are bound to be involved in disputes; and if there were no generally accepted pattern of social control for dealing with such conflict, then chaos would result. There must therefore be a group of people in the community who are trained to have a disinterested attitude with regard to maintaining order and justice on behalf of society at large and, of course, to protect society as a whole against outside attacks and insecurities. This second 'class' Plato called 'the Guardians' and he felt that the function of such a class is not simply a negative one of restraining or suppressing the artisans, but the positive one of providing a stable and secure basis for their proper freedom and the proper fulfilment of their own functions. In short, such 'guardianship' should be not repressive but liberative to a proper degree.

Plato then argued that still a third class of people in a complex community is necessary, and this follows from the supreme difficulty of the art of government. The guardians, who protect society and maintain order, have to act in accordance with certain ideals and principles of justice and morality, but the recognition and understanding of these ideals, and the wisdom to govern effectively in accordance with them, requires very clear vision, very careful deliberation, and very considerable powers of reason, knowledge, and judgment. But the force of Plato's argument may best be seen if we approach it negatively. He put the matter crucially like this.

There are some people, he said, who think that—although it is advisable to go to a skilled cobbler for a good pair of shoes, or to a trained saddle-maker for a good horse's saddle—when it comes to considering the tasks of decision-taking, legislation and administration in *government*, *everyone* in society should have an equal say. But this, surely, said Plato, is absurd. If, in the making of shoes, saddles, and other simple manufactures, specific talents and specific training are necessary for the achievement of excellent standards, how much more must this be true with regard to the most subtle and most difficult art of all—the art of government? Surely this art, more than any, requires many-sided talents of the highest order and the most excellent degree of training in the understanding of all aspects of human nature and society that can be provided. There should, then, be a third 'class' of people—'the Philosophers'—who prove, after many and searching tests, that they possess these many-sided talents and who then devote a very large period of their lives to learning the skills of thought and judgment which will give them the clearest knowledge possible of the moral ideals in the light of which the community should be governed, and the wisest basis of knowledge and judgment whereby the best order of society is to be achieved and sustained. But again it must be noticed that the governing authority of the 'Philosopher Kings' is not thought of by Plato as being repressive or tyrannical. On the contrary, for him the

'Philosopher Kings', too, have a positive function: the necessary, rational ordering of relations in society whereby every sector of society can fulfil its proper task, and its proper kind and degree of functional excellence, with regard to the maximum well-being of the whole. Plato went on to give a very detailed account of how he thought that people in a society should be selected and trained for these various functional skills. For the moment, however, it is enough to see that he gave an account of both the *factual* and the *ideal* nature of society in terms of certain necessary functions and the highest degree of excellence in the fulfilment of them.

Following this, Plato then considered how far this threefold functional analysis of the artisans, guardians and philosophers in society might be of use in understanding the factual and ideal nature of the individual human soul, and he tried to demonstrate that it was of use in this connection. He claimed that the individual human soul, too, can be seen to consist of at least three important elements, and that these have the same functions that are reflected in society as a whole. First of all there is the desiring element: all the specific appetites by which man is driven and which seek their satisfaction by the attainment of specific utilitarian ends—as, for example, hunger and desiring food; sex and desiring consummation in love; fear and desiring security. These appetites in the soul are the equivalent of the artisans in society, and the activities of the artisans are, obviously, closely related to them. But again Plato insisted that if the appetites of a man, though each having its own proper end of satisfaction, were to be submitted to no over-all control whatever, the result would be chaos. In such a situation it would not be the case that a man governed his appetites in such a way that each of them had its proper place, and provided its proper satisfaction in his nature. On the contrary it would be his appetites which *tyrannically dominated him*. It is therefore necessary, secondly, that there should be some kind of government of the appetites in the soul, and Plato argued that it was the rational element in human nature (parallel with the Philosopher Kings in society), which could give man a clear knowledge of the moral ideals in the light of which he could wisely govern his nature and exercise control over his desires and conduct.

There is also, however, a third element in the nature of the human soul which Plato found it more difficult to be clear about, and this he called the spirited element, (equivalent to the role of the guardians in society). He argued that there is some element of feeling in us— equivalent to what we would now call 'conscience'—which *is* a feeling but which, peculiarly, seems always to be on the side of reason in supporting some kind of governing order over the sheer

anarchy of the appetites. And Plato maintained that the best ordering of the nature of the individual soul is achieved when the
rational element, utilizing the spirited element, orders the many
desires of the soul (appetitive and others) in such a way as not to
suppress and negate them, but to achieve a sustained balance or
harmony, within which each of them can satisfactorily fulfil its own
appropriate functions with regard to the unity of the whole. This,
again, is both a *factual* and an *ideal* theory; an account of what the
nature and constitution of the individual human soul both *is* and
ought to be.

There are one or two points which must be emphasized before
leaving this account of Plato.

First of all Plato discussed the political constitution of society in
terms of some blend of the democratic element (the artisans),
the oligarchic element (the guardians), and the monarchic or
aristocratic element (the philosopher kings), and his argument
was that the monarchic or aristocratic constitution, in which the
philosopher kings exercise authority in governing the artisans with
the aid of the guardians, is the best one; that is to say—it is the
constitution most likely to achieve that over-all harmony within
which each group can most satisfactorily and happily find its
appropriate fulfilment. In short, Plato was anti-democratic on
reasoned grounds.

Secondly, it is worth reiterating that Plato's *ideal* model of society
and of the individual soul rested essentially upon his *factual*
analysis of what society and the individual soul *actually* are. In his
view, the understanding of society and the individual required the
recognition of ideals which *exist;* which are definitely entailed in the
nature of human needs; and which are *discovered* by reasoning.
This blend of *actual* and *ideal*, of the factual and the normative, is
still a matter for serious philosophical consideration and which we
have nowadays all too easily rejected.

A third point worth emphasizing is that Plato saw a real dimension
of moral *endeavour* in this clarification of the ideal and the actual.
Recognizing the nature of intellectual, aesthetic, and moral ideals
is not, in itself, enough. With this discovery, this elucidation of
reason, there is a positive desire to approximate to these ideals in
so far as it is possible, and this means a conscious attempt to order
society and one's own nature in such a way as to achieve the ideal
constitution that one has in mind. This again may be an element in
social and individual thinking that we tend nowadays to ignore,
and with loss to ourselves.

A final point to notice is that Plato was not 'academic' in any
orthodox sense. Though he emphasized fully the intellectual in-

vestigation of the nature of the actual and the ideal, and, indeed, the importance of 'the life of the mind' as such, he had, centrally, always a practical end in mind: namely the actual effort in this life as individuals and as members of society to approximate as closely as possible to those idealities of which we became aware. Plato never thought for a moment, either, that the 'idealities' and 'harmonies' of which he spoke were in any sense simple to recognize, or achieve, or that they were 'once-for-all' ends that one could attain. The balance was always precarious. And we sought these things in a perennial and vital 'war of the soul' in which man was always involved.

The Theory of Aristotle (384—322 BC)

It is worthwhile to make a few brief comments on the ideas of Aristotle* but only for our own purposes, to see that, though in some ways similar to and in some ways different from Plato, his theory was essentially of the same nature: still couched within the context of the City State.

First of all, Aristotle's theory was the same as Plato's in that it gave an account of both individual and society in terms of functional excellence. Similarly, he agreed with Plato in wishing to establish that in some sense or other morality is deeply rooted in the nature of man and is not something conventional in any superficial or expedient sense.

Secondly, Aristotle also agreed completely about the importance of clarifying ideals for the purpose of guiding individual and social endeavour. His difference with Plato here was only a difference of metaphysical level. Whereas Plato wished to insist that in some important sense which it is difficult to make clear ideals *actually exist*; that they are implicit in all the actual forms of nature and of human nature and that reason can discover, clarify, and know them; and that all the actual individuals in the world (trees, animals, men) are in a process of active development, seeking to fulfil the ideal form on which they are patterned; Aristotle wished to argue that it is sufficient to think of ideals as being simply standards recognized and clarified within men's minds in contemplating their experience. He did not think it possible or necessary to give them an 'existential'† status beyond this. Even so Aristotle's analysis was still in terms of ideals rooted in certain human needs and in the overall desire for harmony and happiness in social and individual life, and he was not therefore greatly different from Plato in this.

A third point is that Aristotle's theory of man and society was

* See chiefly the *Ethics* and *Politics*.   † Or 'ontological' status.

still in terms of a substantive account of 'the good life'. It was still rooted in a careful analysis of human needs and human ends and in the purposive striving for an overall government of individual and social conduct which would harmonize the needs and functions of men and achieve the highest possible degree of excellence.

Fourthly, however, Aristotle was very sceptical about the place and status of the 'Philosopher Kings' in society. Despite Plato's insistence that the 'philosophers' were men carefully selected for their *all-round* qualities—their physical qualities, their courage, their temperance, their wisdom, as well as for their qualities of intellect proper—Aristotle still argued that philosophers do not necessarily have, and, indeed, cannot possibly get, the practical experience that is required for the successful organization of social affairs. His own emphasis with regard to the achievement of effective government was upon the importance of the *practical sagacity* of the man of affairs. The role of the philosophers with their intellectual enquiries should be to explore fully and in detail all the implications of political issues in order to give men of 'practical sagacity' the best context of information within which to exercise their judgment. The philosophers, in short, should serve and supplement this practical sagacity. Aristotle wished to achieve in society the most excellent qualities of judgment resting upon a *knowledge* of human affairs and he believed the practical sagacity of the man of affairs to be of equal, if not greater, worth than the intellectual competence of the philosopher.

Finally, Aristotle was more empirically and scientifically orientated in his work than Plato, though, to my mind, this can easily be over-emphasized. Whereas Plato critically reflected upon his own experience of the Greek communities, Aristotle urged the undertaking of a careful comparative study of the varieties of political con-stitutions that existed in the world of his time. He urged upon his students a recognition of the necessity of this kind of comparative empirical study for a knowledge and understanding of human societies, just as he urged it upon students of biology for establishing a knowledge of different animal species. Aristotle was perhaps the most important early scholar to see the necessity of scientific and comparative sociology, as distinct from, or in addition to, the speculative discussion of 'idealities' which underlay the entire thought of Plato. Aristotle was also very 'sociologically' orientated in his analysis of social institutions and their interrelations in society as a whole. He gave clear and detailed accounts of the part played by the family as a social group, of the 'village' as a communal group, and of the functions of particular institutions—such as 'property'—in establishing certain kinds of relationships and qualities in society.

And he placed much importance on inter-personal ties such as 'friendship', of which, again, he gave a very full account.

It is quite clear why Comte and others in approaching the making of sociology in more recent times looked to Aristotle as one of their most important 'ancestors'. Aristotle already had quite a clear conception of a science of society—the analysis and comparative study of social systems in order to establish testable knowledge about them; and, within this conception, he had already undertaken a study of some social institutions and relationships in considerable depth.

To summarize: the theories of man and society which were produced in the context of the Greek City State were theories in terms of *functional analysis and excellence*. They were undertaken to refute the Sophists by showing that morality was not expedient, superficial, or 'man-made' in any specious sense, but that it was as much a part of the nature of things and of the nature of man and society as anything else encountered in human experience. They emphasized normative considerations, but these were thought to rest upon and to be implicitly entangled with actualities, so that they also offered accounts of the facts of human nature and human society. And they emphasized the importance of attaining knowledge and wisdom for the practical endeavour of governing individual, social and political life in seeking to approximate to the idealities which were recognized. These theories were obviously rooted in the characteristics, conditions, and problems of the life of the Greek city states that we outlined at the beginning, and they were to change when the city states themselves changed and declined.

Theories of Hellenistic Greece

Plato and Aristotle lived and worked when the Greek city states were already changing considerably, and when they were on the point of decline. The self-containment of these political communities vanished altogether with the campaign of Alexander which set up an empire of tremendous extent. This empire was itself a very short-lived achievement, lasting little longer than the lifetime of Alexander himself, and quickly disintegrated, but the important result was that Greek civilization came to be thinly spread over this very wide area. Although certain local centres such as Alexandria, became important, the old self-contained, 'familial', and independent kind of Greek community was not achieved again. There was, in short, a situation and a period in which men had to live without

107

any clear civic and political unity in mind. There was no longer the clear basis for political citizenship that had existed before.

In this context the old conceptions of the good life for both the individual and society, as being almost two sides of the same coin, were no longer relevant. Instead of thinking of personal morality and political obligation in the same terms—of the fulfilment of individual qualities in a life of loyalty and service to the community, people now came to think in much more individualistic terms. They now thought in terms of some '*natural law*' or some source of morality and ground of moral obligation which existed 'in the nature of things', over and above the particular state in which one lived. This 'moral law' existed universally, and applied universally to all men, transcending political boundaries. The characteristic qualities of this thought can best be described as *individualistic and cosmopolitan*, in clear distinction from the much more 'locally orientated' *functional excellence* in the thought of the Greek city states.

This individualism and cosmopolitanism was expressed in different terms by different 'schools' of philosophy which were founded and developed during this period. The Stoics, the Cynics and Epicureans were all schools of importance, and put forward distinctive points of view, but the Stoics give perhaps the best illustration.

A clear distinction lay at the heart of the Stoics' belief. Some things in the flux of nature were not within the individual's power to control. Some things, however, *were* within his power. For example, the span of human life, the sequence of human growth, being a prey to accidents, diseases, death . . . all these were things beyond personal control. On the other hand the individual *could* control his own behaviour, his own conduct towards others, his own manner of thinking and speaking; the governing and shaping of his own character. Their teaching was, then, that it was sensible to *resign* yourself to the things that were *not* in your power (since it was useless to do otherwise) and to concentrate upon governing in the best way possible the things that *were* within your power. It is the aspect of *resignation* to uncontrollable things which is nowadays taken to be the distinctive characteristic of Stoicism but it can be seen that this was only one emphasis, or one side, of their teaching.

The question arose, however, as to what the *best* or the *right* way of controlling one's conduct was? The Stoics' answer was that the feature which entirely distinguishes man from the brutes is his capacity for reason. Reason is the universally distinguishing attribute of man, enabling him to elucidate the nature of things, to clarify and know the *Natural Law* by which all things in nature are ordered, and to guide his conduct in accordance with this knowledge. A knowledge of *Natural Law* is therefore the most important thing for us, and each individual must recognize his own responsibility for his own reasoning and the government of his own life.

The Stoics did, in fact, outline a good many rules for personal conduct, and outlined certain principles and qualities of character which reason seemed to uphold, but even so, it will be seen that this kind of teaching had a noticeable lack of *content* as far as the *obligations of men as citizens of the state* were concerned. Community life lacked close, centralized cohesion, and therefore the account of the good life was in entirely individualistic terms, and there was a complete absence of consideration of the necessary relations between individual and community which had characterized the theories of the Greek city state. There was no discussion of political constitutions of the Platonic and Aristotelian kind. The Stoic creed was a personal creed, and the same was true (though they were qualitatively different in their details) of the teaching of the Cynic and the Epicurean schools.*

Theories of the Roman Empire

During the third and second centuries before Christ, Rome gradually absorbed, together with other territories, the area of the disintegrated Macedonian empire. The modes of thought that were prevalent in Hellenistic Greece became elements in Roman civilization and continued throughout the period of Roman domination in Europe. The Epicureans, for example, were represented by Lucretius.† Cicero wrote treatises on ethics and government using Plato's familiar titles of *The Republic* and *The Laws*. And the representatives of the Stoics best known to us were men like Epictetus, Marcus Aurelius, and Seneca—the first a slave, the second an emperor. The Stoic philosophy is presented most clearly in their writings.

What is particularly important for our purpose is to note that the conception of *natural law* persisted throughout this period. Roman civilization did not produce any great original philosophers of the

---

* Also of the Peripatetic School.
† Lucretius is worth brief mention here, although he is not central for our present concern. In *The Nature of the Universe* he put forward a most modern interpretation of nature and of man's place in nature. He was a materialist. He postulated a theory of evolution in almost Darwinian terms: of the transmission of characteristics from parent to offspring and the operation of natural selection. He wrote about the origins of human society and put forward a plausible version of the 'social contract' theory of political obligation, and so on. Indeed, of all the writers of antiquity, he was possibly the most 'modern' in his approximation to the way of thinking of modern science.

calibre of those who had arisen in Greece. Roman thinkers studied the Greeks and discussed their ideas both clearly and elaborately. Cicero, for example, has a greater range and power as a thinker than is commonly thought. Still, it is true that they made no major contributions themselves. In the main Rome was most noteworthy and important in the development of Western civilization, including the development of thought, for its contributions in the sphere of *practical law* and *government*. The great achievement of Rome was the successful establishment of a wide network of positive law over the many peoples they conquered, and, during this practical process, the achievement of a systematic, reflective, and progressive *codification of the law*.

One very important aspect of this was that the conception of natural law, as a strictly philosophical idea, now received a basis of practical support from the actual experience of the Romans in dealing with the new complexities and problems of law. *Jus Naturale* for the Romans was that law inherent in the nature of things, including human nature, which could be discovered by reason, and which in some sense underlay the actually existing network of the civil law. In short, *Jus Naturale*, was very similar to the philosophical idea of the Stoics, but was thought also to interpenetrate the actual laws of society.

Another important element of law emerged in Roman affairs, however, which was very similar, but not exactly the same. In the early city states of Rome, as in the early Greek city states, membership of the community was a matter of *blood-membership* or *birth*, and men were subject to the pattern of custom and law within the community into which they were born. With the extension of Roman administration, however, disputes were brought before the courts between men who were members of widely differing societies and patterns of custom. The lawyers found themselves having to judge claims, counter-claims, and specific cases between members of different communities to whom quite different systems of law applied. They therefore looked for the 'common' element in all these systems as an agreed ground for judgment. A body of 'common' law accumulated, and was known as '*Jus Gentium*': the 'law of the people'. In the Roman empire these two elements of law, *Jus Naturale* and *Jus Gentium*, appear never to have been quite identified with each other; were never thought to be quite the same; but nonetheless were thought to lend support and reinforcement to each other. It was felt that natural law, discoverable by human reason, must underlie the common strands of law which actually existed in the law of the people derived from all communities. If reason and natural law were universal, one would expect them to assume a certain common form in the institutions of justice in all societies.

In addition, however, there was a third strand of law: the body of constitutional laws laid down by the decrees of the emperors and the edicts of the praetors as and when they came to power; and this was known as civil law or positive law: *Jus Civile*. A close relationship between all these three elements in law was held to exist, even though the relationship was never thoroughly worked out or made perfectly clear.

In the period of the Roman Empire then, the theory of a 'natural law' underlying the ordering and government of individual and social behaviour, received a kind of 'underpinning' from the actual administration of legal affairs.

Theories of Feudal Society

Following the disruption and decline of the Roman Empire, and the gradual emergence of the new order of Feudal society, a new dimension of law—*Divine Law*—came into being as an ultimate justification of all those other strands of law that had come to be emphasized during the period of the empire. This, of course, rested upon the central importance of the Christian Church in the new pattern of authority. Whereas, before, 'civil law' and the 'law of the people' was justified by 'natural law', which was clarified and understood by reason, it was now believed that, beyond this, there existed the 'divine law' which contained elements not discoverable by human reason.

Christian doctrine came to maintain that whereas reason was God-ordained and could therefore be supposed in its original condition of innocence to contemplate the full nature of the moral law of God, it had been rendered incapable of this by the sinfulness of man and the fall of man from his initial state of grace. This did not mean that human reason was totally incapacitated, and it was still agreed that human reason could, to a degree, clarify certain matters of morality and certain aspects of the will of God, but because of man's fallen nature it had been necessary for God to provide, *by revelation*, a knowledge of his own nature and of his divine law which reason itself could not now apprehend. This 'revealed' divine law came therefore, to proclaim and insist upon certain idealities and moral principles which went beyond natural law, civil law, and positive law.

On the basis of this divine law, but linking with it the rational clarification of natural law which earlier thinkers had achieved, the philosophers of medieval society, perhaps especially St. Thomas

111

Aquinas, outlined an entire theory of the nature of civil society and an entire picture of what 'the good society' was like. This, of course, was cumulatively established and clarified by successive papal encyclicals. Here again, then, was a 'theory' of society which outlined the factual nature of the individual soul and of society, in such a way as also to provide a clear statement of moral and spiritual ideals for man's guidance. But it was this theologically based theory of Christendom which came to be torn asunder with the Protestant reformation and the violent emergence of modern secular nation states.

Theories in the emerging Nation States

The success of feudalism brought about its own downfall, With the new security which the feudal order re-introduced into the chaos following the disruption of empire, there was a renewal and re-establishment of many of the earlier strands of communication between diverse peoples. Travel between various parts of Christendom was now more possible. Roads and sea-routes were opened up again. New commercial contacts and interchanges were established and extended, And with this resurgence and growth of inter-communication came an increasing interchange of knowledge and enquiry. A new spirit of adventurousness in all fields of enquiry and activity awoke. This was linked, in practical terms, with the emergence of competing groups of merchants, all seeking to establish new mercantile organization and their 'national' independence. The universal pattern of Christendom was gradually unsettled and then violently torn asunder. A period of intense conflicts, of an economic, political, and religious nature, brought the disintegration of the feudal order and the emergence of new secular nation states, each insisting upon its own political authority and independence, and upon its own responsibility for its internal organization and its external policies. These struggles towards independent nationhood were reflected in the emergence of new theories about human nature and about the grounds of moral and political obligation.

We have seen that all the earlier theories of man and society had contained propositions as to what men *ought* to be like and how they *ought* to behave. There was always a mixture in them of the *facts* of human nature and the *idealities* which human beings *ought* to observe. One of the most noticeable changes in the new moral and political theories attending mercantilism and the emergence of the independent nation state was that the accent upon the normative tended to be very much diminished, indeed decried, and there was a much greater emphasis upon the *positive* study of man; the study of the facts. This must not be exaggerated too much—the normative was still very strongly there; but it was stressed very forcefully that 'idealities' were figments and delusions with which those who were in power hoodwinked those who were not, and that the only grounds on which morality could reliably rest were to be derived from a knowledge and understanding of what the *facts* of human nature actually were.

Machiavelli (1469–1527) wryly advocated that statesmen should have done with thinking too much about how men ought to behave and should look more scrupulously at the ways in which they *actually do* behave. Only if men had a satisfactory knowledge and understanding of the actuality of human nature could they know successfully how to influence others, and gain and sustain power over them for the pursuit of what they themselves thought worthwhile. All this was laid down in his treatise on *The Prince*. Machiavelli, however, was by no means altogether as sinister as he is now made out to be and in his *Discourses on Titus Livius* he gave some account of the moral principles which ought to be the objective of the statesman's efforts. Machiavelli's real emphasis was that 'ideals' and 'principles' are all well and good, but of no avail if one cannot achieve and sustain *effective* order and government; and for this a thorough knowledge of the ways in which men pursue *power* is necessary.

Similarly in the work of Thomas Hobbes (1588—1679)* there was a firm insistence upon knowing the hard facts of human nature as a basis for knowing wisely what the most just order of society could and should be. It is well known that his ethical theory was not successful in the sense that he could not demonstrate how his ultimate moral principles were derived from the stark 'facts' of human nature in which, he claimed, there were no moral glimmerings at all. Nonetheless, his theory offered a detailed analysis of the psychological propensities of men which led them to fear others and be in conflict with them, to be in a 'state of war' with each other, and thus to be driven to seek some kind of legitimate civil authority which would minimize this conflict and provide a basis for peace, security and harmony. Many of these observations which Hobbes made about human nature, about both the individual and society, are full of remarkable insight, and again it must be said that he was far from being as sinister in his account of the perpetual pursuit of power on the part of all men, as is commonly supposed. For example, his account of the 'passions' which drive men to seek

* *Leviathan.*

'power' include such propensities as benevolence, curiosity, humour and the like, and for him the term 'power' refers simply to the seeking of that degree of control over things and people which is needed to secure the ends which the passions desire. This is by no means necessarily sinister. However, our central object here is not to defend Hobbes, but only to see the kind of theory that he proposed.

One other point that must be noted is that it is with the emergence of the modern nation states that the 'Social Contract' kind of theory came into being. 'Divine law' had come to be suspect, and had to be attacked. With the overthrow of Christendom, however, some new basis of political sovereignty had to be found and this, by these new theorists, was sought by examining the assumed reciprocity of a 'contractual' nature which seemed to underlie all the co-operative behaviour of men in society. Men do, in a political community, seem to act as though they feel bound by reciprocal obligations; as though they had entered into a contract with each other. Why do they feel and act like this? What exactly underlies this 'contractual' behaviour?

Perhaps one of the most important characteristics of this new kind of social theory was that all the metaphysical or theological presuppositions concerning the basis of power and authority were dropped. There was no longer an appeal to *divine law* and *natural law* in the sense that there was something actually there over and above the heads of men, which by reason could be discovered and which gave some kind of 'ultimate' justification to the actual laws of the state. The emphasis was now entirely upon *positive law*. To put the matter simply, law was thought to be *what men decided*; and *nothing else*. Law was simply that set of rules which men made to order their social life. This was enough.

Theories in the maturing Nation States

This vehicle of the 'Social Contract' idea came to be filled with rather different contents as the emerging nation states came to grapple more fully with the making of political constitutions. The detailed elaboration of new patterns of political rights; the detailed working out of constitutional procedures; resting only upon human reason and morality, encountered different problems in different societies. Machiavelli and Hobbes produced their theories in the thick of the rebellions taking place against the order of Christendom; but towards the end of the seventeenth and during the eighteenth centuries, up to the time of the French revolution, those who con-

structed theories of society were now faced with the positive and continuous task of providing a justification for the details of the new
secular political orders. The social contract idea was therefore used
with different emphases by different theorists in the context of
different conditions.

Towards the end of the seventeenth century in Britain, John
Locke, for example, argued, as against Hobbes, that moral
principles were not, and could not be, brought into being by the
creation of a political society. They were not created with the setting
up of a central sovereignty. On the contrary, moral principles were
actively involved in the 'state of nature' of men's ordinary feelings
and conflicts. Men felt and recognized reciprocal moral duties before
any elaborate political apparatus of authority was set up. Furthermore the political constitution, or the apparatus of the state, which
men did set up for the achievement and preservation of a just order
in society, was one which they accepted in order effectively to *secure*
the moral principles they already recognized. If, therefore, this
organ of government came to deny or to abuse these principles of
morality, then the people had a right to overthrow it and to replace
it with something more satisfactory. Locke's theory again, however,
consisted of a psychological account of the nature of man, both
individual and social, from which he then deduced his principles
for the organization of the state.

Jean-Jacques Rousseau also used the social contract theory as a
vehicle criticizing the *ancien régime* in France during the eighteenth
century, and he too used the theory for the strong defence of democracy. He regarded any kind of political apparatus which—whether
from size, complexity, or arbitrary privilege—prevented every
adult individual in the community from participating in the taking
of those central decisions which were to be binding upon them all,
as being totally unjustified. He argued therefore for the relatively
small political community in which all men could participate as
individuals. Again, however, Rousseau's theory included a psychological account of the nature of man and a connected account of
that organization of society which would most lead to the maximization of individual liberty and individual fulfilment.

It is interesting to notice, also, that even the *criticisms* of these
social contract theories were themselves theories of society in what
we would now call psychological and sociological terms. The best
example of this is the theory put forward by Edmund Burke, in his
Reflections upon the Revolution in France as a critique of everything
that the French revolution stood for. Burke argued that the 'social
contract' idea was historical nonsense and, furthermore, that the
idea that the men of one generation could 'rationally' know how to

obliterate the institutional fabric of a society and replace it overnight in a revolutionary manner with a totally new social structure, was a matter of political as well as intellectual lunacy, and deeply dangerous. The fabric of institutions in society as a whole, Burke insisted, is a collective tradition which has grown up over many centuries; to which many generations have contributed; and which has come to be a complex embodiment of all the non-rational and prejudicial, as well as the rational elements of a people's experience in confronting and dealing with its own particular historical circumstances. The social heritage consists of a pattern of institutions which are intricately and intimately interrelated, and which are rooted in the most profound emotions and values of a people which simply cannot be fleetingly and momentarily 'understood' by the rational analysis of one generation. The institutions of a nation are ways of *living*, ways of *feeling* and *doing*, not just abstract administrative procedures which can be 'known' by 'reason' and judged against abstract moral principles. And to tamper brashly in ill-considered social reform with any one element of the social heritage might well produce a degree and range of social disorder that was not envisaged and might bring disaster instead of improvement. One stone in a building may seem to fit badly, but if, without care, it is pulled out, the entire building may collapse.

Burke's theory was therefore a very conservatively toned theory, insisting that reform, if undertaken at all, should only take place after very prolonged and deliberate thought and careful judgment, and even then very guardedly and never in any totalitarian or revolutionary spirit. Again, however, it is to our purpose only to note that this is really a systematic theory of society: a socio-psychological analysis of what is involved in the cumulative development of social traditions in the institutional organization of society as a whole.

New Approaches to Social Theory

During the eighteenth century, however, whilst these new kinds of 'national' social theories were being put forward, a qualitatively new kind of approach to the study of man and society was beginning to emerge, was beginning to disentangle itself from the old, and the crucial distinction which was being clarified in these new approaches was that between a scientific and a moral theory. Some thinkers were coming to be clearly aware that a certain scientific body of knowledge at least about the nature of human societies could be achieved, and that it was necessary to achieve it, quite separately from the statement of any moral theories as to what human society ought to become. And this was a movement of thought which grew throughout the eighteenth century and culminated in a proliferation of theories about the establishment of 'social science' round about the time of the French revolution. For our purposes two theorists are particularly significant: Montesquieu and Condorcet.

(a) *Montesquieu* (1689—1755)

Montesquieu was a man of culture and affairs; a man of wide experience as well as a scholar. He travelled in Italy, Germany, Holland, and stayed for something like three years in England. His work had a wide-ranging air of sophistication, and contained much social commentary and satire quite apart from contributing very substantially to serious and scholarly studies of society. In his Persian Letters, for example, published about 1721, he produced a satire on the nature of French and Parisian life and discussed many ideas of the time—for example Hobbes' account of the 'state of nature'—in an unusual and entertaining way by treating them as they were seen through the eyes of two visiting Persians. His major contribution to the study of society, however, was his book *The Spirit of the Laws* for which he undertook an enormously wide range of reading and research in history, geography, political philosophy, economics and comparative law. The range of this work is best indicated by Montesquieu's full title—*De L'Esprit des Lois, ou du rapport que les lois derivent avoir avec la constitution de chaque gouvernement, les moeurs, le climat, la religion, le commerce, etc.*

The central and most distinguishing feature of Montesquieu's treatment was that he now used the idea of 'natural law' not in the old philosophical sense in which it had been used throughout European history, but in the new sense of a scientific 'law of nature'. He now brought to the fore the idea that each society, each social system as an entirety, has its own 'natural law of development', and that it should be the objective of the student of society to uncover and to establish a satisfactory knowledge of this law. He still believed, like all the other thinkers we have mentioned, that such knowledge should be provided for the use of statesmen but his major belief, rather like that of Burke, was that a statesman can only legislate wisely if he *knows*, very intimately, the nature of the society for which he is legislating, and knows the nature and pace of institutional change which is proper to that society. Only if he legislates within the context of this knowledge of social development will his principles and actions of government be soundly based and such, therefore, as to produce successfully the ends he has in mind. Montesquieu, too, was opposed to the idea of the statesman as a

117

kind of idealist who, with certain moral principles in mind, believes that he can totally reconstruct society in a revolutionary manner. The wise statesman governs within the context of the institutional fabric of his society, of which he has gained a profound knowledge.

In pursuing these 'laws of development' of societies Montesquieu insisted upon and actually used both comparative and historical methods in his study. He classified societies chiefly in terms of the political constitutions that they possessed; into republics, monarchies, and despotisms; but in this classification he took into account not only the differing institutional complexes which were appropriate to each, but also what he called the 'spirit' or the 'principle' which was required among the members of society if the institutions were to function satisfactorily. This 'principle' or 'spirit' really amounted to the kind and qualities of *education* by means of which those values necessary for the functioning of a society were engendered in its individual members. In despotisms the 'principle' necessary to maintain institutional order is always *fear*. In monarchies, which frequently have a nobility surrounding the monarch, the 'principle' on which social order depends is the instilling of *honour*. And in republics, which may be democratic when all people share in the tasks of government or aristocratic when relatively few people participate, the principle whereby appropriate social order is secured and sustained is that of *virtue*. Montesquieu therefore conceived of entire social systems as being collectively different entities but as being the embodiments of certain 'typical' networks of institutions, each of which was sustained by a particular 'ethos' of a psychological nature engendered and sustained by education.

Stemming from all this he also put forward certain political prescriptions. For example he agreed that if liberty is to be maximised in a society there must be a division of powers between legislative, executive and judicial authorities, and that these powers should be undertaken by different bodies of people. These political prescriptions however, were an additional matter.

It should also be mentioned that Montesquieu saw the total institutional complex of a society as coming to assume the shape it did by a process of adaptation to a specific *ecological* setting. One of the most important characteristics of a society's environment he thought, was its climate: its ranges of temperature, and the like. He believed that climatic and other ecological conditions exerted a powerful influence upon the psychological nature of a people and that this was reflected in the nature of their social system. However, the social system—the interconnected institutions of religion, government, education, family—was seen as an entirety *in relation to*

the environment and not, by any means, as being entirely subservient to it. Montesquieu quite readily believed that it was part of
the function of the statesman to reduce this dominant influence of
the geographical environment and society's dependence upon it,
and he believed that as human civilization grew, and as its technology accumulated and advanced, so the social order could have an
increasingly determining influence upon the geographical environment, rather than the other way round.

Montesquieu's theory of society, then, was a theory about the
development of social systems within their ecological settings, and
it involved an entire psychological, institutional and developmental
analysis of the nature of these societies. In all this he also studied
institutions in a way which we would now call sociological and
scientific, quite independent of any ethical or metaphysical questions concerning the truth of their values. A good example of
this is that he discussed the nature of religion in society, and the
social and psychological functions it fulfils, quite apart from the
question as to the truth or falsity of any of its doctrines. In all this
Montesquieu was remarkably modern and a clear precursor of
psychological and sociological theory proper. Like Aristotle,
Montesquieu is one of the 'pre-scientific' students of society to whom
many later sociologists—Comte, Durkheim and others—acknowledge their great indebtedness. The reason is quite clear.

Perhaps, referring again to his consideration of the division of
powers in the exercise of political authority, one final point to be
made is that Montesquieu, though he did not make much of this in
the entirety of his theory, really had an implicit theory of progress.
He hated and despised slavery, domination, tyranny, and it was the
maximization of individual fulfilment that he loved. And his comparative study of 'laws of social development' came to be judged
according to this yardstick of measurement. Those social systems
which maximized liberty were 'better' than those which did not, and
therefore constituted models for political action.

(b) Condorcet (1743—1794)

This mention of the term 'progress' brings us directly to the significance of the work of Condorcet. It was Condorcet who, more
conspicuously and centrally than anyone else, brought the new idea
of progress into the centre of all thought about the nature of man
and society, and this change of orientation was much more considerable than we are nowadays inclined to think. In many of the earlier
systems of social thought, the prevailing assumptions were those of a
kind of timeless eternity. Man, his society, his patterns of historical
change, were all seen within the larger context of the divine eternity

of things within which he had been created. Some theories, like that of the Italian philosopher Vico, argued that there was a cyclical pattern of change in human societies, but that these cycles of change still existed within the external nature of things as created by God, and were, indeed, ways in which man became ever more aware of the divine scheme of the universe. The new conception of man's place in nature came as biological and historical knowledge increased, and the idea emerged that there was no evidence for the earlier 'cyclical' theories, and that human history could simply be regarded as an on-going process in which change was, no more and no less, a matter of society *becoming different from what it had been before*. Ideas of cyclical patterns or eternal purposes tended to be abandoned, and it was thought more correct to conceive of human history as a changing creative process in which human civilization was a cumulative and, in many ways, possibly an advancing thing.

Condorcet, even more than Montesquieu, was very much a man of affairs, distinguishing himself in French academic life, but also, with the French Revolution, involving himself very considerably in political activities. He became responsible, for example, for state education in the early years following the Revolution, and in 1792 it was he who put forward a scheme for State Education. His concern for clarifying the nature of progress in human society had therefore very practical implications for the making of policy in the context of the new political constitution of France, as well as being a matter of theoretical interest.

His main work, and probably his most influential work after his own time (it was published posthumously), was his *Sketch for a Historical Picture of the Progress of the Human Mind*. In this book he analysed the stages of advancement of human civilization from a 'sub-human' or near animal condition to the possibility of an enlightened and virtuous society which had as its objective individual fulfilment and happiness. And in all this he tried to show how the advances of mental experience as experienced by individuals, were closely associated with, and considerably dependent on, the conditions of society at any particular time. In short, his account was an analysis of the progress of mankind from its original 'animal' state towards the most perfect fulfilment of human potentialities, emphasizing throughout the close interdependence of individual and society.

Condorcet maintained that there had been nine great and distinguishable epochs of social development in history. First of all, mankind must have lived in simple hordes. Their economic activity must have been that of hunting, fishing, food gathering, and they must have come to possess some central customary authority, some systematic kinship relationships, and a language—no matter how rudimentary. These, he thought, were the crucial necessary elements for the foundation of human society. A second stage was when men accomplished a pastoral economy—their livelihood depending upon the keeping of large herds. At this stage property as a social institution emerged and, correlated with it, social inequality and slavery. But these developments were responsible, at least, for a certain amount of leisure amongst certain groups of the population, leading therefore to a new development of other aspects of culture, including inventions and the beginning of science. A third stage was when mixed agriculture was accomplished as a basis for the economy. In these societies wealth was greater; the degree of leisure enjoyed by the population was therefore greater; and there was a better, more efficient, and wider-ranging division of labour. But, perhaps more crucial, there was the emergence of literacy. The development of alphabets, written knowledge and records, meant that history proper and clear perspectives of historical consciousness in societies could begin. The fourth and fifth stages were more or less descriptions of Greek and Roman civilization respectively and gave a detailed account of all their scientific, philosophical, technical and artistic advances. The sixth and seventh stages were those of the Middle Ages; the first being more or less the founding of the feudal order, ending in the crusades; the second referring to the development of feudal society ending with the invention and effective use of printing. The eighth stage covered the period from the invention of printing to the emergence of modern critical philosophy marked, for example, by the 'systematic doubt' of Descartes; and the ninth stage covered the period from this to the French Revolution. In this final stage Condorcet discussed the gradual extension of scientific knowledge about all aspects of the world and society; the gradual culmination of the scientific approach to the study of a society; and, following this, the conscious reconstruction of the institutions of society on the basis of a clear moral philosophy and clear scientific knowledge.

The tenth stage to which Condorcet devoted himself very considerably was, of course, the *future* of mankind which was just beginning to be consciously created in his own time. He believed that the conscious reconstruction of society would focus upon the elimination of inequalities between nations, the elimination of inequalities between social classes, and, parallel with this, upon the perfecting—physical, intellectual and moral—of individual human nature. All this meant an elaborate statement of human rights in order to secure and maximize individual freedom in the social order.

Condorcet maintained that no end to the possible progress of mankind could be foreseen; that no limits, could be set upon it;

but that perhaps the most important vehicle for the achievement of advancement was that of *education*. He also, with a kind of rationalistic optimism (though by no means a naive optimism) thought that the kind of feeling that had hitherto been organized by religions in society, about their symbols, rituals, and doctrines, could now be adequately organized about certain important humane ideals and so organized with equal efficacy in the service of human liberty and human improvement. In all this he thought that education could achieve an extension of human sympathy, of social feelings, and reciprocal social concern.

These then were the kinds of social theories presented in the on-going development of moral and political philosophy, and in our discussion of them, two things, at least, have become very clear.

First of all, these theories possessed the same characteristics as the 'religious theories' which we outlined earlier. They can all be seen to have been appropriate to the conditions and problems experienced in the societies in which they were elaborated. They were all pragmatically based; shaped in order to *deal* with these pressing social problems. They were also empirically based, presenting an account of the *facts* of human nature and society. But, related to this, they also sought a *moral* ground of justification of some kinds of social organization as against others. They all included an analysis of the nature of social institutions and their functions, but they also provided an account of the psychology of the individual—clearly believing that this was closely bound up with the pattern of social life and values which the individual experienced in the community.

The difference is only that these theories were constructed on the basis of critical philosophy, whereas the religious theories were a matter of accepted traditional belief, but it is of great interest to see that, in both kinds of theory, the same components were involved. It is almost as though these appear to be *essential* components, which *any* satisfactory theory must, in some way or other, take into account.

The second point, however, is that we have also seen quite clearly that, in the time of Montesquieu and Condorcet, and mirrored especially in their work, these theories of moral and political philosophy were moving towards a clearly seen need for a much more scientifically based approach to the study of man and society: an approach which would be much more systematic and widely inclusive in its comparative and historical studies; much more scrupulous in its ways of accomplishing generalizations and in its clarification of the *criteria* of its knowledge; and much more careful in its distinction between the study of facts and the statement of values, and the problems involved in considering *both* with reference to prescriptions for practical application and the making of political policies. These were dimensions not sufficiently pursued before, and it was these kinds of preoccupation within these theories, which led quite directly, shortly after the French Revolution, to the conscious and deliberate attempts to create sociology—a 'science' of society.

C *PHILOSOPHY OF HISTORY*

There was one other field of philosophical enquiry which produced some very interesting theories about man and society, and this, though to a certain extent distinct from moral and political philosophy, was closely and significantly related to it. This was the Philosophy of History.

'Philosophies of history' differ from specific theories within moral and political philosophy in the sense that they offer a *total* account of the place of man and society within the nature of things. The place of man and the development of historical society *within the entire scheme of things* is rendered 'intelligible' in these systems of speculation, whereas moral and political philosophies tend to be relatively limited accounts of the relations between individuals and the state, and of the ethical principles on the basis of which these relations ought to be organized. There is a perennial desire among men to believe that nature, in its entirety, embodies some kind of purpose which gives meaning and significance to the life of individuals and to the complex events of history. When men see the tragic wars, the conflicts of power, the changing panorama of human affairs in history, in which so much that is deeply felt, noble, and sublime, encounters so much that is evil and abhorrent, it seems an agonizing thought—that all this is nothing more than a dance of transient puppets in a meaningless play. There is a desire to believe in some deep-rooted value and meaning in it all.

Philosophical enquiry into whatever meaning and significance might exist stemmed quite directly from some of the religious theories we have mentioned, and from certain religious persuasions about the nature of man. If God had created the world and man with certain underlying purposes, then these purposes should be revealed by careful study. And even if there was no such ultimate divine purpose, it could still be maintained that since man was in part a rational and purposive creature, the historical story of his life and development in the world would reveal the meaning and purpose of his struggles. Some philosophers, therefore, attempted a detailed examination of the events of history in order to trace the meaningful pattern in them, and these theories were, and remain, among the most interesting that emerged before the development of sociology.

Here I shall concentrate chiefly upon the ideas of Hegel, because it seems to me that his is a philosophy of history which rests most clearly upon what we would now call sociological assumptions, and also, an understanding of his system of thought is essential for any subsequent understanding of the sociological theory of Marx, Hobhouse and others. It is of interest, however, to see how sociological insights pervaded the ideas of one or two other scholars who preceded Hegel.

G. B. Vico (1668–1744): The New Science

The work of Vico is quite astonishing in its range and detail, but also, more particularly, for the many insights it contained which clearly anticipated a systematic science of human society.

Vico saw quite clearly, for example, that it was impossible to understand the nature of human personality without studying individuals within the context of the society of which they were members. He was quite clearly aware of the 'social psychological' dimensions of society and their importance for the making of human individuality. Also, he emphasized religion as a particularly important social influence in this respect. Religion sustained and transmitted the important ideological elements of a community and provided the basis for social cohesion. Vico also insisted clearly that societies and their cultural traditions were slow, cumulative, historical processes and that it was therefore necessary to employ a historical method in seeking an understanding of them.

In order to accomplish such a vast account of man and his social developments in history, Vico deliberately undertook careful comparative studies. He was forced to conjecture about the nature of 'primitive peoples' and their mentality (he emphasized language, mythology and religion as the basic elements in the emergence of the earliest societies); but he then went on to collect and study documentary evidence (from classical literature, biblical studies, and the like) in order to describe and analyse with reliability the subsequent patterns of social change and development.

Following these studies, Vico put forward a theory of social change which was in part repetitive, in part progressive. He thought that all the epochs of civilization were characterized by a *cyclical* pattern of change through three stages.* Firstly, there was a stage in which explanations of society and its origins were couched in terms of the 'divine'; there was a dominance of feeling and emotion as distinct from reason, and political organization was 'theocratic'. Secondly, there was a stage in which explanations were couched in terms of 'heroic *human* action and values'; poetic imagination and insight were the dominant characteristics of thought, and social

* This may be compared with Comte's later 'Law of the Three Stages'. See pp. 168–70.

organization was modelled upon aristocratic excellence. The third stage was one in which explanations of society were couched in purely human terms, resting upon straightforward matter-of-fact knowledge, and entailing an extensive range of political freedom under various forms of monarchies and republics. However, this historical change from epoch to epoch—though each epoch was cyclical in itself—took the form of a 'spiral' of progress. Each epoch, though cylical in its own pattern of change, rested upon the achievements of earlier epochs. Each subsequent epoch therefore moved the human mind to a new and progressive level of fulfilment; achieved a richer awareness of reality and of the nature of human destiny within and in relation to it.

In this way Vico tried to show that the entire process of human history was intelligible as a process of the coming to maturity of the human mind in its understanding of nature and God. And this maturing of the human mind, he showed, was attendant upon the achievement of better and more appropriate social institutions. The achievement of enlightenment in human mentality was in large part a collective matter; a matter of the collective advancement of 'mind' or 'spirit' in which all individuals could participate and share.*

In this way, too, Vico tried to demonstrate the hand of God in society and history and the way in which man came to an even more enlightened and deepened understanding of the nature of God and the world.

A final point of great interest is that, in all this, Vico introduced the idea that a study of man and society in history was significantly different from a study of other phenomena in the world in the sense that it involved *subjective understanding in terms of meaning* as well as a simple set of statements of an 'objective' kind about the external qualities of things—trees, rocks, animals, stars, and the like—such as the other sciences of nature could achieve. In this Vico undoubtedly foresaw the emphasis by Max Weber and other German scholars† upon the distinctive differences of theory and method between the 'natural' and the 'human' sciences which were, of course, only developed fully much later.

Immanuel Kant (1724–1804): A Universal History

Kant, of course, is chiefly known for the exposition of the 'critical'

* This, too, may be compared with Hegel's notions which we shall come to in a moment. See pp. 135–38.
† This was a central and important debate in Germany—but it was also clearly seen and thoroughly discussed among British and American scholars. Lester Ward and Giddings were particularly clear about this. See pp. 475–86, 556–62.

philosophy which has influenced modern thought so profoundly. His major contributions lie in the theory of knowledge and in his attendant discussions of moral philosophy. His contribution to the philosophy of history is, by comparison, very slight. It is put forward in one quite short essay: *The Idea of a Universal History from a Cosmopolitan Point of View.* However, Kant's contribution is of considerable importance as an example of a kind of philosophy of history which does not rest necessarily on the religious or theological persuasions of men like Vico and, later, Hegel.

Kant, again like all those who were interested in the philosophy of history, began his essay with the fundamental question as to whether history could be thought to be completely meaningless, or whether it entailed some kind of *direction;* some kind of moral and intellectual *meaning* for man. His answer seems, at first sight, curious. He decided that a certain pattern of purpose was working its way out in all the complex events of human history, but *without* any clear consciousness or fore-knowledge on the part of all the individuals concerned. In short, he thought that a purposive plan was taking place in history 'over the heads of human individuals'.

The basic cause of all this, the basic factor underlying it, is what he called the 'unsocial sociability of man'. He maintained that human nature in society is paradoxical. Men need each other and are bound to enter into social relations with each other in order to fulfil their many needs, but, simultaneously, they resent the extent to which others intrude upon their privacy. They must enter into social relationships with others, but they also want to keep them at arm's length. Men cannot do without each other, but they want to keep each other at a distance. *Both* sociability *and* unsociability are necessarily involved in the fulfilment of human needs and purposes. It is this peculiarly conflictful interdependency of men, said Kant, which gave rise to the origin of human civilization and to the whole complex pattern of historical conflict, co-operation, change and progress.

Kant believed that it was in the experience of these conflicts and in each institutional resolution of them that society developed and that an increasing fulfilment of what is potential in human nature gradually took place. In the long run this pattern of change must move mankind not only beyond families, clans, and tribes to the creation of large-scale nations and federations of nations, but also to a completely global society, in which men the world over will be bound to recognize the necessity of world government and some kind of international organization which caters for the claims and counter-claims of societies and groups throughout the world.

The ultimate purpose, or plan, which is being worked out in

human history is, therefore, the achievement of a government or society which, in his words:

'Combines with the greatest possible freedom, and (in consequence) antagonism of its members, the most rigid determination and guarantee of the limits of this freedom, in such a way that the freedom of each individual may coexist with that of others.'

Also, Kant wrote:

'The history of the human species as a whole may be regarded as a realization of the secret plan of nature for bringing into existence a political constitution perfect both from the internal point of view and, so far as regards this purpose, from the external point of view also: such a constitution being the sole condition under which nature can fully develop all the capacities she has implanted in humanity.'

This is an all-too-brief account of Kant's ideas, but sufficient to show their relevance for and similarity with the much more fully worked out ideas of Hegel, upon whose work I think it is best to concentrate.

G. W. F. Hegel: An Idealist Philosophy of History

There is no doubt that the most impressive statement of a systematic philosophy of history, and that which brings the subject most clearly to the brink of modern sociology, is that of Hegel. And Hegel's work is best introduced as the greatest exposition of an *idealist* philosophy of history. Two points are worth making immediately about this word 'idealist'.

The first is that the term *idealist* in speculative metaphysics does not mean that the philosopher believes in, or postulates, certain moral ideals, or ideals of any other kind (aesthetic, intellectual), in human experience. A 'materialist' can believe in moral ideals and incorporate them into his system of thought, just as legitimately as an *idealist* or anyone else. The crucial distinction is that an *idealist* philosopher is one who believes in the *primacy* of *spirit* or *mind* in the universe. Spirit and mind (or God), is, for him, the ultimate reality, and the entire fabric of nature, material and otherwise, is held to stem from, to be rooted in, to have been in some way created by, this primary spiritual reality.

The second point is that *anyone* who believes in the existence of God, and believes that God created the world and man—and is therefore in some sense immanent in nature, *must* have an implicit philosophy of history of the same kind as that held by Hegel. If they are not clear about this, it is only because they have not worked

HEGEL: AN IDEALIST PHILOSOPHY OF HISTORY

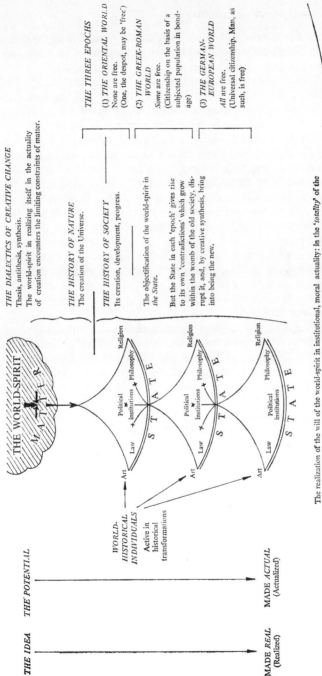

THE IDEA

THE POTENTIAL

WORLD-HISTORICAL INDIVIDUALS
Active in historical transformations

MADE REAL (Realized)

MADE ACTUAL (Actualized)

THE WORLD-SPIRIT — MATTER

STATE — Art, Law, Political institutions, Philosophy, Religion

THE DIALECTICS OF CREATIVE CHANGE
Thesis, antithesis, synthesis.
The world-spirit in realizing itself in the actuality of creation encounters the limiting constraints of matter.

THE HISTORY OF NATURE
The creation of the Universe.

THE HISTORY OF SOCIETY
Its creation, development, progress.

The objectification of the world-spirit in *the State.*

But the State in each 'epoch' gives rise to its own 'contradictions' which grow within the womb of the old society, disrupt it, and, by creative synthesis, bring into being the new.

THE THREE EPOCHS

(1) *THE ORIENTAL WORLD*
None are free.
(One, the despot, may be 'free')

(2) *THE GREEK-ROMAN WORLD*
Some are free.
(Citizenship on the basis of a subjected population in bondage)

(3) *THE GERMAN-EUROPEAN WORLD*
All are free.
(Universal citizenship. Man, as such, is free)

The realization of the will of the world-spirit in institutional, moral actuality: in the '*totality*' of the State. The 'whole' is greater than the parts. The parts realize their character within the whole.

'*Progress*': The emerging freedom of mind and spirit. The joy of mind and spirit in the fully conscious realization of its accomplished, created actuality of the world. The *conscious harmony of mind, spirit, nature and society.*

it out. They have not made fully *explicit* what is *implicit* in their beliefs. Hegel's philosophy of history is therefore of very considerable interest as one detailed example of an 'idealist' position.

It was Hegel's belief in this primacy of spiritual reality (indeed, for him, it was *more* than a belief, in that he was convinced that it permitted of rational demonstration) which enables us to understand what would otherwise be a baffling element in his system.

Believing in this primacy of spirit and mind, Hegel went on to maintain that all the many processes of nature, including all those of human society and history, must be 'intelligible' in terms of it. They must be an embodiment of the progress of God or the 'World-Spirit' in the developing creation of the world. They must manifest a rational direction and pattern, and a study of them must discover and reveal the meaning and purpose of spirit or mind itself.

There were thus two important and connected strands in Hegel's system of thought. First, he discussed *the nature of logical development itself*, the way in which the processes of thought disentangled its problems and moved ever more closely towards the truth, and secondly, he related these logical processes to the *actual events of nature and history*.

The process of logical development; the logical procedures whereby mind moves towards the truth and ultimately discovers it by exact clarification; he termed the 'dialectics' of thought, and his account is similar to the procedures of argument used by the early Greek philosophers. In any discussion or deliberation about the truth of a certain question, we begin with the statement of a proposition about it—a *thesis*. Every such proposition, however, encounters its opposite. Indeed, logically speaking, every thesis entails its own possible contradiction. As Hegel put it, every *thesis* has its *antithesis*. These two contradictory statements are then scrutinized and a partial resolution of them is arrived at. This is the *synthesis* of the two originally conflicting statements. This synthesis, however, then becomes the new thesis for the next stage in the argument. This too will have its own antithesis, and so, in this on-going dialectical way of argument, all the aspects of the question will come to be exposed, explored and clarified, and, progressively, we shall have arrived at the fullest truth possible of the matter under discussion.

Because Hegel thought that mind or spirit (what he called the 'Zeitgeist': the 'World Spirit'; a term which includes the notion of creative *will*) was a real substantive entity, and that Reason* was an actual substantive force working its way towards the creative actualization of truth in the world, he believed that these dialectics of thought and logic were actually at work in the physical order of

---

* One *has* to use capital letters in discussing Hegel.

events in the world, and he therefore identified the dialectics of Reason itself with the dialectical processes of nature and the *dialectics of history*. The phenomena of the natural world and of human history are themselves interpenetrated by substantive Reason and are themselves the manifestations of the dialectics of Reason working themselves out in the actualities of existence.

Now this idea that reason is a substantive entity, an actual reality in the concrete world of events, seems to us in our present climate of scientific thinking a very curious idea, and in order to make it perfectly clear how Hegel himself conceived it we might look at one or two quotations.

First of all, for example, Hegel wrote, when trying to make clear what 'the Great Anaxagoras' meant in his statement that 'reason governs the world':

'It is not intelligence as self-conscious Reason, not a Spirit as such that is meant; and we must clearly distinguish these from each other. The movement of the solar system takes place according to unchangeable laws. *These laws are Reason, implicit in the phenomena in question.** But neither the sun nor the planets, which revolve around it according to these laws, can be said to have any consciousness of them.'

It is perfectly clear from this that Hegel believed that the 'laws' or 'regularities' of nature were, in fact, aspects of substantive reason itself. And he further maintained that this reason actualized in the order of the world was divine providence in the created world, and that this had become manifest in 'religious' truth.

'The world', he wrote, 'is not abandoned to chance and external contingent causes, but *a providence controls it*'.†

The following quotation, however, makes absolutely clear, and in much more detail, what exactly Hegel believed about the nature of reason as such.

'The only Thought which Philosophy brings with it to the contemplation of History, is the simple conception of *Reason*; that Reason is the Sovereign of the World; that the history of the world, therefore, presents us with a rational process. This conviction and intuition is a hypothesis in the domain of history as such. In that of Philosophy it is no hypothesis. It is there proved by speculative cognition, that Reason—and this term may here suffice us, without investigating the relation sustained by the Universe to the Divine Being—is *Substance*, as well as *Infinite Power*; its own *Infinite Material* underlying all the natural and spiritual life which it originates, as also the *Infinite Form*—that which sets this Material in motion. On the one hand, Reason is the *substance* of the Universe; viz. that by which and in which all reality has its being and subsistence. On the other hand, it is the

* My italics.   † My italics.

131

Infinite Energy of the Universe; since Reason is not so powerless as to be incapable of producing anything but a mere ideal, a mere intention—having its place outside reality, nobody knows where; something separate and abstract, in the heads of certain human beings. It is *the infinite complex of things*, their entire Essence and Truth. It is its own material which it commits to its own Active Energy to work up; not needing, as finite action does, the conditions of an external material of given means from which it may obtain its support, and the objects of its activity. It supplies its own nourishment, and is the object of its own operations. While it is exclusively its own basis of existence, and absolute final aim, it is also the energizing power realizing this aim; developing it not only in the phenomena of the Natural, but also of the Spiritual Universe—the History of the World. That this 'Idea' or 'Reason' is the *True*, the *Eternal*, the absolutely *powerful* essence; that it reveals itself in the World, and that in that world nothing else is revealed but this and its honour and glory—is the thesis which, as we have said, has been proved in Philosophy, and is here regarded as demonstrated.'

One can only remark in leaving such a statement behind, that when Hegel is proposing an idea which he thinks difficult of comprehension to relatively ordinary mortals, he simply gives his assurance that this has been *proved* by philosophy and that it can, therefore, be accepted for the rest of the argument. What Hegel thought to be *proved* in philosophy seems now quite incredible,* but we shall return to this in our later criticisms of Hegel. It is at least abundantly clear, however, how Hegel himself regarded the nature of Reason: as a substantive reality interpenetrating the entire world of nature and history.

Hegel then went on to give a detailed account of this dialectical process of Reason in nature and history.

The primary 'thesis' in the creation of the world—in the process of 'becoming of things' in the world—was the World Spirit itself; *THE IDEA* in which all actualization originated. This spirit was the initial *Idea* in which all subsequent creation, all subsequent actualizations of truth in the world, was a *potentiality*. The world spirit, however, encountered the constraints and limitations of its own 'antithesis': MATTER. The conflicts and contradictions between thesis and antithesis, spirit and matter, were thereafter worked out, giving rise to new syntheses, and thus the process of creation began, continued, and continues. What was originally *IDEA*, a potentiality of spirit, came to be made *real* in the world; came to be *actualized* in the created world; as the world of objects, creatures, events as we know it. In such a way, Hegel offered an account of the entire development of universal history; the total process of creation of the physical world; but he then went on to claim that this same actual-

* It also seemed incredible to some people in Hegel's own time. Elsewhere in Europe, for example, Schopenhauer was continually squirming.

ization of the potentialities of the world spirit continued and could be seen in the events of human history and the development of civilization. The 'intelligibility' of history as well as of nature, could be clarified by unravelling the complexity of its events and tracing the dialectical unfolding of the world spirit in the activities and institutions of society.

In giving the same kind of dialectical account of the processes of history, Hegel conceived the World Spirit, still, as being the initial 'idea' or 'thesis' of history, and its antithesis as being the materially rooted desires and passions of mankind, those impulsive appetites over which mind strives to establish adequate control in order to achieve, for all of them, their richest mutual fulfilment.* The ultimate aim and outcome of this dialectical struggle between mind and spirit on the one hand, and materially rooted impulse on the other, was therefore a movement towards order and liberty which, according to Hegel, could only be achieved under the conditions of morality worked out in the form of the state. Hegel wrote as follows:

'Two elements, therefore, enter into the object of our investigations; the first the Idea, the second the complex of human passions; the one the warp, the other the woof of the vast arras-web of Universal History. The concrete mean and union of the two is Liberty, under the conditions of morality in a state.'

Hegel also believed that in this struggle towards formal liberty there was not only an actualization of what was initially potential in spirit, but also that these potentialities of spirit moved from the realm of unconsciousness into the level of human consciousness, so that the ultimate outcome was the full consciousness and enjoyment on the part of the spirit, of its own created freedom.

'The History of the World begins with its general aim—the realization of the Idea of Spirit—only in an *implicit* form in Nature; a hidden, most profoundly hidden, unconscious instinct; and the whole process of History (as already observed), is directed to rendering this unconscious impulse a conscious one.'

And again:

'The realization of freedom is the absolute final aim' of the process of history, and this, he maintained, 'exists for its own sake.'

We must note next how Hegel accounted for this process of historical change in terms of dialectical development. First, it is important to see the way in which he described the idea of *development* itself, for this was to become a central concept in the work of later sociologists, especially, for example, in that of Hobhouse.†

* One can feel the thread of Plato here.
† See *The Making of Sociology*, Vol. 2, Part One, Ch. 3.

Hegel wrote:

'The principle of *Development* involves the existence of a latent germ of being—a capacity or potentiality striving to realize itself. This formal conception finds actual existence in Spirit; which has the History of the World for its theatre, its possession, and the sphere of its realization. It is not of such a nature as to be tossed to and fro amid the superficial play of accidents, but is rather the absolute arbiter of things; entirely unmoved by contingencies, which, indeed, it applies and manages for its own purposes. Development, however, is also a property of organized natural objects. Their existence presents itself, not as an exclusively dependent one, subjected to external changes, but as one which expands itself in virtue of an internal unchangeable principle; a simple essence,—whose existence, *i.e.*, as a germ, is primarily simple,—but which subsequently develops a variety of parts, that become involved with other objects, and consequently live through a continuous process of changes;—a process nevertheless, that results in the very contrary of change, and is even transformed into a *vis conservatrix* of the organic principle, and the form embodying it. Thus the organized *individuum* produces itself; it expands itself *actually* to what it was always *potentially*.—So Spirit is only that which it attains by its own efforts; it makes itself *actually* what it always was *potentially*.—That development (of *natural organisms*) takes place in a direct, unopposed, unhindered manner. Between the Idea and its realization—the essential constitution of the original germ and the conformity to it of the existence derived from it—no disturbing influence can intrude. But in relation to Spirit it is quite otherwise. The realization of *its* Idea is mediated by consciousness and will; these very faculties are, in the first instance, sunk in their primary *merely* natural life; the first objects and goal of their striving is the realization of their merely natural destiny—but which, since it is Spirit that animates it, is possessed of vast attractions and displays great power and (moral) richness. Thus Spirit is at war with itself; it has to overcome itself as its most formidable obstacle. That development which in the sphere of Nature is a peaceful growth, is in that of Spirit, a severe, a mighty conflict with itself. What Spirit really strives for is the realization of its Ideal being, but in doing so, it hides that goal from its own vision, and is proud and well satisfied in this alienation from it.'

'Its expansion, therefore, does not prevent the harmless tranquillity of mere growth, as does that of organic life, but a stern reluctant working against itself. It exhibits, moreover, not the mere formal conception of development, but the attainment of a definite result. The goal of attainment we determined at the outset; it is Spirit in its *completeness*, in its essential nature, i.e. Freedom. This is the fundamental object, and therefore also the leading principle of the development—that whereby it receives meaning and importance. . .'

As to the dialectical nature of this development of spirit in the world, after having written briefly about the complicated contents of world history—'that vast picture of changes and transactions; of infinitely manifold forms of peoples, states, individuals in unresting succession'—Hegel continued:

'The general thought—the category which first presents itself in this restless mutation of individuals and peoples, existing for a time and then vanishing —is that of *change* at large. The sight of the ruins of some ancient sovereignty directly leads us to contemplate this thought of change in its negative aspect. What traveller among the ruins of Carthage, of Palmyra, Persepolis, or Rome, has not been stimulated to reflections on the transiency of kingdoms and men, and to sadness at the thought of a vigorous and rich life now departed—a sadness which does not expend itself on personal losses and the uncertainty of one's own undertakings, but is a disinterested sorrow at the decay of a splendid and highly cultured national life! But the next consideration which allies itself with that of change is, that change while it imports dissolution, involves at the same time the rise of a *new life*—that while death is the issue of life, life is also the issue of death. This is a grand conception; one which the Oriental thinkers attained, and which is perhaps the highest in their metaphysics. In the idea of *Metempsychosis* we find it evolved in its relation to individual existence; but a myth more generally known, is that of the *Phoenix* as a type of life of *Nature*; eternally preparing for itself its funeral pile, and consuming itself upon it; but so that from its ashes is produced the new, renovated, fresh life. But this image is only Asiatic; oriental not occidental. Spirit—consuming the envelope of its existence—does not merely pass into another envelope, nor rise rejuvenescent from the ashes of its previous form; it comes forth exalted, glorified, a purer spirit. It certainly makes war upon itself—consumes its own existence; but in this very destruction it works up that existence into a new form, and each successive phase becomes in its turn a material, working on which it exalts itself to a new grade.'

The next point in Hegel's system which must be made clear is his teaching that the dialectical processes whereby the World Spirit becomes actualized in history (becomes objectified and then borne in upon human consciousness) takes the form of large scale social movements which assume their patterns of institutionalization, over and above the heads of individuals and without awareness or foresight. It is the *State* according to Hegel, which is the vehicle of spiritual advance. It is in the *State*, not in the minds of individuals, that the achievements of the world spirit, at any particular time, come to be objectified. And by the State, Hegel meant the *totality* of the inter-connected social institutions of any particular epoch of civilization. The will and achievement of the world spirit in any period is to be seen in the characteristic institutions of the State, and individuals can only find their fulfilment and historical destiny in so far as they submit themselves to those values and purposes which are manifested in the State of their time. *The whole*—qualitatively as

F

well as quantitatively—is greater than *the parts* (including the individuals) of which it consists. The highest objective spiritual truth of any epoch lies in *the totality of the state*, and individuals realise and fulfil their own nature by virtue of their *participation* in the whole. It is *not* the case that the whole, the totality of institutions, is consciously brought about by the efforts of purposive individuals. The whole makes the parts, not the parts the whole. The qualities of the whole are not simply a sum of the independent qualities of the individual parts. Qualities arise in the creative process of the whole itself, and these qualities are then engendered and created in individuals (the parts) as they enter, and are appreciated in, their consciousness.

There are several important elements in this point of view which need special attention.

Firstly, from the point of view of subsequent sociological analysis, it is important to notice that the conception of a society which Hegel found it necessary to use was already a clear idea of the *social system:* consisting of various institutions which, though existing for specific purposes and having particular functions in relation to some aspect of human nature and human freedom, were nonetheless interdependent in their characteristics, all—together—forming one total society with its own qualitatively distinct ethos. This 'ethos' of the whole society, too, was conceived as having an important determining influence upon the nature and character of the individuals in society. Hegel, in short, had a distinct conception of 'social psychology' in the sense that it was the psychological aspects of the collectivity of society which engendered qualities in individual minds and personalities. But another very interesting point in this connection is that Hegel believed a society to be a *total* phenomenon which, in fact, could not, excepting superficially, be said to consist of separable parts at all. A society, a 'totality of institutions', was a qualitatively new and distinct creative process in nature; it was a 'total' historical and cultural phenomenon and could only be properly understood as such.

It is only from our own point of view, and for purposes of analysis that we can 'separate' aspects of the whole into parts. Thus, we can speak of the 'religion' of a society, the 'economic' organization of a society, the 'political' system in a society, the 'art' of a society, and so on, but this is a matter of analytical necessity only. We find it impossible to understand the whole without some such kind of preliminary analysis and description. Nonetheless, Hegel maintains, a society *is in fact, a totality which does not possess these sharp distinctions.* The religious aspects, the economic aspects, the governmental aspects, the artistic aspects of a society all interpenetrate each other. Together, they all constitute one living creative whole. Hegel wrote, for example, when speaking of the union between the objective manifestation of the world spirit and the subjective will of individual personalities:

'The objective existence of this union is the State, which is therefore the basis and centre of the other concrete elements of the life of a people—of art, of law, of morals, of religion, of science.'

And, he went on:

'A state is an individual totality of which you cannot select any particular side, even a supremely important one such as its political constitution, and deliberate and decide respecting it in that isolated form.'

It is clear beyond doubt then, that Hegel can be said, quite definitely, to have been a 'sociologist' in his way of regarding society and his proposed way of understanding and explaining it. He was perfectly clear in both his conception and his treatment, that the analysis of society had to be based upon the recognition of this intimate interconnection between social institutions; and that it was a positive error to believe that any one institution in a society could be understood in isolation from the rest. He thought of a social system, a set of social institutions interconnected with each other, almost exactly as we now think of it. This is a very important insight, and later we shall see that it has considerable weight and raises difficult problems, from the point of view of distinguishing between concepts we find useful for describing and analysing the constituent parts of a society, and the concepts we require for the *causal explanation* of its nature and changes. But this question must be left until the very end of our study, when we have considered the ways in which many sociologists have thought about it and tried to deal with it.

Before leaving this whole question, however, let us see exactly how Hegel thought about the nature of the state as the *objectification of the world spirit*. First of all, he wrote:

'What is the material in which the Ideal of Reason is wrought out? The primary answer would be,—Personality itself—human desires—Subjectivity generally. In human knowledge and volition, as its material element, Reason attains positive existence. We have considered subjective volition where it has an object which is the truth and essence of a reality, viz. where it constitutes a great world-historical passion. As a subjective will, occupied with limited passions, it is dependent, and can gratify its desires only within the limits of this dependence. But the subjective will has also a substantial life—a reality,—in which it moves in the region of *essential* being, and has the essential itself as the object of its existence. This essential being is the union of the *subjective* with the *rational* Will: it is the moral Whole, the *State*, which is that form of reality in which the individual has and enjoys his freedom, but on the condition of his recognizing, believing in, and willing that which is common to the Whole. And this must not be understood as if the subjective will of the social unit attained its gratification and enjoyment through that common Will; as if this were a means provided for its benefit; as if the individual, in his relations to other individuals, thus limited his freedom, in order that this universal limitation—the mutual constraint of all—might secure a small space of liberty for each. Rather, we affirm, are Law, Morality, Government, and they alone, the positive reality and completion of Freedom. Freedom of a low and limited order, is mere caprice; which finds its exercise in the sphere of particular and limited desires.'

'In the history of the World, only those peoples can come under our notice which form a state. For it must be understood that this latter is the realization of Freedom, *i.e.* of the absolute final aim, and that it exists for its own sake. It must further be understood that all the worth which the human being possesses—and spiritual reality, he possesses only through the State. For his spiritual reality consists in this, that his own essence—Reason—is objectively present to him, that it possesses objective immediate existence for him. Thus only is he fully conscious; thus only is he a partaker of morality—of a just and moral social and political life. For Truth is the Unity of the universal and subjective Will; and the Universal is to be found in the State, in its laws, its universal and rational arrangements. The State is the Divine Idea as it exists on Earth.'

And then:

'Summing up what has been said of the State, we find that we have been led to call its vital principle, as actuating the individuals who compose it,— Morality. The State, its laws, its arrangements, constitute the rights of its members; its natural features, its mountains, air, and waters, are *their* country, their fatherland, their outward material property; the history of this State, *their* deeds; what their ancestors have produced, belongs to them and lives in their memory. All is their possession, just as they are possessed by it; for it constitutes their existence, their being.'

'Their imagination is occupied with the ideas thus presented, while the adoption of these laws, and of a fatherland so conditioned is the expression of their will. It is this matured totality which thus constitutes *one* Being, the spirit of *one* People. To it the individual members belong; each unit is the Son of his Nation, and at the same time—in as far as the State to which he belongs is undergoing development—the Son of his Age. None remains behind it, still less advances beyond it. This Spiritual Being (the Spirit of his Time) is his; he is a representative of it; it is that in which he originated, and in which he lives.'

Hegel then went on to claim that the entire process of history could be divided clearly into certain important *epochs* of civilization, each of which was characterized by a newly emergent form of the state (a new 'totality of institutions)', and each of which constituted an advance of the world spirit. In each epoch there was a distinctive quality of perception, thought, and feeling in religious institutions; of moral and philosophical conceptions in political institutions; of perceptions and insight into the nature of things in artistic creation; and similarly in all aspects of social life and organization. Amongst all these there was an all-pervading consensus, a unified 'ethos', which linked them all together, permeating them with a common quality and character; and all these aspects of this 'totality' of civilized achievement were aspects of that *actualization*, accomplished in that period, of what was originally *potential* in the world spirit. Individuals had the fullest experience of the freedom and fulfilment which their nature allowed, if they were fully aware of this ethos of their own time and dedicated themselves to it.

Hegel then undertook a detailed study of history in order to trace and describe such epochs, and there were, he claimed, three major epochs of human civilization which could be clearly distinguished.

'*The Oriental World*' (of the large, highly centralized civilizations of antiquity) was characterized by central despotic authority. *No-one* therefore, was free. Sometimes Hegel wrote as though only *one* person was free in such a despotism, namely the despot himself; but in his detailed consideration of this he maintained that the despot himself must have been so bound up within the authoritarian network of the 'totality' of institutions that even he himself could not be considered free. The second epoch was that of the *Graeco-Roman* world in which *some* were free (i.e., the *principle* of political citizenship had emerged, and *some* people enjoyed it, but there was still an uncritical assumption that some men were born to slavery and the institutions of society still rested upon an unfree section of the population). Thirdly, there was the *German-European* epoch in which *all* were free; that is, the conception had emerged in this latter epoch that man *as such* (and *universally*) was free, and the institutions of society were changing in such a way as effectively to *secure* this for all citizens.

Each of these epochs manifested (in the creative 'totality' of the state) a new 'thesis' for the subsequent dialectical development of the world spirit. Each, however, gave rise within its own created institutions to its 'anti-thesis'. The institutions of each gave rise to contradictions which grew like the seeds of a new birth within the womb of the old society. Dialectical conflict ensued. The old order of the state was gradually disintegrated, giving rise to the new. Hegel sometimes wrote as though he believed that in the German-European epoch of his own time, the world spirit had, in large part, achieved its task, since this represented a full achievement of human freedom, and, as we have seen, the criterion of spiritual advance which Hegel adopted as the ultimate end of the whole process of history, was the progressive achievement of freedom. But this apparent finality must not be taken too seriously, as we shall see.

Before considering the ways in which Hegel's system is open to criticism, there is one other important aspect of his 'theory' which deserves attention and emphasis. This is the role which he attributed in the 'dialectics of history' to 'World Historical Individuals'. And this can best be introduced by thinking of the relation between the 'totality' of the state as Hegel thought of it, and 'totalitarianism' as it has come to exist in modern political thought and action.

If we think of Hegel's system without reference to recent political events, it may seem an exciting, speculative philosophy which is politically harmless; having little to do with fanaticism or dictatorship. When Hegel spoke of the 'totality' of the state, he was obviously referring to the *gradual unfolding* of a *consensus* in the thought, feeling and institutions of a civilization. He referred to the all-pervading ethos of an epoch as a unified spiritual achievement which emerged gradually and historically. And this seems to have little to do with modern totalitarian dictators. For they—whether Fascist, National Socialist or Communist—have, on the contrary, positively *imposed* the uniformity which they desire upon all the people in society. They have positively *created* a 'totality' of institutions in society: forcing a whole people to accept the values and the 'historical task' which they themselves dictate; forcing thought into certain channels; dictating certain principles for the creation of works of art; forbidding anything which militates against their own ideology. On the face of it, there seems to be a great gulf between a Hegel and a Hitler.

This gap, however, is not as wide as it appears when we consider what Hegel had to say about the nature and task of great men in history; the men he called 'WORLD HISTORICAL INDIVIDUALS'. Although Hegel insisted that the World Spirit was manifested in the 'totality' of society and that this occurred over and above the consciousness and efforts of individuals as such, he nonetheless claimed that some men were specially gifted and possessed a greater and more far-reaching vision than the average individuals in society. They possessed an insight into the dialectical processes of history that went beyond that of ordinary men. They could divine in the bewildering changes which were going on about them the next historical step of the 'World Spirit'. They could see the next important advance in human destiny. Their task, then, was always to act as luminaries, as leaders, to the confused people of their day, clarifying their immediate historic task and helping them to achieve it.

When describing such World Historical Individuals, Hegel tended to write with a certain poetic fervour, maintaining that these men could commit deeds which, to others, would seem unjustifiable, and which might indeed, for other men, be thought immoral and punishable. They, if necessary, could ignore the sufferings of their fellows because their task was so noble and of such crucial importance.

Why it is that the World Spirit, after all these massive aggregate dialectical processes, suddenly needs to make use of eminent individuals of this kind, Hegel does not tell us. But it is clear, on considering what Hegel said about them, that he and the Hitlers of this world are not so far apart as one might have thought at first glance. Neither does it seem so clear that there are the two brands of totalitarianism, which we distinguished at the outset. The two seem to fuse into one.

Having said that world historical individuals are those who direct 'those momentous collisions between existing acknowledged duties, laws and rights and those contingencies which are adverse to this fixed system', and having mentioned men like Caesar and Napoleon as examples, Hegel went on to write:

'Such are all great historical men,—whose own particular aims involve those large issues which are the will of the World-Spirit. They may be called Heroes, inasmuch as they have derived their purposes and their vocation, not from the calm, regular course of things, sanctioned by the existing order; but from a concealed fount—one which has not attained to phenomenal, present existence,—from that inner Spirit, still hidden beneath the surface, which, impinging on the outer world as on a shell, bursts it in pieces, because it is another kernel than that which belonged to the shell in question. They are men, therefore, who appear to draw the impulse of their life from themselves; and whose deeds have produced a condition of things and a complex of historical relations which appear to be only *their* interest, and *their* work.'

'They are thinking men, who had an insight into the requirements of the time—*what was ripe for development*. This was the very Truth for their age, for their world; the species next in order, so to speak, and which was already formed in the womb of time. It was theirs to know this nascent principle; the necessary, directly sequent step in progress, which their world was to take; to make this their aim, and to expend their energy in promoting it. World-historical men—the Heroes of an epoch—must, therefore, be recognized as its clear-sighted ones; *their* deeds, *their* words are the best of that time.'

And as to what can only be called the ethical privileges of such individuals, Hegel wrote:

'A World-historical individual is not so unwise as to indulge a variety of wishes to divide his regards. He is devoted to the One Aim regardless of all else. It is even possible that such men may treat other great, even sacred interests, inconsiderately; conduct which is indeed obnoxious to moral reprehension. But so mighty a form must trample down many an innocent flower—crush to pieces many an object in its path.'

'The deeds of great men, who are the Individuals of the World's History, thus appear not only justified in view of that intrinsic result of which they were not conscious, but also from the point of view occupied by the secular moralist. But looked at from this point, moral claims that are irrelevant, must not be brought into collision with world-historical deeds and their accomplishment. The Litany of Private virtues—modesty, humility, philanthropy and forbearance—must not be raised against them.'

One can only hope, when such Individuals are putting Jews in gas ovens, burning heretics, smashing kulaks, and even forcing upon us a 'choice' between fivepenny and fourpenny mail, that the World Spirit will understand us in entertaining a measure of doubt about their authority, and a certain resentment at their privilege.

In what ways can Hegel's philosophy of history be criticized?

In the first place, Hegel had the merit of seeing the world, and the human situation in the world, as a *process* of ongoing change, and made an awe-inspiring attempt to bring together the earlier absolutism of metaphysics and this new dynamic conception of a changing universe. Those who criticize his grandiose attempt and find his talk of the World Spirit, the Idea and the Real, the Potential and the Actual, the role of World Historical Individuals, confusing, should at least stop and reflect whether their own beliefs and assumptions do not imply similar difficulties. The Christian, for example, who believes in a God who created and sustains the world and who is working his purpose out in history, must meet exactly the same kind of difficulties in bringing his notions of God and spiritual reality together with our modern scientific knowledge of the changing universe and the changes of human society. Hegel may have failed— but is there any other philosophy of history basing itself on the primacy of spirit or mind as the fundamental ground of reality, which has succeeded any better than he did? The answer, as far as I am aware, is—no!

I think it is worth saying too, that we should beware of rejecting Hegel's ideas, and his 'metaphysically toned' way of stating them, too easily. We live in a climate of thought so closely dictated by the immediate empiricism of science, and a very technologically orientated science at that, that we are altogether too prone to assume that our own perspective is the right one. There is also a hectic pressure about our academic thinking that well-nigh precludes the kind of searching thought that an assessment of Hegel, or any of the other great philosophers requires. Speaking personally, and although I find some things in him quite unacceptable, I always feel Hegel to be full of a profundity which one cannot leave unconsidered. There is something so telling in his notions of 'creativity' and 'development' and the significance of 'forms' in nature and history; he seems so intriguingly to bring the central ideas of early metaphysics into the context of our modern 'dynamic' conception of nature and history; that I always feel persuaded that he deserves long and careful study*. Certainly some of the 'materialist' notions which have followed him are brash in comparison. And, after all, it *is* a *possibility* that God exists!

Hegel also had the great merit of introducing *perspective* into historical knowledge. His was not the first attempt; but it was certainly more clear and more detailed than anything that had been attempted before. Furthermore, his lectures on the philosophy of history are full of fascinating observations as, for example, on the intimate relation between religious perception and experience and artistic perception and experience in the various epochs, and many other similar insights. Hegel's work contains a richness to which this kind of brief account cannot possibly do justice. It is also worth bearing in mind that Hegel was one of the first thinkers to reflect, not only upon the *facts* of history, but upon the *methods of writing* history itself, and his observations in the field of historiography are still of the greatest interest.

When all is said in Hegel's favour, however, his system does appear to suffer from some defects and some grave dangers.

In the first place, his notion of reason as a substantive reality in the world (actually existent in the material nature of the world), and his identification of processes of logic with the actual processes of natural and historical events, is not a view which can now be upheld. Nowadays we think of reasoning, thinking, the procedures of logical inference, as an *activity* which men undertake. Reasoning is a matter of men thinking. We can certainly abstract a statement of what constitutes 'rational thought' from the active procedures of men thinking. But reason cannot be said to exist as a substantive fact apart from this. Reason does not exist independently of men reasoning, or clarifying the processes of their reasoning. And though men may make statements about nature and history from which logical inferences may be made, so that their statements may be logically connected, the actual processes of nature and history cannot themselves be held necessarily to be *logically* interconnected. This, if I

---

* One's judgment about men of the stature of Hegel can never be final, even though it might be decisive about some points.

understand it aright, is one aspect of the fundamental point which Hume makes in his theory of knowledge*

For example, suppose that a man is walking under a cliff when a boulder is dislodged by a violent wind, and, in falling, this crushes and kills him. Or suppose that a volcanic eruption spills lava over a small island in the Atlantic and destroys the people who live on it. In both these cases, we can assemble knowledge about all the processes involved: the force of the wind, the force of gravity, the resistance to pressure of the human body; the power of a volcanic eruption, the effect of lava upon human bodies, and so on. We can then provide a wide body of statements which are themselves logically interconnected and from which further inferences can be made to the effect that if such and such happens, then men will be killed and communities will be destroyed. But it cannot be maintained, surely, that *the natural events themselves are logically connected*? That they are the manifestation of substantive reason? They are interconnected *facts* in our experience, but it would surely be very difficult to see such sequences of facts as being rationally meaningful in terms of any substantive reason or spirit? Indeed, if some 'spiritual reality' underlay events of this kind; if it *constituted* interconnections of this kind, and brought them about deliberately; we should be driven to have a very jaundiced conception of it. Men can *reason about* the regular connections between rocks, wind, volcanoes, and human death, but the physical interdependencies cannot, surely, be said to be 'substantive reason'? Nature and history, then, cannot be assumed to be the substantive rational processes that Hegel conceived them to be, and his assertion that this assumption is one already *proved* in philosophy is an assertion that we ourselves cannot possibly accept or adopt.

Secondly, whilst there is merit in Hegel's insistence that reality can only be properly conceived as a process of change; and whilst his conception of 'dialectical' change seems as though it would be useful in analysing the contradictions and conflicting forces in nature and history; it must be said that the *points and methods of transition* in historical change, as described by Hegel, turn out to be extremely vague. In a sense, of course, it is a simple truism that the assumption of a definite form by social institutions and their values necessarily introduces related constraints. These can give rise to conflict, and this can bring about further change whereby the problems are resolved. But this changed institution will create new constraints, and so on. But Hegel nowhere makes very clear the actual mechan-

---

* i.e. That the 'causal laws' of nature do not, at all, possess *logical certainty*, but only psychological regularity; that is to say, men always find them such in their experience.

isms of social change which are at work. In this, as we shall see later, Marx sought to improve upon Hegel.

It has been stated as a third criticism, that Hegel's apparent finality is curious, to say the least. The idea that the task of the world spirit was more or less completed in the Europe of his own day seems, now, rather an odd conclusion. To my mind, however, this is a relatively minor criticism, for one or two reasons.

Firstly, because it is a criticism which is applicable to all thinkers of this kind, who are seeking a 'system' of explanation; and can be understood. There seems to be a powerful inclination in men towards the achievement of certainty, conclusiveness, completeness in the statement of their theories.* There is a certain aesthetic love of rounding off one's own metaphysical system; making it a complete, finished, harmonious whole; which tends to make all thinkers bring their systems to a conclusion. The world itself, however, is never as final as our speculative systems of thought about it. It goes on and changes, and men find their 'completed' systems of thought no longer satisfactory. This is so much so that one might even conclude that any system of thought or any theory of society which claims finality, which claims to explain *everything*, demonstrates at once its weakness and inadequacy.

The statement made by A. N. Whitehead in the preface to his book *Process and Reality*—

'There remains the final reflection, how shallow, puny, and imperfect are efforts to sound the depths in the nature of things. In philosophical discussion, the merest hint of dogmatic certainty as to finality of statement is an exhibition of folly.'

—seems to me altogether salutary.

The second reason, however, why one cannot make this a weighty criticism of Hegel, is that it is altogether doubtful whether he was as final in his conceptions as his work sometimes tends to suggest. The apparent finality is because he confined his analysis entirely to what had already *happened* in history, and explicitly set aside any consideration of what might happen in future. But in what he had to say about the new world of America, it is clear that his mind was by no means altogether closed to the probability of future development and advance. In writing of 'the new world and the dreams to which it may give rise', he said:

'America is therefore the land of the future, where, in the ages that lie before us, the burden of the World's History shall reveal itself—perhaps in a contest between North and South America. It is a land of desire for all those who are weary of the historical lumber-room of old Europe.

* See Pareto, *The Making of Sociology*, Vol. 2, Part Three, Ch. 5.

Napoleon is reported to have said, 'Cette vieille Europe m'ennuie.'
It is for America to abandon the ground on which hitherto the History
of the World has developed itself. What *has* taken place in the New
World up to the present time is only an echo of the Old World,—the
expression of a foreign life; and as a Land of the Future, it has no interest
for us here, for, as regards *History*, our concern must be with that which
has been and that which is. In regard to *Philosophy*, on the other hand, we
have to do with that which (strictly speaking) is neither past nor future,
but with that which *is*, which has an eternal existence—with Reason; and
this is quite sufficient to occupy us.'

It seems obvious that we should not make too much of this
particular criticism of Hegel.

A fourth criticism is that his doctrine of 'the Real Will' of the
World Spirit, and of the role of 'World Historical Individuals' in
serving this will, is dangerous in its totalitarian and authoritarian
implications. How are ordinary mortals to judge which of these—
amongst the many power-seeking leaders who seem desirous of
setting them about their historical task—are the great men possessing genuine insight into the real will of the world spirit? Which
among them is really the servant of the world spirit and which is
merely an upstart? This is an especially pressing question when some
of the 'Leaders' who tramp about the stage of the world do not seem
to have the insight into world-history of an average bus-conductor.
According to Hegel, obviously, ordinary people can have no ground
for judgment. Indeed, it is doubtful whether in his system they can be
said to have a *right* to judge. If one sympathizes with 'World Spirits'
one might be inclined to respond to the grandeur of Hegel's zeal. But
if, on the contrary, one sympathizes with ordinary mortals one might
be strongly disinclined to agree with Hegel on this matter. From this
latter point of view, as soon as a man puts himself forward as a
World Historical Individual, claiming a right to trample upon others
for the purpose of historical destiny, our principle ought always to
be—to trim him down to scale; to put him in prison rather than in
government, in an asylum rather than the House of Lords.

Philosophically speaking, however, it is enough to point out that
there seem to be no criteria whatever for demonstrating the existence
of such a 'real will' independent of the minds of men in society, and
for the belief that there are some great individuals who have been
given a preferential insight into the nature of it.

Closely linked to this is the fifth criticism—that Hegel's notion of
freedom is not easily comprehensible. It has uncomfortable ambiguities. It is certainly intelligible to maintain that a person may
find a rich fulfilment of the many aspects of his nature by devoting
himself to tasks and values which he finds in the society about him,

and even in the values and aims of his social tradition which he feels to be greater than himself. It is also intelligible to speak of the maximization of freedom being only possible in the conditions of morality secured by certain institutions of the state. But to speak of this in terms of *submitting* himself to what is 'objectified' in the 'totality' of the state can surely be a complete abnegation of freedom as we know it. Hegel seems to conceive of freedom and complete submission to the objective qualities and values of the state as being identical. And this seems both philosophically unwarranted and politically highly dangerous.

It is quite clear from these brief accounts that these theories selected from the 'philosophy of history' possessed the same characteristics as the theories in myth and religion, and moral and political philosophy, which we considered earlier. Here again, we find that they were based upon the facts of nature and history; attempted a certain moral justification of the forms of society and authority in history; offered an analysis of the many institutions of society in their interdependence within society as a 'whole'; and clearly thought of the nature of the individual and society as being very closely and reciprocally linked. Perhaps more like the 'religious' theories than the theories of moral and political philosophy, these 'philosophies of history' also placed man and society within the wider context of reality at large, and provided an 'intelligible' account of this reality. The same elements of theory were therefore clearly present.

Our discussion of the ideas of Hegel in particular, however, has indicated one or two important points which ought to be emphasized.

Firstly, it is perfectly clear that Hegel was already employing 'sociological' insight in his conception of the nature of society and social change. His analysis of society as a 'whole' in terms of a pattern of interconnected institutions is scarcely different from that of a modern sociologist. He also saw quite clearly, like Condorcet, Montesquieu, and many later writers, that the development of mind and the growth of knowledge is significantly correlated with changes in all the other institutions of society, and that it can therefore be used as a central measure for comparative studies. He saw perfectly clearly too, the close interdependence between the nature of the individual personality and the symbolic content of the social tradition, and that the two should properly be studied in the closest interrelationship. In short, in his pursuit of a satisfactory 'philosophy of history', a satisfactory account of the nature of man and his place in the world, Hegel had found a 'sociological' analysis of society in history indispensable.

We have seen, however, that in spite of this conception, Hegel's system and method of interpretation was still strongly rooted in dogmatic metaphysics. Many principles which Hegel seemed to accept uncritically, and certainly many of the large-scale pronouncements which he derived from them, were such as to seem philosophically in error, and dangerous for political practice.

And this leads to the final point which has become quite plain: that the very existence of a philosophy of history like that of Hegel, which can become so influential in political thought and practice, and which possesses so much that is dubious and dangerous, demonstrates, perhaps more forcibly than anything else, the *need* for a more reliable science of society. It is only possible to criticize such systems of thought adequately if we can show that we have better methods than they have; if we can show that our judgments and hypotheses rest on more accurate criteria than theirs; if we can provide a better and more reliable (more testable) survey of the facts of history and historical change than that which Hegel and similar thinkers put forward.

One can say, in conclusion, that although Hegel's philosophy of history did not constitute a scientific sociology, it had the great merit of making the development of such a science necessary; of making the need for it starkly apparent. And this, in a way, is the kind of dialectical development of knowledge that he himself had in mind. The contribution he made was certainly a telling and a productive one. So much sprang, by way of criticism, from the systematic statement which he accomplished.

D SCIENCE AND EPISTEMOLOGY

In addition to the later developments of moral and political philosophy and the philosophy of history, there were two other developments of thought during the eighteenth century which were especially important in leading to fundamental criticisms of early social theories, and which culminated, at the same time, in the clear need for a science of society. These were, firstly, the development and extension of the natural sciences: their increasing success in producing a testable and useful body of knowledge about various aspects of the nature of the world; and, secondly, the development in the theory of knowledge (epistemology) attendant upon this.

Little need be said about the developments of science. It is enough simply to note that following the exacting criticisms of the methods of attaining knowledge undertaken by philosophers such as Hobbes and Descartes there had been an extension of the methods of science in investigating all aspects of the nature of the physical world—in physics, astronomy, chemistry, and so on. In all these fields science was proving itself increasingly superior to other and earlier methods of study. It was not only extending man's knowledge of the world, but also bringing about an increasing degree of control over the environment with regard to the better satisfaction of human needs and the increase in human welfare. The chief thing to emphasize, for our purposes, is that this development of the natural sciences gave rise to a totally new perspective, concerning the place of man in nature.

Two sciences in particular were responsible for this. The first was the science of geology which, in its new methods of dating the geological strata of the earth, began to give completely new perspectives of time as far as the origin and history of man in the world was concerned. The place of man in the scheme of creation; of the human species within the context of all other species; could now be dated in a much more exact way, so that early theories concerning the special creation of man were at least thrown open to serious question. But the second and probably more important science was that of biology. There had been many doubts about the possibility of applying the scientific method to the study of man, but once biology became established as a science it could no longer be doubted that the study of at least *some* aspects of man permitted of scientific study. Whatever Man might be besides, he had now to be seen, at least, as one animal species amongst others. This at once gave support to the idea that science could be employed in the study of man and stimulated its further exploration. It also cast severe doubt

149

upon the earlier theories of the origin and development of man and led to a search for a more satisfactory picture. And it led to a growing assumption that the development of human society and human civilization had also to be understood in historical and developmental terms. Just as man seemed to have evolved from some earlier animal condition, so it seemed necessary and feasible to think that human society had developed from some condition of primitive savagery to the latter-day condition of complex and highly sophisticated civilization.

All the older theories of man in society had now to come to terms with these new perspectives which the development of science provided.

Apart from establishing their own particular bodies of knowledge, however, the sciences gave rise, in general, to more exacting demands for standards of accuracy in *any* theories, about anything which claimed to be *true*. These new standards of rigour in 'explaining' events in nature were scrutinized and clarified very carefully in what has come to be called 'The Theory of Knowledge'.* And undoubtedly the two people who contributed most in this direction were David Hume and Immanuel Kant.

The procedures whereby science arrived at testable knowledge were not at all the procedures of inference which had been clarified by logic and metaphysics in the past, and it was Hume more than any other who attempted very carefully to make clear what exactly was meant by 'scientific method' and what exactly was meant by the 'laws of causality' at which it arrived. In doing this he showed the ways in which speculative metaphysics was totally insufficient, when compared with scientific theories, in establishing testable knowledge about the world as we experience it.

David Hume

Hume asked quite directly, in his *Treatise of Human Nature*: what do we understand by causal laws? Or, putting the matter even more simply: when we say that certain factors, in conjunction, *cause* certain events, and that these cause-and-effect relationships are '*laws* of nature', what exactly do we mean? His answer was simply this: that when we speak of certain factors causing subsequent events we mean only (*a*) that these factors are found in a certain spacial contiguity with each other when the subsequent event occurs, (*b*) that they are related to the event in a certain irreversible temporal sequence, and (*c*) that they are *always* so conjoined in our experience.

* i.e. 'Epistemology'.

It is this fact that they are *always* conjoined in our experience which leads us to claim that there is a *necessary connection* between them. In short, causal laws are merely statements of 'uniformities of coexistence' and 'uniformities of succession' which are constant in our experience. They are nothing more than this. They possess no *logical* certainty whatever—indeed logical certainty does not pertain to them. They are simply regularities among phenomena that we find in our experience.

When we say, for example, that putting a match to a vat of petrol causes an explosion we are saying no more than that a certain source of heat in spacial contiguity with petrol is constantly found in our experience to be followed by an explosion; and, furthermore, that the temporal sequence is always in the one direction. It is never the case that an explosion is followed by the appearance of a vat of petrol and the subsequent striking of a match. A 'causal law' comes to be stated, of course, not only about a particular match, vat of petrol, and explosion—but generally in terms of the ignition point of petrol. A particular explosion is then 'explained' in relation to this 'law'. But this is all that is involved. Furthermore, it is all that is necessary for the exact observation and measurement of events in nature and the statement of careful predictions about them.

Hume wrote:

'We have no other notion of cause and effect, but that of certain objects, which have been *always conjoined* together, and which in all past instances have been found inseparable. We cannot penetrate into the *reason* of the conjunction. We only observe the thing itself . . .

Thus, though causation be a *philosophical* relation, as implying contiguity, succession, and constant conjunction, yet it is only so far as it is a *natural* relation, and produces a union among our ideas, that we are able to reason upon it, or draw any inference from it.'

Hume went so far as to say that *all* knowledge consisted of either deductive logical inference (i.e. the explicit clarification of the entailments of premises) or the statement of testable causal laws of the kind he had described. Nothing else constituted *knowledge* at all. At one stroke, then, all the metaphysical and religious theories of the past went into the wastepaper basket.

Immanuel Kant

This doctrine of extreme empiricism was, itself, something of an explosion to all those who had not radically and systematically doubted established religious and metaphysical theories, and

151

Immanuel Kant, the German philosopher was among these. Kant was so profoundly disturbed by Hume's analysis as to feel compelled to undertake his own 'critical philosophy' in order to examine his contentions and to see how far they were correct. It is enough for our purposes to say that although, in his elaborate theory of knowledge, he modified very considerably Hume's views concerning the nature of the mind and the categories it brings with it to 'experiencing' the world and 'knowing' it, he did not so much refute Hume on the matter of his empiricism as take it one degree further.

Kant insisted that the human mind is much more than any kind of naive 'reflection' of facts or objects that exist in the external world, and that it brings categories of its own without which the perception of the world would be quite impossible. At the same time his position was in agreement with that of Hume that all our knowledge of the world is, and can only be, a knowledge of 'phenomena': a knowledge of the world as it *appears to us* through the media of our human senses and human categories. Beyond this we cannot go. We can never know the world as it may actually exist beyond our experience of it. Kant said that we can have knowledge only of 'phenomena'; never of 'noumena'—by which he meant *'things in themselves.'* To put this in another way—it may well be the case that the nature of the world has dimensions that go beyond human perception, but we can never establish *knowledge* of this reality. We can only establish *knowledge* in terms of regularities among *phenomena:* the objects and events of the world as we experience them.

All knowledge, then, is human knowledge, and consists, as Hume maintained, of 'analytical' knowledge (sequences of deductive logical inference) and 'synthetic' knowledge (propositions about the factual nature of the world as we experience it).

The upshot of these developments in science and the theory of knowledge meant quite simply that, henceforth, *any* theory about the nature of man and society had now to contend with the rigour of these new standards. Metaphysical assertion, which could not prescribe any conditions of test could no longer expect to be accepted whether on the grounds of faith, dogma, or anything else, without justifiable challenge. *All* theories now had to produce their credentials. They had to demonstrate the grounds of method on which they rested, and this meant that many of the earlier social theories which we have considered were seen to have considerable short-comings. This was not to say, by any means, that they were worthless. Only that in many respects they fell short of accuracy, and therefore required improvement.

In addition to the trends of thought in moral philosophy and the philosophy of history, powerful in themselves, there was, therefore, this other movement, that could not be gainsaid, towards the need for some theory of man and society which could lay claim to respectability and exactitude in accordance with these new terms.

3
The Need for Sociology

Revolution and the reconstruction of modern society

We have now discussed our common-sense assumptions about the nature of man and society and the several kinds of early 'theories' which put forward certain 'truths' and speculations about them with sufficient thoroughness to see quite clearly how sociology is rooted in them and grew out of them. Both common sense and the various theories of religion and philosophy possess a good deal that is of value, and a good deal which, in fact, constitutes the basis of sociology itself. Sociology is not something totally new which imposes itself in total opposition to them; it is something which grows quite consistently out of them, and which remains rooted in them. But it *does* and *has* to grow out of them, and beyond them, for the simple reason—which we have seen plainly—that they prove to be insufficient in our experience; they prove to be inadequate for our needs. And I would like to emphasize, as a final note in this first section on the 'Beginnings' of sociology, this element of *need*. It cannot be too much stressed for a proper understanding of sociology, that the subject emerged as a 'science' at a particular time when it became positively *necessary*. It was no accident. It was not some new, precious intellectual extravagance dreamed into being at someone's scholarly whim. It was *needed* by men. And it is *still* needed.

In all that we have said, it is quite plain, firstly, that the emergence of sociology—as an attempt to achieve a 'science' of society—was a *necessary intellectual development*. Throughout the eighteenth and in the early nineteenth centuries, there were developments of thought and knowledge in the sciences themselves, in the theory of knowledge, in moral and political philosophy, and in the philosophy of history which were all such as to lead to, and to emphasize the need for, the careful creation and elaboration of a science of society. None of the problems in these fields of thought could be studied at the level of profundity required, unless a scientific study of society as a whole, and of the place of man as an individual within it, was attempted, and, indeed, achieved to that degree of exactitude which proved possible. All these directions of thought were moving towards a point of culmination at which the new standards of scientific rigour were required in order to establish the basis of any new advances, or,

154

indeed, for any satisfactory treatment of problems and questions already encountered.

All this has already been made clear.

Thought, however, does not take place in abstraction from society itself. Men do not theorize excepting in the context of their own life and times. And these changing theories of society were, in fact, part of a rising tide of social change which was to prove probably the most cataclysmic that men have ever experienced in their history, and which, in our own time, is becoming a flood embracing every corner of the world. The widespread commerce which had gradually changed and then disrupted the order of Christendom was now developing into a new industrial capitalism in which science was becoming harnessed to agricultural and industrial technology and in which secular nation states were the established and powerful units of political authority. The old order of institutions—of traditional authority in government; of sacred authority in the Church; of established status and privilege among the 'Estates'—Crown, nobles, commoners; of property and economic organization appropriate to a still predominantly agrarian society, though much changed by mercantilism . . . all this was proving quite inadequate for the new complexity of activity in society. The 'ancien régime' was doomed, and it was to be broken asunder during the revolutionary decades of the end of the eighteenth century. The French Revolution especially was the symptomatic bursting of these many ills of social change.

The point which is central for our purpose is simply this: since the breakdown of society was a *total* breakdown, men experienced the need for a *total* social reconstruction. Since the *entire* fabric of institutions was falling apart, it was no longer thought feasible to reform society in a bit-and-piece manner. It was not enough to change the family here, education there, the political constitution at this point, economic organization at that. A *total* re-making of society was thought to be necessary. And two things followed closely upon this persuasion. With the disruption of traditional authorities and, coupled with this, the disruption of religious belief, men (or at least significant numbers of them) came to believe *that they themselves were responsible for the re-making of society*. This was a conscious assumption of man's responsibility for the making of his own destiny of a kind and a magnitude quite new in history. And the second fact, attendant upon this, was that, needing responsibility to undertake the total reconstruction of their society, men also felt the need for a body of knowledge about the nature of society *as a totality of institutions* to serve as a firm and reliable basis for their judgment and activities.

A science of society was *needed* by the politicians and others who were living within the wreck of an outmoded social order, and who had—in the most detailed and practical way: drawing up new laws of property; working out new constitutions; organizing a new system of education—to make a new one. A *knowledge* of society was therefore of the very greatest urgency and importance.

It is worthwhile to press home this point: that this is a factor which has remained at the heart of sociology from that day to this. With the transformation of human society from the relatively simple conditions of traditional agrarian communities to the vast complexity of the conditions of industrial and urban organization, a new body of knowledge has been, and is, *necessary*—if men are going to exercise any effective control whatsoever over the social forces which these new conditions have unleashed.

But there is another distinctive fact, implicit in all these intense actualities of social change, which was of vital importance then—in this early revolutionary epoch—and which remains so now. This is the awareness of the *international* implications of the social changes which were afoot.

From the age of mercantilism on, men had become increasingly aware of the international fabric of their trading relations and the links between political societies which these entailed. This did not mean that they necessarily *desired* international unity. The mercantilists themselves, with this awareness, had in fact sought separateness and independent nationhood. New ideas of national self-interest, however, were breaking down this simplicity. The free-trade ideas of Adam Smith were pointing to the interdependencies of nations in their trading and manufacturing activities, and, for many reformers, the old orders of power and authority were obstacles in the way of this new international freedom. The thought which accompanied the American and the French Revolutions was certainly already of an international and universal flavour. All the slogans were about the rights of man. Liberty, equality, fraternity—for men everywhere regardless of class, colour, creed—these were the principles on the lips of Tom Paine as well as on those of Jean-Jacques Rousseau. And there was another aspect of this.

Men were becoming aware—not only, now, in terms of ideas, but in terms of the seen and known implications of their economic and political activity—of the inter-linking of all the nations of the world into a *global entirety of 'human society'*. The unity of mankind was no longer an issue for ethical doubt or conviction; it was something—with all its threats and promises, all its difficulties and potentialities of achievement—which was clearly taking place. Commercial and industrial links, with their correlated political negotiations would come, gradually, to create a unity of interest throughout the world at large. The new conception of the responsible self-direction of man was therefore, at once, a conception of a united world.

The concern which emerged at the turning point of the eighteenth and nineteenth centuries with the role of the advanced societies of Europe and America with regard to the less technologically developed societies of the world, became a central preoccupation; and again, of course, it remains so to this day. We shall see that, at the very outset of the making of sociology proper, Auguste Comte was proposing a Council of European States which, utilizing their advanced knowledge and experience in all fields, could aid the under-developed societies of the world. In 1970 we are still preoccupied with the consideration, though not, alas, with the possibility, for many realistic reasons, of the same simple expansiveness of altruistic feeling and effort which Comte had envisaged and hoped for. But again, we see here, in the awareness of a growing internationalism and the problems it entailed, a positive *need* for a scientific body of knowledge about the nature and interconnections of human societies.

In connection with the same point it is also worthwhile and important to note that, from the time of the Renaissance to the time of the French Revolution, the increase and the spread of human knowledge (achieved so much more effectively with the development of printing) had brought about an increased awareness, on the part of Europeans, of other peoples and civilizations. Men's conjectures about human nature and the nature of society had already begun to take into account the apparent diversities of practices between men in different parts of the world; between societies with different patterns of culture. When Montaigne, in his essays, was speculating about the human nature he saw about him in France and about which he read in his classical authors, he was able, rather wryly, to compare this with the practices of men who, apparently, did not wear trousers! Anthropology was afoot. The new theories of society were therefore already taking these new comparative studies into account and it was already seen that the newly needed science of society required broad comparative studies in order properly to consider the actualities of human nature in various kinds of society.*

It is also necessary to remember that, in the intense and many-sided conflicts which these massive social changes represented and brought in their train; in the radical cleavages between traditionalist and revolutionary; the movements and changes of social theory

* It was the same kind of situation as that in Greece—when the comparative accounts of Herodotus had been available, when philosophers were critically speculating about the institutions and political constitutions of their own City States.

were far from being a peaceful matter of 'ivory-tower' scholasticism. The intellectuals were in the wars too. Hobbes had to seek refuge in Holland from Royalist and Roundhead alike; as had Spinoza from the spiky fist of orthodox theology. Tom Paine was imprisoned for his humanity, and Condorcet spent time in prison under threat of execution. His book on the development of the human mind which we now read in relative peace was published posthumously. But the chief point in mentioning this battle of ideas is simply this. The movement towards a 'science of society' was not only not a peaceful thing: it was fought into existence in the teeth of earlier orthodoxies of ideas, and (and this is the crux of the matter) these orthodoxies have never relinquished their claims and their power. They remained when 'sociology' came into being. They remain now.

Theories of human nature and society have been, and are, claims for men's allegiance. Far more is attached to them, and invested in them, than purely intellectual questions as to their truth. All of which means that there are always theories of man and society making competing claims for men's support and loyalty. And it is therefore clear, too, that, in assessing these competing claims—the relative truths and falsities of all these theories—men experience the need for some firm ground of judgment and adjudication between them. In short, the intense dialogue between powerful ideological claims necessarily drives men towards the quest for some criteria of objective knowledge which will provide degrees of resolution.

Of course, though men are powerfully driven in their arguments, it does not follow by any means that they will like, admit, and accept the truth when they find it. And this leads to one final aspect of the felt *need* for a 'science' of society which deserves a good deal of emphasis.

It is simply that, in the throes of these violent changes, these hot arguments, these pressures towards extremism and fanaticism of all kinds, men came to fear 'idealism' in political affairs in the absence of reason, judgment, and a readiness to be tempered by the realism of considered knowledge. Plato had thought extreme democracy next door to tyranny, and, in this modern period of revolution, many men found that their demagogue of today was their dictator of tomorrow. It was this fear which drove Edmund Burke to criticize in the most searching way every procedure that the French Revolution stood for. He was not opposed to the attainment of justice and excellence in society, but he was passionately persuaded that the hot revolutionary method of transforming society overnight was not the right or the effective way to do it. Again, it is enough that we should simply note that some men, at least, came to see the need for knowledge and balanced judgment in approaching the thorny problems of the social transformations that were taking place about them, and this again led to the positive *need* for *the systematic study of society*, as distinct from simply entertaining passionate ideals about its future. We shall see that practically all the major sociologists, from Comte onwards, had at the very heart of their intellectual concerns this awareness of the problems of statesmanship in dealing wisely with the complex political scene of the modern world. They were all aware that man had been overtaken by perhaps the greatest crisis in his history; that the very greatest standards of knowledge, wisdom, and political judgment and action were necessary if he was to survive it; and that 'idealism' alone was not only not enough, but could even be the ground for its own defeat.

Sociology, then, was not only rooted in common sense and in early social theories in any straightforward way. Its development from them was a matter of intense struggle, within the wider context of the political struggle which attended the transformation of limited traditional societies to a modern technological and industrialized society which seemed likely to encompass the whole world. It was not only in common-sense assumptions or in earlier theories, but also in these many, urgent, cumulative, and essentially interrelated needs, that sociology had its troubled 'beginnings'.

Foundations

1
Introductory Note

The period in which sociology emerged teemed with writers of distinction. The 'Physiocrats', rooted in Montesquieu, made contributions of brilliance in many directions. Turgot, Quésnay, Mirabeau: all deserve mention. The 'Scottish School'—including writers such as Lord Kames, with his remarkable *Sketches of World History*, Adam Ferguson, Dugald Stewart, Adam Smith, Hutcheson, and many more—did much to further the making of a science of society.* Our treatment of the directions and developments of social thought has therefore been highly selective—with the single aim in mind of achieving clarity in seeing the major elements and tendencies which constituted the 'beginnings' of sociology.

It must be the same, now, in moving on to make clear the *'foundations'* of the subject.

Other writers than the ones I have selected contributed much that was indispensable. They were important participants in the ongoing argument. Saint-Simon, for example, formed a necessary part of the development of Comte's ideas—even negatively, in his clashes with him, besides contributing much in his own right. De Tocqueville might be said by some to have contributed more, in his substantive study of American society, than did John Stuart Mill whose work he greatly admired and with whom he corresponded. T. H. Huxley and many other fiery Victorians made contributions in discussing the application of the idea of 'evolution' to the study of society and morality and the new assessment of 'Man's place in Nature' as well as Herbert Spencer. Feuerbach, the French Socialists, and many others, as well as Hegel whom we have already mentioned, made contributions which were important in themselves as well as being at the roots of the ideas of Marx and Engels. And many others in philosophy and literature, in politics and economics, in anthropology and history, took part in the surge forward during the nineteenth century of the new exploration of thought and knowledge which was transforming man's picture of his own nature and the nature of the world.

Even so, I believe that it is by a careful selection of certain authors that the nature and elements of sociology which were founded during the nineteenth century can best be laid bare. The ideas of Comte, Mill, Spencer and Marx together with their influences upon certain

* See Appendix (I) p. 645.

163

American writers will tell us all that we need to know for a full and clear comprehension of the system of sociology which was then established; of the basic elements of the new science of society which, by the end of the century, had been successfully founded.

It would be possible to divide these ideas and contributions in various ways. For example, Comte and Mill had much more to say about definitions, concepts, methods—about logic and methodology generally—than did Spencer and Marx; and the latter thinkers might be said to have offered more substantive and detailed theories of the nature of society and social change than did the two former. But any such division, though perhaps expedient for certain purposes, would not be strictly true. Comte, for example, in addition to his methodological discussions, undertook very substantial historical studies. Only Mill, among them all, confined himself specifically to a *logical critique* of sociology; and he did this only in the service of accuracy and, as he himself put it, with a knowledge of his own limitations, and of the limited state of advancement of certain components of the subject (e.g. psychology) at the time. The characteristic which all these men shared, however, and which underlay their concern for accuracy of method in founding a science of society, was their concern about, and involvement in, the social and political dilemmas which men were facing, and their passionate and powerful persuasions about certain theories which, they thought, would help men to understand their situation and so help them towards effective political judgment and action.

In short, they were concerned to understand and explain the facts of human nature, society, history, and social change, in order to judge and to act wisely in relation to them; and their efforts to create a scientific way of 'studying' these facts was part and parcel of this committed quest. They were not men who wanted to be 'social scientists' as such. They were not 'professional' scholars. They were not men to sit in universities fabricating vast skeins of concepts. They wanted a true understanding of the facts of man and society because they *needed* it; and they needed it because they felt themselves responsible, among other men, in grappling with the issues and struggles of human destiny in their own time.

I have therefore thought it the best thing of all to deal with each man's work in its own right, and each in turn. They will be seen to be all connected. And our account will not be a chronological story only. As we proceed, the interconnections, the related developments of conceptions and methods will become clear, and, at the end, we shall be able to see very clearly the firm foundations of the new science of sociology which had been accomplished by the end of the nineteenth century.

164

2

Auguste Comte: Positive Science and Sociology: A First Synthesis*

Comte was born in 1798 during the ferment of the French Revolution, that vast complex of events which heralded the birth of the modern world. He died just over a hundred years ago, in 1857. He was one of the greatest thinkers during this period notable for its great contributions to human thought, and he grappled with the human situation of his day with a power of mind and a dedication which was unsurpassed. His was a great attempt to analyse the nature of, and the reasons for, the decline and disruption of Christendom; to consider the ways in which human society should be reconstituted and revitalized; and to provide that system of knowledge and moral guidance which would make this possible.

To understand Comte's ideas fully, one has to understand clearly those problems which confronted and preoccupied him; about which he was passionately concerned.

Comte lived in the aftermath of the French Revolution. He was continually disturbed and distressed by the disorder of his time, and by the material and cultural poverty of the people. His fundamental and lifelong preoccupation was how to replace disorder by order; how to accomplish the total reconstruction of society. He saw the French Revolution as a crucial turning-point in the history of human affairs. The *ancien régime* was gone, fallen to pieces, shown to be totally inadequate for the new trends and conditions of scientific knowledge and industrialization. There was no adequate order of institutions for the new changes in society. The social action of men was ungoverned and ill-directed. The thought of men was disorientated. There were great cleavages between belief and knowledge. And the feelings of men lacked coherence, confidence, and worthwhile objectives. In the spheres of social loyalty, traditional allegiance, moral purpose, men were adrift.

A new polity—a new order of feeling, thought, and action—was necessary for the new, complex, industrial society. But this social

* This chapter draws considerably on my Comte Memorial Lecture (*Auguste Comte and the Making of Sociology*, Athlone Press) which was delivered at the London School of Economics when I was re-reading Comte, together with other theorists, in preparation for this book.

165

reconstruction needed a reliable basis of knowledge. And—and this was the crucial point for Comte—it rested upon man's assumption of his own responsibility. It was no longer possible to fall back upon Gods, metaphysical forces and destinies, traditional modes of belief and feeling. Man was now responsible for his own destiny. Man must make his own society. Man must consciously and responsibly make himself.

On what basis of knowledge and action could this be done? Religion, too, had been disrupted. What values and beliefs could now provide an adequate bond of co-operative citizenship in the new society?

Comte was convinced of a number of things:

(1) that this juncture of human affairs was by no means a momentary and temporary crisis, nor was it of significance only in France, but that

(2) it was the unavoidable culmination of the long process of change and development in the history of mankind which had now arrived at a qualitatively new level of human thought, experience, and social organization.

(3) It was unlikely, therefore, that the problems raised would be easily solved by political thought and policies previously tried.

(4) New kinds of social action were not likely to be effective unless they rested upon a new and more reliable knowledge of human nature and human society, and

(5) the desired changes in human institutions would not come about of themselves. They would not be achieved unless there was a positive moral desire, commitment, and effort on the part of the people. Social reconstruction would only be possible, Comte thought, if supported by the moral convictions, even the religious feeling of the people. This could only be achieved, given the decline of traditional religion, by the clarification and acceptance of a new 'religion of humanity'—in which the improvement of human conditions, the qualities of culture and the qualities of individual character should be the goals of man's endeavours and aspirations.

Comte's work, in its entirety, dealt with these preoccupations. It was a thoroughly worked out answer to the question: how are we to deal with this qualitatively new situation that faces mankind? The relevance of his work to our own time, the relevance of sociology to ourselves, is—at once—perfectly clear. For those are the problems which still confront us. They are not, by any means, over yet. We have still not solved them.

It was in the work of Comte more than in that of any other single writer, that all the many earlier lines of thought which we have considered were brought together into a unified, systematic statement. In doing this, Comte achieved a synthesis which was, and is, without any question, of great and permanent value.

In his statement of the nature of 'positive science' he drew upon the epistemological ideas of Hume and Kant, and, indeed, upon the substantive knowledge of all the individual sciences. His range of knowledge in philosophy and in all fields of science was extraordinarily wide. In creating Sociology, and providing a new basis for social and political thought and practice which has, even yet, not been fully worked out, he brought together the work of Aristotle (who, as we have seen, had attempted an empirical comparative study of political constitutions), Montesquieu (who had done the same, and had also explored and developed the notion of 'laws' of society and social development), and Condorcet (who had written his history of the progress of the human mind in the context of stages of institutional development). But he was also thoroughly acquainted with the contributions to the philosophy of history of Vico, Kant, Hegel and Turgot. He knew the many-sided contributions to social science and social philosophy of the Scottish School. He was familiar not only with the work of Hume, but also with that of Adam Smith (he valued highly Adam Smith's treatment of the division of labour; indeed, Smith was the only economist with whom he had much patience) and that of Adam Ferguson—whom he commended for some of his accounts of the historical changes of social institutions. In working out the ritualistic aspects of his new religion, Comte also made much use of De Maistre, especially his 'Du Pape'; not—one might think—the happiest of influences, but, nonetheless, indicative of Comte's wide scholarship.

The work of Comte was thus a great synthesis in the history of human thought. Bringing together important contributions in Moral and Political Philosophy, the Philosophy of History, Epistemology and the history and methods of the particular sciences—he worked these into a new systematic statement which was, at once

(*a*) a unified system of knowledge, inclusive of the methods required for its attainment, maintenance and expansion.

(*b*) a systematic basis for social analysis and social action, and

(*c*) a systematic basis for religious feeling and moral effort.

Furthermore, there was no finality about Comte's statement—a fault in many other large 'systems' of thought. It was a system that carried within itself the necessity of continual testing, the prospect of continual expansion, and the prospect of a continuing increase in man's control over his material and social environment, which itself entailed, Comte argued, the increasing possibility of moral progress:

G

the extension of distinctively human qualities (reason, knowledge, social co-operation, and altruistic feeling) over man's animal qualities (limited, self-centred impulse).

This 'synthesizing' nature of Comte's work should not blind us to his originality. Originality is rarely pure innovation. As human thought develops, there are many and continuous changes of degree, but—on occasion—various existing contributions are brought together to produce changes so considerable as to constitute a difference in *kind*. Comte's contribution was of this order. Before his work, as we have seen, many areas of human inquiry were still open to unchecked speculation and religious dogma; and none more so than the realm of human nature and human society. After his time—these areas were, and are, open to such unchecked dogma and speculation no longer. Theology still fusses, but is all the time trying to clothe itself in scientific dress so that it can walk respectably through the streets of the twentieth century. Everyone now has to come to terms with the kinds of methods which Comte laid down. His work, as he himself would rightly appraise it, is representative of a crucial point of historical development in human thought, feeling, activity, and social organization.

It is impossible to do justice to Comte's many-sided contributions in summary fashion, but I shall outline as clearly as possible the chief ideas in his system, then touch upon and emphasize certain important aspects of his work which, I believe, are nowadays scarcely known, and rarely, if ever, attributed to him, but which I believe to have been of essential importance in the making of the subject.

The Three Stages of mental and social development: the co-ordination of feeling, thought and action in individuals and society

There are three important aspects of our nature, Comte said, which, in our individual lives, must be brought into some sort of satisfactory working relation with each other:

1. *Our feelings*—the impulses and emotions which prompt us to, and are attendant on, activity.
2. *Our thought*—which is undertaken in the service of our feelings, but helps also to govern them, and
3. *Our actions*—which are undertaken in the service of our feelings and in the light of our thought.

Also, as it is with our individual—so it is with our social life and behaviour. For the existence and continuity of *society* (a system of shared and regulated behaviour amongst individuals) there must be some order of institutions, knowledge, values, and beliefs which successfully relate the *feelings, thought,* and *activity* of its members.

In the history of mankind—during which the social order bringing these elements into relation with each other has been worked out—three 'types' of solution, three 'stages' of development, can be distinguished. The first is what Comte called the *Theological Stage.* It is characterized by the fact that feeling and imagination dominate in man's search for the nature, causes, and ends of things. Explanations take the form of myths concerning spirits and supernatural beings. Comte discussed three levels of mental development within this stage.

1. Fetishism—when everything in nature is thought to be imbued with life analogous to our own,
2. Polytheism—in which unrestrained imagination peoples the world with innumerable gods and spirits, and
3. Monotheism—in which a simplification of many gods into one god takes place, largely in the service of awakening reason, which qualifies and exercises constraint upon the imagination.

In this stage of thought (the theological), social organization is predominantly of a military nature. It is military power which provides the basis of social stability, and conquest which enlarges the bounds of social life. It is important to realize that Comte did not, in relegating this stage to the past, deny its value. He believed that feeling and imagination were (and are) the chief elements of experience moving men to inquiry; it was they that pressed for understanding and explanation in the condition of human experience before any accumulation of systematic knowledge could have taken place. Once the philosophical (reflective) tendencies leading to monotheism have taken place, however, they cannot be held in check. They lead to a second stage of critical thought, which is transitional.

This is the *Metaphysical Stage,* and it is characterized by the dominance of 'ratiocination'. Indeed, ratiocination plays a much more unbridled role here than in the later stage of science proper. Just as in the theological stage, feeling and imagination are unrestrained and undisciplined, so in the metaphysical stage, speculative thought is unchecked by any other principle. Men now pursue meaning and the explanation of the world in terms of 'essences', 'ideals', 'forms'; in short, in conceptions of some 'ultimate reality'. The institutional changes correlated with this stage of thought are, chiefly, the development of defensive militarism and the extension of established law which lays down a more secure basis for co-operative civil life.

Neither of these two ways of relating feeling, thought and action in society, however, is stable or adequate; they are found to be wanting as society changes. Intellectually, they show themselves inadequate in that, over many centuries, they move no nearer to conclusiveness; they never resolve problems. Their problems, in fact, turn out to be incapable of solution. But they also fail when brought to the test of practical experience. As human society becomes in all respects more complicated (particularly because of industrialization) theological and metaphysical systems of thought become increasingly inadequate. They cannot provide the basis of reliable knowledge which—for their manifold purposes: technical, economic, political, etc.—men need. Men therefore abandon them, and they are superseded by the third 'stage' of thought and social development: the *Positive stage*.

At this stage of thought, men reject as useless all supposed 'explanations' in terms either of gods or essences. They cease to seek 'original causes' or 'final ends' because (*a*) it becomes clear that these are *not* explanations at all (Comte mentioned as an example of such pseudo-explanation Molière's satire that opium causes sleep because of its 'dormitive virtue' or its 'soporific essence'), and (*b*) they can neither be checked against facts nor utilized to serve our needs. Men cease looking for 'causes' of any kind, and seek merely '*laws*'. And it is very important to see that, by 'laws', Comte merely meant statements about the ways in which, in our experience, we find facts to be connected with each other; *that is all*. The crucial factor distinguishing the propositions which go to make up 'positive knowledge' is that in addition to possessing logical validity, they should all be submitted to the test of careful observation, and, where possible, to exact experiment.

For Comte, all knowledge is inescapably *human* knowledge; a systematic ordering of propositions concerning our human experience of the world. The *only* knowledge we can have, as distinct from unsupported conjecture, is knowledge of observed facts. Our practice in both individual and social life, if it is to be effective and reliable, must rest upon theories about the interconnections of facts. To go beyond this is pointless. Questions raised about the nature of the world beyond our experience of it cannot possibly be answered.

Positive Science and Positive Philosophy

Comte has been much criticized for his dogmatism, his assertiveness, his sweeping claims on behalf of positive science and his equally sweeping rejection of theology and metaphysics, but a careful examination of his work shows that he was not only right, but also that his claims on behalf of positive science were, in fact, modest rather than overweening. His claim concerning the nature of positive science was only a common-sense admission of human limitations and a philosophical clarification of them; and then, on this basis, a claim that this—after all—is all that we require for our effective action and fulfilment in the world.

Theological and metaphysical questions, said Comte, are set aside simply because they cannot be answered; that is all.* Positive Science confines itself to seeking the 'laws' of *phenomena:* statements of the ways in which facts are linked.

These are (1) *laws of co-existence*—statements about the universally found interdependence of elements which distinctively comprise the phenomena being studied (e.g. planetary systems, biological species, human societies, etc.) and (2) *laws of succession*—statements about concrete historical changes, or about facts as they are connected in temporal sequence. Every subject thus has its 'statical' and 'dynamical' aspects, both of which are necessary and both of which are closely dependent upon each other.

In stating these 'laws', however, Positive Science is very careful never to claim completeness, comprehensiveness, or certainty. Comte, indeed, went to great lengths to demonstrate the *limitations* of the claims of science.

All human knowledge, he insisted, *must* be considered limited for two simple reasons:

(1) because of our 'organization' and 'situation' as a species. Our knowledge can only deal with the world as we experience it through the media of our own human senses, and from our own position in the natural world and in society. If we had *different* natural endowments (for example, if we did not possess the sense of sight) the world would appear differently to us, and consequently our knowledge would be different. And:

(2) because social change and the cumulative nature of human knowledge make final certainty extremely unlikely, if not impossible. At the same time, since it permits of continuous growth and systematization, and is continually subjected to the checks of observation and experiment, positive science provides us with the most reliable basis we can obtain for 'prevision' or 'prediction'. Though limited, therefore, it nonetheless provides (and this—without

---

* i.e. *Not* because they are *disproved.* For Comte, for example, atheism is just as much a belief as other theological and metaphysical positions; equally incapable of demonstration. And this holds for any doctrine which states propositions going beyond the range of our experience.

question) the only reliable basis for effective *action* in the world and in society, in the pursuit of all our ends.

Before moving on from this simple outline of Comte's description of positive science. I want to pick out and emphasize several aspects of his treatment. He is often misrepresented as having proposed a simple-minded method of 'induction' in scientific method.* He is often thought to be guilty of 'historicism': his conception of 'laws' concerning social facts being said to be grandiose predictions of 'inevitable trends of history'.† He is often thought to be guilty of some peculiar kind of finality. And, because of his egotism, and his assertive style, he is often thought to be dogmatic in all his intellectual work. Comte could be defended against all these and many other criticisms. Here I shall stress what I think are some of the more important points for our own purposes—namely, to see what dimensions he clarifies in his conception of science in general, and of the new science of society.

(a) *Feeling and imagination in science*
Though Comte said that feeling and imagination become 'necessarily subordinate to observation' in positive science, it is certainly not true that his account of 'positivism' discounted the role of imagination in science and came to think of science only as a simple, colourless collection of facts. Comte said quite definitely:

'Nevertheless, there is always plenty of important work for imagination to do in positive speculation; for it has to form and improve the hypotheses, definitive or provisional, by which phenomena are to be connected.'

Furthermore, he attacked the 'erroneous interpretation' of the subordination of imagination to reason as having:

'. . . been most improperly used to degrade real science into a sort of barren accumulation of unrelated facts, with no merit except that of accuracy. It is therefore important to understand that the true positive spirit is at bottom quite as far removed from empiricism (*i.e.* mere fact-collection) as from mysticism . . . Science really consists in the laws of phenomena. Facts themselves, however exact and numerous they may be, can only furnish the indispensable *materials* of science.' '. . . true science, far from consisting of bare observations, always tends to dispense as much as possible with direct exploration, and to substitute for it that rational

---

* See P. B. Medawar, *The Art of the Soluble*, Chapter on 'Hypothesis and Imagination' pp. 130–155. In this chapter a simple notion of 'Induction' is attacked in the form of John Stuart Mill's ideas—but there is no awareness that Comte, earlier, had had something very clear and significant to say about the role of hypothesis in science.
† See K. Popper. *The Poverty of Historicism.*

prevision which is, in all respects, the principal characteristic of the positive spirit . . .'

Clearly, Comte thought of science as a questing, imaginative, hypothetical study exactly as modern philosophers of science do.

(b) The Role of Hypothesis in Science

Comte was perfectly clear, also, about the part played by hypothesis in science. In *no* sense did he hold a naive notion of 'induction' or 'empiricism'. At the very beginning of his 'Course of Positive Philosophy', he said:

'If it is true that every theory must be based upon observed facts, it is equally true that facts cannot be observed without the guidance of some theory. Without such guidance, our facts would be desultory and fruitless; we could not retain them; for the most part we could not even perceive them.'

But consider the following, bearing in mind the modern exposition of scientific method. Discussing the nature of hypothesis, Comte said that neither inductive nor deductive procedures would help us:

'. . . even in regard to the simplest phenomena, if we did not begin by anticipating the results, by making a provisional supposition, altogether conjectural in the first instance, with regard to some of the very notions which are the object of the inquiry. Hence the necessary introduction of hypotheses into natural philosophy . . . without it all discovery of natural laws would be impossible in cases of any degree of complexity; and in all, very slow. But the employment of this instrument must always be subjected to one condition, the neglect of which would impede the development of real knowledge. This condition is to imagine such hypotheses only as admit, by their nature, of a positive and inevitable verification at some future time—the precision of this verification being proportioned to what we can learn of the corresponding phenomena. In other words, philosophical hypotheses must always have the character of simple anticipations of what we might know at once, by experiment and reasoning, if the circumstances of the problem had been more favourable than they are. Provided this rule be scrupulously observed, hypotheses may evidently be employed without danger, as often as they are needed, or rationally desired . . . if we try to reach by hypothesis what is inaccessible to observation and reasoning, the fundamental condition is violated, and hypothesis, wandering out of the field of science, merely leads us astray.'

Again, when discussing methods appropriate to Biology, Comte wrote:

'It is permissible to form the most plausible hypothesis as to the unknown functions of a given organ, or the concealed organ of a manifest function. If the supposition be in harmony with existing knowledge, if it be held provisionally, and if it be capable of a positive verification, it may contribute to the process of discovery, and is simply a use of a right of the human mind . . .'

And, having upheld the worth of the hypothetical method in a particular piece of work by Broussais, he went on:

'Whether he was mistaken or not, is not the question. His hypothesis being open to unquestionable confirmation or subversion, it gave a great impulse to the study of pathology in a positive manner . . .'*

All that Professor Karl Popper is now saying about 'conjectures and refutations' and the 'hypothetico-deductive method'; all that Talcott Parsons is now saying (in Sociology) about 'theory before empirical investigation'; was stated with perfect clarity by Comte.

(c) The Nature and Importance of Prediction

It is often thought too, or appears to be thought by some sociologists and philosophers, that Comte thought of 'prediction' purely in a historical fashion—as a matter of 'predicting the future', and especially in sociology, of predicting 'future states of society'; as though he wished sociology to possess a kind of historical 'clairvoyance'. But his notion of 'prevision' or 'prediction' was in every way the same as that of contemporary science.

'Prevision', he says, 'is a necessary consequence of the discovery of constant relations between phenomena, and it is the unfailing test which distinguishes real science from that empty erudition which mechanically accumulates facts without aspiring to deduce them from one another . . . Thus the true positive spirit consists above all in seeing for the sake of foreseeing; in studying what *is*, in order to infer what *will be*, in accordance with the general dogma that natural laws are invariable.'

But such prevision is not confined in any simple-minded sense to the foretelling of future events, natural or social.

'The truth is', wrote Comte, 'that whether the aim is to explain or to foresee, in either case it is the establishment of a connection. Every real connection, whether statical or dynamical, discovered between any two phenomena enables us both to explain them and to foresee them, each by the means of the other. For prevision, in the scientific sense of the word, is not confined to the future; it may evidently be used also of the present and even of the past. It consists in the knowledge of a fact indirectly, by virtue of its relations with other facts already known, without needing to explore it directly . . .'

* These quotations are taken from the 2-volume translation and condensation of Comte's *Course of Positive Philosophy* by Harriet Martineau, but similar points about the nature and dimensions of 'positive science' are to be found in Comte's *General View of Positivism*, which is printed as the opening work of Vol. I of the *System of Positive Polity* (Longmans Green, 1875)

This, surely, is perfectly clear. And Comte maintained, of course, and rightly, that this scientific 'prevision' is the firmest basis for our actions and policies in dealing with either the material world or the institutions of society.

'From science comes prevision: from prevision comes action.'

But we must now consider Comte's conception of the *content* of Positive Science and Positive Philosophy.

The Hierarchy of Sciences

Comte maintained that an examination of the growth of the several established sciences showed not only that human thought in general had passed through the three stages we have mentioned, but also that each particular subject had developed in the same way. This appeared, therefore, to be a necessary order of the unfolding of human inquiry; three stages in the development of the human mind in seeking knowledge of the world and of itself. Now that science (i.e., in his time) had been successfully applied to the study of organic life (biology), and now that the extension of science to the study of man and society was seen to be necessary, it was possible to arrange the sciences systematically in a way which coincided with:

(*a*) the order of their historical emergence and development,

(*b*) the order of their dependence upon each other ('each rests upon the one that precedes it, and prepares the way for the one that follows it'),

(*c*) their decreasing degree of generality and the increasing degree of complexity of their subject-matter, and

(*d*) the increasing degree of modifiability of the facts which they study.

His final arrangement of the sciences on this basis (elaborated in the 'Positive Polity') was: Mathematics, Astronomy, Chemistry, Physics, Biology, Sociology, and, finally, Morals—by which Comte really meant a study of Man the Individual (a study which followed upon sociology and was a mixture of psychology and ethics).

Certain points in Comte's discussion of this 'hierarchy' are worthy of note.

(*a*) Comte thought that each science came into being not arbitrarily, but in order to seek the 'laws' of a particular kind, or level, of facts which man had encountered in his experience of the world; which could not be adequately analysed or explained in terms of the 'laws' of the other already existing sciences; and which were seen to require particular methods for their study.

(b) This meant that Comte—though he passionately sought a systematic arrangement of the sciences which would give a reliable picture of man's total situation—was also led to guard jealously the independent sphere of each science, and to oppose rigorously the naivety of what we now call 'reductionism'.

(c) It led him also to insist upon the freedom of each science to consider and develop methods appropriate to its own subject-matter. Consequently, he had no naive notion of one 'scientific method' which was the same in all sciences, neither did he naively equate it with the methods employed in one particular (the most exact) science.*

Finally,

(d) since he has been criticized for the inadequacy of his 'hierarchy', on the grounds that other border-line sciences have emerged since his time, it might be noted that Comte was extremely modest and tentative about the proposed 'hierarchical scheme' and did not suggest any finality in this respect. Since 'Man's very feeble intellect has to be applied to a very complex universe', and since it seems likely that the phenomena of the several sciences will never be brought under one universal 'law', the 'hierarchy' which he proposed had, he said, the merit at least of utility and convenience. It did at least serve to bring scientific knowledge together in a systematic whole, and to give rise to speculative inductions and deductions between the sciences.

(e) A fifth point of both interest and importance is that Comte considered the study of 'Man—the Individual' the most complex study of all (more complex than the psychological attributes that are *common* to all men, and more complex, even, than the study of 'social structures'), and thought that it waited upon the achievement of adequate sciences of Psychology and Sociology, but required elements of Philosophy too. This, in my opinion, is a more satisfactory point of view than that held by many psychologists and sociologists now.

Sociology

It is now necessary to see in what ways Comte conceived of the new Science of Society (Sociology—he chose to call it), and in what ways it was important to him.

First, it is clear in terms of objective fact that the other sciences,

* It can be clearly seen that the modern interpretation of 'positivism' as a simple application to the study of man of the methods of the natural sciences is a complete misunderstanding.

176

even including biology, do not, and cannot possibly explore at their own level, the 'laws' (i.e., interconnections of social facts) of human society. The subject-matter of all these other sciences are certainly involved in, and certainly affect, the nature of man and society, but their 'laws' cannot give an adequate account of this new complex level of societal facts in human experience. Biology, said Comte, studies 'man—the animal', but does not take into account the complex cumulative institutions and traditions of his social life. The chief thing distinguishing man from other animals (besides greater intelligence and adaptability) is the growth and development of a historical tradition. Human society is a cumulative process of institutions, knowledge, skills, traditions, values, beliefs, and neither biology nor any other natural science can study these. Neither can the changing nature of these social phenomena be simply deduced from the nature of man as a biological individual. Sociology is necessary, therefore, as a new science, because man has become aware of a new level of phenomena which cannot be adequately studied by existing sciences. It emerges because man recognizes a new level of objective facts which he cannot explain, but which he needs to explain in order to deal effectively with them.

Comte was quite clear then that the distinctive subject-matter of sociology was the 'social system', and the varieties of social systems in the world. A society was a system of interconnected parts. This system was something more than, something other than, the individuals within it, and therefore it required special study. Indeed, individuals could be understood only within the context of the societies of which they were members. Comte was very definite about this. 'Sociology', he wrote, 'consists in the investigation of the action and reaction of the different parts of the social system . . . This view condemns the practice of contemplating social elements separately as if they had an independent existence; and it leads us to regard them as in mutual relation, and forming a whole which compels us to treat them in combination.' Sociology was, then, the scientific study of the nature and the different forms of societies; of social systems.

And Sociology, in addition to the methods appropriate to the other sciences—observation and experiment—must also, because of the peculiar nature of social facts, use both the *comparative* and the *historical* methods.

When discussing the comparative method, Comte quite distinctly meant:

'The comparison of the different co-existing states of human society on the various parts of the world's surface—those states being completely independent of each other. From the wretched inhabitants of Tierra del Fuego

177

to the most advanced nations of western Europe, there is no social grade which is not extant in some point of the globe, and usually in localities which are clearly apart.'

This knowledge might suggest some ideas concerning social change and evolution, said Comte, but then, the careful use of the historical method could supplement these ideas and check them. And by the historical method, Comte was far from meaning simple chronological narrative. He spoke, for example, of 'the rational use of social series'. And again, drawing upon Condorcet, he said that—for clearness—we may suppose a single nation to which we may refer all the consecutive social modifications actually witnessed among different peoples. This, he said, is a 'rational fiction', but, 'as a scientific artifice merely', he would 'employ this hypothesis, and on the grounds of its manifest utility'. In short—Comte both used and advocated the construction of models, of ideal types, for the exploration of hypotheses.

These methods are appropriate for the statement of sociological 'laws' (i.e. connections between social facts).* If, further, these 'laws' pertaining to social aspects of human nature could also be supported by deductions from the 'laws' pertaining to the biological facts of human nature, they could then be regarded as being as certain and reliable as we could manage to attain—though, let it be remembered, they would never be held to be final, but still open continuously, to test.†

Like other sciences, sociology should be divided into 'statics' and 'dynamics'. It must be remembered here that Comte thought that the 'consensus' or the 'nature of the interdependence' of the phenomena being studied should be borne in mind in deciding upon the most appropriate methods of study to be employed.

In organic studies, it might be possible to study 'parts' or 'bits' of material data, and then move towards knowledge of the whole in an 'additive' way. In Biology, however,—in studying the living organism; or in sociology—in studying systems of social institutions; the 'consensus' of facts immediately required that 'the whole' should

---

* It is worth noting that those who maintain that 'laws of society' are impossible are usually completely misconceiving what Comte is trying to do. It is they themselves who are still thinking of 'laws' in theological and metaphysical ways. They are 'pre-Comtian'. Usually, of course, they have not read Comte, and do not realize that what he means by 'laws' is simply the statement of regularities of connection between facts—in Sociology, regularities of connection between social facts.

† It may be noted that, according to Comte, the 'Law of the Three Stages' is such a 'law'. It is historically and comparatively traced as an empirical generalization, but it also permits, he maintained, of support by deduction from what we know of the psychological 'laws' of the human mind.

be the focal concept (the governing orientation) of study, since the parts could only be properly investigated and understood in terms of their interdependence in the whole system. It was of the very *nature* of the 'parts' that they co-existed in certain ways in the 'whole'. 'Statics' in sociology thus consisted of clarifying the interconnections between those social facts which appear to be universally necessary for the existence of a society of any kind: the nature of, and connections between, the family, the division of labour, property, government, religion, morality, and so on. 'Dynamics' then consisted of studying and tracing the interconnections between these many aspects of society as they actually existed and changed in the many types of society in the cumulative processes of history. It was a study, that is, of the actual varieties of societies existing in the world. 'Statics' is therefore chiefly 'analytical,' 'Dynamics' is chiefly 'empirical'. 'Dynamics' applies the analysis of 'Statics' to the study of actual societies.

Sociology was necessary, firstly, then, because of the existence of a distinctive level of objective facts which required study.

Secondly, however, sociology was also a matter of objective necessity for Comte as a body of testable knowledge on which reliable policies for social reconstruction could be formulated.

But there is a third interesting aspect of the place of Sociology in Comte's system which brings to a head much that had been said earlier—especially by Hume, and, in Comte's own time, by John Stuart Mill—and this is the role it plays in the 'subjective' orientation of all the sciences.* We know, said Comte, that the hierarchy of sciences reflects the nature of the 'objective' world only in the most sketchy and tentative way. But there is another way of conceiving and arranging the sciences which provides a certain and unassailable unity of order. This is what Comte called the 'subjective' way of regarding them. *All* knowledge, in *all* the sciences, is *human* knowledge. All the sciences have had a complex historical development within the growth of human society. Consequently, it is clear that all the other sciences fall into place in this one unifying science. Just as all the data of the several sciences are involved in the phenomena of man and society, and all the sciences are necessary for a full understanding of the situation of man, so all these sciences have developed within human society and are themselves part of the full scope of the science of man.

'It is quite otherwise', said Comte, having discussed difficulties of the 'objective' ordering of the sciences, 'when we consider scientific knowledge from the subjective point of view, that is to say when we look at human

* See quotation from Hume, p. 81.

theories as having their origins in ourselves, and regard them as naturally resulting from the mental evolution, both in individuals and society, and as having for their aim the normal satisfaction of our cravings of every kind. When thus regarded in relation not to the universe but to man, or rather to Humanity, the diverse branches of real knowledge have on the contrary an evident and natural tendency towards a complete systemization not only logical but scientific.'*

It is easy to see, therefore, why Comte maintained that this full system of positive science and philosophy provides the intellectual basis for the unity, order and progress of the life of man in the modern world. His system brought into a unified whole all the many directions of human science and thought which had hitherto developed in what one might call an 'inarticulated' way. On the basis of this system alone, Comte claimed, could man understand his place both in the natural world and in historical society, and proceed, consciously and effectively, to reconstruct his social and individual life.

It is worthwhile to note here, too, that when Comte spoke of Sociology as the 'crowning edifice' of the hierarchy of sciences, he had this general unifying and orientating nature of the science in mind. He did not mean that it is in any sense 'superior' to any other science; but only that it serves to bring all other sciences into relationship with each other, in the overall intellectual history of man. With Psychology and Sociology, man finally comes to establish positive knowledge not only about the world about which he thinks, but also about his own mind which is doing the thinking. The framework of knowledge is thus rounded out and complete.

It was Comte's further contention that this growing system of knowledge and attendant institutions which can give each individual the opportunity for his greatest fulfilment, is clearly a cumulative product of many generations throughout history and of all contemporaneous human groups and nations. It is a co-operative product of mankind at large—what he liked to call 'Humanity'—a collective reality which is greater than individuals themselves. And this led him to other considerations.

For Comte, this achievement of a system of positive science including the science of man in society, was only the solution to *one* aspect of the problem of man in the modern world—that aspect relating to thought and knowledge. But, in itself, it is not enough for the reconstruction of a social order whose old foundations have gone. In order that it should be effectively employed in active reconstruction, it has to be coupled, he said '. . . with two other fundamental

* This is the beginning, really, of a conception of the 'Sociology of Knowledge'.

conditions—*a sufficient conformity of feeling*, and *some convergence of interests.*'

Social Interests

Comte saw the required convergence of interests in the growth and spread of industrialization. In particular, he placed much hope in the working class—the proletaries. Industrialization forces men to accept the viewpoint of positivism and inclines them to reject theological and metaphysical explanations of nature. The day-to-day activities of life in industrial society, he said, are directed to the practical improvement of man's conditions; and this industrial life, devoted to mundane interests, 'is at bottom in direct contradiction with all providential optimism, since it necessarily assumes that the order of nature is so imperfect as to require incessant amendment by man . . .' Also, in all industrial operations, 'we must needs regard the external world not as directed by arbitrary wills of any kind, but as subject to laws enabling us to exercise a sufficient foresight, without which we should have no rational warrant for exerting ourselves at all.'

Comte thought that manual workers were more likely to be won over to positivism than 'managers', because they were working directly upon material nature, whereas 'managers' or 'capitalists' were much more engaged in taking decisions with regard to people. Comte thought also that working men, though having little leisure, had, nonetheless, minds which were free from the preoccupations which burdened a busy bourgeoisie, so that they could come with fresh minds to positivistic ideas. Also—a very important point for Comte—their minds had not been spoiled by the stupidities of formal education: bedevilled by classical inanities, squeezed small and petty by the narrow absurdities of specialization, or, above all, unfitted for life and thought by the academies.

Much of this, of course, smacks of Karl Marx. Marx did, in fact, read Comte's work. How much he was influenced by Comte it is difficult to say.* What is certain, however, is that Marx's emphasis upon the importance of the role of the proletariat in the shaping of the modern industrial world is far from being as original as is commonly supposed.

Comte had also much of value to say about education—to be based upon systematic instruction in the hierarchy of sciences—but it is impossible to discuss this element of his thought satisfactorily here.

* But see Z. A. Jordan, *The Evolution of Dialectical Materialism.*

Religion and Morality

The aspect of *feeling* which would inspire and sustain co-operative activity and citizenship in the reconstituted industrial society, could be provided, Comte thought, by the 'Religion of Humanity'. It is on this score that Comte has been most attacked, even by many who are prepared to accept the rest of his system. One cannot help but feel, however, that, in rejecting his ideas about positive religion so completely, they have not taken sufficient care to distinguish between two aspects of Comte's thought.

On the one hand, there are Comte's views concerning the worthwhile objectives of human effort and aspiration—indeed, human devotion. On the other, there are the over-elaborate ritualistic prescriptions connected with all this in the 'Positive Polity'—which was clearly saturated with his obsessive devotion to Madame de Vaux. One can, it seems to me, readily accept the one without the other.

To put the matter as briefly as possible (and, it must be confessed, by so doing to eliminate many of his extravagances), Comte believed that—now that the inadequate foundations of the existing religion had been exposed and displaced—the true core of religious feeling and duty remained. Indeed, it was now freed from its supposed dependence upon dubious doctrines, and made much more clear. And this was no more and no less than a compassionate concern for mankind; an aspiration towards the achievement of the highest human ideals; and a direction of one's efforts to the improvement of both the conditions of man and his nature. 'Love is the principle', reads Comte's slogan, 'Order is the basis, Progress is the end.' It is the moral commitment, in feeling, thought, and activity, to the service of mankind, which is the true core of religion.

'It is', says Comte, 'the only religion which is real and complete; destined therefore to replace all imperfect and provisional systems resting on the primitive basis of theology.' It is '. . . the substitution of Love of Humanity for Love of God . . . To love humanity may be truly said to constitute the whole duty of man.'

It is true that this essential core of his teaching is obscured by the detailed prescriptions in the 'Polity'. Indeed, it is perfectly clear that in this last exercise of zeal, Comte—always extreme; unstable in mind and temperament—was carried away by the power of his feelings, his love, for Clotilde de Vaux. George Henry Lewes, for example, wrote:

'It was in the early days of this attachment (i.e. to Madame de Vaux) that I first saw him, and in the course of our very first interview he spoke of her with an expansiveness which greatly interested me. When I next saw him he was as expansive in his grief at her irreparable loss; and the tears rolled down his cheeks as he detailed her many perfections. His happiness had lasted but one year. Her death made no change in his devotion. During life she had been a benign influence irradiating his nature, for the first time giving satisfaction to the immense tenderness which slumbered there . . . Her death rather intensified than altered this influence . . . The remainder of his life was a perpetual hymn to her memory. Every week he visited her tomb, every day he prayed to her and invoked her continual assistance. His published invocations and eulogies may call forth mockeries . . .'*

Well, the mockeries have come. It is this, chiefly, that has given rise to distaste amongst all serious critics. For the same obsessive reason, Comte was led to write in far too fulsome a way about the whole matter, parading his private love in the public enunciations of his system.

Nonetheless, the core of what he had to say is true enough, and I am convinced that it is the ground of morality of the majority of people in the mid-twentieth century. Comte's major error, perhaps, lay in thinking that since this concern for human welfare and human values was, at heart, a religious feeling, its dissemination depended upon ritualistic trappings akin to those of the old religions, whereas, in fact, with the temper of positive science and appropriate education, perhaps anything redolent of the old religious trappings strikes false, is such as to engender distaste rather than make an appeal, and the required elements of humane feeling can better be inculcated with less pomp and more quietness. Still, the last word has not been said on this matter.

Comte said much about the nature of the positive priesthood, and about the special role of women, which now seems to verge on the absurd, and, indeed, to contain some elements of reaction—as with regard to the status of women in society. Still, if one has patience, even in the most extreme ideas there is always sufficient in what he said to make a critical reconsideration worthwhile. Besides, Comte had an unhappy knack of writing about these elements of sublime feeling with such direct naivety and exaggeration as almost to *force* a sense of distaste upon the reader. He tried to unburden his intense poetic feeling in severe, exacting, meticulously argued prose, and the result is frequently embarrassing. The truth which lies at the heart of what he had to say about religion was obscured, spoiled, and even made unpalatable by the melo-dramatic way in which it was stated. It was a great pity.

These, then, were the essential ideas which Comte elaborated

* 'The History of Philosophy from Thales to Comte', 3rd Edition, 1867, p. 581.

and wove together in his system of knowledge (including the science of sociology), and though we have dealt with each as briefly and clearly as possible, I hope that their interrelatedness, as parts of a *system* of ideas, has been made quite evident. Comte was, in fact, one of the most systematic of thinkers. From his diagnosis of the problems of his time, throughout the critical construction of his whole scheme of knowledge, throughout the creation of his science of sociology, right up to the devising of an actual polity and the making of proposals for an extensive international programme of political action, all Comte's ideas were dovetailed into each other with a fantastic degree of rational inter-connectedness and articulation. And, as we have seen, this included not only a system of his own devising—in the sense of something which was concocted purely from his own ideas, but a systematic bringing together of all the many contributions to scientific and social thought whose significant relationships with each other he had clearly seen.

Indeed, his pride, towards the end of his life, lay in the fact that he did indeed accomplish the gigantic task of intellectual synthesis which he set himself early in his youth. His Course of Positive Philosophy outlined the systematic way of achieving the knowledge on the basis of which social reconstruction could take place. His System of Positive Polity extended this, elaborated the nature of sociology in particular, and set out the outlines of a new polity which, established first among the nations of the West, could ultimately be extended to embrace all the nations of the world—bringing material security, peace, justice, and the conditions for continual improvement—and so achieve the unity of mankind.

It was, in fact, a great achievement.

These essential ideas aside, however, Comte has many other far from incidental merits and contributions which deserve critical reappraisal. These we cannot fully explore because they are not central to our purpose, but a few of them should at least be indicated because they have some relevance to the ideas and purposes which were taken up by subsequent sociologists, and to which we shall refer later.

First of all, it is worthwhile to note that Comte adopted a very definite position with regard to the relations between psychology and sociology, and that this position had certain distinct merits, and posed important problems, even if it was not altogether free from ambiguity. Comte's views lie decidedly on the side of those whose dictum is: 'All psychology is *social* psychology'—at least as far as man is concerned. Biology (and psychology related to this) can provide us with a basic knowledge of the elements of experience and behaviour attendant upon the facts of anatomy, physiology, and the like, which comprise the inherited endowment of human nature. These alone, however, cannot possibly explain the many differing qualities of experience and behaviour which are brought into being *in* individual lives by virtue of their membership of a social and cultural tradition. They do not explain the detailed differences of religious experience, political experience, language, aesthetic experience, among individuals from society to society. For the explanation of *these* elements of perception, feeling, motivation, thought, action, an analysis of *society* is necessary. However, two other points must be made perfectly clear.

Though emphasizing the *social* context of human experience and behaviour, Comte by no means wished to exclude, or to deny the importance of, the fundamental bio-psychological elements of human nature. On the contrary, he wished to establish the 'fundamental laws of life and mind' at this level so that they could be related—deductively and hypothetically—with 'laws' at the *societal* level. It is worth remarking very clearly that Comte insisted upon the close relationship between the two levels in order to achieve as complete as possible an explanation and understanding of man in society.

The other very important point is that Comte insisted upon the necessity of a close relationship between not only psychology and sociology, but also between these two and moral philosophy, in any satisfactory study of 'Man the Individual'. He was surely right in maintaining that the *social* framework of reference is necessary for the psychological study of the individual, and that sociology and psychology should work in the closest combination; but this additional point, that neither sociology nor psychology can properly understand the actuality of human nature in isolation from the study of moral and social philosophy, is one which—though unfashionable—is well worth consideration. Here, we can only note that Comte stated and developed this persuasion very fully.

It is also important to note that, in his analysis of the chief components of 'social systems', Comte emphasized especially the central significance of the 'Division of Labour' in society. Indeed, his entire analysis of the nature of society: its 'units', its elements of 'structure', its 'apparatus', and their inter-relationships within the 'system' of society as a whole; and his entire analysis of the changes and developments of societies; rested upon the central fact of the 'division of functions' and the 'combination of efforts' which came into being as a community came to terms with its environment. Comte's account was a completely clear 'structural-functional' analysis of the nature of social order and social change in relation to environmental circumstances.

Comte claimed that Aristotle was the first to lay down this basis for the analysis of society.

'Aristotle,' he wrote, 'laid down the true principle of every collective organism, when he described it as the distribution of functions, and the combination of labour. Strangely enough, our modern economists claim the discovery of this luminous conception, whilst narrowing it, with metaphysical empiricism, to a mere law of industry. The first of philosophers repudiated this particular application of the theory. In its original form, he gave it the wide extension required for its systematic use . . .

. . . when society is organized in active co-operation, and this is the characteristic of civil society, this itself becomes a constant source of differences, mental and moral. And these would ever tend to destroy the association altogether, were it not preserved by some apparatus adequate to maintain the organization. Accordingly, the ground plan of Social Statics as a whole ultimately rests on the principle of the distribution of functions . . . Thus sociology is finally furnished with an invaluable centre for its Statical work, and its Dynamical will be in reality nothing but the development of this central principle to its necessary conclusions. In fact, the principle of distribution of functions usually employed to explain the earliest rise of civil society, has now been shown to be the ground on which we may ultimately construct our entire theory . . .'

This particular emphasis in Comte's scheme of sociological analysis is worth noting, not only because it demonstrates with the utmost clarity the outlining and adoption of a 'structural-functional' analysis of social systems at the very foundation of the subject, but also because it will serve later to demonstrate the clear continuity in the development of the subject. We shall see that Emile Durkheim made his own contributions to the making of sociology by taking up certain of these fundamental points of emphasis stated by Comte, and developing them further. This is true both of Comte's emphasis upon 'social psychology' and his emphasis upon the 'division of functions' and the 'division of labour' in society.

Indeed with this prospective reference to Durkheim in mind there is one other special aspect of Comte's 'structural-functional' analysis of social systems which is worth mention: that is his suggestion that (as in biology, so in sociology) the 'normal' functions of the parts of a society might well be clarified by a study of their 'pathology'. As we can become more clearly aware of the function which a part of the body is normally performing within the organism as a whole, when it breaks down, or ceases to function, or comes to be diseased in its functioning, so we may be able more clearly to know the function which a social institution normally performs in the social system as a whole by studying the consequences of its breakdown, or its degrees of 'mal-functioning', brought about by various causes.

The study of the 'pathological' as well as the 'normal' was therefore given a special place in sociological method by Comte, and this too was seized upon by Durkheim and developed in his own rules of sociological method. The *raison d'être* for this method—namely, the progressive clarification of the functions of the units, or parts, of the social system—has not commonly been fully appreciated.

Comte was also extremely jealous of the central persuasion of sociology, that all the institutions of society had to be seen in their interrelatedness, in their 'consensus', if any one of them, or all of them, or any changes in them, were satisfactorily to be understood. He was strongly opposed to any facile development of supposed 'specialisms' in sociology. He wrote as follows:

'There can be no scientific study of society, either in its conditions or its movements, if it is separated into portions, and its divisions are studied apart. The methodical division of studies which takes place in the simple inorganic sciences is thoroughly irrational in the recent and complex science of society . . . It is no easy matter to study social phenomena in the only right way—viewing each element in the light of the whole system. It is no easy matter to exercise such vigilance as that no one of the number of contemporary aspects shall be lost sight of. But it is the right and the only way . . .' and '. . . by any other method of proceeding, we shall only find ourselves encumbered with special discussions, badly instituted, worse pursued' and 'accomplishing no other purpose that that of impeding the formation of real science.'

With this, as with every point one makes about Comte, his relevance for the problems of sociology in our own time becomes patently clear.

It is the same with his strictures on an ill-considered 'empiricism'. Though the collection of information is obviously important, Comte opposed altogether the idea that an 'empirical' sociology was a kind of 'social arithmetic'; that it consisted of collecting and counting *facts* in contemporary society; that it was empirical because you actually went out, with notebook and pencil in hand, and looked through your eyeballs at what was *there now*; that it was *scientific* in that it was accurate.

Comte would have made two points: first, as we have seen, that this conception of empiricism is a misconception of science as such, and second, again, that social facts are essentially historical, and that the idea that you can observe and understand contemporary social facts independent of historical perspective is an illusion. No history, says Comte, no sociology, and it is perfectly clear what he meant.

Even in his concern for morality and political action, which, as we have seen, was so extravagantly overlaid and overdressed by his proposals for the ritual ordering of his new religion, Comte made points of considerable importance, and took the trouble to apply himself to the working out of a definite programme of political reform which foreshadowed much of what is only now coming into being.

Comte argued that in the past social sympathy had been too much restricted to the idea of the Nation, and that it would become the duty of the nations of Western Europe in particular to move beyond their nationalities to form a European Union as a preliminary step in seeking the union of humanity as a whole.

'Wise and generous intervention of the West on behalf of our sister nations who are less advanced, will form a noble field for Social Art, when based on sound scientific principles. Relative without being arbitrary, zealous and yet always temperate; such should be the spirit of this intervention; and thus conducted, it will form a system of moral and political action far nobler than the proselytism of theology or the extension of military empire. The time will come when it will engross the whole attention of the Positive Council . . .'

It is this, of course, which is now coming increasingly to engross the attention of our councils, in Europe and in the United Nations.

The work of Comte, then, quite apart from providing the first systematic statement of the foundation of sociology as a science, positively bristles with ideas which are both relevant to, and correctives of, many conceptions and practices of our time.

It is perfectly true that Comte was unbalanced as a person in many respects; that he was precocious, egotistical in the extreme, and possessed of an almost boundless megalomania. It is true that his personal qualities and personal affairs led him to quite outrageous extravagances in his elaboration of some of his ideas.* Yet, if we have the patience and fair-mindedness to set these elements aside, there is a core of very considerable importance in his work. Edward Beesly, one of Comte's translators, wrote:

'I am not sure that the intelligent reader has always the patience to consider whether he has really grasped Comte's full meaning. Never was there a writer whose every word requires to be so carefully weighed.'†

And Gilbert Murray, a man of the soundest judgment, was of the same opinion.

'Whatever the failures and imperfections of his actual statement,' he wrote, 'I cannot but feel, first, that his system forms a wonderful achievement of

* See Appendix 2. p. 652.
† Introduction to 'A Discourse on the Positive Spirit'.

sincere and constructive thinking and, secondly, that the thing he is trying to say, if only he could succeed in saying it, is not only sublime, but true.'*

These judgments, I believe, are wholly sound.

It is only fair, too, to say that Comte encountered personal difficulties, and possessed personal qualities, which were such as to do much to offset the less fortunate aspects of his nature which are commonly emphasized by critics who wish to derogate his ideas by pointing a finger of scorn at him.

Comte was, of course, mentally ill, and extremely so, during some periods of his life, and experienced family and other circumstances that explain much.

He was the son of Royalist and Roman Catholic parents. Grappling, with desperate honesty, with the radical changes of thought in the revolutionary situation, he had continually to resist parental wishes and criticisms as boy, youth, and man. His mother, in particular, must have exerted powerful emotional pressure upon him, hoping to see him remain within the religion of his birth. The extent of the parental pressures he encountered may be conjectured from an incident relating to his marriage. Comte, because of his beliefs, had resisted his parents' wish to solemnize his marriage by a religious ceremony. During a period in which he was suffering severe mental illness, whilst he was still violently unbalanced, his mother, with the aid of a zealous Abbé and the Archbishop of Paris, contrived to have her son and his wife undergo the ceremony of marriage—conducted by a priest—before leaving the asylum. It is a shocking, harrowing story; an almost unbelievable instance of how far maternal love (if that is the right word) and clerical malpractice (if that is a sufficient word) can go.

And on his side in the matter of personal qualities two things might be remembered.† First, he was not a man only to talk. He did not only advocate, for example, the free scientific education of working men. From 1830 to 1848, on Sunday afternoons and without fees, he delivered annually a course of lectures to them. Second, his compassion for the unfortunate among mankind was deeply and genuinely felt. As a young man of eighteen and nineteen, wandering about the streets of Paris during the time of carnival, his wonder and comment was—how it was possible that people could so forget that thirty thousand human beings around them had barely a morsel to eat. Similarly, at the very end of his life, living very frugally, and, again, with an almost absurd asceticism, 'at the close

---

* *'Stoic, Christian and Humanist'* (Ch. iv. 'What is Permanent in Positivism').
† It may be of interest to note, too, that he took pains to analyse his own experiences of mental derangement in discussing the nature of the mind.

COMTE'S SYSTEM OF ANALYSIS*

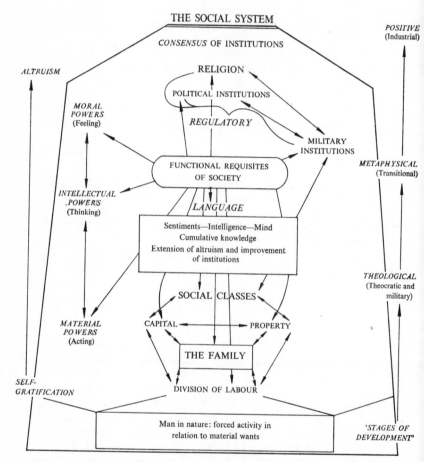

* This is a very insufficient diagram—but serves to indicate the systematic detail of Comte's analysis of the social system, and its similarity to later writers (e.g. Marx—on the importance of work, capital formation, property, and social class, etc.). For a full appreciation of this, readers can only go to Volume II of the 'System of Positive Polity' where all this is set out very clearly. I have introduced Mill's term 'functional requisites' since it is fully in keeping with Comte, and it is not worth while to attempt a similar diagram for Mill since it would be inappropriate for his 'logical critique', and, in any case, would be similar in all essentials.

of dinner he daily substituted for dessert a piece of dry bread, which he ate slowly, meditating on the numerous poor who were unable to procure even that means of nourishment in return for their work'.

'The world,' said John Morley, 'has strong self-protecting qualities. It will take what is available in Comte, while forgetting that in his work which is as irrational in one way as Hegel is in another.' This is true. But the world might, at the same time, be gracious in its understanding of the probable causes of such irrationality, and exercise some magnanimity in considering the work of a man who dedicated himself to the service of mankind more than most. Despite its great extravagances, Comte's contribution is one of considerable and enduring worth. The foundation of the new science of sociology —seen to be so necessary, by so many, for so long—was clearly and firmly accomplished at his hands. This was a great achievement.

Summary

With the aim of complete clarity in mind, let us summarize the chief elements of the first systematic statement of Sociology by Comte in order to see the ways in which it constituted an advance upon the early social theories and common sense in which it was rooted. If we follow this practice in relation to each contributor, we should finally achieve a clear picture of the nature, scope, and main elements of the subject as it had been created by the end of the nineteenth century.

(a) Scientific knowledge: a clear delimitation

(I) THE LIMITATION OF SCIENTIFIC KNOWLEDGE

Following the ideas of Hume and Kant, Comte achieved a very clear statement of what science could achieve, and should attempt. The scope of scientific knowledge was precisely delimited. Scientific knowledge consisted of such propositions about the regularities of connection between phenomena as could be subjected to test. Anything going beyond this, even the idea of 'causes' as being something lying 'behind' phenomena, forcing them to be what they were, was abandoned. Knowledge consisted of statements of regularities found in the world of our experience.

(II) SCIENTIFIC 'LAWS'

These propositions were of two kinds: (a) 'uniformities of co-existence' (about the interdependence of parts in the phenomena one was studying), and (b) 'uniformities of succession' (about the actual changing varieties of such phenomena in the world, which we sought to explain).

(III) STATICS AND DYNAMICS

Statics was that part of a science devoted to the careful analysis of its subject-matter, the analysis of the 'consensus' of parts in the whole, (i.e. in the 'organism' in Biology, or the 'social system' in Sociology), thus producing 'uniformities of co-existence'.

Dynamics, applying this analysis, was the study of the actual changing forms of the subject-matter existing in the world, thus producing 'uniformities of succession'.

(IV) A CLASSIFICATION OF THE SCIENCES

All sciences were of this nature, and could be classified in accordance with the order of their emergence and development, the order of their dependence upon each other, the degree of complexity of their subject-matter and the degree of exactitude possible, and the degree of modifiability of the facts which they studied. There was no *one* kind of scientific method and technique. Each science uncovered 'laws' appropriate to its subject-matter; at its own 'level' of facts. The propositions of no science could be 'reduced' to another, though deductions from knowledge in one could furnish hypotheses for another; and the levels could therefore be connected.

(V) A BASIS FOR PREDICTION AND ACTION

Such knowledge, though circumscribed and limited, was bounded by clear criteria. It was, therefore, just because of its prescribed limitations, the most exact and reliable basis for (*a*) *prediction* and (*b*) the *guidance of action*

(VI) SCIENTIFIC KNOWLEDGE NEVER FINAL

Such knowledge was not final, but 'relative' to human nature and its circumstances. Though 'relative', however, it was not *arbitrary*. It rested on the most carefully considered criteria of which man was capable at any particular time.

(b) *Scientific knowledge of society: Sociology*

(I) SOCIOLOGY: A SCIENCE

Sociology was one science among others, so defined. It had become necessary because a specific 'level' of facts had become recognized in human experience which existing sciences could not sufficiently explore or explain.

(II) THE EXISTENCE OF 'SOCIAL SYSTEMS'

It had become recognized that groups and institutions existed in some relationship of interdependence in societies as wholes, and that they could only be properly understood within this perspective. Sociology was necessary, therefore, as the scientific study of 'social systems'.

(III) THE NECESSITY OF THE METHODS OF SCIENCE

Testable knowledge (as distinct from opinion or speculative conjecture) about 'social systems', as about any other facts in our experience, could only be achieved by using the methods of science.

(IV) THE ABANDONMENT OF 'METAPHYSICAL' EXPLANATION

Sociology therefore abandoned explanations of social systems in terms of 'final ends' or 'ultimate purposes', or even 'causes' which 'lay behind' social phenomena.

(V) THE DELIMITATION OF SOCIOLOGY

Sociology deliberately confined itself to discovering and stating regularities about the nature of social systems; the interconnections between their parts in whole societies; and the relations between such societies themselves. 'Whole societies' were related to each other to some extent and in certain ways within 'human society' as a whole throughout the world, and had come to be what they were within the cumulative processes of history. Sociology was concerned to establish knowledge about this entire fabric of social interdependency.

(VI) SOCIOLOGICAL 'LAWS'

The propositions of sociology would state regularities of at least two kinds: (a) 'uniformities of co-existence' (about the nature of the 'social system' as a subject-matter, and the relations between the parts of society and the whole; about the kind of 'consensus' of facts a 'social system' was) and (b) 'uniformities of succession' (about the changing nature of actual societies in history).

(VII) SOCIAL STATICS AND SOCIAL DYNAMICS

Sociology was (like all sciences) divided into Social Statics: devoting itself to the conceptual analysis of the nature of social systems; their parts, their functions, their interrelations; and Social Dynamics: devoting itself to the application of this analysis to achieve an understanding and explanation of the varieties of societies in the world. Statics and Dynamics were *not* distinguished as having separate subject-matters, they were only two different aspects of method and theory.

193

(VIII) SOCIAL STATICS (1): STRUCTURAL-FUNCTIONAL ANALYSIS

The complex nature of a society could be analysed in terms of 'structures' and their 'functions'. Its 'units' (groups and institutions) and their 'apparatus' could be described and analysed and their functions clarified. The normal functions of units might be illuminated by studying 'pathological' conditions of social systems, when institutions had, by the aggravation and intensification of certain normal processes, broken down; or for some reason had been brought into disorder and disorganization.

(IX) SOCIAL STATICS (2): SOCIAL INSTITUTIONS
AN ORDERING OF FEELING, THOUGHT, AND ACTION

These elements of 'structure' and 'function' could be understood by focusing upon the central fact that they brought the *feeling*, *thought*, and *action* of men into satisfactory relationship with each other whilst, as members of the community, they were dealing with the material and organizational problems related to their environmental situation.

(X) SOCIAL STATICS AND SOCIAL DYNAMICS LINKED: THE CONSTRUCTION OF MODELS

This kind of analysis could provide the framework for a detailed study of the varieties of societies and the processes of historical change, by facilitating the construction of clear 'models' or 'types' of social system. The 'theological', the 'metaphysical', the 'positive' stages of social organization were three such 'types' of social order (three kinds of institutionally patterned organization of feeling, thought, and action) in terms of which the actual changes of society in history could be illuminated and understood.

(XI) SOCIAL DYNAMICS: A TYPE OF HISTORICAL SEQUENCE

These 'types' did not exist as pure, actual societies. Every society, at different periods, could be understood as a blend of them. Also, societies in history were interconnected in wide cultural movements and epochs in which changes from a predominance of one 'type' to the predominance of another, took place. It was possible, therefore, again conceptually, to employ the 'scientific artifice' of conceiving of human history as a 'rational series', or a 'rational fiction', drawing upon the many actual societies and their modifications which we can observe, and by this means understanding the sequence of social change through the three types. The 'models' of social order also implied a 'model' of social change—and was of the nature, therefore, of a hypothesis.

(XII) TYPES OF SOCIAL ORDER AND SOCIAL CHANGE
FOCUSED UPON MIND AND KNOWLEDGE IN SOCIETY

The construction of these types of social order and social change was focused upon the development of thought and feeling, of mind and knowledge, in society, because these could be seen to be crucial for the orientation of the institutional activities of men; and therefore all social institutions could be expected to be correlated with them.

(XIII) DEDUCTIONS AND HYPOTHESES, SUPPORTING
EMPIRICAL GENERALIZATIONS, YIELDED EXPLANATIONS

Also, these 'types' of social order and social change rested *both* upon deduction from what was known about the biological and psychological aspects of human nature, *and* upon empirical generalizations about the actual interdependence of social institutions found in history. Deduction and hypotheses therefore supported empirical generalizations to provide 'explanations'.

(XIV) METHODS OF SOCIOLOGY

The methods of sociology, in this entire task, included those of the other sciences: observation, description, classification, comparison; experimentation in so far as it was possible; and, in addition, and uniquely, the historical method. The historical method was necessary because human societies were different from other 'facts' in nature in being historical, cumulative, cultural sequences of feeling, thought and action. The classificatory and comparative method and the historical method thus supported each other.

(XV) THE KNOWLEDGE OF SOCIOLOGY NEVER FINAL
KNOWLEDGE

The knowledge established by Sociology would not, and could never claim to be, 'final' or 'absolute'. It would always be 'relative' to the nature of man and his circumstances. At the same time it would not be 'arbitrary', but based always upon the clearest criteria of testable truth which men could achieve in their time. As in all positive sciences, it would be continuously open to objective test. It would be capable of continuous extension in range, and improvement in accuracy. And only if this was so could the degree of men's responsible and effective control over their environment and social organization be capable of improvement.

(XVI) A BASIS FOR PREDICTION AND SOCIAL PRACTICE

The knowledge of sociology would, therefore, though deliberately limited by its own criteria, be the most exact and reliable basis we

195

could achieve for *prediction*, and for the making of *practical policies* in society.

The nature and scope of sociology was now outlined with meticulous clarity. The nature of its subject-matter, and the nature of its methods were laid out in a completely systematic fashion. A mode of analysing social order and, thereafter, of investigating and explaining social change was clearly outlined. And social theory was linked with the practical tasks of politics with which men were confronted. Properly pursued, sociology promised a basis of the most reliable knowledge possible on which practical judgment and decision could rest.

Sociology, then, even in this—its first statement—could clearly be seen to go beyond the assumptions and dilemmas of common sense, and beyond the earlier theories of man and society. It provided not only a new perspective on the nature and development of society, but also a framework for the testing of its own pronouncements; a basis for the continuous growth of its knowledge.

Out of the many roots which had preceded it, the science of society was, at last, *made*: clear and complete as a system of analysis. All the main components for a satisfactory knowledge of society— the study of government, of religion, of education, of property, of social classes and their conflicts, of all those institutions which were the sources of men's troubles—now found their place within this new perspective: *the only perspective within which they could be understood.* From this point on, the sociological perspective was *the only satisfactory perspective.* Those who rejected it, had to provide one more reliable. So far, in the century that has followed, they have raised only a great cloud of dusty argument which still drifts across our vision, but an alternative and more reliable perspective has not yet been produced.

Meanwhile, the foundation so successfully laid by Comte has been built upon and enriched in many ways.*

* See Appendix 3 for one other important contribution to the making of sociology in France during the nineteenth century.

3
John Stuart Mill: A Logical Critique of Sociology

John Stuart Mill, one of the greatest and most humane thinkers of the nineteenth century, indeed of any century, is very well known for his contributions to ethics, political philosophy, economics and logic, to mention but a few of the subjects to which he devoted himself. Curiously, however, his contribution to the making of sociology is little known and has been considerably under-estimated. Unlike Comte, Mill did not even attempt a substantive theory of man in society. He was conscious of the fact that the human sciences were too little advanced, in his own time, for any complete statement. Instead, he undertook a logical clarification of the methods most properly to be employed in these sciences, and the kinds of generalization and the degree of exactitude which it was reasonable to expect them to attain.

In a correspondence with de Tocqueville, for example, Mill refused his invitation to construct the science of society whose methods he had (so de Tocqueville thought) so clearly proposed, because, he said, it was so difficult and so little advanced. And in the sixth book of his own *System of Logic* he said that he was quite well aware of how little could be done towards the substantive creation of this science in what was, as he put it, a *mere* treatise on logic. However, he thought that something could be done to suggest the outlines of such a science; to make clear the kinds of methods that were most appropriate to it and the kinds of methods that ought, from the outset, to be rejected.

Mill approached the study of the social sciences from at least three points of view.

Firstly, like Comte, he was persuaded that the problems peculiar to human society since the French Revolution—the disruption of the old social order, the new problems created by complex industrial development, the problem of replacing the established traditional authority of both religion and Government by some more rationally based morality, and the like—could only be dealt with effectively on the basis of a new body of *knowledge* about man and society, and this could only be achieved by the use of scientific method. In the preface of his book on logic, Mill said that the last section of his work (Book VI: On the Moral Sciences) was:

'an attempt to contribute towards the solution of a question which the decay of old opinions and the agitation that disturbs European society to its inmost depths, render as important in the present day to the practical interest of human life as it must at all times be to the completeness of our speculative knowledge—whether moral and social phenomena are really exceptions to the general certainty and uniformity of the course of nature, and how far the methods by which so many of the laws of the physical world have been numbered among truths irrevocably acquired and universally assented to, can be made instrumental to the formation of a similar body of received doctrine in moral and political science.'*

Mill's primary object then, in considering the establishment of a science of man and society, was that of being in a position to deal adequately with the problems confronting mankind in the modern world. His concern, like that of Comte, and most previous philosophers, was ethical and practical, as well as being speculative in a purely intellectual sense.

Secondly, however, Mill was also much aware of and much in sympathy with the desire of Hume to see a science of man formulated, and at the end of his book on logic, having considered the application of scientific method to the study of man, he commented in the following way.

'Notwithstanding', he said, 'the extreme generality of the principles of method which I have laid down, I have indulged the hope that to some of those on whom the task will devolve of bringing those most important of all sciences into a more satisfactory state, these observations may be useful. Should this hope be realized, what is probably destined to be the great intellectual achievement of the next two or three generations of European thinkers will have been, in some degree, forwarded.'†

Thirdly, Mill was amongst the first thinkers in Britain, or in any other country for that matter, to be thoroughly acquainted with the work of Comte, and to concern himself with a critical assessment of his ideas, and the furthering of his proposals for a science of sociology. In this sense, Mill was responsible for giving the work of Comte wide publicity in Britain and, indeed, he was one of a number of Englishmen who actually helped to maintain Comte financially during a particular, important and problematical period of his life.

Much emphasis, however, must be placed not only upon Mill's methodology of social science as such, but also on his study of logic proper.

Mill was concerned with a very specific problem here. The natural sciences had developed over the previous two centuries, and had,

* Preface to the First Edition.
† *A System of Logic, Ratiocinative and Inductive.* People's Edition. Longmans Green, 1884, p. 622. All subsequent references are to this edition.

without any question, demonstrated their worth in producing testable and reliable knowledge about all aspects of the nature of the physical world. Curiously, however, the kind of *logic* which men still considered as being productive of truth, the only kinds of *inference* which they still considered to constitute a pattern of clear thinking, was the syllogistic logic which had been little changed since the time of Aristotle. There was an odd gap between the procedures of inference which men actually used in science, and the philosophical account of such logic as could be employed. Mill was therefore very much concerned to clarify the new procedures of inference used in the natural sciences. He wanted to discover, and to state as clearly as possible, the ways in which men actually produced testable knowledge of the world of their experience.

His main emphasis in his whole study of logic was that the earlier conviction that knowledge of the world could be produced from completely *a priori* assumptions and propositions, was false, and that—no matter how conjectural some generalizations or hypotheses might appear—*all* of them, without any question, were derived from human *experience*. They were, that is to say, *inductive*, rather than *a priori* and *deductive*, in origin. This is not to say, by any means, that Mill thought deduction played no part in science and its procedures of inference. On the contrary, he thought it was extremely important. His chief point was only that the propositions and generalizations which men established about the nature of the world—whether produced by clear and systematic methods, by the deliberate assembling of as many facts of a particular kind as possible, or whether purely by a rough-and-ready analysis of our common sense experience—were all *drawn from experience*. As we shall see later, however, this does not mean that Mill, as many critics have said, was guilty, in any sense, of a naïve notion of induction or of 'inductive logic'.

In addition to insisting upon this experiential basis of all human knowledge; the foundation in empirical experience of all worthwhile procedures of inference; Mill then went on to undertake a detailed examination of all those procedures of experimentation or comparison, all those procedures of inference, of handling data in order to produce conditions of test, of judging evidence, whereby scientists actually attained their results. Having clarified these procedures as they had, in fact, been developed, and as they were, in fact, used in the natural sciences, Mill then, in the final book of the *Logic*, applied them to the study of man and society, in order to see whether and how far, they could be fruitfully employed in this kind of study. Mill's concern in the *Logic* then, though having a very important bearing upon the development of sociology, a 'general science of

H 199

man in society', was much wider than this. His book on logic can be said to be among the most important contributions in this field since the time of Aristotle.*

For *our* purposes, however, it is Book VI of the *Logic* which is of the greatest importance, and it will be most rewarding, for understanding the development of sociology, to analyse Mill's main proposals and arguments in this book.

The state of 'knowledge' concerning man and society

Mill began by claiming how backward, when compared with the degree of exactitude established in the natural sciences, was man's knowledge about his own nature and the nature of his own society. Having shown how successful the various sciences which establish 'laws' about the natural world had become, Mill claimed that the laws of mind and, to an even greater degree, those of society, were so far from having attained an even approximate degree of certainty in their formulation, and an even partial degree of recognition among scholars, that it was still an open controversy whether they were capable of becoming subjects of science at all in the strict sense of the term. And, he claimed, those who were agreed on this point disagreed on almost every other!

'If a more general agreement is ever to exist among thinkers,' he wrote, 'if what has been pronounced the proper study of mankind is not destined to remain the only subject which philosophy cannot succeed in rescuing from empiricism, the same process through which the laws of many simpler phenomena have by general acknowledgement been placed beyond dispute must be consciously and deliberately applied to those more difficult enquiries.'†

Man's knowledge concerning his own nature and his own society was still very much, even in the mid-nineteenth century, in the realm of *opinion* rather than that of testable knowledge, and the only way in which this situation could be improved was that the methods of science should at least be applied as far as this proved possible.

* Peter Medawar, in recent talks and essays, has emphasized the importance of Whewell in this connection. In my opinion, however, he over-simplifies Mill's notion of 'induction'. What is certain is that, though Mill was aware of Whewell's arguments, and took them into account, both he and Comte had quite independent things to say about the role of 'hypothesis' in scientific method. As an example of such criticism, see Medawar: *The Art of the Soluble*; chapter on 'Hypothesis and Imagination', pp. 131–155. In *Auguste Comte and Positivism* (p. 55), as well as in his *Logic*, Mill especially emphasizes, as one of Comte's major contributions, his discussion of 'the proper use of scientific hypotheses'.
† *System of Logic*, Book VI, p. 546.

The only thing it is salutary to notice, before leaving this, is that Mill's words are almost as applicable to our own time as to the time in which he was writing. The situation is not too different some hundred and twenty-five years afterwards. This alone should cause us to stop and take very seriously the question Mill was raising.

A first objection: the freedom of the will

Before trying to clarify the methods most appropriate to the study of man and society, Mill first dealt with what he thought was a genuine obstacle to many people; a problem which, for many, seemed altogether to preclude the possibility of a scientific study of man. And it is worthwhile to look at his discussion of this problem very closely, since it is a source of disquiet to many people still. It is the old question of the freedom of the will.

If, as many people believed, Mill said, human individuals possessed free will; if they could exercise deliberate choice; how was it possible to establish generalized knowledge about them which would allow *predictions* to be made? How could a *scientific* knowledge of men and societies be possible? If people could exercise choice, no matter how carefully we made predictions about them, they would always be able to act differently if they so wished, and thus confound our predictions. Furthermore, if a man possessed free will and could exercise choice, how was it possible to claim that his nature was causally determined; was the outcome of *causes*?

Mill treated this question in what seems to me an admirable and well-nigh conclusive way.

He began by arguing that it was an error to discuss the question of free will in too abstract a way. No one believes, for example, that a human being 'possesses' a 'will' in the same sense that he possesses a brain or heart or lungs or any other part of his body. When we use the word 'will', we are speaking not of some part of man, but of his capacity for exercising choice; the ability to exercise conscious deliberation, and, subsequently, to control his conduct. Similarly, when we want to maintain that human beings possess *'free'* will we never think that, in their exercise of choice, they are *completely* free; free without any reference to limitations. The idea of freedom, indeed, can never really be held as a complete abstraction. It is always a question of being free *to do* something, or being free *from* something; and it is always *to some extent*.

To put the matter briefly, Mill maintained that the best way of considering this question was to reduce it to more modest and sensible terms. Instead of asking: do men possess free will? it is better to ask: can men exercise choice? And, if so, does this prevent us from claiming that human nature and conduct are the outcome of causes about which we can establish scientific knowledge?

His first point was then the straightforward one that there is no inconsistency whatever in maintaining *both* that man's character is the outcome of causes *and* that he is capable of exercising choice, for the simple reason that, in human experience and behaviour, the choices that men make are themselves among the causes of their subsequent character and behaviour.

It is true that a man is born into a particular social environment; a complex set of circumstances. He is brought up within a family and is educated in a certain school. He grows up surrounded by the beliefs, values, ideals, institutions of society. His nature is therefore, quite obviously, to a very large extent shaped by these influences. But, throughout his experience of these influences, as he is growing to maturity and afterwards, he reflects upon them to some extent, changes his ideas about them to some extent, and chooses ways of behaving which, upon reflection, he has to some extent worked out for himself. Without at all pressing the matter so far as to argue that the individual can achieve *entire* self-determination, it is quite clear that the choices he makes have a determining influence upon the ways in which he behaves and the kind of character he becomes afterwards. For example, if a boy, on leaving school, chooses to follow one career rather than another, this will have an enormous determining influence upon the circumstances which will exert subsequent influences upon him for many years to come; and this will therefore have a determining influence upon aspects of his behaviour and character. If he chooses to become a soldier, a civil servant, a university student, each of these choices will have a very different effect upon his behaviour, his habits, his mode of life, and his character in future.

It seems clear then, Mill argued, that the choices a person makes are among the causes of his behaviour, and, therefore, that if we could know *all* the antecedents of a man's present character, it would be possible to give a causal account of his whole development; since his deliberations and his choices were themselves causes (among other kinds of causes) of the ongoing changes in his nature. It turns out, then, that there is no inconsistency whatever in saying that, to some extent, a man can shape his own character, but, also, that his character is the outcome of causes.

Mill claimed that the discussion of the 'free will versus determinism' issue in the past had been bedevilled by an unwarranted element of 'necessitarianism' in the idea of 'causal determination'. It had come to be thought that to say that a causal account could be given of a man's character and behaviour, was to say that the causes, including his choices, of a man's life and conduct were, in some sense, *inevitable*. The choices were only *apparent* choices, because, in fact, they could not possibly have been any different.

Mill completely rejected this 'necessitarian' idea as an undemonstrable and unnecessary metaphysical assertion, and claimed that a man could reflect and choose in his life, but, nonetheless, that these reflections and choices were among the causal influences shaping his subsequent nature, and that if we knew all about them we could give a full causal account of his development. The reason why we are always unable to give such a complete causal account of any individual is simply that we do not, and cannot, know all the factors and events which were antecedent to his present nature. We shall return to this point later.

Having clarified this, however, Mill went on to make his second important point. This is that—although a man may exercise choice, and although we need not deny some degree of freedom of the will—his choices are nonetheless, in fact, very considerably circumscribed by at least two factors. A man's choices are never completely free; they are always exercised within constraints which can be specified and known.

First of all, from the beginning of his life, an individual gradually develops a *settled character*. His inclinations, his dispositions, his attitudes, his habits, are never completely arbitrary. They come to have a certain stable and settled form, a certain pattern, in his character. This character will be partly the outcome of his responses to all that he imbibes from his social environment; but it will also be the outcome of his own efforts to achieve the kind of character which other people desire of him, or that he himself, in the context of other people's judgments, desires. We do find, in fact, that when we know a man's character sufficiently well, we can predict with a large measure of accuracy how he will exercise his choice, and how he will conduct his deliberation upon various matters. We can predict how he will choose. And this is not because he is not free to choose. It is simply that, knowing him well enough, we know *how* he will exercise his freedom. Taking Mill's earlier point into account, it is important to see that the man we know will, in fact, be judging freely, in accordance with his own convictions, his own principles. He *could* choose to do something else if he wished to do so; he could deliberately flout our predictions if he wished; but he will not, in fact, do anything else because of the particular nature of his character.

We do not, therefore, need to regard a man as a machine, as an automaton, before we can predict about him. Of course, a man may do something totally unexpected; incalculable; but, in our experience, this is so exceptional as usually to astonish us. And, if it happens, we conclude that, after all, we did not know this person's character as well as we had thought. We frequently say of a person who has done something unexpected: 'I never knew that he had it in him'. But in the normal, usual, sequences of a man's life we can, in fact, predict a good deal about him. We all know that when we know a person intimately, it is possible to predict in this manner and, furthermore, all our expectations in social intercourse are based upon such predictions.

Also, without being at all cynical, it is surely true that none of us are rational and reflective to the point of totally disentangling ourselves from our earlier experience. Our qualities of character have been very considerably engendered by the influences and pressures of our early environment. Even the most reasonable and reflective of us are aware of deep-rooted dispositions which more or less have their own way with us; which almost insist upon themselves in our behaviour, and determine our reactions, even when we think we have achieved rational control over them. Indeed, it is possible to be perfectly conscious that we possess some disposition in our nature and still be unable ourselves to govern it. Again, it is the case that the exercise of choice is a matter of degree, and thus this degree is within the context of settled dispositions of character.

Mill's second circumscribing factor is the immediate set of circumstances in which a person is placed. We are never able to exercise choice among an *infinity* of alternatives. We can exercise choice only among those limited alternatives which actually confront us in a given situation; and it is perfectly obvious that all social situations carry constraints which limit the things we would like to do. To give a simple example: if a man is employed in a factory which recognizes the practice of the 'closed shop', he can exercise choice only in a very limited number of ways. He can either leave the factory, or join the trade union, or work at the factory, not join the trade union, and put up with the misery and discomfort of being, say, 'sent to Coventry'. He is not free to do *anything* that he likes. The range of his choices is *finite*. His choices are always limited in accordance with the immediate circumstances.

Mill claimed firstly, then, that though a man can choose, this does not preclude a causal account of his nature, since the choices are themselves causes; and, secondly, that a knowledge of a person's character and of those social and physical circumstances in which he is placed, enables us to predict to a specifiable degree about the way in which, in fact, he will exercise his choices.

Many other things, of course, could be said about this issue between free will and determinism, but it seems to me that Mill treated it with an adequacy completely sufficient for his purpose, and for ours, which is that of showing that the fact that man can choose does not stand in the way of establishing testable scientific knowledge about him. It will be noted that—so far—this argument has been entirely concerned with individuals, though the specific study of social circumstances has entered. However, social facts, elements of social organization themselves, such as the legal system, the governmental system, the religious system of a community, can obviously be observed and described even more easily than individuals, and therefore, on the face of it, there seems to be no obstacle whatever in applying science either to the study of men as individuals or to the study of the institutions of their social life. Freedom of the will does not stand in the way of a science of man and society.

Before leaving this point, it is important to notice that Oxford historians, theologians, and others, who maintain that freedom of the will *does* stand in the way of science of society are obliged to come to terms with Mill's argument and to say, clearly, on what grounds they do not accept it.

The natural sciences and the human sciences

Having shown that a scientific study of man was, in principle, possible, Mill's next argument was to show that the human sciences (and their problems) were not so different from the physical sciences as was commonly supposed. To do this, he compared them briefly with three physical sciences—meteorology (the science of the weather), tidology (the science of the tides) and astronomy.

In meteorology and tidology he showed that even though the underlying laws which govern the weather and the tides are known with considerable exactitude (the relationships, for example, between pressure and temperature: the influence exerted by the moon on the seas, etc.), it is still, nonetheless, beyond the power of the meteorologist and the tidologist to predict with precision what the weather or the level of tides will be at any particular spot and at any particular time. This is because they do not know, in sufficiently exact detail, all the antecedents of the particular instances about which they are making predictions. We may know exactly the 'laws' of temperature and pressure which produce particular kinds of weather, but we cannot predict with exactitude what the weather will be like in East Anglia next August 3rd at 4.0 in the afternoon, simply because we cannot possibly know all the antecedents before that occasion. Similarly, though we may know exactly the extent of the attraction of the moon upon the sea and the way in which this produces the tides, we find it extremely difficult to predict what the level of the tide will be at Clacton on the second Thursday in May a year hence because we do not know all the other detailed circumstances that may be involved: the force of the wind at that time, or the local irregularities of the ocean bed (which may have changed before that time). What this amounts to, then, is that even in some physical sciences, though the underlying laws which govern the behaviour of the facts which they study are exactly known, and can be exactly demonstrated in laboratory conditions, it is still impossible to predict certain specific events of nature because, in any such particular situation, all the relevant antecedent facts cannot possibly be known.

Astronomy, on the other hand, is a precise science because *both* the general laws of the movements of the planets *and* the specific antecedents which cause the local perturbations in the orbits of particular planets are known. In this case, there has been sufficient time, and the phenomena are sufficiently simple, to allow knowledge of all the particular antecedents to particular planetary movements to be known as well as the general laws which govern the large-scale movements of the planets.

Logically, therefore, said Mill, there is no reason at all why the human sciences should be considered fundamentally different from these natural sciences. There may well be universal characteristics about human nature and human society. There may be similarities in all human societies, in certain institutions—let us say in the family, or religion. There may be universal laws of character development in human nature. But none of these would, in themselves, enable us to predict precisely about any particular person at any time, or about a specific change in any particular society. For precision, for exactitude, here, we would need as detailed a knowledge as we could get of all the peculiar local circumstances of the individual, or of the social order we were concerned to study, and this we can never hope to achieve completely. Mill maintained then, that the human sciences are in the condition of meteorology and tidology—where general laws may be ascertained but where precise exactitude in particular predictions seems likely to remain impossible.

However, the *degree* of exactitude of our particular predictions will become greater as our knowledge of the antecedents of these events increases. We can, that is to say, move the human sciences ever more closely to the kind of exactitude that astronomy has achieved, though without ever hoping to achieve the same degree of precision. This *im*precision of our knowledge of human nature, however, is *not* because the thinking, feeling, acting of individuals are not consequent upon causes. It is only because we cannot possibly foresee all the particular *circumstances* in which individuals or societies will be placed, and because we cannot know with complete detail all the dimensions of the *characters* of the individuals and groups involved. These aspects of individuals and social behaviour are never altogether alike in different cases. Hence, a science of man and society can only, at the best, consist of empirical generalizations ('general laws') and statements of tendencies. Even so, our knowledge of these tendencies will, and can, be more or less exact, depending upon the methods of study we use. Furthermore, some aspects of human nature may be common to all of us even though other aspects may differ considerably.

'Inasmuch,' said Mill, 'however, as many of these effects which it is of most importance to render amenable to human foresight and control are determined (like the tides) in an incomparably greater degree by general causes than by all partial causes taken together, depending in the main on those circumstances and qualities which are common to all mankind, or at least to large bodies of them, and only in a small degree on particular or peculiar idiosyncrasies, it is evidently possible with regard to all such effects to make predictions which will almost always be verified, and general propositions which are almost always true.

'And whenever it is sufficient to know how the great majority of the human race or of some nation or class of persons will think, feel and act, these propositions are equivalent to universal ones.'*

It would not be enough, however, simply to state these generalizations concerning the common aspects of human nature and human behaviour. They would, in addition, have to be explained.

Psychology: the essential basis of a science of man

Having thus shown that a scientific study of man and society was, in principle, possible, and was not, in principle, different from some natural sciences, Mill then proceeded to examine the possible nature of a science of man, and undertook an exacting discussion of the methods most appropriate to it.

The starting-point of his views, and one which was very distinctive and on which he insisted, was the fundamental persuasion that all *social* phenomena are rooted in the nature of human *individuals*; that all phenomena of *society* are, when properly considered, phenomena of human psychology.

* *System of Logic*, p. 554.

'All phenomena of society', he says, 'are phenomena of human nature generated by the action of outward circumstances upon masses of human beings ... The laws of the phenomena of society are, and can be, nothing but the laws of the actions and passions of human beings united together in the social state. Men in a state of society are still men. Their actions and passions are obedient to the laws of individual human nature. Men are not, when brought together, converted into another kind of substance with different properties as hydrogen and oxygen are different from water.'*

Mill's first point, then, was that psychology was of the most fundamental importance for any kind of social explanation. He said relatively little about the actual nature of psychology, knowing very well that the subject was very much in its infancy, and being too sensible to attempt the establishment of knowledge when no knowledge really existed. However, he had some very interesting points to make about a science of psychology.

His first point of importance was that the science of psychology must be a science of observation and experiment. We could not, he claimed, know anything with any degree of certainty about human nature, human experience, and human behaviour, unless we followed the methods of observation and experiment. For too long, suppositions about human psychology had rested upon unsubstantiated opinion. Rigorous observation and rigorous experiment were therefore necessary.

Secondly, Mill had interesting points to make about the relationship between physiology and psychology. Clearly, he said, our psychological experiences—our emotions, motives, thoughts, purposes, sensations and the like—depend upon and rest upon certain bodily states. A knowledge of such bodily states is therefore necessary. However, he claimed, no amount of knowledge of the physical basis of psychological experiences can ever make an investigation of these experiences themselves unnecessary. Physiological knowledge is knowledge additional to that of psychology; it is necessary and useful knowledge; but it is an error to think that it can altogether replace it. To put this in another way, Mill argued firmly that psychological knowledge can never be *reduced* to 'explanations' in terms of physiological processes, and this, I think, is a point which deserves much emphasis at the present day in view of some developments of so-called 'Physiological psychology' which, strictly speaking, are nothing more than physiology proper.

A third point which Mill made clearly, was that environmental

* *System of Logic*, pp. 572–3. It may be noted that Mill's conception, very clearly and definitely, was that sociological generalizations included essentially. generalizations about *social action*, and *motivation* within the context of institutional regularities.

influences play a very great part in shaping or engendering qualities of human experience. He was strongly persuaded that, among human beings, differences in family circumstances, education, in all outward social situations, were capable of affording an adequate explanation of a considerable portion of personality and character formation, but he thought that if we knew more about inherited differences, about differences in the acuteness of the senses and perception, about differences in the inherited instincts and emotions, among individuals, that these might well yield a greater explanation of some differences of qualities of personality than we now think. For example, he thought that a great acuteness of the senses (a quick and subtle susceptibility to sense impressions) may lead to such qualities in personality and character as a love of the beautiful and moral enthusiasm, whereas a mediocre sensibility may be connected with a love of scientific or abstract truth; and a person with such a limited sensibility might be deficient to some extent in artistic feeling and taste, and in moral fervour. It is important to say, however, that Mill did not *assert* these matters—he simply suggested them as possible examples of his view that if we knew more about these fundamental aspects of human sensation, impulse, emotion, they might be able to add a good deal to our explanations of human nature in addition to our knowledge of those environmental circumstances which play upon it.

The chief point of importance here, however, is simply that Mill was quite firmly convinced that psychology is an essential basis for the construction of a science of human society, and this was a very definite and basic component in his outline of such a science.

The scientific study of society

In addition to the study of individuals, Mill then said, it is obviously also necessary in any adequate science of human nature to study the facts of *social* life: 'the actions of collective masses of mankind, and the various phenomena which constitute society'.

In addition to our knowledge of individual feeling, thinking and acting, we need also, by observation and experiment, in so far as this proves possible, to establish a knowledge of the social institutions, the forms of social organization, within which men find themselves. Later, as we shall see, Mill described what he considered to be the main elements of social structure in any society when he spoke of the basic conditions for the existence of a society. For the moment, however, we can simply note that he believed a knowledge of social structure, of the institutional organization of society, to be a necessary component in a science of man, in addition to a knowledge of the nature of the individuals who live within it. However, it is very important to note here that Mill still maintained his strong belief that institutions do not exist, and cannot be said to exist in any sense, independently of individuals.

'All phenomena of society', he wrote, 'are phenomena of human nature generated by the action of outward circumstances upon masses of human beings: and if, therefore, the phenomena of human thought, feeling and action are subject to fixed laws, the phenomena of society cannot but conform to fixed laws, the consequence of the preceding. There is no hope that these laws, though our knowledge of them were as certain and complete as it is in astronomy, would enable us to predict the history of society like that of the celestial appearances for thousands of years to come. But the difference of certainty is not in the laws themselves, it is in the data to which these laws are to be applied.'*

It is quite clear, then, that Mill required in his science of man *both* a knowledge of the structure of social institutions within which men carry on their social life and activities, *and* a knowledge of the psychological characteristics of individual human nature. Having insisted on this, he then went on to argue, however, that some *other* component is necessary in any science of human nature to investigate and explain the interaction between these two.

Ethology: the science of personality and character formation and of 'collective' psychological facts

This third component Mill called Ethology, and, as he described it, it is what modern psychologists would think of as a compound of personality psychology and social psychology. It is the scientific study of the way in which (given a basic knowledge of perception, motivation, emotion and other basic endowments of human nature) character and personality is developed by the influence of the groups and institutions within which individuals are born and brought up to maturity, and within which they continue to pursue their associational activities as adults. Mill believed that ethology was predominantly, indeed wholly, a deductive science.

On the one hand, observation and experiment can give us a basic knowledge of the psychological endowment of individuals. On the other, observation can give us a clear knowledge of the structure of groups and institutions within which individuals are born and

* *System of Logic*, p. 572. It may be noted—in view of Popper's criticism of Mill's supposed 'Historicism', to which we shall come later—that Mill explicitly set aside all hope of predicting the history of society.

grow to maturity. Ethology studies the way in which character formation takes place through the action of the institutional setting upon the basic psychological endowment. Mill believed, therefore, that ethology should follow deductive procedures in the sense that it should be possible to deduce, from a knowledge of psychology, what kind of character development would be likely to take place if certain specified conditions of social life were given. The validity and truth of this deduction could then be tested against our observations as to whether, in these specific social circumstances, this kind of character was, in fact, brought into being.

The science of ethology provides, therefore, what Mill called the 'middle principles', the '*axiomata media*', linking the observational sciences at either extreme.

An adequate science of human nature must therefore include these three necessary components: (1) a basic psychology, (2) a descriptive and analytical knowledge of social structure, and (3) a hypothetical study of social psychology and personality and character development, linking the other two.

To put this in a slightly different way, in order to point to other important dimensions, ethology would be necessary in order to show how the individuals within a community came to possess certain settled dispositions of character and personality; settled ideals, beliefs, attitudes, social purposes; and this knowledge would be necessary in order, further, to explain how changes in *some* institutions reacted upon people's dispositions in such a way as to bring about changes in others. This is an extremely important point to which we shall come back later.

In all this, it is most important to bear in mind that Mill certainly did not expect ever to be able to achieve the degree of exactitude in the human sciences that was possible in the natural sciences. He was only concerned to say that we should try to achieve the greatest degree of exactitude that lay within our power. And he was continually reiterating that an amount of knowledge quite insufficient for prediction may be most valuable for guidance. The science of character—Ethology—may not permit of absolute precision. Nonetheless, it is the science on which the most important art of education rests, and Mill was always pointing out that, in spite of inexactitude, people in society *do* have very definite opinions as to what kind of family upbringing, what kind of school experience, what kind of instruction and training is most likely to bring about certain ends and qualities of character. Now these suppositions must rest upon implicit 'theories' about character development, and the only thing that we can possibly do to make our suppositions as reliable as we can, is to make these 'theories' as explicit and exact as possible, and to test them. Only on our most reliable *knowledge* of the facts of character-development can our arts of family upbringing and education be reliably based and effective. Only if they rest upon reliable knowledge are the methods we use in upbringing and education likely to bring about the ends that we desire. More broadly speaking, this same knowledge is necessary for the wise exercise of the art of government.

Having briefly outlined this three-fold nature of a general science of man and society, Mill then turned to the question as to what its methods should most properly be: which methods were obviously inappropriate, and which methods, on the other hand, would have to be followed if knowledge was to be established.*

Methods appropriate to a study of man and society: (1) Methods rejected

In one of the most important sections of his work, Mill then critically considered the extent to which the various methods of inductive study which he had earlier elaborated in his *Logic*, could be effectively applied to the study of man. Some of these methods he rejected outright, others he qualified, arriving finally at a conception of method in sociology which was closely in agreement with the one already elaborated by Comte. First of all let us look at the methods he rejected.

* Before leaving this consideration of Mill's conception of a science of man, and the three components of it, it is worthwhile to notice one point whose importance will be seen much later.

It is quite clear that Mill did *not* regard a science of man, and even a science of personality development, as being purely a *deterministic* thing; one purely of mechanistic causation. He clearly thought in terms of *character* development as well as *personality* formation; or, to put it more clearly, he believed that we can understand the development of character, and to some extent the *self-determination* of character, and the social purposes that men pursue, in terms of their own conscious thought, their own conscious and deliberate self-direction, their own conscious aims to achieve certain ends in individual and social activity. This will be most important when we come to consider the addition of a new dimension of sociological analysis which Max Weber (among others) introduced. Here we may simply, but emphatically, note that Mill was *not* 'deterministic' in thinking of the application of the methods of the sciences to the study of man, but that he recognized the necessity of incorporating into scientific method this possibility of the understanding of human action in terms of deliberation and rationality. However, it is also necessary to emphasize that Mill failed to see the important relevance of this point for the development of distinctive sociological methods of analysis and explanation. For clearly, a causal explanation in terms of deliberations and choices is something qualitatively different from anything arising in the 'natural sciences'. This is a point, however, to which we must return in much detail later, and it is one of great importance.

(a) The Chemical (Compound) Experimental Method

The first method which Mill completely, emphatically and, indeed, hotly rejected was what he called the 'chemical' or 'compound' method in social science, including the various 'experimental' methods attendant upon it.

Now this precise heading of Mill's chapter—which appears to equate the 'chemical' and the 'experimental' in speaking of this particular method—has, I believe, given rise to a considerable degree of misunderstanding of Mill's position. Furthermore, I believe that the point Mill was at pains to make in this section is of the very greatest importance, and I therefore think it is necessary to make it luminously clear. Later, we shall see that Durkheim, in criticizing Mill, actually falls into the error which Mill here warns against, and gives rise to much ambiguity as a result. The understanding of this matter here will be a valuable basis for understanding much that comes later.

Firstly, let us consider this term—the 'chemical' method; which seems rather curious in our modern ears. It seems odd to use the word 'chemical' to refer to a particular scientific method. What Mill essentially meant by this term was this.

There are some social scientists, indeed people in all walks of life, economists, politicians, clergymen and the like, he maintained, who speak as though they believe that social institutions or any other actualities of political and economic affairs (such as, for example, a tariff barrier or the bank rate) have an actual existence, as entities, over and above the heads of individuals, and are actually involved in a network of cause-and-effect relationships between each other without involving men and women as individuals—as, as it were, mediators of social experience and action—at all. Mill was concerned to attack this idea root and branch! He thought it was a completely false way of conceiving the nature of society, and that it gave rise to a completely false method of exploring human interactions in the context of social structure and social change.

Let me try to make this absolutely clear.

Mill was *not* saying that elements of social structure such as a form of government, a form of industrial organization, an administrative structure of the Health Service, a form of the family and marriage, a system of education, and so on, which have characteristics other than those of individual psychology, do not exist. This he was perfectly ready to admit, and indeed, as we have already seen, he believed that empirical generalizations could be made about social organization, at this level of 'social' facts. What he was particularly concerned to make clear and emphasize beyond doubt, however, is that these elements of social organization cannot, by any stretch of imagination or any stretch of scientific methodology, be conceived as having cause-and-effect relationships between each other as self-existent entities. If a change in one of these institutions is followed by changes in other institutions, it is not that *it* has caused *them*, though we may sometimes speak in a convenient, shorthand way, as if this were the case. It can only be because the first change has been mediated through the experience and action of *people* in such a way as to bring about the subsequent changes. The first change has an impact, an influence, upon the settled dispositions, ideas, qualities of character of the individuals living in that society. It is then through their responses to this influence in relation to other aspects of their lives, that changes in other kinds of social institutions have occurred. Again, to be perfectly clear, let us think of an example.

If—a thing common in our experience now—the bank rate is reduced and this is followed by an expansion in productivity in the economy, it is not, Mill would say, that some entity called the 'bank rate' (existing independently of individuals) has *caused* an increase in another entity called the 'level of production in the economy' (also existing independently of individuals), though, in a shorthand way we may conveniently speak like this. What, in fact, has occurred, is that an alteration in the bank rate has influenced the calculations, the expectations, the decisions of the men and women involved in economic activity. The grounds for economic decisions have been changed. It may now be more profitable to borrow cheaper money and to invest capital in productive industry. Manufacturing activities in many directions may be stimulated. And it is because of these reactions of individuals and groups of associated individuals to the change in the Bank Rate that changes in the level of production throughout the economy have subsequently taken place. Mill himself used the example of 'protective tariffs' and whether or not they caused 'prosperity' in society; a question that was much discussed in his time; but any example of this kind makes the point perfectly clear.

What this amounts to, Mill was trying to say, is this.

The kind of view which a chemist might have of the compounds which he is studying—namely that certain molecular *compounds* are qualitatively distinct from the separable components of which they consist, and that they can be studied in terms of causal interconnection at their own level—is quite fundamentally and quite definitely incorrect and false when applied to the phenomena of human society. Though society has a framework of interconnected institutions which have qualities other than those of individual psychology; and though these institutions certainly do have their kinds and degrees of causal influence upon the personality and character formation of individuals; it is still not the case that society is some kind of 'compounding of individuals' into something totally different from and independent of individuals. Individuals, in the context of all the influences which play upon them, remain people—men and women who calculate their modes of life as persons—and any explanation of changing 'institutional regularities' must take this fact into account.

Mill put it like this:

'The laws of the phenomena of society are and can be nothing but the laws of the actions and passions of human beings united together in the social state. Men, however, in a state of society are still men. Their actions and passions are obedient to the laws of individual human nature. Men are not, when brought together, converted into another kind of substance with different properties as hydrogen and oxygen are different from water or as hydrogen, oxygen, carbon and azote are different from nerves, muscles and tendons. Human beings in society have no properties than those which are derived from and may be resolved into the laws of the nature of individual man. *In social phenomena the composition of causes is the universal law.*

'. . . the method of philosophizing which may be termed chemical, overlooks this fact and proceeds as if the nature of man as an individual were not concerned at all or were concerned in a very inferior degree in the operations of human beings in society.'*

It may be specially noted before leaving this point, that it is on these grounds of thinking (i.e. that a consideration of individuals must necessarily be involved in social explanation) that Mill has been charged with what Karl Popper has called 'psychologism'. It is also the case that attempts to elaborate the complex patterns of explanation involved in bringing psychology and sociology properly together, are condemned as 'abstract theory' by those who have not the patience, or qualities of mind, to confront the actual intricacies of human nature and human society. It is interesting to note, therefore, that Mill himself—already, when making this point—ridiculed those who objected to it as 'abstract theory'. The errors of 'abstraction' he claimed, lay rather with those guilty of this unwarranted 'objectification' of institutionalized regularities.

Mill's point about this 'chemical' or 'compounding' conception of society is therefore perfectly clear. Let us turn now to the second term in his title—'The Experimental Method'.

Mill quite definitely rejected the appropriateness of the experimental method in a science of man and society. For this, too, he has been criticized. But again it is of the utmost importance—and this also must be emphasized very greatly—to see that *Mill rejected*

* *System of Logic*, p. 573 (Ch. VII).

the experimental method only in relation to this 'chemical', 'compound' conception of the nature of society.

It is the idea that—given that societies exist as sets of inter-connected social institutions, we can then conduct experiments: comparing total societies with each other in order to test the causal efficacy of isolated institutional variables in bringing about certain social effects—that Mill emphatically rejected. This section of his work was extremely complicated, but we must do our best to become quite clear about these experimental methods which he rejected, and about his grounds for rejecting them. This is important not only for its own sake (though, of course, it *is* important simply from the point of view of achieving an accurate understanding of Mill's own ideas) but also because in the subsequent development of sociological theory, some thinkers, without the logical clarity of Mill, nonetheless employed some of the methods he rejected. It is important to understand these methods, and Mill's objections to them, as clearly as possible, so that we can properly assess in the development of the subject many of the contributions (such as those of Emile Durkheim and Max Weber) which followed. This is not, by any means, to say at this stage, that the contributions of Durkheim and Weber were to any great extent erroneous; only that some of their proposed methods had already been critically assessed by Mill, and had been shown to be questionable. We therefore need to understand this.

Mill elaborated five experimental methods:

   (i) The method of difference.
  (ii) The indirect method of difference.
 (iii) The method of agreement.
 (iv) The method of concomitant variations.
  (v) The method of residues.

His objections to all these methods were much the same, but it is important to define each method as clearly as possible.

(I) THE METHOD OF DIFFERENCE

The method of difference, Mill said, is that in which we compare two particular instances which are alike in every respect except the one which is the subject of enquiry. If we could conduct this kind of experiment, we should be able to isolate the effect of this one difference. Applying this to the study of societies, Mill says:

'If two nations can be found which are alike in all natural advantages and disadvantages, whose people resemble each other in every quality, physical and moral, spontaneous and acquired, whose habits, usages of opinions, laws and institutions, are the same in all respects except that one of them

216

has a more protective tariff or in other respects interferes more with the freedom of industry, if one of these nations is found to be rich and the other poor or one richer than the other, this will be a crucial experiment, a real proof by experience which of the two systems is most favourable to national riches.'*

Mill then went on to say, however, that though this method might be applicable to the subject-matter of the natural sciences, the supposition that two *nations*, or two total *societies*, possessing such a complete degree of similarity could ever be found, was manifestly absurd. There was, therefore, an undoubted and demonstrable impossibility of obtaining in Sociology the conditions required for the most conclusive form of scientific enquiry. This 'direct' method of studying specific differences and their consequences was out of the question.

Because of this inadequacy, Mill then considered the second possibility, which he called 'the indirect method of difference'.

(ii) THE INDIRECT METHOD OF DIFFERENCE

This method is that in which, instead of comparing two *specific instances* which differ in nothing but the presence or absence of one particular circumstance, the investigator compares two *classes* of instances which agree in nothing excepting the presence of the specific circumstances in the one class, and its absence in the other.

For example, we might compare two sets of societies—one which differed in all characteristics excepting that they *possessed* protective tariffs; the second which also differed in all characteristics excepting that they *lacked* protective tariffs. The attempt in comparing these two sets of societies might be to see what effect the presence or absence of protective tariffs had upon the prosperity of these societies.

At first glance, supposing the societies possessing the protective tariff were prosperous and those lacking it were all impoverished, it would seem to be plausible that the tariff barrier had *caused* prosperity. On further thought, however, Mill maintained, it is clear that this result is quite inconclusive, for the simple reason that the prosperity of the one set of countries and the poverty of the other might be due to any one or any group of those other social factors which differed amongst them all. In short, the multiplicity and wide-ranging difference of the factors involved makes any such conclusion, by employing the indirect method of differences, impossible.

Mill then considered a third method: the 'method of agreement'.

* *System of Logic*, p. 575.

(III) THE METHOD OF AGREEMENT

This third method rests upon the canon that:

'If two or more instances of the phenomenon under investigation have only one circumstance in common, the circumstance in which alone all the instances agree is the cause of the given phenomenon.'

For example, if we found two or more cases, two or more societies* which were characterized by prosperity and which possessed tariff protection, but which differed in all other social institutions, then it would be proved—according to this method—that the existence of tariff protection was the *cause* of prosperity.

Mill's objection to this method rested upon the simplicity of its assumptions. There always exists in human societies, he insisted, a *multiplicity* of causes and effects, extremely difficult to disentangle. In the example given, there are so many and various causes which contribute to, and result in such large social 'effects' as 'prosperity' (for example military security, political freedom, stable government, industrial activity, industrial relations, good education, and so on) that no one of them, even if it is a common feature in the societies being compared, can be claimed to be solely responsible.

'No one cause', Mill wrote, 'suffices of itself to produce any of these phenomena whilst there are countless causes which have some influence over them and may co-operate either in their production or in their prevention. From the mere fact, therefore, of our having been able to eliminate some circumstance, we can by no means infer that this circumstance was not instrumental to the effect in some of the very instances from which we have eliminated it. We can conclude that the effect is sometimes produced without it, but not that, when present, it does not contribute its share.'†

What Mill was saying here, is that in social matters we always have a plurality of causes, various combinations of which may have a similar result. Now this is a point which merits much argument and criticism, and later we shall see that Durkheim takes Mill to task for it. Let us simply note, however, before leaving it, that Mill is thinking of arguments concerning the causes of large scale social effects such as prosperity, security, poverty, and it is these circumstances of *societies*, as whole *systems of institutions*, which he thinks it impossible to explain in terms of any *single* cause, and especially any single cause in terms of an institutional or aggregate 'entity' without reference to the experience and behaviour of people.

* i.e. We are again, here, comparing *specific instances, specific societies*, not *classes*, as in the second (indirect) method.
† *System of Logic*, p. 576.

218

The same kind of objections, Mill thought, had to be raised against the fourth method: the method of 'concomitant variations'.

(IV) THE METHOD OF CONCOMITANT VARIATIONS

This is the method of establishing statistical correlations between aggregates, and it is important in assessing Mill's discussion of this method to notice that he did *not* maintain that correlations between aggregates cannot be achieved, nor did he maintain that these are of *no* value. Indeed, Mill was well aware of the new developments of social statistics and the curious constancies of human behaviour over long periods of time within the same society which they revealed: rates of marriage, murder, suicide, posting letters without stamps, leaving umbrellas in hotel foyers, and so on. Mill was perfectly well aware that, in the aggregate, constancies and correlations of human behaviour could usefully and clearly be established by statistics.

What he was concerned to argue, however, (and I believe that most modern statisticians would uphold him) was that a statistical correlation is always and only a correlation, and a correlation between *aggregates*. It can never claim to be a *causal* statement. Mill emphasized that the aggregates between which statistics establishes its correlations, all consist of individual cases. Since there is such a multiplicity of causes in individual behaviour and social affairs, different causes might be operative in each particular individual case, even though an aggregate correlation bound all these cases together.

To give an illustration: it may be that there is a constancy in the rate of suicide from year to year, and it may be that this constant rate of suicide may be correlated, let us say, with the stability of the economy. That is to say, if there are great instabilities and fluctuations in economic circumstances (whether of sudden prosperity or sudden poverty), the suicide rate may be shown, invariably, to increase. With continued stability, perhaps the suicide rate remains low. But Mill would say that this is only a very general correlation indeed and not, by any means, a sufficient causal statement. For it may be that if we considered Mr Jones, Mr Smith, Mr James and so on, who committed suicide, the actual causes in each case might be very different, and refer to other factors, even though they might be connected with economic circumstances. For example, one man may have committed suicide because he thought he had cancer; another because he had lost his life-savings; another because his wife had left him and taken off his children; another because he was deeply depressed in a new social class with which he was unfamiliar; and so on. Now all these individual causes may be *connected* with, and even attendant upon, the stability or instability of economic circumstances yet the statistical correlation at the aggregate level would not be a detailed uncovering of all the many causes that were involved. For a *full* causal analysis, the factors in each individual case would have to be examined. Mill simply maintained that the multiplicity of causes in human affairs is so great that the method of concomitant variations is limited, though useful, for the exploration of them.

Mill himself wrote:

'Every attribute of the social body is influenced by innumerable causes, and such is the mutual action of the co-existing elements of society that whatever affects any one of the more important of them will by that alone, if it does not affect the others directly, affect them indirectly. The effects therefore, of different agents not being different in quality, while the quality of each is the mixed result of all the agents, the variations of the aggregate cannot bear a uniform proportion to those of any one of its component parts.'*

Now it may be that Mill over-emphasized the objections against the method of concomitant variations and underestimated its use in uncovering significant connections in which causal relationships might lie, and we shall return to this method when we consider the work of Durkheim. Let us only note, however, in order to be perfectly clear about this, that Mill was *not* maintaining that empirical generalizations about social aggregates cannot be established by statistical methods. He was only claiming that this is *all* that statistics can do; and that, for a causal explanation of these empirical generalizations, something more, and something more detailed and specific is required. Indeed, empirical generalizations, Mill insisted, are not themselves explanations at all. They are simply descriptive statements of general fact which themselves require explanation. Statistical generalizations, such as that the rates of suicide in different societies are related significantly to variations in certain other factors, themselves require explanations of a kind which statistical method itself cannot provide.

A simple example of an empirical generalization in another science would be that in the autumn all leaves, or acorns, or apples, fall to the ground; but this in itself, though a regularity in the behaviour of nature, is not an explanation of anything. It is a generalization which intrigues us and leads us to *look* for an explanation, and this explanation would be found to have many aspects, having something to do, say, with the maturing of fruit, the establishing of a layer of cork between twigs and leaves, the methods of reproduction and dispersal of seeds by trees, the force of gravity, and so on. The same is the case

---

* *System of Logic*, p. 577.

in society. The fact that a rate of suicide is constantly concomitant with certain other elements of social life is not in itself an explanation; it is a generalization which itself requires explanation. Mill was only maintaining this, but we shall look at this point again when we come to consider the ideas of Durkheim.

(v) THE METHOD OF RESIDUES

Mill then considered a final experimental method: the 'Method of Residues'. In this method, he claimed, we examine one instance of a phenomenon only; in sociology—one instance of a human society. We then eliminate all those effects of the causes of which we already possess a clear knowledge. We must then be left with a limited number of effects and causes. And we shall then be able to concentrate on clarifying the relationship between these residual causes and effects, thus being more likely to achieve an elucidation of what is still lacking in our knowledge.

Again, however, Mill maintained that this method was inappropriate for sociology; his reasons being again the wide-ranging multiplicity and the varying combinations of causes in the production of social effects.

This then, though a brief résumé, is what Mill had to say about the five kinds of experimental method; and he rejected them all for the study of society, for sociology.

Again, however, it is most important that we should note that he rejected these methods solely with reference to the experimental study of *total societies*, of institutions and *systems* of institutions, which are held to have some kind of cause-and-effect interdependency without reference to individuals. Mill *insisted* upon the experimental method for psychology, and I believe that he would have been prepared to consider the experimental method, though with qualifications, if it were conducted at a limited level of individuals, and groups of individuals in specified social situations. It is only this large 'chemical, compound' conception of society which he was attacking here, and it was in relation to this that he thought the experimental method false and useless.

One final point may just be mentioned in this place; again a point to which we shall return. Mill has frequently been criticised for what has come to be called 'holism'.* He has been said to be guilty of considering societies as 'wholes', and believing that societies

---

* See Appendix (4) on some aspects of Sir Karl Popper's criticisms of Mill, and of 'psychologism' and 'historicism'.

as wholes have destinies and move in certain directions with historical inevitability—indeed, with an inevitable *progress* in their historical destiny. I hope it is absolutely clear from what has been said, that this criticism of Mill is sheer nonsense. It is totally unfounded. If ever anyone was concerned to maintain the place of the individual, not only in moral philosophy and in political behaviour of a practical kind, but also in the explanation of the most complex social events, it was Mill. No one can possibly have stressed the importance of the place of the individual more than he. This criticism, then, is completely unfounded; and this will be even more clear a little later.

(b) *The Geometrical or Abstract* (*Deductive*) *Method*

The second method of study which Mill completely, and without qualification, rejected, was the 'geometrical' or 'deductive' method. This is much easier to be clear about than the various kinds of 'experimental' method, and little time need be spent upon it. By the geometrical method, Mill meant the method of pure deduction: clarifying the conclusions entailed in particular premises, without any resort to empirical testing; the kind of reasoning one gets in a geometrical theorem. It is quite unwarranted, he thought, to offer a whole theory of society which is no more than a set of deductions drawn from some simple premise. Even the premise itself, which may have been drawn from careful personal observation, and may have been established with some care, should never be accepted and adopted without wide and careful checking against the facts of experience. But, and perhaps more important, the corollaries deduced from the premise should never be accepted without empirical checking either.

To give one or two examples: Thomas Hobbes gave an account of the emergence and nature of political sovereignty which was nothing more than a process of logical deduction from what he considered to be the primary motive in human nature—that is, fear, and the suspicion and conflict between human individuals and societies to which it gives rise. Given this fundamental feeling of fear and the 'state of war' which it entails in the absence of social regulation (in the absence of a central political authority) Hobbes then deduced a whole theory as to what the nature of political society should be like. Clearly, this is not, in any sense, a scientific method. Such a process of deduction from some premise (whether a guess, or careful observation, or from whatever source it might have come), would be perfectly all right if it were subsequently submitted to specified conditions of test. But, as we well know, many philosophical theories about the nature of society have lacked this last and crucial element of empirical testing. They have been elaborate systems of pure deduction.

Mill is surely right in casting this method aside, as being not in any sense scientific or reliable. With this method, it is open to anyone to provide any kind of premise and deduce any kind of theory from it. If this is never to be checked against facts, then it is obviously without a vestige of precision. This method, then, can be dispensed with readily.

Methods appropriate to a study of man and society: (2) Methods accepted

Having eliminated what he considered to be unsatisfactory methods, Mill then turned to those which he thought appropriate and correct in the study of man and society. In order to do this as clearly and fully as possible, he began by stating the problems of sociological explanation as he saw them, and in the analysis which follows it will be seen that he was in very close agreement with Comte.

(a) Two kinds of sociological enquiry

There are, he said, two fundamental questions which face a science of society.

The first is: 'What are the causes which produce and the phenomena which characterize states of society generally?'

The second is: 'What effect will follow from a given cause, a certain general condition of social circumstances being presupposed?'

That part of sociological analysis dealing with the first of these questions is 'Social Statics'. Social statics is the theoretical understanding of the very nature of society; what its main components are; the needs and functional problems in which they are rooted, in any type of society. It clarifies, as Mill put it, 'the conditions of stability in the social union'. The empirical 'laws' or 'generalizations' appropriate to this branch of sociology will be *uniformities of co-existence*. They will be statements about the nature and interconnections of institutions which actually *constitute* a society and make a stable society possible.

That branch of sociological analysis which deals with the second kind of question is 'Social Dynamics'. Social dynamics is the theoretical understanding of the progressively changing nature of the actual historical societies of all kinds which exist in the world; it elucidates the causes of social change. As Mill put it 'The fundamental problem . . . is to find the laws according to which any state of society produces the state which succeeds it and takes its place. The empirical laws of society produced by social dynamics will be *uniformities of succession*'.*

Two points must immediately be made clear:

The first point is that when Mill spoke of 'empirical laws', (a) uniformities of co-existence, and (b) uniformities of succession, he did not mean that these generalizations were causal laws in the sense of constituting 'explanations'. They were purely descriptive generalizations which themselves required explanation. Moreover, Mill believed that it was a very important aim, or should be an important aim of sociological enquiry, simply to discover and establish such generalizations. And it was for this purpose, for example, that he thought statistical correlations particularly useful and important, and he welcomed statistical methods from this point of view.

'In statistics' he said, 'it is evident that empirical laws may sometimes be traced and that tracing them forms an important part of that system of indirect observation on which we must often rely for the data of science ...' And again: 'To collect, therefore, such empirical laws from direct observation is an important part of the process of sociological enquiry.'†

As we shall see later, Mill believed that empirical generalizations of this kind were important, both for stimulating the formulation of hypotheses *and* for testing such hypotheses as might be made.

The second point which must be clarified at once, is the way in which Mill used the word 'progress' and 'progressive'. When he was insisting that social phenomena are always in process of change; that societies are essentially characterized by historical change; and when speaking of the task of social dynamics; Mill argued that the processes of history are 'progressive'. But it is most important to note that Mill quite explicitly said that he did *not* mean, by this word, that social change necessarily entailed *moral betterment*.‡ He did think it likely that the developments in history could be shown to entail moral betterment, and that they would be likely to entail moral betterment in future, but he did *not* think that this could be at all *assumed*. This is decidedly *not* what he was meaning when he used the word progressive here.

All he was arguing here was that social change is simply *an ongoing process of difference*. That is to say, the facts in the sequences of historical change are simply *different from what they were before*; and there is no evidence to suggest any cyclical movements in history such as had been claimed by earlier thinkers. Social change,

---

* This mention of 'uniformities of co-existence and succession' demonstrates the clear continuity of ideas from Hume, through Comte, and into the work of Mill.
† *System of Logic*, p. 592.   ‡ See Appendix (4).

he said, by way of contrasting illustration, is not cyclical, but moves always forward with a kind of *trajectory* movement. Society *changes* and becomes *different*. That is *all*. Social change does not return upon itself.

It is very important to notice this point, because Mill has been charged with the same error as Comte and others in claiming the inevitability of human progress. This charge, as can be seen, is a totally false one. Mill made this claim concerning the nature of historical change purely in order to clarify the nature of the essential historical method that sociology must employ.

Having criticized the cyclical theory of history offered by Vico, Mill wrote:

'The words progress and progressiveness are not here to be understood as synonymous with improvement and tendency to improvement. It is conceivable that the laws of human nature might determine, and even necessitate, a certain series of changes in man and society which might not in every case or which might not, on the whole, be improvements. It is my belief that the general tendency is, and will continue to be, saving occasional and temporary exceptions, one of improvement, a tendency towards a better and happier state. This, however, is not a question of the method of the social science, but a theorem of the science itself. For our purpose, it is sufficient that there is progressive change, both in the character of the human race and in their outward circumstances so far as moulded by themselves, that in each successive age the principal phenomena of society are different from what they were in the age preceding.

'The progressiveness of the human race', Mill says, 'is the foundation on which a method of philosophizing in social science has been of late years erected far superior to either of the two modes which had previously been prevalent, the chemical or experimental and the geometrical modes.'*

Clearly, Mill was referring here to the 'progressive' account of institutional changes offered by Condorcet and borrowed and developed by Comte.

Before clarifying the method which Mill proposed for the study of these questions, let us look firstly at his conception, not only of the nature of social statics, but also of the facts of the social order with which social statics had to concern itself. In the following passages, we shall see that Mill had a very clear conception of the nature of a society, of the major institutions which comprise it, and of their close interconnection. Furthermore, he saw clearly that a functional analysis of the interconnections of these institutions and the ways in which they are rooted in human needs and problems, is necessary. Again, like Comte, he had a completely clear notion of a

---

* *System of Logic*, p. 596. See Appendix (4). Mill was not, in any sense (as Popper has claimed), mistaking a 'trend' or 'tendency' for a 'law' here.

'structural-functional' analysis of social systems. The language that he used in these passages as, for example, when speaking of the institutional 'requisites' of a society, are completely modern and thoroughly anticipate such terms as the functional 'pre-requisites' of modern theorists such as Parsons, Merton, and others. Also, in noting Mill's point of view here, let us remember that it is exactly the same kind of conception of the nature of a society, and the social facts of which it consists, as that put forward earlier by Comte, and, as we shall see, that put forward later by Spencer, Marx, Hobhouse, Durkheim, Weber, and others. Indeed, it is the conception put forward by every sociologist of note from the very first foundation of the subject.

Firstly, when introducing the scope of social statics, Mill said that since this analyses what constitutes a 'state of society', it is necessary to fix clearly the ideas attached to the phrase 'a state of society'. He wrote as follows:

'What is called a state of society is the simultaneous state of all the greater social facts or phenomena. Such are the degree of knowledge, and of intellectual and moral culture, existing in the community, and of every class of it; the state of industry, of wealth and its distribution; the habitual occupations of the community; their division into classes, and the relations of those classes to one another; the common beliefs which they entertain on all the subjects most important to mankind, and the degree of assurance with which those beliefs are held; their tastes, and the character and degree of their aesthetic development; their form of government, and the more important of their laws and customs. The conditions of all these things, and of many more which will readily suggest themselves, constitute the state of society or the state of civilization at any given time.

When states of society, and the causes which produce them, are spoken of as a subject of science, it is implied that there exists a natural correlation among these different elements; that not every variety of combination of these general social facts is possible, but only certain combinations; that, in short, there exist Uniformities of Co-existence between the states of the various social phenomena. And such is the truth; as is indeed a necessary consequence of the influence exercised by every one of those phenomena over every other. It is a fact implied in the *consensus* of the various parts of the social body.

States of society are like different constitutions or different ages in the physical frame; they are conditions not of one or a few organs or functions, but of the whole organism. Accordingly, the information which we possess respecting past ages, and respecting the various states of society now existing in different regions of the earth, does, when duly analysed, exhibit uniformities. It is found that when one of the features of society is in a particular state, a state of many other features, more or less precisely determinate, always or usually co-exists with it.'*

* *System of Logic*, Ch. X, p. 595.

226

A second important passage of the same kind begins as follows:

'As already remarked, one of the main results of the science of social statics would be to ascertain the requisites of stable political union. There are some circumstances which, being found in all societies without exception, and in the greatest degree where the social union is most complete, may be considered (when psychological and ethological laws confirm the indication) as conditions of the existence of the complex phenomenon called a State. For example, no numerous society has ever been held together without laws, or usages equivalent to them; without tribunals, and on organized force of some sort to execute their decisions. There have always been public authorities whom, with more or less strictness, and in cases more or less accurately defined, the rest of the community obeyed, or according to general opinion were bound to obey. By following out this course of inquiry we shall find a number of requisites which have been present in every society that has maintained a collective existence, and on the cessation of which it has either merged in some other society, or reconstructed itself on some new basis, in which the conditions were conformed to. Although these results, obtained by comparing different forms and states of society, amount in themselves only to empirical laws, some of them, when once suggested, are found to follow with so much probability from general laws of human nature, that the consilience of the two processes raises the evidence to proof, and the generalizations to the rank of scientific truths.'*

It is most important to see, before leaving this initial treatment by Mill of the nature of society, that he regards the generalizations that can be made at the level of functional analysis as being *laws* and *scientific truths* in the fullest sense. They are not only empirical generalizations at the 'societal' level (about the associations, institutions and forms of organization in the social order), but also can be shown to stem from the basic psychological nature of man, the ethological requirements for the growth of human character, and the necessitous social problems which must be confronted and dealt with by all communities. A deductive element of high probability is found to support the empirical generalizations. This we shall come to later when, in speaking of 'functionalism', it will be necessary to criticize those who believe that the premises of functionalism cannot be said to possess any theoretical basis at all.

We must now clarify that method of studying *both* social statics *and* social dynamics which Mill thought most appropriate and correct. Having dispensed with methods he thought false and dangerous, he then outlined the only method which he thought correct and worth pursuing.

* *System of Logic*, p. 600.

227

(b) The Concrete Deductive Method

Mill declared that the only correct method for a 'general science of society' was what he called the concrete deductive method and this is very close to what is now known, in the philosophy of science, as the 'hypothetico-deductive' method. 'The social science', said Mill, 'is a deductive science, not indeed after the model of geometry but after that of the more complex physical science'. It is most important to emphasize the nature of this hypothetico-deductive method by Mill, since his analysis of inductive *procedures* has been so travestied by critics as being an extremely naive notion of 'inductive logic'.

The concrete deductive method, said Mill, consists of three operations, the first of direct induction, the second of ratiocination, the third of verification. Mill believed that more often than not the first induction, as he called it, stems from some direct observation in our experience, whether an outcome of common experience or of a more meticulous collection of facts undertaken systematically. The essential thing, however, upon which Mill insisted, is that the first step in the concrete deductive method is that we have *some kind of knowledge of facts which we consider significant* from which we then proceed to infer or deduce that, if this is so, then certain other facts should be such and such. This procedure of inference is the second step of ratiocination or deduction. The third step of verification is simply the testing of *both* our initial assumptions *and* our deductions in discovering whether, in fact, our predictions are borne out.

This use of the term 'direct induction' as the first procedure of reliable scientific method ought not to lead us to think that Mill thought of this procedure of induction as merely a collecting of facts without any kind of theoretical presuppositions. The idea that Mill had a naive notion of inductive logic is totally false. When he spoke of 'direct *induction*', he was simply meaning that our initial premises are always drawn from some kind of *experience* and are not completely '*a priori*' axioms as had been thought to be the case in earlier classical syllogistic thinking. His emphasis really derived from his concern to attack 'a priori' metaphysics as being unproductive of knowledge; and to insist that those axioms or premises which *seemed* of an 'a priori' nature, were, in fact, rooted in our *experience*.

Denying this simple and naive notion of induction as being a collecting of 'facts' without theoretical presuppositions and *condemning* both Bacon's account of it and Kepler's practice of it, Mill claimed that, for him, induction consisted purely in drawing inferences from known facts to those at present unknown. As he put it, induction, 'as distinguished from those mental operations sometimes improperly designated by the name', can be summarily defined as generalization from experience. It consists in inferring from some individual instances in which a phenomenon is seen to occur, that it probably occurs in all instances of that certain class, namely, in *all* those which resemble the instances already observed. When Mill spoke of inductive *procedures* of establishing knowledge, then, he was chiefly concerned to attack the *a priori* syllogistic mode of reasoning of earlier times and to insist that all our knowledge of the world is experiential.

In order to make Mill's conception of the concrete deductive method completely clear, it is necessary to quote what he had to say about the use of hypothesis in science, and, in my opinion, these passages vindicate him completely against the misinterpretations of many of his modern critics.

'An hypothesis', he wrote, 'is any supposition which we make (either without actual evidence, and on evidence avowedly insufficient) in order to endeavour to deduce from its conclusions in accordance with facts which are known to be real; under the idea that if the conclusions to which the hypothesis leads are known truths, the hypothesis itself either must be, or at least is likely to be, true. If the hypothesis relates to the cause or mode of production of a phenomenon, it will serve, if admitted, to explain such facts as are found capable of being deduced from it. And this explanation is the purpose of many, if not most, hypotheses. Since explaining, in the scientific sense, means resolving a uniformity which is not a law of causation into the laws of causation from which it results, or a complex law of causation into simpler and more general ones from which it is capable of being deductively inferred; if there do not exist any known laws which fulfil this requirement, we may feign or imagine some which would fulfil it; and this is making an hypothesis.'

'Any hypothesis being a mere supposition, there are no other limits to hypotheses than those of the human imagination.'

'According to the foregoing remarks, hypotheses are invented to enable the Deductive Method to be earlier applied to phenomena. But in order to discover the cause of any phenomenon by the Deductive Method, the process must consist of three parts—induction, ratiocination, and verification. Induction, (the place of which, however, may be supplied by a prior deduction), to ascertain the laws of the causes; ratiocination, to compute from those laws how the causes will operate in the particular combination known to exist in the case in hand; verification, by comparing this calculated effect with the actual phenomenon. No one of these parts of the process can be dispensed with.'

'Now the Hypothetical Method suppresses the first of the three steps, the induction to ascertain the law, and contents itself with the other two operations, ratiocination and verification, the law which is reasoned from being assumed instead of proved.'

'This process may evidently be legitimate on one supposition, namely, if the nature of the case be such that the final step, the verification, shall

amount to and fulfil the conditions of a new complete induction. We want to be assured that the law we have hypothetically assumed is a true one.'
'It appears, then, to be a condition of the most genuinely scientific hypothesis, that it be not destined always to remain an hypothesis, but be of such a nature as to be either proved or disproved by comparison with observed facts.'
'The hypothesis, by suggesting observations and experiments, puts us on the road to that independent evidence if it be really attainable; and till it be attained, the hypothesis ought only to count for a more or less plausible conjecture.'
'This function of hypotheses is one which must be reckoned absolutely indispensable in science. When Newton said "Hypotheses non fingo", he did not mean that he deprived himself of the facilities of investigation afforded by assuming in the first instance what he hoped ultimately to be able to prove. Without such assumptions, science could never have attained its present state; they are necessary steps in the progress to something more certain; and nearly everything which is now theory was once hypothesis.'
'The process of tracing regularity in any complicated, and at first sight confused set of appearances, is necessarily tentative: we begin by making any supposition, even a false one, to see what consequences will follow from it; and by observing how these differ from the real phenomena, we learn what corrections to make in our assumption. The simplest supposition which accords with the more obvious facts is the best to begin with, because its consequences are the most easily traced. This rude hypothesis is then rudely corrected, and the operation repeated; and the comparison of the consequences deducible from the corrected hypothesis with the observed facts suggests still further correction, until the deductive results are at last made to tally with the phenomena.'
'The vortices of Descartes would have been a perfectly legitimate hypothesis, if it had been possible, by any mode of exploration which we could entertain the hope of ever possessing, to bring the reality of the vortices, as a fact in nature, conclusively to the test of observation. The vice of the hypothesis was that it could not lead to any course of investigation capable of converting it from an hypothesis into a proved fact.'
'Nevertheless, I do not agree with M. Comte in condemning those who employ themselves in working out into detail the application of these hypotheses to the explanation of ascertained facts, provided they bear in mind that the utmost they can prove is, not that the hypothesis *is*, but that it *may* be true.'*

* I do not know how far readers will agree with me that these passages are meticulously clear and sensible. I must confess that I am totally at a loss to understand how anyone can have possibly believed that scientific method was in a kind of 'fog' of naïve inductivism, until Sir Karl Popper came along. This is not to disagree basically with Popper's outline of scientific method; but only to say that the 'hypothetico-deductive' method was quite clearly understood and stated by both Comte and Mill. Peter Medawar's writings are really a persisting echo of Popper, though a brilliant echo for all that.

All these passages are to be found in Paragraphs 4 and 5 of Ch. XIV (*System*

This, then, was the 'concrete deductive method', the most reliable method of science according to Mill, and, in the 'science of society' it would proceed as follows: Possessing (1) knowledge (derived from observation and experiment) of the laws of *psychology*, and (2) empirical generalizations (derived from observation and comparative and historical studies) concerning the *regularities of society* (of associations and institutions and their interconnections in society), the investigator would (3) state a hypothesis in terms of the middle principles of Mill's science of ethology (*personality and social psychology and the exercise of deliberate choices*) as to how certain social circumstances had acted upon the nature of the individuals in society in such ways as to bring about the subsequent event, set of circumstances, or social change, which was being studied, and for which an explanation was being sought. The method is exactly that followed in the other natural sciences, but is applied appropriately with regard to the qualitatively different psychological and social facts which are under investigation, and about which testable knowledge is desired.

In this application to the study of man and society, however, Mill saw that the method encountered two fundamental difficulties, and he examined these carefully.

(*c*) *The multiplicity of causes and effects, and the compounding of laws*
As he had argued when rejecting other methods of study, Mill again insisted that the phenomena of man and society are characterized by their great complexity of causes and effects and by their continuous change. It follows from this that deductive propositions of the kind mentioned are very difficult to frame. To put the matter as simply as possible—in the analysis of any social event, there will always be several, and frequently many, factors to encompass, and we shall have to weigh many causes and effects in arriving at the explanation which seems most satisfactory. An 'explanation' of any social event, or set of social events, in terms of one cause and one effect, as outlined by the relatively simple form of the concrete deductive method, seems completely out of the question. Indeed, when the utmost care has been taken to review all the multiplicity of causes, a realistic appraisal of the difficulties involved leads us to think that our result is likely to be at best, only a *meticulously careful approximation*, a statement of *tendency*, rather than a clearly demonstrable explanatory law. Still, an awareness of those difficulties does

of Logic) pp. 322–31, entitled 'Of the Limits to the Explanation of Laws of Nature, and of Hypotheses'. It contains also a good deal of discussion of Dr Whewell. See also p. 606 for a very clear discussion of the 'Law of Three Stages' (of Comte)—misunderstood by Whewell.

not mean that we should abandon the scientific method. We have no alternative but to seek the best degree of exactitude that we can, and if we follow the concrete deductive method as rigorously as possible, bringing all causes and effects together in our investigation, and paying the closest attention both to the correctness of our modes of inference and to the empirical testing of our hypotheses, then we shall attain the best results possible. 'The ground of confidence', Mill wrote, 'in any concrete deductive science, is not the 'a priori' reasoning itself but the accordance between its results and those of observation 'a posteriori'.'

'The effect produced', said Mill, 'in social phenomena by any complex set of circumstances amounts precisely to the sum of the effects of the circumstances taken singly, and the complexity does not arise from the number of the laws themselves, which is not remarkably great, but from the extraordinary number and variety of the data or elements of the agents which, in obedience to that small number of laws, co-operate towards the effect. Sociology infers the law of each effect from the laws of causation on which that effect depends, not, however, from the law merely of one cause, as in the geometrical method, but by considering all the causes which conjointly influence the effect, and compounding their laws with one another.'*

(d) Problems of contemporary and historical study

The second fundamental difficulty in the way of using the concrete deductive method in social science is the extreme difficulty of studying strictly contemporaneous events in society, and many points of the very greatest importance are attendant upon this consideration.

The first point which is very simple but frequently ignored by many sociologists, is that it proves to be almost impossible to observe a strictly contemporaneous event in such a way as to have a full knowledge of all that is involved. People who speak of direct 'observation' of contemporaneous social facts or events are in danger of deceiving themselves. Indeed, social events which are occurring in the *present* are often the most difficult to know. It is only, sometimes, long after the events have taken place, when various documents and other items of evidence have become available, that we can satisfy ourselves that we have, at least, an objective, balanced, and detailed knowledge of them. Curiously, then, the fact seems to be that it is easier, sometimes and in some respects, to observe an event of the past than an event that is occurring in the present. Historians, of course, have long accepted this fact. Furthermore, one's own *personal observation* of a current event must be extremely limited. Only with a later consideration of, and reflection

* *System of Logic*, Ch. IX, p. 583.

upon, all the factors involved, as can be obtained through scrutiny and interpretation of documents, can one have anything approaching a full coverage of the nature of a social event. What this amounts to then, is that *sociological method* cannot avoid a dimension of *historical method*. The concrete deductive method in sociology must always be concerning itself, in very large part, with events that have already taken place, with data drawn from the past.

This leads to a second important aspect of this question which is, simply, that very frequently, the examples of those social circumstances and problems which most trouble us, which are most important to us, and which we most wish to understand and explain, *have already occurred*. It is during the course of their happening that we have come to realize their urgency, and we are interested in analysing and understanding them in order to be able to deal with them more effectively should they happen to us again. Indeed, we may wish to understand the causes of the events concerned in order to prevent their recurrence. The other examples which we can draw together for comparative study will be, however, chiefly historical examples in other societies which we must cull from the past. Again then, it is clear that sociological analysis must concern itself essentially with a study of historical events, as constituting a very large part of its task, and possibly a larger part of its task than studies strictly of the present moment.

Mill argued, therefore, that it is necessary to qualify the concrete deductive method in its application to the study of man and society in a way which led him to call it the '*inverse*' deductive method.

(e) The Inverse-Deductive Method

Because of this peculiar nature of the data of sociology, that it consists chiefly of past events drawn from various societies, it is usually the case that we have certain empirical generalizations about them before we have made or constructed any hypotheses, and before we have inferred any kind of explanation of them. This means that we have to undertake the concrete deductive method in an inverse manner. Instead of clearly stating our hypotheses, making inferences from them, and then verifying our predictions by submitting them to conditions of test of the nature of an artificial manipulation of facts (as in the laboratory experimentation of the natural sciences), the reverse order has to be followed. We already *have* certain empirical generalizations; and we have to try to produce hypotheses and deductions from them which will satisfactorily explain the empirical generalizations about events that have already happened. By using this 'inverse deductive' method alone can we arrive at causal explanations of social processes. Mill further argued that it is only in this way that we can come to have any confidence in our ability to understand and predict events for the future.

The nature of historical events, and the substantial place they must occupy in a science of society, makes necessary, therefore, this inversion in the way in which we conduct the concrete deductive method.

'Instead,' Mill said, 'of deducing our conclusions by reasoning and verifying them by observation, we in some cases begin by obtaining them provisionally from specific experience and afterwards connect them with the principles of human nature by *a priori* reasonings, which reasonings are thus a real verification.'

Mill went on to point out that this was, in fact, the method proposed by Comte, who had regarded it as an inescapable and essential component in the nature of sociological theory.

In order to be as clear as possible, I shall try to summarize Mill's understanding of the nature, and essential parts of a 'science of society' with the aid of a few diagrams.

In the scientific study of society, it is false, he claimed, to think that elements of a social system are entities which have cause and effect relationships with each other without reference to the individuals in society.

We can make empirical generalizations about the way in which elements of social structure are connected with each other in any situation, and the ways in which changes in some follow upon changes in others, as indicated in level (1) SOCIOLOGY, in Diagram (1), but these do not give us a sufficient *causal* explanation. They are purely empirical generalizations at the social level. Similarly, we can establish generalizations about the basic psychological elements of human nature, on the basis of observation and experiment, as indicated in level (2) PSYCHOLOGY. But these two levels are quite distinct and, in this state, unconnected. It is also obviously insufficient to suppose that we can explain the complex changes in social institutions by any simple reference to the psychological qualities of individuals in abstraction from their social experience— as in Diagram (1) (ii).

Interrelated changes in the elements of social structure (at level (1)) can only be correctly traced, understood, and explained, by investigating the impact which one change has upon the settled personality and character dispositions of individuals (at level (3) ETHOLOGY) and which therefore gives rise to subsequent changes in other institutions. Diagram (2) is the better indication of the actual kinds of interconnection between institutional changes, individuals

234

DIAGRAM (1)

SOCIETY

(1) *SOCIOLOGY* — Empirical generalizations about interconnections of elements of social structure — GOVT ←→ LAW ←→ RELIGION ←→ ECON. ←→ FAMILY ←→ EDUC. (etc.)

(2) PSYCHOLOGY — Experimental science. 'Laws' of experience and behaviour of: — INDIVIDUALS

DIAGRAM (1) (ii)

SOCIETY

N.B. ALSO INSUFFICIENT

(1) *SOCIOLOGY*   GOVT.   LAW   RELIGION   (ECON.)   FAMILY   EDUC.

(2) *PSYCHOLOGY*   INDIVIDUALS

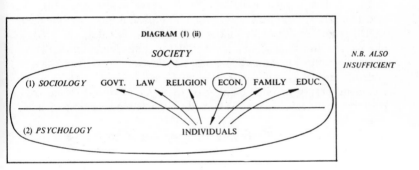

DIAGRAM (2)

SOCIETY

(1) *SOCIOLOGY* — Empirical generalizations about interconnections of elements of social structure — GOVT. ←→ LAW ←→ RELIGION ←→ (ECON.) ←→ FAMILY ←→ EDUC. (etc.)

(3) *ETHOLOGY* — Science of personality and character formation + social psychology — Deductions + hypotheses

Settled dispositions of character and personality formed through association + play of institutional influences. [Ideals, beliefs, attitudes, etc.]

(2) PSYCHOLOGY — Experimental science.

INDIVIDUALS

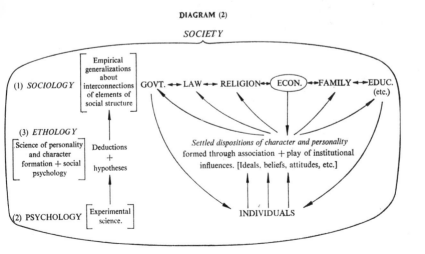

235

as the outcome of their social and collective experiences, and their basic human psychology, than is either version of Diagram (1). To support and explain the empirical generalizations at level (1), we need hypothetical and deductive propositions as to what we would expect the reactions of people to be to specified change in circumstances; and these would be based upon our knowledge of psychology (level (2)), and our derived hypotheses at the level of social psychology (level (3)).

Supposing, for example, a change in economic institutions takes place—say the large-scale development of industrialization, with new forms of property, company organization, factory methods of production, and a complex division of labour; and supposing that this change always seemed to be followed (in all societies which experienced it) by related and distinctive changes in other institutions: in the family, education, political organization, religion, and so on. It would be an *error*, Mill maintained, to say—as indicated in Diagram (1)—that the changed 'Economic Institutions' *caused* changes in the family, education, religion, and government. Statements of institutional interdependence of this sort are only 'empirical generalizations' which *require* explanations. And it would not be sufficient simply to refer blankly to basic 'laws' of individual psychology, as at level (2), as indicated in the second version of Diagram (1).

The only correct procedure of explanation would be by the incorporation of level (3) ETHOLOGY. We should aim at a body of knowledge as to how the institutional patterns of society (level (1)) operate upon the basic elements of human psychology (level (2)) to bring into being the settled dispositions and qualities of personality and character, and their patterns of deliberation and choice, in individuals as members of society. With this, we should then explore how the changes in 'Economic Institutions' (Industrialization and its specified characteristics) have an impact upon individuals, and how, mediated in their experience, deliberation, and action, *subsequent* changes in the family, education, government, religion, are brought about. The arrows in Diagram (2) seek to indicate this sequence of explanation.

Mill's essential understanding is that all *these three components are necessary in a satisfactory science of man and society*. There can be no such thing as an 'autonomous' sociology; no such thing as an 'autonomous' psychology. *All* are necessary in this kind of inter-relationship for a satisfactory scientific study of all the dimensions of human experience and behaviour in the context of social relationships, which have their own structured interdependencies in the framework of society's organization as a whole. The isolation of any one component is a *wrong* isolation. It is an *error*. And, within this conception, Mill's chief emphasis is that institutions do not exist as entities independent of people and that the changes in one which bring about changes in others are always mediated through the experience, behaviour, deliberation, and action of individuals, and can only be sufficiently explained in these terms.

It may be very strongly noted here, that in Mill's whole system of sociological analysis, it is *the middle principles*, the hypotheses and deductions in terms of 'ethology' or 'social psychology', which are considered to be of the greatest importance for explanation. *'The laws of collective character'*, he wrote, *'are by far the most important class of sociological laws.'** The important hypothetical explanations of social facts are rooted in these middle principles. 'The middle principles,' said Mill, 'the *axiomata media*, of every science, principally constitute its value.' It is these hypotheses which link, in an explanatory way, the empirical generalizations at the level of psychology on the one hand, and the empirical generalizations at the level of social institutions and social regularities on the other. Without them no complete sociological explanation is possible.

Having considered these quite fundamental problems of method, Mill then discussed in more detail the nature of historical facts, the development of societies and social institutions in history, in order to see how far we could have confidence that, apart from other considerations, the subject matter was *manageable* and that we might expect to be able to establish systematic knowledge about it. In all this, he followed very closely the treatment of Comte, and the following points are those which he accepted and emphasized as being important for the making of a science of man and society.

Firstly, Mill accepted Comte's generalization about the 'three stages' of social development, the three 'types' of social order, and he clearly regarded this generalization as being a useful *classification* of 'types of society' for purposes of comparative study.

'Speculation Comte conceives to have, on every subject of human enquiry, three successive stages; in the first of which it tends to explain the phenomena by supernatural agencies, in the second by metaphysical abstractions, and in the third or final state confines itself to ascertaining their laws of succession and similitude. This generalization appears to me to have that high degree of scientific evidence which is derived from the concurrence of the indications of history with the probabilities derived from the constitution of the human mind. Nor could it be easily conceived, from the mere enunciation of such a proposition, what a flood of light it lets in upon the

---

* This emphasis may be noted for our later discussion of the relation between the ideas of Durkheim and Mill.

whole course of history, when its consequences are traced, by connecting with each of the three states of human intellect which it distinguishes, and with each successive modification of those three states, the correlative condition of other social phenomena.'*

Secondly, Mill accepted that the *consensus* of institutions in human society, and the continuity of this consensus from period to period, or, more specifically, as he put it, from generation to generation, is such as to give us confidence that a systematic and orderly knowledge of institutional development can be achieved.

Thirdly, however, having emphasized the extreme difficulty of seeing some grounds of systematic order in these detailed institutional developments, Mill said that it would be very useful if we could find that there was *some one element* in the complex nature of society which was pre-eminent over all others as the prime agent of social change and social development. Fortunately, he claimed, there was one such factor which we could take as being of central importance; as constituting a central line of development in human society; and about which we could correlate the changes which had taken place in all other social institutions. This central factor was the growth of human knowledge, the development of the 'speculative faculties of mankind', and this again, of course, was the point made by Comte.

Mill, however, made this point very clearly indeed and with far greater brevity than Comte. He wrote as follows:

'Now, the evidence of history and that of human nature combine, by a striking instance of consilience, to show that there really is one social element which is thus predominant, and almost paramount, among the agents of the social progression. This is the state of the speculative faculties of mankind, including the nature of the beliefs which by any means they have arrived at concerning themselves and the world by which they are surrounded.

'It would be a great error, and one very little likely to be committed, to assert that speculation, intellectual activity, the pursuit of truth, is among the more powerful propensities of human nature, or hold a predominating place in the lives of any, save decidedly exceptional, individuals. But, notwithstanding the relative weakness of this principle among other sociological agents, its influence is the main determining cause of the social progress; all the other dispositions of our nature which contribute to that progress being dependent on it for the means of accomplishing their share of the work. Thus (to take the most obvious case first) the impelling force to most of the improvements effected in the arts of life is the desire of increased material comfort; but as we can only act upon external objects in

* It will be seen that this generalization of the 'three stages' is one in which the knowledge of psychology and the empirical generalizations of sociology lend support to each other, and is therefore the kind of generalization which both Comte and Mill were looking for. See *System of Logic*, Ch. X, p. 606.

proportion to our knowledge of them, the state of knowledge at any time is the limit of the industrial improvements possible at that time; and the progress of industry must follow, and depend on, the progress of knowledge. The same thing may be shown to be true, though it is not quite so obvious, of the progress of the fine arts. Further, as the strongest propensities of uncultivated or half-cultivated human nature (being the purely selfish ones, and those of a sympathetic character which partake most of the nature of selfishness) evidently tend in themselves to disunite mankind, not to unite them,—to make them rivals not confederates; social existence is only possible by a disciplining of those more powerful propensities, which consists in subordinating them to a common system of opinions. The degree of this subordination is the measure of the completeness of the social union, and the nature of the common opinions determines its kind. But in order that mankind should conform their actions to any set of opinions, these opinions must exist, must be believed by them. And thus the state of the speculative faculties, the character of the propositions assented to by the intellect, essentially determines the moral and political state of the community, as we have already seen that it determines the physical.

'These conclusions, deduced from the laws of human nature, are in entire accordance with the general facts of history. Every considerable change historically known to us in the condition of any portion of mankind, when not brought about by external force, has been preceded by a change of proportional extent in the state of their knowledge or in their prevalent beliefs. As between any given state of speculation and the correlative state of everything else, it was almost always the former which first showed itself; though the effects, no doubt, reacted potently upon the cause. Every considerable advance in material civilization has been preceded by an advance in knowledge; and when any great social change has come to pass, either in the way of gradual development or of sudden conflict, it has had for its precursor a great change in the opinions and modes of thinking of society. Polytheism, Judaism, Christianity, Protestantism, the critical philosophy of modern Europe, and its positive science—each of these has been a primary agent in making society what it was at each successive period, while society was but secondarily instrumental in making *them*, each of them (as far as causes can be assigned for its existence) being mainly an emanation not from the practical life of the period, but from the previous state of belief and thought. The weakness of the speculative propensity in mankind generally has not, therefore, prevented the progress of speculation from governing that of society at large; it has only, and too often, prevented progress altogether, where the intellectual progression has come to an early stand for want of sufficiently favourable circumstances.

'From this accumulated evidence, we are justified in concluding that the order of human progression in all respects will mainly depend on the order of progression* in the intellectual convictions of mankind, that is, on the law of the successive transformations of human opinions.'†

* Our earlier comments on the way in which Mill used the word 'progress' and 'progressive change' should be borne in mind here.
† *System of Logic*, Ch. X, pp. 604–5.

Fourthly, Mill also accepted Comte's point that human and social facts, as a corollary of their more complicated nature, are not less, but *more*, modifiable than mechanical and chemical facts. Consequently, with our knowledge of sociology, we should have considerable power to alter them. In this, Mill agreed with Comte that the advancement of sociological knowledge should be of use to men in enabling them to formulate effective social policies for the attainment of those kinds of improvements in society that they desired.

Fifthly, Mill also agreed with Comte that history was a cumulative process and that the longer it continued, the more interdependent the various societies of the world would become. Consequently, there would be an increasing similarity in the pattern of institutions throughout the world, and again consequently, the firmer the foundation for sociological generalization would become. He wrote as follows:

'The longer our species lasts and the more civilized it becomes, the more, as Comte remarks, does the influence of past generations over the present, and of mankind *en masse* over every individual in it, predominate over other forces; and though the course of affairs never ceases to be susceptible of alteration both by accidents and by personal qualities, the increasing preponderance of the collective agency of the species over all minor causes is constantly bringing the general evolution of the race into something which deviates less from a certain and preappointed track. Historical science, therefore, is always becoming more possible; not solely because it is better studied, but because, in every generation, it becomes better adapted for study.'*

Also:

'. . . since both the natural varieties of mankind, and the original diversities of local circumstances are much less considerable than the points of agreement, there will naturally be a certain degree of uniformity in the progressive development of the species and of its works. And this uniformity tends to become greater, not less, as society advances; since the evolution of each people, which is at first determined exclusively by the nature and circumstances of that people, is gradually brought under the influence (which becomes stronger as civilization advances) of the other nations of the earth, and of the circumstances by which they have been influenced. History accordingly does, when judiciously examined, afford Empirical Laws of Society. And the problem of general sociology is to ascertain these, and connect them with the laws of human nature, by deductions showing that such were the derivative laws naturally to be expected as the consequences of those ultimate ones.'†

* *ibid.*, p. 615.
† We shall see, much later, the relevance of these ideas to the current themes of 'modernization' in sociology.

240

By these methods then, Mill maintained that a reliable knowledge of man in society could be established. He realized to the full the great difficulties in the way of achieving precise testable knowledge by the application of scientific method; indeed, he is probably the most painstakingly honest and the most modest theorist in the whole development of sociology; but he pointed out that it is better to pursue that degree of exactitude in knowledge that we find we are capable of, than to leave the study of man and society in the realm of completely unwarranted and unchecked conjecture. And, as we have said before, he continually reiterated: 'An amount of knowledge quite insufficient for prediction may be most valuable for guidance'. If we wish to govern society as wisely and effectively as possible, even though *exact* knowledge is beyond our power to achieve, it is still necessary to secure as reliable a degree of accuracy in knowledge as is humanly possible.

'The aim of practical politics', Mill said, 'is to surround any given society with the greatest possible number of circumstances of which the tendencies are beneficial, and to remove or counteract, as far as practicable, those of which the tendencies are injurious. A knowledge of the tendencies only, though without the power of accurately predicting their conjoint result, gives us, to a considerable extent, this power.'*

The making of social policy: science, philosophy and practical experience

There is one final aspect of Mill's work which deserves attention.

When Comte had outlined his science of society, he proposed that a kind of 'council of social scientists', those who possessed an expertise in the new science, should be the responsible advisers and governors of the modern state, indeed, of the modern world. Mill was much more modest, and much wiser than Comte in this connection. He saw quite clearly that the knowledge of the social sciences cannot of itself demonstrate *moral* truths. It cannot determine the ends we *ought* to seek or the moral values in the light of which we *ought* to govern society. It is therefore necessary, said Mill, that the knowledge of the social scientist and the deliberations of the moral philosopher should be considered together and in relation to each other; that *both* should be taken into account. The moral philosopher can do something to clarify the ends and values which ought to guide our legislation; the social scientist brings such knowledge as he can of the means whereby these ends might be successfully

* *System of Logic*, p. 586.

achieved, given the present context of social circumstances. But Mill went even further than this, and it is the mention of the 'present social circumstances' which leads us on to this.

Besides the contributions of social scientists and moral philosophers, Mill thought it vitally necessary that those who practise the appropriate arts in society should be consulted too. Those men who are practically engaged in the management of human relationships; in the practice of the several arts—the judge, the doctor, the politician, the artisan; are likely to have qualities of judgment, practical assessments of immediate problems, and spontaneous notions about the means by which they can best be dealt with, which neither the social scientist nor the moral philosopher may possess. If all *three* contributions are carefully considered and taken into account in the making of social policies, then we can at least be as sure as possible that the best approach to the taking of decisions has been made.

In this, as in his purely methodological thought, Mill seems to me to have been admirably qualified, guarded and wise. His contribution to the making of sociology was very great indeed. He publicized, critically assessed, developed, and used, the best of the work of Comte; but his own methodological outline, his own logical critique of what seems unwarranted and what seems possible and worthwhile in sociological theory, remains of the utmost importance, even at the present time. His work certainly constituted a great consolidation and advance in the making of sociology.

Many later sociologists owed much to Mill; many committed the errors against which he had already warned; and many who are thought to have advanced the study of sociology considerably have, in fact, said little, if anything, more than Mill in this preliminary logical outline of the subject. All students of the social sciences would benefit from coming to terms with his work, and considering his various points in meticulous detail. After a profound study of Mill, no-one would be likely to be jejune in his approach to sociological explanation. And even this, if it could be accomplished, would be a great advance.

Summary

Mill's exacting logical critique led him, then, into complete agreement with Comte that a science of man and society was both necessary and possible.* Again, in order to achieve a completely

* Mill did not, of course, agree with all the extravagances of Comte's system; indeed he was highly critical of many of them. These criticisms, and their severity,

clear picture of the development of the subject, let me try to summarize his main conclusions as follows.

(a) The need for a science of society

(I) TO ESTABLISH KNOWLEDGE AS DISTINCT FROM OPINION

A science of society was necessary if *knowledge*—as distinct from opinion, or untested conjecture—about it, was to be achieved.

(II) TO PROVIDE A RELIABLE BASIS FOR JUDGMENT AND PRACTICE

A science of society was also necessary in order to achieve the most reliable basis possible for the discussion of political practice; for the weighing, taking, and implementing of important political decisions.

(III) TO CONTRIBUTE TO THE GREATER EFFECTIVENESS OF 'FREE WILL' (OF DELIBERATE CHOICE AND SOCIAL ACTION)

A scientific study of society did *not* deny 'freedom of the will' and did *not* presuppose 'determinism'. A *science* of man and society was logically and actually possible even if men *did* 'possess free will'. Furthermore, if it was successful in establishing 'laws' of human behaviour, or of the regularity of institutional connections in society, it did not in any sense strip men of their free will or divest them of a basis for deliberate action. On the contrary, sociology explored the actual dimensions, conditions, and possibilities of the exercise of deliberate judgment and action, and therefore provided a basis of knowledge for their greater effectiveness.

(b) Methods of science appropriate to sociology

(I) METHODS OF SCIENCE CLARIFIED AND ACCEPTED

The careful delimitation of the methods of science—of observing, describing, classifying a specified range of facts; of establishing 'laws' of interconnection among them by means of hypothesis, deduction, and crucial experimental test—were the means of attaining demonstrable knowledge. Such methods alone could produce *knowledge* of society, as well as of nature. And such knowledge alone could form a basis for reliable prediction, and, therefore, for reliable judgment and action.

(II) SOCIAL SCIENCE NOT DIFFERENT FROM NATURAL SCIENCE

A science of man and society was not significantly different from the sciences of nature in encountering difficulties of achieving precise

may be seen in *Auguste Comte and Positivism*. But see Appendix 2 in the present volume, p. 652.

prediction about empirical complexities, even if general 'laws' could be established. Sciences which *had* established general 'laws', could still only achieve precise prediction in so far as they improved to a point of exactitude their methods of attaining information about all the antecedents of the particular events they sought to predict. A science of society was not different from other sciences in any sense of logical principle in this respect; only, perhaps, with regard to the greater complexity of the antecedents with which it had to deal.

(III) AN ERROR TO REGARD 'SOCIAL FACTS' AS 'COMPOUND ENTITIES' INDEPENDENT OF INDIVIDUALS IN THEIR CASUAL CONNECTIONS

Social 'institutions' or 'societies' as wholes, were not to be regarded as definite entities, whose causal interdependencies could be adequately known and stated independent of individuals with their particular dispositions of personality, character and will. Experimental methods referring to 'social entities' of this kind were to be rejected as being conceptually and methodologically incorrect; as being mistaken with regard to the very nature of social facts, social processes, and their interconnections.

(IV) AN ERROR TO PERSIST IN PAST METHODS OF PURE DEDUCTION

Methods of pure deduction (whether from completely 'a priori' or from experiential premises) which made no use of careful empirical procedures of study, and no reference to conditions of empirical test, were also to be completely rejected, as being totally inappropriate to the pursuit of knowledge.

(V) METHODS PROPER TO SOCIOLOGY:

EMPIRICAL GENERALIZATIONS AND THEIR EXPLANATION

The methods proper to sociology were, as in other sciences, observation, description, the establishing of empirical generalizations, and the explanation of these by hypotheses and deductions which were subject to conditions of test. Such generalizations would certainly include statements about 'societies' as wholes, about 'institutions'— the articulation of their parts, and their kinds and degrees of interdependency in both order and change; but they would also include statements about the individuals and groups who pursued sequences of social action and the attainment of certain ends within the context of them.

THE COMPOUNDING OF A MULTIPLICITY OF CAUSES
AND EFFECTS

The many causes and the many effects which were simultaneously at work in even the most apparently simple social event, must always mean for sociology a complex task of compounding them in any full and satisfactory explanation. An 'explanation', in sociology, could never be a *'weighting'* of one institutional *entity* within the context of others. It was always more complicated than that.

THE COMPARATIVE METHOD: THE ALTERNATIVE TO
EXPERIMENT

In view of the great and probably insurmountable difficulties of artificial experiment (i.e., of close approximation to laboratory experiment) in the study of society, sociology could do no other than employ, as carefully as possible, the comparative method. This, clearly, also involved the *classification* of societies and social institutions.

THE HISTORICAL METHOD

Since societies, social institutions, and the sequences of action of men in society, were essentially historical phenomena; involving persistence and change in time; the scientific study of society must, *necessarily*, include a historical method. The absence of this would mean an insufficient understanding of the nature of the facts being studied; a falsification and superficial treatment of them; and therefore the great probability of error in the conclusions.

THE INVERSE-DEDUCTIVE METHOD

Because of the nature of society and history, and the limited position of the investigator in the context of his own age and circumstances, the hypothetical-deductive method would have to be of an 'inverse' nature in sociology. We were unavoidably in a position of having to seek the most satisfactory hypotheses possible for 'facts' we could already establish, or which were already established, at the level of 'empirical generalizations'. In sociology, therefore, the empirical, comparative, classificatory, historical methods of study were almost bound to be employed in this 'inverse' context. We were almost bound to deduce backwards from empirical generalizations already fairly well established to get at the hypothesis which best explained them. Contemporary comparative studies seemed necessarily to involve the manipulation of historical data.

(c) The nature and components of a science of society

(I) THREE ESSENTIAL ELEMENTS AND LEVELS: THE PSYCHOLOGICAL, SOCIETAL, AND SOCIAL-PSYCHOLOGICAL

A satisfactory science of society must comprise: (*a*) a basic experimental Psychology to establish knowledge of the psychological endowment of human beings, (*b*) a study of social systems; the nature and interconnections of institutions in societies as 'wholes' at the level of societal organization, and (*c*) a 'personality and social psychology' (ethology) to provide middle principles of knowledge concerning the reciprocal influences obtaining between institutions and groups (at the one level) and the psychological endowment of individuals (at the other): manifested in the formation of personalities, the establishment of character dispositions, and the exercise of deliberation and will by individuals in their roles in institutions and as members of groups. Explanations of interconnected changes at the institutional level (i.e., changes in some institutions brought about by changes in others) would then be mediated in terms of the influences of the institutional changes upon the collective dispositions and wills of the individuals involved. Hypotheses and deductions (and any necessary compounding of these to account for complex situations) would be drawn from the levels of psychology and social psychology as well as from the study of institutional interconnections, and *all* these, taken together, could 'explain' the empirical generalizations at the level of institutional regularity and change. The 'middle principles' of social psychology therefore played a central role in Mill's understanding of 'explanation' in sociology.

(II) SOCIAL STATICS AND SOCIAL DYNAMICS

Sociology should, as Comte had suggested, be logically divided into the two parts: Statics and Dynamics; the one providing a detailed analysis of the essential nature of 'society' as the distinctive subject of study; the other consisting (in the light of this analysis) of a detailed empirical study of the concrete varieties of societies in the world and attempts to establish specific theories about them.

(III) STATICS: A STRUCTURAL-FUNCTIONAL ANALYSIS

Social Statics could provide a detailed analysis of social systems (of societies), in terms of those institutional elements which were necessary to satisfy certain functional 'requisites' rooted both in the psychology of human beings and in determinate problems encountered and experienced in communal relationships. The high degree of consonance between these analytical and deductive generalizations and the empirical fact of the universality of these institutions in human societies gave even these the logical status of 'laws' of human nature and human society.

(IV) DYNAMICS: CLASSIFICATION, COMPARISON, AND HISTORICAL STUDIES

Using the guiding framework of analysis provided by 'Statics', the study of the concrete varieties of societies in the world should then be undertaken by the classificatory, comparative, and historical methods already mentioned. Mill agreed that, in this task, the construction of models, and, specifically, Comte's 'three types' of social order and the attendant sequence of social change which they theoretically emphasized, was of great utility. Mill agreed that the 'Law of the Three Stages' as outlined by Comte had much to support it; and he thought that it provided a great unifying thread for comparative and historical studies and was a first great generalization for the understanding of social change.

(V) THE PROGRESSIVENESS OF SOCIAL CHANGE

Mill discarded earlier 'cyclical' (and other philosophical) assumptions underlying the study of social change, and held that sociology could best proceed on the assumption that social change was no more than a certain temporal 'progression': namely that things simply *became different from what they were before.* There were no assumptions here—whether of moral betterment, of cyclical patterns, or of any other expectation—at all. Any such tendencies that might exist would only be *discovered* by empirical study, not introduced by assumption beforehand. This scientific study of the nature of social change would be bound to be more accurate and more reliable than earlier theories.

(VI) KNOWLEDGE IN SOCIETY: A CENTRAL CRITERION

Mill also agreed with Comte that the selection of the development of *knowledge* in society as the central 'yardstick' about which other institutional change could be correlated, was correct and well-justified. He agreed that, of all aspects of society, this, especially, was accessible to clear description. It permitted of analysis in terms of clear criteria: of knowledge as such, and also of the degrees of control over the social and natural environment which it provided. Since it was the basis of all man's activities, it was also likely to permeate and affect literally *all* the institutions of society.

(VII) SOCIAL KNOWLEDGE, SOCIAL JUDGMENT, SOCIAL PRACTICE

A very clear picture was also provided by Mill of those relations between the social scientist (with his knowledge), the moral and social philosopher (with his clarification of moral principles and moral ends), and the man of practical experience (with his understanding of the immediate actuality and possibility of things) which were necessary if the best deliberations, the best judgments, and the best political decisions and actions on social issues were to be achieved. The knowledge of sociology was seen therefore not only as something in and for itself, but as a necessary and important contribution within the context of social judgment and utility.

The making of Sociology as proposed and outlined by Comte was therefore defended, validated, and further clarified by this searching logical critique of Mill. Indeed, Mill established the groundwork of the new science much more firmly. He eliminated conclusively what had been thought to be insuperable objections to it—as, for example, the doctrine of 'the freedom of the will'. He showed convincingly that it was in no crucial way different from the natural sciences, or any less valid than they in dealing with its subject-matter. He clarified and exposed certain possibilities of error (such as the attaching of misplaced concreteness to 'institutions' or 'societies' as aggregate 'entities' independent of people).* And he explored in much more satisfactory detail the several levels of investigation necessarily involved in a science of society: the psychological, the social psychological, and the societal. It is as good a point as any on which to leave our outline of Mill's most excellent and thorough work to note and to emphasize that—for him—*there could be no possible separation of psychology from sociology, or any conflict between them, if they were properly conceived.* Properly understood, a science of man and society *included* psychological, social psychological, and societal studies as *indispensable and co-operating components: no one of which could be sufficient in itself.* This is a point of view which, I shall argue at the end of our study, is altogether correct, and there is no clearer statement of it in the entire literature than that accomplished by John Stuart Mill. The work of Mill was not only a great contribution to the making of sociology; it is something from which we can still learn much which is of the most fundamental importance in our subject.

Mill, however, and from his own considered choice, confined

---

* Let us note again, as an important point which we shall have to reiterate and emphasize later, that this is *not* to say that institutions do not involve elements and attributes *other* than, and *more* than, individuals; it is only to insist that they are not existent *entities independent* of individuals. This is a distinction of the utmost importance.

himself to the study of logical analysis and method. He explicitly withheld himself from any attempt to offer substantive theories of society. He thought that such an attempt would be untimely and impossible, since the state of some of the necessary components (such as psychology) was insufficiently advanced. We turn now to certain nineteenth century thinkers who not only accepted the necessity and importance of a science of society, and who not only attempted to found it, but who also offered substantive theories on the basis of it which were, in their view, vital for the understanding of modern industrial society and the problems which men confronted. These theories were stated within the context of the newly dominant perspective of the nineteenth century—the perspective of 'evolution'. First we shall examine the contribution of Herbert Spencer who, more than any other single figure, was the exponent of 'evolution'. Then we shall examine one very specific theory within this same context—that of Karl Marx.

4

Herbert Spencer: Structure, Function and Social Evolution

A unified scheme of knowledge. Influences of Comte and Mill

Spencer's work was very similar to that of Comte in that he sought to achieve and present a unified scheme of knowledge resting upon a clear philosophical position and embracing *all* the sciences. Spencer was therefore much more than a sociologist. He was a philosopher and a scientist in the widest sense, concerned with as complete an understanding as possible of the nature of things and of the place of man within nature, and he achieved an astonishing body of work.

First Principles clarified the philosophical basis for all the rest of his work, and presented his approach to all the sciences. This outline was then filled out by a *Principles of Biology*, a *Principles of Psychology*, a *Principles of Sociology*, and, subsequently, a *Principles of Ethics*. In addition to these—all of which were very voluminous works—he published a separate book on *The Study of Sociology* and essays of both a slight and a substantial nature on many themes: moral and political theory, practical social questions such as education and state-education, the changing nature of the political parties, the purpose of art, the origin of music, vaccination, dying, gymnastics, and so on. On every theme, large and small, important and unimportant, Spencer wrote clearly, entertainingly, and always with something stimulating and original to say.

His work could, in one sense, be regarded as a detailed filling-out (in terms of substantive knowledge) of the skeleton 'schema' which Comte had indicated in his 'hierarchy of sciences', were it not for the fact that Spencer himself claimed, and most emphatically, that his work was developed independently of the ideas of Comte, and rested on at least some ideas which were significantly different.

There is little point in arguing whether Spencer did or did not borrow very largely from the work of Comte. Three things, however, may be said.

Firstly, it is clearly quite wrong to think of Spencer as being simply a *successor* to Comte, or a *successor* to the logical critique of Mill. Spencer was, in fact, an early contemporary of both Comte and Mill.

His own work was developed at much the same time though, of course, he outlived both of them and continued his writing on sociology and on political questions a good deal longer than they did.

Secondly, there is no doubt whatever that Spencer did know of the work of Comte; knew also of the critical assessment of his work in Mill's book on *Logic;* and utilized the ideas of both men extensively. That this is so may be clearly seen in the actual phrasing of many of his ideas. A good example of this can be taken from his essay on education. In his extremely interesting discussion of the inadequacies of the study of history in his time, Spencer argued that a *sociological* study of history was the only kind of history worth while.

'The thing it really concerns us to know', he wrote, 'is the natural history of society. We want all facts which help us to understand how a nation has grown and organized itself.'

Amongst these social facts, said Spencer, would be the government—its structure, principles, methods, and not only central but also local government; the ecclesiastical organization in society; superstitions and myths; the system of social classes—including the titles, salutations, and forms of address that accompany it; leisure activities; the nature of the family, the regulation of the sexes; the relations between parents and children; the economic system—including the division of labour, guilds, associations between employers and employees, the means of producing and distributing commodities; the means of communication in society; the nature of art, literature and the mode of daily life of the people; and also, finally, the system of morals in society. Having briefly indicated the kinds of facts that would go into a natural history of society, he then continued:

'These facts, given with as much brevity as consists with clearness and accuracy, should be so grouped and arranged that they may be comprehended in their *ensemble*, and contemplated as mutually-dependent parts of one great whole. The aim should be so to present them that men may readily trace the *consensus* subsisting among them; with the view of learning what social phenomena co-exist with what others. And then the corresponding delineations of succeeding ages should be so managed as to show how each belief, institution, custom, and arrangement was modified; and how the *consensus* of preceding structures and functions was developed into the *consensus* of succeeding ones. Such alone is the kind of information respecting past times, which can be of service to the citizen for the regulation of his conduct. The only history that is of practical value, is what may be called Descriptive Sociology.

'And the highest office which the historian can discharge, is that of so narrating the lives of nations, as to furnish materials for a Comparative

Sociology; and for the subsequent determination of the ultimate laws to which social phenomena conform.

'But now mark, that even supposing an adequate stock of this truly valuable historical knowledge has been acquired, it is of comparatively little use without the key. And the key is to be found only in Science. In the absence of the generalizations of biology and psychology, rational interpretation of social phenomena is impossible. Only in proportion as men draw certain rude, empirical inferences respecting human nature, are they enabled to understand even the simplest facts of social life; as, for instance, the relation between supply and demand. And if the most elementary truths of sociology cannot be reached until some knowledge is obtained of how men generally think, feel and act under any given circumstances, then it is manifest that there can be nothing like a wide comprehension of sociology, unless through a competent acquaintance with man in all his faculties, bodily and mental. Consider the matter in the abstract, and this conclusion is self-evident. Thus: Society is made up of individuals; all that is done in society is done by the combined actions of individuals; and therefore, in individual actions only can be found the solutions of social phenomena. But the actions of individuals depend on the laws of their natures; and their actions cannot be understood until these laws are understood. These laws, however, when reduced to their simplest expressions, prove to be corollaries from the laws of body and mind in general. Hence it follows, that biology and psychology are indispensable as interpreters of sociology. Or, to state the conclusions still more simply: all social phenomena are phenomena of life—are the most complex manifestations of life—must conform to the laws of life—and can be understood only when the laws of life are understood.'*

There is absolutely no doubt of the fact that these paragraphs were written with the ideas of Comte and with Mill's *System of Logic* in mind. The insistence upon a recognition of the interdependence of social facts in societies as 'wholes'; the tracing of the kind of 'consensus' that exists among them; the clear acceptance of a 'social statics' and 'social dynamics' and of the methods of classification and comparison; the desire to support empirical generalizations about *social* facts by deductions based upon biology and psychology; are all clearly rooted in these two writers. The phraseology, let alone the ideas, are almost exactly the same. We can be quite clear in our minds then that Spencer did, in fact, consider critically the ideas of Comte and the ideas of Mill, and that, to some extent, his own work was additional to them and a development of them. Indeed, in addition to such textual knowledge of Spencer's indebtedness to Comte and Mill, we know that he was a friend of people like George Henry Lewes and George Eliot, also of T. H. Huxley, some of whom were among the first people in Britain,

* *Education—Intellectual, Moral, and Physical.* Thinker's Library Edn., 1945, pp. 33–4.

together with Mill, to appreciate the work of Comte and to do everything in their power both to publish and to publicize it, though not, of course, uncritically.

The third point, however, is that no matter how extensive Spencer's indebtedness to Comte, Mill, and others might have been, there is no doubt whatever that, from the beginning of his thought, he had been moving towards a similar conception of a science of society, and, furthermore, that he had a power of mind, a power of sustaining long, serious, painstaking study in the development of his system, which was itself a source of great originality and independence. In this sense, his work is not derivative but shows an originality, a thoroughness, a clarity, and a tenacity of mind which are altogether to be admired.

As with so many of the thinkers we have already considered, Spencer has been much caricatured. His point of view, or indeed his many points of view, have been much over-simplified, and then criticized adversely on this false basis. A full understanding of Spencer's treatment is such as to enhance one's admiration of the detailed way in which he worked out his systematic comprehension of things.

Furthermore, Spencer's initial statement of the foundation of philosophy, the distinction between religion and philosophy, and, within this context, the place and the nature of science, was profound, clear, and in some ways preferable to that of Comte. It was perhaps less dogmatic than the position of Comte, though I would not want it to be thought that I was making this a major distinction.

Comte, of course, denied the fruitfulness of metaphysical and theological speculation once positive science had come to be established, even though he readily acknowledged their utility in science, in the sense that the exercise of imagination and speculation within them might furnish important insights and hypotheses. Spencer agreed that positive science was the only method whereby testable knowledge could be achieved, but, nonetheless, he maintained that men would continue to ponder, and quite understandably, about the more fundamental questions concerning the nature of the universe and man which scientific knowledge could not possibly solve. He did not maintain that we could establish *knowledge* about these questions, but, simply, that we could not stop thinking about them, and that *something* of the nature of metaphysical speculation, *something* of the nature of religion, would always continue to exist in human thought and feeling.

A little later we shall see what he had to say about the development of ecclesiastical institutions, the place of religion in society, and the state of agnosticism to which he thought religious development in a scientific age must lead. This, I believe, is one of the clearest statements of the present culmination of the religious quest that has been given. Apart from being true, it is very apposite to the problems which we face now, in our own time.

Spencer, then, was a great original thinker of the nineteenth century—one of the great Victorians—and there is no doubt whatever of the importance of his contribution to the making of sociology: both as a system of analysis in its own right, which can still hold its own against any other system within sociology, and as a system of concepts and ideas which had a tremendous influence on subsequent thought.

The position which Spencer held with regard to what constitutes '*knowledge*', and the kinds of methods by which we can arrive at it, was in complete agreement with that of Comte and Mill, and with the earlier notions of Hume and Kant, though he worked it out and expressed it rather differently.

Everything in our experience, he thought—the regularity and order of everything in nature, the necessitous relationships and the orderly processes of the world—led us to be persuaded that there did, in fact, exist some *actuality*, some fundamental *reality*, in which everything was rooted, out of which all things proceeded, or *of* which all things were changing forms and manifestations, which possessed dimensions and qualities going beyond our own perceptions of it. We could not bring ourselves to believe that our own *experience* of the world really exhausted or fathomed all aspects of the actual nature of the world. Furthermore, all the ways in which we spoke of our 'knowledge' were such as to confirm this persuasion. When we recognized that our experiences or propositions were 'partial' or 'relative', our language implied that there was some 'whole' or 'entirety' of which we could see only a 'part', or some 'absolute' reality of which we could have only a 'relative' view. It was at least plausible, then, that there was some inscrutable reality the full nature of which transcended our own partial experience.

However, the simple truth was that we could find no way whatever of stating propositions about this reality excepting in terms of *how it appeared to us:* as a world of objects, people, relationships conveyed by our senses and systematically connected by our reasoning. We could do no more, then, than admit that there was a realm of the 'Unknowable', but then confine our attention to the 'Knowable'.

We could make accurate statements about all the aspects of the world as we experienced them, and we could arrange these statements to form a coherent, systematic and testable body of knowledge. Commonsense began with a disconnected set of statements. The various sciences went beyond these in a reflective and more accurate way, but each science was still a 'partial' segment of knowledge. Philosophy brought all the sciences into relation with each other and provided a 'unified' scheme of knowledge embracing all the dimensions of our experience.

'Knowledge of the lowest kind', wrote Spencer, 'is *un-unified* knowledge; Science is *partially-unified* knowledge; Philosophy is *completely-unified knowledge.*'

Spencer's aim, therefore, was to produce a new unification of all knowledge which the new developments of science had made possible, and this included a scientific knowledge of man in society. He claimed that, following the emergence of the methods of science, man could only provide himself with a true and satisfactory perspective of his place in the wider nature of things; a true picture of his place and destiny in the world; if he undertook and achieved a 'Synthetic Philosophy' of this kind.

The central enthusiasm at the heart of Spencer's effort towards this system of knowledge, however, the central significance of the 'system' which he offered, was that he believed he had discovered a conception which did, in fact, pervade the whole of nature and unify the whole of knowledge. His 'unifying' or 'synthetic' philosophy was by no means simply a 'collection' of the knowledge of all the special sciences. It was an illumination of the actual unity, connectedness, and coherence of all knowledge by the use of a conception which pointed to, and then analytically explored, the central process which lay at the very heart of, and characterized all the actualities and transformations of nature, human nature, and human society. This was the concept of 'Evolution'.

The Concept of Evolution

Spencer's entire schema of knowledge rested upon this persuasion that 'evolution' was the key concept for the understanding of the world as a whole and of man's place within it, and it is therefore absolutely essential to achieve a full understanding of what he meant by it. Spencer's system of 'explanation' in all sciences, including sociology, simply *cannot* be understood without a primary understanding of his concept of evolution—because his principles and grounds of explanation are rooted in, and derived from it.

It is because of this wide employment of the concept of evolution that Spencer's work has been subjected to much criticism that is quite fundamentally erroneous. A chief criticism, entirely trivial, is that Spencer falsely extrapolated from the biological theory of evolution for the purpose of sociological explanation. That is, it is commonly thought that Spencer *derived* his theory of social evolution from the *biological* theory of evolution, and that this was therefore a false application of the concept of evolution in sociological explanation. This criticism is totally unfounded; it is a complete misunderstanding of Spencer; and, because of it, it is necessary to make completely clear what the fundamental basis of Spencer's evolutionary conception actually was.

We must bear in mind Spencer's basic persuasion that the *origins* and the '*ultimate*' nature of the reality which forms the basis of all our experience are inscrutable and remain in the realm of the unknowable. Science can do no more than deal with a careful analysis and exploration of our actual experience of nature without ever being able to plumb the fundamental depths of how that nature came to originate in the first place or what its ultimate purposes, if any, might be. For Spencer, then, scientific knowledge consisted simply of careful, systematic, testable propositions about all aspects of the world of our experience.

When we consider all the varieties of objects in nature of which we do have perceptual experience—planetary systems, oceans and mountain-ranges, storms and earthquakes, trees and grasses, fishes, reptiles, birds and men, and the civilizations of men in history—we realise, as a fact of the most fundamental nature, that all these phenomena are *forms* and *transformations* of the same basic material substance. Nature consists of a vast variety of continuing forms into which its basic substance and energy is compounded. Furthermore, all these forms—differently according to their nature—are sequences and processes of creation, growth, development, death and dissolution in time. The forms of the world emerge out of the basic substance of existence, have their pattern of growth and change, and are then dissolved into their original basic elements. The very nature of the variety of things in the world is an appropriate pattern of transformation of the basic substance of which the world consists

In some sense, then, an explanation of all aspects of the world as we experience it must consist in an understanding of what these processes of transformation are: what are the components, sequences, and grounds of their occurrence; how, and according to what principles, do they occur? A knowledge of the world will be a systematic and testable body of propositions about these several *patterns of transformation:* which *are* the world, as we experience it.

In all this, Spencer had two fundamental ideas. Firstly, that since all forms of nature were transformations of material substance, the pattern of them must be evident in the processes of material substance, and evidenced, then, in the basic postulates of physics. Secondly, though the world manifested many *forms* of transformation, *the basic process of transformation itself* was common to them all, and was the central characteristic of the entire nature of things. Whitehead's later dictum that 'reality' is 'process' and that 'existence' consists of the actualization of 'forms' of process, is right at the heart of Spencer's thinking—as, indeed, it has been a central philosophical persuasion from Plato, to Bergson, and Whitehead himself.

The basic process of transformation, at the heart of the nature of all things, Spencer called 'Evolution', and the clarification of it, and what was involved in it (and in a satisfactory explanation of it), could only, he maintained, be gained by examining the basic formulations of physics.

It can be seen already, and at once, how totally absurd is the notion that Spencer simply borrowed the idea of biological evolution for use in sociology. His position was rooted in a far more fundamental philosophical persuasion than that.

It would be too detailed a task to go into all the ramifications of Spencer's explanation of the laws of physics, but a simple statement of the propositions he accepted and used, is this:

(1) There is a persistence of force in the world; a persistence of some sustaining energy in which all phenomena are rooted, upon which all phenomena rest, but which itself lies beyond our knowledge. This is a major, irreducible fact which we cannot explain, but which we are obliged simply to accept.

(2) The basic elements of matter and energy in the world are neither created, nor destroyed, but 'conserved'. There is a basic 'indestructibility' of the elements of matter.

(3) There is a perpetual continuity of motion in the world. All things continue in motion.

(4) There is a persistence of certain relations among forces in the world.

The force, the elements of matter, the continual motion in the world is not a chaos. There exists a uniformity or regularity of relationships among *defined phenomena* in the world.

These are ordered, recurring manifestations of events in the natural world, and the forces, elements of matter, and relations of motion existing among them have a definite regularity.

The world is an *order* of elements.

(5) Changing manifestations of these regular forms and processes of nature take place as a transformation and equivalence of forces.

The force, the elements of matter, the motion, are never lost or dissipated entirely in a process of change, but are

257

merely transformed into the manifestation of some other event or some other form of existence.

(6) The directions of change and movement among the phenomena of the world; the direction of motion of the elements of phenomena; are a resultant of the fact that all forces and elements move along the line of least resistance, or greatest attraction.

(7) All phenomena in nature have their own particular rate and rhythm of movement; of duration and development.

Each has its appropriate pattern of transformation; this is attendant upon the nature of the organization of its force, elements of matter, and pattern of motion.

Phenomena are manifestations of certain rhythms of motion.

These basic propositions are stated very simply here, bare of detail, but it will be clearly seen that they entail a pattern of explanation. The defined phenomena of the world rest upon certain dispositions of force, elements of matter, and patterns of motion, and all exist in a condition of interdependence. A certain 'equilibrium' of forces and elements obtains within and among them. The explanation of *each phenomenon*—a planetary system, a tree, a species of animal, a civilization—will consist of an analysis and clarification of that disposition of forces and elements which constitutes its 'order' and sustains its equilibrium. This order, of course, will itself be a 'moving equilibrium' since all phenomena are in a continuous condition of interdependence in motion. The explanation of *changes* in and among phenomena will consist of an analysis and clarification of the factors which have brought about a disruption or alteration of the normally persisting disposition of forces and elements, and a tracing of the new *re-ordering* of forces and elements which takes place as a new disposition of them, in a new condition of equilibrium, is arrived at.

Whatever phenomena we are analysing, then—physical, chemical, biological, psychological, social—this yields a very clear system of description, analysis, and explanation. But Spencer went considerably beyond this.

First of all, he derived from these basic propositions his 'law' of evolution. When we examine the nature of both order and change in any kind of phenomena in the world, we find, he insisted, that the pattern of transformation is the same, and could be formulated like this:

'Evolution is an integration of matter and concomitant dissipation of motion, during which the matter passes from relatively indefinite, incoherent homogeneity to a relatively definite coherent heterogeneity and during which the retained motion undergoes a parallel transformation.'

According to Spencer, all the phenomena of nature—the stars and planetary systems, the earth and all terrestrial phenomena, biological organisms and the development of species, and all the changing psychological and sociological processes of human experience and behaviour—followed this definite pattern of change. All processes of change are similar, in that they emerge out of the physical stuff of the world, have their own patterns of transformation and change, and, according to these patterns, in due course decline and dissolve. In this, they move from a condition of simplicity to a condition of organized complexity; from a condition of indefiniteness to a condition of definiteness; from a condition in which their parts are relatively undifferentiated to a condition of increasing specialization, in which their parts are characterized by a complex differentiation of structure and function; from an unstable condition consisting of a large multiplicity of very similar units, relatively incoherent and disconnected in their behaviour, to a stable condition consisting of relatively fewer phenomena now so intricately organized and articulated that their behaviour is regular, coherent and predictable.

All phenomena in nature are what they are in the context of reciprocally interacting environmental conditions. They change within such a context of forces, and appropriately. In this process of accommodation, all phenomena, without exception, grow and change from relatively simple units and processes which are very similar to each other and relatively incoherent in their connections and relations with each other, to more complicated forms which, though developing internal differentiations of structure and function, also manifest a greater degree of articulation in the organization of their parts, and of regularity of behaviour—both among their internal parts, and, externally, in relation to the elements and conditions of their environments.

This was how Spencer conceived and described his 'law' of evolution, and it can be seen that it is perfectly clear; providing a universally applicable *system* of analysis and knowledge, linking all the phenomena in the world of our experience and the orientations of all the sciences in exploring them. There is no doubt or ambiguity whatever, then, in what Spencer meant by a 'unified scheme of knowledge' or a 'synthetic philosophy' which the sciences and critical philosophy could now provide.

Following this initial statement, this outline of his framework, Spencer then proceeded to apply it in his investigation of all fields of knowledge, actually trying to achieve the scheme of knowledge which he had proposed. Naturally, he failed. One lifetime is not enough for such a project, and Spencer's accomplished work was chiefly within the range of the biological and human sciences—psychology and sociology—which were more at the centre of his concerns. The fact that Spencer could not exhaustively *complete* his scheme is not, however, any criticism of the nature and validity of the scheme itself. As with Comte's proposals for a system of positive knowledge, so with Spencer's scheme, it is arguable that it is, indeed, this kind of systematization of knowledge alone which can provide man, today, with a meaningful picture of his place within the scheme of things and with a reliable basis for responsible action in changing the nature of the world and of society. If such a scheme is beyond the capacity of one man to complete in all its detail—which it most certainly is—it is not beyond the capacity of many co-operative scholars; and perhaps it is still something at which we should aim in an effort to prevent the fragmentation and disorientation of specialist knowledge as our society becomes ever more complicated.

With regard to this question of the *validity* of Spencer's scheme, one or two other preliminary points must be made before leaving this brief outline of his concept of 'evolution'.

First of all, it will be seen how supremely important it is *not* to make the error of thinking that Spencer simply extended any particular theory of biological evolution to other fields of study in which it was not applicable. And it is worth noting that Spencer's outline of the centrality of 'evolution' in the nature of things was stated *before* Darwin's *Origin of Species* was published. It is also worth noting that though Spencer *did* conceive of any phenomenon as being continuously in a condition of having to accommodate itself to its environment, and sometimes spoke of the 'struggle for existence', he was *not* committed to the strictly Darwinian account of biological evolution in terms of genetic transmission and 'natural selection', and the application of this account in fields going beyond biology. On the contrary, Spencer's conception was *broader* than that of Darwin, and provided for the exploration of the patterns of transformation *appropriate* to all kinds of phenomena—plants, planets, people, societies—as they accommodate themselves to their environmental contexts.

And this leads to a vital point: that, even if Spencer's particular description of 'evolution' is found to be insufficient or inaccurate in this or that detail, it is still the case that his unified scheme of analysis for relating the sciences, and the knowledge they provide, holds good. Phenomena of all kinds *are* forms of material substance, persisting as certain concatenations and dispositions of elements.

They *do* exist in a 'moving equilibrium' of inter-dependence with their environments. They *do* have appropriate sequences of transformation of their elements in their pattern of emergence, growth, development, and dissolution. The changes that beset them, or occur to or among them, *are* related to changes in environmental conditions and *do* consist of a re-ordering of their elements into a qualitatively changed form.

It is important to see, then, that the scheme of analysis which Spencer provided still offers a luminously clear programme for the pursuit and unification of knowledge, even if his own particular notion of 'evolution' fails before certain criticisms. Having said that, however, it is doubtful—once Spencer's notion of 'evolution' is freed and disentangled from that of Darwin—whether it does fail to withstand criticism, and I will come back to this later.

One other very important point, however, remains to be made.

It might be said, by way of criticism of Spencer, that—even if 'evolution' as he described it is central to the processes of nature—it is still the case that his 'law' of evolution is *not* an *explanation* of anything at all. It is, in fact, simply a *descriptive* statement, an *empirical generalization* only, which itself requires explanation.

Now in so far as we have described it already, this criticism would appear to have weight, even though, as we have seen, Spencer's conception did imply quite a clear system of analysis and explanation. In fact, however, Spencer went far beyond the descriptive account we have given (what he called the 'inductive' grounds for his statement), to consider principles of deductive explanation which make this criticism quite beside the point. Here, we need only note these grounds of explanation, but—when we come to consider Spencer's account of the nature of society and social evolution—we will return to them to give this criticism and the rebuttal of it, full weight.

It is enough now simply to note that, having described this centrality of 'evolution' in nature, Spencer did in fact search for grounds of explanation rooted in the fundamental proposals he had outlined. Given the persistence of force, the indestructibility of the basic elements of material substance, the continuity of motion, and the like: *why* were the changes of phenomena from the homogeneous to the heterogeneous? from the relatively incoherent to the relatively coherent? from the simple to the complex? from the undifferentiated to the differentiation of specialized structure and functions? The following are the more important factors which he emphasized.

Explanations of Evolution

(a) The instability of the homogeneous

The condition of homogeneity, Spencer argued, is, in fact, a condition of unstable equilibrium.

When an aggregate of many similar units exists, and extends its number over a larger area, two factors making for changes and differentiations among them are present. Firstly, they cannot maintain their arrangements unaltered: they have to change their relations to one another. Secondly, the several parts of the aggregate are exposed to different forces, different conditions (whether of kind, or quantity, or intensity) and are therefore differently modified.

'The homogeneous', said Spencer, 'must lapse into the non-homogeneous . . .' and he gave illustrations drawn from all phenomena. For the moment, let us note briefly what he said about the differentiation of species in biology.

'We have abundant materials for the induction that each species will not remain uniform—is ever becoming to some extent multiform; and there is ground for the deduction that this lapse from homogeneity to heterogeneity is caused by the subjection of its members to unlike circumstances. Tending ever to spread from its original habitat into adjacent habitats, each species must have its peripheral parts subject to sets of forces unlike those to which its central parts are subject, and so must tend to have its peripheral members made different from its central members.'*

Spencer gave excellent examples of the same principle at work in human societies, too, but we can come to these later. It is enough for now to see that the movement from initial homogeneity to relative heterogeneity is not only described but *explained*.

(b) The multiplication of effects

Secondly, Spencer argued, once differentiation and diversity begins; once it emerges; a cumulative rapidity of increasing diversity and differentiation is set in motion. Diversity feeds upon itself, so to speak, and makes for increasing complexity. A brief quotation makes Spencer's conception completely clear:

'Each differentiated division of the aggregate becomes a centre from which a differentiated division of the original force is again diffused. And since unlike forces must produce unlike results, each of these differentiated forces must produce, throughout the aggregate, a further series of differentiations.

'This secondary cause of the change of homogeneity to heterogeneity,

---

* *First Principles*. Thinker's Library Edn., p. 379.

obviously becomes more potent in proportion as the heterogeneity increases. When the parts into which any evolving whole has segregated itself, have diverged widely in nature, they will necessarily react very diversely on any incident force—they will divide an incident force into so many strongly contrasted groups of forces. And each of them becoming the centre of a quite distinct set of influences, must add to the number of distinct secondary changes wrought throughout the aggregate.

'Yet another corollary must be added. The *number* of unlike parts of which an aggregate consists, is an important factor in the process. Every additional specialized division is an additional centre of specialized forces, and must be a further source of complication among the forces at work throughout the mass—a further source of heterogeneity. The multiplication of effects must proceed in geometrical progression.'*

Again, Spencer gave illustrations from all fields of knowledge, and later we will look at those he selected to illustrate social processes in particular.

(c) Segregation

This is not easy to clarify briefly, but it is enough for our immediate purposes to say that, once differentiation occurs within the units of an aggregate, a tendency towards the 'specialization' of parts will develop. To any particular influence, units which are alike will respond in a similar fashion, whereas units which are different will respond differently. A process of internal 'selection' or 'segregation' of specialized parts will be set afoot.

'If,' wrote Spencer, 'in an aggregate containing two or more orders of mixed units, those of the same order will be moved in the same way, and in a way that differs from that in which units of other orders are moved, the respective orders must segregate . . . the mixed units must under-go a simultaneous selection and separation.'

The movement from homogeneous to heterogeneous, with the increasing rapidity and complexity of differentiation attendant upon the multiplicity of effects, will therefore not be arbitrary. A pattern of specialized differentiation is likely to occur. This will be better clarified when we consider Spencer's sociological examples.

(d) Equilibration

A fourth element of explanation is the outcome of Spencer's consideration of the *limits* of heterogeneity, differentiation, and complexity in the transformations of phenomena. Are the kinds and degrees and paces of evolutionary change in nature unlimited, unbounded, uncircumscribed? They most certainly are not, said Spencer.

* *First Principles*. Thinker's Library Edn., pp. 392–3.

There is, of course, or so it seems in all natural phenomena, the ultimate of dissolution. But, a long way before that, and all the way before that, the changes of all phenomena are bounded by the conditions of their environments. Their nature is constrained by their environments both in the sense that changes in them cannot go beyond certain limiting conditions in their environments, and in the sense that they cannot avoid responding in some appropriate way to forces imposed upon them by their environments. They are constrained, that is to say, to establish some manageable 'equilibrium'.

All phenomena are in a process of adjustment and accommodation until a 'moving equilibrium' is reached; a situation in which the 'ensemble' of its parts and their total functioning is nicely adjusted to the interplay of forces in the environment; and the limitations of change and differentiation will be when such an equilibrium is reached.

'Every evolving aggregate', wrote Spencer, 'must go on changing until a moving equilibrium is established . . .

'Respecting the Structural state simultaneously reached, it must obviously be one presenting an arrangement of forces that counterbalance all the forces to which the aggregate is subject. So long as there remains a residual force in any direction—be it excess of a force exercised by the aggregate on its environment, or of a force exercised by its environment on the aggregate, equilibrium does not exist; and therefore the re-distribution of matter must continue. Whence it follows that the limit of heterogeneity towards which every aggregate progresses, is the formation of as many specializations and combinations of parts, as there are specialized and combined forces to be met.'*

This fourth principle, therefore, according to Spencer, means that the explanation of the nature and limitations which any phenomenon undergoes in its 'evolution'; in its movement from simplicity to complex differentiation, from homogeneity to heterogeneity and the like; can be sought and uncovered in an 'equilibrium—disequilibrium' analysis.

(e) Dissolution

A fifth and final aspect of explanations is rooted in the process of 'dissolution', to which, ultimately, every phenomenon must submit. 'Evolution' is a process whereby elements are brought together in a certain form of growth and organization. 'Dissolution' is the *reverse* process: of the *undoing* of these forms, and the disengagement and dissipation of the elements of which they consist. Dissolution is the undoing of evolved forms.

* *First Principles*. Thinker's Library Edn., p. 379.

Spencer, it is important to notice, does not regard 'evolution' and 'dissolution' as two totally separable 'stages'. On the contrary, he insists that, in the 'equilibrium—disequilibrium' adjustments to internal and environmental forces in which any phenomenon is continuously engaged, forces making *both* for integration *and* disintegration are always involved, and what happens is always a *resultant* of these forces.

Spencer put it in this way:

'. . . neither of these two antagonistic processes goes on unqualified by the other, and a movement towards either is a differential result of the conflict between them . . . '

In any evolving aggregate:

'. . . after the integrative changes have ceased to predominate, the reception of motion . . . constantly tends to produce a reverse transformation, and eventually does produce it. When Evolution has run its course—when an aggregate has reached that equilibrium in which its changes end, it thereafter remains subject to all actions in its environment which may increase the quantity of motion it contains, and which in course of time are sure, either slowly or suddenly, to give its parts such excess of motion as will cause disintegration. According as its size, its nature, and its conditions determine, its dissolution may come quickly or may be indefinitely delayed—may occur in a few days or may be postponed for billions of years. But exposed as it is to the contingencies, not simply of its immediate neighbourhood but of a Universe everywhere in motion, the time must at last come when, either alone or in company with surrounding aggregates, it has its parts dispersed.'

One part of the 'explanation' of any phenomenon, then—in its origins, growth, change and disintegration—will be the uncovering of those forces which lead to its dissolution; those factors which lead to the undoing of its nature, the decline of the equilibrium situation which it had attained, and the dispersal of those parts and elements which had been bound together, in organized fashion, within it. Again, it will be best to leave any illustration of this until we come to look at Spencer's suggestions when considering the dissolution of *societies* especially.

There is no doubt whatever, then, that Spencer provided not only a 'descriptive generalization' of 'evolution', but also a systematic approach to the *analysis* and *explanation* of it; and this will be seen to be quite vital in his system of sociology.

It is well worth emphasizing, too, before leaving this point, that Spencer, in proposing this scheme of knowledge which was focused upon the unifying concept of 'evolution', was *not* guilty of a 'naive inductivism' any more than Comte and Mill had been before him.

Throughout, he sought hypotheses and deductive support for the empirical generalizations (the 'inductions') gleaned from experience.

Having clarified this pattern of evolutionary change, and having maintained that it applied to all phenomena, Spencer then proceeded to test his law, by empirical observation, in the sphere of each science. We are only concerned here with what he had to say about society, but before turning to this, let us simply note that Spencer was quite clear in his mind about the method he was pursuing. He had clarified his supposition that the pattern of 'evolution' was central to all natural processes; derived a set of hypotheses as to the explanation of this from the fundamental laws of physics; made deductions from them as to what the behaviour of other, and more complicated phenomena in nature would be, and, following that, he wrote:

'Deduction has now to be verified by induction.'

There was clearly no lack of clarity with regard to inference and method here.

If all that I have said is true, however—and it is; the question arises: why has Spencer been thought to have been guilty of borrowing the evolutionary explanations of *biology*, in particular, and applying them inappropriately in sociology? The answer lies in a central feature of Spencer's treatment: the considerable (some would say the inordinate) use he made of the analogy between the nature of a biological organism and the nature of a society.

The analogy between a society and an organism

Spencer used this analogy to make it perfectly clear what he meant by analysing a society in terms of 'structure' and 'function', and the 'functional interdependence' of parts in the social system as a whole. It may be true that Spencer used this analogy in much greater detail than most other thinkers. In fairness, however, it must be insisted that Spencer was always quite explictly aware that he was dealing with an analogy only. He *never* believed that societies *were* organisms, that organisms *were* societies. He *never* believed that the relationship between the two was homologous rather than analogous, and later we shall see exactly what he said about this.

Even at the start of his argument, however, he took care to point out that when discussing the 'evolution' of human societies he was *not* thinking of this in terms of *organic* evolution, but what he called *super-organic* evolution. Human societies, though having some characteristics similar to those possessed by organisms, were something *more* than biological organisms as such. They consisted of forms of social organization which were *other* than the characteristics of biological organisms; and any change that took place in them was therefore a kind of change over and above organic change proper. Hence his term '*super-organic evolution*': a kind of evolutionary change which occurred in addition to, and over and above, the changes peculiar to biological organisms.

Let us look at the nature of the analogy which he drew, and, in order to be as clear as possible, elucidate first the *similarities*, and then the *differences* between societies and organisms to which he drew attention.

(a) Similarities

Societies and organisms are *similar*, Spencer maintained, in the following ways:

1. They both differ from inorganic phenomena in that they *grow* in size.
2. As they grow in size, so there takes place, in both, a differentiation of internal elements of structure, and their total internal organization becomes more complicated.
3. In both, this differentiation of structure is concomitant with a differentiation of functions. The internal specialization of structures and functions develops together.
4. In both—and this is an important point for Spencer—the differences in size, structure, and functions brought about by evolutionary change are not *arbitrary*. They are *definitely related* differences resulting from adjustments to environmental factors. Both organisms and societies encounter environmental problems, environmental challenges, and the changes of size, structure and function which come into being are not *arbitrary* changes, but a definite outcome of adaptations to these problems.
5. Even though their whole unity, as such, may be destroyed, the individual parts—in both—may continue to live for some time afterwards. The parts of both possess a certain independence and continuity. For example, when an organism dies, certain parts continue to grow even though they no longer perform their appropriate function in the life of the organism as a whole. Similarly, if a human society is destroyed as a total independent entity—by conquest, earthquake, economic absorption into a larger power, or some other disaster—nonetheless, even in this context of overall disorganization, certain parts and components of the society may continue to function. For example, family groups may continue to exist, some local

267

communities may retain their entity, religious practices may survive, and so on.

(b) Differences

Having outlined these similarities in much detail, Spencer then, however, spent a good deal of effort in pointing out the very important ways in which societies and organisms *differed* from each other. There were three chief differences which he emphasized. We may note before glancing at these, that Spencer pointed them out very carefully, because he was clearly aware of the *dangers* that could attend the analogy between societies and organisms when used irresponsibly by philosophers or statesmen of authoritarian persuasions.

Societies and organisms are *different*, Spencer argued, in the following ways:

1. In an organism, the parts, the internal units, form—together—a united living whole; a concrete physical entity. The parts are bound together in actual physical connection with each other. In a society, however, the parts are separated and dispersed. For example, families are disconnected from each other and widely dispersed throughout a country. Similarly, schools, industrial firms, political parties, and other groups and institutions, though all interrelated, are nonetheless all distinct and separate entities, whereas, in an organism, the brain, the lungs, the heart, are actually in physical interconnection with each other.

2. In an organism, the internal differentiation of structures and functions results in the fact that particular functions are fulfilled by specific organs alone, and by no other. For example, the brain may be said to be the 'organ of thought', and no other organ in the body can fulfil that function. Similarly, the stomach may be said to perform certain specific functions of digestion. Other parts of the organism do not have these special functions at all, and are, in these particular respects, insensitive. This, Spencer emphasizes, is *not* true of a human society. It is *not* the case that the government of a society is the sole 'organ of thought' or the sole 'seat of authority', or that the religion of a society, for example, is the sole 'seat of feeling or belief'. *All* human beings in a society, and as members of *all* institutions, to some extent share *all* these functions amongst each other. Specialization occurs among forms of social organization, but the specialization is different in kind from that which takes place among the parts of an organism.

In making this point, Spencer was emphasizing very carefully that he did *not* believe (as certain other thinkers had believed) that, in a society, there was such a thing as a *group mind* (one of the dangers of this analogy which has given rise to a great deal of criticism).

3. In an organism, Spencer maintained, the parts function with regard to the good of the whole, whereas, in a society, the entire 'ensemble' of institutions, exists only for the good of its parts—its individual members. In this point, too, Spencer wished to make it perfectly clear that his use of this analogy did *not* entail the idea that the individual was subordinated to the state.

It is surely perfectly clear—beyond all doubt whatever—that, having taken the differences, as well as the similarities, of the analogy into account:

(*a*) Spencer was perfectly clear that he was drawing *an analogy only*, and

(*b*) he specifically rejected those aspects of the analogy which might possibly carry unwarranted implications of totalitarianism.

It is true, however, that Spencer employed this analogy on almost every page of his treatise on social institutions. It is as though he felt compelled by the demands of systematization—having given an account of the way in which social institutions in certain types of society had developed—to illustrate this, in much detail, with reference to similar organic changes in particular biological species. This was done so frequently, and in such great detail, that it is perfectly understandable that many people should think he was interpreting social institutions and their changes in terms of biological evolution. Nonetheless, it is clear that this is an incorrect interpretation. Certainly the elaborate use of this analogy gave a decided biological flavour to Spencer's treatment. But we have seen perfectly clearly, that the fundamental 'law' of evolution which formed the basis of all his discussion was rooted not in biology but in the more fundamental (as he thought them) laws of physics.

Actually, however clumsy and unnecessary we may now judge this element of Spencer's treatment to have been, it was the employment of this analogy between a society and an organism which enabled him to give what was undoubtedly the clearest 'structural-functional' account of society that had been produced up to his day.

It was not totally new. Comte had used the same analogy extensively, and had also offered a 'structural-functional' analysis of the 'consensus' of institutions in the total social system. But Spencer's analysis of the process of differentiation of structures and functions in the pattern of evolutionary change gave his account a far greater clarity. It also enabled him to construct very clear models of certain *types* of society, and thus to make very clear indeed what he meant by the process of social evolution.

Just as the evolution of forms of organic life is characterized by the emergence of *species* which have a greater differentiation of structure and function, and are thus better fitted to survive in their natural environments, so the evolution of societies is characterized by the emergence of new *types of social system* which have a greater differentiation of structure and function and are thus better fitted to survive in their natural and social environment. Spencer's notion of social evolution, then, was that of an ongoing pattern of change in the structure and functions of social institutions which emerged to deal with newly encountered conditions and problems, and came to form distinctive 'types' of society. These changes, and these 'types', he claimed, were no more *arbitrary* than those which occurred in the evolution of biological species. They were distinctive and determinate social forms quite definitely related to particular problems and particular sets of environmental circumstances.

'The many facts contemplated,' Spencer wrote, 'unite in proving that socia evolution forms a part of evolution at large. Like evolving aggregates in general, societies show *integration*, both by simple increase of mass and by coalescence and by re-coalescence of masses. The change from *homogeneity* to *heterogeneity* is multitudinously exemplified up from the simple tribe alike in all its parts to the civilized nation full of structural, functional unlikenesses. With progressing integration and heterogeneity goes increasing *coherence*. We see the wandering group dispersing, dividing, held together by no bonds, the tribe with parts made more coherent by subordination to a dominant man, the cluster of tribes united in a political plexus under a chief with sub-chiefs, and so on up to the civilized nation, consolidated enough to hold together for a thousand years or more. Simultaneously comes increasing *definiteness*. Social organization is at first vague. Advance brings settled arrangements which grow slowly more precise. Customs pass into laws which, while gaining fixity, also become more specific and their applications to varieties of actions and all institutions at first confusedly intermingled slowly separate, at the same time each within itself marks off more distinctly its component structures, thus in all respects is fulfilled the formula of evolution. There is progress towards greater size, coherence, multiformity and definiteness.

'The inductions arrived at,' he claimed, 'thus constituting in rude outline an empirical sociology, show that in social phenomena there is a general order of co-existence and sequence and that, therefore, social phenomena form the subject matter of a science reducible in some measure at least to the deductive form.

'Guided then by the law of evolution in general and in subordination to it, guided by the foregoing inductions, we are now prepared for following out the synthesis of social phenomena.'*

It is quite plain, then, how and why Spencer used the analogy between an organism and a society, and we are now in a position to see what exactly this analogy led him to say about the nature of a society and the processes of social evolution. Before moving on to this, however, I think it is worthwhile to make it clear beyond doubt that *this is not simply my own interpretation* of Spencer. It must be insisted that *this is his own view* which he himself makes quite plain for all who will read him. Let us see what Spencer said about this analogy towards the end of the second section of Volume 1 in *The Principles of Sociology*, in which he discussed this matter. Having pointed out the inadequate uses of the analogy in the work of some earlier thinkers, such as Plato and Hobbes, he went on to say:

'Here let it once more be distinctly asserted that there exist no analogies between the body politic and the living body save those necessitated by that mutual dependence of parts which they display in common. Though in foregoing chapters, sundry comparisons of social structures and functions to structures and functions in the human body have been made, they have been made only because structures and functions in the human body furnish familiar illustrations of structures and functions in general . . .'
'But now,' he says, 'let us drop this alleged Parallelism between individual organizations and social organizations. I have used the analogies elaborated, but as a scaffolding to help in building up a coherent body of sociological inductions. Let us take away the scaffolding, the inductions will stand by themselves.'†

Nothing, surely, could be clearer than this. All those who criticise Spencer on this count can clearly be seen to be wrong.

In the same way, it may be worthwhile to see how Spencer himself thought of 'Evolution' as a universal process of transformation, of which social transformations were an example and a part, rather than as essentially a *biological* theory which could be applied in sociology.

'While we think of Evolution', he wrote, 'as divided into astronomic, geologic, biologic, psychologic, sociologic, etc., it may seem to some extent a coincidence that the same law of metamorphosis holds throughout all its divisions. But when we recognize these divisions as mere conventional groupings, made to facilitate the arrangement and acquisition of knowledge —when we remember that the different existences with which they severally deal are component parts of one Cosmos; we see at once that there are

* *Principles of Sociology.* 3rd Edn., 1893, Vol. I, pp. 584–5.
† *Ibid.*, p. 580.

not several kinds of Evolution having certain traits in common, but one Evolution going on everywhere after the same manner.

'So understood, Evolution becomes not one in principle only, but one in fact. There are not many metamorphoses similarly carried on, but there is a single metamorphosis universally progressing, wherever the reverse metamorphosis has not set in . . .

'. . . In any locality, great or small, when the occupying matter acquired an appreciable individuality, or distinguishableness from other matter, there Evolution goes on; or rather, the acquirement of this appreciable individuality is the commencement of Evolution. And this holds regardless of the size of the aggregate and regardless of its inclusion in other aggregates . . .'*

Having made Spencer's position clear beyond question, let us now examine his conception of the nature of a society, and the nature of social evolution, which he illuminated by this analogy, because on these matters too he has been very strangely and falsely criticized.

The nature of a society

Following upon the discussion of his analogy, and his conclusion that there is something of an 'organic' nature about a society, Spencer quite decisively rejected two ideas. He quite explicitly insisted that 'a society', as an entity, is something more than, and other than, an 'organism', even though human 'organisms' (individuals) are members of it. It is a total system of elements of social organization and their interdependent functions within which individuals pursue their courses of social action. It is a *super-organic* entity; an *organizational entity* over and above the level of the 'organism'.

Also, Spencer just as emphatically rejected the idea that a 'society' was no more than a collective name for a number of individuals.

The nature of a 'whole', he maintained, was quite distinguishable from a mere collection of its parts, or its elements, by virtue of 'the permanence of relations among its component parts'. Thus, a house is not only a collective name for a heap of bricks, wood, stones, and other bits and pieces—it is a certain ordering and connecting of these parts in a distinctive total form.

Similarly, he wrote:

'We consistently regard a society as an entity, because, though formed of discrete units, a certain concreteness in the aggregate of them is implied by the general persistence of the arrangements among them throughout the

* *First Principles*, pp. 490–1.

SPENCER'S SYSTEM OF ANALYSIS

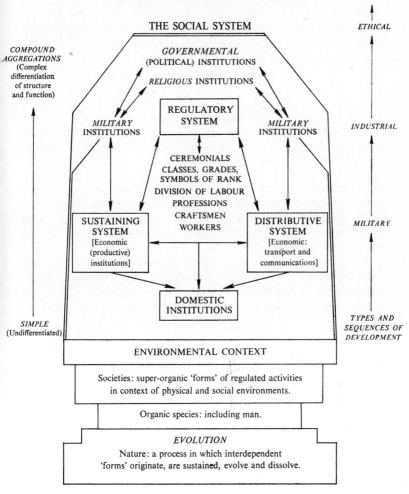

THE SOCIAL SYSTEM

ETHICAL

COMPOUND AGGREGATIONS (Complex differentiation of structure and function)

GOVERNMENTAL (POLITICAL) INSTITUTIONS

RELIGIOUS INSTITUTIONS

REGULATORY SYSTEM

MILITARY INSTITUTIONS

MILITARY INSTITUTIONS

INDUSTRIAL

CEREMONIALS
CLASSES, GRADES,
SYMBOLS OF RANK
DIVISION OF LABOUR
PROFESSIONS
CRAFTSMEN
WORKERS

MILITARY

SUSTAINING SYSTEM [Economic (productive) institutions]

DISTRIBUTIVE SYSTEM [Economic: transport and communications]

DOMESTIC INSTITUTIONS

SIMPLE (Undifferentiated)

TYPES AND SEQUENCES OF DEVELOPMENT

ENVIRONMENTAL CONTEXT

Societies: super-organic 'forms' of regulated activities in context of physical and social environments.

Organic species: including man.

EVOLUTION
Nature: a process in which interdependent 'forms' originate, are sustained, evolve and dissolve.

area occupied. And it is this trait which yields our idea of a society. Withholding the name from an ever-changing cluster . . . (of individuals) . . . we apply it only where some constancy in the distribution of parts has resulted from settled life.'*

When clarifying the 'scope of sociology' as a scientific study of 'societies', Spencer was also meticulously clear in specifying what the parts of a 'society' were.

* *Principles of Sociology*, Vol. 1, p. 436.

First of all, there was the family and kinship system, whereby 'successive generations are produced, reared, and fitted for co-operation'. Secondly, there were the many aspects of the political organization—central and local; military (for offence and defence); regulatory over internal aspects of social organization; and the relations between all these and such other aspects of authority as the law and ecclesiastical institutions, and other aspects of social co-ordination, such as 'communications'. Thirdly, there was religion itself: its doctrines and rituals and its ecclesiastical organization. Fourthly, there were all aspects of social control: law, custom, morality, and all the many symbols and insignia of ceremonial connected with them. Fifthly, there were the several distinctive aspects of the economic system: the organization of production, distribution, and of the procedures of industrial arbitration. Sixthly, there were the distinctive social classes which were attendant upon this entire division of functions. And seventhly, there were all the determinate aspects of the social life of the people within this complex of institutions: their language, knowledge and education, art and entertainment, and morals.

A 'society' was an organizational entity consisting of these parts in interrelationship, and an analysis of a 'society' would consist of a clear description of them. But it would *not*, said Spencer, consist of a description of each part in isolation from the others.

'We have', he wrote, 'to consider the inter-dependence of structures, and functions, and products, taken in their *totality*. Among these many groups of phenomena there is a *consensus*; and the highest achievement in Sociology is so to grasp the vast heterogeneous aggregate, as to see how the character of each group at each stage is determined partly by its own antecedents and partly by the past and present actions of the rest upon it.'

Spencer's conception of a 'society', and of the nature of the 'Sociological analysis' of a total society was perfectly clear; but his discussion of the 'organic' analogy enabled him to go even further. It is not our purpose to explore the analogy itself, but the points which Spencer drew from it are important.

Of all the totality of parts in a society, he claimed, it was possible to distinguish three clear 'systems'. All societies had to deal with their physical and social environments, and during the course of this, three major differentiations took place. In order to organize a society for effective conflict with the environment, groups especially responsible for authoritative control—both with regard to the regulation and co-ordination of internal resources and with regard to the organization of military offence and defence—came to be differentiated from groups chiefly responsible for economic productivity. Spencer spoke of the differentiation, sometimes, as being one between responsibility for 'Outer' protection and security, and 'Inner' sustenance. A 'Regulating System' was clearly differentiated from the 'Sustaining System' of societies, and this was a fundamental differentiation of functions and appropriate structures. These two systems, however, especially as they became larger in scale and more complex, had to be linked together by an efficient network of communications and a determinate distribution of resources. This third differentiation of functions and structures gave rise to the 'Distributive System'.

Spencer analysed each society, then, into all its specific elements of social structure; all its 'organs' of social organization; but he then emphasized especially these differentiations of the 'Regulating', 'Sustaining', and 'Distributive' systems, and examined the nature of societies in terms of the relative preponderance of each.

All the major aspects of 'evolutionary' change—of growth in size; of structural-functional differentiation; of the change from the homogeneous to the heterogeneous, from the indefinite to the definite, from the incoherent to the coherent, and in various conditions of 'equilibrium'—were then studied with the use of this analytical model. And this leads us to consider how Spencer went about the comparative study of societies in order to establish a body of descriptive knowledge about them.

Before leaving this point, however, let us simply note that when a modern American sociologist writes: 'Superorganic evolution is a beautiful term, but it has meaning only if it denotes a clear conception of the nature of society—a matter that unfortunately Spencer never clarified'—he is writing sheer stuff and nonsense. As we have seen, Spencer was completely clear about his conception of the nature of society, the parts of which it was composed, and what constituted a 'sociological analysis' of it. It is also important, in readiness for criticisms which will arise much later, to note that in this 'structural-functional' analysis of a 'society', Spencer was quite clear that the elements of structure to which he referred were organizations of the '*combined actions*' of men in their associations with each other. In short, Spencer was quite clearly analysing the '*social action*' of men in his '*structural-functional*' analysis of *social systems*. The reason why this should be borne clearly and emphatically in mind will be seen later.

However, having clarified the nature of societies as entities, Spencer then argued:

'But now before trying to *explain* these most involved phenomena, we must learn by inspection the relations of co-existence and sequence in which they stand to one another. By comparing societies of different kinds, and societies in different stages, we must ascertain what traits of size, structure, function, etc., are associated. In other words, before deductive interpretation of the general truths, there must come inductive establishment of them.'

It can be seen that Spencer followed the comparative and historical method in the way advocated by Comte and Mill, and—like Mill especially here—thought it of primary importance to *undertake empirical studies of societies*; to establish *empirical generalizations* about them. Adequate explanations could then be considered. And it is interesting to notice that such empirical generalizations about societies, and the 'consensus' of parts within them, were, according to Spencer, 'relations of co-existence and sequence'. Here again, we see the strand of empirical, causal analysis which had continued from Hume onwards. And here again, too, we see Spencer's way of employing the kind of distinction which Comte had called 'Statics' and 'Dynamics'. Spencer's conceptual analysis of the nature of society as one kind of consensus of facts in our experience—his 'Social Statics'—was based upon his conception of 'Evolution'. With this analysis, he then approached the study of the many varieties of societies in the world in order to establish empirical knowledge about them and the ways in which they changed: his 'Social Dynamics'.

Types of society: classification and comparison

His clear conception of the nature of a society enabled Spencer to construct very clear models for the classification and comparison of societies. Two methods arose quite directly from his analysis.

First: his evolutionary 'law' suggested that societies would change in terms of growth, aggregation, and an increasing differentiation of institutions. Small, simple aggregates became 'clustered' or 'compounded'—as a result of many factors—into larger, more complex aggregates. Societies could be classified, then, on the basis of their '*degree of composition*'.

Secondly, however, the actual and detailed processes of this 'aggregation' might be illuminated by a supplementary method of classification: the method of constructing 'models' or 'types' of societies in terms of the relative preponderance of one or other of the 'Regulating', 'Sustaining' and 'Distributive' systems. A society which subordinated its entire pattern of life to its 'Military' security would have a very different 'consensus' of institutions from one which subordinated its entire social life to the extension of wealth and welfare by developing its 'sustaining' (economic) system. And the patterns of aggregation which societies have undergone in historical change might prove to be significantly related to the changing predominance of one or other of these 'systems'. 'Models' of this kind would therefore provide another dimension of interpretation and understanding.

It is very important to notice two things about Spencer's methods of classification. Firstly, the two methods are quite different. The classification according to the 'degree of composition' rests upon an *empirically determinate set of characteristics of social organization* which can be *observed*. It can be *seen* whether the society one is studying is a 'tribe', or a 'confederation of tribes', or a 'confederation of nations'; and societies of the same level of aggregation can be grouped together accordingly. The classification according to 'typologies' or 'models' does *not* rest upon empirically determinate facts—though it *refers* to them in attempting *interpretation*. These 'types' or 'models' are hypothetical constructs. Spencer does not claim, or wish to claim, that societies *actually exist* in the extreme form which his models may take. All societies will have *some* blend of the 'Regulating, Sustaining, and Distributive systems' and our understanding of *this actual blend* may be aided by our construction of analytical extremes. We shall see what Spencer had to say about the specific 'types' which he constructed in a moment.

The second point to notice here is that Spencer quite clearly introduced into comparative sociology this method of the construction of 'types' of society: which were 'structural-functional' models of societies in which certain predominant traits were assumed, and emphasized, in such a way as to give a total picture of the pattern of social action in that society, and to provide an understanding of it (including the close relationship between the institutional structure of the social order and the pattern of life and character of its individual members). All this we shall come back to again, but this insight and this method of Spencer's must be noted and emphasized now, because later we shall see that some modern critics argue as though the subjective understanding of social *action*, and the construction of 'types' for this purpose, had been absent from sociology until very recently—whereas, as we can see, they had been firmly incorporated into sociology during the nineteenth century.

*(a) Classification by 'degree of composition'.**

Spencer's first method of classification can best be made clear by referring to the following diagrams which he provided:

* *Principles of Sociology*, Vol. 1, pp. 539–42.

(1) SIMPLE SOCIETIES

HEADLESS.

Nomadic: (hunting) Fuegians, some Australians, Wood-Veddahs, Bushmen, Chépángs and Kusúndas of Nepal.

Semi-settled: most Esquimaux.

Settled: Arafuras, Land Dyaks of Upper Sarawak River.

OCCASIONAL HEADSHIP.

Nomadic: (hunting) some Australians, Tasmanians.

Semi-settled: some Caribs.

Settled: some Uaupés of the upper Rio Negro.

VAGUE AND UNSTABLE HEADSHIP.

Nomadic: (hunting) Andamanese, Abipones, Snakes, Chippewayans, (pastoral) some Bedouins.

Semi-settled: some Esquimaux, Chinooks, Chippewas (at present), some Kamschadales, Village Veddahs, Bodo and Dhimáls.

Settled: Guiana tribes, Mandans, Coroados, New Guinea people, Tannese, Vateans, Dyaks, Todas, Nagas, Karens, Santals.

STABLE HEADSHIP.

Nomadic:

Semi-settled: some Caribs, Patagonians, New Caledonians, Kaffirs.

Settled: Guaranis, Pueblos.

(II) COMPOUND SOCIETIES

OCCASIONAL HEADSHIP.

Nomadic: (pastoral) some Bedouins.

Semi-settled: Tannese.

Settled:

UNSTABLE HEADSHIP.

Nomadic: (hunting) Dacotahs, (hunting and pastoral) Comanches, (pastoral) Kalmucks.

Semi-settled: Ostyaks, Beluchis, Kookies, Bhils, Congo-people (passing into doubly compound), Teutons before 5th century.

Settled: Chippewas (in past times), Creeks, Mundrucus, Tupis, Khonds, some New Guinea people, Sumatrans, Malagasy (till recently), Coast Negroes, Inland Negroes, some Abyssinians, Homeric Greeks, Kingdoms of the Heptarchy, Teutons in 5th century, Fiefs of 10th century.

STABLE HEADSHIP.

Nomadic: (pastoral) Kirghiz.

Semi-settled: Bechuanas, Zulus.

Settled: Uaupés, Fijians (when first visited), New Zealanders, Sandwich Islanders (in Cook's time), Javans, Hottentots, Dahomans, Ashantees, some Abyssinians, Ancient Yucatanese, New Granada people, Honduras people, Chibchas, some town Arabs.

279

(III) DOUBLY COMPOUND SOCIETIES

OCCASIONAL HEADSHIP. {
Semi-settled:

Settled: Samoans.
}

UNSTABLE HEADSHIP. {
Semi-settled:

Settled: Tahitians, Tongans, Javans (occasionally), Fijians (since fire-arms), Malagasy (in recent times), Athenian Confederacy, Spartan Confederacy, Teutonic Kingdoms from 6th to 9th centuries, Greater Fiefs in France of the 13th century.
}

STABLE HEADSHIP. {
Semi-settled:

Settled: Iroquois, Araucanians, Sandwich Islanders (since Cook's time), Ancient Vera Paz and Bogota peoples, Guatemalans, Ancient Peruvians, Wahhàbees (Arab), Omán (Arab), Ancient Egyptian Kingdom, England after the 10th century.
}

(IV) CIVILIZED NATIONS

'There remain to be added the great civilized nations which need no tabular form, since they mostly fall under one head—trebly compound. Ancient Mexico, the Assyrian Empire, the Egyptian Empire, the Roman Empire, Great Britain, France, Germany, Italy, Russia, may severally be regarded as having reached this stage of composition, or perhaps, in some cases, a still higher stage. Only in respect of the stabilities of their governments may they possibly require classing apart—not their political stabilities in the ordinary sense, but their stabilities in the sense of continuing to be the supreme centres of these great aggregates. So defining this trait, the ancient trebly-compound societies have mostly to be classed as unstable; and of the modern, the Kingdom of Italy and the German Empire have to be tested by time.'

'As already indicated,' Spencer insisted, 'this classification must not be taken as more than an approximation to the truth.'

It will be readily seen that this is a clear, systematic, and comprehensive scheme of classification within which all societies known to us can be compared.

The 'degrees of composition' are defined quite clearly. Simple societies, Spencer wrote, are those 'which form simple working wholes unsubjected to any other and of which the parts co-operate with or without a regulating centre for certain public ends'. 'Compound societies are those in which the simple groups of which they are compounded have their own respective chiefs under a supreme chief.' 'Doubly compounded societies are those formed by the federation of these compound groups, giving rise to more settled complex forms of social organization with stable and more elaborate forms of government.' And trebly compounded societies are all the 'great civilized nations' and large-scale empires or federations of nations, whether of ancient or modern times.

It will be noticed, too, that Spencer introduced two subsidiary categories of classification into this scheme—namely that of stable or unstable 'headship' and whether the society was 'nomadic, semi-settled, or settled'; but these do not require particular comment. Two or three other points, however, deserve brief emphasis.

Firstly—it will be seen that the societies drawn together under these categories are *both* historical *and* contemporary. In short, this is a *classificatory scheme* into which *all* societies of which we have knowledge can be manageably drawn. Secondly, its objective is no more than to *arrange* empirical knowledge of societies under certain headings so that further, detailed comparative study can be undertaken, and so that, as an outcome, generalized (systematic) knowledge can be arrived at about the 'consensus' of institutions in each category and the pattern of institutional change which characterizes the development of one 'consensus' out of another. Uniformities of co-existence and sequence can be established. This classification of knowledge does not, of itself, *explain* social order or social change, it is simply a way of *gaining* and *extending* systematic (descriptive) knowledge,* which we shall then *seek* to explain; and this is exactly how Spencer regarded it.

Thirdly, however, it is worth noting that Spencer put his scheme forward *tentatively* rather than *dogmatically*. It was the best he felt able to do given the basis of the evolutionary conception and the 'status' of the empirical knowledge he had at his disposal.

'This classification', he wrote, 'must not be taken as more than an approximation to the truth. In some cases the data furnished by travellers and others are inadequate; in some cases their accounts are conflicting; in some cases the (degree of) composition is so far transitional that it is difficult to say under which of two heads it should come . . .'†

---

* It is highly significant that the several volumes of comparative knowledge drawn together as a result of Spencer's scheme were entitled *Descriptive Sociology*. † *Principles of Sociology*, Vol. 1, p. 542.

But still, he argued, this was the best scheme of classification available, and it rested upon, and revealed, certain generalizations which could be quite safely accepted. Spencer also poured scorn on those critics who with glib and Oxford-historian-like facility, made much of the uncertainty of his data, and the fact that much was drawn from 'travellers' tales'.

'I am aware', he wrote, 'that in the eyes of most, antiquity gives sacredness to testimony; and that so, what were "travellers' tales" when they were written in Roman days have come, in our days, to be regarded as of higher authority than like tales written by recent or living travellers. I see, however, no reason to ascribe to the second-hand statements of Tacitus a trustworthiness which I do not ascribe to the first-hand statements of modern explorers; many of them scientifically educated—Barrow, Barth, Galton, Burton, Livingstone, Seeman, Darwin, Wallace, Humboldt, Burckhardt, and others too numerous to set down . . .'*

Spencer was very well aware—indeed, much better aware than his critics—of the limitations of the data at his disposal.

(b) *Classification by the construction of 'types'.*
Using the second of his two methods, Spencer thought it most useful to construct two extremely dissimilar types—*so* dissimilar as to constitute a 'polarity'—the 'Militant' and the 'Industrial'. The first was a type in which the 'Regulating System' was dominant over all other aspects of society. The second was one in which the 'Sustaining System' was emphasized, and all other aspects of society were subordinated to its service. The 'Distributing System' was, of course, significantly different in the differing 'consensus' of the two types.

Here again it is necessary to insist how clear Spencer was in the *tentative* nature of his approach. He was quite clear that, excepting for some of the simplest societies which occupied territories where they were quite safe from invasion, *both* regulating *and* sustaining systems always existed in some conjunction; *both* militant *and* industrial aspects existed in some combination in *all* societies.

'But,' he wrote, 'while the two systems in social organisms co-exist in all but the rudimentary forms, they vary immensely in the ratios they bear to one another. In some cases the structures carrying on external actions are largely developed; the sustaining system exists solely for their benefit; and the activities are militant. In other cases there is predominance of the structures carrying on sustentation; offensive and defensive structures are maintained only to protect them; and the activities are industrial.'†

* *Principles of Sociology*, Vol 1, see footnote, p. 683.   † *ibid.*, p. 544.

He also put it in the following way:

'Much less definite (i.e., than that based upon degree of composition) is the division to be made among societies according as one or other of the great systems of organs is supreme . . .

'Nevertheless, as the militant type, characterized by predominance of the one, is framed on the principle of *compulsory co-operation*, while the industrial type, characterized by predominance of the other, is framed on the principle of *voluntary co-operation*, the two types, when severally evolved to their extreme forms, are diametrically opposed; and the contrasts between their traits are among the most important with which Sociology has to deal.'*

This was therefore a construction of two polar 'types' for the sake of a clearer understanding of societies which possessed a relative preponderance of one or other of the two systems. It is interesting to notice that, in his conviction that the exploration of the contrasts between these two types is possibly the most important task for Sociology, Spencer was again very much in agreement with Comte. Spencer's distinction between the 'Militant' and 'Industrial' types of society was, really, the same as Comte's distinction between the 'Theological' and the 'Positive' types; and the agreement between these two men—and others to be mentioned later—points to the crucial distinction we have already touched upon between the 'Traditional' societies of the past and the 'Modern Industrial' societies which have developed since the French Revolution. We shall see that this is the central, continual, preoccupation of Sociology.

Spencer described his two 'types' of society as follows:

(I) THE MILITANT SOCIETY

The militant society is a type in which organization for offensive and defensive military action is predominant. It is one, said Spencer, 'in which the army is the nation mobilized and the nation is the quiescent army', and, consequently, in which the entire structure of society is closely moulded about its military structure, reflecting its military organization.

Such a society has the following marked characteristics:

There is firstly, a highly centralized pattern of authority and social control. The military head is also the political head, and he has a despotic power over the life and property of all his subjects. The absolute control of the ruler makes necessary a clear, precise, and rigid hierarchy of power throughout society, in which each level of officials has to be completely subservient to that above, and com-

* *Principles of Sociology*, Vol. 1, p. 562

pletely in power over those below. 'All are slaves', wrote Spencer, 'to those above and despots to those below.' And this rigid hierarchy of power necessarily involves a precise and rigid grading of social status and social ranking and thus gives rise to rigid social classes in economic life. The distribution of property, the distribution of material rewards in society, is meticulously linked with the order of social ranks.

But this authoritarian and hierarchical nature of the society is also reflected in the prevailing system of ideas and beliefs. There exists also a set of doctrines, myths, and attendant rituals which portrays a similar form of supernatural authority and government. The gods themselves, and their divine agencies, are pictured in terms of a hierarchy of power, and as being closely concerned with the destiny of society. 'Ever in antagonism with other societies,' Spencer said, 'the life is a life of enmity and the religion a religion of enmity.'

This hierarchical power of the gods as pictured in doctrine and myth is also reflected, indeed embodied, in the hierarchical form of the actual ecclesiastical organization. The religion itself is a hierarchical organization, and the Ecclesiastical Head himself possesses supreme, despotic authority. Furthermore, in such a society, the despotic head is, at one and the same time, not only the Military and Political, but also the Ecclesiastical head. His central power over government, army, and all civil and economic affairs, is sanctified and given justification by religion.

It follows that the whole tenor of life in such a society is characterized by rigorous discipline and by a close identity between private and public life. No element of the private life of the citizen is closed to the state. The state can invade and interfere in the private lives of citizens whenever it is felt necessary or desirable to do so. Indeed, the word 'citizens' is hardly appropriate. The great majority of the population are completely subjected to the regulatory purposes of the central authority. And this lack of individual rights in the relationship between individual and state is supported by the belief 'that its members exist for the benefit of the whole and not the whole for the benefit of its members. The loyalty of the individual to the state has to be unquestioning.'

'Human relationships', said Spencer, 'are characterized in this kind of society by a state of "*compulsory co-operation*".'

Clearly (without elaborating this point here) Spencer's Militant 'type' of society is applicable, as a basis of interpretation, not only to the despotic societies of antiquity, but also to totalitarian societies in the contemporary world. It is intriguing to consider his analysis in relation to the Soviet Union, or China, Nazi Germany, or Fascist Italy. As a 'type', the 'militant society' can be seen to be of wide use for the purpose of comparative studies, being relevant to societies of both the past and the present.

(II) THE INDUSTRIAL SOCIETY

Spencer's 'Industrial Type' of society is one in which military activity and organization, though it still exists, is carried on at an increasing distance from the civilian life and concerns of the community. It takes place on the periphery of the society; and the greater part of social organization is peaceful, concentrating upon the increase and improvement of all aspects of human production and welfare; upon economic and civil activities.

The characteristics of such a society contrast strongly with those of the 'militant' type.

First of all, there is a clear and firm recognition, on the part of all its members, of *personal rights*, which they hold as citizens of the community. On this basis there is a continual exercise of the making of mutual claims and counter-claims, and a voluntary submission on the part of individuals to impartial procedures for the resolution of them. There is also an active concern for the maintenance of these rights by an insistence upon effective means of representative government.

In this society, too, the 'sustaining system' possesses a large degree of freedom, a large degree of disengagement, from the 'regulatory system'. The control and government of economic affairs is largely and deliberately divorced from the political government. It is, indeed, assumed by the government, as well as by everyone else in society, that intelligent individuals concerned with their own economic activities will be better capable of making their own decisions than remote administrative officials. And, indeed, they are not only *allowed*, they are actively *encouraged*, to do so.

With the growing complexity of agriculture, commerce and industrial manufacture, within the peaceful context of an area bounded, at the distant periphery, by military security, there is therefore a growth of free associations and institutions. In all such forms of association, there comes to be a growth of *committee* procedures for the government of affairs, and, within this context, the appointment of officers by *election*. These factors bring about a much less rigid and less tyrannical class structure, which rests increasingly upon human relationships which are contractual and free, and in which gradations of status and rank are less precisely marked. There is a growth, as Spencer put it, of 'combinations of workmen and employers' to resolve particular disputes, quite separately from central authority and law.

Similarly, religious organization and religious beliefs lose their hierarchical structure and absolute power. Individual faith, individual and sectarian discrimination, enters into religion. In place of the doctrine that the members of society exist for the good of the state, emerges the idea that it is the will and the well-being of the individual citizens which is of supreme importance in society, and that the organ of government, and, indeed, all forms of organizational control, exist merely to manifest their wishes and to serve them.

In such a society, then, it is not only thought that despotic government is wrong; it becomes a positive duty on the part of citizens to *resist* irresponsible government. There is always a tendency to *disobedience* amongst minorities and individuals, and such a critical tendency is positively encouraged. Human relationships in the industrial society are, therefore, wholly different from those in the militant society. Free, responsible, contractual relationships between individuals require *voluntary co-operation*, not the compulsory co-operation which characterizes relationships in the militant type.

It must be emphasized again that Spencer did not believe that societies actually existed in the world with the sharp clarity of distinction that he described in drawing up these two 'models'. He merely thought that comparison between these two specially constructed types was useful in conjunction with his other mode of classification (on the basis of degrees of composition) in order to interpret and understand some of the crucially important trends of social evolution, and, especially, those trends which were of importance as traditional societies were being radically transformed by the processes of industrialization.

Having provided these modes of classifying societies, Spencer then undertook a very detailed comparative study of each major social institution within each 'type' of society; arranging an enormous range of descriptive facts into this classificatory framework in order to establish the main characteristics and trends of social evolution. This gave him a picture of what, in the whole field of social institutions had actually occurred in the past, and what was happening in the present.

This comparative study was carried out with meticulous clarity and consistency. Each chief element of social structure, and each of the major 'systems' of institutions in society—Domestic, Ecclesiastical, Political, Industrial institutions—were studied in turn, and the nature of these was examined firstly in societies according to their 'degrees of composition' and secondly in accordance with their contrasting nature in societies which approximated to the 'militant' or 'industrial' types. In each case, too, Spencer summarized his findings in a section in 'Retrospect and Prospect' so that a clear perspective of contemporary changes in society was provided. A remarkably systematic and well-ordered body of knowledge about the nature of societies; about the 'consensus' of institutions in each type, and the patterns of change which they experienced in coming to terms with different situations; was thus provided. And this, it must be noted, was not only an ordered body of descriptive knowledge (though it *was* that), but also a system of knowledge resting upon certain *explanations* deductively derived from an analysis of 'systems' within their context of 'evolutionary transformation', and utilized to provide certain *interpretations* of the structures of social action in societies of different types.

Spencer's contribution to the making of sociology was a remarkable achievement. He has been much criticized for using library materials and documentary data, and having other people carry out researches for him; but on what other sources of materials could Spencer have drawn in his time? And, in any case, Spencer was chiefly concerned to achieve a clear scientific fabric within which *any* relevant data could be most reliably studied. As we have seen, he was well aware of the limitations of much of the material on which he could lay his hands. Furthermore, the data which Spencer amassed is still extremely useful, and much knowledge and illumination is still to be gained from a reading of the volumes of the *Principles of Sociology*.

However, the outcome of Spencer's efforts in these wide comparative studies was the provision of a very clear picture of the nature of social evolution as he saw it. And it would be a pity to leave Spencer having pointed out only the methodological and theoretical schema which he created, and not the substantive knowledge in which his methods resulted. Also, I would like especially to demonstrate the way in which Spencer was attempting to *explain* the several aspects of social evolution, because I believe he is very much underrated, misunderstood, and misrepresented in this, and his ideas really deserve much critical attention. Let us look, then, at the picture of social evolution which Spencer's studies provide—as briefly as is commensurate with sufficiency for purposes of understanding.

The nature of Social Evolution

No summary statement of Spencer's over-all picture of the facts of social evolution could be better than that which he himself provided.

'Societies', he wrote, 'are aggregates which grow. In the various types of them there are great varieties in the growths reached. Types of successively larger sizes result from the aggregation and re-aggregation of those of

287

smaller sizes; and this increase by coalescence, joined with interstitial increase, is the process through which have been formed the vast civilized nations.

'Along with increase of size in societies goes increase of structure. Primitive hordes are without established distinctions of parts. With growth of them into tribes habitually come some unlikenesses; both in the powers and occupations of their members. Unions of tribes are followed by more unlikenesses, governmental and industrial—social grades running through the whole mass, and contrasts between the differently-occupied parts in different localities. Such differentiations multiply as the compounding progresses. They proceed from the general to the special. First the broad division between ruling and ruled; then within the ruling part divisions into political, religious, military, and within the ruled part divisions into food-producing classes and handicraftsmen; then within each of these divisions minor ones, and so on.

'Passing from the structural aspect to the functional aspect, we note that so long as all parts of a society have like natures and activities, there is hardly any mutual dependence, and the aggregate scarcely forms a vital whole. As its parts assume different functions they become dependent on one another, so that injury to one hurts others; until, in highly-evolved societies, general perturbation is caused by derangement of any portion. This contrast between undeveloped and developed societies, arises from the fact that with increasing specialization of functions comes increasing inability in each part to perform the functions of other parts.*

'The organization of every society begins with a contrast between the division which carries on relations, habitually hostile, with environing societies, and the division which is devoted to procuring necessaries of life; and during the earlier stages of development these two divisions constitute the whole. Eventually there arises an intermediate division serving to transfer products and influences from part to part. And in all subsequent stages, evolution of the two earlier systems of structures depends on evolution of this additional system.

'While the society as a whole has the character of its sustaining system determined by the character of its environment, inorganic and organic, the respective parts of this system differentiate in adaptation to local circumstances; and, after primary industries have been thus localized and specialized, secondary industries dependent on them arise in conformity with the same principle. Further, as fast as societies become compounded and recompounded, and the distributing system develops, the parts devoted to each kind of industry, originally scattered, aggregate in the most favourable localities; and the localized industrial structures, unlike the governmental structures, grow regardless of the original lines of division.

'Increase of size, resulting from the massing of groups, necessitates means of communication; both for achieving combined offensive and defensive actions, and for exchange of products. Faint tracks, then paths, rude roads, finished roads, successively arise; and as fast as intercourse is thus facili-

---

* This entire account may be compared with Durkheim's distinction between Mechanical and Organic types of society in his *Division of Labour in Society*.

tated, there is a transition from direct barter to trading carried on by a separate class; out of which evolves a complex mercantile agency of whole-sale and retail distributors. The movement of commodities effected by this agency, beginning as a slow flux to and re-flux from certain places at long intervals, passes into rhythmical, regular, rapid currents; and materials for sustentation distributed hither and thither, from being few and crude become numerous and elaborated. Growing efficiency of transfer with greater variety of transferred products, increases the mutual dependence of parts at the same time that it enables each part to fulfil its function better.

'Unlike the sustaining system, evolved by converse with the organic and inorganic environments, the regulating system is evolved by converse, offensive and defensive, with environing societies. In primitive headless groups temporary chieftainship results from temporary war; chronic hostilities generate permanent chieftainship; and gradually from the military control results the civil control. Habitual war, requiring prompt combination in the actions of parts, necessitates subordination. Societies in which there is little subordination disappear, and leave outstanding those in which subordination is great; and so there are produced, societies in which the habit fostered by war and surviving in peace, brings about permanent submission to a government. The centralized regulating system thus evolved, is in early stages the sole regulating system. But in large societies which have become predominantly industrial, there is added a de-centralized regulating system for the industrial structures; and this, at first subject in every way to the original system, acquires at length substantial independence. Finally there arises for the distributing structures also, an independent controlling agency.

'Societies fall firstly into the classes of simple, compound, doubly-compound, trebly-compound; and from the lowest the transition to the highest is through these stages. Otherwise, though less definitely, societies may be grouped as militant and industrial; of which the one type in its developed form is organized on the principle of compulsory co-operation, while the other in its developed form is organized on the principle of voluntary co-operation. The one is characterized not only by a despotic central power, but also by unlimited political control of personal conduct; while the other is characterized not only by a democratic or representative central power, but also by limitation of political control over personal conduct.

'Lastly we noted the corollary that change in the predominant social activities brings metamorphosis. If, where the militant type has not elaborated into so rigid a form as to prevent change, a considerable industrial system arises, there come mitigations of the coercive restraints characterizing the militant type, and weakening of its structures. Conversely, where an industrial system largely developed has established freer social forms, resumption of offensive and defensive activities causes reversion towards the militant type.'*

It is worthwhile to notice, before leaving this, that Spencer did *not* predict that industrial societies would inevitably be *peaceful*.

* *Principles of Sociology*, Vol 1, pp. 581–4.

It can be seen in the last paragraph above that Spencer saw quite clearly that even when industrialization was extensively developed, an involvement in military activities would bring about some degree of 'reversion' towards an authoritarian social structure. We shall return to this point later. However, just as Spencer's over-all summary of the *facts* of social evolution is admirably clear, so also is his summary statement of how these facts can be seen to be in accordance with the general principles of evolutionary transformation which he had outlined earlier. He wrote as follows:

'The many facts contemplated unite in proving that social evolution forms a part of evolution at large. Like evolving aggregates in general, societies show *integration*, both by simple increase of mass and by coalescence and re-coalescence of masses. The change from *homogeneity* to *heterogeneity* is multitudinously exemplified; up from the simple tribe, alike in all its parts, to the civilized nation, full of structural and functional unlikenesses. With progressing integration and heterogeneity goes increasing *coherence*. We see the wandering group dispersing, dividing, held together by no bonds; the tribe with parts made more coherent by subordination to a dominant man; the cluster of tribes united in a political plexus under a chief with sub-chiefs; and so on up to the civilized nation, consolidated enough to hold together for a thousand years or more. Simultaneously comes increasing *definiteness*. Social organization is at first vague; advance brings settled arrangements which grow slowly more precise; customs pass into laws which, while gaining fixity, also become more specific in their application to varieties of actions; and all institutions, at first confusedly intermingled, slowly separate, at the same time that each within itself marks off more distinctly its component structures. Thus in all respects is fulfilled the formula of evolution. There is progress towards greater size, coherence, multiformity, and definiteness.

'Besides these general truths, a number of special truths have been disclosed by our survey. Comparisons of societies in their ascending grades, have made manifest certain cardinal facts respecting their growths, structures, and functions—facts respecting the systems of structures, sustaining, distributing, regulating, of which they are composed: respecting the relations of these structures to the surrounding conditions and the dominant forms of social activities entailed; and respecting the metamorphoses of types caused by changes in the activities. The inductions arrived at, thus consituting in rude outline an Empirical Sociology, show that in social phenomena there is a general order of co-existence and sequence; and that therefore social phenomena form the subject-matter of a science reducible, in some measure at least, to the deductive form.'*

Nothing could be clearer than these statements. What I would now like to do, however, is to take certain elements of the *explanations* of evolution which we clarified earlier, and show as clearly as possible how Spencer thought of these as possible *explanations* of

* *Principles of Sociology*, Vol. 1, pp. 584–5.

social evolution. I do not want to claim too much for Spencer here, but it is of the utmost importance to see that his scheme of analysis resting upon the concept of 'Evolution' *did* contain definite elements and dimensions of *explanation*, and that these were not all nebulous and vague. I will take some of the more important of these in turn.

Explanations of Social Evolution

(*a*) *Society is a co-ordinated system of institutions going beyond individuals, but always exists within a determinate physical context.*

The first source of explanation of the changes which occur to a society is that of the variations in the physical resources from which the society draws its sustenance. A society comes to assume a form which goes beyond particular individuals, and exercises a vast system of control over the physical environment in which it exists. But this control is never complete, and changes in the nature of the social system can sometimes be accounted for in terms of the consequences of changes in this environment. Spencer wrote as follows:

'Whatever takes place in a society results either from the undirected physical energies around, from these energies as directed by men, or from the energies of the men themselves.

'While, as among primitive tribes, men's actions are mainly independent of one another, social forces can scarcely be said to exist: they come into existence along with co-operation. The effects which can be achieved only by the joint actions of many, we may distinguish as social. At first these are obviously due to accumulated individual efforts, but as fast as societies become large and highly organized, they acquire such separateness from individual efforts as to give them a character of their own. The network of roads and railways and telegraph wires—agencies in the formation of which individual labours were so merged as to be practically lost—serve to carry on a social life that is no longer thought of as caused by the independent doings of citizens. The prices of stocks, the rates of discount, the reported demand for this or that commodity, and the currents of men and things setting to and from various localities, show us large movements and changes scarcely at all affected by the lives and deaths and deeds of persons. But these and multitudinous social activities displayed in the growth of towns, the streams of traffic in their streets, the daily issue and distribution of newspapers, the delivery of food at people's doors, etc., are unquestionably transformed individual energies, and have the same source as these energies—the food which the population consumes.

'The correlation of the social with the physical forces through the inter-mediation of the vital ones, is, however, best shown in the different amounts of activity displayed by the same society according as its members are supplied with different amounts of force from the external world. A very bad harvest is followed by a diminution of business. Factories are worked half-time; railway traffic falls; retailers find their sales lessened; and if the scarcity rises to famine, a thinning of the population still more diminishes the industrial vivacity. Conversely, an unusually abundant supply of food, occurring under conditions not otherwise unfavourable, both excites the old producing and distributing agencies and sets up new ones. The surplus social energy finds vent in speculative enterprises. Labour is expended in opening new channels of communication. There is increased encouragement to those who furnish the luxuries of life and minister to the aesthetic faculties. There are more marriages, and a greater rate of increase in population. Thus the society grows larger, more complex, and more active. When the whole of the materials for subsistence are not drawn from the area inhabited, but are partly imported, the people are still supported by certain harvests elsewhere grown at the expense of certain physical forces, and the energies they expend originate from them.'*

This is an element of explanation stemming from Spencer's general principle of the 'Equivalence of Forces'.

(b) Social growth and its directions

It would be too long a task to show in substantive detail how Spencer described the processes of the *growth* of society in such a way as to demonstrate that it was accompanied by the other characteristics of evolution: integration, differentiation and specialization, definiteness, coherence, and the like; but it is worthwhile to see in some detail how Spencer thought the *directions* of social growth could be *explained* by the principle that, following upon the 'equivalence of forces', changes 'took the direction in which they encountered least resistance'.

The *direction* of a society's growth, wrote Spencer, was that 'in which the aggregate of opposing forces is least':

'Its units have energies to be expended in self-maintenance and reproduction. These energies are met by various antagonistic energies—those of geologic origin, those of climate, of wild animals, of other human races with whom there is enmity or competition. And the tracts the society spreads over, are those in which there is the smallest total of antagonism while they yield the best supply of food and other materials which further the genesis of energies. For these reasons it happens that fertile valleys where water and vegetal products abound, are early peopled. Sea-shores, too, supplying much easily-gathered food, are lines along which mankind have commonly spread. The general fact that, so far as we can judge from the traces left by them, large societies first appeared in those warm regions where the fruits of the earth are obtainable with comparatively little exertion, and where the cost of maintaining bodily heat is but slight, is a fact of like meaning. And to these instances may be added the allied one daily furnished by emigra-

* *First Principles*, p. 197

tion, which we see going on towards countries presenting the fewest obstacles to the self-preservation of individuals, and therefore to national growth.

'Similarly with that resistance to the movements of a society which neighbouring societies offer. Each of the tribes or nations inhabiting any region, increases in numbers until it outgrows its means of subsistence. In each there is thus a force ever pressing outwards on to adjacent areas—a force antagonized by like forces in the tribes or nations occupying those areas. And the wars that result—the conquests of weaker tribes or nations, and the overrunning of their territories by the victors, are instances of social movements taking place in the directions of least resistance. Nor do the conquered peoples, when they escape extermination or enslavement, fail to show us movements which are similarly determined. For, migrating as they do to less fertile regions—taking refuge in deserts or among mountains —moving in directions where the resistances to social growth are comparatively great; they still do this only under an excess of pressure in all other directions: the physical obstacles to self-preservation they encounter, being really less than the obstacles offered by the enemies from whom they fly.

Internal social movements also may be thus interpreted. Localities naturally fitted for producing particular commodities—that is, localities in which such commodities are got at the least cost of energy . . . become localities devoted to the obtainment of these commodities. Where soil and climate render wheat a profitable crop . . . the growth of wheat becomes a dominant industry. Where wheat cannot be economically produced, oats, or rye, or maize, or potatoes, or rice, is the agricultural staple. Along seashores men support themselves with least effort by catching fish, and hence fishing becomes the occupation. And in places which are rich in coal or metallic ores, the population, finding that labour expended in raising these materials brings a larger return of food and clothing than when otherwise expended, becomes a population of miners.

'This last instance introduces us to the phenomena of exchange, which equally illustrate the general law. For the practice of barter begins, as soon as it facilitates the fulfilment of men's desires, by diminishing the exertion needed to reach the objects of those desires. When instead of growing his own corn, weaving his own cloth, sewing his own shoes, each man began to confine himself to farming, or weaving, or shoemaking; it was because each found it more laborious to make everything he wanted, than to make a great quantity of one thing and barter the surplus for other things . . .

'The process of transfer which commerce presupposes, supplies another series of examples. So long as the forces to be overcome in procuring any necessary of life in the district where it is consumed are less than the forces to be overcome in procuring it from an adjacent district, exchange does not take place. But when the adjacent district produces it with an economy that is not outbalanced by cost of transit . . . transfer commences.

'Movement in the direction of least resistance is also seen in the establishment of the channels along which intercourse takes place. At the outset, when goods are carried on the backs of men and horses, the paths chosen are those which combine shortness with levelness and freedom from ob-

293

stacles—those which are achieved with the smallest exertion. And in the subsequent formation of each highway, the course taken is that which deviates horizontally from a straight line so far only as is needful to avoid vertical deviations entailing greater labour in draught. The smallest total of obstructive forces determines the route, even in seemingly exceptional cases; as where a detour is made to avoid the opposition of a landowner. All subsequent improvements, ending in macadamized roads, canals, and railways, which reduce the antagonism of friction and gravity to a minimum, exemplify the same truth. After there comes to be a choice of roads between one point and another, we still see that the road chosen is that along which the cost of transit is the least: cost being the measure of resistance.

'When there arises a marked localization of industries, the relative growths of the populations devoted to them may be interpreted on the same principle. The influx of people to each industrial centre is determined by the payment for labour—that is, by the quantity of commodities which a given amount of effort will obtain. To say that artisans flock to places where, in consequence of facilities for production, an extra proportion of produce can be given in the shape of wages, is to say that they flock to places where there are the smallest obstacles to the support of themselves and families; and so growth of the social organism takes place where the resistance is least.

'Nor is the law less clearly to be traced in those functional changes daily going on. The flow of capital into businesses yielding the largest returns, the buying in the cheapest market and selling in the dearest, the introduction of more economical modes of manufacture, the development of better agencies for distribution, exhibit movements taking place in directions where they are met by the smallest totals of opposing forces. For if we analyse each of these changes . . . we see that all these commercial phenomena imply complicated motions set up along lines of least resistance.'*

The *explanation* of certain social changes and social developments may also be sought, in part, then, in the analysis of the forces and circumstances which the society, or the group within society, faces. This was part and parcel of Spencer's conviction that the transformations of a society will be explicable in terms of its process of 'adaptation' to its environmental circumstances, and we may note that this element of explanation is applicable *both* to societies as total entities *and* to *parts* of societies.

(c) The instability of the homogeneous
We might ask, however, what initiates this vast process of social growth, complexity, specialization in the first place? Why do not small simple groups of men stay as they are? Why do societies tend to grow into large, different systems of complex institutions, which,

* *First Principles*, pp. 214–18.

though containing more highly specialized parts are nonetheless more integrated and coherent in their articulation?

It is here that Spencer emphasized the 'instability of the homogeneous' as an explanatory principle. It is, he argued, well-nigh impossible for a large number of very similar units to *remain* very similar. For their reactions to each other *give rise to differences* among them, which tend to be perpetuated, and, in any case, some may be exposed to different sets of circumstances, which, again, may produce differences among them.

Spencer emphasized five different factors which must tend to initiate and develop differences among men who, in their simple groups, are originally relatively similar to each other.

First: men have to act in relation to each other in their various activities, and this must give rise to struggles between them. In this, some differences of 'supremacy and subordination' must come to be established.

'So long as men are constituted to act on one another, either by physical force or by force of character, the struggles for supremacy must finally be decided in favour of some class or some one; and the difference once commenced must tend to become ever more marked. Its unstable equilibrium being destroyed, the uniform must gravitate with increasing rapidity into the multiform. And so supremacy and subordination must establish themselves, as we see they do, throughout the whole structure of a society, from the great class-divisions pervading its entire body, down to village cliques, and even down to every posse of school-boys.'*

Secondly, though men may be very similar, their modes of life, circumstances and experience are bound to encounter and therefore to engender differences.

'. . . an aggregation of men *absolutely* alike *in their endowments*, would eventually undergo a similar transformation. For in the absence of uniformity in the lives severally led by them—in their occupations, physical conditions, domestic relations, and trains of thought and feeling—there must arise differences among them; and these must eventually initiate social differentiations.'†

Thirdly, even completely accidental circumstances are likely to bring about differences:

'Even inequalities of health caused by accidents will, by entailing inequalities of physical and mental power, disturb the exact balance of mutual influences among the units; and the balance once disturbed, will inevitably be lost.'‡

* *First Principles*, p. 383.
† *First Principles*, p. 383.   ‡ *Ibid.*

Fourthly, though men may be similar, they are likely to have different aptitudes and desires, and to develop different interests and abilities—which is likely to give rise to some differences of specialization. But these:

Fifthly, will be much emphasized when, as a people inhabit an ever more extensive area, quite different local and regional conditions and circumstances come to play upon them. Different occupations and different problems will be forced upon them.

'A community,' Spencer wrote, 'which, by conquest, or otherwise, has overspread a large tract, and has become so far settled that its members live and die in their respective districts, keeps its several sections in different circumstances; and then they no longer remain alike in their occupations. Those who live dispersed continue to hunt or cultivate the earth; those who spread to the sea-shore fall into maritime occupations; while the inhabitants of some spot chosen, perhaps for its centrality, as one of periodic assemblage, become traders, and a town springs up. In the adaptations of these social units to their respective functions, we see a progress from uniformity to multiformity caused by unlike incidence of forces. Later in the process of social evolution these local adaptations are greatly multiplied. Differences in soil and climate, cause the rural inhabitants in different parts of the kingdom to have their occupations partially specialized, and to become known as chiefly producing cattle, or sheep, or wheat, or oats, or hops, or fruit. People living where coal-fields are discovered are transformed into colliers; Cornishmen take to mining because Cornwall is metalliferous; and iron-manufacture is the dominant industry where ironstone is plentiful. Liverpool has taken to importing cotton, because of its proximity to the district where cotton-goods are made; and for analogous reasons Hull has become the chief port at which foreign wools are brought in. Thus in general and in detail, industrial heterogeneities of the social organism primarily depend on local influences.'*

There are several factors in the 'instability of the homogeneous', then, which are *explanations* of the beginnings of social change and differentiation.†

(d) The multiplication of effects
All these initial tendencies to differentiation are then *reinforced* in various ways. Once differences exist they breed *more* differences of stimulus and response, and cumulative experience in relation to diversities of environments. Social differences feed upon themselves,

---

* *First Principles*, p. 384.
† It is worthwhile to note that Spencer never claims that social organization and social change are 'caused'—in any simple sense—by a teleological 'utilitarianism' (a position attacked by Durkheim and others). His analysis, even of the earliest origins of differentiation in human societies, takes many factors into account— many of them going quite beyond human desire as such.

so to speak, and tend to be ever more rapid and extensive in their developments. Again Spencer gave specific examples.

First of all, the specialization of skills and occupations, once it has emerged, tends to establish itself.

'Consider the growth of industrial organization. When some individual of a tribe displays unusual aptitude for making weapons, which were before made by each man for himself, there arises a tendency towards the differentiation of that individual into a maker of weapons. His companions, warriors and hunters all of them, severally wishing to have the best weapons that can be made, are certain to offer strong inducements to this skilled individual to make weapons for them. He, on the other hand, having both an unusual faculty, and an unusual liking, for making weapons (capacity and desire being commonly associated), is predisposed to fulfil these commissions on the offer of adequate rewards: especially as his love of distinction is also gratified. This first specialization of functions, once commenced, tends ever to become more decided. On the side of the weapon-maker, continued practice gives increased skill. On the side of his clients, cessation of practice entails decreased skill. Thus this social movement tends to become more decided in the direction in which it was first set up; and the incipient heterogeneity is, on the average of cases, likely to become permanent for that generation, if no longer.'*

Secondly, this relatively simple specialization implies a system of barter and exchange, so that a wider impetus is given to additional specializations.

This extension of specialization is accentuated, thirdly, by the increase of population, which again is a cumulative process.

'An *addition* to the number of citizens', Spencer wrote, 'involving a greater demand for every commodity, intensifies the functional activity of each specialized person or class; and this renders the specialization more definite where it exists, and establishes it where it is nascent. By increasing the pressure on the means of subsistence, a larger population again augments these results; since every individual is forced more and more to confine himself to that which he can do best, and by which he can gain most. And this industrial progress opens the way for further growth of population which reacts as before.'†

The extraordinary ramifications which such specialization ultimately comes to have for the entire structure of a complicated society is very colourfully given by Spencer's illustration of the effects of the invention of the 'locomotive engine'.

'Let us confine ourselves to the latest embodiment of steam-power—the locomotive engine. This, as the proximate cause of our railway-system, has changed the face of the country, the course of trade, and the habits of the people. Consider, first, the complicated sets of changes that precede the

* *First Principles*, p. 408.   † *Ibid.*, p. 409.

making of every railway—the provisional arrangements, the meetings, the registration, the trial-section, the parliamentary survey, the lithographed plans, the books of reference, the local deposits and notices, the application to Parliament, the passing Standing-Orders Committee, the first, second, and third readings: each of which brief heads indicates a multiplicity of transactions, and a further development of sundry occupations, (as those of engineers, surveyors, lithographers, parliamentary agents, share-brokers), and the creation of sundry others (as those of traffic-takers, reference-makers). Consider, next, the yet more marked changes implied in railway construction—the cuttings, embankings, tunnellings, diversions of roads; the building of bridges, viaducts, and stations; the laying down of ballast, sleepers, and rails; the making of engines, tenders, carriages, and wagons: which processes, acting upon numerous trades, increase the importation of timber, the quarrying of stone, the manufacture of iron, the mining of coal, the burning of bricks; institute a variety of special manufacturers weekly advertised in the *Railway Times*; and call into being some new classes of workers—drivers, stokers, cleaners, plate-layers, signalmen. Then come the changes, more numerous and involved still, which railways in action produce on the community at large. The organization of every business is modified. Ease of communication makes it better to do directly what was before done by proxy; agencies are established where previously they would not have paid; goods are obtained from remote wholesale houses instead of near retail ones; and commodities are used which distance once rendered inaccessible. Rapidity and economy of carriage tend to specialize more than ever the industries of different districts—to confine each manufacture to the parts in which, from local advantages, it can be best carried on. Cheap distribution equalizes prices, and also, on the average, lowers prices: thus bringing divers articles within the reach of those before unable to buy them. At the same time the practice of travelling is immensely extended. People who before could not afford it, take annual trips to the sea, visit their distant relations, make tours, and so are benefited in body, feelings, and intellect. The prompter transmission of letters and of news produces further changes—makes the pulse of the nation faster. Yet more, there arises a wide dissemination of cheap literature through railway book-stalls, and of advertisements in railway carriages: both of them aiding ulterior progress. So that beyond imagination are the changes, thus briefly indicated, consequent on the invention of the locomotive engine.'*

Here again, then, Spencer sought to provide *explanatory* principles in his elaboration of the 'Multiplication of Effects'.

(e) Segregation
Once these differences have been established, a certain 'selectivity' also takes place in the ways in which they will develop. A certain 'segregation' of specialist groups and classes and organized associations takes place, and here Spencer attempted to introduce

---

* *First Principles*, pp. 410–11.

certain factors which could explain the 'composition' of society, or the 'distribution' or 'localization' within it of particular groups. To some extent these elements of explanation were further aspects of his earlier discussion of the 'direction of social growth'.

Firstly, Spencer argued that geographical factors determined a certain 'segregation' of mankind in the world.

'Of the forces which effect and maintain the segregations of mankind, may first be named those external ones classed as physical conditions. The climate and food which are favourable to an indigenous people, are more or less detrimental to an alien people of different bodily constitution. In tropical regions the northern races cannot permanently exist: if not killed off in the first generation, they are so in the second, and, as in India, can maintain their footing only by the artificial process of continuous immigration and emigration. That is to say, the external forces acting equally on the inhabitants of a given locality, tend to expel all who are not of a certain type, and thus to keep up the integration of those who are of that type.'*

Secondly, however, these kinds of groupings tended to give rise to 'segregations' *within* any particular society in which they might reside.

'The other forces conspiring to produce these national segregations, are those mental ones shown in the affinities of men for others like themselves. Units of one society who are obliged to reside in another, generally form colonies in the midst of that other—small societies of their own. Races which have been artificially severed, show tendencies to re-unite . . . The feelings characterizing a member of a given race, are feelings which get complete satisfaction only among other members of that race—a satisfaction partly derived from sympathy with those having like feelings, but mainly derived from the adapted social conditions which grow up where such feelings prevail.'†

Thirdly, similar 'segregations' arose from specialist groups and classes within each society.

'During the development of each society we see analogous segregations caused in analogous ways . . . Those most important ones which constitute political and industrial organizations, result from the union of men in whom similarities have been produced by training. Men brought up to bodily labour are men who have had wrought in them a certain likeness— a likeness which, in respect of their powers of action, obscures and subordinates their natural differences. Those trained to brain-work have acquired a certain other community of character which makes them, as social units, more like one another than like those trained to manual occupations. And there arise class-segregations answering to these super-

* *First Principles*, p. 431.
† *Ibid.*, p. 431. Compare all these points with Giddings on the 'Consciousness of Kind', p. 544.

induced likenesses. More definite segregations take place among the more definitely assimilated members of any class who are brought up to the same calling. Even where the necessities of their work forbid concentration in one locality, as among artizans happens with masons and bricklayers, and among traders happens with the retail distributors, and among professionals happens with the medical men, there are not wanting Operative Builders' Unions, and Grocers' Societies, and Medical Associations, implying a process of sifting out and grouping. And where, as among the manufacturing classes, the functions discharged do not require the dispersion of citizens who are artificially assimilated, there is an aggregation of them in special localities, and a consequent increase in the definiteness of industrial divisions.'*

And fourthly, particular local conditions in a large society—the existence of resources suitable to the pursuit of a certain trade, for example—led to a 'localization' of industries and the 'clustering' of distinctive communities.

'If there be any locality which, either by its physical peculiarities or by peculiarities wrought on it during social evolution, is rendered a place where a certain kind of industrial action meets with less resistance than elsewhere, it follows from the law of direction of motion that those social units who have been moulded to this kind of industrial action, will be segregated by moving towards this place. If, for instance, the proximity of coal and iron mines to a navigable river, gives to Glasgow an advantage in the building of iron-ships—if the total labour required to produce a given vessel, and get its equivalent in food and clothing, is less there than elsewhere; there is caused a concentration of iron-shipbuilders at Glasgow, either by detention of the population born to iron-ship building, or by immigration of those elsewhere engaged in it, or by both. The principle equally holds where the occupation is mercantile instead of manufacturing. Stock-brokers cluster where the amount of effort to be severally gone through by them in discharging their functions, and obtaining their profits, is less than elsewhere. A local exchange having once been established, becomes a place where the resistance to be overcome by each is smaller than in any other place; and, being like units under stress of common desires, pursuit of the course of least resistance by each involves their aggregation around this place.'†

(f) Equilibration
Spencer also introduced the tracing of cause and effect relationships in the changing nature of societies in his 'equilibrium—disequilibrium' analysis. The structural-functional pattern of institutions which constituted a society would change in accordance with changes encountered in its total external environment, and with changes in its internal conditions. There would be a changing

---

* *First Principles*, p. 432.   † *Ibid.*, p. 433.

disposition of the parts of a society until some appropriate 'equilibrium' was reached. A few of the factors discussed by Spencer can be briefly mentioned.

First of all, he argued that the population of a society was continuously in process of adapting itself to its material subsistence.

'Each society,' he wrote, 'displays the process of equilibration in the continuous adjustment of its population to its means of subsistence. A tribe of men living on wild animals and fruits, is manifestly, like every tribe of inferior creatures, always oscillating from side to side of that average number which the locality can support. Though, by artificial production unceasingly improved, a superior race continually alters the limit which external conditions put to population; yet there is ever a checking of population at the temporary limit reached.'*

Secondly, he discussed the many ways in which the many aspects of the economic, or industrial system, of a society are continuously adjusting themselves to the forces of 'supply and demand'. In this the 'equilibrium' analysis of economics is seen as part of a wider sociological explanation. This is clear enough, but Spencer had interesting things to say about the changing nature of such economic 'equilibrium situations' as a society developed towards the maximal use of its known resources. One example might be given:

'During early stages of social evolution, while the resources of the locality inhabited are unexplored and the arts of production undeveloped, there is never anything more than a temporary and partial balancing of such actions. But when a society approaches the maturity of that type on which it is organized, the various industrial activities settle down into a comparatively constant state. Moreover, advance in organization, as well as advance in growth, is conducive to a better equilibrium of industrial functions. While the diffusion of mercantile information is slow and the means of transport deficient, the adjustment of supply to demand is very imperfect. Great over-production of a commodity is followed by great under-production, and there results a rhythm having extremes that depart widely from the mean state in which demand and supply are equilibrated. But when good roads are made and there is a rapid diffusion of printed or written intelligence, and still more when railways and telegraphs come into existence—when the periodical fairs of early days grow into weekly markets, and these into daily markets, there is gradually produced a better balance of production and consumption: the rapid oscillations of price within narrow limits on either side of a comparatively uniform mean, indicate a near approach to equilibrium.'†

Thirdly, Spencer discussed political institutions in 'equilibrium-disequilibrium' terms in a very interesting way, and in a way

---

* *First Principles*, p. 457.　　　　† *Ibid.*, pp. 458–9.

remarkably reminiscent of Kant's principle of the 'Unsociable-Sociability of man'.

'On the one hand,' he wrote, 'there is in each man more or less of resistance against restraints imposed on his actions by other men—a resistance which, tending ever to widen each man's sphere of action, and reciprocally to limit the spheres of action of other men, constitutes a repulsive force mutually exercised by the members of a social aggregate. On the other hand, the general sympathy of man for man and the more special sympathy of each variety of man for others of the same variety, together with allied feelings which the social state gratifies, act as an attractive force, tending ever to keep united those who have a common ancestry. And since the resistances to be overcome in satisfying the totality of their desires when living separately, are greater than the resistances to be overcome in satisfying the totality of their desires when living together, there is a residuary force that prevents separation. Like other opposing forces, those exerted by citizens on one another produce alternating movements which, at first extreme, undergo gradual diminution on the way to ultimate equilibrium.'*

Again, Spencer had interesting things to say about the gradual development of institutions in dealing with such 'oppositions' in society, and his view was that a 'moving equilibrium' can be reached when political institutions reflect these oppositions so effectively as to make necessary adjustments ever more marginal.

'Each primitive nation,' he wrote, 'exhibits wide oscillations between an extreme in which the subjects are under rigid restraint, and an extreme in which the restraint fails to prevent rebellion and disintegration. In more advanced nations of like type, we always find violent actions and reactions of the same essential nature: "despotism tempered by assassination", characterizing a political state in which unbearable repression from time to time brings about a bursting of bonds. Among ourselves the conflicts between Conservatism (which stands for the restraints of society over the individual) and Reform (which stands for the liberty of the individual against society), fall within slowly approximating limits; so that thie temporary predominance of either produces a less marked deviation from the medium state—a smaller disturbance of the moving equilibrium.'†

The close approximation between many of the policies of the 'opposed' political parties in contemporary Britain is a good example of what Spencer had in mind.

Societies as total entities, then, and the parts of any society in their interrelationships, could be analysed in relation to environmental conditions, and changes in them could, in part, be *explained* by 'equilibrium—disequilibrium' adjustments.

(g) Dissolution
Sometimes, however, societies are overcome by conditions which

---

* *First Principles*, p. 460.　　　　† *Ibid.*, pp. 460–1.

destroy them. Sometimes, the power of the forces making for 'disequilibrium' is such that there is a failure to adapt to them. Then there follows an 'undoing' of the coherent, definite, integrated pattern of institutions which had existed, and a sequence of incoherence, indefiniteness, and disintegration follows in its place. Even this process of *dissolution*, however, Spencer argued, can be systematically analysed and *explained*.

'. . . social disorder,' he wrote, 'however caused, entails a decrease of integrated movements and an increase of disintegrated movements. As the disorder progresses the political actions previously combined become uncombined: there arise the antagonistic actions of riot or revolt. Simultaneously, the industrial and commercial processes that were co-ordinated throughout the body politic, are broken up; and only the local, or small, trading transactions continue. And each further disorganizing change diminishes the joint operations by which men satisfy their wants, and leaves them to satisfy their wants, as best they can by separate operations.'*

Sometimes, this disorder may be brought about by direct conquest; but sometimes it is an outcome of being drawn suddenly under the influence of quite different environmental circumstances and pressures. Spencer gave the highly interesting example of Japanese society, and we might note that this was written in 1867.

'Of the way in which such disintegrations are set up in a society that has evolved to the limit of its type, and reached a state of moving equilibrium, a good illustration is furnished by Japan. The finished fabric into which its people had organized themselves, maintained an almost constant state so long as it was preserved from fresh external forces. But as soon as it received an impact from European civilization, partly by armed aggression, partly by commercial impulse, partly by the influence of ideas, this fabric began to fall to pieces. There is now in progress a political dissolution. Probably a political reorganization will follow; but, be this as it may, the change thus far produced by an outer action is a change towards dissolution—a change from integrated motions to disintegrated motions.'†

In general, however, a developed society can become so rigid as not to be able to accommodate itself with sufficient flexibility and speed to new competitive pressures from outside, and then, too, gradual decline and disintegration can occur.

'Decline of numbers is, in such case, brought about partly by emigration; for a society having the fixed structure in which evolution ends, is one that will not yield and modify under pressure of population: so long as its structure is plastic it is still evolving. Hence the surplus population is continually dispersed: the influences brought to bear on the citizens by other societies cause their detachment, and there is an increase of the uncom-

* *First Principles*, p. 466.   † *Ibid.*, p. 466.

bined motions of units instead of an increase of combined motions. Gradually as the society becomes still less capable of changing into the form required for successful competition with more plastic societies, the number of citizens who can live within its unyielding framework becomes positively smaller. Hence it dwindles both through continued emigration and through the diminished multiplication that follows innutrition.'*

Even, then, when societies *fail* to come to terms with their environments and are either gradually or suddenly dissolved, grounds of *explanation* can be given within Spencer's conceptual scheme of the 'evolution' of 'systems' in the contexts of their environments.

It is totally beyond doubt, then, that Spencer's elaborate account of social evolution was one of systematic *explanation* as well as one of detailed *description*. A few special points in connection with this deserve quite firm and distinctive emphasis, but these can be delayed for a moment in order to note the kind of thing Spencer had to say about *particular* social institutions within his *general* scheme of comparative study.

Specific Institutions: Examples

We have already seen quite clearly that, within his classificatory schema, Spencer studied each major social institution (each 'part' of society) and each major 'system' of institutions ('regulating', 'sustaining', etc.,) in detail: examining the nature and functions of each in each 'type' of society (*both* in terms of social 'composition' *and* in terms of whether they approximated to the Militant or Industrial types) and clarifying the changes which characterized the 'transformations' from one type to another—especially the changes attendant upon industrialization. It is important to emphasize how *consistent* Spencer was in this. Every element of social structure was dealt with in turn according to his schema, and no study could have been carried out more systematically than his. This, again, needs emphasis because of much misleading criticism to the contrary.†

---

* *First Principles*, pp. 466–7.

† For example, Timasheff (*Sociological Theory: Its Nature and Growth*, Double-day, 1955 pp. 30–42) quotes Spencer: 'We must learn, by inspection, the relations of co-existence and sequence in which social phenomena stand to one another. By comparing societies of different kinds and societies in different stages, we must ascertain what traits of size, structure, function are associated with one another.' —and then goes on to say: 'This principle, however, did not guide his own procedures . . .' and, '. . . as material he used mainly illustrations from ethnology.' Such criticism is purely assertive, and totally unfounded. Spencer, in addition to ethnological data, used the widest range of historical and contemporary material,

What I think it important to do, however, is to give at least some indication of the kinds of comments his studies led him to make about just one or two particular institutions. This will give at least some impression of the quality of his observations and insights and the value of his analysis in providing a perspective within which the contemporary changes of institutions can be judged. Here, I select some of Spencer's comments on 'Domestic Institutions' and 'Ecclesiastical Institutions', but equally telling comments could be selected from every institutional field.

(a) The Family and Marriage in society

Here are a few of Spencer's *predictions* about the changes in the nature of marriage and of the relations between parents and children in the family which are attendant, in his view, upon the processes of industrialization and the many social conditions—of scientific knowledge, urbanization, etc., which go with it.

(i) Firstly, he maintained that as the conditions of industrialization spread throughout the world, there would be a spread of 'monogamy'. Furthermore, the growth of disapproval of many earlier practices—of the abduction of women, the practice of marriage for money, or status, or the arrangement of marriage by elders, and the like— could be expected, he said, to 'purify' the monogamous marriage by making it, in all cases, *real*—a *chosen* union between two parties of equal status, and resting upon personal affection—rather than, in many cases, nominal.

(ii) Secondly, he wrote:

'As monogamy is likely to be raised in character by a public sentiment requiring that the legal bond shall not be entered into unless it represents the natural bond, so perhaps it may be that maintenance of the legal bond will come to be held improper if the natural bond ceases. Already, increased facilities for divorce point to the probability that whereas, while permanent monogamy was being evolved, the union by law was regarded as the essential part of marriage, and the union by affection as non-essential, and whereas at present the union by law is thought the more important and the union by affection the less important, there will come a time when the union by affection will be held of primary moment, and the union by law as of secondary moment, whence reprobation of marital relations in which the union by affection has dissolved.'*

referring to societies of all types, and his actual studies followed his proposals of method precisely. One can only ask students to *read* Spencer and judge for themselves. Indeed, the explanations of social change and differentiation we have already mentioned—briefly though we have dealt with them—many be compared with one of the most recent accounts of social evolution: that of Talcott Parsons —*Society: Comparative and Evolutionary Perspectives.*

* *Principles of Sociology*, Vol. 1, p. 753.

When making this point, Spencer was by no means under any illusion that it would be understood, popular, or well-received.

'That this conclusion will be at present unacceptable,' he said, 'is likely, I may say certain.'

(iii) This view did not lead Spencer to think pessimistically about any decline in the stability of marriage or the family. He wrote:

'those higher sentiments accompanying union of the sexes, which do not exist among primitive men, and were less developed in earlier European times than now, may be expected to develop still more as decline of militancy and of industrialism foster altruism, for sympathy which is the root of altruism is a chief element in these sentiments. Moreover, with an increase of altruism must go a decrease of domestic dissension, whence, simultaneously, a strengthening of the moral bond and a weakening of the forces tending to destroy it, so that the changes which may further facilitate divorce under certain conditions, are changes which will make those conditions more and more rare.'*

(iv) Spencer also said that a strengthening of the bond between husband and wife resting upon their joint interest in their children might be anticipated. This factor, he said, must become stronger as the solicitude for the care and education of children becomes greater and more prolonged, as we have seen that it does with progressing industrial civilization, and will doubtless continue to do. The implication, he maintained, was that 'welfare of offspring must hereafter determine the course of domestic evolution'.

(v) Concerning the status of women, he said that a continual movement towards the equality of status between the sexes would take place. With the development of industrialism, with a decrease of compulsory co-operation and an increase of voluntary co-operation, with a strengthening sense of personal rights and an accompanying sympathetic regard for the personal rights of others, there must go, he thought, a diminution of the political and domestic disabilities of women until there would remain only those resting on differences of personal constitution.

'That in time to come,' he said, 'the political status of women may be raised to something like equality with that of men, seems a deduction naturally accompanying the preceding ones.'†

(vi) Having considered the changing nature of parental authority, which was resting increasingly upon responsible concern, Spencer also concluded that relationships between parents and children

---

* *Principles of Sociology*, Vol. 1, p. 754.　　　　† *Ibid.*, p. 757.

would come into being which would need no external control to ensure their sensitive, reciprocal concern and their good working.

These predictions, made in 1879 require, I think, no detailed comment. The qualities of Spencer's analysis are borne out by their aptness. Every one is sound. Every one has occurred as he supposed. Indeed, the judgments underlying them are more acute and advanced than many people in our own day are capable of. The new Divorce Law Reform Bill (1968) and the new 'Family Law' proposals (1969) rest exactly upon the judgments Spencer made clear, and the arguments advanced by opponents of these reforms of the law rest upon assessments of social change which have still not caught up with the contributions of Spencer's analysis. At least *some* of the Great Victorians, a hundred years ago, possessed a social knowledge and a progressive judgment which was far more soundly based than those of many politicians, churchmen, and administrators in the nineteen-sixties.

(b) Religion in society

The same aptness can be demonstrated in what Spencer had to say about the nature, functions and development of religion in society.

In his study of 'Ecclesiastical Institutions', Spencer offered a far more detailed analysis of the effects of industrialization upon the nature, organization, and changing functions of religion than anyone before him, and, indeed, a more comprehensive analysis than that offered by Durkheim a good deal later, (and Durkheim is, according to some, the scholar of greatest originality in the sociological analysis of religion).

Spencer offered a theory of the 'origins' of religion in 'ancestor-worship'; in the fear and love felt by the living for the dead, (and hence accounted for the 'compound' emotion of 'awe' which was at the heart of religion). But also, going far beyond this, he discussed the distinction between magic and religion, the tendencies to move from polytheism to monotheism with the growth of knowledge and, especially, the emergence and nature of 'ecclesiastical hierarchies' and the social functions which they—in conjunction with the doctrines and rituals they served—performed. In short, he studied the *organization* of religions, and traced their connections with political, military, judicial, and other organizations in society. His was, in fact, a truly *sociological* analysis of religion.

In all this, he analysed religion as a 'supplementary regulatory' system, reinforcing the political and judicial systems, and as a system of doctrines and rituals insisting on obedience to authority and reinforcing the 'social bond' in society. He clarified the ways in which 'ecclesiastical hierarchies' had been involved in military, political and judicial authority and its maintenance; how, in educative functions, they were important elements in instilling 'socializing disciplines'; how they were essentially conservative in their social influences: preserving 'verities', defending the 'cult' and 'institutionalized religion', sustaining reverence for existing authority, upholding the existing nature of 'property', and engendering appropriate sentiments by their modes of collective worship. His analysis was detailed and his comparative study was very wide in its range.

Again, however, we might best gain an impression of the quality of his treatment by considering what he had to say about religion in modern industrial society, and what the tendencies of development were.

Spencer thought that although Ecclesiastical Institutions held a less important place in industrial societies than in traditional societies of a simpler kind, they were not likely to disappear, but to change.

First of all, he thought that the tendency towards the separation of ecclesiastical institutions from the political institutions with which they had been initially fused would, in industrial society, become complete. There would be a very considerable extension of secularization. Spencer thought, as part of this tendency in Britain, for example, that there would be a growing pressure towards the disestablishment of the Church of England. Religion and priests would lose their earlier 'coercive' authority.

Secondly, he thought that with the growth of knowledge and critical reflection upon earlier dogmas, there would be an increase in the *number* of religious bodies, independent of the State, with respective differences of belief and practice. There would tend to be a growth of 'sects' in society; a multiplicity of points of view in religious belief and behaviour.

Thirdly, he thought that within the government and organization of the larger churches and religious bodies there would be a strong tendency for *central* power and authority to decline; and for the relative autonomy of local groups and individuals (priests or lay members) to increase. This would be a continuity of a marked trend towards the 'relinquishment' of central priestly (or ecclesiastical) power which was already considerably advanced among the 'Dissenters'.

However, Spencer did not think this 'de-centralization' *inevitable*. If there was a 'recrudescence of militancy'—which he thought might well be the case—then there could also be a simultaneous reversal of this tendency.

In all this, too, Spencer thought that there would be a marked shift of emphasis in the functions of the churches and priests in society.

In the past, the chief priestly duty was that of 'officiating' in modes of worship, and the insisting on rules of conduct was related to this. With the development of a scientific, industrial, secular society the first function, Spencer said, would become of much diminished importance, and the second—the detailed concern about morality in society—would greatly increase.

'The insistence on duty . . .' Spencer wrote, 'may be expected to assume a marked predominance and a wider range. The conduct of life, parts of which are already the subject-matters of sermons, may hereafter, probably be taken as subject-matter throughout its entire range. The ideas of right and wrong, now regarded as applying only to actions of certain kinds, will be regarded as having applications coextensive with actions of every kind. All matters concerning individual and social welfare will come to be dealt with; and a chief function of one who stands in the place of a minister, will be not so much that of emphasizing precepts already accepted, as that of developing men's judgments and sentiments in relation to those more difficult questions of conduct arising from the ever-increasing complexity of social life.'*

The concern for morality in all directions of personal life and social welfare would therefore come to supersede the emphasis upon modes of ritual and worship, and the emphasis upon doctrines about the nature of God and theological 'truths' as such.

Spencer, then, had much of interest to say about the fate of the religious *doctrines* of the past, and the effects of scientific ways of thinking and knowing upon the nature of the 'religious consciousness'.

On the one hand he thought there was no doubt whatever that the specific religious theories or doctrines of the past were doomed. The growing sophistication of thought would increasingly show the 'anthropomorphic' nature of earlier doctrines. Higher moral sentiments would make it increasingly repugnant to continue to attribute to God motives which no decent human being ought to be guilty of. And, in general, these early doctrines would be revealed as the relatively crude pictures of reality which they really were.

Notions of original sin, atonement, hell and damnation, in Christianity, for example, would be rejected as men came to see the crudity and injustice of the old orthodox story.

'The visiting on Adam's descendants,' Spencer wrote, 'through hundreds of generations, of dreadful penalties for a small transgression which they did not commit; the damning of all men who do not avail themselves of an alleged mode of obtaining forgiveness, which most men have never heard

* *Principles of Sociology*, Vol. III, p. 157.

of; and the effecting a reconciliation by sacrificing a son who was perfectly innocent, to satisfy the assumed necessity for a propitiatory victim; are modes of action which, ascribed to a human ruler, would call forth expressions of abhorrence; and the ascription of them to the Ultimate Cause of things, even now felt to be full of difficulties, must become impossible.

So, too, must die out the belief that a Power present in innumerable worlds throughout infinite space, and who during millions of years of the Earth's earlier existence needed no honouring by its inhabitants, should be seized with a craving for praise; and having created mankind, should be angry with them if they do not perpetually tell him how great he is. As fast as men escape from that glamour of early impressions which prevents them from thinking, they will refuse to imply a trait of character which is the reverse of worshipful.'*

The new methods and knowledge of science would properly move men away from such doctrines to a responsible 'agnosticism', Spencer thought. At the same time this did not mean that men would cease to feel the 'religious consciousness'; would cease to be perplexed and moved by the enigma of the world; would cease to feel wonder at the very existence of things. On the contrary—and this is a very important point which Spencer rightly emphasized— the scientific picture of the world is such, really, as to *increase* man's sense of amazement. The man of science, far *more* than the untutored man, realizes the complex nature of the world; he realizes much more profoundly, too, the *limitations* of his knowledge. Science therefore *enlarges* rather than *reduces* the range of the 'religious consciousness'; it is only the dogmas about it that it can no longer accept. Indeed, it cannot accept these dogmas *because* of an enlarged consciousness of the nature of things. It is religious men, one might almost say, who most emphatically reject religions.

Even within religious bodies, and among priests, this element of sustaining the religious consciousness will therefore remain, despite absence of convincing dogma.

'. . . it does not follow,' said Spencer, 'that there will lapse all observances tending to keep alive a consciousness of the relation in which we stand to the Unknown Cause, and tending to give expression to the sentiment accompanying that consciousness. There will remain a need for qualifying that too prosaic and material form of life which tends to result from absorption in daily work, and there will ever be a sphere for those who are able to impress their hearers with a due sense of the Mystery in which the origin and meaning of the Universe are shrouded. It may be anticipated, too, that musical expression to the sentiment accompanying this sense will not only survive but undergo further development. Already protestant cathedral music, more impersonal than any other, serves not unfitly to

* *Principles of Sociology*, Vol. III, pp. 166–7.

express feelings suggested by the thought of a transitory life, alike of the individual and of the race—a life which is but an infinitesimal product of a Power without any bounds we can find or imagine; and hereafter such music may still better express these feelings.'*

Both the sense of wonder and the sense of moral duty which mankind possesses are therefore likely to be increased and to become more sophisticated in modern scientific society, but man's ability to be *certain* about matters of spiritual and metaphysical dogma will necessarily be much diminished, and honesty and integrity demand that this should be recognized. No harm is necessarily done by this. We can do nothing better than to devote ourselves, with careful scepticism, to a pursuit of the truth. 'The highest truth he sees,' said Spencer (about 'modern man') 'he will fearlessly utter, knowing that, let what may come of it, he is thus playing his right part in the world knowing that if he can effect the change he aims at—well; if not—well also; though not so well.'

But Spencer wanted to emphasize that, quite beyond religious organizations as such, the religious consciousness could be enlarged, not diminished, by science.

'Those who think,' he wrote, 'that science is dissipating religious beliefs and sentiments seem unaware that whatever of mystery is taken from the old interpretation, is added to the new. Or rather, we may say that transference from the one to the other is accompanied by increase; since, for an explanation which has a seeming feasibility, science substitutes an explanation which, carrying us back only a certain distance, there leaves us in presence of the avowedly inexplicable.

'Under one of its aspects, scientific progress is a gradual transfiguration of nature. Where ordinary perception saw perfect simplicity, it reveals great complexity; where there seemed absolute inertness, it discloses intense activity; and in what appears mere vacancy it finds a marvellous play of forces.'†

'This awareness,' he said, 'possesses: . . . an accompanying feeling as much beyond that of the present cultured man as his feeling is beyond that of the savage. And this feeling is not likely to be decreased, but to be increased by that analysis of knowledge which, while forcing him to agnosticism, yet continually prompts him to imagine some solution of the Great Enigma which he knows cannot be solved. Especially must this be so when he remembers that the very notions, origin, cause and purpose, are relative notions belonging to human thought, which are probably irrelevant; and when, though suspecting that explanation is a word without meaning when applied to this Ultimate Reality, he yet feels compelled to think that there must be an explanation.

'But one truth must grow ever clearer—the truth that there is an Inscrutable Existence everywhere manifested, to which he can neither find nor

* *Principles of Sociology*, Vol. III, p. 157.   † *Ibid.*, pp. 171–2.

conceive either beginning or end. Amid the mysteries which become the more mysterious the more they are thought about, there will remain the one absolute certainty, that he is ever in presence of an Infinite and Eternal Energy from which all things proceed.'*

Again, everything that Spencer said about the changing nature of religion in industrial society can be seen to be most apt with regard to what has happened since his day, and, indeed, with regard to what is happening *now*. Modern theological writings such as those—to take one example—of the Bishop of Woolwich bear out all the tendencies of doctrine to which Spencer pointed. And the tensions within even the Roman Catholic Church over the matter of birth control is evidence of the increasing pressures against central power and authority and towards the discrimination of individual priests and lay members.

These two examples, at any rate—on the Family and Religion in society—substantiate the modernity of Spencer, and the continued utility and validity of much that he had to say about specific social institutions.

Points of special emphasis

There remain a number of points about Spencer's entire system of analysis which need special emphasis with regard to our central concern to clarify the making of sociology.

(a) Spencer and Comte: the similarity of concern
The over-all similarity between Comte and Spencer in terms of their conceptions of scientific knowledge and 'laws'; their conceptions of societies, the parts of which they consisted, the classificatory, comparative and historical methods by which they should be studied, and the like, are already so apparent as to need no further elaboration: excepting simply to note this strong continuity in the making of the subject.

One element of their treatment does, however, deserve special remark—and that is the same persuasion and concern which is apparent in their classification of 'types of society'. To be brief, Comte's 'Theological' and 'Positive' types are almost exactly the same as Spencer's 'Militant' and 'Industrial' types (it being remembered that, for Comte, the 'Metaphysical' type was a 'Transitional' and not a stable type between the Theological and the Positive). And this similarity not only refers to a substantive agree-

* *Principles of Sociology*, Vol. III, p. 175.

ment about the historical transitions of human society—which is very important, and which, as we shall see, is borne out in the work of many other scholars—but also to a shared concern: the concern, that is, for understanding the recent and present transition from traditional agrarian to modern industrial society in such a way as to make political action as wise and effective as is possible in dealing with its many complex problems.

The crucial concern of both men was that a transition of unprecedented scale and dimensions had overtaken mankind, and that a new systematic *knowledge* of society was necessary in order to deal with it.

(b) Spencer and Comte: the Future

This central agreement can be reinforced further by a brief indication of a third 'type' of society which Spencer only mentioned, but then put aside because it was really only a possibility for the future.

It will be remembered that Comte envisaged a global unity of mankind, as all societies, of all levels of development, were drawn together by the connecting influences of industrialization. Also, that he elaborated a 'Council of Europe' which would assist undeveloped countries in coming to achieve and enjoy the new and shared level of material and moral civilization in the world. In a very similar way, Spencer, too, foresaw a global drawing together of societies—not, by any means, in any simple-minded, jejune way, as we shall see later—and the possibility of what he called an 'Ethical' type of society.

The spreading interconnections of industrialization, he thought, would lead to wider areas of social co-operation; going beyond nation states to federations of states, for example. And as basic economic and political problems were dealt with in an ever more satisfactory way, men would be able to concern themselves increasingly with cultural activities—with the more refined arts of living.

'Were this the fit place,' he wrote, 'some pages might be added respecting a possible future social type, differing as much from the industrial as this does from the militant, a type which having a sustaining system more fully developed than any we know at present, will use the products of industry neither for maintaining a militant organization, nor exclusively for material aggrandizement, but will devote them to the carrying on of higher activities* As the contrast between the militant and the industrial types is indicated by inversion of the belief that individuals exist for the benefit of the state into the belief that the state exists for the benefit of individuals, so the contrast between the industrial type and the type likely to be evolved

---

* This was a persuasion later adopted by John Maynard Keynes.

313

from it, is indicated by inversion of the belief that life is for work into the belief that work is for life.'

With characteristic realism, however, Spencer went on,

'But we are here concerned with inductions derived from societies that *have been* and *are* and cannot enter into speculations respecting societies that may be.'*

This is all that Spencer had to say about the ethical type of society, but it is enough to see that his analysis of social evolution did not pretend to finality, and that it led him to a consideration of a kind of social life which, he thought, was possibly on the point of coming into being after the full development of industrialization, when a level of productivity of wealth had been achieved far greater than that possible in the society of his own time. And this was very similar both to the vision of Comte before him, and to the vision of Marx whose ideas we shall be considering shortly.

(c) The increase of Functional Coherence in society
A further agreement of substance and emphasis between Comte and Spencer is also worth noting, as it is one of the central points of all the major theories of society during the nineteenth century, and, as we shall see, is now receiving renewed emphasis in contemporary sociology. Spencer's system of analysis and explanation led him to full agreement with Comte that the more societies developed in their structural-functional complexity, and the more that all societies became drawn together in economic, political, and cultural involvement in common problems and concerns, the more *coherent* and *definite* they became, and—therefore—the more *predictable*. The more differentiated societies became in their global interdependency, the more they moved towards a similarity and predictability of institutionalization. Paradoxical though it may sound, then, both writers maintained that sociological analysis yielded *more precise* descriptions and explanations when studying more complex but more highly articulated social systems than it could when studying a multitude of simple but homogeneous groups.

Properly understood, this point is of great importance, because it is a telling argument against the criticism that sociology must grow more and more incapable of managing its subject-matter as societies become more complex. Both Comte and Spencer agreed in arguing that the reverse was the case.

In Spencer, of course, this point took the form of demonstrating the greater *functional coherence* of the interdependent parts of

* *Principles of Sociology*, Vol. I, p. 563.

society as structural and functional differentiation took place, and as this proceeded between and among, as well as within, societies as wholes.

Concerning political interdependency, Spencer wrote:

'Of the European nations it may be remarked that in the tendency to form alliances, in the restraining influences exercised by governments over one another, in the system of settling international arrangements by congresses, as well as in the weakening of commercial barriers and the increasing facilities of communication, we see the beginnings of a European federation —a still larger integration than any now established.'*

And this extension of political interconnection would grow, he thought, throughout the world. And of functional differentiation and 'segregation' among all societies of the world, he wrote:

'. . . beginning with a primitive tribe, almost if not quite homogeneous in the functions of its members, the progress has been, and still is, towards an economic aggregation of the whole human race; growing ever more hetero- geneous in respect of the separate functions assumed by separate nations, the separate functions assumed by the local sections of each nation, the separate functions assumed by the many kinds of producers in each place, and the separate functions assumed by the workers united in growing or making each commodity . . .'†

In short, all societies in the world were moving towards an in- creasing degree of interdependence—taking the form of a vast network of functional differentiation embracing them all. And the more this developed, the more definite the sociological analysis and knowledge of them could be.

This is a point of considerable interest which tends, firstly, to be borne out, in the sense that modern sociologists now draw up many of their generalizations in terms of the correlates of industrialization: 'education in an industrial society', 'the family in an industrial society', 'law in an industrial society', and so on. There is a wide agreement that the process of modern industrialization has certain predictable institutional concomitants, no matter what the nature of the traditional society in which it develops, and which it transforms. Indeed, many contemporary generalizations about social change are focused upon the transition brought about in 'Traditional' societies by the process of 'industrialization', and, more recently, 'moderni- zation'. But secondly, it is an encouraging point, in the sense that it allows us to expect, not purely in terms of optimistic desire, but on reasonably firm intellectual grounds, that we may be able to establish a body of reliable knowledge about the regularities of our institutions

---

* *First Principles*, p. 282.   † *Ibid.*, p. 311.

and problems in the context of industrialization, and thus be able to deal adequately and effectively with them.

(*d*) *Spencer's account of Evolution* not *unilinear* or *inevitable* or *of total uniformity*

These first three points of emphasis have immediately, however, to be qualified by, and seen within the context of a fourth, which is, perhaps, the most important point of all.

Spencer has been massively and militantly criticized on certain supposed aspects of his theory of evolution. He has been criticized for advancing a *unilinear* theory of social evolution: that the line of evolution is always in the one direction from simplicity to complexity, from homogeneity to heterogeneity, and the like. He has been criticized for claiming that this *unilinear* direction of evolution was *inevitable*, and, on the grounds of this inevitability, for '*prophesying*' what, in future, it would be like, and for being inconsistent in— at one and the same time—predicting the *inevitable* course of change and proposing that statesmanship was able to do something responsibly to *qualify* it. He has been criticized for claiming that all societies, in this unilinear evolution, must inevitably pass through the same determinate *stages*, or '*types*', and must move from the 'militant' to the 'industrial'. And, sometimes, he has been thought guilty of claiming an ultimate *uniformity* of social institutions throughout the world as the ultimate pattern of differentiation and coherence comes to be achieved.

Now a detailed reading of Spencer will show that he was open to *none* of these criticisms; that his fundamental position was quite different from that suggested in them; and that his statements on all these matters were far more qualified and careful than they suggest.

It is true, as we have seen, that Spencer described a certain process of evolutionary change which characterized all the kinds of 'aggregates' known in nature—from planetary systems to societies; and it is also true that he maintained that the directions and the extent of this process (of increasing differentiation, definiteness, coherence, etc.) in any aggregate would accord with the extent of environmental influences, and would pass through a certain sequence in its adjustment to an 'equilibrium' situation within the context of these influences. He did not think, for example, that a simple social aggregate of clans within a tribe would be likely to become a highly industrialized society—manufacturing aeroplanes and locomotives—overnight. He thought a certain sequence of social, intellectual, economic, political development was necessary between the two kinds of 'social aggregation', and, in fact, that all developed societies in the world bore evidence of this.

But—Spencer's position did not at all entail all these other supposed errors with which he has been charged. Let us dispense with them in turn.

Firstly, Spencer distinctly did *not* couch these ideas in terms of a *prophecy* of a *unilinear* pattern of change which *all* societies would in fact undergo. He simply maintained that societies, like all other kinds of aggregates in nature, assumed a nature as they encountered and dealt with environmental problems. He clarified a system of analysing and explaining the nature of 'social systems' in this process of adaptation; and this gave a basis of *scientific prediction* (as *distinct* from prophecy). His analysis allowed him to make propositions of the kind: '*IF* the conditions and circumstances of a society (or a part of a society) are such and such . . . *THEN*, in accordance with such and such 'sociological law' (i.e., an explanatory hypothesis so far borne out by empirical generalizations) such and such is likely to be the case.' And all the procedures of inference and method and the truth or falsity of the actual predictions could be submitted to test. But Spencer did *not* maintain that *all* societies would undergo the entire sequence of evolutionary change his analysis provided.

On the contrary, he quite explicitly held that each society would change only according to some equilibrium position appropriate to its own environmental conditions. So that some societies might forever be simple aggregates of clans or tribes.

Right at the end of the *Principles of Sociology*, for example, Spencer wrote:

'The cosmic process brings about retrogression as well as progression, where the conditions favour it. Only amid an infinity of modifications, adjusted to an infinity of changes of circumstances, do there now and then occur some which constitute an advance: other changes meanwhile caused in other organisms, usually not constituting forward steps in organization, and often constituting steps backwards. Evolution does not imply a latent tendency to improve, everywhere in operation. There is no uniform ascent from lower to higher, but only an occasional production of a form which, in virtue of greater fitness for more complex conditions, becomes capable of a longer life of a more varied kind. And while such higher type begins to dominate over lower types and to spread at their expense, the lower types survive in habitats or modes of life that are not usurped, or are thrust into inferior habitats or modes of life in which they retrogress.'*

What holds for evolution in general, also holds, Spencer argued, for types of society.

'Social evolution throughout the future, like social evolution throughout the past, must, while producing step after step higher societies, leave out-

---

* *Principles of Sociology*, Vol. III, p. 599.

317

standing many lower. Varieties of men adapted here to inclement regions, there to regions that are barren, and elsewhere to regions unfitted, by ruggedness of surface or insalubrity, for supporting large populations, will, in all probability, continue to form small communities of simple structures. Moreover, during future competitions among the higher races there will probably be left, in the less desirable regions, minor nations formed of men inferior to the highest: at the same time that the highest overspread all the great areas which are desirable in climate and fertility.'*

It is also perfectly clear, of course, that in introducing his analysis of 'Dissolution'—the undoing of social systems which failed to come to terms with their environmental problems—Spencer quite consciously drew attention to the fact that societies could *decline* as well as develop; *cease* to be, as well as come into being. And between large-scale development manifesting *all* his characteristics of evolutionary change and the disaster of final dissolution and destruction —was a wide gamut of societies evolving to this or that degree, in accordance with this or that set of circumstances.

The idea of a definite, unilinear evolution of societies through which all must inevitably pass is therefore foreign to Spencer's system. And the idea of *prophesying* some *inevitable* course of social change is also foreign to him. He provided a schema for the description, analysis and explanation of social systems, and his supposed 'prophecies' were tentative 'predictions' of an 'IF . . . THEN . . .' nature.

A second point to insist upon is that although Spencer thought that each society would undergo a certain sequence of change in accordance with its circumstances (e.g., the 'primitive society' would not jump to becoming an 'industrialized society' overnight), he was not so foolish, of course, to suggest that *all* societies would go through *all* the *same* stages in their own pattern of development. He was well aware that a simpler society could be absorbed by conquest into a larger one; that a society with rude techniques could suddenly encounter a society with advanced technological skills and so be rapidly and radically changed by it; and also, indeed, that once a certain sequence of development had occurred, it could well be consciously introduced by men in other parts of society, as in other parts of the world, *in the reverse order*! To think that Spencer was guilty of such an inflexible view with regard to the sequence of stages for *all* societies is really to attribute to him a degree of idiocy that he was very far from possessing. Indeed, all such cricticms are almost beyond academic belief. Spencer's only insistence here, of course, was that the 'jumping' of various stages of differentiation on the part of such societies was possible only because they had encountered

* *Principles of Sociology*, Vol. III, pp. 599–60.

societies which had already experienced and assimilated these sequences of change themselves.

A third, and similar, and attendant point is that though Spencer thought that the spread of industrialization throughout the larger societies in the world would bring about an increasing 'functional coherence' and a growing similarity in *cardinal* aspects of institutionalization—he very explicitly did *not* maintain that all societies would become *uniform*. On the contrary, he argued that in this coming to terms with a common interdependency, each society would make *cardinal* adjustments—in political constitutions, in economic organization, etc.—but would obviously have to do this by altering its *existing* pattern of institutions, so that variety would still, nonetheless, remain. Here, I will give only one example—but a completely clear one—from what Spencer had to say about the adjustment of political constitutions to the conditions of industrialization. Spencer wrote:

'It seems likely that hereafter, as heretofore, the details of constitutional forms in each society, will not be determined on *a priori* grounds, or will be but partially so determined. We may conclude that they will be determined in large measure by the antecedents of the society; and that between societies of the industrial type, there will be differences of political organization consequent on genealogical differences. Recognizing the analogies furnished by individual organizations, which everywhere show us that structures evolved during the earlier stages of a type for functions then requisite, usually do not disappear at later stages, but become remoulded in adaptation to functions more or less different; we may suspect that the political institutions appropriate to the industrial type, will, in each society, continue to bear traces of the earlier political institutions evolved for other purposes; as we see that even now the new societies growing up in colonies, tend thus to preserve marks of earlier stages passed through by ancestral societies. Hence we may infer that societies which, in the future, have alike become completely industrial, will not present identical political forms; but that to the various possible forms appropriate to the type, they will present approximations determined partly by their own structures in the past and partly by the structures of the societies from which they have been derived.'*

Nothing, surely, could be clearer than that. It is worthwhile to notice, to make a fourth important point, that Spencer followed this passage by saying:

'Recognizing this probability, let us now ask by what changes our own political constitution may be brought into congruity with the requirements.'*

* *Principles of Sociology*, Vol. III, pp. 650–1. The relevance of this to modern questions concerning the 'convergence' of societies in the process of industrialization in the modern world is perfectly clear.

And two points may be seen with complete clarity in this:—first, that Spencer analysed this tendency as a *probability* (not as an *inevitability* or as a *prophecy*),* and secondly, that, following it, he was concerned to ask *what the members of society could do, and should do to amend their institutions in such a way as to make them 'congruous' with 'constraining requirements'*. There is nothing of the brash 'historicist' or 'determinist' here; and no inconsistency whatever in these attempts to foresee the probable exigencies attendant upon certain constraining tendencies in such a way as to be able to act wisely in relation to them.

Whenever Spencer attempted to 'foresee the future'—which he certainly did try to do—it was always tentatively in terms of the 'IF . . . THEN . . .' grounds of prediction of his system of analysis; always in terms of carefully qualified 'probabilities'; and always with reference to understanding society for the pressing purposes of wise political deliberation and action.

It is of the utmost importance, too, on this point, to realize that Spencer's emphasis in the sphere of statesmanship was always, and very powerfully, to *understand* BEFORE *acting*, and—very frequently— in terms of this understanding, *not to act at all*. Very unlike the other great sociologists of the nineteenth century, Spencer was on the side of an extreme liberalism. I do not want, here, to enter into any ethical consideration as to whether this position was right or wrong, good or bad, defensible or indefensible. It is only necessary here to see that Spencer most definitely and powerfully believed that men, by study, deliberation, and wise action, could affect the changes to which their societies and institutions were constrained by changing pressures and circumstances. As John Stuart Mill would have put it: there was no misconceived 'necessitarianism' in Spencer's conception of the 'cause and effect' analysis of things; of scientific knowledge and its application to the affairs of society.

As to the 'inevitability' of the 'industrial type' of society and its corollary of 'peacefulness'—on which Spencer has been so strongly denounced for being in error; a *reading* of Spencer will show that he not only maintained that conditions of increased militancy might lead to the growth of new totalitarian powers of a collectivist kind in highly industrial societies, but also actively feared that such totalitarian forms of authority and power were actually taking place in his time. Again, it was a matter of an 'IF . . . THEN . . .' prediction, and a detailed reading of Spencer will show how astonishingly correct his prediction was.

If ever there was a stark and true warning against the powers and dangers of modern bureaucracy, of modern totalitarianism and

* See Appendix 4 for similar considerations with regard to Mill.

its ramifications throughout all the institutions of society, it was that delivered by Herbert Spencer, and I can only say that, for my part, his analysis and the insights it contains seem to have become *more* rather than less relevant as the political experience of the twentieth century has worn on. The various kinds of 'collectivism' proposed, were, Spencer thought, all modes of replacing the social system resting increasingly on 'contract' by an earlier kind of social system resting on 'status'. They were likely to produce complex systems of power in which: 'The individual withers and the State is more and more.'

'There seems no avoiding the conclusion,' he wrote, 'that these conspiring causes must presently bring about that lapse of self-ownership into ownership by the community, which is partially implied by collectivism and completely by communism . . .*

'In what way the coming transformation will be effected is of course uncertain. A sudden substitution of the *régime* proposed for the *régime* which exists, as intended by bearers of the red flag, seems less likely than a progressive metamorphosis. To bring about the change it needs but gradually to extend State-regulation and restrain individual action. If the central administration and the multiplying local administrations go on adding function to function; if year after year more things are done by public agency, and fewer things left to be done by private agency; if the businesses of companies are one after another taken over by the State or the municipality, while the businesses of individuals are progressively trenched upon by official competitors; then, in no long time, the present voluntary industrial organization will have its place entirely usurped by a compulsory industrial organization.'†

'As shown in multitudinous ways throughout this work, a society organized for coercive action against other societies, must subject its members to coercion. In proportion as men's claims are trampled upon by it externally, will men's claims be trampled upon by it internally. History has familiarized the truth that tyrant and slave are men of the same kind differently placed.'‡

'Men thus constituted cannot maintain free institutions. They must live under some system of coercive government; and when old forms of it lose their strength must generate new forms . . .'

'Instead of restraints and dictations of the old kinds, new kinds of restraints and dictations are being gradually imposed. Instead of the rule of powerful political classes, men are elaborating for themselves a rule of official classes, which will become equally powerful or probably more powerful—classes eventually differing from those which socialist theories contemplate, as much as the rich and proud ecclesiastical hierarchy of the middle ages differed from the group of poor and humble missionaries out of which it grew.'§

* *Principles of Sociology*, Vol. III, p. 594.   † *ibid.*, p. 595.   ‡ *ibid.*, p. 596.
§ *ibid.*, pp. 596–7.

However, far from regarding this as inevitable, Spencer powerfully argued for ways of preventing it, and advocated a struggle on the basis of a modestly conceived optimism for the maintenance and extension of such freedoms as man had achieved within the context of industrial society.

'The function of Liberalism in the past,' he wrote, 'was that of putting a limit to the powers of kings. The function of true Liberalism in the future will be that of putting a limit to the powers of Parliaments.'

And, contemplating the large variety of societies drawn together in the modern world, and their functional diversities, he wrote also:

'While the entire assemblage of societies thus fulfils the law of evolution by increase of heterogeneity—while within each of them contrasts of structure, caused by differences of environments and entailed occupations, cause unlikenesses implying further heterogeneity; we may infer that the primary process of evolution—integration—which up to the present time has been displayed in the formation of larger and larger nations, will eventually reach a still higher stage and bring yet greater benefits. As, when small tribes were welded into great tribes, the head chief stopped inter-tribal warfare; as, when small feudal governments became subject to a king, feudal wars were prevented by him; so, in time to come, a federation of the highest nations, exercising supreme authority (already foreshadowed by occasional agreements among "the Powers"), may, by forbidding wars between any of its constituent nations, put an end to the re-barbarization which is continually undoing civilization.'*

All his own efforts and desires were towards the formation of 'this peace-maintaining federation.'

These several criticisms of Spencer's position are therefore simply not true, and I can only hope that, during the course of this discussion, the true nature of Spencer's scientific analysis and explanation of social systems has been made completely clear. As we shall see, it is most important to have a correct appreciation of this when we come to consider and judge the so-called 'systems analysis' of our own day.

A few remaining points of emphasis can very rapidly be made.

(e) Spencer did not use only Ethnographic data

It must be emphasized again, in defence of Spencer's classificatory and comparative studies, that it is simply not true that he used only, or even chiefly, ethnographic data. He did, in fact, draw on a very wide range of historical and contemporary material drawn from societies of all types. His studies were not in this way 'slanted' in any one direction, therefore, as has been suggested.

* *Principles of Sociology*, p. 600.

(f) The nature of Spencer's 'types' of society

It is necessary for future reference, simply to note that Spencer's 'Militant' and 'Industrial' *types* of society were constructed in terms of (*a*) the total 'structural-functional' pattern of institutions (*b*) the 'social psychological' aspects of the relationship between the institutional structure of society and the concomitant qualities of personality and character required in its individual members, and (*c*) an *understanding* of all this in terms of *a system of social action*—both at the collective and at the individual level. It will be seen that this 'typological' method is closely in accord with Comte's types—constructed in terms of institutional patterns of thinking, feeling, and acting; and with Mill's conceptions of the three levels of 'social structure', 'social psychology,' and 'individual psychology', and, in all this, the exercise of deliberate choice in individual and social action. But it will also be seen later, that it is also in accord with the construction of 'types' for the interpretation of social change through different levels of social complexity by all subsequent important scholars in sociology—Tönnies, Durkheim, Weber, and others up to the most recent theorists such as Becker, Parsons and others.

(g) Spencer's basis of 'Materialism'

A final point of emphasis is that Spencer's entire system of analysis rested upon a 'materialistic' basis. This is not at all to say that Spencer was a 'materialist' in any metaphysical sense; indeed he explicitly was not. Neither is it to say that he 'reduced' his explanations of all levels of phenomena to 'materialistic' terms; again he explicitly did not. And in these and similar ways he was more properly qualified in his thinking than Marx—and others—who held a 'materialist' position. But it is *just because of this*, that this point needs emphasis, and again it is a point on which both Comte and Spencer were agreed.

Spencer insisted that all 'aggregates' in nature were indeed material aggregates (whatever other emergent qualities they possessed) and therefore had to be understood and explained in the context of their relationship with their material environment—consisting of other aggregates of many kinds. Furthermore, he insisted that all this was a *process*. No phenomenon could be understood or explained as an *object* in isolation; every phenomenon in our experience was itself a PROCESS *of transformation assuming a certain form in relation to internal accommodation to external* PROCESSES. What this really amounts to is that Spencer was as good a *'dialectical materialist'* as you are likely to find, BUT that his system did NOT suffer from any naive historicism or from any metaphysical dogma and reductionism.

At the end of this entire section on 'The Foundations of Sociology' I will try, by way of both substantiation and summary, to bring together some of the statements of Comte, Spencer and Marx on this subject, in such a way as to show how much error has crept into it by some curious insistence that Marx was the most important exponent of it. In fact, Marx was by far the *least* adequately qualified in his handling of the *material basis* or the *material aspects* of human society among all the three of them. But here this may be simply entered and emphasized as a point to be noted.

Some Criticisms

Many criticisms of Spencer's system of sociology have been raised and dealt with as we have clarified each point in his argument. In order to be as complete as possible in our present assessment of his contribution to the making of sociology, however, a few others must be mentioned.

(*a*) *Criticisms of the concept of evolution*
These need not be elaborated as they have been sufficiently dealt with. We might simply note, however, that we have demonstrated:

(i) That Spencer's 'law' of evolution was *not* only a descriptive generalization but also a system of *explanation*,

(ii) That it was *not* an application of the *biological* theory of evolution in the field of sociology, but something much more than this,

(iii) That Spencer was quite clear and consistent in his use of the analogy between an organism and a society; that he did not misunderstand it; and, indeed, that he dispensed with it when he thought fit: i.e., when he thought his meaning had been made sufficiently clear,

(iv) That it was not a *unilinear* theory of evolution,

(v) Nor *inevitable*,

(vi) Nor inconsistent with the advocating of positive political deliberation and action,

(vii) That it did not imply that all societies passed through identical determinate stages,

(viii) And that it did not specify any ultimate uniformity.

And these are really quite a lot of points to be getting on with. Other attendant criticisms, however, have also been made.

(*b*) *Criticism of the range of relevance of the concept of Evolution*
Going beyond the concept of evolution itself and its utility in

sociology, many critics have claimed that Spencer was at fault in thinking that it could be relevant to all phenomena—astronomical, physical, chemical, biological, psychological, sociological, and all else. Such a view, they claim, could not nowadays be advanced.

I do not wish to deal with this criticism exhaustively here, but will be content simply to raise a question about it. On what evidence, one wonders, do the critics make this claim? For in all fields of science the concept of evolution still seems quite central.

Consider cosmology. Professor Fred Hoyle writes as follows:

'Let me tell you a few words about what we mean by stellar evolution. A star does not stay the same all the time. It changes and the reason why it changes is because nuclear processes take place within its interior . . .

'Many stars have grown very much brighter than they originally were: they not only grow brighter but they change their size, their physical dimensions, and when we look in these clusters we can see stars at all stages of this evolutionary development. Notice particularly that we do not see them actually evolve, because to do that you would have to live for thousands of millions of years actually to see the evolution taking place. Perhaps I can give you a simple analogy here that may be helpful. Suppose you went into a factory and you saw a motor car being assembled, or rather you saw an assembly line in a motor car factory. You might see if you looked along the line, all the stages through which a car is assembled, and it would be quite clear to you from what you saw, just how a car is put together. This would be so even if you did not see a single operation actually take place, as long as you saw all the stages of development laid out one by one before you, and this is the situation for the astronomer in these clusters. He sees the evolution laid out before him at all its stages.

'This again is a development of very recent times, indeed of the last five years. It is only within five years that observational astronomers, particularly at the Mount Wilson and Palomar Observatories, have been able to measure and to determine these various evolutionary states with great precision. The observations do not in themselves reveal how fast the stars pass from one evolutionary stage to another. They simply tell us what these evolutionary stages are, but they do not tell us how fast the star passes through those stages. This last piece of information can, however, be supplied by calculation. Knowing the evolutionary stages and knowing how fast they pass along them it is possible whenever we see one of these groups, these clusters of stars, to give some sort of an estimate of how old that particular cluster is. So far, neither the observations nor the calculations have been or are anything like complete, but a very good beginning has been made.'*

And, it seems, this picture of the 'evolution' of stars holds good whatever theory one may hold about the *origins* of the stars.

In the study of astronomical phenomena then—of stars and

* 'The Time Scale of the Universe' 47th Conway Memorial Lecture, Dec. 1956, pp. 7–8.

planetary systems—and of the physical and chemical processes involved, 'evolution' still seems a central concept. In biology it goes without saying that evolution is still quite fundamental, and it is increasingly relevant in the connected studies of the behaviour of organisms and comparative psychology. Thus the classification of 'behaviour patterns' characterizing particular species is now as definite a matter as the classification of anatomical and physiological details, and the explanation of all the genetic and environmental processes involved is still rooted in the fundamental concept of evolution.

Within sociology, too, 'evolution' is far from being as redundant a concept as some very myopic critics appear to think. Here, I will give only a curious example.

In relatively recent times, the supposed 'school' of Functionalism has been thought by some to dispense with the concept of evolution, and, indeed, not to concern itself with 'social change' at all. And one of the most eminent 'founders' of 'Functionalism' was Radcliffe-Brown. But what do we find Radcliffe-Brown himself saying about 'social evolution'? We find him saying this:

'Evolution, as I understand the term, refers specifically to a process of emergence of new forms of structure. Organic evolution has two important features: (1) in the course of it a small number of kinds of organisms have given rise to a very much larger number of kinds; (2) more complex forms of organic structure have come into existence by development out of simpler forms. While I am unable to attach any definite meaning to such phrases as the evolution of culture or the evolution of language, I think that social evolution is a reality which the social anthropologist should recognize and study. Like organic evolution, it can be defined by two features. There has been a process by which, from a small number of forms of social structure, many different forms have arisen in the course of history; that is, there has been a process of diversification. Secondly, throughout this process more complex forms of social structures have developed out of, or replaced, simpler forms.

'Just how structural systems are to be classified with reference to their greater or less complexity is a problem requiring investigation. But there is evidence of a fairly close correlation between complexity and another feature of structural systems, namely the extent of the field of social relations. In a structural system with a narrow total social field, an average or typical person is brought into direct and indirect social relations with only a small number of other persons. In systems of this type we may find that the linguistic community—the body of persons who speak one language—numbers from 250 to 500, while the political community is even smaller, and economic relations by the exchange of goods and services extend only over a very narrow range. Apart from the differentiation by sex and age, there is very little differentiation of social role between persons or classes. We can contrast with this the systems of social structure that we observe today in England or the United States. Thus the process of human history to which I think the term social evolution may be appropriately applied might be defined as the process by which wide-range systems of social structure have grown out of, or replaced, narrow-range systems. Whether this view is acceptable or not, I suggest that the concept of social evolution is one which requires to be defined in terms of social structure.'*

Such are the curiosities of fashion in academic thought! One's only possible conclusion is that critics do not *read*! There is no other explanation. Even so, it is very odd to find Radcliffe-Brown writing like this, because one would suppose, on reading him, that no work whatever had been done on the 'classification of structural systems' with reference to their 'greater or lesser complexity', whereas Spencer had produced several very clearly written volumes on the subject, as had Comte and Mill before him.

At any rate—I have said enough to question the assertions of the critics. Evolution *does* still seem a concept central to all processes of change, rather as Spencer conceived it to be. The critics, then, may well be wrong.

One final and very curious work which might be mentioned in considering the supposed redundancy of Spencer's ideas is *the Phenomenon of Man* by Teilhard de Chardin, (who was a French Roman Catholic thinker). In this book, which was given an excellent reception by the press only a few years ago, and has since been very influential and highly thought of,† all the main propositions of Spencer are sombrely laid out and clothed with a fantastic kind of mystical philosophizing. Herbert Spencer, in short, has almost been taken to Church. Almost, but not quite!—since Chardin himself was not accepted. But in this book there is scarcely anything about the theory of evolution which Spencer had not already laid down and, indeed, said much better. It is one of the curiosities of our time that some people are criticized for being outmoded, their ideas thought dead and buried, whilst at the self-same time, new thinkers are thought to be making a great contribution to scholarship by reiterating the self-same ideas! Herbert Spencer's ideas are dead for many people. Yet, trailing clouds of obscurantist, theological glory, they are greeted with enthusiasm in the work of Chardin. The modern intellectual scene is very strange indeed.

(c) The illustration rather than the testing of hypotheses
A further criticism is that though Spencer's methods of classification

* *Structure and Function in Primitive Society*, Cohen & West, 1952, pp. 203–4.
† Excepting by Sir Peter Medawar who has got its proper measure and sees that its proper place is in the waste paper basket.
See 'The Phenomenon of Man', *The Art of the Soluble*, Methuen, 1967, pp. 71–81.

and comparison, of hypothesis and deduction to explain empirical generalizations, seemed, logically speaking, acceptable, and though they had the *appearance* of science, they were not *really* scientific at all. Spencer *began* (it is said) with his conviction as to the trends of social evolution. His 'Law of Evolution' was an 'a priori' generalization. He then gathered (or had gathered for him) an enormous amount of documentary evidence, and proceeded to *select* those elements of this evidence which *illustrated* and *supported* his presupposed laws. This criticism, though it requires a more careful statement than this, has a degree of weight.

There is nothing illegitimate, scientifically speaking, about having a hypothesis in mind before approaching the study of data. Indeed, it is now thought that any study, even the most simple observation or description of data, involves *some* selective hypothesis—implicit or explicit. In science, however, the crucial thing is that the hypothesis should be made both clear *and vulnerable* in the sense of exposing it to test under certain specified conditions. And though Spencer does speak as though he is *testing* his hypotheses and deductions (against empirical generalizations) it must be conceded that he does not anywhere prescribe precise conditions under which his hypotheses could be subjected to crucial test. Within his work there is no clear way of checking whether or not he has *illustrated* his hypotheses by *selecting* from all the available data those examples which will support it. Spencer is, therefore, open to criticism on these grounds.

How serious a criticism this is, however, it is difficult to decide. My own judgment is that, firstly, though not providing a procedure of crucial experiment (remembering Mill's arguments, it is questionable whether this is possible), Spencer did nonetheless set up a clear schema of classification and comparison within which empirical generalizations could be gathered, arranged, explored, and explained; and within this framework itself, the adequacy of Spencer's own propositions can be checked. It is possible for the student to place specific societies within Spencer's classificatory scheme and to see whether or not the 'consensus' of its institutions accords with that which he proposed. Putting this in another way: given the difficulty of crucial experiment in sociology (perhaps, even, its impossibility) Spencer's methods of classification and comparative study must be critically assessed in terms of whether they are the most satisfactory *alternative methods of testing* generalizations and hypotheses that can be achieved. It is not enough simply to say that they do not constitute crucial experiment.

The second point, also, is that there is no doubt whatever that Spencer did survey the facts he could assemble with a critical eye.

Indeed, he would have liked to have provided more data in relation to his many points than it seemed feasible to publish. And, in fact, he deleted much empirical detail from his chapters—some of which were first printed in the *Fortnightly Review*—when he came to publish them in *The Principles of Sociology*. This was to meet some criticism as to the 'readability' of his work. However, he did not cut material unduly. He wrote in a preface:

'That with a view to improved effect I have not suppressed a large number of illustrations, is due to the fact that scientific proof, rather than artistic merit, is the end to be here achieved. If sociological generalizations are to pass out of the stage of opinion into the stage of established truth, it can only be through extensive accumulations of instances: the inductions must be wide if the conclusions are to be accepted as valid. Especially while there continues the belief that social phenomena are not the subject-matter of a Science, it is requisite that the correlations among them should be shown to hold in multitudinous cases. Evidence furnished by various races in various parts of the world, must be given before there can be rebutted the allegation that the inferences drawn are not true, or are but partially true. Indeed, of social phenomena more than all other phenomena, it must, because of their complexity, hold that only by comparisons of many examples can fundamental relations be distinguished from superficial relations.'*

There is no doubt that 'scientific proof' was the end that Spencer kept continuously before him.

(d) Evolution and Progress: ethical ambiguities
A final criticism of Spencer is that he was unclear and, indeed, ambiguous in what he had to say about the *facts* of evolution and the grounds of his *ethical* judgments of them. He spoke of the 'progress' of evolution; of 'higher' and 'lower' types of social evolution; sometimes in a purely technical sense but sometimes, also, in an ethical sense. And, clearly, to speak of the 'advance' of social evolution simply in the sense of moving through certain sequences of differentiation and complexity is a very different thing from judging the 'more developed' societies as being 'better' in a moral sense than the less developed.

There is nothing wrong or incorrect in exercising ethical judgments about the facts of social evolution *so long as the two processes of thought and judgment* (i.e., the scientific study of facts and the philosophical clarification of ethical principles) *are clearly distinguished and studied appropriately and sufficiently*. But it *is* incorrect to assume that ethical principles can simply be drawn from

* 1879 Preface to Part IV.

the facts; or to confuse propositions about facts with propositions about evaluative judgments.

It can be readily agreed that Spencer was ambiguous about these matters, and that he did not sufficiently clarify them. This problem was one left over for later scholars, and we shall see that to deal more successfully with it was an important part of the contribution of L. T. Hobhouse. And we might also notice that Spencer seemed to slip unwittingly into a mixture of fact and value in some of his work. For example, we have seen that he feared the 'recrudescence' of militancy among industrial societies which, he thought, would bring about a 'reversion' to a 'militant' type of society. Now we may well share his fears and his moral judgments here—for it is clear that his ethical principles rest firmly upon the maximization of individual liberty within the state—but, even so, in terms of the *facts* of social change, why should he not think that some degree of collectivization in the nature of industrial societies was one more evolutionary change as such societies adapted themselve to qualitatively new and different environmental conditions? And indeed—to be extreme—if totalitarian societies are better fitted to survive in the process of adaptation to these changed conditions, what is wrong with that *in terms of the scientific analysis of social change alone*?

I hope it is clear that I myself do not accept any reliance upon scientific analysis alone. My concern here is only to point out the difficulties in the problem, and the kind of ambiguity in which Spencer was involved.

This criticism of Spencer, then, is a correct one.

At the same time, it is worth our while to note that there is something in Spencer's view which deserves a good deal of thought. The differentiation of institutions in societies, he maintained, were not arbitrary. They were causally related to newly emergent social and environmental problems. They were an embodiment of the greater ability, on the part of man, to exercise effective control over nature and over the organization of society. And within this context, the development of moral ideas may not have been arbitrary either. Men may have been constrained to consider, unravel, clarify, their moral issues as their societies and the nature of their social problems changed. In this sense, moral ideas and the direction of philosophical reflection concerning them, may have been intimately connected with these new problems. Morality and moral progress, like other aspects of human endeavour, may have been more closely connected with necessity than we commonly think. Necessity may have been the mother of ethical concern, acuteness, and heart-searching deliberation, just as it has been the mother of thought, discovery, and action in other spheres. It is *possible* then, that the actual historical growth of civilization has been accompanied, factually, by a more elaborate and progressive consideration of the moral problems attendant upon them, and by a progressive clarification of moral criteria. Certain directions of social change *may*, therefore, have been morally progressive. Though recognizing completely that ethical criteria cannot be simply drawn from a survey of facts, it is, nonetheless, not self-evident in any easy sense that Spencer is altogether wrong. There is a difficult problem here.

I think it is worthwhile to point out, too, that Spencer was more aware of the moral 'malaise' attendant upon the rapid transitions of society from a 'traditional' to a scientific, technological and industrialized condition than many other thinkers. He saw the 'anomie' which Durkheim later emphasized with great clarity and concern. He wrote, for example:

'The growth and spread of exact knowledge, changing as it is now doing men's ideas of the Universe and of the Power manifested through it, must increasingly modify the regulative action of ecclesiastical institutions. A necessary concomitant is the waning authority of the associated system of morals, now having an alleged supernatural sanction; and before there is accepted in its place a scientifically-based ethics, there may result a disastrous relaxation of restraints. Simultaneously with progression towards more enlightened conceptions, we see going on retrogression towards old religious beliefs, and a strengthening of the sacerdotal influences associated with them. The immediate issues of these conflicting processes appear incalculable. Meanwhile men's natures are subjected to various disciplines, and are undergoing various kinds of alterations. The baser instincts, which dominated during the long ages of savage warfare, are being invigorated by revived militancy; while the many beneficent activities distinguishing our age, imply a fostering of the higher sentiments. There is a moral struggle of which the average effect cannot be estimated.'*

However, it still remains perfectly true that before we can reliably judge all questions of an evaluative kind, we have to possess criteria of moral judgment, ethical standards, which are themselves philosophically clarified and justifiable, and which are not simply 'taken' from a study of facts, and this Spencer did not sufficiently make clear.

These then are the more important criticisms of Spencer, and though some of them can be seen to have grounds which must be considered seriously, others rest on misconceptions or an insufficient knowledge of what he said. None of them is seriously damaging with regard to the over-all system of sociological analysis which Spencer contributed to the making of the subject.

Spencer's work, of course, has dimensions of interest which

* *Principles of Sociology*, Vol. III, p. 581.

go far beyond his contributions to sociological theory. His essay on 'Education' is still a remarkably modern and valuable piece of work. His essays on political philosophy, though framed in terms of nineteenth century Liberalism, are still exciting and highly relevant to contemporary political life, no matter what the extent to which one agrees or disagrees with him. His comments on many slight and incidental issues in the social life of his own day, particularly in the latter half of the nineteenth century, also make fascinating reading now. However, our concern here must be centrally with his contribution to the making of sociology as a science, and his clarification of elements of theory and method.

In this, as we have seen, he made a very considerable contribution which added much to the work of Comte and Mill. Within the changed perspectives of the knowledge of his time; the new perspectives brought about by the upsurge of science and its extended application to all aspects of human experience; he did indeed produce a new systematic approach to knowledge which provided a new picture of 'Man's place in Nature'. And, as with Comte and Mill, this system of knowledge was consciously seen as a necessary foundation for deliberation and action as society encountered the grave and complex problems attendant upon the rapid transformations of industrialization.

He carried the analysis of social systems, the comparative study of societies within a classificatory scheme, and the outline of a systematic approach to the explanation of them, to a greater level of clarity, precision, and detail than Comte, Mill, or any of the earlier philosophers of history and historians had achieved before him. Also, by his enormous collection of data on every kind of social institution in all kinds of human society, he brought together, in a systematic way, a far greater amount of information than had been gathered together hitherto within the context of sociological analysis, and, in so doing, emphasized the fundamental importance of *empiricism*. His contribution was very great indeed, and his influence, during the latter half of the nineteenth century, was equal to that of Comte.

I cannot withhold a final remark that Spencer was well aware, at the end of his life, of the criticisms, and in some cases, the misrepresentations of his ideas, and also of the wide reputation he had of being a 'theoretician', and that he regarded them all with a certain balanced humour and cynicism.

When writing of an afternoon visit to T. H. Huxley, for example, he said that Huxley had greeted him with the words:

'. . . "Come upstairs; I want to show you something which will delight you—a fact that goes slick through a great generalization!" His ironical expression (Spencer continued) was prompted by his consciousness that being so much given to generalizing I should be disconcerted.''*

And when explaining, in a preface to *First Principles* (in 1880†) that his theory of evolution was *not* derived from Darwin, and that it had, in fact, been stated in his writings *before* Darwin's publication of the *Origin of Species*, Spencer nonetheless resignedly wrote:

'I do not make this explanation in the belief that the prevailing misapprehension will thereby soon be rectified; for I am conscious that, once having become current, misapprehensions of this kind long persist—all disproofs notwithstanding. Nevertheless, I yield to the suggestion that unless I state the facts as they stand, I shall continue to countenance the wrong conviction now entertained, and cannot expect it to cease.'

Spencer had obviously learned a lot in a long life, but, come what may, correctness would be insisted upon and observed. Spencer was a great, consistent, and indefatigable scholar, and his system of sociology, his contribution to the making of sociology, was one of the greatest to be produced during the nineteenth century, or indeed, at any time.

Summary

The great similarities and agreements between the ideas of Comte and Mill and those of Spencer are already quite plain. However, with our ultimate objective in mind of seeing the interrelationship between all their contributions with complete clarity, let us briefly summarize the main elements of Spencer's system.

(a) Scientific knowledge: a clear delimitation
(I) THE LIMITATIONS OF SCIENTIFIC KNOWLEDGE

Like Comte, Spencer insisted that science was productive of knowledge exactly because of its very careful and precise delimitation. Reality no doubt had many dimensions going beyond our awareness, but we could achieve an intellectually justified position of clear agnosticism. Scientific knowledge was the establishing of testable

---

* Some very interesting comments on Spencer as a person are to be found in *Society in the Country House*, T. H. S. Escott, Fisher Unwin, 1907, pp. 132–4, in which he is pictured as a very genial, generous, and tolerant person: praising T. H. Huxley's style (of writing), for example, and acknowledging George Eliot as his teacher rather than his pupil. 'She is my senior in age, and immeasurably so as regards knowledge and power. She was always much more widely read and better informed than myself.' See also: Beatrice Webb—*My Apprenticeship*.
† To the 4th Edition.

'laws' about the interconnections of *the facts of our experience*. It explicitly *confined* itself to stating regularities of *phenomena*; propositions about the interrelations among elements of the world *as we experienced them*. *This* was knowledge; *this* could be clear; whatever the riddles of reality which might lie beyond.

(II) SCIENTIFIC LAWS

Scientific 'laws' were such statements of interconnection: 'uniformities of co-existence and succession'; and here again, Spencer was in agreement with Hume, Kant, Comte and Mill. Explanation was a matter of stating hypotheses and deductions which provided a satisfactory (testable) account of empirical generalizations.

(III) SCIENCE ROOTED IN COMMON SENSE, AND PHILOSOPHY ROOTED IN SCIENCE

Science sprang, by critical reflection, from the insufficiencies of common sense—which was *un-unified* knowledge. The many special sciences were systems of *partially-unified* knowledge. But all these could be brought together in an entirety of *completely-unified* knowledge—and, for Spencer, this latter was the task of philosophy. For Spencer, as for Comte, then, all the sciences could be brought together to provide a unity of knowledge.

(IV) SCIENCE A BASIS FOR FORESIGHT AND ACTION

As with Comte and Mill too, Spencer maintained that scientific knowledge alone provided a reliable basis for prediction, and therefore for sound judgment and effective action in relation to both nature and society.

(b) *Evolution: a central guiding concept*
(I) EVOLUTION: A UNIFYING CONCEPTION

The unity of science, the relatedness of its findings in *all* fields, and the clarification of its appropriate methods in *each* field, could be centrally illuminated, Spencer held, by the concept of 'evolution'. Evolution was a universal process. Nature consisted of a multiplicity of finite living forms in a continuous process of transformation. All these forms manifested definite regularities and definite relationships with the elements of their environments in the context of which they came into existence, grew, developed, and went out of existence. Change in all these forms was a re-ordering of elements in a necessary adjustment to seek equilibrium in the context of constraining forces. The course of evolutionary change manifested a certain pattern: from indefiniteness to definiteness; from simplicity and sameness, through a differentiation of parts and functions, to complexity and difference; but also from incoherence and simple connectedness of parts, to a complex coherence of organization (or articulation) of parts. All forms in nature permitted of clear scientific analysis in these terms.

(II) EVOLUTION: GROUNDS FOR EXPLANATION

The concept of evolution was not only a unifying *description*; an empirical generalization; it also provided clear grounds for systematic *explanation*. Such grounds were: the instability of the homogeneous; the multiplicity of effects—once differentiation had begun; factors making for specialization and segregation of parts; adjustments to achieve equilibrium; factors making for destruction and dissolution. A 'schema' of *both* analysis *and* explanation was therefore provided by the concept of 'evolution'.

(III) EVOLUTION: APPLICABLE TO 'SOCIETIES'

Evolution could also prove a unifying concept in the making of *Sociology*—for *societies* were forms in nature, organizational systems, which were shaped, and which grew and developed, in the process of coming to terms with constraining and challenging environmental factors. Societies, therefore, could be systematically studied in accordance with the same 'schema' of analysis and explanation. A science of society was possible, and its nature and methods could be made perfectly clear.

(c) *Sociology: statical analysis: the nature of a society*
(I) SOCIETY: AN ENTITY: AN ORGANIZATIONAL SYSTEM

Societies, Spencer held, were definite organizational entities, institutional systems which had specifiable and determinate attributes just as clearly as had any other forms in nature. They were 'superorganic' systems. They did not exist independently of individuals; they did not obliterate individuals; they did not compound individuals into some new metaphysical 'collective entity'; but they were *systems of institutions* which were something *more* than, and *other* than individuals, possessing clearly discernible attributes. Sociology was, therefore, *the scientific study of such social systems.*

(II) STRUCTURAL—FUNCTIONAL ANALYSIS

Societies, like all other forms, could be analysed into their component parts and the functions they fulfilled in relation to the whole. Institutions possessed discernible *structures* of organization, and they fulfilled discernible *functions:* both in dealing with a specific social task, a specific set of social problems and in operating interdependently with other institutions in the entire society. The structures and functions of institutions should therefore be explored in relation to their place in the 'totality' of the social system.

(III) A 'CONSENSUS' OF INSTITUTIONS

This structural-functional interdependence of the institutions of a society meant a certain 'consensus', a determinate interconnectedness of all the parts of the society as a whole, which could be uncovered by study. The 'consensus' of institutions, the kind of interconnectedness among them, would be different in societies of different types. These similarities and differences could also be uncovered and made clear by careful study.

(IV) THE NATURE OF A SOCIAL SYSTEM TO BE ANALYSED AND EXPLAINED IN TERMS OF ITS HISTORY AND ITS ACCOMMODATION TO ENVIRONMENTAL PROBLEMS

Like all other forms, societies too were essentially *processes*, continuously involved in the transformations of elements, energies and resources, and continuously constrained by environmental conditions. The patterns of change, growth, and development—or change, diminution and dissolution; the differentiations of structures and functions which characterized them, could be analysed and explained in terms of their historical accommodation to the conditions and challenges they had experienced. *Structural-Functional analysis* would therefore, simultaneously, be an analysis of *social and historical change.*

(V) SIGNIFICANT GROUPINGS OF INSTITUTIONS

In addition to the analysis of structure, functions, and their patterns of change as outlined so far, Spencer also maintained that institutions could be significantly *grouped* with regard to the *predominant* social functions which they *shared*. Regulative, Sustaining and Distributive groups of institutions could be distinguished, and the kind of *consensus* existing in a society at a particular period of its history could be illuminated and explained by the relative dominance of one or other of these groups. Sometimes the Sustaining (Economic) institutions might be predominant; sometimes the Regulative (Political and Military). This grouping of institutions therefore provided a basis for the analytical construction of 'types' of society.

(d) Sociology: Dynamics: the empirical study of societies
This statical (in Comte's terms) analysis of the nature and com-

ponents of social systems could then be consistently applied in the empirical study of the actual variety of societies in the world in order to achieve substantive, testable knowledge, and specific testable theories, about them.

(I) OBSERVATION, CLASSIFICATION, COMPARISON, AND HISTORICAL STUDIES TO ESTABLISH DESCRIPTIVE KNOWLEDGE

The methods of *observation*; of the *classification* of *types* of society (on the observable basis of the degree of social aggregation, or on the basis of the theoretical construction of 'models'); of careful *comparison;* and of *historical* study were all proposed, and held to be necessary by Spencer—as they had been by Comte and Mill—in the undertaking of satisfactory empirical studies. It is uneccessary to elaborate again each one of these methods—though each one is of vital importance.

Spencer insisted that all these methods were necessary even to establish—in a systematic, satisfactory, and manageable form—a body of *descriptive* knowledge about societies. But this was not the *end* of empirical studies. The aim of science, and of sociology, was to establish *explanatory theories*.

(II) GROUNDS OF EXPLANATION

The analysis of social systems derived from the concept of 'evolution' could also be applied in seeking the *explanation* of the *descriptive generalizations* about specific societies, their similarities, their differences, their institutions, the 'consensus' of institutions appropriate to particular types, the sequences of structural-functional differentiation discovered in them, and, in short, all the known or supposed 'uniformities of co-existence and succession' which descriptive studies had provided.

These grounds of explanation were, again, the consideration of societies always in relation to the constraining conditions of their environments; the unstable condition of the homogeneous'—exposed, in different settings, to different conditions and influences; the multiplicity of effects once differential change had begun; the factors making for specialization and segregation of parts in the development of differentiation; the struggle of adaptation in relation to 'equilibrium-disequilibrium' stresses; and the factors making for disintegration and dissolution if the environmental conditions could not be met.

Spencer's system therefore specified a schema for the stating of specific *explanatory theories* about the many aspects of the nature of social order and social change; it was by no means the simple 'blanket-like' dogma of unilinear and uniform evolution as has been commonly supposed.

Sociology, then, in Spencer's conception, was a completely clear science of society, of social systems, which provided a meticulously clear analysis of the nature of its subject-matter, and an equally clear set of methods and directives whereby, within the context of this over-all analysis, specific empirical studies and theoretical explanations could be pursued.

Other things could be said by way of summary: Spencer's agreement with Comte and Mill on many other important points—the prospect of a future in which men could eliminate gross economic problems and devote themselves more freely to improved ethical and cultural qualities of living; the persuasion that the increasing functional coherence of human societies on a global scale would make sociological generalizations and understanding *more* rather than *less* possible; the conviction that sociology could provide men with a basis for sounder judgment and more responsible and effective action; and the like. But here, it is best to concentrate only upon the major conceptions which Spencer put forward for the making of sociology, and in which his agreement with Comte and Mill was so clearly apparent.

We turn now to a man whose theory has often—and very militantly —been thought to offer a theory of society and social change vastly *different* from those we have considered so far: a quite distinctive theory of *revolutionary*, not *evolutionary*, change; of *conflict* and violent antagonism in the relationships of society, not of consensus and order. But we shall see that, like most other simple juxtapositions and exaggerations, these, too, are no more than a kind of hectically coloured vapour.

5

Karl Marx: Economy, Class, and Social Revolution

I have chosen to follow our discussion of Comte, Mill, and Spencer with a study of the work of Marx for a number of quite definite reasons. Marx was, of course, one other of the great Victorian thinkers who was dedicated the making of an adequate science of society for the purpose of changing and improving the society he saw about him. For many reasons , however, he has come to be thought a *heretic* among intellectuals: a heretic among economists, a heretic among philosophers, a heretic in politics . . . in short, just about the most conspicuous and disastrous 'enfant terrible' of the nineteenth century; and one who has sown more trouble than any other single figure for the twentieth. In terms of the political up-heavals which followed in his train, there are, no doubt, under-standable grounds for this reputation, but in what follows I hope to show that, when the polemical cloud that hangs about him is cleared, and. even when quite basic disagreements with him are clearly stated, his conception of the science of man and society was, in very large part, the same as that of others who were engaged in the making of sociology, if not presented with anywhere near the same clarity.

Our concern here, of course, is not to accomplish a definitive assessment of the work of Marx, or of 'Marxism', in all its aspects, but essentially *only to clarify Marx's contribution to the making of a science of society*; and this must be strongly borne in mind. Even so, a proper estimation of Marx (that is, an assessment in which one can be thoroughly satisfied that one has done him justice) is very difficult to achieve, and I would like to explore these difficulties a little in stating, in an introductory way, why I have chosen to attempt a study of him here.

Like all the other men we have considered, Marx was far from being only a 'scholar', and was certainly most not a 'professional' scholar. His intellectual efforts sprang from a deeply and genuinely felt humanity, and his entire work was the outcome of a complete and unswerving moral commitment to all those qualities that add up to the freedom and dignity of the human person. His social science was undertaken for humanitarian purposes, and many things are connected with this emphasis. The first thing, however, that must be said is that Marx was thoroughly likeable and admirable as a man in this fundamental respect. He was devoted to his intellectual and political causes, but all these were rooted in a sensitive concern for people at the *personal* level. We have seen that Comte, Mill, and Spencer also had this fundamental concern for humanity and for those standards of material well-being, social and cultural enrichment, and political liberty which would do most to ensure individual fulfilment, but it is worth remarking that in certain ways Marx had a more immediate and personal humanity than them all. This is not to derogate *them*, by any means, but only to say that Marx's humanitarianism had essentially *personal* qualities which were different, and which must not be forgotten. Whatever one may come to think about his ideas, or about the uses to which they have been put, this fundamental fact of his sensitive and staunch humanity must be appreciated and cannot be denied. Whatever one's intellectual disagreements with him, this firm moral stand for certain qualities of humanity and human dignity, and his insistent efforts to achieve them in the day-to-day relations of society, must be admired.

Later we shall emphasize the particular quality which this humanity lent to his interpretation of 'materialism' and other elements of his system which it is all too easy to caricature, and thus improperly estimate. For now, however, it is enough to note that, though always involved in intellectual work and political agitation on a broad cosmopolitan scale, he was always, also, a man of warm personal relationships—as husband and father in his family, and as friend and colleague with all those among whom he worked.

'I make bold to say,' said Engels at his graveside, 'that though he may have many opponents he has hardly one personal enemy.'

Also—when attacking, with a passionate disgust and anger, the harshness of the treatment and conditions of wage-earning people in the context of industrial capitalism, it was always the very concrete examples of savagely over-worked children, women, and men to which he referred; it was always the humiliations, the indignities to which individuals were subjected, as well as the gross physical poverty, toil, illness, and ugliness which they suffered, against which he protested. And when he advocated freedom, he thought firstly, and always very practically, of such measures as the shortening of the working day. Contrary to many present-day conceptions of him, Marx was in fact opposed to a vulgar notion of 'Communism' in which public ownership might simply bring a certain equality in '*having*' things, and, instead, desired the creation of '*human*' society in which the qualities of creative social life among *persons* could, at last, be achieved.

Let me stress again, to prevent any misunderstanding, that this insistence upon the quality of Marx's humanitarianism is far from being a kind of litany of his virtues for its own sake. Besides this—important in itself—this quality has a quite basic relevance for a correct appreciation of many of his ideas.

A second important point on which his persuasions were in considerable agreement with the other thinkers we have discussed was that his concern was centrally upon the problems of *industrial* society. Like them, he was convinced not only that the vast social transformations brought about by science, technology and manufacturing industry constituted a radical movement from traditional agrarian society to something qualitatively new in human history, but also that—when its turmoils were over—it would provide the basis for a new and improved condition of human life such as had not been experienced before.

Like other thinkers too, he believed that the efforts to undsrstand the social processes which were afoot, and the political efforts to create such a society, required a rigorous *scientific* study of man and society.

His central desire to *change* society rather than simply to *understand* it, led to what is one of the greatest complicating factors for the study of Marx—namely, that he was a journalist and committed political agitator; very much an activist in his writing and organrzing; and *not* only concerned to work out a satisfactory intellectual system. Indeed, he failed to complete a systematic account of his ideas. Of all the thinkers we have mentioned so far, Marx is the *least* satisfactory in this respect. Furthermore, the scope and quality of his writing is very variable: depending on whether he was really working out his reflections or whether he was writing a manifesto for the guidance of political action. Some of his writing in the *Economic and Philosophical Manuscripts of 1844* is the outcome of genuine, exploratory, profound study and thought, and is most compelling—again, despite disagreements!—and there is brilliance in his essays of a historical nature—as, for example, in *The Eighteenth Brumaire of Louis Bonaparte*, whereas the *Communist Manifesto* and similar writing contains the most insufficiently worked out notions, the most sweeping and unqualified statements; whilst sections of *Das Kapital* contain the most fantastically *over*-worked notions which do not carry any conviction whatever. But a greater complication is attendant upon this.

Because Marx did not complete much of his work, and because many of his ideas were not developed beyond a certain point; because, too, he was involved with colleagues in his political activities; the fact is that many of his ideas came to be argued through, and even prepared for publication, by others. During, and immediately after, his own lifetime, it was Engels who most contributed to this 'supplementary' argumentation and explanation. Since then, however, the process has been never-ending. Lenin undertook extensive works of 'interpretation' of Marx's ideas, and of the application of them in a new situation of 'socialist' power. And this was followed to a lesser, but still important extent, by the writings of Stalin and others. It therefore becomes very difficult to disentangle Marx's notion of (let us say) 'materialism' and its application to the study of history, from the interconnected ideas of Engels, and, later, of Lenin and Stalin. And this, again, is not necessarily to *derogate* the writing of these other authors. Stalin, for example, was a much better and clearer thinker and writer than is commonly thought, and showed himself very painstaking and systematic in endeavouring to present the ideas of Marx and Engels in a compact and coherent form.* It is simply that it is difficult always to know whether one is interpreting Marx (himself) aright, or whether one is attributing to *him* an emphasis which was introduced or pressed by others. However, one can only do one's best to be accurate in this, and the problem is, after all, not of such grave consequence for us, since our concern is chiefly to become clear as to how Marx went about the making of a science of society, not to chase all the ambiguities of his political propositions.

Despite this, however, this is a point on which *much* care must be exercised. Engels, for example, in both good ways and bad, was (it seems to me) much more of a variable and 'opportunist' polemicist than Marx, and one can never be quite sure whether he qualified Marx too far, or, sometimes, interpreted him too narrowly. Though both writers vouched for a good deal of agreement between themselves, Marx's writing on the nature of 'materialism', for example, was distinctively different from that of Engels: being couched in much less orthodox philosophical language, and much less philosophically 'pedantic'. It seems to me to claim much *less*, philosophically, than did the argument of Engels. Yet both treatments, both sets of arguments, form part of the theory of 'dialectical materialism' and 'historical materialism' which is central for the Marxian explanation of the nature of society and social change. So there are real problems here. Engels, too, tended on some occasions to use the techniques and standards of a platform-orator in his writing, which sometimes gave a decided bias and flavour to his judgments without advancing substantive *arguments*. For example, he praised Feuerbach (as did Marx) for being the first great writer

* Which is something that they themselves did not achieve.

since Hegel to demolish 'idealism' and to achieve a convincing statement of 'materialism', but—in then criticizing what he thought were limitations of Feuerbach—he went on to speak of the '*rank* materialism' of Feuerbach as against that of Marx; and elements of derisiveness creep into his attack. The clarification of the serious elements in the writing of Marx and Engels has therefore to grapple with this task of distinguishing and casting aside much of a specious polemical nature.

It is the same with regard to the question of 'economic determinism' in the explanation of social change. Engels so qualified the determining influence of the 'economic basis', or the 'productive forces', of society upon the nature of all other social institutions as to seem to strip the 'hypothesis' of any distinction, of any 'cutting edge' for purposes of analysis, whatever. And yet he wished to *retain* it as the distinguishing feature of the Marxian system of social explanation. How far Marx was in agreement with the extent of such qualifications is very difficult to decide.

We are, in short, faced with a body of ideas riddled with ambiguities, intensified by the excitement of polemics and political practice, and vexed by a multiplicity of interchanges of argument coming from many—and equally dogmatic—sources. So problems—in plenty—confront us.

An immediate question which arises is: is this tangle of ideas and ambiguities really worth bothering with? If Marx, Engels, and many of their followers chose to stride round Europe declaiming vehemently about this and that; asserting themselves over all other notable thinkers in history; all well and good. But if the intellectual wares they were selling comprised a bundle of ill-assorted and insufficiently connected bits of brash and arrogant nonsense . . . which were politically dangerous in the highest degree: why bother to give them serious consideration? Why not drop them into the waste-paper basket where they belong, and get on with something serious? And this leads to another group of very important reasons why we should try, in this place, properly to estimate the nature and value of Marx's 'system' among all the other contributions to the making of sociology.

The most immediate and obvious reason why we cannot leave Marx and his ideas unexamined is that, whether rightly or wrongly, justifiably or unjustifiably, they have come to form the basis of the largest and most radical political movement in the modern world. The *importance* of these ideas for what is happening in social science and the 'understanding' of the nature and destiny of man, and what is happening on the world's vast stage of political power, can neither be denied nor escaped. Furthermore, even if we come to decide that these ideas are wrong, incorrect, and must be rejected, we are still left with the fact that, over great stretches of human society through-out the world, they have clearly been thought to be relevant to the economic, social, and political struggles attendant upon the trans-forming influences of industrialization, and they have, without any doubt whatever, become the effective focus for political effort and political organization. Why is this? Even if the ideas of Marx them-selves are insufficient on various clear intellectual grounds, they may well be rooted in some very important and significant ways with the conditions of rapidly changing industrial society. They may—almost in Marx's own terms—be functioning as a powerful 'ideology' in modern society, even if they are something of a 'false consciousness' and intellectual error underlies them; and, if this is so, then this is a fact of great importance both for social science and for our estimation of concrete political events in the world.

Given this great prominence of Marx's 'system' in the prevailing struggle for power and the re-shaping of societies, it is also of the greatest importance that we gain a *true* and satisfactory understand-ing of this system. If there are dimensions of truth in it, then we must accept them. If there are grave errors in it, then we must *know clearly* what they are, and be able to demonstrate them. It is not enough—whether in *support* of the ideas of Marx or *against* them—simply to vituperate. It behoves everyone to seek clear knowledge and known grounds of judgment in an area of thought on which so much now hangs.

But a further aspect of this point is one on which I have come to feel very powerfully indeed. It is this. In the developing of these several approaches to the study of society, for the purpose of under-standing and governing society, the all-pervading tendency has seemed, and still seems to be one of emphasizing *differences*. Every-body has wanted, and still wants, to set up a *new* theory. And, furthermore, everybody wants—in setting up their *own* theory—to denounce (critically) all others. Everybody wants their own theory to be *the* theory which supersedes all others. So that there appears to be a continuous fight between diametrically opposed theories: 'dialectical materialist' against 'metaphysical'; 'revolutionary' against 'evolutionary'; 'functionalist' against 'evolutionary'; and so on. Now by and large these antitheses are *bogus*! And I want especially to show that this is true concerning Marxism and its relations with other nineteenth-century theories. The titles given to this chapter and the last: 'Structure, Function, and Evolution' with regard to Spencer, and 'Economy, Class, and Revolution' with regard to Marx, point to the *marked distinction* which is commonly thought to differentiate the two kinds of theoretical positions. Now, I want to demonstrate beyond doubt that this is a false appraisal of the development of sociological theory. I want to show that Marx, like Spencer, provides a structural-functional model of society for the analysis of both social order and social change, and that his theory is one of social *evolution*,* completely the same, in form, as that of Spencer, and, indeed, as that of Comte. It is, in my view, most important to see that the supposed 'dichotomies' between these theories are false, and, especially, that all these thinkers, despite differences of emphasis *within* their scheme of description, analysis, and explanation, nonetheless adopted the *same kind of scheme*. In the making of sociology they all agreed as to the over-all framework and components of the science they were so concerned to construct and use.

Marx did *not* offer a qualitatively different science of society from that which we have seen taking shape at the hands of others. He was subject to the same intellectual influences which had played upon others in his time—the emergence of the scientific method and the new perspectives resulting from the work of the natural sciences; the new perspective (especially) of evolution; the insufficiencies of moral and political philosophy, the philosophy of history, and the like— and he made his scientific study of man out of the stuff of these same influences. He was aware of the same historical juncture in human society which had dominated the concerns of others: the crucial turning point of technological and industrial change; and confronted these dilemmas constructively and creatively as others had done. He was couched within the same context of thought and action—and was by no means the isolated heretic he is sometimes thought to be. But this raises a final source of difficulty we might note.

Like other theorists, Marx brought together many strands of earlier thought and worked them into a new synthesis. One's estimation of him depends to quite a large extent upon which of these influences and which element of this synthesis one considers to have been the most important. The position I shall adopt here is quite clear. There is no doubt, it seems to me, that there were two main roots in Marx's thinking. First, he was a scholar of the philosophy of history, and his central orientation here was a critique of the 'Idealist' philosophy of history of Hegel and the replacement of it by a 'materialist' philosophy stimulated in very large part by the work of Feuerbach. Marx was rooted firmly in Hegel; his way towards a science of society was that by way of a critical amendment of the

---

* As a matter of interest, it may be noted—using Spencer's terms—that whereas Spencer argues that differing sets of institutions—the 'regulating', the 'sustaining', the 'distributive'—have differing degrees of determining influence in differing material and historical circumstances, Marx argues that it is *one* set of institutions, the 'sustaining', which has the dominant determining influence throughout. But the *form* of their institutional and historical analysis is the same.

MARX: A MATERIALIST PHILOSOPHY OF HISTORY

THE CREATIVE
PROCESS OF NATURE.   *DIALECTICAL*
UNIVERSAL HISTORY.   *MATERIALISM*

HISTORICAL MATERIALISM

MATTER : *PRIMARY REALITY*

NEW EMERGENT REALITIES

LIFE, MIND,
SPIRIT : *SECONDARY* ('REFLECTIONS')

QUANTITATIVE
→
QUALITATIVE
CHANGE

Man's practical activities in relation to material environment: *Primary Reality*.
All other institutions.
Govt, law, religion, etc.: *Secondary* ('Reflections').

→ *SOCIETY*

(1) Basis = means of production: products, property, techniques. — *The Productive Forces*
(2) Relations of men to means of production. — The *Material Basis* of Society
(3) Established system of social classes.
(4) The 'Super-structure' of legal, political, military, religious (etc.) institutions, + ideologies. — Alienation — 'Reflect' the Material Basis
(5) The *State*: organ of ruling class.

SOCIAL CHANGE

(6) Quantitative change in productive forces becomes disruptive of old order. Changes class relations.
∴ class struggle and revolution to qualitative change.

(7) This has produced types of society characterised by productive forces and nature of social classes. With the revolution of the industrial proletariat (the dictatorship of the proletariat): no new subjected class.
∴ classless society.
∴ state unnecessary: withers away.

TYPES OF SOCIETY (EPOCHS)

(1) *PRIMITIVE COMMUNAL* (Simpler societies)

(2) *ANCIENT (SLAVERY)*

(3) *FEUDAL (SERFDOM)*

(4) *CAPITALIST* ('Wage-slavery')

(5) *SOCIALIST* (Transitional)

(6) *COMMUNIST* (A 'human' society)

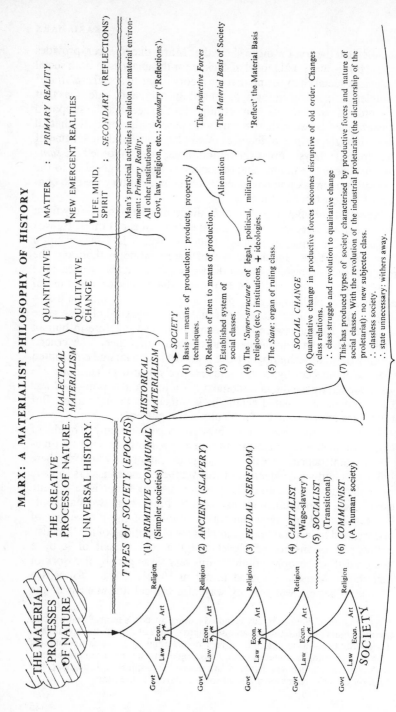

THE MATERIAL PROCESSES OF NATURE

Religion   Art
Govt   Law   Econ.

SOCIETY

PROGRESS: Man's Spiritual freedom = a progressively emergent thing: won from man's struggles with the material processes of nature and society.

philosophy of history; and he cannot be understood apart from this. Second, he was a scholar of political economy, and his study of Adam Smith, Ricardo, Jean-Baptiste Say, and others, led him into a detailed analysis of the relationships involved in industrial capitalism. It was this root of thought which led him to set 'labour' and 'capital' against each other as the chief source of class conflict and the main lever of social and political change. And Marx, in bringing together his philosophy of history and his analysis of the fundamental economic relationships of capitalism, created a *sociology*. He produced, without any doubt, a scientific study of societies as wholes—a theory of the nature of social order and of social change. And this is the pattern of ideas which we shall trace here.

It is true that a third source of influences was the large and varied body of writings of the French 'socialists'; and these ideas were obviously at work in influencing the way in which he brought together the philosophy of history and his analysis of industrial capitalism. However, it is these two latter components which, together, formed his system of analysis, and, in his hands, they were fused to create a sociology—a systematic science of society.*

Bearing in mind these several important introductory points, and the difficulties they entail, let us now try to clarify, in turn, each component of Marx's sociological system.

Remembering our brief analysis of Hegel's system, it may be helpful, for purposes of complete clarity, to attempt a condensed diagrammatic summary of Marx's ideas along the same lines. As the text proceeds, it will gradually fill in and elaborate each specific item; but a study of the diagram itself may prove useful as an initial guide.

The necessity and the nature of science in the study of Man

In the first place it is worthwhile to establish the fact that Marx and his several 'interpreters' were quite emphatic about their theory of knowledge, and their persuasion that scientific methods were the *only* methods productive of testable knowledge. But the position

---

* Later we shall consider one other powerful influence at work in the mind of Marx that tends, by and large, to be ignored (though noted in biographical sketches of him), and that was the dominant ideas of certain great literary figures such as Shakespeare and, perhaps especially, Goethe. The humanistic emphasis in Marx's work is closely related to his appreciation of the exploration and judgment of human nature and its destiny to be found in the work of writers such as these. However, this was one strand among others, and can simply be noted here, though it is of considerable importance.

adopted has certain interesting dimensions, all of which it is important to note.

(a) The necessity of the Scientific Method

The dimension with which we can begin is that both Marx and Engels were insistent upon the fact that they advocated and employed *the scientific method* in the study of nature and human society; they declared themselves 'empiricists'; but in no place whatever did they offer a detailed analysis of what they considered 'scientific method' to be. Some things were said: there were continual *assurances* that the methods of science were employed throughout their work and formed the firm basis of all their propositions; that empirical *facts* were the bed-rock of their theories; yet no clear conception or outline of this 'scientific method' was ever presented with satisfactory clarity or detail.

Marx felt it important, for example, '. . . to assure the reader conversant with political economy' that *his* results had been 'won by means of a wholly *empirical* analysis . . .'* and, furthermore, that he welcomed 'every opinion based on scientific criticism'. He also took pains to make it clear that his accounts of English factory legislation (and of the conditions of work in the factories) in *Das Kapital* were based upon a detailed study of 'blue-books' which were themselves the results of the empirical investigations of factory inspectors and commissioners undertaking governmental enquiries. He had, indeed, a great respect for the competence and lack of bias of these inspectors and for the accuracy of British social statistics. In all this he emphasized his empiricism and his concern for the accuracy of his empirical 'sources'.

The claim was made that the new system of analysis formulated by Marx was to be distinguished completely from the 'metaphysical' systems of the past in that it rested clearly and fundamentally on *science*, and found its generalizations in the *facts* which were empirically studied, whereas they did not.

Thus, according to Engels, philosophy 'came to an end' with Hegel, but, because Hegel had developed the old metaphysics to their fullest extent:

'. . . he showed us the way out of the labyrinth of "systems" to real positive knowledge of the world.

'One leaves alone "absolute truth", which is unattainable along this path or by any single individual; instead one pursues *attainable, relative truths along the paths of the positive sciences* . . .'†

---

* *Economic and Philosophical Manuscripts of 1884*, Lawrence and Wishart, p. 15.
† *Ludwig Feuerbach and the Outcome of Classical German Philosophy.* See

'It is no longer a question anywhere of inventing interconnections from out of our brains, but of discovering them in the facts.'*

With this development, science alone produced testable knowledge about all aspects of nature, man, and history, and philosophy was totally displaced. Philosophy was now stripped of any substantive subject-matter.

'For philosophy,' wrote Engels, 'which has been expelled from nature and history, there remains only the realm of pure thought (so far as it is left): the theory of the laws of the thought-process itself, logic and dialectics.'† Dialectical Materialism, as a scientific study and knowledge of nature and history . . . "no longer needs any philosophy standing above the other sciences".'‡

Indeed, later, Lenin was to echo this position in his claim that the 'philosophy' of Marx, 'Dialectical Materialism', was all-sufficient as a *'perfected philosophic materialism'*.§

Lenin also emphasized the scientific basis of Marx's system of thought, when he claimed that Marx's application of dialectical materialism to the study of man and history:

'. . . represented the greatest conquest *of scientific thought*. Chaos and arbitrariness, which reigned until then in the views on history and politics, were replaced by *a strikingly consistent and harmonious scientific theory*, which shows how out of one order of social life another and higher order develops . . .'‖

It was 'historical materialism', he maintained, which:

'. . . first made it possible to study *with scientific accuracy* the social conditions of the life of the masses and changes in these conditions.'**

Engels, too, emphasized that Marx's system was an extension of the methods of science into the study of man and society.

'For we live not only in nature but also in human society, and this also no less than nature has its history of development and its science. It was therefore a question of bringing the *science of society* into harmony with the materialist foundation, and of reconstructing it thereupon.'††

Karl Marx: Selected Works, Vol. I, p. 425. The strong similarity with the ideas and the language of Comte may be noted.
* *Ibid.*, p. 468.   † *Ibid.*, p. 468.   ‡ *Anti-Dühring.*
§ V. I. Lenin. *The Three Sources and Three Component Parts of Marxism.* See *Marx: Selected Works*, Vol. I, p. 56.
‖ *Ibid.*, p. 56.
** *Karl Marx.* (Article) *Selected Works*, Vol. I, pp. 19–53.
†† *Ludwig Feuerbach. Ibid.*, p. 439.

Marx himself was quite definite about the all-embracing nature of science in securing such knowledge as man could achieve.

'*Sense-perception* must be the basis of all science. Only when it proceeds from sense-perception in the two-fold form both of *sensuous* consciousness and of *sensuous* need—that is, only when science proceeds from nature—is it *true* science.

'All history is the preparation for "*man*" to become the object of *sensuous* consciousness, and for the needs of "man as man" to become (natural, sensuous) needs. History itself is a *real* part of *natural* history—of nature's coming to be man. Natural science will in time subsume itself the under science of man, just as the science of man will subsume itself under natural science: there will be *one* science.'*

There is no doubt whatever, then, about the scientific pretensions and claims of Marx and Marxism. Before leaving this initial and simple noting of their basic emphasis upon science, and before moving on to ask what Marx and his followers considered the *nature* of this science to be, it is worthwhile simply to point out how ambiguities had raised their heads even in these apparently straightforward assertions. Only a few points need to be mentioned at this stage.

Firstly, when Marx spoke of 'science *proceeding from nature*'—what exactly did he mean? And when he claimed that only this science is *true* science: did he think that there were kinds of science which did *not* proceed from nature? And that, therefore, there were criteria in accordance with which one could distinguish *true* science from *false* science? Later, we shall see that the *relativity* of its propositions is one characteristic distinguishing science from 'metaphysics', but, given relativity, the question of distinguishing *true* from *false* science raises large problems.

Secondly, it can be seen in these few quotations that the extension of 'science' in the study of nature, man and society seems to be not so much closely associated, as *identified* with the acceptance of 'materialism', 'dialectical materialism', 'historical materialism'. To accept something called 'materialism' (as against the 'idealism' of 'metaphysics') and to adopt a 'scientific' approach to the study of any kinds of facts, seem to be considered synonymous. But why? No good reasons are given. In this, 'science' seems to be identified with the acceptance of one metaphysical assertion (*not* argument, let it be noted!) rather than another. And this seems rather an odd and questionable assumption.

These ambiguities are seen to entail even greater elements of con-

* *Economic and Philosophical Manuscripts of 1844*, p. 111. Again notice the similarity with Comte's conception of the science of man as the 'crowning' edifice in the entire 'hierarchy of sciences', and the totality of 'positive science' as being, alone, productive of testable knowledge.

fusion when the testability of 'science' is in some way strongly associated, if not equated, with 'practice' or 'pragmatism', and the 'relativity' of systems of ideas, bodies of knowledge, or 'ideologies' is seen in relation to the 'material' basis of social classes and political movements: so that we are quickly transported from a 'scientific study of nature, man, and society' (i.e. involving, presumably, testable theories about various kinds of facts) to something called 'scientific communism' or 'scientific socialism' which now, somehow, gives scientific guarantees and justifications for the destinies of certain socio-political groups.

'Scientific' communism or socialism, it may be noted, is forthrightly contrasted (by both Marx and Engels) with 'Utopian' socialism—as put forward by many of the earlier French socialists; and the 'search after a new social science' on the part of these scholars was denigrated (though not entirely) because *their* social science was not satisfactorily founded on the developing proletariat and its developing material conditions.* There are hints here as to how one distinguishes 'true' science from 'false'—but they are rather disquieting ones.

The extent of this ambiguity must not be under-estimated or under-emphasized; it is a very real, important, and unresolved ambiguity, and needs to be seen clearly.

Perhaps the most stark statement is to be found in the systematic exposition of Stalin. Having stated the materialistic and scientific basis of Marxism:

'Marxist philosophical materialism holds that the world and its laws are fully knowable, that our knowledge of the laws of nature, tested by experiment and practice is authentic knowledge having the validity of objective truth, and that there are no things in the world which are unknowable, but only things which are still not known, but which will be disclosed and made known by the efforts of science and practice.'†

And having explained the extension of this scientific procedure to the study of society and history, Stalin then pronounced the fact that:

'Hence Socialism is converted from a dream of a better future for humanity into a science.'

It is important to see that Stalin did *not* say: 'With this scientific knowledge of society, Socialism will be better equipped to achieve its ends', (and, of course, *any* political movement should be in such a position armed with accurate knowledge), but that 'Socialism' *itself* was 'converted into a science'.

Similarly, V. Adoratsky, in his preface to the selected works of

* See *The Manifesto of the Communist Party*, Section 3.
† *Dialectical Materialism and Historical Materialism.*

351

Marx (and Engels) described these works as being 'permeated by the integral world outlook of scientific communism'.

'The struggle of the proletariat', he wrote, 'cannot be successful without a revolutionary theory which completely reflects and explains the whole complicated process of historical movement and serves as a guide in changing the world. Scientific communism includes practical revolutionary activity as an indispensable constituent part. But this activity must be guided by scientific theory . . .'*

Ambiguity on ambiguity! 'Science', it seems, is by some strange logic transmuted into the ideology of the proletariat, the content of which accords with, or is relative to, its practice within its own material conditions. This may seem a strange position, as indeed it is, but it will be seen to derive quite directly from the actual, and very definite propositions of Marx himself as well as his followers. It is enough here, however, to see that the basic insistence upon a *scientific* approach to the study of man and society was a very much more ambiguous matter than it was in the work of the other men we have discussed.

Since *science* was so fundamental to this new approach to the study of society, one would have expected Marx to be meticulously careful in making clear the *nature* of science, and, especially, the *nature* of his *science of society*. In fact, however, he says astonishingly little about this. Much is *said* about the importance of science and empiricism, but hardly anything about its nature. Some of the ambiguities creep in here because, as we shall see, such discussions as take place about the distinctive approach of science tend to take the form of a defence of 'materialism' and its suppositions. Even so, some of the assumptions—whether correct or not—of Marx and Engels about the nature of science, can be drawn from their indirect remarks. And some of these are of considerable importance for a critical assessment of their system.

(b) The nature of the scientific method and basic epistemological assumptions
Practically all the points which I wish to emphasize in this section occurred in the discussion about the nature of 'dialectics', 'materialism', and the like, and were so closely connected with them as to be almost inseparable from them. Even so, I think it better to consider these larger ingredients of Marx's thought later, and I believe each of these points about the nature of science and epistemology to be important in their own right—both for a correct appreciation of Marx, and, more important for our purposes, for seeing the contri-

* *Karl Marx, Selected Works*, Vol. I, Preface, p. xv.

bution of Marx in clear relation to that of other scholars of the nineteenth century.

(I) SCIENCE PROVIDES KNOWLEDGE OF 'NATURE': EXPERIENTIAL, TESTABLE, RELATIVE, NEVER FINAL: AKIN TO POSITIVISM

The first thing which is completely clear from the various writings of Marx and Engels is that they rejected earlier 'theological' and 'metaphysical' conceptions of 'truth' as radically as Comte had done. In this, their position was like that of all nineteenth-century thinkers who accepted the new criteria of testable truths adopted in the natural sciences as against any kind of speculative assertion or 'argument' for which there were no kinds of 'experiential' conditions of test. This also entailed for them, as for others, a conscious awareness of the 'delimitation of knowledge' in accordance with the concepts, techniques, and methods of science. In this position it is not too much to say that they simply accepted a Comtean account of the nature and limitations of 'positive science'.

Engels wrote, for example:

'. . . the demand for *final* solutions and *eternal* truths ceases once for all; one is always conscious of the necessary *limitation* of all acquired knowledge, of the fact that it is *conditioned* by the circumstances in which it was acquired.'*

This, as the earlier quotation on page 348, could well have come straight from the pages of Comte.

However, both Marx and Engels were more extreme and philosophically less cautious than Comte in the extent to which they conceded, or rather insisted upon, the 'relativity' of knowledge. Comte, it will be remembered, recognized that there were grounds and conditions of 'relativity' in knowledge, but, nonetheless, did not think that the criteria of knowledge which had been, and could be, set up, were 'arbitrary'. Engels, however, could write as sweepingly as this:

'. . . one no longer permits oneself to be imposed upon by the antitheses, insuperable for the still common old metaphysics, between true and false, good and bad, identical and different, necessary and accidental. One knows that these antitheses have only a relative validity . . .'†

—and he never appeared to see what enormous, indeed impossible problems this position opened up before him when he might wish for example, to insist on definitive 'criteria' for the testing of 'truths within science (let alone metaphysics), or when he might wish to maintain that science is *true* as against metaphysics, or that 'scientific

---

* *Ludwig Feuerbach. Ibid.*, p. 453.   † *Ibid.*, pp. 453–4.

communism' possesses more accurate degrees of 'truth' than does, let us say, 'bourgeois reaction'.

If the antitheses between truth and falsity, identity and difference, necessity and contingency, have disappeared, one wonders what science can possibly be about!

What this amounts to is that Marx and Engels adopted and accepted 'positive science' as a method of achieving knowledge, but paid insufficient attention to clarifying its nature, and were careless to (quite literally) an unspecified degree with regard to its 'relativity'.

(II) SCIENTIFIC KNOWLEDGE IS KNOWLEDGE OF 'REALITY'— WITHOUT PHILOSOPHICAL LIMITATION

There was one important sense, however, in which the claims made by Marx and Engels for the nature and extent of 'scientific knowledge' went far beyond the claims of other nineteenth-century thinkers. Comte, Mill, and Spencer, for example, accepting the 'de-limitations' of scientific knowledge and rejecting the claims of 'truth' of metaphysical speculations about the nature of things, nonetheless recognized a necessary limit of 'philosophical agnosticism'. In one way or another, they all accepted the fact that we can ask more questions about the nature of things than we can answer, and that there are, most probably, dimensions of 'reality' that man—with the limitations and confining characteristics of his nature and conditions —can never know. He can, at least, never be sure that he has knowledge of all dimensions of the world because he knows that he perceives, observes, connects, generalizes, thinks, through the conditions of his own nature. In one way or another, they all accepted that, though we cannot go beyond 'scientific knowledge', we cannot, either, claim that such 'scientific knowledge' as we have is to be taken without qualification, as knowledge of 'reality'. Indeed, they all chose not to speak of 'reality' in this sense—because it was, in its own way, a metaphysic!

Marx and Engels, however, in strong opposition to the 'reality' of the metaphysician, seemed to want to juxtapose a 'material reality' of their own. Whereas the other scholars we have mentioned took heed of the caution of Hume (in his sceptical empiricism) and Kant (in his limited knowledge of 'phenomena' and his recognition of unknowable 'noumena'—'things-as-they-are-in-themselves'), Marx and Engels outrightly rejected them, but again, it must be said, with a cavalier setting aside of anything approximating to philosophical argument.

Agnosticism, or Neo-Kantian agnosticism, was no more, Engels wrote, than 'shame-faced' materialism, whatever that was supposed to mean.

There is no doubt whatever that though his 'materialism' in his theory of society was a complicated and much qualified matter, Marx quite definitely conceived 'matter' to be the primary 'reality' in 'nature', and the human mind and the knowledge it produced to be a 'secondary reflection' of it. It was this, indeed which formed the basis of his opposition to Hegel. Engels too, was agreed about the primary 'reality' of matter, but the essential point here is that both believed that science could produce direct and exhaustive knowledge of such reality.

Drawing upon Hegel himself, for example, Engels wrote:

'If you know all the qualities of a thing, you know the thing itself; nothing remains but the fact that the said thing exists without us; and when your senses have taught you that fact, you have grasped the last remnant of the "thing-in-itself" . . .'*

But nowhere did he even begin to say by what criteria we can know that 'all' the qualities of a thing have been brought into our knowledge; and nowhere did he begin to apprehend the philosophical problem attendant upon the recognition that the 'qualities' of a thing may be dependent on the 'qualities' peculiar to the perceiver, and that the 'knowledge' pertaining to 'human' perception may be limited on these grounds.

He agreed that the problems raised by Hume and Kant seemed 'undoubtedly hard to beat by mere argumentation' (why *mere*, one wonders?), but he readily brushed this aside with the remark: 'but before there was argumentation, there was action', and then proceeded to show that our sense-perceptions could be checked and tested by 'putting them to use'.

'Not in one single instance, so far, have we been led to the conclusion that our sense-perceptions, scientifically controlled, induce in our minds ideas respecting the outer world that are, by their very nature, at variance with reality, or that there is an inherent incompatibility between the outer world and our sense perceptions of it.'

But, of course, neither Kant nor Hume wanted to claim that our perception of things or relations of things in the world were at variance with 'reality' or 'incompatible' with it. Hume was only concerned to show that knowledge of the world was knowledge of our experience of this kind, and that it did not possess logical certainty, and Kant was only concerned to claim that such knowledge was not (and had no grounds for claiming that it was) the whole of the story. Engels did not see that his several arguments were simple repetitions of Dr Johnson-like 'kicks against the lamp-post' to

* (On Historical Materialism), *ibid.*, p. 400.

prove it was there. But this was no philosophical basis for an un-qualified 'realism' of empirical knowledge.

This 'over-stated' claim for the extent of 'scientific' knowledge may not seem a particularly important point to emphasize, but it *is* of the greatest importance when, attached to a 'materialistic' dogma, it comes to insist that only 'scientific knowledge at a certain level' (i.e. the basic level of 'material reality') constitutes a 'real' explanation. We are then at the point of a new metaphysical dogma of 'scientific materialism'.*

(III) SCIENTIFIC KNOWLEDGE: A SHEER EMPIRICISM

A third characteristic of the nature of scientific knowledge which was closely connected with this 'over-statement' of its claim and the acceptance of the 'objective facts of material reality' was what can be called a 'sheer' empiricism, or what some philosophers of science would call a 'naive inductivism'. It was the view that the generaliza-tions of science, the 'laws' of nature and society, were simply *there* in the facts. No speculation was necessary, the straightforward study of the facts revealed them. As we have seen, Engels argued that, with the abandonment of philosophy, it was no longer a question:

'... of inventing interconnections from out of our brains, but of discovering them in the facts.'

No detailed examination was undertaken as to what methods such a process of 'discovery of interconnections' involved.

* The extent to which this insistence upon the primacy of 'material' reality and upon the total sufficiency of 'scientific knowledge' can go may be seen in the following passage from Stalin:

'Contrary to idealism, which asserts that only our mind really exists, and that the material world, being, nature, exists only in our mind, in our sensations, ideas and perceptions, the Marxist materialist philosophy holds that matter, nature, being, is an objective reality existing outside and independent of our mind; that matter is primary, since it is the source of sensations, ideas, mind, and that mind is secondary, derivative, since it is a reflection of matter, a reflection of being; that thought is a product of matter which in its development has reached a high degree of perfection, namely, of the brain, and the brain is the organ of thought; and that therefore one cannot separate thought from matter without committing a grave error ...

'Contrary to idealism, which denies the possibility of knowing the world and its laws, which does not believe in the authenticity of our knowledge, does not recognise objective truth, and holds that the world is full of "things-in-themselves" that can never be known to science, Marxist philosophical materialism holds that the world and its laws are fully knowable ... that there are no things in the world that are unknowable, but only things which are still not known, but which will be disclosed and made known by the efforts of science and practice.'

These, of course, are travesties of idealism and its claims.

Short History of the Communist Party of the Soviet Union (Bolsheviks), Cobbett Publishing Co. 1938, pp. 100–1.

(IV) SCIENTIFIC KNOWLEDGE: THE RIGIDITY OF 'LAWS'

A similar, connected conception in the mind of Marx, Engels and all
their followers was that of the 'laws' which scientific knowledge
discovered. These were not only thought of as 'interconnections' or
'regularities of relationship' among phenomena, but also as determinate, constraining forces in nature. Marx, for example, when
arguing about the usefulness of the knowledge of a developed
industrial society for foreseeing the problems of those which were
undeveloped, wrote:

'It is a question of these laws themselves, of these tendencies working with
iron necessity towards inevitable results. The country that is more developed
industrially only shows, to the less developed, the image of its own future.'*

Whether this is a true or false conception of scientific 'laws' we
need not here try to decide. What is certain is that this language is
unmistakable. It is, without doubt, the language of determinism
(what Mill called 'necessitarianism'); the language of 'inevitability'.

(V) SCIENTIFIC KNOWLEDGE: THE LIMITED CONTROL PROVIDED BY FORESIGHT

This 'deterministic' emphasis was also reflected quite clearly and
definitely in the fact that Marx believed that, even with the foresight
which a knowledge of scientific 'laws' provided, the extent to which
man could control or change the expected events was decidedly
limited.

'One nation can and should learn from others,' he wrote. 'And even when
a society has got upon the right track for the discovery of the natural laws
of its movement, it can neither clear by bold leaps, nor remove by legal
enactments, the obstacles offered by the successive phases of its normal
development. But it can shorten and lessen the birth-pangs.'†

Like Comte, Marx clearly thought that in the pursuit of science,
we seek 'to see, in order to foresee', but, even when we *could* foresee,
the extent of our controlling action was very limited.

(VI) SCIENTIFIC KNOWLEDGE: EXPERIMENT AND PRACTICE

The nearest that either Marx or Engels came to a clarification of
what they took scientific method to be was the emphasis that they
placed upon 'experiment' and 'practice' as modes of testing theories.
With regard to both notions, however, what they said was very

* Preface to 1st Edition of *Capital*. (Tr. by Moore and Aveling, Wm. Glaisher
Limited, 1918.)
† Preface to 1st Edition of *Capital*, p. xix.

limited, and, in what they said about 'practice' in particular, the issues became clouded again in ambiguity.

Marx undoubtedly thought 'experiment' to be crucial in the scientific method, and it is interesting to see how he himself thought he was using this in his study of society. Though Marx saw his 'materialist' conception and method as having application to all kinds of societies, his chief focus of concentrated study was the nature of 'industrial capitalism', the laws of which he sought to 'lay bare'. In undertaking this study, however, his focus was even more concentrated than that. In fact, he devoted himself chiefly to the study of industrial Britain. He outlined, in *Capital* his 'theoretical laws' by a process of definition and analysis, and then exemplified them in what might be called a specific 'case study' of capitalistic Britain. But he quite consciously regarded this as a specific 'experimental' instance, and, indeed, as an approximation to the experimental method of the natural sciences.

'The physicist', he wrote, 'either observes physical phenomena where they occur in their most *typical form* and most free from disturbing influence, or, wherever possible, he makes experiments under conditions that assure the occurrence of the phenomenon *in its normality*.

'In this work I have to examine the capitalist mode of production, and the conditions of production and exchange corresponding to that mode. Up to the present time, their classic ground is England. That is why England is used as the chief illustration in the development of my theoretical ideas.'*

As we have seen earlier, having clarified the 'laws' of this 'type' of social system, Marx went on to say that they served as a guide to those societies which were 'developing' towards it.

What this amounts to is that in his 'science of society', Marx quite distinctly maintained that societies could, like other phenomena, be classified into 'types'—each having its own 'laws' of relationships between its parts—and that these 'typical' characteristics could be clarified by considering in detail the most 'normal' case. Again, we see that the *experimental* and the *comparative* method were conceived as being part of each other in the science of society, and, of course, since the whole force of Marx's 'dialectical materialism' was to the effect that societies, like all other phenomena, were *processes* in relation to their material conditions, the *historical* method was also essentially involved in experiment and comparison. All these considerations of the elements of a science of society, though never clearly stated and elaborated, can be seen to be common to the writers we have already discussed, and to others who were to follow.

Considerable difficulty was introduced, however, by the further

* Preface to 1st Edition of *Capital*, p. xvii.

element of testability—namely, 'practice'. Marxism is in some essential way 'pragmatic' in its emphasis, and the scientific implications of this seem far from clear. Everyone after Marx used the same kind of phraseology. Engels wrote of: 'practice—viz. experiment and industry'. Stalin later wrote of the laws of nature and society—'tested by experiment and practice'. And one meaning of this is, of course, quite clear. In so far as men put their knowledge to use in their technology, in their practical methods of industry, they will have continuously to be relying upon, and continuously testing, its truth and adequacy. It was in this same sense, for example, that Comte believed that the new industrial proletariat would be more receptive to the knowledge and methods of 'positive science'—because they were quite directly involved in *using* them; the effectiveness of their working activity *depended* upon them. This can be both understood and accepted; but it is quite clear that this is no more than saying that those who must continuously *use* and *apply* the knowledge of empirical science will be most sensitive to its adequacy. There is no problem here; practice is simply a kind of extension of 'experiment'.

Marx himself, however, raised conceptual problems here which are much more difficult to understand. He clearly wished to distinguish a conception of science as an intellectual effort to establish knowledge of the world and so *understand* it, from a conception of science as part of a sensuous activity of man, in creatively *changing* the material conditions of nature and society in a process of gradually and progressively creating his own, distinctively human nature. This, I shall try to be as clear as possible about, later; but here we might simply note the great difficulty and ambiguity of this point. The most simple statement of this (though not the best*) is to be found in Marx's often-quoted 'Theses on Feuerbach', of which the most relevant are:

(I)

'The chief defect of all hitherto existing materialism—that of Feuerbach included—is that the object, reality, sensuousness, is conceived only in the form of the *object* or *contemplation* but not as *human sensuous activity*, *practice*, not subjectively. Thus it happened that the *active* side, in opposition to materialism, was developed by idealism—but only abstractly, since, of course, idealism does not know real sensuous activity as such. Feuerbach wants sensuous objects, really differentiated from the thought-objects, but he does not conceive human activity itself as activity *through objects*. Consequently, in the *Essence of Christianity*, he regards the theoretical attitude as the only genuinely human attitude, while practice is conceived and fixed only in its dirty-Jewish form of appearance. Hence he

---

* The fullest account of this 'sensuous, creative activity' interpretation of materialism, as far as I am aware, is in the *Economic and Philosophical Manuscripts of 1844*.

N

does not grasp the significance of "revolutionary", of practical-critical, activity.'

(II)

'The question whether objective truth can be attributed to human thinking is not a question of theory but is a practical question. In practice man must prove the truth, i.e., the reality and power, the "this-sidedness" of his thinking. The dispute over the reality or non-reality of thinking which is isolated from practice is a purely scholastic question.'

(VIII)

'Social life is essentially *practical*. All mysteries which mislead theory to mysticism find their rational solution in human practice and in the comprehension of this practice.'

(XI)

'The philosophers have *interpreted* the world in various ways; the point however is to *change* it.'

These, really, are garbled and confused statements. It is quite clear in them that a 'theoretical' attitude to the 'understanding' of 'objective' facts in the world and society is set against 'human sensuous activity' or 'revolutionary, practical-critical activity' which somehow 'proves the truth in practice' not by 'theoretically understanding', but by 'changing' the world. But what on earth does all this mean? What are the *criteria* whereby truth is proved in practical sensuous activity? And in what ways do they differ from the scientific criteria of 'theoretically understanding' the world? We are never told this, not by Marx himself, or the many from Engels, Lenin, Stalin to hundreds of thousands who quote from these 'theses' as though they contained the light of the ages. But until we *are* told this, these notions can only be regarded as nonsensical.

Their assertiveness, too, however, needs noting. Whoever asks about the 'reality or non-reality of thinking'? Who says that social life is *essentially* practical; or that *all* mysteries find their rational solution in practice? And there *may* be a *point* in *changing* the world —but to whom? Some people who *understand* some aspects of the world may see *no* point in changing them. On what criteria are they held to be mistaken?

Apart from its immediate intellectual ambiguity, this particular emphasis of Marx has increased the ambiguities which have drawn together the 'scientific' pretensions and the 'pragmatic' aims of Communism. By this twist, 'scientific' validity is claimed for the pragmatic programme of a political movement. It is surely very clear too, and patently dangerous, that there is an 'anti-intellectual' element in this position. I think there are elements in Marx's emphasis upon the 'sensuous creative activity of man' which can be understood, and with which one can very deeply sympathize, and this we shall come back to later; but there seems to me no doubt that to introduce *this* dimension of practice as something significantly qualifying the nature of scientific method and knowledge is both obscuring and dangerous in its outcome.

(VII) SCIENTIFIC KNOWLEDGE: CLASSIFICATION

One aspect of the last point is worth selecting for brief special emphasis. We saw that Marx—when thinking of experiment and comparison—insisted upon a central concern in science for the clarification of 'types', or, indeed, 'typical forms' which could exist 'in their normality' or affected by 'disturbing influences'. It is worthwhile simply to stress the fact that—upholding their 'dialectical materialism' (which saw the world as an interdependent multiplicity of forms of process) as against 'metaphysics' (which—as they thought —saw the world as an arrangement of distinct, separate objects)— Marx and Engels emphasized this procedure of *classification* in scientific method. Engels, for example, wrote:

'. . . while natural science up to the end of the last century was predominantly a *collecting* science, a science of finished things, in our century it is essentially a *classifying science*, a science of the processes, of the origin and development of these things and of the inter-connection which binds all these natural processes into one great whole.'*

As we shall see, Marx's 'materialism' led to the classification of certain 'types' of social system; but here it is enough to see that with Marx and Engels, as with Comte, Mill, and Spencer, the methods of science included classification as well as observation, description, analysis, comparison, experiment, and a historical account of process and development.

(VIII) SCIENTIFIC KNOWLEDGE: PROBES BEYOND SURFACE APPEARANCE TO 'HIDDEN LAWS'

One other point which deserves very brief mention here is especially relevant to the science of society. It is enough, for now, simply to say that both Marx and Engels thought it necessary that realistic science should seek those motives, forces, 'laws' which lay *hidden behind* what *appeared to be* a teeming multiplicity of disconnected facts.

Society *appears* to be complex, accidental, in many ways a prey to chance, but *really* 'it is always governed by inner, hidden laws and

---

* *Ludwig Feuerbach. Marx: Selected Works*, Vol. I, p. 454.

it is only a matter of discovering these laws'. (Engels) Also, men *appear* to act in society according to their views, or ends, or principles of a moral, religious, political, etc., nature—but *really* there are *class-interests behind* these motives which must be discovered by analysis for any realistic and satisfactory explanation. Again, Engels attacked the 'old materialism' for taking the 'ideal driving forces which operate there (in history) as ultimate causes'. Instead, he argued, one should investigate '. . . what is *behind* them, *what are the driving forces of these driving forces*'.

Now obviously, science delves below appearance, and may well discover deeper connections where, on the surface, there appear to be none. Even so, one does not have to be a genius to smell both a dogmatic metaphysic and an infinite regress here, unless care is exercised.

What this conception could amount to is that one continues to uncover the 'driving forces behind the driving forces' until one arrives at the *kind* or *level* of driving forces which one considers to be 'ultimate'—i.e., which is stipulated by one's metaphysic. It only needs someone with a *different* metaphysic to arrive on the scene, however, for the proposition to be made: 'Ah, no! I beg to differ! We must uncover *the* driving forces behind the driving forces behind the driving forces . . .'

Ultimately, one may get back to the first flip of God's finger—and then one might have an *explanation*.

Certainly the Marxian dogma of 'materialism' lends itself to the danger of this error.

(IX) SCIENTIFIC KNOWLEDGE: THE SIGNIFICANT CHARACTERISTICS OF NINETEENTH-CENTURY DEVELOPMENTS

Finally, it is worthwhile to see clearly that—whether they expressed it clearly or not—the emphasis upon the scientific method and its nature adopted by Marx and Engels was seen, by them, in exactly the same context as that recognized by the other thinkers we have considered. There is one passage in Engel's essay on Ludwig Feuerbach which sets out with complete clarify a perspective of nineteenth-century scientific influences and developments which might well have been set out by Herbert Spencer. It is this:

'Above all, there are three great discoveries which have enabled our knowledge of the interconnection of natural processes to advance by leaps and bounds: first, the discovery of the cell as the unit from whose multiplication and differentiation the whole plant and animal body develops—so that not only is the development and growth of all higher organism recognized to proceed according to a single general law, but also, in the capacity of the cell to change, the way is pointed out by which organisms can change their species and thus go through a more than individual development. Second, the transformation of energy, which has demonstrated that all the so-called forces operative in the first instance in inorganic nature—mechanical force and its complement, so-called potential energy, heat, radiation (light or radiant heat), electricity, magnetism and chemical energy—are different forms of manifestation of universal motion, which pass into one another in definite proportions so that in place of a certain quantity of the one which disappears, a certain quanitity of another makes its appearance and thus the whole motion of nature is reduced to this incessant process of transformation from one form into another. Finally, the proof which Darwin first developed in connected form that the stock of organic products of nature surrounding us today, including mankind, is the result of a long process of evolution from a few original unicellular germs, and that these again have arisen from protoplasm or albumen which came into existence by chemical means.

'We have now arrived at the point where we can demonstrate as a whole the interconnection between the processes in nature not only in particular spheres but also in the interconnection of these particular spheres themselves, and so can present in an approximately systematic form a comprehensive view of the interconnection in nature by means of the facts provided by empirical natural science itself. . . .

'But what is true of nature, is also true of the history of society in all its branches and of the totality of all sciences which occupy themselves with things human.'*

This attempt to sift through the many comments made by Marx and Engels on the importance and nature of the scientific method which they sought to apply to the study of society may well have seemed rather painstaking. However, it is undoubtedly necessary if we are properly to assess their theory of society, and, apart from this, I hope it has shown conclusively that the elements involved in their approach to the making of sociology were very much the same in Marx and Engels as in the other thinkers who were seeking the same objective. The 'Marxian' attempt to construct a 'science' of society took place in the same context of nineteenth-century influences, was one attempt among others—and similar to them, and utilized many similar conceptions of theory and method. I hope it has also been made clear, however, how insufficiently Marx's 'scientific assumptions' were worked out, when compared with those of Comte, Mill, and Spencer, and what awkward and potentially dangerous ambiguities were used, though unclarified and unresolved.

We are now in a position to move to the substantive theory of nature and society which Marx, with all the corollaries of Engels, put forward.

* *Marx: Selected Works*, Vol. I, pp. 454–5.

Dialectical Materialism

Marx's entire theory of nature and society, his whole 'system' of thought, can best be introduced and presented as a *contradiction* to that of Hegel. Whereas Hegel is the best representative of an 'IDEALIST' philosophy of history, Marx is the best representative of a 'MATERIALIST' philosophy of history. Our first step in understanding Marx must therefore be to become clear about his disagreement with Hegel, and what exactly he meant by 'materialism' and 'dialectical' materialism.

In this, as in every item of Marx's thought, there are ambiguities. Because of this, it is possible to give, on the one hand, a superficial interpretation which is open to caustic criticism and outright rejection, or, on the other, a sympathetic and profound interpretation—which takes care to delve beyond the ambiguities—and which, though extremely difficult to assess, seems to contain elements, insights, reorientations, emphases, of very great importance. There is a sense in which Marx is genuinely like an intellectual iceberg. The one fifth, which stands starkly above the surface is brilliant and striking, but it is also disturbing and disquieting because one is aware of the large and labyrinthine nature of the four fifths which lie, as the supporting reality, below—every single part of which presents considerable difficulties of exploration and navigation in moving towards a full and accurate knowledge of the whole. In this presentation, I shall try to give a clear and fair outline of each necessary component—trying to indicate both its superficial and profound aspects, the ambiguities that attend it, and the different interpretations which arise. But the concentration will be upon *clear exposition*. Our *critical assessment* can follow in a separate section.

What, then, were Marx's disagreements with the dialectical account of nature and history from an 'Idealist' point of view put forward by Hegel?

In a complete and radical manner, Marx first of all rejected the 'idealist' basis of Hegel's system. For him, there was no evidence whatever to suggest the existence of a 'World Spirit' prior to the existence of the material reality of nature; or that the vast, changing panorama of the world and of man's history within it were an 'actualization' of this previously existing 'Idea'. On the contrary, all our evidence was to the effect that the material reality of nature existed prior to the emergence of man, and prior to the subsequent emergence, within nature, of all those qualities of life and mind which, active in all men's activities—in art and music and literature, as well as in the making of societies—we have come to call 'spiritual'. This meant a complete over-turning of Hegel's system which had many very important dimensions.

First of all, the *material reality of nature* was *primary* in the nature of the world and history, and *'mind'* or *'qualities of the spirit'* were *secondary*. In *some* way, *matter* had given rise, in its intricate processes, to the emergence of animal organisms, the human species, human society and its historical transformations, and the conscious, creative activities of *mind*. Because of this order of the facts, the order of *explanation* and *understanding* was the same. It was a knowledge of the nature, conditions, and processes of *material reality* which could *explain* the subsequent qualities of life, mind, and conscious human creativity, *not* vice versa. Hegel had got *both* the order of the facts, *and* the necessary order of the explanation, the wrong way round.

Secondly, however, this error of Hegel's also entailed a false attributing of qualities of *'reality, truth, eternity'* to *'mind and spirit'*, and a relegating of the actual activities of natural processes, and the actual struggles of men in history to a level of *contingency* only. The *real* qualities had existed from eternity in the 'Idea' of the 'World Spirit', and the vast scene of nature and history, with all its vicissitudes and tribulations, was no more than a fabric of *means*, whereby the 'World Spirit' came to enjoy the full consciousness, in created actualities, of its original potentialities. Nature and men were borne upon a kind of vast tide of divine intentions and divine realities. Once this perspective was overturned, however, many interpretations were fundamentally changed. The 'ideas' of the human mind and spirit, and the concepts (such as 'beauty', 'truth', 'justice') which were implicit in them, no longer possessed 'reality, absoluteness, eternity', but were seen to be relative to man's actual activities in nature and society; they were 'reflections' of the material reality of nature and society and relative to men's historical conditions in that context. Man's actual activities in changing nature and society were seen to be the creative *reality* of human affairs, and 'ideas' and 'knowledge' were a relative part of these. Qualities of mind, though not absolute and eternal, were, nonetheless, in *this* perspective, seen to be *won* from the struggles with material nature. They therefore had a new status and dignity, despite the 'lower' or 'lesser' metaphysical claims that could be made for them.

This might especially be seen if one considers a particular 'idea' and 'actuality' such as 'Freedom'. Both Hegel and Marx 'measure' the dialectical 'advances' of history in terms of ever-increasing degrees of 'Freedom'. With Hegel, however, 'Freedom' is an initial 'Idea' within the potentiality of the World Spirit, and, after all the swirls of historical conflict, comes to be 'conscious' of its actualization when men, in the morality of the state, experience it. The atoms and organisms of the world have been woven in a kind of jazz about the underlying theme, or melody, of 'Freedom', which was stated at the outset by the 'World Spirit'. With Marx, 'Freedom' is an achievement of consciously worked out creative, personal activity in society, which men have *won*, have *struggled for*, have *accomplished*, in suffering, learning about, and then directing the material conditions and vicissitudes of nature and history. This is a very different perspective.

There is another element of this which Marx thought important. The Hegelian 'Idealist' system, of interpreting 'reality' in terms of certain 'categories' or 'ideas' and their (logical) dialectical unfolding in the actualities of nature, led to the imposition of a demand for theoretical understanding in terms of *'abstractions'*. 'Actualities' in nature and history were *'externalizations'* of *'ideas'*, and therefore to *'understand'* them was to uncover the *'abstract idealities'* which interpenetrated them. Marx radically opposed such 'theoretical understanding' in terms of 'abstraction', too. The *actualities* are the *material struggle*, he argued. The *practicalities* of nature and society are the basically real facts, and the 'ideas' are an outcome of, and can only be understood in terms of, the *practical* activities. Marx, then, advocated a fundamentally opposed method of understanding and explaining nature and history in terms of practical activities within a context of material conditions and processes, including an understanding of men's 'ideas', 'knowledge' and 'theories' as part of this. And it is clear that there really was, and is, something vitally important in this 'overturning' of the earlier philosophical approach. This was a viewpoint which not only proposed a vast reversal of order in philosophy and science itself, but was also of very basic importance for the making of sociology, and the statement, and criticism, of sociological theories.

Again, the sharp difference between Hegel's and Marx's position here can be made meticulously clear by briefly considering one matter—the nature of 'alienation'—which both men took to be of central importance for understanding the conflicts and contradictions at the heart of society and its many relationships. For Hegel— 'alienation' is a matter of the mind, or spirit (i.e., the World Spirit itself, and its partial actualization in man in any historical epoch) feeling separated from, and distanced from, the 'objectification' of its real 'essence' in the institutions of 'civil society' and the 'state' (and other 'actualizations' of nature). This experience of 'estrangement' is an important factor in the ongoing struggle in nature and history until the full conscious experience of the essence in the actuality is accomplished. For Marx—'alienation' is the distance and estrangement man comes to experience in the limiting, constraining conditions of his practical creative activity in the context of nature and society. In working on nature, he creates necessary material objects and material conditions and relationships (with other men) of labour. These themselves constrain his 'essential' activity—i.e. of creativity—and especially because, in history, they include the necessary emergence of 'property relations' which not only set man at a distance from the objects of his creativity, but also set man against man in relationships of exploitation, conflict, and power. These material, economic, and social aspects of 'alienation' are the mainsprings of historical struggle for Marx. The difference between the 'Idealist' and the 'Materialist' positions therefore seems very fundamental.

One other important dimension of this is difficult to state, but a great deal hangs upon it, and the perspective it provides is, properly understood, of the highest importance for understanding the historical significance of the 'modern revolution' of the past two hundred years or so, and is entirely compatible with the viewpoint of Comte, Spencer, and others who attempted to place the period, and the human dilemma to which it gave rise, in perspective. It is this:

The Hegelian 'Idealist' position rested on the unquestioned assumption that the spiritual 'essence' of man existed prior to his emergence in the world, and that there was therefore a kind of ultimate spiritual bedrock of absolute truth on which the entire fabric of the universe and human society was solidly based. In the smoke and confusion of history, men saw through a glass darkly, but, behind the troubled obscuring details, behind the 'temporal' sufferings, the rock-like eternity was there. The Marxian 'materialist' position—one among several which emerged with the questioning of modern science—maintained not only that there was no such rock, but that the true perspective contained dimensions which it was most important to realize in properly estimating man's contemporary dilemmas of destiny. Marx's position really maintained that the intricate material processes of nature and history were really the ground out of which *man made himself. Man did not have a nature prior to history*. On the contrary, man, as one species amongst others, emerged in a material nature over which he had no control, but in which he had to struggle. *The historical conditions of this struggle, which were the complex developments of societies, were actually the long process of creation of man's own nature.* The material conditions of historical change, too, have hitherto been beyond man's control, but with the emergence of modern science and modern industrial technology, man is increasingly conscious of his historical perspective, increasingly able to direct the future of his own creative efforts, and thus able to *make himself*, consciously and freely. In this way,

Marx regarded the entirety of previous history, during which man had been subordinated to his material conditions, as the 'PRE-HISTORY' of man. Only from this point on could man impose his own spiritual values and purposes upon history.

It will readily be seen that this view is strongly in keeping with Comte's picture of the culmination of history in the 'positive' stage, in which man must assume responsibility for the direction of his own affairs, and also with Spencer's idea of the 'Ethical' condition of society now before us—when the more mundane, economic problems of mankind have been resolved. But it will also readily be seen how firmly such a system of ideas provides a programme for *progressive political action*, whereas Hegel's system—with its eternal verities to uphold—leads itself to political conservatism and reaction. It is easy to see how and why Marx became a plank for political revolution; but it is also clear that—whatever one may ultimately accept or reject in his system—Marx was one very important voice among others stating a vast change of perspective—both of thought and action—in the modern world.

I may say that, in my opinion, both Marx and Engels either misunderstood or misrepresented some aspects of Hegel. For example, to argue that, for Hegel, the actualities of nature and history were simply *'externalizations'* (which is not the same as 'objectifications') of the 'World Spirit', and that 'matter' was a kind of secondary vehicle only, which Spirit used to 'externalize' itself, is a misunderstanding. For Hegel, matter itself is a creation of Spirit, always in a creative turmoil in the actualization of its forms; there is no 'externalization' in it; the entirety of existence is a creative process in which spirit is *itself-becoming*. Consequently, to think that the understanding of all this is a matter of 'abstractions' at the level of logic and 'rational theory' in the ordinary sense, is, itself, not to do justice to Hegel; not to penetrate his language and conceptions sufficiently. In short, Hegel himself is much more involved in the 'practical, sensuous activity' of nature and history than Marx gives him credit for; he is no cardboard figure of metaphysics. It can also be argued that—no matter how Hegel himself might have been *used* ideologically, consciously or otherwise, by various groups and social classes—there is nothing *necessarily* conservative or reactionary in an 'Idealist' philosophy of history. Neither, by the way, is there *necessarily* anything progressive in a 'materialist' one. At any rate, these issues are still open to debate at the deepest philosophical level and we must touch upon them again at the end of this chapter; but this need not prevent, or hold up, our exposition of Marx's 'materialism' *as if it were* a completely valid *opposite* to the system of Hegel.

It is necessary, now, to look with care at specific aspects of this in order to see all the elements of Marx's position, and, especially, to see where the ambiguities, superficialities, and profundities show their several faces.

(a) The over-turning of Hegel

It is perfectly clear that Marx himself, Engels, and all who followed, regarded the position of 'Dialectical Materialism' as a complete reversal of Hegel. Marx wrote, in the preface to the second edition of *Capital*:

'My dialectic is not only different from the Hegelian, but is its direct opposite. To Hegel, the life-process of the human brain, i.e., the process of thinking, which, under the name of "the Idea", he even transforms into an independent subject, is the demiurgos of the real world, and the *real* world is only the *external, phenomenal form* of "the Idea". With me, on the contrary, the ideal is nothing else than the material world *reflected* by the human mind, and translated into forms of thought.'

The italics in this passage are mine, and seek to emphasize firstly, the superficial conception of Hegel which we have noted earlier, and secondly—an important point to which we shall return—Marx's quite definite conception that the human mind *reflects* the material world, which is itself *real*. This too, of course, is a philosophically superficial and unwarranted position.

At the same time, we must notice that Marx did not *reject* Hegel, as did many critics of the time. On the contrary, he defended him against those who, as he put it, treated Hegel as 'a dead dog'. Though he *reversed* Hegel's 'Idealism', he nonetheless upheld and praised the 'dialectical' conception of nature and history—the conception of all the elements of nature and history as parts of a vast, interdependent, conflictful, developmental *process* of things—which Hegel had put forward and examined so systematically. In opposition to the totally destructive critics, he wrote:

'I therefore openly avowed myself the pupil of that mighty thinker, and even here and there . . coquetted with the modes of expression peculiar to him. The mystification which dialectic suffers in Hegel's hands, by no means prevents him from being the first to present its general form of working in a comprehensive and conscious manner. With him it is standing on its head. It must be turned right side up again, if you would discover the rational kernel within the mystical shell.'

There is no lack of clarity here. The 'dialectical' conception was retained, but its 'Idealist' basis was rejected. *Reality* was *material* reality, and out of *this* had all secondary qualities of life and mind emerged; by *this* were all qualities of life and mind determined. To see the clear, didactic way in which this position came to be held, it is interesting to note the statement of Stalin.

'Contrary to idealism, which regards the world as the embodiment of an "absolute idea", a "universal spirit", "consciousness" . . . Marx's philosophical materialism holds that the world is by its very nature *material*, that the multifold phenomena of the world constitute different forms of matter in motion, that interconnection and interdependence of phenomena . . . are a law of the development of moving matter, and that the world develops in accordance with the laws of movement of matter and stands in no need of a "universal spirit" . . .'*

It is when one comes to consider in detail the actual nature and processes of '*material reality*' and the ways in which it is thought to be causally '*determining*' of the nature and content of mind that difficulties and ambiguities arise.

(b) *Materialism: Matter and Mind*

It seems, to my mind, completely correct and fair, despite qualifications which were made later in their thinking, to say that the position of Marx and Engels was quite emphatically that the material processes of nature constitute the objective reality of the world, and that mind—in all its forms—is, and remains, a 'reflection' of this; and is '*determined*' by it. Indeed, I want to show, at the outcome of our argument, that if this position is qualified to the extent that they later wished to qualify it, it ceases to be a distinctive theory of 'materialism' in the radical sense that they claimed.

Matter is the primary reality, and it brings into being, and determines the nature and changing content of mind. For any satisfactory explanation of any events in nature, we must look for the causal factors in material reality. Mind is always secondary and dependent; a reflection of this. This was the definite and undeniable position of Marx and his followers.

We have already seen his own words:

'With me, the ideal is *nothing else* than the material world *reflected* in the human mind, and *translated* into forms of thought.'

Similarly, though I do not want to introduce too much, as yet, the consideration of the *material reality* of *society*, Marx also wrote:

'The mode of production in *material* life *determines* the social, political and intellectual life processes in general. It is not the consciousness of men that determine their being, but, on the contrary, their social being that *determines* their consciousness.'†

* Stalin. *Short History of the Communist Party of the Soviet Union* (*Bolsheviks*), p. 100.
† Preface to '*A Contribution to the Critique of Political Economy.*'

These are completely definite statements, and they were much reiterated in varying forms and emphases throughout the writing of Marx. Engels, as always, was much more pedantic, and very specific indeed.

'The real unity of the world,' he wrote, 'consists in its materiality . . .'*
'. . . the material, sensuously perceptible world to which we ourselves belong is the only reality; and our consciousness and thinking, however supra-sensuous they may seem, are a product of a material, bodily organ, the brain. Matter is not a product of mind, but mind itself is merely the highest product of matter.'†
'. . . the dialectic concept of the concept itself becomes merely the *conscious reflex* of the dialectical motion of the *real* world, and the dialectic of Hegel is placed upon its head . . .'†
'*It is impossible to separate thought from matter that thinks*. This matter is the substratum of all changes going on in the world . . .'‡

Again, there can be no doubt about this position. In attacking the 'Idealist' emphasis upon the *primacy* of mind, it was thought necessary to demote the role of mind in nature, and to insist upon the primacy, the totally dominant determining powers, the reality, of *matter*. Both Marx and Engels emphasized too, that all the 'theoretical outlooks' of men were 'derived from their material conditions'.

'Does it require deep intuition,' they wrote in the Communist Manifesto, 'to comprehend that man's ideas, views and conceptions, in one word, man's consciousness, changes with every change in the conditions of his material existence . . . ?'

No, one might reply, but it requires a good deal more than deep intuition, and something much more susceptible to test, to demonstrate that it is always the latter that *determines* the former; and that only the latter is *real*, whilst the former is no more than a '*reflection*' of it. It is apparent at once where ambiguities rush in upon a position of this kind. For though it *may* be plausible to reject an 'Idealist' metaphysic, and though it *may* be plausible to argue that mind has emerged in the world in the context of prior material processes, and remains to some extent constrained by them, it does *not* follow that mind is totally subservient to them, determined by them, or ineffective in 'causing' change. Neither does it follow that mind is, in any sense, less 'real' than matter. It may be that protoplasm emerged in the world *after* atoms and molecules, but no-one would say it was 'less real' than they: it is one quality of the world as we are aware of it, and so are aspects, efforts, purposes, and powers of mind. To replace

* *Anti-Dühring*. p. 54.
† (Ludwig Feuerbach) *Karl Marx: Selected Works*, p. 435.
‡ Marx and Engels: '*The Holy Family*.'

'Idealism' by 'Materialism' in the sense stated above, is no more than to *assert* one metaphysic against another.

Again, to see the extent of the solidifying of this metaphysic, we might look briefly at the culminating statements of followers such as Lenin and Stalin. Lenin, for example, wrote:

'Materialism in general recognizes objectively real being (matter) as independent of consciousness, sensation, experience . . . Consciousness is only the reflection of being, at best, an approximately true (adequate, ideally exact) reflection of it.'*

And:

'Matter is that which, acting upon our sense-organs, produces sensation; matter is the objective reality given to us in sensation . . . Matter, nature, being, the physical—is primary, and spirit, consciousness, sensation, the psychical—is secondary.'†

Stalin, with his methodical precision and care, wrote as follows:

'Contrary to idealism, which asserts that only our mind really exists, and that the material world, being, nature, exists only in our mind, in our sensations, ideas and perceptions, the Marxist materialist philosophy holds that matter, nature, being, is an objective reality existing outside and independent of our mind; that matter is primary, since it is the source of sensations, ideas, mind, and that mind is secondary, derivative, since it is a reflection of matter, a reflection of being; that thought is a product of matter which in its development has reached a high degree of perfection, namely, of the brain, and the brain is the organ of thought; and that therefore one cannot separate thought from matter without committing a grave error.'

We have noted the ambiguity attending this question of what is, or is not, *real*, and the 'determining' powers of matter, and all that need be said further, here, is that the great importance of realizing these ambiguities will be seen when we come to consider their place in theories about 'Historical Materïalism'. They are far from being philosophical, or conceptual issues alone, but lie at the heart of our assessment of Marx's sociology. Before leaving this initial aspect of 'materialism', however, one other point must be emphasized strongly —and this refers to a 'trivial' or 'profound' interpretation of Marx, even though it is, again, but a pointing out of indefiniteness and ambiguity. It is this.

It seems to me true to say that Marx himself always wrote with a broader, richer, vision of things before him than many of the rather narrow, repetitive, parrot-like systematizers who came after him; who rode to prominence and power on his philosophical band-

* Lenin, *Selected Works*, p. 377.   *Ibid.*, pp. 207, 208.

wagon. It is easy to see how 'matter' and 'mind' can be juxtaposed in the most simple-minded of ways, following from the above kinds of statement, and how a naive notion of material 'determinism' can be stated, criticized and totally rejected. And this may be a valid criticism of many Marxists. Marx himself, however, never wrote in quite such naked terms. By and large, Marx did not oppose 'matter' and 'mind'—which, for him would be 'abstractions'; but really thought always of man being involved in practical, sensuous, creative activities *in nature*; and thought of man's 'feeling', 'thinking', 'theorizing' as always being concomitant with these activities—arising in and from them, serving them, and being tested in their application. It was really 'man creatively active in nature; suffering the constraints of material circumstances in nature and society; but coming ultimately to govern them and direct them in the light of knowledge and with the effective power of industrial technology',* and this gives a very different picture, allowing for a full appreciation of all the qualitative richness of nature; the qualitative richness of 'material reality'. It is also less doctrinaire in its dogmatism. Marx, for example, wrote in this way:

'The worker can create nothing without *nature*, without the *sensuous external world*. It is the material on which his labour is manifested, in which it is active, from which and by means of which it produces . . .'†

To say that: '. . . Man *lives* on nature—means that nature is his *body*, with which he must remain in continuous intercourse if he is not to die. That man's physical and spiritual life is linked to nature means simply that nature is linked to itself, for man is a part of nature.'‡

It is at least obvious, and this is all we need note for now, that an account of man's creative activity in nature, and an account of the historical making of societies and of systems of thought, belief, and artistic imagination which are significantly related to this activity is a much richer and more acceptable programme of description, analysis, and explanation, than a simple 'matter-versus-mind' determinism. And this must be borne in mind. Some insights and dimensions of Marx may be more true and important than some criticism of the determinism which can be constructed from his statements would seem to suggest. And yet we must note that this, even so, is really a defence of profundity in terms of ambiguity—which is an odd kind of defence, and really leads to nothing firm. For it means, really, that in so far as Marx can be interpreted as asserting a metaphysic of narrow 'materialistic determinism' he can be shown to be philosophically shallow; but in so far as he can be interpreted as possessing

* This is *not* a quotation, merely an indication of Marx's way of thinking.
† *1844 Manuscripts*, p. 70.   ‡ *Ibid.*, p. 74.

insights of profundity, he can be shown *not* to be putting forward a tight 'materialism' at all. The problems of deciding upon 'superficial' or 'profound' interpretations, and the ambiguities which vex any attempt at fair and correct judgment, begin to swarm about us!

So much, at any rate, for materialism and its emphasis upon the 'determinism' of mind by material reality.

(c) *Dialectical Materialism: contrary to 'Metaphysics'*

One other claim made on behalf of Dialectical Materialism by Marx, Engels and their followers which contains ambiguity, and should be seen clearly, was that it is somehow (by insisting upon the basic reality of material processes) contradictory to, and an advance upon, 'metaphysics'.

Thus, when writing of the application of (Hegel's) dialectics to the 'materialist conception of nature', Engels maintained that:

'. . . modern natural science . . . has proved that in the last analysis nature's process is *dialectical* and not *metaphysical*.'*

We need not dwell on this point since it is so obvious an error, but, again, to emphasize how far the error has gone in doctrinaire expositions, let us briefly note some of the repeated statements of Stalin:

'Dialectics is the direct opposite of metaphysics.

'Contrary to metaphysics, dialectics does not regard nature as an accidental agglomeration of things . . . unconnected with, isolated from, and independent of each other, but as a connected and integral whole . . .

'Contrary to metaphysics, dialectics holds that nature is not a state of rest and immobility, stagnation and immutability, but a state of continuous movement and change . . .

'Contrary to metaphysics, dialectics does not regard the process of development as a simple process of growth . . .'

And so—on and on. In this way of arguing (if that is the right word) something called 'metaphysics' is derogated as a kind of musty old lumber-room full of old ideas of 'reality' as being 'static', 'stagnant', 'accidental, isolated collections of objects', and the like, whereas 'dialectical materialism' shines by its side as all that is scientific, seeing 'reality' as a rich, ceaselessly changing, growing, progressive process of things.

But this, of course, is completely misguided. 'Metaphysical' theories (which are about the nature of 'reality') as distinct from scientific theories (which are about the testable interconnections among the facts of our experience) do *not* necessarily assert 'static' accounts of 'discrete, isolated' objects, etc. *Some* metaphysical theories

* *Anti-Dühring.*

might, but certainly not all; and the term 'metaphysical' is certainly not to be *equated* with the holding of such notions. But also —Dialectical Materialism *is itself* a theory of reality; indeed, a very pugnacious one, attacking the 'Idealist' account of 'reality' and seeking to replace it very definitely with another. There must, then, be no doubt or confusion whatever about this. 'Dialectical Materialism' was a new *Metaphysical theory*; and it will be important to see that its supposed '*scientific theories* of society' are in large part no more than an assertive insistence upon the adoption of *this* metaphysic rather than others.

We are clear, then, about 'Materialism' as a new, ambiguous metaphysic; but we have come to use the adjective 'dialectical'. What, exactly, was meant by this? And why, and in what ways, was it thought to be an 'advance'?

(d) Materialism: Dialectics
Dialectical Materialism was distinguished from what Marx and Engels called the 'Old' Materialism by two important characteristics, both of which were held to imply fundamental differences in what constituted scientific 'explanations' of events in nature and history. These two features were therefore new features of *method*, as well as new conceptions of the nature of reality. First—Dialectical Materialism regarded all the 'entities' or 'events' of the world *not* as disparate, concrete 'things', existing in a set of eternal, external, spatial relations to each other, but as mutually interpenetrating and interdependent parts of one vast, continuous process. Objects (and their 'distinctive natures') could only be understood in their close interdependence with surrounding objects, and, essentially, as part of an all-pervading *process*, in continuous interaction and change. Second—Dialectical Materialism specified the nature, the determinate characteristics, *of this process of change*; it was, in fact, a process in which sequences of *additive, quantitative* change gave rise, at certain specific 'nodal' points to *qualitatively* new forms of reality. These two features, taken together, however, led to a third point which I wish especially to emphasize: namely that Dialectical Materialism was, in fact, a materialistically based *theory of evolution*: scarcely distinguishable from that of Spencer. Its claims to be distinctive in this respect were, as we shall see, unfounded. It was, in fact, one expression among others of the nineteenth century evolutionary perspective. It also contained exactly the same ambiguities concerning 'evolution' and 'progress'.

The new insistence which was placed upon *process* has already been noted in the fact that Marx, whilst rejecting Hegel's 'Idealistic' basis, nonetheless accepted his 'dialectics' as being a reorientation of the greatest importance. The same emphasis is to be found in all the expositions of Engels.

'What distinguished Hegel's mode of thought,' he wrote, 'from that of all other philosophers was the enormous *historical sense* upon which it was based . . .

'He was the first who attempted to show an *evolution*, an *inner coherence* in history . . .

'This epoch-making conception of history was the direct theoretical prerequisite for the new materialistic contemplation . . .'*

The fundamental contribution which Marx and he had made in 'rescuing' Hegel's dialectical conception and applying it to the materialist conception of nature, was, claimed Engels:

'The great basic thought that the world is not to be comprehended as a complex of ready-made *things*, but as a complex of *processes*, in which the things apparently stable no less than the mind-images in our heads, the concepts, go through an uninterrupted change of coming into being and passing away, in which, in spite of all seeming accidents and of all temporary retrogression, a progressive development asserts itself in the end . . .'†

And in this dialectical conception of materialism, he maintained:

'. . . nothing is final, absolute, sacred. It reveals the transitory character of everything and in everything; nothing can endure before it except the uninterrupted process of becoming and of passing away, of endless ascendancy from the lower to the higher.'‡

This, it is very clear, is almost exactly the endless process of 'transformation of forms' put forward by Spencer; and the terms 'progressive development', 'endless ascendancy' from 'lower to higher' make the implicit *evaluative* element in Engels' conception clear beyond all doubt. In order to make this identity (I do not think this is too strong a word) between Engels and Spencer meticulously clear, we might look at the statement which Engels made when trying to emphasize the difference between 'dialectical' and 'old' materialism by insisting that *matter* simply could not be conceived independently of *process*, of *motion*. In *Anti-Dühring*, he wrote:

'*Motion is the mode of existence of matter*. Never anywhere has there been matter without motion, nor can there be. Motion in cosmic space, mechanical motion of smaller masses on the various celestial bodies, the motion of molecules as heat or as electrical or magnetic currents, chemical combination or disintegration, organic life—at each given moment each individual atom of matter in the world is in one or other of these forms of motion, or in several forms of them at once. All rest, all equilibrium, is

* *On Karl Marx's 'Contribution to the Critique of Political Economy.'* Section (11)
† *Ludwig Feuerbach.*   ‡ *Ibid.*

only relative, and only has meaning in relation to one or other definite form of motion. A body, for example, may be on the ground in mechanical equilibrium, may be mechanically at rest; but this in no way prevents it from participating in the motion of the earth and in that of the whole solar system, just as little as it prevents its most minute physical parts from carrying out the oscillations determined by its temperature, or its atoms from passing through a chemical process. Matter without motion is just as unthinkable as motion without matter. Motion is therefore as uncreatable and indestructible as matter itself; as the older philosophy expressed it, the quantity of motion existing in the world is always the same. Motion therefore cannot be created; it can only be transferred.'*

The first distinctive feature of 'Dialectical Materialism'—the insistence on a perspective of *interdependence* and *process*—is therefore very clear, and we shall emphasize again, later, that this was, in fact, the nineteenth century theory and perspective of 'evolution'. The second feature, however—the 'quantitative-qualitative' process of change in material reality—is even more important for our critical assessment of Marx's theory of nature and society. And it is important to insist that this central conception of the transformation of 'quantity' into 'qualitative difference' was, in fact, held by Marx himself (not only by Engels) and did, in fact, constitute a basic principle of analysis and explanation in all his work. It is sometimes held that it was the *followers* of Marx, rather than Marx himself, who made much of this conception, and this principle of explanation, and it is true that Engels (and later Lenin and Stalin) articulated it much more pedantically than he did. Still—he stated, accepted, and adopted it fully himself, and his system is based upon it, and open to criticism in terms of it.

In fact, Marx derived the conception from Hegel—that, in nature and history, additive elements of a *quantitative* nature reached certain 'nodal points' at which they became *qualitatively* newly emergent substances, forms, entities. The *essential* nature of change and creation in material reality was this emergence and unfolding of qualitative difference, out of cumulative quantitative change. And in *Capital* Marx wrote of social transformations of this kind, and also referred to the same kinds and sequences of change as uncovered in the molecular theory of chemistry.

It was Engels, however, who—in his *Dialectics of Nature* and his polemics against Herr Dühring—amassed examples to illustrate these 'quantitative-qualitative' dialectical processes, and it is most important to see these examples clearly and to see the mode of explanation which they clearly imply, and insist upon.

In the *Dialectics of Nature*, Engels wrote:

* *Anti-Dühring*, Engels, (Martin Lawrence Limited, Tr. Emile Burns), p. 71.

'In physics . . . every change is a passing of quantity into quality, as a result of a quantitative change of some form of movement either inherent in a body or imparted to it. For example, the temperature of water has at first no effect on its liquid state: but as the temperature of liquid water rises or falls, a moment arrives when this state of cohesion changes and the water is converted in one case into steam and in the other into ice . . . A definite minimum current is required to make a platinum wire glow; every metal has its melting temperature; every liquid has a definite freezing point and boiling point at a given pressure, as far as we are able with the means at our disposal to attain the required temperatures; finally, every gas has its critical point at which, by proper pressure and cooling, it can be converted into a liquid state . . . What are known as the constants of physics are in most cases nothing but designations for the nodal points at which a quantitative (change) increase or decrease of movement causes a qualitative change in the state of the given body, and at which, consequently, quantity is transformed into quality.'

And in *Anti-Dühring*:

'This is precisely the Hegelian nodal line of measure relations, in which, at certain definite nodal points, the purely quantitative increase or decrease gives rise to a *qualitative leap*, for example, in the case of water which is heated or cooled, where boiling-point and freezing-point are the nodes at which—under normal pressure—the leap to a new aggregate state takes place, and where consequently quantity is transformed into quality.'

In *Anti-Dühring*, too, Engels gave examples of a number of acids—formic acid, acetic acid, propionic acid, butyric acid, and valerianic acid—which, he showed, constituted:

'. . . a whole series of *qualitatively* different bodies, formed by the simple *quantitative* addition of elements and in fact always in the same proportion . . . Each new member comes into existence through the addition of one atom of carbon and two atoms of hydrogen, to the molecular formula of the preceding member, this *quantitative* change in molecular composition produces at each step a *qualitatively* different body.'*

Again, to see how firmly this doctrine of conception and explanation came to be laid down, let us see how Stalin framed it:

'Dialectics,' he wrote, 'does not regard the process of development as a simple process of growth, but as a development which passes from insignificant and imperceptible quantitative changes to open, fundamental changes, to qualitative changes; a development in which the qualitative changes occur not gradually, but rapidly and abruptly, taking the form of a leap from one state to another; they occur not accidentally but as the natural result of an accumulation of imperceptible and gradual quantitative changes.'†

* *Anti-Dühring*, p. 145.
† *Short History of the Communist Party of the Soviet Union*. p. 96.

This conception, and this principle of explanation in 'Dialectical Materialism' are undeniably clear. Material reality is primary; qualities of life and mind are dependent, and secondary. All particular elements or aspects of material reality can only be understood and explained as interdependent parts of a continuous process of transformation and change. And in this process, change is brought about by a sequence of cumulative, additive, quantitative changes which, at certain points, undergo, or manifest a 'qualitative leap' to a newly emergent entity. The explanations of 'Dialectical Materialism' rest upon the fundamental foundation of this conception.

Here, we will not stop to enter into criticism, but move forward to see some other ways in which this 'Dialectical Materialism' was thought to constitute an advance.

(e) Materialism: Dialectics an advance on 'Old' Materialism

We have already noted, in passing, the ways in which 'dialectics' was thought to have surpassed the 'old' materialism, but, for the sake of precision, let us simply note that there were *three* of these. First, the 'old' materialism was thought to be 'mechanistic', whereas the new conception saw reality as a complex, interwoven process. Second, the 'old' materialism had a 'static', 'eternal', frame of reference (the 'metaphysical' conception) whereas the new perspective was one of dialectical, quantitative-qualitative change, essentially historical and developmental, and, as Lenin put it later, applied 'the standpoint of evolution consistently and all-sidedly'. Third, the 'old' materialism conceived of men still in 'abstract' terms, and focused its efforts upon 'understanding' and '*interpreting*' the world, whereas the new conception saw historical man in his essentially practical activities, and focused its efforts upon '*changing*' the world.

We need not note again the ambiguities attending some of these points. The other claims for the *advancement* over earlier theories of 'dialectics' are more interesting.

(f) Materialism: Dialectics an advanced Theory of Evolution

Already, we have seen, and have argued, that the Marx-Engels formulation of 'Dialectical Materialism' was, in fact, a Spencerian theory of evolution in (in many respects) scarcely distinguishable terms. But it is worthwhile to note quite specifically that this is how followers of Marx themselves came to regard it. Indeed, this is what they insisted on claiming for it. The best example, after Engels, was Lenin, who wrote as follows:

'In our times, the idea of development, of evolution, has almost fully penetrated social consciousness, but it has done so in other ways, not through Hegel's philosophy. But the same idea, as formulated by Marx

379

and Engels on the basis of Hegel's philosophy, is much more comprehensive, much more abundant in content than the current theory of evolution. A development that repeats, as it were, the stages already passed but repeats them in a different way, on a higher plane; a development, so to speak in spirals, not in a straight line; a spasmodic, catastrophic, revolutionary development; "breaks of gradualness"; transformation of quantity into quality; inner impulses for development, imparted by the contradiction, the conflict of different forces and tendencies reacting on a given body or inside a given phenomenon or within a given society; interdependence, and the closest, indissoluble connection between all sides of every phenomenon (history disclosing ever newer and newer sides); a connection that provides the one world-process of motion proceeding according to law—such are some of the features of dialectics as a doctrine of evolution more full of meaning than the current one.'*

This, with absolute clarity, claims not only that 'Dialectical Materialism' is a theory of evolution, but that it is a *better*, more thorough, more comprehensive, theory of evolution than others of the time. But, equally clearly, it speaks in almost complete ignorance of the evolutionary theories of men like Comte and (especially) Spencer which were, in many ways, very similar. As I have said earlier, I want to emphasize this very strongly because, on the one hand, many recent critics have tended to deplore the insufficiencies of 'evolutionary' theories, and have held up Marxism as a 'revolutionary' theory which has sharper explanatory 'teeth', so to speak. And they do not seem to realize that Marxism was, and is, one 'evolutionary' theory among others. But also, on the other hand, 'Dialectical Materialism' has come to be thought, by many, quite a unique, startlingly new outlook of 'process and change', and quite a distinctive basis for the making of a satisfactory sociology—different from all others. And this, of course, is simply untrue, and cannot be upheld for a moment. 'Dialectical Materialism' is not distinctively different from the evolutionary perspective of Spencer *except* that it asserts, within—indeed, in the heart of—this context, a materialist, quantitative-qualitative metaphysic and dogma. And this turns out to be its most vulnerable, indeed its insupportable, component.

(g) *Materialism: Dialectics an advanced Social (as well as Natural) Science*

Finally, we may simply note that one claim made on behalf of 'Dialectical Materialism' was that it provided a completely new basis and perspective for the creation and development of a 'science of society' which was an improvement on anything achieved before. Lenin has stated this claim very clearly, but all 'Marxists', from

* *Marx: Selected Works*, Vol. I, p. 28.

Marx and Engels to the present day, have shared it. In his encyclopaedia article on 'Karl Marx', Lenin wrote:

'*At best*, pre-Marxist "sociology" and historiography gave an accumulation of raw facts collected at random, and a description of separate sides of
the historic process. Examining the *totality* of all the opposing tendencies,
reducing them to precisely definable conditions in the mode of life and the
method of production of the various *classes* of society, discarding sub-
jectivism and arbitrariness in the choice of various "leading" ideas or in
their interpretation, showing how all the ideas and all the various tendencies, without exception, have their roots in the condition of the material
forces of production, Marxism pointed the way to a comprehensive, an
all-embracing study of the rise, development, and decay of social economic
structures.'*

Though one would agree that it was an improvement in the
scientific approach to the study of society to study 'all sides' of the
historic process, the 'totality' of social facts in their interdependence,
and the like, it is, of course quite false to think that pre-Marxist
'sociology', and historiography ignored these things. The outlook of
'Dialectical Materialism' was simply *not* new in these respects at all.
What it *could* claim was to have laid specific emphasis upon the
primacy of *material* conditions in nature and society. Even here, it
was not new in being 'materialistic'; it was new and different only in
specifying the quantitative-qualitative process of change, and the
primacy in this cause and effect determinacy of the *material* facts.

So much, then, for 'Dialectical Materialism' as a conceptual
approach to the analysis of, and statement of theories about '*Nature*'.
For Marx and his followers, the 'World Spirit' was totally removed
from the scheme of things and from the apparatus of explanation.
The entirety of 'Nature' was a *material* process which changed in
accordance with quantitative additions and accumulations, and
qualitative 'leaps', and which was simply '*reflected*' in the emergent
processes of life and mind.

The most interesting matter, from our point of view, is the way in
which this clear 'analytical apparatus' of Dialectical Materialism
then came to be applied to the study of society and history—thereby
coming to be called 'Historical Materialism'. This, especially, was the
contribution of Marx to the making of sociology, and we are now
completely ready both to state this theory and to achieve a critical
assessment of it. In this section especially, I want first of all, to confine myself to the fairest *exposition* of Marx's theory, and, only
secondly, after this, to come to a scrupulous *criticism* of it. Before
launching into this, however, one point must be made. In Marx
himself, of course, there was, strictly speaking, no distinction be-

* *Marx, Selected Works* Vol. 1, p. 30.

tween 'Dialectical Materialism' and 'Historical Materialism'. It was one of Marx's major emphases that man was a part of nature; that human society was a developmental outcome of the material activity of man in nature; and that the history of society was a determinate sequence of these material activities and the institutional fabric built about them. So this must be borne in mind. It is really, again, the Marxian *'expositors'*—Engels, Lenin, Stalin, who clarify *firstly* 'Dialectical Materialism' as a system of conceiving and explaining the world ('nature'), and then *secondly* 'Historical Materialism' as a system of conceiving and explaining society and its development. However, in my opinion, this 'pedagogic' dichotomy has, in fact, done a great service, because, in trying to be meticulously clear, it has meticulously clarified the *analogies* which, in Marx, are taken to be real *identities* (e.g., between the material aspects ('basis') of natural processes, and the 'material conditions' of society; between the 'quantitative' addition of molecules in the changes of nature, and the 'quantitative' additions of technological inventions in history; etc.) and the conceptual and terminological inexactitudes (ambiguities) which lead, in my view, to theoretical—and even descriptive and analytical—falsity. All this may well sound unnecessarily complex, but I do not think it is. These ghosts really do need laying, and I want to do my best to lay them.

Let us move then, to Marx's theory of society, his 'Historical Materialism', and let us work through his argument systematically both in order to be exact in our understanding of it, and to make clear all those components of analysis and theory which are common to those other theoretical positions we have considered so far.

Historical Materialism

(*a*) *As matter is the primary objective reality in Nature, so Man's relations to the material world, Man's material conditions of life, are the primary objective reality in Society.*
This was the first major principle of the application of 'Dialectical Materialism' to the scientific study of society, and there were really two aspects of it—not, strictly speaking, identical with each other—which are emphasized by Marx and Engels.

The first of these was a stated priority of need: that man had, of necessity, to sustain himself economically, to win a livelihood from the material resources of nature, and so survive—before he could devote himself to 'secondary' social experiences and activities: religion, art, family organization and the like. In his speech at Marx's graveside, Engels said:

'Marx discovered the law of evolution in human history; he discovered the simple fact, hitherto concealed by an overgrowth of ideology, that mankind must first of all eat and drink, have shelter and clothing, before it can pursue politics, science, religion, art, etc.; and that therefore the production of the immediate material means of subsistence and consequently the degree of economic development attained by a given people or during a given epoch, form the foundation upon which the state institutions, the legal conceptions, the art and even the religious ideas of the people concerned have been evolved, and in the light of which these things must therefore be explained, instead of *vice versa* as had hitherto been the case.'*

Also, the same point was emphasized in Engels' biographical note on Marx:

'History was for the first time placed on its real basis; the obvious but previously totally overlooked fact that men must first of all eat, drink, have clothing and shelter, therefore must *work*, before they can fight for domination, pursue politics, religion, philosophy, etc.'†

This, strictly speaking, was simply a statement of historical *order*; of temporal *sequence*: that the wresting of a livelihood from the material resources of nature had to come *before* the development of the more complex fabric of social organization.

The second aspect of this point was distinctively different, though it might be said to be inclusive of it. It was that, quite apart from historical sequence alone, it could be shown to be *always* the case in society that man's practical activity in making products from the material resources of nature formed a basic set of social and (especially) property relations which *determined* the nature of all the other institutions—of law, government, religion, education, etc.—which came into being to serve its particular pattern of interests and power. In this sense, man's practical relations with the material world were the *primary, objective* reality in society, and all other institutions were *secondary reflections* of it; the former constituted the *material basis* of society, the latter—the *'super-structure'* of institutions.

Marx wrote that when criticizing Hegel's philosophy of law, he was driven to the conclusion:

'. . . that legal relations such as forms of the state are to be grasped neither from themselves nor from the so-called general development of the human mind, but rather have their roots *in the material conditions of life* . . . the anatomy of civil society is to be sought in *political economy*.'

Also, in the first volume of *Capital*, he insisted:

'*Technology* discloses man's mode of dealing with nature, the process of production by which he sustains his life, and thereby also lays bare the

* *Marx: Selected Works*, Vol. I, p. 16.   † *Ibid.*, p. 12.

mode of formation of his social relations, and of the mental conceptions that flow from them.'

But here it is best to look carefully through Marx's own 'classical' statement of his theory*—because it contains, both implicitly and explicitly, practically all the elements which we shall want to draw out, examine, and emphasize as separate points.

'In the social production which men carry on they enter into definite relations that are indispensable and independent of their will; these relations of production correspond to a definite stage of development of their material forces of production. The sum total of these relations of production constitutes the economic structure of society—the real foundation, on which rises a legal and political superstructure and to which correspond definite forms of social consciousness. The mode of production in material life determines the social, political and intellectual life processes in general. It is not the consciousness of men that determines their being, but, on the contrary, their social being that determines their consciousness. At a certain stage of their development, the material forces of production in society come in conflict with the existing relations of production, or—what is but a legal expression for the same thing—with the property relations within which they have been at work before. From forms of development of the forces of production these relations turn into their fetters. Then begins an epoch of social revolution. With the change of the economic foundation the entire immense super-structure is more or less rapidly transformed.

In considering such transformations a distinction should always be made between the material transformation of the economic conditions of production which can be determined with the precision of natural science, and the legal, political, religious, aesthetic or philosophic—in short, ideological forms in which men become conscious of this conflict and fight it out. Just as our opinion of an individual is not based on what he thinks of himself, so can we not judge of such a period of transformation by its own consciousness; on the contrary this consciousness must be explained rather from the contradictions of material life, from the existing conflict between the social forces of production and the relations of production. No social order ever disappears before all the productive forces for which there is room in it have been developed; and new higher relations of production never appear before the material conditions of their existence have matured in the womb of the old society itself. Therefore, mankind always sets itself only such tasks as it can solve; since, looking at the matter more closely, we will always find that the task itself arises only when the material conditions necessary for its solution already exist or are at least in the process of formation.

In broad outlines we can designate the Asiatic, the ancient, the feudal, and the modern bourgeois modes of production as so many epochs in the progress of the economic formation of society. The bourgeois relations of

* *A Contribution to the Critique of Political Economy.*

production are the last antagonistic form of the social process of production—antagonistic not in the sense of individual antagonism, but of one arising from the social conditions of life of the individuals; at the same time the productive forces developing in the womb of bourgeois society create the material conditions for the solution of that antagonism. This social formation constitutes, therefore, the closing chapter of the prehistoric stage of human society.'

In this statement it is perfectly clear that the materialist basis of society was held to determine all other 'secondary' qualities of it, and that the dialectical process of change in the history of society, as in nature, was one of accumulative quantitative additions in the material basis of society, accompanied, at certain points, by 'qualitative leaps'—revolutionary transformations—to new 'super-structures' of institutions. Each of the components of this theory must now be separately stated.

(b) Man's practical relations with the material world are man's 'economic' relations. The economic structure is the material basis of society

This is a distinctive step of argument which is not always made clear in Marx's theory. To speak of man's sensuous practical activity in nature, or man's relations to the material world, is *one* thing; to equate all this with man's *'economic'* relations; the 'forces of production'; and then to claim that the nature of the *latter* determines all the dimensions of the *former*—is quite definitely another; but in Marx these are not at all distinguished. We shall come back to a criticism of this point later, but here it is enough to note and emphasize that the *'primacy of material reality'* in nature maintained by dialectical materialism, is, in its application in 'Historical Materialism', interpreted as the principle that, *in society, men's relations to the material world are the primary reality which determines all the rest*; and, further, that these relations to the material world are men's *economic* relations.

Marx treated the two terms—'material' and 'economic'—as being synonymous. Thus, in a letter to Annenkov,* he wrote, concerning the 'social history of men':

'Their *material relations* are the basis of *all their relations*.'

And in the first paragraph of the last quotation, he maintained that the sum-total of the 'definite relations' of 'social production':

'. . . constitutes the *economic structure* of society—the *real foundation*, on which rises a legal and political superstructure . . .'

* Letter to P. V. Annenkov, December 1846. *Marx: Selected Works*, Vol. I, p. 373.

Men's material relations with each other and with the material world were clearly identified with the *economic* structure of society—which was the material basis; the real foundation; which determined all the institutions of the super-structure. And this material, 'economic' basis of society consisted, according to Marx, of the *'forces of production'*.

(c) The Economic Structure of Society: The 'Productive Forces'

By the 'material forces of production', Marx meant a number of specific and closely related things.

(I) PRODUCTS, AND INSTRUMENTS OF PRODUCTION

In working upon the material resources of nature to satisfy their needs, men created material products (houses, roads, vehicles, 'commodities') which formed a material basis of regulated social life. These products were a material embodiment, a material 'objectification' of the social labour of the population in a community, and, as members of the community, men had to be related in some regulated way to them. Also, in working upon their material environment, men developed certain *'instruments'* or *'means'* of production; a certain technology which was of a definite material nature at any given period in society. The energy and activities of men in working upon nature were always 'patterned' or 'channelled' through this technology. The *products* of a communal labour and the *means of* production therefore constituted a fundamental material basis of society.

(II) THE RELATIONS OF MEN TO THEIR PRODUCTS AND INSTRU-MENTS OF PRODUCTION

This definite nature of the products and the instruments of production in society meant, also, equally definite ways in which *men were related to them*. The making and distribution of *products* meant some necessary *'property relations'* among men. The existence of definite *means of production* meant that men must be related to these means of production in definite ways: again, in certain *'property relations'*, but also in a specified *'division of labour'*. The members of a small community of Bushmen in the material conditions of the Kalahari Desert with limited techniques for seeking water and such sources of food as were available; the Lord of a medieval village and the peasants who worked the land with limited techniques of farming; the Manager, administrative staff and colliers who operated a modern coal-mine, with specific techniques of mining; would obviously all have a different set of relations to their material conditions and means of production. The distinctive division of work; the distinctive regulations of property; would be related to the technical apparatus of the society.

The definite relations of men to their products and means of production in any social and historical situation were held to be a corollary of, to be concomitant with, the material products and techniques themselves; and they patterned the material activities and energies of men into certain, determinate forms. The relations of men to their products and means of production were therefore a determinate part of the material 'productive forces'.

(III) THE RELATIONS OF MEN TO EACH OTHER: SOCIAL CLASSES

Since men were related to their products and means of production in determinate ways, it followed, of necessity, that they were related to each other in definite ways. In their division of labour and in their property relations—in short, in their relations to the means of production—men held definite positions: of power or lack of power; of status or lack of status; of property or lack of property. Men sharing the same positions in this economic order would also share an identity of interests. The relations of men to the means of production led directly to the formation of *class relations*, and to *class conflict*. The 'social being of men determines their consciousness', Marx claimed, and therefore the different interests which arose from being differently placed in relation to the means of production, gave rise to '*class consciousness*'.

On the basis of their material products and means of production, then, men came to have determinate relations to these means of production, and thus to have determinate class relations. A system of social classes was established as a necessary concomitant of each system of technology (each 'economic system'); and this system of classes was therefore a part of the 'productive forces' of society; a part of the material, 'economic' foundation of society.

The material basis of society, then, the primary objective reality forming the foundation of the social order, was the 'economic' structure, consisting of the 'productive forces'—and these consisted of (*a*) the material products and the means of production, (*b*) the relations of men to them (the property relations and the organized relations of labour), and (*c*) the system of social classes. This basic reality then came to be 'reflected' in the 'secondary' superstructure of institutions.

(d) The 'Super-structure' of Social Institutions

Just as the material reality of nature came to be 'reflected' in the qualities of life and mind which were 'secondary', so—in 'Historical Materialism'—the material basis of society (its productive forces) came to be 'reflected' in the qualities of a super-structure of institutions. Legal institutions were built upon the fundamental property relations and reflected the interests of social classes. Institutions of marriage and family relationships reflected the nature of personal relationships within the system, and indicated the 'level' of sensitivity reached in such relationships. Religious institutions reflected the material structure of society and sanctified property and the hierarchy of authority in economic relationships. The institutionalization of art, philosophy, education provided an 'ideological' reflection of class interests and a systematization of the 'knowledge' underlying the technical skills and practical degrees of control over nature in society.

That the 'super-structure' of other institutions was regarded as the qualitative reflection of the material, economic basis, subordinate to it in terms of causal determination, was made perfectly clear by Marx and all who followed him.

'The mode of production in material life *determines* the social, political and intellectual life processes in general,' he wrote. 'It is not the consciousness of men that determines their being, but, on the contrary, their social being that determines their consciousness.'

Again:

'. . . the economic structure of society is the *real* foundation, on which rises a legal and political superstructure and to which correspond definite forms of social consciousness.'

Engels was equally definite—though we shall consider his qualifications to this later. He quite specifically refers to legal, political, and all 'ideological' institutions and conceptions as being only *'reflexes'* of the material basis of society.

'. . . the jurist imagines he is operating with *a priori* principles,' he wrote, 'whereas they are *really only economic reflexes* . . .'*

In the same letter he wrote of the:

'. . . political, legal and moral reflexes' of the economy.

And in his essay on Ludwig Feuerbach, he also wrote of the 'state' as being:

'. . . only a reflex . . . of the economic needs of the class controlling production . . .'

The same emphasis has continued to be a firm plank of the Marxist position. Lenin, for example, in his essay on the 'Sources and Com-

---

* Letter to Conrad Schmidt, October, 1890. *Marx: Selected Works*, Vol. I, p. 383.

ponent Parts of Marxism', made this standpoint of Historical Materialism very clear:

'Just as the cognition of man reflects nature (i.e. developing matter) which exists independently of him, so also the *social cognition* of man (i.e., the various views and doctrines—philosophic, religious, political, etc.) reflects the *economic order* of society. Political institutions are a super-structure on the economic foundation.'*

This is a perfectly clear example of the application of the persuasions of dialectical materialism to historical materialism.

Before leaving this point, it is worthwhile to remind ourselves that the relations of men in the 'material basis' of society, as part of the 'productive forces' of society, were held by Marx to be:

'. . . *indispensable* and *independent of their will* . . .'

If this is so, and if the qualitative elements of the super-structure are so specifically determined by the material base—then all the qualitative characteristics of the life, mind, and institutions of men in society are held to be completely determined by the material means of production. This is a social determinism resting solely on material products and the technological means of producing them. It is an economic and technological determinism.

(e) The 'State' as the central institution in the 'Super-structure'

It needs to be emphasized, as the next component in the argument, simply that among all the institutions of the super-structure, the 'State' is the one most central and of greatest importance. Indeed, it is, in a sense, the collective embodiment of all the others; or, better, all the others are parts, dimensions, of its whole nature. Thus the law, in all its detail, is centrally upheld in the form of the State. The doctrines, values, and practices of Religion centrally serve the form and stability and sanctity of the State; and so with each major element of the super-structure. But since all these are 'reflections' of the economic basis and the established 'class-system', the State is, crucially, the embodiment of the interests, ideology, values, and power of the ruling class. It is the focal point of all these institutions which reflect, justify, protect, serve, and uphold the existing material basis of society.

Thus, in the Manifesto of the Communist Party, Marx and Engels wrote:

'The executive of the modern state is but a committee for managing the common affairs of the whole bourgeoisie.'

---

* *Marx: Selected Works*, Vol. I, p. 56.

And, again:

> Political power, properly so called,* is merely the organized power of one class for oppressing another.'

Engels himself, too, in *The Origin of the Family*, wrote that the State is the organ of:

> '. . . the most powerful, economically dominating class that, with the help of this state, becomes also the politically dominating class, and thus acquired new means of subduing and exploiting the oppressed masses. The ancient state was thus the state of the slave-owners for subduing the slaves, just as the feudal state was the organ of the nobility for subduing the serf-peasants, and as the modern representative state is a tool for the exploitation of wage-labour by capital.'

The State, then, becomes the political organ serving class-domination, and is the central element in the entire superstructure which reflects the economic order, the material base.

(f) A Structural-Functional Model of Society

It will be clearly seen that Marx had outlined, in this analysis, a very clear model of the nature of society, of the 'social system' as a whole, and that this was in 'structural-functional' terms. In Comte's terms, Marx provided a very clear analysis of 'Social Statics': an analysis of the main elements of a social system and the functional interdependency between them. The clarity of this model might be emphasized with the aid of the accompanying diagram. (See opposite)

After our earlier discussion, I do not think this diagram requires any comment. The main components of the social system and their close functional interconnections with each other are luminously clear. Only two brief points may be added.

The first is that Marx himself was quite explicitly aware that he was conceiving 'the social system' as a functionally interdependent set of parts in this way, and had quite clear definitions of the nature of a 'society' in his work. A clear definition of this kind is to be found in his letter to P. V. Annenkov on the nature of Historical Materialism.

'What is society,' he wrote, 'whatever its form might be? The product of men's reciprocal action. Are men free to choose this or that form of society for themselves? By no means. Assume a particular state of development in the productive forces of man and you will get a particular form of commerce and consumption. Assume particular stages of development in production, commerce and consumption and you will have a corresponding

* This expression—'properly so called' is *so* reminiscent of Comte's phraseology and style as to lead one to think there was a greater influence of Comte on Marx than is ever consciously and openly acknowledged.

social order, a corresponding organization of the family and of the ranks and classes, in a word a corresponding civil society. Presuppose a particular civil society and you will get particular political conditions which are only the official expression of civil society . . .

It is superflous to add that men are not free to choose their *productive forces*—which are the basis of *all* their history . . .'

MARX: A STRUCTURAL-FUNCTIONAL MODEL OF SOCIETY

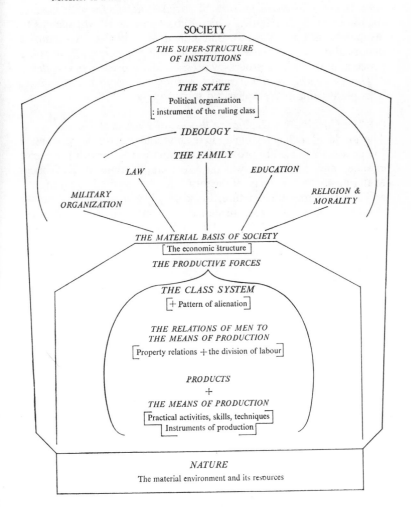

The structural-functional model of society is perfectly clear in this statement,* as also is the conception of 'types' of societies resting on differing stages of development of the productive forces—a separate point to be separately emphasized shortly.

The second point worthy of additional emphasis is that this structural-functional model was outlined by Marx in such a way as especially *to explain the nature of social conflict, social transformation, and social change*. And these aspects of conflict and change were not *contingent* or *additional*—when looking at actual societies; they were seen as *essential characteristics* of social systems. As with Comte, the model of 'Social Statics' which Marx constructed was such as to lay emphasis upon the fact that human society was *essentially* a historical process; *essentially* a *changing* and *cumulatively* developing process; and that this process was *essentially* a process of *conflict*.

The structural-functional model was one of conflict and change. This point cannot be emphasized too strongly.

(g) *The Quantitative-Qualitative Process of Historical Change*

This model of society resting upon the material basis of the productive forces was then used to provide an explanation (a 'theory') of social change, and again this was a direct application of Dialectical Materialism to the facts of history. Just as gradual, quantitative additions accumulate in nature, and suddenly give rise to determinate 'qualitative leaps' into new substances or forms, so in history, gradual quantitative additions accumulate within society, suddenly compelling 'revolutionary leaps' to qualitatively new total social systems. The argument of Marx was this.

Since the basic reality of society was its material, economic foundation, the factors making for change were to be sought in these productive forces. Gradually, over a long period, changes were brought about in the means of production. Technological changes occurred. These material changes in the means of production were additive and cumulative. In ways unforeseen by the people who brought them about, however, these many cumulative changes came gradually to *transform* the relations of men to the means of production, and thus their class-relations. The material basis of society became transformed within the ever more constraining system of an old super-structure of institutions. At a certain point however, this old set of institutions could no longer adequately contain, or deal with, the new productive forces and the new class interests they

---

* As a matter of interest, this conception of social systems in which the parts are not by any means arbitrary, but assume specific patterns of interrelationship, may be compared with that of John Stuart Mill: page 226, though Mill, of course, would reject the 'economic determinism'.

entailed. A 'revolutionary' situation suddenly forced radical changes; the old super-structure was burst asunder and overthrown, and a qualitatively *new* super-structure came into being, adequately reflecting the new material basis.

Several extremely important aspects of this quantitative-qualitative explanation of Historical Materialism need to be separately made clear and emphasized.

(I) SOCIETY, AND ANY ADEQUATE EXPLANATION OF IT, ESSENTIALLY HISTORICAL

It is important to see that Marx was in agreement with all the other theorists we have considered in his persuasion that *society was essentially a historical process, and that the explanation of it essentially required a historical method.* Furthermore, Marx clearly insisted that social *development* was a reality that had to be noted and explained. Change was *not* only *subsequent difference*, it was also the cumulative emergence of new *levels* of technical achievements and social organization which *grew* on the basis of past achievements and *advanced* beyond them. Marx's theory was, therefore, a theory not only of change, but also of *development* and *progress*.

(II) SOCIAL EVOLUTION

A second important aspect of Historical Materialism is that it was essentially a theory of social *evolution*. It explained the emergence of determinate types and levels of society which *gradually* developed and succeeded each other, and only changed finally into new forms of society when the new material conditions had become so far developed, so thoroughly developed, as to make the old superstructure no longer (in *fact*, not in *moral principle*) tolerable. This too, is a point deserving emphasis, because the stress laid, for political progress, upon the 'revolutionary' point of social change (the climax of social transformation), has been such as to lead some theorists to assert that the Marxian theory was something radically different from evolutionary theories. Stalin is a particularly good example of this.

'If the world is in a state of constant movement and development, if the dying away of the old and the upgrowth of the new is a law of development . . . we must not base our orientation on the strata of society which are no longer developing, even though they at present constitute the predominant force, but on those strata which are developing and have a future before them . . .

'In order not to err in policy, one must look forward, not backward.

'If the passing of slow quantitative changes into rapid and abrupt qualitative changes is a law of development, then it is clear that revolutions made by oppressed classes are a quite natural and inevitable phenomenon. 'In order not to err in policy, one must be a *revolutionary*, not a *reformist*.'*

The clear identity of the theoretical analysis of 'qualitative leaps' and the political directive of 'revolutionary' commitment could not be plainer; nor could the quite unqualified identity of 'progress' with 'technological advance'.

A much more careful and judicious thinker—Werner Sombart— saw things very differently and insisted that Marx's was a wiser perspective than that of some idealistic socialists *exactly because* he saw 'revolutions' as the culminations of long 'evolutionary' sequences.

'Marx,' he wrote, 'applies the evolution idea to the social movement. Other conspicuous men have tried to consider socialism and the social movement as in the flow of historic life. But no-one has so clearly, illuminatively, effectively shown these historical relations. That political revolutions and agitations are fundamentally great displacements of social classes . . . The idea was decisive that revolutions could not be forced, but were the outgrowth of specific economic antecedents . . . thus for the social movement the idea of "revolution" passes into the thought of "evolution" . . .'†

Sombart also quoted some of the last writing of Engels (published shortly before his death as the introduction to *The Struggle of Classes in France*) who claimed of those who had tried to force a proletarian revolution in Europe round about the mid-nineteenth century:

'History has proved wrong us and all who thought similarly . . . We, "revolutionaries", succeed far better by means legal than illegal and destructive.'

Our point here is not, of course, to recommend Marx's specific mode of explanation in all this, but only to emphasize that his theory *is* a theory of social *evolution*. Indeed it could be demonstrated that this conception of social evolution had almost all the same characteristics as those laid down by Spencer: from simplicity to complexity, and the like.‡

(III) TYPES OF SOCIETY: CLASSIFICATION AND COMPARISON

A third important point is to see that, following upon his particular model of society, Marx sought a systematic study of all known societies and their process of historical development by exactly the

---

* J. Stalin, *Dialectical Materialism and Historical Materialism*.
† W. Sombart, *Socialism*, Putnam & Sons, 1898, pp. 100–111.
‡ '. . . in history,' Engels wrote (*On Marx's Critique of Political Economy*), 'development as a whole proceeds from the most simple to the more complex relations . . .'

methods recommended by Comte, Mill, and Spencer—namely the methods of careful description, classification and comparison. Again we see the historical and comparative method proposed and used in necessary relation with each other. The difference in Marx was only that, with a different conception of the significant causal factor in social change (i.e., the central hypothesis for 'social dynamics')—in his case the 'material basis' of society—he classified 'types' of society in terms of this criterion, and, more especially, in terms of the class-system which characterized them. He distinguished 'primitive communal' societies which had a minimal social differentiation, and then societies characterized by slavery, serfdom, and wage-slavery (Capitalism) followed by a 'transition' through 'socialism' to 'communism'. Each of these 'types', however, was only *designated* by the criterion of technology and class; each of them consisted of a determinate 'complex' of interrelated institutions which could be uncovered by historical and comparative study.

(IV) EQUILIBRIUM-DISEQUILIBRIUM ANALYSIS

A fourth important characteristic of the method of analysis and explanation employed by Historical Materialism—and again a proposal shared by Comte and Spencer especially—is that of the 'equilibrium-disequilibrium' analysis of social order and social change. The development of a certain set of productive forces gradually brings into being about it an appropriate super-structure of institutions, and this is an achievement of an 'equilibrium' condition, a condition of integration and stability. Within this framework, however, material changes occur, class relations are gradually transformed, class interests are changed, new struggles are born, and so 'disequilibrium' conditions are cumulatively brought into being. These are 'resolved' by the qualitative leap to a new and appropriate 'equilibrium'. The sequence of social and historical change thus permits of analysis in these 'equilibrium-disequilibrium' terms.

Marxian 'Historical Materialism' is, in fact, an 'equilibrium-disequilibrium' analysis of the historical sequences of social order and social change, and the *explanation* of this process in terms of material change, attendant social conflict, and its resolution.

(V) SOCIAL PSYCHOLOGY

A fifth quite fundamental and integral component of 'Historical Materialism' is the particular position adopted concerning the *psychological* aspects of human nature in society; the place of psychology in the scheme of sociological explanation; and, indeed, the very conception which is implied of 'psychology' as a science.

These points were not worked out systematically by Marx, and can be dealt with only briefly, but his position concerning them was both patently clear and important.

First of all, Marx—in a way more complex, and more fully conceived than can possibly be sufficiently conveyed here—believed that though one could postulate clearly the 'essence' of man in the sense of indicating the qualities that characterized the *human* as distinct from other animal species, it was quite impossible to speak of a substantive '*human nature*' independent of the creative, cumulative, cultural activity of *society*. As to the 'essential' nature of man distinguishing him from other species, it was the necessity and ability to 'work up', creatively, the resources of nature in such ways as to satisfy *and* explore needs. But this itself meant that man was a 'maker': his nature was not something *there* which filled the moulds of 'society'; his nature was something he progressively made, explored, expanded, enriched in the creative, co-operative work with his fellows which essentially constituted the making of history, the creative adventure of history. In short, man's 'essence' necessitated the making of historical society; but this making of historical society was itself the making of '*human nature*'. Also—the creativity of man was *necessarily* a *social* process in which countless other men were involved; in which any generation of men rested initially upon the achievements of earlier generations; and in which 'unintended consequences' of action had aggregate social effects going beyond men's individual wills. So that the making of *individual human nature* was essentially a process of *society*.

The implications of this viewpoint, and this conception, are of enormous range and importance, but again it is worthwhile to see the fullest agreement between Marx and Comte on this point. To 'Know Thyself', said Comte, it is necessary to study the history of society. All psychology, other than a knowledge of relatively simple concomitants of biology, was, for him, 'Social Psychology'; and it may be remembered that he believed that the fullest study of 'Man the Individual' could only come after our fullest exploration of the science of society. Marx was equally definite about all this, and some special implications deserve the strongest, sharpest emphasis.

It is quite impossible, from Marx's point of view to 'explain' society in terms of something called '*Individual* Psychology'. On the contrary, the explanation of the substantive nature of the individual's experience and behaviour can only be achieved in sociological terms. *Society* is the creative process—going far beyond the individual—within which the individual comes to be what he is.

Marx takes this point much further, and much more radically, however. It is not only that, conceptually and methodologically

396

speaking, one cannot explain society in terms of individual psychology, but, radically and fundamentally, *there is no such thing as individual human nature, or indeed simply 'human nature' (whether individual or otherwise) in abstraction from the creative process of society.* Society makes and shapes the most basic attributes of man. It might be argued, for example, as against this, that at least *some* things—such as the simple *senses* (sight, hearing, taste, touch, scent) —are *basic* in human nature . . . But no!—said Marx—they are *not*! And to get this perspective right is fundamental. He wrote insistently as follows:

'Just as music alone awakens in man the sense of music, and just as the most beautiful music has *no* sense for the unmusical ear—for this reason the *senses* of the social man are *other* senses than those of the non-social man. Only through the objectively unfolded richness of man's essential being is the richness of subjective *human* sensibility (a musical ear, an eye for beauty of form—in short, *senses* capable of human gratifications, senses confirming themselves as essential powers of *man*) either cultivated or brought into being. For not only the five senses but also the so-called mental senses—the practical senses (will, love, etc.)—in a word, *human* sense—the humanness of the senses—comes to be by virtue of its object, by virtue of *humanized* nature. The *forming* of the five senses is a labour of the entire history of the world down to the present.'*

It follows from this that any 'psychology' must be couched within this context of the full and rich appreciation of the creativity of society and history—otherwise it will be 'abstracted' out of all realistic awareness of its subject-matter. A science of psychology abstracted from this detailed awareness of society and history in the making of man *is an academic impossibility.* This again is a point so important, and so deserving of our consideration as to merit the utmost emphasis.

'A *psychology*,' Marx wrote, 'for which this, the part of history most contemporary and accessible to sense, remains a closed book, cannot become a genuine, comprehensive and *real* science. What indeed are we to think of a science which *airily* abstracts from this large part of human labour and which fails to feel its own incompleteness, while such a wealth of human endeavour unfolded before it means nothing more to it than, perhaps, what can be expressed in one word—"*need*," "*vulgar* need"?'†

This emphasis of Marx is one which was perhaps never more needed than now. The study of human nature must lie within the study of society and history; otherwise it is a vast mistake.

---

* *1844 Manuscripts*, p. 108. Later this may be compared with Durkheim (see *The Making of Sociology*, Vol. 2) and his insistence on the *creativity* of society.
† *1844 Manuscripts*, p. 110.

(VI) THE STUDY OF SOCIAL ACTION

Moreover, Marx argued, the psychological and sociological study of man cannot regard men as 'passive agents' in the determinate flow of events. Though men's activities in society are constrained, limited, determined by aggregate forces and material conditions which lie beyond their individual wills, still—they are *activities*. Men are continuously involved in practical, creative action in society. Men make their own history, though within determinate constraints. They work consciously, actively, in conflict, among the interests, attitudes, values and relationships, of the time within which they live. A full understanding and explanation of 'society' and its 'dialectical' processes cannot be achieved therefore excepting by a full understanding of the *social action* of men. This again is a most important emphasis—both in reiterating a point on which Comte, Mill and Spencer had also insisted, and in showing that the emphasis upon the 'understanding of social action' later stressed by Weber was already fully recognized among these nineteenth century thinkers —even though they did not look with sufficient sophistication into the conceptual and methodological problems involved.

Engels, perhaps, put this point most clearly and forcibly. In his essay on 'Ludwig Feuerbach', he wrote:

'When it is a question of investigating the driving forces which—consciously or unconsciously, and indeed very often unconsciously—lie behind the motives of men in their historical actions and which constitute the real ultimate driving forces of history, then it is not a question so much of the motives of single individuals, however eminent, as of those motives which set in motion great masses, whole peoples, and again whole classes of the people in each people; and here, too, not the transient flaring up of a straw-fire which quickly dies down, but a lasting action resulting in a great historical transformation.

'To ascertain the driving causes which here in the minds of acting masses and their leaders—the so-called great men—are reflected as conscious motives, clearly or unclearly, directly or in ideological, even glorified form—that is the only path which can put us on the track of the laws holding sway both in history as a whole, and at particular periods and in particular lands. Everything which sets men in motion must go through their minds; but what form it will take in the mind will depend very much upon the circumstances.'*

The study of the 'psychological aspects of men in society' was not, then, a study only of their 'conditioning' by material and historical circumstances, but also an understanding of their considered actions in the detailed working out of events. In insisting upon this point, Marx was also very concerned to *avoid* the conception of *society* as

* *Marx: Selected Works*, Vol. I, p. 459.

some abstract '*totality*', or some '*entity*' independent of the manifold activities of actual men in their work and their social relationships.

'What is to be avoided above all,' he wrote,* 'is the re-establishing of 'Society' as an abstraction *vis-à-vis* the individual. The individual is *the social being*. His life, even if it may not appear in the direct form of a *communal* life carried out together with others—is therefore an expression and confirmation of *social life*. Man's individual and species life are not *different*.'

The 'dialectics' of history therefore clearly involved *men* in their *actions*.

(VII) UNINTENDED CONSEQUENCES

An additional point which is of importance, and which should be made clear, is that when both Marx and Engels argued that the material changes in the basic economic structure of society *determined* the relations of men and the institutions of the superstructure, what they had very largely in mind was the vast play of 'unintended consequences' in society. This too seemed to underlie what they meant by claiming that these great social transformations were 'independent of men's wills'. The substance of the point is that when countless men make small alterations and improvements in the particular jobs they are doing; when they gradually change their technical means of production; they have nothing further in mind. They are simply wanting to ease their task, or improve the efficiency of their effort, or improve the quality of their product. They have no social transformation in mind. But—in the entirety of society, and over periods of time—these many specific changes accumulate to such proportions as to have aggregate effects which were unforeseen. The entire fabric of the means of production has been cumulatively transformed, and men find that their relationships have been changed accordingly, and that old institutions no longer fit their needs; no longer serve their interests satisfactorily. This 'lack of fit' of institutions becomes increasingly conflictful until a new super-structure is created.

Again, Engels stated this persuasion very clearly. Arguing (in 'Ludwig Feuerbach') that the 'dialectics of nature' were paralleled in the 'dialectics of history', he nonetheless found it necessary to explain the ways in which the dialectical processes of history contained, so to speak, the 'conscious aims and intentions' of men. He wrote in this way:

'In one point, however, the history of the development of society proves to be essentially different from that of nature. In nature—in so far as we

† *1844 Manuscripts*, p. 105.

399

ignore man's reactions upon nature—there are only blind unconscious agencies acting upon one another and out of whose interplay the general law comes into operation. Nothing of all that happens—whether in the innumerable apparent accidents observable upon the surface of things, or in the ultimate results which confirm the regularity underlying these accidents—is attained as a consciously desired aim. In the history of society, on the other hand, the actors are all endowed with consciousness, are men acting with deliberation or passion, working towards definite goals; nothing happens without a conscious purpose, without an intended aim. But this distinction, important as it is for historical investigation, particularly of single epochs and events, cannot alter the fact, that the course of history is governed by inner general laws. For here, also, on the whole, in spite of the consciously desired aims of all individuals, accident apparently reigns on the surface. That which is willed happens but rarely; in the majority of instances the numerous desired ends cross and conflict with one another, or these ends themselves are from the outset incapable of realization or the means of attaining them are insufficient. Thus the conflict of innumerable individual wills and individual actions in the domain of history produces a state of affairs entirely analogous to that in the realm of unconscious nature. The ends of the actions are intended, but the results which actually follow from these actions are not intended; or when they do seem to correspond to the end intended, they ultimately have consequences quite other than those intended. Historical events thus appear on the whole to be likewise governed by chance. But where on the surface accident holds sway, there actually it is always governed by inner, hidden laws and it is only a matter of discovering these laws.

'Men make their own history, whatever its outcome may be, in that each person follows his own consciously desired end, and it is precisely the resultant of these many wills operating in different directions and of their manifold effects upon the outer world that constitutes history.'

Similarly, in a letter to Joseph Bloch, Engels wrote:

'History makes itself in such a way that the final result always arises from conflicts between many individual wills, of which each again has been made what it is by a host of particular conditions of life. Thus there are innumerable intersecting forces, an infinite series of parallelograms of forces which give rise to one resultant—the historical event. This again may itself be viewed as the product of a power which, taken as a whole, works *unconsciously* and without volition. For what each individual wills is obstructed by everyone else, and what emerges is something that no one willed. Thus past history proceeds in the manner of a natural process and is also essentially subject to the same laws of movement.'*

In this conception it is again evident how 'Historical Materialism' must seek the 'hidden' patterns of social and historical interconnection which may not be 'apparent' on the surface of events, or in the consciousness of men who are being borne along by them. Much

* *Marx: Selected Works*, Vol. I, pp. 456-8.

later, we shall see how this has been incorporated into 'modern' sociological analysis under the term 'latent', as distinct from 'manifest' functions.

(VIII) ALIENATION AND IDEOLOGY

There is this further dimension of Marx's analysis in terms of 'Historical Materialism', and it concerns the question: *how* do the aims, intentions, and powerful motives of men come to be intimately related to the material processes of social change, to class-conflict and political struggle? The answer lies in Marx's 'materialist' (as distinct from Hegel's 'idealist') account of 'alienation' and the ideologies which are rooted in this experience. This is an incredibly difficult matter to be both brief and clear about—but still, let us try. The effort is necessary because some sociologists have gone so far as to ask 'What has all this to do with sociology?' But this reflects a very profound lack of understanding of Marx, because this notion of man's 'alienation' and the resolution and elimination of it was not only the basic strand underlying his sociology; it also provided one of the central 'mechanisms' of human motivation in social action. Briefly, Marx argued as follows—his ideas being rooted in the conceptions of both Hegel and Feuerbach.

Hegel had introduced the idea of 'alienation' in a 'spiritual' sense in order to provide an understanding of the felt incompleteness of human experience and the striving for completeness amid the actualities of creation. For him the continuous process of creation in the world was an unfolding of the actualizing of spirit and mind in the concrete forms of nature and history, and each particular step of this—each 'form' being a particulate, limited actuality; a partial 'objectification' of spirit; a partial 'realization' of the 'idea'—entailed a certain 'distancing' of spirit from its degree of objectification, a certain 'estrangement' in that the spiritual essence was not yet fully, richly, realized in the actuality. And the motives of men in their historical struggles (including philosophy, art, religion as well as the political and legal making of societies) were moved, compelled, by this undertone of divine discontent, seeking the fullness of spiritual realization in their creative life in the world. The 'dialectics' of mind and spirit continuously sprang from this spiritual unrest of 'alienation', and this human 'alienation' was rooted in the larger creative entirety of the 'World Spirit'.

Feuerbach, in his *Essence of Christianity*, rejected this large 'Idealist' perspective, and argued simply that the sublimities of religion in society—the ideologies which portrayed spiritually satisfying aims and ends and conditions of human destiny—were simply rooted in human insufficiencies and dissatisfactions. The

Gods were wish-fulfilments. Man, in his actual conditions of life in nature and society, suffered a many-sided tragedy—of transience, of continual limitation and frustration, frequently of injustice, and ultimately of death. The creation of a religious ideality—of Gods, doctrines, rituals—was the outcome of man's desire to seek a resolution of his dilemmas, a healing of his wounds, a salvation from his limitations and his evils. A religious ideology was, in short, a reflection of the needs of man in the actuality of his conditions.

Marx and Engels had rejected Hegel's 'Idealist' system, and found Feuerbach's more direct explanation a release from it, indeed a kind of deliverance from it, but they needed to take it further: to show, in detail, how 'ideology' in society could be explained in terms of their own dialectical and historical materialism, and how these ideological experiences and motives of men could be shown to be rooted in an 'alienation' accompanying man's practical activities in nature and society. Their explanation of 'alienation' and 'ideology' thus provided a basic understanding of the motivation which underlay 'class-struggles' and the political activity which arose out of it. It *linked* the material basis of society and changes in it with the clash of ideas, values and beliefs at the level of the 'super-structure'. It was therefore a necessary component of the 'dialectical' explanation of history. Marx's explanation was this.

Man's 'essence'—the characteristic which distinguished him, as a species, from all others in nature—was his *social creativity*; the co-operative activity with his fellows in working creatively upon nature. Beginning in the necessitous struggle for survival, this then became the historical creation of culture, within the context of which man made the very stuff of his own individual nature. Man the maker; Man the creator; Man who works the manifold qualities of nature into an increasingly rich fabric of culture, and, in so doing, creates in the world, and out of the stuff of the world, the distinctive qualities of the human spirit: this was Marx's picture. Properly understood, Marx's picture of man in the world was one of Creative Humanism. This, then, was Man's 'essence'—to create richly and freely in nature.

'It is just in the working-up of the objective world, therefore,' he wrote, 'that man first really proves himself to be a *species being*. This production is his active species life. Through and because of this production, nature appears as *his* work and his reality. The object of labour is, therefore, the *objectification of man's species life*: for he duplicates himself not only, as in consciousness, intellectually, but also actively, in reality, and therefore he contemplates himself in a world that he has created.'*

* *1844 Manuscripts*, p. 76.

And, again:

'In creating an *objective world* by his practical activity, in *working-up* inorganic nature, man proves himself a conscious species being. Admittedly animals also produce. They build themselves nests, dwellings, like the bees, beavers, ants, etc. But an animal only produces what it immediately needs for itself or its young. It produces one-sidedly, whilst man produces universally. It produces only under the dominion of immediate physical need, whilst man produces even when he is free from physical need, and only truly produces in freedom therefrom. An animal produces only itself, whilst man reproduces the whole of nature. An animal's product belongs immediately to its physical body, whilst man freely confronts his product. An animal forms things in accordance with the standard and the need of the species to which it belongs, whilst man knows how to produce in accordance with the standard of every species, and knows how to apply everywhere the inherent standard to the object. Man therefore also forms things in accordance with the laws of beauty.'*

In this creativity 'essential' to his nature, Man actively *needed* objects in nature; indeed, part of his *own* nature was this need to be objectively related to nature for the possibility and fulfilment of this activity. Marx insisted upon this inextricable and intimate relationship between 'human nature' and 'nature' (as constituting the 'essence' of man's nature) in the following way.

'*Man* is directly a *natural being*. As a natural being and as a living natural being he is on the one hand furnished with *natural powers of life*—he is an *active* natural being. These forces exist in him as tendencies and abilities— as *impulses*. On the other hand, as a natural, corporeal, sensuous, objective being he is a *suffering*, conditioned and limited creature, like animals and plants. That is to say, the *objects* of his impulses exist outside him, as *objects* independent of him; yet these objects are *objects* of his *need*— essential *objects*, indispensable to the manifestation and confirmation of his essential powers. To say that man is a *corporeal*, living, real, sensuous, objective being full of natural vigour is to say that he has *real, sensuous, objects* as the objects of his being or of his life, or that he can only *express* his life in real, sensuous objects. To be objective, natural and sensuous, and at the same time to have object, nature and sense outside oneself, or oneself to be object, nature and sense for a third party, is one and the same thing. *Hunger* is a natural *need*; it therefore needs a *nature* outside itself, an *object* outside itself, in order to satisfy itself, to be stilled. Hunger is an acknowledged need of my body for an *object* existing outside it, indispensable to its integration and to the expression of its essential being. The sun is the *object* of the plant—an indispensable object to it, confirming its life—just as the plant is an object of the sun, being an *expression* of the life-awakening power of the sun, of the sun's *objective* essential power.'†

* *1844 Manuscripts*, pp. 75–6.   † *ibid.*, pp. 156–7.

The essentially 'naturalistic' or 'materialistic' nature of Marx's conception of man's 'essence', as against Hegel's 'idealist' or 'spiritual' conception, was therefore perfectly clear. And, given this, his conception of 'alienation' was also clear.

Just as, in Hegel, the objectification of the thing created was a certain constraining delimitation upon the larger potentiality of spirit itself, so, in Marx, the sensuous, practical activity of man in 'working-up' the materials of nature took the form of 'material objects'; of 'products'. The labour of men in a community became *embodied* in *products*. A material order of objects was created. But this, in itself, had a certain delimiting constraint upon their creative energies. They were, to a new degree (and a *growing* degree as the material order and the material instruments of production became more complex) set at a distance from the pristine conditions of their creative activity. A certain 'estrangement' was brought about. But this 'alienation' was especially intensified by the fact that, in the conditions of communal production, the individuals who created 'products' did not themselves 'own' them. A new problem of the relation of men to the means of production and to the products created, and to the exchange of these products, arose. In short— production, exchange, and the division of labour in society entailed *property* relations. The objects which men produced, the means of production which they had to use to produce them, did not belong to *them*; they did not themselves have direct control over them; they were owned, controlled, by *others*. Men were therefore 'alienated' from the *essential* conditions for the fulfilment of their *essential* nature not only by the material process of production, but by the complex *relations of production* which set some men over against others and therefore in conflict with others. *Property-relations* were conflictful *class-relations*. *Property* was *power*.

With this picture, the entirety of Marx's scheme of explanation becomes at once apparent. Each distinctive 'technological' stage in history, each distinctive 'material, economic, basis' of society constituted a distinctive set of property relations, of class-relations in which a certain class 'owned' and controlled the means of production and the 'commodities' produced, and in which the other, subordinate classes were 'alienated' from the conditions necessary for their 'essential' human activity and fulfilment. Class-conflict is therefore endemic to human society. The super-structure of institutions reflects (and effectively serves) the domination of the property-owning class over those classes which are 'alienated'. And 'ideologies' in society are the sets of ideas, values, and aims (including the 'wish-fulfilment dimensions' of Feuerbach) which reflect these different complexes of class conditions. In this entire sense, Marx and Engels believed that:

'The history of all hitherto existing society is the history of class struggles.'

It is very important to insist here that, for Marx, this entire historical process of kinds and degrees of 'alienation', and of man's struggle to overcome all forms of 'alienation', was not a kind of morally blameworthy sequence of man's chosen cruelty to man, but, on the contrary, a necessary historical process of the making of man; the necessary sequence of conditions whereby man came to a full creative achievement of his 'essence' as a distinctive species. Thus, *private* property (and its several forms related to certain modes of production) was necessary in the stages of man's social creativity; just as it was also necessary, following upon the emergence of industrial capitalism, to supersede it.

'Precisely in the fact,' wrote Marx, 'that *division of labour* and *exchange* are embodiments of private property lies the twofold proof, on the one hand that *human* life *required* private property for its realization, and on the other hand that it now requires the *supersession* of private property.'*

This entire process of property-relations, class-relations, alienation, and ideological struggles, Marx regarded as the *'pre-history'* of mankind; the long period of struggle in which man had gradually won the recognition and the conditions of his 'essence'. The *future* of man would be his self-directed history. In this picture, and this emphasis, can be seen (again) both Marx's 'turning upside down' of Hegel—in insisting that man's spiritual essence, his creative individual freedom in nature and history, is something that man has *creatively achieved*, rather than something that was initially *there* in the world spirit; and the agreement of this position with Comte's conclusion that Man now had to confront responsibly a self-directed future, and Spencer's conclusion that Man could now create a new 'ethical' society.

However, there is one further point that must be made about the nature of 'ideology' in all this. On the one hand, we have seen that 'ideology' was thought of as 'reflecting' material conditions and real conditions of alienation. The 'general consciousness' of men was:

'. . . only the *theoretical* shape of that of which the *living* shape is the *real* community, the social fabric . . .'

In this sense, it would appear that the several 'ideologies' in society would be considered *true*—in the sense of corresponding with definite aspects of social reality; but, curiously, Marx and Engels tend definitely to regard 'ideologies' as kinds of *'false* consciousness'; as kinds of pictures of social reality which one has got

* *1844 Manuscripts*, p. 134.

to question and reject—probing, instead, *behind* them with scientific analysis which gets at the deeply hidden *truth*. Engels wrote in a letter to Franz Mehring:

'Ideology is a process accomplished by the so-called* thinker consciously indeed, but with a *false consciousness*. The *real* motives impelling him remain unknown to him, *otherwise it would not be an ideological process at all.*'

This is a very odd, assertive point; but here we will not argue with it, only note it. It is necessary to notice briefly just one further dimension of 'alienation' and the conflicts to which it points.

(IX) VALUE, CAPITAL, AND THE CONFLICT BETWEEN WAGE-LABOUR AND CAPITAL

It has already been evident that, in Marx's conception, 'alienation' and 'class-conflict', though *subjectively experienced* things, were also actual material relations, and it is important simply to make clear the way in which Marx analysed this material basis in his explanations of historical change.

We have already seen that, for Marx, 'material products' were the embodiment of human relations. Products of human labour were not just 'things' as other objects in nature were; it was a kind of 'fetishism' so to regard them; they were objectifications of particular sets of productive relationships among men. 'Alienation' too was a reflection of a division of the value of products between the classes concerned. The *value* of a product was the amount of human labour which went into the making of it. The *owner* of the product, however, made a *profit* when *exchanging* the product on the economic market. This 'margin' of difference (the profit) between the price the owner received for the product on the market, and the price he paid the workers for their labour (wages) was therefore thought to be '*expropriated*'. Competition was such as to lead the owner to pay only the *minimal* level of wages (that sum necessary to provide the worker with his *necessary subsistence*) in seeking to *maximize* his profit. And so the conflict between the owner and the alienated took the form of a conflict between capital (stored and expropriated value) and wage-labour . . . and, in capitalism, between *capitalists* (the owners of the means of production) and the *proletariat* (the property-less wage-earners).

A final aspect of this is that Marx believed that with the changing 'composition of capital', the development of industrial capitalism

---

* Notice the term 'so-called'. Those who produce 'ideologies', are 'so-called' thinkers. Those who use the analysis of 'dialectical materialism' are, presumably, 'real' thinkers.

would lead to a falling rate of profit, and, therefore, to an increasingly intense conflict between 'capital' and 'labour'. Perhaps, too, it is necessary to note that Marx believed that industrial capitalism—whilst leading to larger-scale production—would also become increasingly restrictive on the expansion of production, and the employment of new inventions and new techniques, since these would tend to despoil the markets for their 'successful products'. Conflict would also, therefore, intensify here between 'capital' and 'labour' since the narrow defence of private property and enterprise served the interests of one class, whereas the movement towards the collectivization of property and larger-scale production seemed to be in the interests of the other.

(X) THE PROLETARIAN REVOLUTION: SOCIALISM, COMMUNISM, AND THE CLASSLESS SOCIETY: THE WITHERING AWAY OF THE STATE

In the entire process of history, hitherto, the 'qualitative leaps' of political revolution whereby new super-structures of society had replaced the old, had been accomplished, according to Marx, by rising social classes which had come to power on the basis of changed conditions of production. Hitherto, also, each new dominant class, on achieving power, had found beneath it a subjected class, lower than itself in the economic structure, and which, in the new pattern of material relationships, it had proceeded to exploit. There was, however, a great difference in the specific case of industrial capitalism and its transformation to a collectivized society. It was this.

In the case of industrial capitalism, the productive forces and the property relations were such as to produce a basic conflict between only *two* social classes, as we have seen: between those who owned the means of production—the capitalists; and those who owned none—the wage-earning proletariat.* There were professional 'middle-classes', but Marx thought these were related to the means of production in the same way as the proletariat, and would therefore become a part of the new collectivized order as the conflict intensified and the resolution of it became clear.

Consequently, when the industrial proletariat accomplished the revolution—demolishing private property and collectivizing the means of production—*there would be no subjected class beneath them.* All the members of society would be related to the means of production *in the same way.* There would be no class-exploitation. The enormously increased productivity of collectivized industry, and the unrestrained application of science and technology to industry,

---

* Comte's new industrial 'proletaries'.

would eliminate conditions of 'alienation'. Men could now experience their 'essential' creativity freely. Through the transitional period of Socialism, under the guidance of the 'dictatorship of the proletariat', a Communist society would be achieved in which productivity would make it possible to *distribute* wealth in accordance with *need*, whilst asking of men that contribution to society of which they were *capable*. This, it is important to see, would be the *reversal* of inequalities, and a complete transformation in the tone and human values of society.

This is worth much emphasis. Marx—and some may be surprised at this—was *opposed* to what he called a *crude communism*. Simply to transform 'private property and enterprise' into 'public property and enterprise'—whilst retaining the old emphasis of values upon competitive 'getting' and 'having' was, he thought, a travesty of the aims of socialism. The transformation of the material means of society should be to accomplish those new relations among men which could lead to man's experience of his 'essential nature', his creative activity in nature freely enjoyed with his fellows. It was, Marx insisted, a *'human'* society we should achieve, in which all the alienating conditions of material and social organization which had limited the achievement of this had been overcome. Marx's utopian vision has much in it to warm the heart, whether or not one agrees with his explanatory system on which it rested.

At any rate, in *this* revolution—from industrial capitalism to communism—a *classless* society could be achieved, indeed *would* be achieved, and the further corollary of this was that—since the 'State' was the organ of the ruling class, and, now, no social classes existed— the 'State' was no longer necessary, and would 'wither away'. Both Marx and Engels were very emphatic about the several aspects of this. Marx, for example, in trying to make very clear what his own specific contribution had been; what was *not* new, and what *was* new in his own work; wrote in a letter to Joseph Weydemeyer (March, 1852):

'. . . And now as to myself, no credit is due to me for discovering the existence of classes in modern society, nor yet the struggle between them. Long before me bourgeois historians had described the historical development of this class struggle and bourgeois economists, the economic anatomy of the classes. What I did that was new was to prove: (1) that the *existence of classes* is only bound up with *particular, historic phases in the development of production*; (2) that the class struggle necessarily leads to the *dictatorship of the proletariat*; (3) that this dictatorship itself only constitutes the transition to the *abolition of all classes* and to a *classless society* . . .'*

* *Marx: Selected Works*, Vol. I, p. 377.

There are no half-measures about this statement. Similarly, there are no half-measures about what Engels said concerning the fate of the 'State' following the proletarian revolution. In *Anti-Dühring*, he wrote as follows:

'*The proletariat seizes the State power, and transforms the means of production in the first instance into State property*. But in doing this, it puts an end to itself as the proletariat, it puts an end to all class differences and class antagonisms, it puts an end also to the state as the state. Former society, moving in class antagonisms, had need of the state, that is, an organisation of the exploiting class at each period for the maintenance of its external conditions of production; that is, therefore, for the forcible holding down of the exploited class in the conditions of oppression (slavery, villeinage or serfdom, wage labour) determined by the existing mode of production. The state was the official representative of society as a whole, its embodiment in a visible corporation; but it was this only in so far as it was the State of that class which itself, in its epoch, represented society as a whole; in ancient times, the state of the slave-owning citizens; in the Middle Ages, of the feudal nobility; in our epoch, of the bourgeoisie. When ultimately it becomes really representative of society as a whole, it makes itself superfluous. As soon as there is no longer any class of society to be held in subjection; as soon as, along with class domination and the struggle for individual existence based on the former anarchy of production, the collisions and excesses arising from these have also been abolished, there is nothing more to be repressed which would make a special repressive force, a state, necessary. The first act in which the state really comes forward as the representative of society as a whole—the taking possession of the means of production in the name of society—is at the same time its last independent act as a state. The interference of the state power in social relations becomes superfluous in one sphere after another, and then ceases of itself. The government of persons is replaced by the administration of things and the direction of the process of production. The state is not "abolished", *it withers away*.'*

Nothing could be clearer or more emphatic.

In this way, then, a classless, stateless society will be created on the basis of the new material conditions now possible. And in this way, Marx and Engels completed this application of 'dialectical materialism' to the study of society and history: producing a systematic theory of the way in which man, in the making of both his society and himself, has moved creatively out of the early bondage of material necessity, through the many constraining, alienating conditions of the various stages of 'pre-history', to a self-directed society in which individual men can freely enjoy the creative activity in nature and human relationships which is their distinctive essence. Spiritual freedom, out of long suffering and struggle, has been

* *Anti-Dühring*, pp. 314–15.

achieved, and can form the basis for man's future consciously directed life.

(XI) SPECIFIC HISTORICAL AND COMPARATIVE STUDIES

It remains only to say that both Marx and Engels undertook specific and searching studies of particular historical situations in various societies in order to demonstrate the utility and validity of their system of analysis. The extent to which Marx studied the many reports on the material conditions and the productive relations existing in Britain may be seen in sections of *Capital*, but also, in very telling fashion, in his address to the Working Men's International Association in September 1864 (at St Martin's Hall in London). His studies of the 'Eighteenth Brumaire of Louis Bonaparte', of 'The Civil War in France', of the 'Class Struggles in France: 1848–1850,'* are very substantial examples of his analysis of the 'social action' of men pursued within the context, within the grip, of changing, aggregate conditions larger than themselves. And, to a more limited extent, both Marx and Engels, had quite substantial comments to make about material conditions, class-relations, and political situations in Ireland, India, and even Russia. So that historical and comparative studies were entered into and achieved to some considerable extent.

So much, then, by way of systematic exposition of Marx's 'Dialectical and Historical Materialism'. We must now turn to the task of critical assessment.

Criticisms

I shall try to be quite exhaustive in enumerating the several criticisms of Marx, though some of them are of relatively minor and others of major importance. We are now in a position to assemble and to judge these criticisms quite fully and clearly, and we must try to make our critique as definitive as possible so that we can properly assess the place of Marx in the making of Sociology.

(a) Dialectical Materialism: Not New

A first criticism levelled at Marx was that the 'Dialectical Materialism' with which he countered 'Idealism', was not *new*. Heraclitus, it has often been said, and other scholars of the past, had already put forward the idea of the world as a continuous material process; an ongoing, ever-changing flux of events. Marx had therefore made no contribution here.

* All these examples are to be found in Vol. II of *Karl Marx: Selected Works*.

This criticism, of course, is of no consequence whatever. A theory is not to be judged according to its age, or, indeed, according to the number of times it has been stated in history. If Heraclitus was *right*; if his theory was *true*; then it was a contribution of Marx to have re-stated it. But, of course, Marx's 'system' of explanation of the world in materialistic terms was quite different in its detail from the views of thinkers in earlier historical periods. As such, it was undoubtedly a contribution. The question is—is it true or false? And this cannot be decided by noticing that other people have said something similar before.

This criticism is, in short, pointless and trivial, as well as being, in quite basic respects, untrue.

(b) Dialectical Materialism: too simple a theory of nature

A second criticism, often associated with the first, is that 'Dialectical Materialism' was not only not new, but that it was so large-scale and simple a theory as not really to explain anything much. On the surface, to speak of 'quantitative changes' leading to 'qualitatively new substances and forms' in nature, seems very factual, measurable, scientific, and especially when the illustrations given—such as an additional molecule of hydrogen leading to a qualitative change from a gas into a liquid—seem so telling. But as soon as this apparently clear statement is *questioned*, and as soon as the processes of nature are examined in more detail, the more questionable becomes this *dictum* that all 'qualitative' change is brought about by a number of gradual, additive, quantitative changes. Consider, for example, the explanation of the emergence of a new biological species offered by the 'theory of evolution'. It seems true that a small accidental change in the genetic constitution of the germ cell of an animal brings into being a qualitatively new offspring, and if this offspring is favoured by the natural environment, it may give rise to a qualitatively new species; but it does *not* seem true that this process is characterized by a long sequence of gradual, cumulative, quantitative additions (a kind of 'incremental' material process) which, at a certain 'nodal' point suddenly gives rise to a qualitatively new phenomenon. Genetic changes, genetic 'mutations', seem rather to be unusual, arbitrary changes which are, immediately, qualitatively new phenomena. And many of them, of course, are *unfitted* for survival, they are, in fact, fatal for the offspring which results from them. Dialectical materialism, as stated by Marx and Engels, with its basic process of 'quantitative-qualitative' change, is therefore far too large-scale and simple, far too all-embracing a theory, to give us a really satisfactory explanation of all the processes of change in nature. Whereas it *seems* to fit with changes such as the quantitative additions of

411

molecules, or with the increase in the temperature of a liquid which will bring it to the condition (i.e., at boiling point) of a vapour, it certainly does not fit *all* kinds of change in nature. Strictly speaking, Dialectical Materialism is the large-scale assertion of a specific philosophical (a metaphysical) viewpoint; it is *not*, in itself, a scientific theory.

(c) *Dialectical Materialism: the distinction between 'Quantitative' and 'Qualitative' change questionable*

This questioning of the scientific utility and accuracy of 'Dialectical Materialism' also leads to a third criticism which *appears* (and indeed *is*, though not wholly so) *terminological*, but which is of quite basic importance. It is this. Is there not something fundamentally questionable about the whole distinction between the *'quantitative'* and *'qualitative'* elements of change, and, consequently, upon the whole weight which comes to be placed upon the 'quantitative' (as being *'material'*, the *'primary* reality', the fundamentally *'real'*) basis in that *order* of causal explanation which, alone, is taken to be satisfactory? Consider this carefully.

In the simplest case—if I add one molecule of a certain chemical element to an acid, and thereby produce another acid, is it strictly correct to say that a quantitative addition has produced a 'qualitative leap' to a new substance? Or is it more correct to say that the addition of the molecule is, *simultaneously, both a quantitative and a qualitative* kind of change; and that the use of the words 'quantitative' and 'qualitative' refer only to *the ways in which we regard* that change: 'quantity' being used when we are thinking of the measurement of the unity of 'analytical components', and 'quality' when we are referring to 'perceptual differences' or 'properties' (in some perceptual sense). But, strictly speaking, the change is *both* quantitative *and* qualitative simultaneously.

This is more apparent if we take other examples given by Engels— let us say the boiling or freezing of water (or liquids). If we increase the temperature of water, for a long time nothing happens excepting a quantitative increase (parallel with the units of temperature) in the rapidity of circulation of the molecules. When a certain temperature is reached, however, ('boiling point', and 'nodal' point), any further quantitative change brings about the *qualitative* change from a liquid to a vapour. But let us think about this carefully. Why should the *heating* of the water (because we can *measure* it in *degrees*) be termed a *quantitative* change? Why should the increasingly rapid circulation of the molecules of water be termed only a *quantitative* change? Are not the *heating* and the more rapid circulation of molecules simultaneous *qualitative* changes too? We certainly think so if we put our fingers in the water; or if, for example, we are heating a baby's feeding bottle or a tin of soup. But also—why should we speak of '*qualitative* change' *only* at the point when the water changes to steam? Surely, all we are doing here is taking *the most evident perceptual difference*, from the point of view of our own sense-experience, as a qualitative 'nodal point' in nature. Perhaps the difference in terms, of 'heat' or 'rapidity of circulation of molecules' is still only a gradual, incremental change; and it is only that *from the viewpoint of our own (human) perceptual awareness* that a qualitatively striking change has, with relative 'suddenness', occurred.

Certainly to speak of something *quantitatively additive causing* something *subsequently qualitative* is a questionable, indeed highly dubious, way of describing what is happening. Again, it can be seen, really, to be of the nature of a metaphysical *assertion*. The arguer *wants* to insist that what he takes to be *qualitative attributes* are not objectively or basically real, but are only subjectively experienced phenomena which are *dependent* upon, *secondary* to, more fundamental *quantitative* facts which *are* objective and *are* real; and therefore he conceptually separates quantitative and qualitative attributes, and *asserts* that it is the former which always *cause* the latter. It is a metaphysical sleight of hand!

This may seem, when arguing about water and acid, to be only a small, even a petty, linguistic point, but we shall see that when we come to the distinctions drawn between the 'material, quantitative' elements of *society*, and the 'qualitative' elements of the super-structure, it is a point of the most fundamental importance.

(d) The Transition from Dialectical Materialism to Historical Materialism: too simple

The fourth criticism is with regard to the supposed *application* of Dialectical Materialism to Historical Materialism, and is—that the transition from the one to the other is conceived and undertaken in far too simple-minded a manner: without a satisfactory appreciation of either the different levels of subject-matter involved or the conceptual and methodological problems of studying them.

It is one thing to speak of molecules of various acids, or the circulation of molecules of water, and quite another to speak of human beings—thinking, feeling, purposefully acting beings—involved in complexities of social relationships. These are two quite different levels of phenomena; *the nature of the subject-matter is so qualitatively different* that the *same* concepts and methods *do not* apply; or, at least, are not *immediately seen to apply*.

Some detailed consideration of the *appropriateness* for the more complex level, of the concepts and methods which are satisfactory for the more simple level, is clearly necessary. Yet these matters are never worked out satisfactorily by either Marx or Engels. Comte, it may be remembered, had *insisted* upon the importance of recognizing *levels* of facts, and qualitatively different *kinds* of *consensus*, for the proper formulation of the methods appropriate to the several sciences. Marx and Engels well-nigh ignore all this.

It is true that they recognize, as we have seen, that men are consciously active in changing both nature and society; that material reality is actively reflected in their minds; and that the explanation of social change at least includes the understanding of men's interests and purposes; and yet the basic assertion of *materialism*; of the sequence and weighting of '*quantitative-qualitative*' change remains the same with regard to men in society as with regard to molecules and cells in nature. We shall elaborate the many deficiencies of this position in the separate points which follow, but one crucial point might be noted and emphasized here.

Bearing in mind this difference in level between the compounding of molecules in various substances, and of men grappling with their material environments in various societies, it is quite clear that any discussion of the *material reality* or the *material conditions* of both must be *only an analogy*. If we speak about the 'quantitative basis of material reality' which underlies the emergence of vapour as a phenomenon qualitatively distinct from a liquid, that is one thing. If we then speak of the *quantitative basis of the material conditions* of the activities of men in seeking to satisfy their needs in nature and society, as (for example) giving rise to capitalist society, as a phenomenon qualitatively distinct from feudal society, that is quite another thing. If we seek to emphasize the role of the *material basis* of one (in bringing about qualitative difference) by illustrative reference to the other, we are *employing an analogy*. No more.

If we regard the two sets of phenomena as examples of *the same materialistic process*, then we are indeed mistaking an *analogous* for a *homologous* relationship, and are in error. And in applying their metaphysical assertion of materialism to explain equally *both* natural *and* social and historical processes, it seems to me beyond doubt that Marx and Engels committed this error—which was even more powerfully and didactically reinforced by later teachers such as Lenin and Stalin.

Spencer, it may be noted, had at least been meticulously clear about the analogies which he used, but Marx and Engels seemed blind to theirs, and so have been most of their followers. The force of this point can be more fully seen as we explore all the more *specific* doctrines of 'Historical Materialism'.

(e) The Material Basis of Society: The Identity between men's 'Relations with the Material World' and men's 'Economic Relations' unwarranted

The first set of vaguenesses which terminate in an unjustified dogma are Marx's considerations as to the 'material conditions' of men's 'sensuous, practical activities' which constitute the 'basic reality', the 'objective reality', the 'economic structure' which is the foundation of society. It is best to state this criticism quite baldly, and to say that it is an error to equate men's 'relations to the material world' with men's 'economic relations' and, thereafter, to claim that these 'determine' everything else in society.

It is a truism that men act in relation to *'nature'*, or the *'material world'*, in seeking to satisfy their needs or in exploring the many dimensions of their experience and their purposes. But let us stop at once and consider all that this involves. Surely, it covers, in fact, almost every element in human experience.

When men are bewildered by the magnitude and apparent infinity of the world; when they are afraid of all its powers that can be so destructive of security and happiness; when they are both amazed at its grandeur but distressed at its lack of meaning for them; and when they enter into both collective and private rituals, practices, beliefs, speculations about the nature of it all—surely all this is one aspect of their relations to the material world? When men lose those they love in death, and are aware of their transience, and are afraid of death for themselves and others, and desire beliefs and rituals to give some meaning to personal life, this is surely part of their relations to nature? When men and women form sexual relationships and know love, affection, loyalty; and when, in parenthood, they share concern and responsibility for their children; surely these, too, are aspects of their relations to the material world? When men feel aesthetically excited, moved, calmed, by the various moods of skies, landscapes, seas, and the varieties of living forms in the world, all this artistic experience and activity is surely part of their relation to the material world? But none of these can be said, as such, to be men's *'economic relations'*. To say that men's relations to the material world, or even men's *activities* in relation to the material world, are the same as men's economic relations is an absurd over-simplification and quite an unwarranted identity. And yet it slips into Marx and Engels almost unnoticed.

This is where the looseness of Marx's language leads to real difficulty. For to speak of men's 'sensuous, practical activity' in *'nature'* can easily be held to be *inclusive* of all these qualitative details, and I am sure that Marx *did* wish to include them. But to speak of 'the material world' and men's 'economic relations' as determining all the qualitative aspects of human experience gives a different kind of picture; and it also gives rise to quite a false premise for the analysis and understanding of social institutions and the explanation of social change.

(*f*) *The Material Basis of Society: The 'Primacy' of the 'Material' or the 'Economic' relations in society: an error of causal sequence*
The first aspect of error here may be called the error of historical order, or of causal sequence. We have seen that, with this false identity between men's activities in relation to the material world and men's *economic* relations in their minds, both Marx and Engels maintained that men's *primary economic problem* had to be solved *first, before* other aspects of experience and activity could be pursued. *First*, it was argued, men must eat and drink, have shelter and clothing; and *then, thereafter*, they could pursue politics, science, religion, art. The *first* economic achievements formed the foundation for all which followed. The politics, science, religion, art, *reflected* the primary material, economic reality, and were therefore to be explained in terms of it.

Something regarded as a material economic problem was clearly regarded as being *primary* in this sense of historical order. And though this seems, on the face of it, to be plausible, it is, in fact, quite false.

Clearly, human groups must struggle for survival; to win material sustenance from nature is necessary; *but*—it is a marked error to assume that there are certain 'material needs', or 'economic needs' *independent of all other human needs* which are in some sense more basic than they, which constitute an economic problem prior to them, and in terms of which they can be explained in a relationship of *subsequent dependence*. Men's 'economic activity', even in the earliest pre-historical periods would already be patterned in accordance with the many simultaneously felt facets of their experience. For example, men do not have 'raw' (so to speak) individual needs for food, drink, shelter; they exist in *groups* bound together by ties of sexual involvement, parenthood, relations and dependencies of kinship, so that what we might call their *familial* bonds actually pattern their activities in relation to nature. They experience the need for food, drink, shelter *for their families*. Similarly, men are aware of death and the dead; they come to bury the dead in certain ways; they bury food, weapons, implements with the dead in accordance with some conceptions of life beyond the grave; they may colour the corpse with red powder in order to recover the semblance of life; and all these will be activities undertaken in relation to nature; they constitute (among other elements of experience) a certain *patterning*

416

of 'economic' activity. Men allocate certain resources to the dead!

What this amounts to is that man's 'economic problem' is *always* a problem of utilizing the resources of nature in seeking to meet a *multiplicity* of needs and desires.* Familial needs, religious needs, aesthetic needs, needs for material sustenance and shelter . . . *all* are experienced simultaneously; and men's activities in relation to the material world are always *patterned* accordingly. It is not true, therefore, that some *primary* economic problem has to be resolved *before* other, secondary, needs can be entertained. *All* needs are experienced, and the 'economic problem' is itself always shaped by the simultaneity of competing needs; it is itself woven of these manifold needs.

Any question of 'explanation' must therefore be pursued by an analysis of this 'interdependency of factors', *not* by the asserted dominance of one factor over others. But it is also very important to notice here that there are no grounds at all for distinguishing something called '*economic* needs' or '*economic* relations' from all other needs and relations in human society. *All* human needs and desires— sexual, parental, artistic, religious, etc.—are of telling importance *in their own right;* they all involve relations with the material world; they all affect the patterning of economic activity; but they are not *subsidiary* to, or *subordinate* to, or *determined by*, some more basic necessity called '*economic reality*'.

It is interesting to notice that historically—in terms of all that is known in archaeology and anthropology—this seems to be borne out without question. The earliest archaeological records, not only of *homo sapiens*, but even of earlier groups such as the Neanderthalers, show that, besides having a simple technology, they wore magical charms of fertility; produced art of a ritual and utilitarian kind; practised burial rites; and appear to have lived in family groups. The 'economic' activities of these communities were permeated by, and patterned in relation to, this entire complex of experience and behaviour. With this continuous, simultaneous, interdependency of social elements in mind, all talk of 'primary' and 'secondary'; of 'substructure and super-structure'; can be seen to be fundamentally questionable, and indeed, to be really the outcome of metaphysical assertion. It declares the presence of an 'a priori' assumption which is not explicit, and not warranted.

There are two other points worth making before leaving this. The one is that a 'materialist' theory such as that of Marx and Engels,

---

* Resources are *always* limited, and have alternative uses, in relation to almost *unlimited* wants. It is this which gives rise to the fundamental problem of 'SCAR-CITY' which lies at the heart of the economists' definition of 'the economic problem'.

if it is really consistent, faces a very difficult question. If material conditions *determine* the qualitative super-structures of societies, how is the theory to explain the fact that the *same* material conditions are often accompanied by *widely differing* super-structures? But this is a *question* which may simply be noted.

The second point is more important, indeed of the greatest importance, and we shall return to it as a matter of crucial concern in sociological analysis: namely, that *the material, institutional life and activity of a people in a community is, in fact, interpenetrated by values; it is an organized embodiment of values.* In some way, it has come to be thought that to speak of *material* activities, or *organized* activities is somehow concrete, factual, real, measurable, whereas to speak of *values* or *morals* in society is to speak of something relatively vague, evanescent, secondary, of no real efficacy in the pressing tide of historical events. What we are now saying is that this might well prove to be an unwitting supposition stemming from a false dichotomy. It may be that the structural institutions of a society, including its 'economic' relations, *are* the actual embodiment of a simultaneous definiteness of values, springing from multiple sources of group experience. But this we shall come back to later. It is an issue of crucial importance: to assess the place of values in society, and later, we shall see that there are good grounds for assuming the *centrality* of values in society.

For now, we have seen that the *historical order* of economic and material primacy held by Marx and Engels, and the *causal sequence* which they rest upon it, is without basis. But this point needs to be pressed home in one additional way, so that its full and quite definitive force can be seen.

(g) *The Material Basis of Society: The 'Primacy' of the 'Material' or the 'Economic' relations in society: also an error of conception*

So far, we have emphasized that the 'economic' basis of society does not possess the 'primacy' attached to it by Marx and Engels in the sense of *historical order*, but it needs to be clearly seen (as has implicitly become clear in what we have said) that, quite apart from any question of temporal sequence, this 'primacy' of the 'economic order' in society is a *fundamental conceptual error*.

There is a sense in which it is true that the religious, educational, political, artistic, legal institutions (the 'super-structure') of a society always *reflect* the 'economic structure' of society. They are all closely involved in the allocation of resources in society, and their manifest nature and development is shaped and constrained within this context. But it is a simple conceptual error to assume, from this, that the 'economic structure' *determines* them. On the contrary, the fact that all institutions are 'reflected' so intimately in the economic life of society—in its division of labour, in its rules of property, in its corporate organization—is due simply to the fact that *every institution has its economic aspects, and must engage in demands for resources among the demands arising from all other institutions.* Religion is not just a matter of mystical hot air: it requires buildings, and symbols, and vestments and books and instruments of music. Art itself is not aesthetic contemplation *in vacuo*: it *makes* statues, pictures, and harmonious sounds on sinews and hair and wood and taut leather. The Law is not only a list of rules: it is a set of courts and court procedures, and a profession which requires long and careful education and training. In short, it is *not* something *basic* called the '*economic structure*' which determines all these other institutions, which can then be said to 'reflect' it. On the contrary, the 'economic structure' of society *is* the actual embodiment of the many simultaneous demands upon resources actively made by all these institutions. Of course the 'economic system' reflects the many institutions of society, and *vice versa;* it is called into being and shaped according to their many-sided activity; it *is* one aspect of their many-sided creative activity.

Now this is an extremely important conceptual point, and it makes it clear that to abstract *one part* of the entire, interwoven complexity of a social system and to say that *it* determines all the rest is an absurd procedure. It is a determinism by assertion which *appears* to be supported because 'reflections' of it in society at large can easily be indicated. But there is a conceptual error at the heart of this. Later, we shall look at the efforts made by Marx and Engels to extricate themselves from this bald error of 'economic determinism', but we shall see, too, that these proposals, if accepted, only mean the entire abandonment of their theory. Meanwhile, however, there are one or two further aspects of this point which require separate and special emphasis.

(h) The 'Quantitative-Qualitative' account of social change is untenable

This, in my opinion, is one of the most fundamental criticisms of Historical Materialism and it follows upon the points made so far and is a very important additional dimension of them. We have seen that the 'quantitative-qualitative' distinction is of very dubious validity and value even as a basis for a 'materialist' account of 'nature'. We have seen, too, that to equate the 'material basis' of *natural* phenomena with the 'material conditions' of *social* phenomena is an analogy of dubious validity and value. And we have seen that to equate the 'material activities of men in relation to nature' with men's 'economic' relations, and then to claim that this 'economic structure' determines all other institutions in the 'qualitative' super-structure is both historically and conceptually unjustified. But the insufficiency of Marx's and Engels's system of explanation is revealed with a total and overwhelming clarity when we look with exacting care at what constitutes the supposed *'quantitative change'* which, as the primary change in the material basis of society, is of the utmost importance and determines all else.

What are these basic 'material', 'quantitative' changes? What are these 'material' mainsprings of history? They are, in fact, *inventions*. They are no more and no less than the *application of man's ingenuity and knowledge to his practical activities*. They are changes in the 'productive forces' which men, in their ongoing experience and cumulative knowledge, bring about. Gradually, the theory continues, these primary changes, in a long, cumulative process, and with unintended consequences, come to change men's 'relations' in production, therefore changing their 'class relations' and their class-interests, until ultimately a new, entire super-structure of institutions becomes necessary.

But let us stop and consider the exact nature of this point, and the other clear points which immediately arise.

First: why is this proclaimed a *'material'*, *'quantitative'* change, as distinct from any other kind of change in any other kind of institution? It is, in fact, a *qualitative* matter, and a *qualitative* change entirely. It is the application of man's cumulative *knowledge* to the *improvement* of his tasks. It is with complete astonishment that one has to conclude that Marx, no less than Comte and Mill, offers an explanation of social change in terms of *the cumulative achievements of human knowledge and the increasing degree of control over the environment which it makes possible*. There is nothing *materialistic*, nothing *quantitative*, about this. But several things immediately follow.

It might be said that Marx is distinctively and justifiably 'materialist' in his emphasis because he insists that it is the application of knowledge to *practical, material, economic* tasks which turns out to be the mainspring of social change. Also, that he is justified in speaking of 'quantitative' change in the sense that these many technical changes *quantitatively accumulate* over periods of time. And he is justified in saying that the *quantitative* precedes and determines the *qualitative* changes in society in the sense that the qualitative effects or consequences of these cumulative changes are *not foreseen*. But then—what a strange tissue of ideas, assumptions, assertions, this has become, and in what tell-tale concepts it has been dressed.

420

First, knowledge applied in technology is, as we have seen, a *qualitative* matter. Never mind, we are told, it is concerned with the *material* conditions of society, with *economic* reality. But *why* should this be asserted? And on what grounds should we accept it? As we have seen: *every* human, institutionalized activity—religious, artistic, etc.—has its economic aspects. And if men can effectively apply their knowledge and experience to *some* activities, they can apply them to *all*. They can think and act inventively in their family relationships, in their political constitutions, in their churches, and so on; and these changes may all have economic implications . . . But *why* is the one application of knowledge *material* and *quantitative* and the others not? And why must we suppose that the changes in other institutions are bound to wait upon changes in the material, economic sphere, and never in any other order? There is, of course, no reason whatever. And as to 'unintended consequences'—no one would want to deny that social change is full of these, but (*a*) to say that the application of knowledge has unintended consequences is very different from asserting 'economic or material determinism', and (*b*) why should it be only the unintended consequences of '*techno-logical*' knowledge which are emphasized? The changes which men make in other institutions may have their unforeseen repercussions on the rest of social organization too.

Futhermore, though men may never be able to foresee *all* the consequences of the immediate changes they bring about, and though they *may* not be concerned even to *try* beyond the range of their present interests, *nonetheless* it cannot be assumed that men may not foresee *some* consequences, and that they, or some of them, may not come to wish and seek to see the consequences of change beyond the range of their *own* interests and institute certain social and political provisions accordingly. There is also reason to suppose, according to this conception of the ingenuity and inventiveness of men, that, as knowledge accumulates, such foresight and conscious control might be extended.

Quite plainly, the 'quantitative-qualitative', 'materialist' account of social and historical change dissolves, upon critical reflection, into a mere verbal mist, and, again, we can see clearly that, through all the details, it is the assertion of the strong *materialist metaphysic* which persists. Historical Materialism is not a scientific theory of society; it is a metaphysical dogma dressed up in appropriate concepts and select illustrations. No more.

(*i*) *Institutions of the 'Super-Structure' important in their own right:*
    even as determining influences on 'economic activity'
It follows clearly from all the points we have made that it is quite

421

untenable to claim that some institutions—those in the 'super-structure'—only 'reflect' the material reality of society and are determined by it. There is no reason why we should not suppose that each institution—family, religion, law, education, etc.—is of importance in its own right in society; contributing something distinctive in the entire nature of society; and, indeed, having some determining influence upon the structuring, the patterning of economic activity.

(*j*) *The entire structure of society interpenetrated by interests and values: not only 'Economic'. The understanding of Social Action for purposes of social explanation should take account of* ALL *these.* It also follows clearly from the points made so far that the Marxian insistence on looking *'behind'* stated values and interests (including 'ideological' ones) to the *'real'* material, economic, or class interests which underlie them requires considerable modification. It may be, of course, and often is, that the ostensible aims and reasons offered by men to explain or justify their pursuit of certain actions are specious (whether consciously so or not) and that we have to consider what lies behind these. However, to claim that the only *'ultimate'* data concerning aims and reasons which we can accept as social scientists are *'economic'* ones, is simply the re-assertion of the metaphysical dogma to which we have pointed before. It is just as possible for an overt 'economic' end to be a 'reflection' of an underlying 'religious' persuasion, as vice versa. It follows from our insistence that all institutions may have their own distinctive *raison d'être* in society; that all the ends which are important for men in society—their religion, familial, political objectives, beliefs, and motives, etc.—should be fully considered in their own right. It *cannot* be assumed, apart from the materialist dogma, that the *only real* interests are economic, and that, *on intellectual principle*, one must look *behind* all other interests until one can locate (or conjure up!) some economic motives in which they are *really* rooted. If one *does* assume this, then one is embarked on Engels' infinite metaphysical regress of seeking '. . . the driving forces behind the driving forces'.

Lest this should be thought a small point, let us see how strongly Lenin wrote about it. In his essay on the *Sources and Component Parts of Marxism* he stated his position like this:

'People always were and always will be the stupid victims of deceit and self-deceit in politics, as long as they have not learned to discover the *interests* of one or another of the classes *behind* any moral, religious, political and social phrases, declarations and promises. The supporters of reforms and improvements will always be fooled by the defenders of the old, as long as they will not realize that every old institution, however absurd and rotten it may appear, is kept in being by the forces of one or the other of the ruling classes. And there is *only one* way of breaking the resistance of these classes, and that is to find, in the very society which surrounds us, and to enlighten and organize for the struggle, the forces which can and, by their social position *must* form the power capable of sweeping away the old and of establishing the new.'*

It is quite starkly clear in this passage that *any* moral, religious, political ideas of an old order, defended by *anybody*, *must* be regarded as only the specious defences of class and economic interests. And it is held always to be *stupid* to be misled by them. The ideas have no worth or validity in themselves. One has to get to the *reality behind* them. It is also starkly clear in this passage that what is a *new* economic and class interest must be regarded, without question, as being *better* than any institutional or ideological aspects of the *old*. The political naivety of such a point of view, and the political dangers of it, are, of course, colossal.

(k) A basic error of sociological analysis and 'explanation'

It is time, I think, to draw some of these criticisms together to show how Marxism commits a basic error in sociological analysis and explanation, and is an excellent and informative illustration of it: from which, if we are perfectly clear about it, much can be learned.

We have seen that, for purposes of conceptual clarity, analysis, and description, a certain 'model' of society was adopted by Marx and Engels. The 'social system' as a whole was sub-divided into the 'economic basis', the system of class-relations, and then all the institutional elements of the 'super-structure'—the family, religion, law, government, and the like. A 'structural-functional' analysis was adopted, and specific institutions were analytically defined. Then, however, a *causal explanation* came to be conceived, as a specific '*weighting*' of *one* of these institutional components. It was the '*economic basis*' (the 'productive forces') of society which changed, and, in its changing, determined changes in all the rest.

Now Marx himself especially argued that one should not make the mistake of attributing a misplaced concreteness to 'societies' or 'social institutions' and went so far as to emphasize *individuals* as *social beings* always involved in their many-sided practical activities. And yet, this error of stressing one institutional sector of society as the determining cause of other institutional sectors is one into which the Marxian system fell. Marxism *is* a *mono-causal* theory of institutional change if we treat its arguments and assertions seriously

---

* *Marx: Selected Works*, Vol. I, p. 59.

and consistently. As such, it is an error. I would like to be very clear about certain specific aspects of this.

Firstly—having postulated this institutional definiteness: that the material conditions of productive and class relations are indispensable and independent of men's will, and that they determine other social relationships, Marx then clearly regards the quantitative changes in this material basis as being the application of men's ingenuity and knowledge to their practical tasks. In short, the institutional definiteness becomes a many-faceted application of knowledge and skill by many individuals to their many tasks. The fundamental explanation resides therefore in man's *knowledge* and *creative inventiveness*.

Secondly—there is therefore no reason to suppose that the same knowledge and creative inventiveness should not be applied in *other* institutional areas—in religion, government, law, etc.—so, as we have seen, we are therefore in a position of regarding *all* institutions as being of importance in their own right.

Thirdly, therefore, sociological analysis cannot be a vast 'a priori' statement about one specific, 'necessary', cause and effect relation between these institutional elements in all societies and at all times. The relations between all these institutions of society may vary. It is feasible to suppose that in *some* periods, the technological changes in society may have a dominant importance; in *some* periods military conquest may have a dominant importance; in *some* periods the detailed establishment and development of law; in *some* periods great changes in religious ideas and groupings; in some periods the development of education; and so on. In short, the specific relations to be found among the several institutions of society may well differ among types of society, and from one historical period to another. The exploration of them waits upon detailed empirical study. The *weighting* of *one* institution to explain sequences of change amongst all others *may* be entertained as a *hypothesis* to be *tested*—but not as an overriding metaphysical dogma to be defended by selective illustration.

But fourthly—it is highly dubious, and here we come to the crux of this problem, whether, *for purposes of social explanation* the *weighting* of one institutional component of society as being a dominating determining *cause* of others, *can* be entertained. There are two points. On the one hand, the 'institutional definiteness' can be seen always to consist of men acting within the framework of organization, so that change is always 'mediated' by them, and the explanation of change must therefore always take them into account.

This is a recognition of John Stuart Mill's emphasis—and an acceptance of his rejection of the idea that 'institutions' can have 'causal relations' between each other independently of individuals; BUT, and this must be noted, it is NOT a *reduction* of the explanation of social change to '*individual*' psychology. But also, though 'institutional sectors', 'elements of social structure', may be conceptually distinguished for purposes of social analysis and description, *men in their social activities participate in them all*. The actuality of human action is always a many-faceted pattern of behaviour in which all these institutional aspects are involved. A man, for example, works for his family, in which he is a father, who brings up his children in certain ways because he is a Methodist, and encourages them to take political thought seriously, and to pursue their education devotedly, and so on. In his nature and conduct he is *continuously* drawing upon values, aims, attitudes, constraints, etc., from *all* these institutions simultaneously. He is never *separately* familial, religious, political, educational, etc; he is *always* acting as a kind of summation of all these in his own individual experience. And when men collectively support (say) one political party, this is, at once, in relation to concerns for family, education, welfare services, religious belief, etc. The *social action* of individuals and groups derives from *all* institutional influences and is something more than the institutional entities themselves.

The upshot of all this is that: *the concepts necessary for the careful* ANALYSIS *and* DESCRIPTION *of the institutional organization of society may not be sufficient for* CAUSAL EXPLANATION. *For* EXPLANATION, *other concepts, such as the understanding of sequences of social action may be necessary, and this may always have to include a consideration of individuals and the ends for which they strive.*

This is a most important point to which we must ultimately return at the end of our study, but I hope it is sufficiently clear that, though certain concepts may be necessary for *descriptive* and *analytical* purposes, it is an error to think that *causal* explanation can be satisfactorily achieved by a process of *weighting* any one of them. Thus, it is not only the *mono*-causal emphasis of Marx which is an error, but even the *nature* of his explanation: i.e., the attributing of causal determinacy to an institutional component of society as such.

Marx has often been praised for achieving an 'autonomous' sociology; for having lifted sociological explanation to an institutional level in its own right, and to have avoided any 'reductionism' in terms of individuals or 'psychology'. Karl Popper, for example, so praises him. But Marx is at fault here. In so far as he insists upon an 'institutional' causal explanation, he is in error. In so far as, in fact, his explanation turns out to be one in terms of the application of knowledge by individuals, his error, true, evaporates— but so does his distinctive theory.

Much later, when we have critically assessed the ideas of Durkheim in particular, we will consider this entire question of 'institutional' versus 'individual', 'sociological' versus 'psychological', explanation down to the roots. It is a difficult issue, into which ambiguities easily creep. For now, however, our concern is specifically with Marx and his theory.

(l) The negative, conflictful aspects of Social Class too much emphasized

To return to Marx's specific doctrines concerning social change: once the deterministic tie between 'economic basis' and 'super-structure' is radically questioned and rejected, then the further corollary must also be seen: that the Marxian metaphysic places its emphasis almost entirely on the *negative, conflictful,* economically *repressive* aspects of any hierarchy of class and status in society. Any positive functions which class and status distinctions may serve in the social order: of achieving a certain distribution (allocation) of authority and responsibility, of establishing a beneficial organiza-tion of the division of labour in society, of sustaining an appropriately differential system of education, training and recruitment in society, come to be regarded as inhumane and repressive. They *must* be so regarded, because the foundation of each ruling class is secured by *exploiting* the classes beneath it; by *expropriating* the products of their labour.

Now in this, one does not want to seem to be upholding all the evils that have been attendant upon class divisions in society; but it *is* the case—as soon as one recognizes that the establishing of political order, legal provisions, religious institutions, education and training, and the like, are activities having ends, motives, functions which are *not* to be identified with *economic* interests, and which are something *more* than a *reflection* of them—that distinctions of status and class in society can be said to make positive and worth-while contributions. They may, indeed, be such as to *qualify* and *govern* the raw economic and class interests which might otherwise ride roughshod over all considerations of justice and morality. This is not a popular view—but it is true.

That: 'The history of all hitherto existing society is the history of class struggles' is an absurdly over-simplified statement, and one that emphasizes 'the oppressor' and 'the oppressed'. It could equally well be written that all societies, past and present, have had their appropriate orders of status; that these divisions of social class have often entailed inhumanity; but, also, that frequently those of higher status in society have contributed as much to the benefit of those of lower status, as those lower in the hierarchy have contributed to those more highly placed. Members of *all* classes may be creative in their own ways and in relation to different functions, and sometimes those of a higher class may create conditions of security, stability, and wealth which positively benefit those lower in the social scale. In this sense, Spencer's analysis of ranks, classes, and the insignia of status in society may be said to be better balanced than that of Marx —which, again, really derives from his all-pervading metaphysical dogma.

(m) *Alienation: too much emphasized*

In exactly the same way, Marx can be said to erect 'alienation' into a metaphysical overstatement of a useful idea, and, by so doing, to give it an unwarranted and peculiarly one-sided emphasis. It is obviously the case that the productive activity of men can come, and does come, to create a material order of property, with established rules of property, which place some men in the power of others. In this, property-owners can ill-treat the property-less whom they employ; the property-less can feel that they are being denied their essential human dignity and are being used as units of labour to create profits for their employers. Problems of power, virulent feelings of grievance, and of hatred at the humiliations and the sheer sufferings and hardships involved, are certainly there in plenty. In this context, the sense of 'alienation' from the essential conditions of human dignity has a real meaning for men so placed. And yet—fully and readily agreeing with this—it must be said that Marx's conception of 'alienation' goes *beyond* this, and, in so far as it does, seems unwarranted, and such as to give a one-sided slant to the analysis of the relations of men in production (and in classes and in society).

As we have seen earlier, Marx definitely opposed Hegel's 'Idealist' notion of 'alienation of spirit' in the process of creation with his own 'materialist' notion of man's alienation from his essential ('species-distinctive') condition of needing creative activity in and upon the natural world to accomplish the fulfilment of his own nature. In this sense, every new technological stage in the development of the productive forces of society, every new set of property and class relations, was (despite increased productivity) a new repressive expropriation, until, in industrial capitalism, the worker was property-less—stripped of all the conditions necessary for his essential fulfilment; a de-humanized unit of mechanical manufacture; geared up to the maximization of profit and therefore suffering the minimal return for his work.

Now apart from the fact that there seems *never* to have been a condition of society in which man enjoyed a life *free* from alienation

427

(for Marx claimed that in the very production of *objects*, man created a material order which 'alienated' him, and so began the long trek to history—or 'pre-history') it is surely possible that the enterprise of some men (let us say the 'Merchant Adventurers' towards the end of the Middle Ages, or present-day oil companies exploring the rescources of Alaska) may create totally new conditions and relations of production which may be positively beneficial in every way to wage and salary earners. To put this even more baldly: may it not be that enterprise based upon a joint aggregation of capital can be such *not* as to benefit the entrepreneurs *at the expense of*, and *to the humiliation of*, wage-earning employees, but, quite literally, to the improved benefit of all concerned? Once the *dogma* of Marx is discarded, there seems no reason whatever why this should not be so. But the *negative* dogma only sees the *end* (ie. the termination) of such 'alienation' in the collectivization of property. But here one enters Marx's 'Utopia' which is as perplexing as any other.

(*n*) *Marx's 'Theory of Value': false*

A final point to be touched in on this entire matter of 'class-conflict', 'alienation', 'expropriation', etc., as a set of concepts for the materialist explanation of social change, is with regard to the 'underpinning' basis of economic theory which Marx thought firm and conclusive: namely his 'Labour Theory of Value'. We have seen that, following upon a critique of the work of Adam Smith, Jean Baptiste Say, Ricardo, and others, Marx adopted a 'Cost of Production' theory of the value of commodities—maintaining that the value of a commodity was the amount of labour which went into the making of it. 'Profit' was the amount expropriated by the entrepreneur after he had paid 'wages' to the labourer, which had, at least, to be equal to his cost of subsistence. 'Capital' was 'stored labour' put to use by entrepreneurs. The entire system of production, distribution and exchange was therefore a war for the products of labour (accumulated or otherwise); a war between 'profit' and 'wages', between the 'owners' of the means of production and the 'property-less' proletariat.

The fact is that this theory of value put forward by Marx was false. And on this, there is little to be said. The 'value' of commodities is as much a function of the effective demand for them, as of the cost of the factors which have gone into their production, so that, to be brief, the 'profit' derived from the production and sale of a commodity is *not* a margin subtracted from the labour embodied in it. This can become a complex matter of economic analysis, but it seems perfectly clear, without going further, that this theory of value does not provide the explanatory plank for a fundamental conflict of interest between capitalist and proletariat that Marx thought it did. A basic factor underlying 'alienation' and 'class-conflict' therefore disappears; and it becomes possible, at least, that a certain *identity*, as well as *difference*, of interest can exist between owner and non-owner of the means of production.

This part of Marx's system was criticized and rejected quite definitively by Professor Böhm-Bawerk in his essay*: *Karl Marx and the Close of his System*. In this essay, Böhm-Bawerk showed himself quite sympathetic to Sombart's careful and constructive appraisal of Marx, but even so, was quite definite in his detailed rejection of the 'Labour Theory of Value' and all its entailments in Marx's system.

With this critical rejection of Marx's one-sided emphasis upon class-conflict, his overstated claims concerning the nature of 'alienation', and, finally, his labour theory of value, it can be seen that Marx's entire conceptual apparatus for explaining the sources of essential conflict and change in the economic order proved inadequate, and falls to the ground.

(o) *The relations between mind and matter, between ideology and material reality, dubiously conceived*

We have seen in their entire system that Marx and Engels relegated 'mind' to a 'secondary' role in nature and society. In nature, the experiences and concepts of life and mind only 'reflect' material reality. In society and history, 'ideas, beliefs', all that constitute the 'ideological' element in the social order, 'reflect' the basic material conditions, the productive forces. They are not of importance in their own right, but derive their nature and virility from 'the driving forces *behind*' them; and, furthermore, they are 'false' ideologies, because they stem from hidden relations, conditions, and historical accumulations of which even those who are driven by them may not be aware. Always, mind and its ideas are subjected to the more powerful determining influence of 'material reality'.

This conception can be criticized on many levels. The first thing is that neither Marx nor Engels ever considered seriously the critical philosophy of Kant which presents very telling grounds for the view that—Idealism aside—the human mind does not by any means simply 'reflect' something 'external to it' called 'objective reality', but, on the contrary, that it brings with it *to* experience certain categories—such as time, space, etc.—which do not appear to be *provided* by experience but without which perceptual and conceptual experience would be impossible. Without in any sense leaving the rigorous and sober level of critical philosophy and empirical science

* 1896. English translation, by Alice Macdonald. Fisher Unwin, 1898.

(i.e. without taking flight into questionable Idealist metaphysics) the Marxian conception of mind as being 'reflective' *only* seems very ill-considered and superficial.

The second point is that, although it may readily be agreed that forms of life and mind have emerged in nature *after* the existence of material processes, and that the explanation of this emergence must be, in some sense, in terms of these material processes; and though, indeed, it may be readily agreed that mind, as far as we know it, only operates upon a basis of materially existing organic life; nonetheless *it does not follow that mind, given its accumulation of knowledge, remains subservient to material reality and 'determined' by it.* Once mind has emerged; once it has become conscious *of* its context in nature and society; once it has accumulated knowledge and attendant degrees of control; then it may *govern* nature and society increasingly in accordance with its own needs and purposes. It can become *directive*, and *self-directive*, at least to some degree.

Thirdly, all we have said about the importance in their own right of all the specific areas of institutionalized life in society—religion, art, law, government, education, family, and the like—makes it clear that the development of knowledge, ideas, plans, and purposive social action can all result in growing degrees of control of mind *over* material reality; even to the point of consciously changing the structure of property relations, class relations, and forms of economic organization (e.g. company organization) in important respects.

The determining influence of matter over mind, of economic relations over ideology, is therefore much over-emphasized by Marx and Engels. And again, it is odd to recall that their 'material' changes in the 'economic structure' of society turn out to be nothing less than the ingenuity of mind in achieving technical improvements. There are quite radical inconsistencies here.

(p) The social relations of men are NOT *independent of their will*
It follows from all we have said that the social and economic relations of men are *not* independent of their will as Marx and Engels claimed. It is true enough that when children are born into a society and grow to adulthood in it, they find the productive forces of society *there already*, with a definite nature and set of constraints; and it is true that by a simple effort of will they cannot change them. But this is *not* to say that the consciousness of men is *determined* by these material conditions, and that they are independent of their will in any final, or crucial sense. Men can and do learn about their conditions; they strive to change them, and they *do* change them. Gradually, no doubt; with much resistance, no doubt; with much

frustration and disillusionment certainly, but, nonetheless, men are not only and always determinate pawns on a kind of chess-board of history, placed here or there willy-nilly by irresistible economic forces.

In this respect, of course, Marxism itself has encountered its own inconsistencies—for if men are *determined*, how can it be worthwhile to exhort them to support the proletariat and the Communist Party? —especially if they are products of the professional middle classes— like Marx and Engels and Lenin! It is an impossible inconsistency.

(q) *The State cannot wither away: it creates the conditions of man's freedom*

The strange naivety consequent upon their economic and class determinism is further shown in the conclusions of Marx and Engels as to the future of 'the State' (the organ of government) in society. For them, since 'the State' was that element in the super-structure which functioned as the organ, or 'committee', of the ruling class, once a classless society was achieved the State would no longer be necessary and would 'wither away'. But to contemplate a society (whether with or without social classes) in which men did not make claims and counter-claims on each other, did not enter into disputes, did not have to create and preserve generally acceptable procedures for ensuring order over factions, is to be Utopian indeed. For my part, I find even Hegel himself, certainly Kant, much more convincing when they speak of the freedom of the individual as being something only possible within the objective conditions of morality achieved in the State. The achievement of individual freedom (*including* economic justice) *requires* the achievement of a just form of the State; the State is creative of the conditions (*including* the qualification of economic power) which alone make individual freedom possible; nothing of freedom can be accomplished by waiting for the State to wither away.

It also follows from all we have said about the importance and forcefulness of all the institutions of society *other* than economic institutions alone, that the creation of the State is, at all times, a constructive activity involving *all* these dimensions, and, at all times, going far beyond a simple 'reflection' of economic or class interests alone. The state is a necessary component of society. It has always existed (even, in rudimentary form, in the most simple societies), and it must always exist.

This naivety of Marx and Engels concerning the nature and necessity of the 'State', indicates their lack of attention to, or sympathy with, political theory and philosophy going beyond the bounds of their own doctrine. Although it is true that the organ of government in any society will be much influenced by the power and interests of the privileged class in that society, it is too simple to say that it is nothing more than the 'instrument' of the ruling class in carrying out its exploitation. In modern 'bourgeois' societies of Western Europe, the principle of political citizenship and the extension of representative government is linked to the idea that the organ of government must undertake the task of balancing the claims and counter-claims which are made by, or on behalf of, all groups and classes in the community, and, indeed, that it must establish and secure the apparatus whereby all such claims can be freely and frankly made known. Even in a classless society, these claims and counter-claims would still have to be made and dealt with; so that some organ of central government will always be necessary to discuss them and to legislate as equitably as possible in accordance with them; and the central power of the state will always be necessary to deal with the struggles for power and privilege of contending groups and factions within the community.

We might note here, as a very important point, that it is a mistake to identify a *privileged* class in a society with a *ruling* class in any simple sense. It may well be that a privileged class exists in the society and that it has a great influence in affairs, but there may also be a system of representative government and a constitutional set of checks and balances against the abuse of power, which constrains and minimizes the political power of this class and ensures that the claims of all other sections of the community are justly treated. Privilege is not necessarily *arbitrary* privilege. Inequality is not necessarily *arbitrary* inequality. Supreme power is not necessarily vested in privileged groups.

(r) The classless society: the naive expectations of proletarian rule

In exactly the same way, the Marxian analysis of the 'post-proletarian-revolution' society shows the naivety of the simple conception of class as being a kind of division in society resting solely on men's relations to the means of production, or their place within the productive forces. According to Marx once the private ownership of the means of production is abolished, and the collectivization of the means of production is instituted, then men will be related to the means of production, and therefore to each other, in the same way; and therefore no further basis for class divisions and class expropriation will exist. The productivity of the newly organized productive forces will be greatly increased so that, increasingly, men can be provided for in accordance with their needs, *not* their unequal place in society.

On the one hand, as we have seen, the distinctions of status in society have functional elements other than those stressed by Marx—so that the disappearance of class is not by any means a thing to be readily expected. Even in a society in which there is a common ownership of the means of production, there will have to be some necessary distribution of authority (in the sense of differing degrees of responsibility in decision taking), and this itself will give rise to a hierarchy of statuses and the danger of the concentration of power in the hands of particular groups. It is a commonplace nowadays that power in society resides, not only with those who *own* property, but perhaps to a greater degree with those who exercise *control* over it. The training for the differential exercise of responsibility will also involve differential educational requirements—and this too will be a source of status distinctions. Educational *opportunity* may be equal, but the many provisions of education cannot be equal. There are, then, important determinants of social status and social class other than economic factors, and it follows that the emergence of a society in which all men are similarly related to the means of production does not make inevitable the elimination of social class. The problems of power are likely to remain in other forms.

Perhaps even more important, however, is the strange naivety of the faith placed by both Marx and Engels in the 'dictatorship of the proletariat', and this, together with the rejection of 'bourgeois democracy', has hardened into a dangerous creed which has brought all the worst elements of uncontrolled totalitarian power in its train; a totalitarian ruthlessness which seems, if anything (consider, for example, the recent subjugation of Czechoslovakia) to be gaining strength in the world.

What form the dictatorship of the proletariat was to take, Marx and Engels never made clear, but, in effect, it has become the 'dictatorship of the Communist Party'—the 'advanced' party of the working classes. This party, of course, is not deluded, as many members of the working classes are, into accepting 'reformist' or 'moderate' policies which are foisted on them by capitalist propaganda. This party, based upon the science of Historical Materialism, can see 'behind' these ideological façades to the 'driving forces behind the driving forces', to the *'real interests'* of the working class—not those they *think* are their interests at any given moment. This, of course, especially if one smashes 'bourgeois democracy', is *sheer* dictatorship; it is no less than the abandonment of democracy; and I, for one, find myself at a loss to distinguish between the 'World Historical Individual' of Hegel who knows the 'real will' of the 'World Spirit', and the leader of a Communist Party who knows the 'real interests' of the proletariat. The machine-gun bullet which each of them puts into lower mortals for the sake of the historic destiny of man does not, one suspects, feel much different to those who are destroyed by it.

If, in the pursuit of the 'classless' society, men destroy 'bourgeois democracy', the 'representative' form of the State, but then find that the classless society is not forthcoming, and that divisions of power remain, they may find that they have destroyed the only political means of safeguarding society from the exercise of such arbitrary power. They may still have a class society, but without, any longer, the political means of dealing with its conflicts. These errors, then, are not by any means of a *conceptual* nature only; they are errors of the greatest potential political danger.

(s) *Material and economic determinism: The Qualifications of Marx and Engels*

All these criticisms have been made of the doctrine of Dialectical and Historical Materialism as we have seen it outlined by Marx and Engels. It must be said, however, that both men tried to deny the kind and degree of 'determinism' which our interpretation of their writings has assumed. Attacking this notion of 'economic determinism', Engels insisted of himself and Marx: 'our conception of history is above all a *guide to study*, not a lever for construction after the manner of the Hegelians,' and he vituperated against:

'. . . the fatuous notion of the ideologists that because we deny an independent historical development to the various ideological spheres which play a part in history, we also deny them *any* effect upon history.'

In a letter to Joseph Bloch, he stated his position in this way:

'According to the materialist conception of history the determining element in history is *ultimately* the production and reproduction in real life. More than this neither Marx nor I have ever asserted. If therefore somebody twists this into the statement that the economic element is the *only* determining one, he transforms it into a meaningless, abstract and absurd phrase. The economic situation is the basis, but the various elements of the super-structure—political forms of the class struggle and its consequences, constitutions established by the victorious class after a successful battle, etc.—forms of law—and then even the reflexes of all these actual struggles in the brains of the combatants: political, legal, philosophical theories, religious ideas and their further development into systems of dogma—also exercise their influence upon the course of the historical struggles and in many cases preponderate in determining their *form*. There is an interaction of all these elements in which, amid all the endless *host* of accidents the economic movement *finally* asserts itself as necessary.'*

This appears to be a qualification of some substance, and yet,

* *Marx: Selected Works*, Vol. I, p. 381.

when one examines it carefully, it is simply a way of asserting the dogma more moderately. It still insists upon the distinction between the *economic basis* and the *super-structure*, and it still insists that the economic basis of production is *ultimately* the *determining* element in history; the element which *finally* asserts itself. In many other places Engels makes much of allowing a full consideration of other institutions such as the law, political institutions, and even morals, but still he speaks of them all as '*reflexes*' of the economic order and claims that it is the economic conditions of society which are '*finally decisive*'.

There are really two critical responses to be made to this kind of 'apologia'. The first is simply that if nothing has been modified, excepting to insert the words 'ultimate' or 'final' here and there, then the theory remains open to all the criticisms we have stated—and it remains true that the 'material reality' on which all else rests is simply the application of human knowledge to practical tasks: a peculiarly thin basis for a fundamental distinction between the 'material' basis of society and the rest.

The second response is: that if the economic determinism is abandoned—then *there is no distinctive theory of Historical Materialism at all.* There is simply a theory of social change in terms of cumulative knowledge; its application in all institutional spheres; and the tracing of its many unforeseen consequences; with special emphasis upon property relations and class relations as important sources of social conflict and important factors in social change. But in such a theory, all institutions would have to be given full consideration in any analysis of society so that no distinctive 'materialist' hypothesis arises.

These attempts to qualify the claims of 'Historical Materialism' are therefore of very little consequence however they are taken.

Such, then, are the criticisms of the substantive doctrines of 'Dialectical and Historical Materialism'. The verdict arrived at by Professor Acton—that Marxism is a 'philosophical farrago'—is correct. Any searching criticism shows that the hotch-potch of concepts drawn together in an apparent 'system' simply do not hang together. And there are, of course, other kinds of criticism which we have scarcely mentioned. Marx and Engels did not avoid the entanglement of 'fact and value', for example, any more than did Comte and Spencer. Their theory encounters, but does not satisfactorily consider, or resolve, the same problems of ethics. Most of us may well agree very strongly with Marx's humane sympathies and his desire to see the arbitrary subjection of man by man ended and removed from society, but still, it is necessary to see that his moral ends and moral principles are in no way derived from his 'scientific system', and some curious problems and dangers of Marxist ethics result.

For example, Marx speaks of the many changes in economic and class relations throughout history as constituting an 'advance'. They are 'progressive' changes which are part of the 'pre-historic' making of man; they are a necessary process of winning ultimate freedom from 'alienation'. Marx was in a position of having morally to approve of the 'advances' which had brought about slavery, serfdom, wage labour, each in its turn. But also, Marx claims that these movements in history are inevitable and that the consciousness of men within them is *determined* by their class interests. If this is so—no one in history is either praiseworthy or blameworthy. Men cannot be said to be moral agents. They are not responsible for their moral judgments and social actions. A capitalist cannot help having the views and values he has. In any case, he will inevitably be overthrown by the tide of social change. Why then bother to blame him with the most vituperative language that one can command as an evil exploiter and why, on the other hand, extol the values of the worker? He cannot help being a proletarian, any more than the capitalist can help being a capitalist. Why exhort the members of the bourgeoisie to see the errors of their ways? Why exhort the workers to exert themselves in bringing the revolution to a successful outcome? Why, indeed, exhort anybody to do anything? Their consciousness is determined by their social situation. It is all inevitable; and morality is only relative to material and class conditions.

Marx himself is quite definite about this. In the first preface to *Capital*, he wrote:

'I paint the capitalist and the landlord in no sense *couleur de rose*. But here individuals are dealt with only in so far as they are the personifications of economic categories, embodiments of particular class-relations and class-interest. My stand-point, from which the evolution of the economic formation of society is viewed as a process of natural history, *can less than any other make the individual responsible for relations whose creature he socially remains*, however much he may subjectively raise himself above them.'*

These are very curious inconsistencies. If one maintains that historical processes are inevitable, and that the attitudes of men are determined by their social circumstances, then one removes all grounds for moral praise or blame and all point from moral effort. All that can be said is that the values of one class are on the ascendancy over others in a particular historical situation, but there are no grounds for calling them better or worse and for saying that

* Preface, p. xix.

they constitute a moral 'progress'. Furthermore, there are no ethical grounds for fighting on the side of what is *new*. What is *new* is not necessarily what is *better* in terms of ethical standards.

Marxism and Communism also raises difficulties over the distinction between a long term and an interim ethic. In the 'long term' achievement of a communist society, certain ends are held to be not only morally justifiable, but positively sacred. Meanwhile, however, in the struggle which has to be carried on against capitalism, many things are held to be justified as being necessary means to achieve these desired ends. This distinction can, it is clear, justify any kind of immoral behaviour; any kind of deceit, any kind of expediency, any kind of manipulation of others. But, apart from the fact that, if this is so, capitalists are just as much justified in smashing communists as are communists in smashing capitalists, the distinction between means and ends in morality and in political action is never so clear-cut as this. The continuous practice of dubious means may make the character of a political movement, let alone one's personal character, into something far different from the noble conception which the ideal upholds. The 'end' may never be reached. Its character may have been despoiled and destroyed unwittingly in the exercise and the condoning of certain means.

The doctrines of Marx and Engels and the theoretical system which was built upon them contain, therefore, many difficulties. Indeed, far from being 'theoretical' issues alone, they pose, if they have not in part created, some of the gravest political dilemmas and problems of our age; problems which are yet very far from being solved. Again we are brought up against this ever-pressing and ever-important fact: that the making of sociology has not been an 'intellectual' pursuit alone, but has been one activity among others at the heart of the making of modern society; it has been the making of a science which must serve as a necessary basis for dealing with the many-dimensional problems of industrial society. In Comte and in Spencer, and in Mill in more moderate fashion, we saw how their sociological systems were used as a basis for positive political proposals. In the case of Marx and Engels, the practical political involvement of their theory was, and remains, even more marked. It is written deeply into the very fabric of peace and war in the twentieth century, and for this reason any 'intellectual' refutation of it will not easily lead to its rejection. The assessment of Böhm-Bawerk was very sound.

'What will be the final judgment of the world?' he wrote. 'Of that I have no manner of doubt. *The Marxian system has a past and a present, but no abiding future.* Of all sorts of scientific systems those which, like the Marxian system, are based on a hollow dialectic, are most surely doomed.

A clever dialectic may make a temporary impression on the human mind, but cannot make a lasting one. In the long run facts and the secure linking of causes and effects win the day. In the domain of natural science such a work as Marx's would even now be impossible. *In the very young social sciences it was able to attain influence, great influence, and it will probably only lose it very slowly, and that because it has its most powerful support not in the convinced intellect of its disciples, but in their hearts, their wishes, and their desires.* It can also subsist for a long time on the large capital of authority which it has gained over many people. In the prefatory remarks to this article I said that Marx had been very fortunate as an author, and it appears to me that *a circumstance which has contributed not a little to this good fortune is the fact that the conclusion of his system has appeared ten years after his death, and almost thirty years after the appearance of his first volume.* If the teaching and the definitions of the third volume had been presented to the world simultaneously with the first volume, there would have been few unbiased readers, I think, who would not have felt the logic of the first volume to be somewhat doubtful. Now a belief in an authority which has been rooted for thirty years forms a bulwark against the incursions of critical knowledge—a bulwark that will surely but slowly be broken down.'*

However, the 'final judgment of the world' will be some time yet in coming. The ideological hold of this theory in vast areas of the modern world is rooted not most conspicuously in 'oppressed classes', though this certainly is one contributing factor, but in the massive propagandist education which has been institutionalized in nations of enormous population, and now indoctrinates hundreds of millions of previously uneducated people. The battle in the modern world is still, in one large and crucial dimension, a battle of ideas, and will need, for a long time yet, to be fought vigorously and with vigilance. The making of sociology is still at the heart of the making of society.

A Final comment on Marx

I cannot leave this critical study of Marx without making a final comment arising from a point introduced at the outset. The exposition and criticism of Marx's ideas given here seems to me wholly fair. Even so, I am deeply conscious that much of the writing of Marx contains a qualitative richness, and, especially, a deeply moving humanity, which one cannot properly catch in the snare of critical analysis. In a curious way, some of Marx's ambiguities, though not altogether eluding logic, are qualitatively worthwhile. Thus—to take the most obvious example—though one can logically

* *Karl Marx and the Close of his System*, pp. 218–20.

dismantle, and disprove the validity of, the detailed conceptual apparatus, and the metaphysical assertions which it hides, with which Marx insists upon the basic determining importance in society of 'material conditions' and 'class-relations', even so, when one has done this, one finds that Marx's *emphasis* upon these factors has been such as to make one consider them more fully, more seriously, more richly, in sociological analysis than one would otherwise have done. Even when the metaphysical underpinning is discarded, and one resumes sociological analysis in its full sense, giving all elements of society their full place, one finds oneself taking more seriously, regarding as a more telling component, the sum-total of men's practical, technological activities; the property relations they involve; and their close tie with law, politics, religion, and the like, in society. In short, Marx enriches and deepens sociological analysis, even when one has thrown all his dogmas to the winds. And this is a matter worth noting. It is almost as though, with men of peculiarly profound genius, the question of the truth or falsity of their notions is not what supremely matters. It is as though the quality of their outlook, their dimensions of thought, vision, feeling, is something much more than the logical and conceptual apparatus in which they try to snare it. So that, when you have worked with honest judgment through the complex of their work, and in such a way, perhaps, as to have rejected much of its logical shell, you find, nonetheless, that they have *affected* you. Their quality has deepened you. So that you now look with an enriched awareness, a deeper and more many-dimensioned perception, at the same subject-matter you had contemplated before. I cannot put this better. I only know that it is so, and that this deepening of certain dimensions of human nature and human society comes from a study of Marx, even when one has come to discard much of his system.

The humanity of Marx must be apparent to all who trouble to read him, but there are some aspects even of this on which I feel inclined to place much emphasis. His detailed concern for the personal degradation of men in harsh and disgusting situations of economic and social subjection need no further comment; but they were deeply felt beyond a doubt. But it is also worth stressing that the vision Marx had of the kinds and qualities of human relationship and human experience which would come to be possible once a communist society had become 'humanized' was not absurdly 'Utopian' and was as high in its moral standards as those of any other moralist, or even 'idealist'. Though riddled with philosophical dilemmas of 'ethics', the substantive quality of Marx's 'morality' was high. I will give only one example here: the example of Marx's conception of the personalized, 'humanized', relationship of *marriage*.

It is commonly thought (following 'Communist' teaching) that Marx thought 'marriage' a bourgeois institution, and wished to abandon it with the abolition of other forms of 'private property'. In fact, however, Marx only thought in these terms in the sense of desiring the moral *improvement* of the relationship between the sexes. Indeed, he felt that it was in this most intimate of relationships between persons that the entire quality attained by society was reflected. The following passage speaks for itself.*

'In the approach to *woman* as the spoil and handmaid of communal lust is expressed the infinite degradation in which man exists for himself, for the secret of this approach has its *unambiguous*, decisive, *plain* and undisguised expression in the relation of *man* to *woman* and in the manner in which the *direct* and *natural* procreative relationship is conceived. The direct, natural, and necessary relation of person to person is the *relation* of *man* to *woman*. In this *natural* relationship of the sexes man's relation to nature is immediately his relation to man, just as his relation to man is immediately his relation to nature—his own *natural* function. In this relationship, therefore, is *sensuously manifested*, reduced to an observable *fact*, the extent to which the human essence has become nature to man, or to which nature has to him become the human essence of man. *From this relationship one can therefore judge man's whole level of development.* It follows from the character of this relationship how much *man* as a *species being*, as *man*, has come to be himself and to comprehend himself; the relation of man to woman is the *most natural* relation of human being to human being. It therefore reveals the extent to which man's *natural* behaviour has become *human*, or the extent to which the *human* essence in him has become a *natural* essence—the extent to which his *human nature* has come to be *nature to him*. In this relationship is revealed, too, the extent to which man's *need* has become a *human* need; the extent to which, therefore, the *other* person as a person has become for him a need—the extent to which he in his individual existence is at the same time a social being. The first positive annulment of private property—*crude* communism—is thus merely one *form* in which the vileness of private property, which wants to set itself up as the *positive community, comes to the surface*.'

A final point I feel it worthwhile to make is that Marx is often thought to have been purely a 'social scientist' and 'political agitator'; a 'materialist' who moved between his study and the British Museum or the working men's political platform. It is not commonly considered that he had a great love of literature, that he saturated himself in Shakespeare and Goethe in particular, and that his 'humanism' had deeper cultural dimensions than was apparent. In this, I myself believe that there lies a very important, indeed a basic, element in Marx's feeling and thinking which has tended always to go unnoticed. And it lies crucially in Marx's love of

* *1844 Manuscripts*, pp. 100–1.

Goethe. In my opinion, though I do not possess the detailed knowledge to substantiate this, Goethe had an influence of the most telling importance upon Marx.

It must be remembered that the period with which we are concerned—from about the French Revolution to the present day—has not only been significant with regard to the making of sociology; it has also been of crucial significance for the making of modern literature; indeed the two developments have been, and are (properly understood) part of one entire development. They are both a part of man's attempts to come to grips with a new and rapidly changing society, and they constitute a grappling reinterpretation of human nature, experience, relationships, and destiny within this radically changed context. Much could be said about this, but here we may simply note that the beginning of this revolutionary period witnessed the emergence of the 'Romantic' movement in literature; and the great significance of Goethe, as a European figure, was that, in his own mind and work, he himself accomplished a well-considered, well-rounded, well-digested perspective in all this. In all the details of his work, he ranged from classical to modern times; he assessed the strictly modern romanticism within this entire context, and he balanced wonderfully within his thought the several approaches of science, art, and philosophy in man's exploration of the nature of things. But the central thing I have in mind is this.

In 'Faust', the great, long-term, culminating work of his life, it seems to me that Goethe stated his final judgment, following upon his wide-ranging exploration of all the intellectual positions which man might adopt. By using the device of the compact with the Devil, Goethe—in Faust—was able to range through all the many dimensions, all the nuances, all the heights and depths of human experience; through all the possibilities which man might dare beyond his ordinary boundaries; and through all the many mythologies and *kinds* of mythologies—including *sheer intellectualism*—which man had tried. From the ruin of his first considered insufficiency of human love, Faust moves majestically through all the many kingdoms of man's mental and historical experience.* And, as his quest ranges on for something in experience which he values so much that he would love to see it continuing, all these many avenues of the searching mind in abstraction from humanity become hollow and wearying to him. Ultimately, the judgment of Faust, and

---

* In a way, 'Faust' is an enormously more intellectual version of a 'Peer Gynt'. It moves from the early insufficiency of human love, through the vast kaleidoscope of possible experiences and their threadbare story, to the ultimate sufficiency of love. But in Goethe's case, it is a judgment on the history of civilization, not purely a personal, biographical drama.

Goethe, is that the fullness, the richness, of man's life is to be found not in abstract theorizing or mythologizing at all; not in going *beyond* humanity at all; but in the *realization of all the actual dimensions of our humanity in the ordinary, ongoing, shared creative activity of our distinctively human society within the actual richness of nature.* In the acceptance of a distinctively human life of shared, social, creativity in nature; in the acceptance of our human boundaries; in the exploration of our ordinary tasks of working together in society upon a nature of which, properly seen, our own nature is a part; in this lies the true fullness, greatness, beauty of human destiny.

Towards the end of the drama, Faust is still dogged by the images of Want, Guilt, Need, and Care which have driven men into the false direction of turning away, in despair, from the human condition, and seeking their salvation in colourful, mythical, ideological systems which, in fact, are false, misleading, and prevent men from seeing the true basis for their fulfilment—namely the creative improvement of their human lot.

> 'Could I but break the spell,' Faust cries, 'all magic spurning,
> And clear my path, all sorceries unlearning,
> Free then, in Nature's sight, from evil ban,
> I'd know at last the worth of being man.
> Such was I once, before dark ways I sought
> And with fell words a curse on living wrought.
> Now teems the air with many a spectral shape,
> So thick that none can shun them or escape.'

Harried still by 'Care' who seeks to divert him, Faust persists in his new vision of humanity; in his effort to break through the created clouds of false ideologies, to pierce the veil which keeps man from a clear sight of his true nature.

> 'My way has been to scour the whole world through.
> Where was delight, I seized it by the hair;
> If it fell short, I simply left it there,
> If it escaped me, I just let it go.
> I stormed through life, through joys in endless train,
> Desire, fulfilment, then desire again;
> Lordly at first I fared, in power and speed,
> But now I walk with wisdom's deeper heed.
> Full well I know the earthly round of men,
> And what's beyond is barred from human ken;
> Fool, fool is he who blinks at clouds on high,
> Inventing his own image in the sky.
> Let him look round, feet planted firm on earth:
> This world will not be mute to him of worth.
> Why haunt eternity with dim surmise?
> Things he perceives are his to realize.'

'Clear light within my mind shines still;
And what I framed in thought I will fulfil.
Ho, you my people, quickly come from rest:
Let the world see the fruit of bold behest.
Man all the tools, spade, shovel, as is due,
The work marked out must straight be carried through.
Quick diligence, firm discipline,
With these the noblest heights we win.'

And then, with the 'clash of spades' in his ears, Faust seeks to win, by labour, a fertile land (by draining a marshland on a mountain-side) on which men will be able to live the continuous, creative life of a human community.

'I work,' he declares, 'that millions may possess this space,
If not secure, a free and active race.
Here man and beast, in green and fertile fields,
Will know the joys that new-won region yields,
Will settle on the firm slopes of a hill
Raised by a bold and zealous people's skill.
A paradise our closed-in land provides,
Though to its margin rage the blustering tides;
When they eat through, in fierce devouring flood,
All swiftly join to make the damage good.
Ay, in this thought I pledge my faith unswerving,
Here wisdom speaks its final word and true,
None is of freedom or of life deserving
Unless he daily conquers it anew.
With dangers thus begirt, defying fears,
Childhood, youth, age shall strive through strenuous years.
Such busy, teeming throngs I long to see,
Standing on freedom's soil, a people free.'

And then, with this final judgment, he commits himself to death by declaring, as had been agreed in his pact with the Devil, that here was something he wished to see continuing because of its worth and beauty.

'Then to the moment could I say:
Linger you now, you are so fair!
Now records of my earthly day
No flight of aeons can impair—
Foreknowledge comes, and fills me with such bliss,
I take my joy, my highest moment this.'*

This, of course, is not by any means a total interpretation of 'Faust', but, even going beyond it, it is significant that Faust finds his

* These quotations are taken from the translation by Philip Wayne (Penguin Classics).

ultimate spiritual sublimity in and through this acceptance of the *essentially human*, and *not* through some intellectualized grandeur which has denied it and sought a realm of ideality unconnected with it. Whatever is possible of sublime experience and attainment for man is rooted in, and created of, the *essentially human*; it is created out of nature by the shared activities of man.

Goethe's ultimate, then, is a 'creative humanism', and my point is that this is essentially the vision and perspective and basis of all value in Marx. I believe that one enormously important strand, perhaps the central strand, in Marx's system of thought is this 'creative humanism'. It contains the same cultural and spiritual qualities as the vision of Goethe. It contains the same considered rejection of all the theoretical mythologies, all the abstract intellectualisms, which have stemmed from man's need, but only serve to hide from him the true basis for his possible fulfilment. It contains the same emphasis upon the ordinary creative activities of man within and upon nature, and the social and historical creation of his own distinctive nature. It sees the sublime in the essentially human; rooted in ordinariness, but stripped of all social falsities which despoil its nature. Whether it was derived from Goethe's influence, or an independent vision shared with it, there is a oneness in the judgments and perspectives of the two men which reveals a quality at the heart of Marx's thinking which is different from that normally attributed to him in terms of his heavy coating of 'materialist', economic, and social scientific concepts.

It is this, I think, which accounts for the ambiguity of feeling which men have in relation to Marx. Sometimes, men see Marx's scientific concepts and theories and are intrigued but yet perplexed by them. Sometimes, however, they catch the flavour of this strong, idealistic, conviction as to the powerful truth of 'creative humanism'—and they are won by it. So that followers of Marx are always well-nigh bound to manifest a passion for all that is humane, couched within a tangle of ideas out of which they try, but fail, to make systematic sense.

For my part, it seems to me that one can do no other than reject the apparatus of Marx's 'system', but that, even so, one can appraise the deepening of one's analysis and understanding of human nature and society that his emphases bring, and—especially—that one can approve entirely of his core emphasis upon 'creative humanism'. But again, it seems to me that this can most valuably be seen within the perspective we are emphasizing in this essay—not as one system of thought satisfactory in itself, but as one very important contribution among others in the making of sociology, the making of modern literature, the making of a new kind of society in this modern era of science and industrialization.

Summary

It will have become increasingly apparent, as our analysis of Marx has proceeded, that his conception of the nature and elements of a science of society, and certain aspects of his approach to the making of it, were similar in all basic ways, to those of Comte, Mill and Spencer. We can now make a brief summary statement to make these similarities clear. We have seen that Marx's 'system' was clouded with ambiguities, and riddled with extreme assertions resting on unclarified and unresolved metaphysical assumptions, but here—for the purposes of summary—these can largely be ignored, though they may be noted, in passing, as seems necessary. Our grounds for rejecting them have already been made sufficiently clear.

Scientific knowledge: a clear delimitation

(a) The necessity and nature of science

Like Comte, Mill and Spencer, Marx insisted that it was the methods of science alone, as distinct from speculative opinion and dogma which were productive of *knowledge*. Science was to be adopted, and metaphysical philosophy rejected. Marx was also agreed that a scientific knowledge of society was necessary as a basis for effective political action and the remaking of modern industrial society. Science was necessary for knowledge and action.

The methods of science were essentially *empirical*. They rested upon the observation and close study of the *facts*, and resulted in the clear, tested statement of *laws:* invariable regularities of interconnection among the facts. Such scientific knowledge was not final or absolute, but relative to men's practical activities, level of advancement, and their material, cultural and historical situation.

(I) AKIN TO 'POSITIVISM'

As a general conception of the nature of science, this was obviously closely akin to the 'positive science' of Comte and others. It lacked, however, any detailed analysis of concepts and methodology of the kind that Comte and Mill had provided.

(II) KNOWLEDGE OF 'REALITY'

Its claims also went far beyond theirs. It claimed, indeed, that science provided knowledge of *'reality'*—without philosophical qualification.

(III) SHEER EMPIRICISM: THE 'LAWS' TO BE FOUND IN THE FACT S

It was also a sheer empiricism in that it regarded the 'laws' of science

445

as being 'there in the facts'. The mind (which did no more than 'reflect' them) simply uncovered them.

Marx put forward therefore a far more radical and unsophisticated conception of 'empirical science' than that offered by others.

(b) Prediction: but limited control

Marx also agreed that science made possible prediction, and that' on the basis of foreknowledge, effective action could be undertaken to achieve human advantage. However, he viewed 'laws' and 'historical tendencies' as possessing such a degree of rigidity, of inevitability, that the degree of control which men could exercise, even *with* foreknowledge, was distinctly limited. Men could not eliminate, for example, the conflictful changes from one society to another, they could, at best, only 'lessen the birth-pangs'.

(c) Experiment and practice: the objective being not to nuderstand but to change

Marx agreed, too, that scientific knowledge rested crucially upon factual *testing*, and that this could be accomplished in experiment, and in the trial and error of practice. Here again, he offered no detailed analysis, but his emphasis was upon the testing of theories in *practice* because of his conviction that the primary objective of men was not to *understand*, but to *change* the world. Knowledge was achieved *in* and *for* action. Marx's conception of science was therefore one of 'pragmatism'.

(d) The clarification of hidden laws

One important characteristic and function of science was that it probed beneath the apparent complexities and disparities of the surface of things (of surface phenomena) and produced knowledge of those unsuspected, hidden interdependencies, the 'laws' of a deeper level, by which the interrelatedness of all things could be clearly seen and explained. Science, therefore, gave new, additional, and deeper insights into the nature of things than other kinds of speculation could provide.

Dialectical Materialism and Evolution: guiding conceptions

(a) Basic and unifying conceptions

Exactly as was the case with Spencer, Marx's conception of the actual, fundamental nature of things provided a basis for understanding the necessary components of science, and a basic schema for unifying all the sciences. All phenomena in nature—inanimate processes, organic processes, animal and human species, human societies—were interrelated parts of an ongoing process of material change which manifested a certain developmental and evolutionary pattern. Any specific phenomenon must be seen, and studied, within its actual context of other phenomena; and all were *processes* of material transformation. From relatively simple material processes, more complex forms emerged and developed. Qualitatively new forms rested upon quantitatively changing material processes. Science necessarily operated, therefore, within this over-all perspective of Dialectical Materialism and Evolution.

(b) *The classification of the sciences*
Within this over-all perspective, all the sciences had a distinct nature and place in that each dealt with a specific field of phenomena—physics, chemistry, astronomy dealing with inanimate phenomena, biology with organic processes and forms, and the science of society with developing systems of social institutions. All science was unified by these guiding conceptions, and all the sciences could be classified in relation to each other within the context of them. An 'arrangement' of the sciences—like the classifications (the 'hierarchy' of the sciences) of Comte and Spencer was clearly implicit in Marx: though more specifically articulated by Engels.

(c) *Grounds of 'explanation'*
The over-all perspective of Dialectical Materialism and Evolution also gave certain basic principles of 'explanation' in science. In particular: (*a*) because 'mind' emerged from more basic material processes and was a 'reflection' of them ('secondary' to their 'primary' reality) the *explanation* of mental phenomena, ideas, ideologies, must be in terms of the material reality which underlay and determined them. And (*b*) this process of explanation should always take the form of cumulative quantitative changes giving rise, at certain points, to qualitatively new forms. In this sense it was a 'materialist' explanation of 'material' change.

(d) *Dialectical Materialism and Evolution equally applicable to the study of society and history: an 'advanced' theory of evolution.*
Men and societies were part of nature, and the over-all perspective of Dialectical Materialism and Evolution applied to them too, and provided a firm basis to the scientific study of them. In the study of man and society, as well as in the study of all other aspects of nature, Dialectical Materialism was thought to provide a more *advanced* analysis of the processes of evolution.

The scientific study of society

(a) Society: The Social System

Exactly as Comte, Mill and Spencer, Marx conceived of a society as an entire 'system' of interconnected institutions; of elements of social structure or 'organization'; distinct from 'systems' of phenomena at other levels—such as the levels of inanimate or organic processes. The scientific study of societies was a science of 'social systems', not *just* a study of amalgamations of *individuals*.

(b) A Structural-Functional model of society: Marx's 'Social Statics' and portrayal of the 'consensus' of institutions

In his study of societies, Marx employed a clear structural-functional model of the essential nature of a society, or a 'social system'. This gave a clear picture of the structural components of a society—the material, technological basis; the division of labour and property relations; the system of social classes with the attendant pattern of alienation and ideologies; and the elements of the super-structure: the family, the law, military institutions, religion, and the State—and an equally clear picture of the nature of their functions and their functional interdependence. This was Marx's equivalent of a 'social statics'—as the other thinkers had conceived of it; and it gave a clear analysis and description of the nature of the 'consensus' which, in Marx's view, obtained among the institutional elements of society.

(c) Structural-Functional Analysis: a significant grouping of institutions

Just as Spencer, within his own structural-functional model of society, proposed a significant grouping of institutions—into Regulatory, Sustaining and Distributive—for the purpose of analysing particular patterns of social change, so Marx also proposed such a significant grouping. In his case, it was the significant distinction between those institutions which comprised the *material basis* of society, and those which comprised its *super-structure*. A point which we might simply note here, is that each theorist emphasized those components in his 'social statics' (in his model of society) which he felt to be most important for the hypothesis of explanation which he wished to employ in his empirical ('Dynamic') studies. If explicitly done, this is a perfectly proper procedure in the construction of theories, and it is a point to which we shall return later. Here it is important only to note that Marx, like Spencer and others, did this.

(d) The Structural-Functional model for the analysis and explanation of social change

With this model, and with this significant emphasis within the model,

Marx then studied specific societies and their sequences and patterns of change. Concentrating chiefly on the study of societies undergoing 'modern industrial capitalism', he nonetheless, by historical and comparative reference, indicated the application of his model to other kinds of societies. The point which it is important to emphasize here is that Marx's structural-functional model was explicitly constructed on the conviction that society was a *changing process*, and that the *order* it assumed was the outcome of *conflicts*. It was constructed especially to accomplish a satisfactory analysis and explanation of conflict and change, as well as of *order*, in societies. These empirical studies of change were what others would have termed the 'Social Dynamics' of Marx, and his treatment of them emphasized several specific points.

(e) Society essentially historical

Clearly, Marx believed that society was essentially of a historical nature, and that a satisfactory science of society necessarily contained historical dimensions of analysis. Sociology should include the 'historical method'; it should incorporate detailed historical studies.

(f) Society also an evolutionary, developmental and progressive process of change

Marx held, too, not only that society was a process of *change*—in that the emerging forms of society were *different* from what had existed before; but also that this process of change assumed a *definite pattern in history*. Social *evolution*—the gradual unfolding of new and more complex societies out of earlier and more limited forms—was a *fact* of history. At the heart of this was the reality of *development*: new knowledge, new skills, new techniques, new class systems, and new 'super-structures' of institutions, grew *cumulatively* on the basis of *earlier achievements*. And thirdly—these evolutionary and developmental changes were *progressive*, and in two important ways. They were *technically* and *practically* progressive in that they provided an ever-increasing degree of accuracy of knowledge and range of control over the resources of the environment. And they were *morally* progressive in that they were part of the historical *making of what was distinctively human*, and moved towards the ultimate elimination of human alienation and the achievement of a 'humane' civilization. Marx was therefore committed to all these conceptions.

(g) Types of society: classification and the Comparative Method

Marx's insistence on historical studies was not, however, a request

449

for the study of the chronological events of specific societies; it was a request for *analytical* and *comparative* studies which took the essential historical nature of societies into account. It was in fact, the application of his analytical model to the explanation of societies of particular types (and changes in them.) And this clearly entailed the *classification* of *types* of society for the purposes of *comparative study*. In keeping with his analytical model and his hypothesis, Marx classified societies according to the basic criterion of the *material basis*, or the nature of the *productive forces*, which they possessed.

(h) Equilibrium-Disequilibrium Analysis
The study of the sequences and patterns of order, conflict, and change which attended societies, took the form, in Marx, of an *equilibrium-disequilibrium* analysis. This is so clear as to require no further comment—except to add that it also took the form of the *quantitative-qualitative* sequence of dialectical change mentioned earlier.

(i) Social Psychology
We may note too, as a special point, that Marx was very (indeed decisively) sceptical about a science of psychology. His own persuasion was that distinctively *human* attributes of mind were the outcome of long historical and social processes, and that sociological perspectives were therefore required for their understanding and explanation. Very much like Comte, Marx was convinced that 'all (human) psychology is social psychology'.

(j) The study of social action essential within the context of the Structural-Functional model and historical studies
It was also a fundamental insistence of Marx that 'societies' and 'social institutions' should not be regarded as 'entities' in their own right. They were forms of regulation attendant upon the practical activities of men in pursuit of their interests. In the *explanation* of changing societies, then, it was necessary to study the *social actions* of men—to analyse the ends they sought, the means they employed, the interests which motivated them, the tangle of relationships in which they worked out their affairs in any historical period. Again, it is chiefly important to note that *the study of social action* was insisted upon by Marx *within the necessary context of a structural-functional model*. There was no conflict between the two: but, on the contrary, an indispensable and contributive place for each of them within sociological analysis as a whole.

(k) The study of unintended consequences
A final point of importance emphasized in Marx's analysis of society

was the necessity of tracing the unintended consequences of particular inventions or particular changes in any aspect of the 'productive forces'. The social actions of men terminated, for them, in the furtherance or satisfaction of their own interests. But these actions, and their achievements, had cumulative repercussions throughout the entire fabric of society which were unforeseen, and probably quite different from what anyone in society had consciously intended. This, as we know, was tangled up with the 'quantitative-qualitative' sequence of 'materialist' change in Marx's and Engels' thinking; but it stands as an important point apart from this.

By way of summary, this is enough at this stage. It is clear that the 'conceptual apparatus' which Marx had in mind in his attempt to make and to apply a science of society was in all essentials the same as that put forward by the other men we have considered. There was a great similarity among all of them in their notions concerning the 'nature and elements' of a satisfactory sociology.

As we have seen, many criticisms can be made of Marx's emphasis upon the 'materialist' basis of his system, but again, as a final point of summary, we might note that, despite all these well-founded and well-justified criticisms, it was probably true that Marx's emphasis was such as to enrich sociological analysis in this one dimension. The part played in the changing nature of societies by men's practical, technical activities; by their property relations and class relations; and the extent to which the many interests of men which went into the shaping of 'political' society generally were rooted in, or were the unintended consequences of, their 'material' interests; certainly became focuses for sharper, deeper study as a result of Marx's work. The whole extent to which property relations in particular became a firm crystallization of power in society; a constraining force of power which became vested with respectability and authority, and which had to be broken before new progressive forces (which could liberate larger sections of men and women in society) could find their effective expression and development, received a more powerful statement in Marx's sociology than anywhere else. It was not a *new* element in the making of a science of society, but it was a powerfully new *over*-emphasis upon this one dimension. As such, it was of considerable importance and worth.

6

The Early Americans: Evolution, Knowledge, and Conscious Control

We have seen how, rooted in the insufficiencies of commonsense assumptions and early social theories, the making of sociology took shape in Europe.* And we have seen that the intellectual task of creating a new science of society was also essentially rooted in the disruption of the old traditional order of society, marked most conspicuously by the French Revolution, and in the many problems which sprang up with the rapidity of industrial change. The making of sociology was part of the task of making a new society.

It is time now to remember, and indeed to emphasize, that America was as much at the heart of this vital transformation as any part of Europe, and shared this same perspective. The distinction between the 'Old' World and the 'New' was, strictly speaking, a geographical apportionment. In a historical sense, the same sweep of events with the same significances of meaning embraced the revolt in America and the revolt in Paris. America had its revolution as well as France; and Tom Paine, so to speak, attended both. In a real sense, England and France were no longer in Europe alone, but bestrode the Atlantic, and the blood of Europe's history flowed through living veins into these new distances. In America, too, and with a declared political independence based upon the same 'Rights of Man' for which men fought in Europe, men were embarked upon the task of making a new society. For them too, therefore, a knowledge of society, a science of society, became a great and growing need.

It is worthwhile to note, now, that all those elements in the making of sociology which we have seen to be characteristic of Europe, were also characteristic of scholarship in America. The roots of European, British, and American sociology were, and are, *the same*, and the strong, close interdependence of this common tradition has been continuously in evidence throughout the shaping and the development of the subject.

In sociological thought, however, as in politics, it was no straightforward *borrowing* from Europe that we have to look for here.

* Unlike contemporary politicians, incidentally, but in keeping with historians and geographers, let us think of Britain *as a part of Europe*. In terms of the making of sociology, this is a salutary perspective to bear in mind.

452

Certainly the influences of European thought upon the foundation of sociology in America were massive, detailed, and fundamental, but they were influences received into an already existing creative development of certain directions of thought which were themselves strongly rooted in the 'early social theories' we have mentioned, and which were themselves grappling with the new perspectives brought about by the natural sciences: by biology, for example, and the new perspective of 'evolution'. I wish to emphasize, and make abundantly clear, the continuous interdependence of European and American scholarship in the making of sociology, but this must not be done at the expense of belittling, or under-emphasizing, the *independence* of many of the intellectual efforts that were made; and therefore a few careful points are worth making before we look at the ideas of some of those American thinkers who were most responsible for the founding of sociology there. Here, these points will be made very briefly, but they will be developed, and their significance will be seen with full clarity when we come to examine the idea of each man.

The first point of quite basic importance is that the making of sociology in America began under the enormous stimulation of the ideas of Comte and Spencer especially. This influence was powerful and quite fundamental. The 'foundations' of sociology in America were, in this quite direct sense, *the same* as those in Europe. At the same time, it needs to be emphasized, as we have just noted, that this was no 'passive borrowing', but an active, critical co-operation with ideas from Europe which were already being worked out in what we might call 'native' American thinking. Of course it is only the 'geographical apportionment' we have talked about which leads us to talk like this. Actually, a man like Lester Ward in exactly the same way as Comte, Mill, Spencer, Marx and Engels, inherited the same intellectual tradition. American scholars felt the philosophy and science of Europe at their own roots as much as European scholars did. However, this does need quite strong emphasis in these days when what is thought 'American' is thought to be quite qualitatively distinct from what is 'European'. The fact was that American scholars were, during the nineteenth century, working out their own systems of thought in coming to terms with the new perspectives of knowledge, and their ready acceptance of certain dominant European influences was a constructive and critical activity not at all a bowing before Gods from the old world.

The second point worth special emphasis follows directly from this, and has a dual nature. On the one hand, as one would expect, the early Americans did agree with all the major components of the new science of society which these European scholars had outlined.

They accepted the methods of science in place of speculative meta-physics; they accepted the delimited precision of science; they accepted the evolutionary perspective; they accepted the materialist context of scientific thinking—to an extent far greater than is now commonly supposed; they accepted all the major concepts of the nature of sociology : the necessary use of classificatory, comparative, historical methods of study; the distinction between 'statics' and 'dynamics'; the employment of a 'structural-functional' model of analysis combined with 'social-psychological' studies and the understanding of purposeful social action. They accepted all these things and much more besides; *but*—and this is the important other aspect of this—they introduced their own particular *emphases* of theory, and placed their own particular *stresses* upon certain *dimensions* of analysis, which were quite distinctively important. Two particular things deserve forthright mention. In the analysis of society they emphasized, and discussed far more extensively than European scholars had done, the *psychological* dimensions of social processes. And secondly, they moved very definitely away from too metaphysically-toned a preoccupation with the '*hidden causes*' of society and its changes (though they were very far from ignoring these), and emphasized much more the *conscious, deliberate, purposeful actions* of men in society, and the element of *conscious control* based upon the transmisssion and advancement of *knowledge*.

There was, then, both strong similarity and significant difference between the early Americans and their dominant European influences, and these need to be made clear. And from this a third point follows: that the *different emphases* of the Americans were not simply a number of slight 'riders' to the European foundations; they constituted a quite definite contribution to the founding of the subject; and this contribution formed a definite and traceable link with the subsequent developments which took place, both in Europe and America, early in our own century. Perhaps the emphasis worth making here is that the ideas of the early Americans had a strong influence upon much of the work in social psychology and sociology which took place in Europe in the early part of the twentieth century.* European and American influences were therefore *reciprocal* in the making of the subject.

* We shall see that their emphasis upon knowledge, values, and conscious control in society had a marked influence upon Hobhouse and others; but it is worth remarking that much of the *social psychology* in Britain and Europe probably stemmed from their influence. McDougall's book on *Social Psychology*, for example, which was regarded as possessing such startling originality in Britain, was preceded and anticipated very thoroughly by the work of Lester Ward on the psychologically (and, sometimes instinctually) based 'social forces' which provided the motives and drives of much social action.

This mention of the links between nineteenth and twentieth century work in both Europe and America—which we shall note in some detail, and quite deliberately in the next chapter—indicates a fourth point on which some clarification is required. The work we have discussed so far—of Comte, Mill, Spencer, Marx and Engels—does, in fact, bring us almost exactly to the end of the nineteenth century, and, as we shall see, a distinctively new departure, a quite conscious attempt to develop sociology from the nineteenth-century foundations which had been laid, began immediately after the death of Spencer. There was, in short, quite a definite 'point of arrival and point of departure' here which we shall later remark, and must not be under-emphasized. At the same time, the making of sociology during the two or three decades at the end of the nineteenth century in America took place in the context of so many developments that any sharp distinction in time, or in the play of ideas, would be misplaced, and such as to falsify our picture of the situation. There are three aspects of this which I would like to mention and stress clearly.

We have, so far, clarified the ideas of the most influential nineteenth century thinkers as constituting the 'Foundations' of sociology and in the next book we shall be considering the 'Developments' constructed on the basis of these foundations by other, more-or-less 'second generation' scholars, such as Tönnies, Hobhouse, Westermarck, Durkheim, Simmel, Weber, and others. And this is a perfectly valid procedure. However, it is very important to note that when the early Americans—such as Ward, Giddings, Sumner (whom I have specially selected)—were working upon their own statements of the 'foundations' of sociology, and utilizing the ideas of Comte and Spencer especially, the work of some of these 'second generation' scholars in Europe was already becoming known and already being taken into account by the Americans.* And again, these 'second generation' ideas were by no means simply borrowed, or accepted; they were critically digested, together with the earlier and more basic ideas of Comte and Spencer, in constructing a clear statement of the nature and elements of sociology. The situation was, in short, very complex, but this, of course, is no problem for us. It is simply that we need to note it, so that we do not over-simplify the picture that arises from our discussion. And, especially, it leads us to give reasons for selecting *some* early Americans rather than others. This I shall come to in a moment.

* I do not want to complicate this unnecessarily—i.e., beyond the requirements of our own purpose—but it might be noted that a man like Lester Ward not only took the views of Durkheim, Simmel, Gumplowicz, Ratzenhofer, and others into account, but also played an active part in influencing some of them. This was quite directly so in the case of Gumplowicz.

Q

The second aspect of this complexity of the American-European interchange and interdependency of ideas from about 1880 onwards, I will mention only briefly here—because it is a question to which we shall return at the end of our entire study. It is simply that we need to be *very careful indeed* in our estimation of these developments of American and European sociology, if we are going to avoid very considerable error in our perspective of judgment as to what the important developments and contributions of American sociology, in particular, have been. To exaggerate a little, but scarcely too much, there are people who think that light dawned upon the vast darkness of the American continent with the first page of Talcott Parsons' 'Structure of Social Action'. Before this glorious dawn of grand theory, that continent had been hid in nature's dark night of directionless empiricism. Only with the penetrating revelation of this new light did American sociology proper begin. Only after this were sociological studies illuminated by a new theoretical radiance. There are some (young) British sociologists who build their entire courses of instruction in universities on this radiance, and on this perspective. How far this is so in America it is difficult for an outsider to judge; but one can only hope and trust that American sociologists know the development of their subject in their own country much better than this. However, my sole point here is that there has been a detailed interconnection, in sociological theory, between the ideas of European and American scholars from the very earliest foundation of the subject in America. And this intimate interdependency needs much emphasis. But to this, we shall return.

The third aspect of this complex development in America which has infinitely greater importance for the making of sociology than can possibly appear in a brief statement of this kind, is that—in America—almost as soon as the early statements of the subject were achieved; indeed in part concurrently with the writing of them; the subject was involved in what can only be called 'professionalization'. Sociology was established as a 'subject' in colleges and universities; and courses of instruction, the writing of text-books, the undertaking of research, came to be organized in these terms. Men like Albion Small, Giddings, and others, founded the subject as an academic discipline. Now I do not want to comment on this fact, critically or otherwise, at this stage, but only to note it. Clearly, this development was of the greatest significance for the spreading influence of sociology and was bound to have quite crucial determining constraints on the directions of development of the subject from that point on. I would, at this stage, like only to note two points. Firstly, that *none* of the thinkers we have discussed so far were 'academics', and *none* of them devoted themselves to the subject as something which could be established as a 'discipline' in the universities. Their central concern was to achieve a science of society for the making of a new society. Secondly, that the 'professionalization' of a 'subject' as a department in academic institutions; especially in our modern universities with their planned teaching courses, determinate specializations, and the like; raises problems *for the very nature of the subject* to an extent, and in profound ways, that we are only just beginning to realize. It is still not sufficiently realized that this *academic professionalization* of *subjects* is something almost entirely new, and something which could as much lead to the death of the intellect as to its stimulation and vitality; which could as much despoil and destroy, inflate and distort, a 'subject' as it could further its progress. Such 'professionalization' not only brings with it organizational constraints which might force bogus divisions and claims upon a subject; it also gives rise to an altogether new set of motives for study—administrative motives, 'power' motives, career motives; all of which may not only be foreign to intellectual pursuits proper, but—*and this is the supreme danger*—such as to lead to a positive *denial* of the basic *raison d'être* of the subject. Instead of a situation in which men study sociology because of its direct and deep-rooted connections with man's historical dilemmas, with the important judgments and actions which men now have to take, this 'professionalization' could produce a situation in which a set of 'academics' positively construe it as their duty to *deny* any such concern, and, meanwhile, professionally deny scientific status to anyone outside their 'degree-substantiated' boundaries. It was Bernard Shaw, who said somewhere that 'professions' were 'conspiracies against the public'—and how disastrously dangerous this could be if it turned out to be true in this case!

Later, I shall argue that, in our own time, these grave dangers have indeed fallen upon us, and that many of the difficulties and divisions of the subject that bewilder the public and underpin some very high salaries, are contrivances of these professional pressures. Here, however, I am only noting that this professionalization followed close upon the heels of the earliest statements of the 'foundations' of sociology in America, and that, as soon as it began, some of its attendant difficulties began to make themselves apparent. We shall come back to this point with much vigour later on.

This handful of considerations which preface our study of the early Americans are necessary not only for their own sake—i.e., to indicate the complexity of the scene through which we shall stride boldly—but also, and particularly, to explain why, out of all the scholars involved in early American sociology, I have chosen Ward, Giddings and Sumner. The reason is that, as far as I am able to judge, these men were most clearly representative of the ways in which, in American sociology, the great impact and influence of Comte and Spencer were critically worked into a distinctively American perspective. The three men also represent a kind of spectrum of theoretical points of view—ranging from an almost entirely conservative and 'laissez faire' point of view in the implications of Sumner's system, to the equally powerful reformist note— and zeal!—to be found in that of Ward. The work of these three men can give a good, clear picture of the laying of the foundations of sociology in America, so long as we remember always that their work was couched within the context of increasingly complicated developments as the turn of the century approached.

A *LESTER F. WARD*

Lester Ward, in terms of his personal character, his passionate concern for the radical reform of industrial society as he knew it, and his wide grasp of the subjects within which his attempt at the making of sociology was rooted, was a man akin to, and of similar stature to the men we have considered so far. He was not a professional 'academician' in any orthodox sense. He had little introductory education, and pursued his later education in a part-time way whilst working as a clerk. From the age of about forty, he worked as a palaeontologist with the United States Geological Survey, and though he did a little teaching in sociology in a visiting capacity at one or two colleges, it was not until he was about sixty-five years of age that he became a full-time university teacher. But he had the great distinction of being elected president of the International Institute of Sociology in 1903, and the first president of the American Sociological Society in 1906. He was undoubtedly the central figure in the making of sociology in America.

He was also, in his own person and in his own work, a living embodiment of all the points we have made by way of introduction. His point of departure was the great influence upon him of Comte and Spencer. But his acceptance of their dominant importance was by no means uncritical. He both accepted and rejected elements of each. Indeed, his pages are made all the more interesting in that they contain actual correspondence that he undertook with Spencer, following upon Spencer's criticism of him. But also, Ward's grasp of all the other subjects which went into a full understanding of the new perspective was broad, detailed, profound and admirable. He understood the issues at stake between earlier philosophy, even critical philosophy,* and the new procedures of science very well. His discussions, for example, of Bishop Butler in relation to ethics and the nature of ideals, and of Kant in relation to the empirical knowledge of science, showed a very clear grasp of them. His position was by no means a superficial echo of the views of others. His knowledge of the natural sciences, of biology especially, and of the important figures in it—such as Lamarck, Darwin, Romanes, Huxley—was extraordinarily detailed and exact. And his awareness of other scholars of the time—in history, anthropology, law, and other departments of social science—was remarkable. He commented critically and soundly, for example, on various aspects of the work

* I mean Kantian and post-Kantian philosophy.

of Lecky, Sir William Hamilton, Sir John Lubbock, John Fiske, Sir Henry Maine, Tylor, Sidgwick, Littré, Lewis Henry Morgan, James Bryce—to mention only a few. He was also critically aware of the work of Gumplowicz, Ratzenhofer, Simmel and Durkheim, and, in his discussion of (these) strictly contemporary issues he introduced the work of men like Sidney Webb, Dr Henry Maudsley, Grant Allen, and Havelock Ellis. Ward was a scholar of the greatest ability, and his judicious discussion of the many aspects of the making of sociology, including the careful and pleasing style in which he expressed all this, was of the very highest standard of excellence.

There were important ways, too, in which Ward, in accepting and agreeing with some of the major ideas and perspectives of these European thinkers, nonetheless managed to avoid some of their extremes which, as we have seen, were open to criticism. And he managed to adopt mid-way positions which were much sounder. But this we can see clearly as we look at each of the main ideas of his system.

The Scientific Study of Nature, Man, Society: Evolution and Progress

(a) Science against speculative philosophy as being productive oj knowledge

As much as any of the European scholars we have considered, Ward was forthrightly opposed to the continuity of theological and philosophical speculation, and strongly upheld science alone as being productive of knowledge. And, very powerfully, he argued that this new departure in the approach to the acquisition of knowledge was far from being simply a matter of the *quantity* of knowledge that was possible by these different methods, but, on the contrary, was a matter of adopting fundamentally different assumptions, of assuming a quite basically different perspective. This was true with regard to the study of nature, and equally true with regard to the study of man.

Nothing could lead man further astray, Ward argued, than speculative or dogmatic reason undisciplined by the need *to study facts*.

Men must first orient themselves', he wrote, 'before they can expect to go aright. A man lost in a forest, or a pilot at sea in a fog without a compass, is as likely, in obeying his notions of the direction he should go, to go in the opposite direction or at right angles to the true direction as to adopt that only course which can bring him to safety. The chances of going wrong are vastly against him. So is it with ignorant humanity in the fogs and forests of

460

philosophy. Increasing intellectual power often serves to lead men further astray than pure animal instinct could do. False ideas are reached by reasoning from false premises consisting of deceptive appearances.'*
'From this point of view it is extremely interesting to note to what extent the rational faculty of man, instead of serving him as a compass to point out his safe course, has, in fact, guided his hapless bark upon shoals and rocks, and into storms and whirlpools.'†

The only orientation towards nature that could yield reliable knowledge was that of disciplined science, and this had two aspects. Man had to approach nature firstly as a *student*, and secondly as a *master*. In terms of his needs, his problems, his sufferings, his curiosity, man had to establish knowledge about the world and his own place and nature within it; but this, he held:

'. . . can only be done by study. The phenomena that lie on the surface are of little value. They mislead at every turn. Not only must the deep-lying facts, difficult of access, be sought out with great labor and perseverance, but *they must be co-ordinated into laws* capable of affording *safe and reliable guides* to human operations. To do this requires a vast amount of patient study . . .
'In the domain of physical forces and chemical substances he is able to exercise prevision in many ways to secure advantages and avert evils, but in most of the higher fields of vital, mental, moral, and social phenomena, these relations are either utterly ignored or but dimly suspected, so that his knowledge of them avails him nothing. The great work before him, therefore, still is study.'‡

Only the methods of science could provide such testable *laws* which could be a reliable basis of *prediction* and *guidance* of action, and these methods, demonstrated in the so-called 'natural' sciences should be extended to the study of man. And Ward was especially intent on emphasizing that man was a part of nature and as much a subject for scientific study as anything else.

'Nature stands to man', he wrote, 'in the relation of the whole to a part. Man is an integral part of the universe, and, in order to be correctly conceived and properly studied, he must be conceived and studied as an objective phenomenon presented by nature. Neither the animal and vegetable forms, nor the rock formations, nor the chemical elements, are more to be regarded as natural objects for scientific study than are individual men or human societies. The laws governing the migrations of birds, or the geographical distribution of plants, or the movement of storms, or the elective affinities of chemicals, are not more the legitimate subjects of scientific investigation than are the individual or collective actions of men or the changes that take place in human opinions and public sentiment.

* *Dynamic Sociology*, Vol. II, 2nd Edn., p. 44.
† *Ibid.*, p. 287.   ‡ *Ibid.*, p. 21.

From the scientific point of view, all phenomena are equally legitimate objects of study.'*

It was as proper, then, philosophically speaking, to consider a science of man as it was to think of a science of any other aspect of nature, and, indeed, only by the creation of such a science could *knowledge* about the nature of man be arrived at. We shall see in a moment the conception of man's place in nature which underlay Ward's system, but here, we can simply note what, for him, were the crucial methods of science.

First of all, he insisted, scientific questions were solved by the painstaking study of facts.

'Nothing in concrete science is demonstrated *a priori*. The practical truths of the universe are established *a posteriori*—by massing the evidence.'

And Ward argued very strongly that this establishing of testable empirical knowledge by science had become so dominant as to sweep even critical philosophy (such as that of Kant) before it. Even the vestiges of teleological explanations of nature—of seeing divine purposes or final ends behind the actual processes of nature—were attacked by Ward as being positive and remaining hindrances to a proper approach to knowledge.

'Eternal matter,' he wrote, 'with its eternal activities suffices to account for all the phenomena of the universe, which are as infinite in causation as in duration or extent. All departments of science confirm this truth. Like many other once useful hypotheses, that of *theo-teleology* has outlived its usefulness, and, where still called in, becomes a burden to the advancement of science.'†

What has been accomplished in the scientific revolution, he insisted:

'. . . is nothing less than the establishment of the antitheses, or empirical propositions, of Kant's antinomies. They have been removed from the domain of transcendental philosophy, subjected to scientific methods, such as are applied to all other problems, and proved as other propositions are proved by the inductive method. The eternity of matter and motion and the infinitude of space have passed into scientific postulates, while the uninterrupted and unlimited causal dependence of all phenomena in their relation of antecedence and sequence is the fundamental axiom from which all scientific investigation now proceeds. The entire self-sufficiency of the universe is the great truth which advancing intelligence is daily perceiving more clearly.'‡

It will be seen from this passage that for Ward, as for Comte,

---

* *Dynamic Sociology*, Vol. II, 2nd Edn., p. 3.
† *Ibid.*, p. 29. ‡ *Ibid.*, p. 30.

Mill and Spencer, scientific knowledge consisted not simply of accumulating quantities of facts, but of discovering and stating *laws* of the interconnections (of contiguity and sequence) among them. And indeed Ward was very specific in saying that: 'a knowledge of facts is of very little use to us unless by such knowledge we can establish some *law*'.

Against all the dubious systems of dogma and metaphysics, this discovery of the regularities, or laws, of nature stood firm as a:

'. . . consistent philosophy of causal circumstances. The necessity of nature is a rational necessity. Its truths are such, not because they have been willed or decreed, but in and of themselves. By necessity it is only meant that phenomena are uniform and unvarying. The same circumstances must produce the same effect. If truths were not necessary, they could not be relied upon. If they were not unvarying, they could not be traced, discovered, or utilized.'*

And it was not only the broad regularities of nature, but also the specific *irregularities*, or the apparent *exceptions* to 'laws' which could be explained by science. Ward gave, here, many examples, as in astronomy, where even the apparently unique perturbations in planetary orbits had come to be quite thoroughly known, and in this he was making essentially the same point as Mill: that a science advances towards exactness of prediction as all its 'antecedents' become known. But perhaps Ward's main emphasis when claiming the reliability of science as against earlier philosophy was that it enabled us to lay down a confident programme of work, the results of which—we could be sure—would be the most exact and the most useful for our many purposes that we could possibly obtain.

'Truth', he claimed, 'is no longer a privileged commodity; it is the common property of all who want it. The pursuit of knowledge is no longer the pursuit of a phantom. It is a safe investment of time and talent. In learning that all truth is necessary, we have also learned that it is obtainable. For, if whatever exists or happens has and can have but one definite, necessary cause, without which it could not exist or happen, and with which it could not but exist or happen, then it only remains to ascertain that cause. And, since all causes consist of real and tangible circumstances or combinations of circumstances, they can in most cases be reproduced or prevented in future according as they produce beneficial or injurious results. If we can create the same conditions, we may be sure of the same result; if we can break up those conditions, we can avoid the result. In this way we may in time reach the antecedent causes of the most subtle truths of nature.'†

We have noted that a second important aspect of Science which

---

* *Dynamic Sociology*, Vol. II, 2nd Edn., p. 40.   † *Ibid.*, pp. 43-4.

Ward emphasized was that of *control;* of *mastery* over nature—but it is best to leave our consideration of this until we have seen fully his conception of the *materialistic context* of man's place in nature.

(b) *The materialistic basis of Man's place in nature, and of science*

We have said much about Marx's 'materialist' conception of nature and human society, and we have noted that Herbert Spencer might be said to be an even more consistent 'Dialectical Materialist' than he. But now it may be a matter of surprise to discover that the first great exponent of sociology in America was as much of a 'Dialectical Materialist' as either of these two thinkers. And this is far from being a rather whimsical, or contrived interpretation of Ward: it is the fundamental basis of his system; and it is in the way in which he treats it that there is a positive advancement of conceptualization and clarification on his part.

Let us see, first of all, how completely Ward was in agreement with Marx concerning man's place in nature; how completely he agreed with the materialist (as opposed to the 'Idealist') conception of the emergence of life and mind from the material processes of the universe; how completely he agreed with the persuasions of both Marx and Spencer that the forms of nature and society could only be analysed and explained as processes adapting themselves to environmental circumstances; and how important he felt this materialist conception to be—both as a necessary and correct perspective for any reliable study of man and society, and as a perspective which actually required certain specific assumptions and procedures of science.

We have already seen that Ward accepted a philosophical view of the sufficiency of the actualities of nature for any explanations which we required of it—without seeking any kind of transcendent 'purposes' outside or beyond it; a view in which—'eternal matter with its eternal activities suffices to account for all the phenomena of the universe . . .' We can now note further that he agreed with the conception that all the 'forms' of nature were the outcome of material processes in continuous relationship with each other, in a continuous process of reciprocal adaptation to each other; that the universe was, in fact, a continuous process of 'transformation' in which 'objects' or 'forms' were different kinds of 'aggregations' of matter. And he thought that the attributes of these qualitatively different forms could be analysed in more-or-less Spencerian terms.

Within this material universe, on the basis of certain kinds of aggregation and process, forms of organic life, and man, had emerged; and the definiteness of the order and perspective of this was of the utmost importance for a science of man.

It was not only the case that man was a part of nature, but also that:

'Nature presents the relation of *progenitor* of man. Man is not only a part of nature as a whole, but *nature antedated him and has produced him*. This, however, is true only in the sense that it is true of every other part of nature, every other object in the universe.

'Man, too, has been slowly evolved out of materials which have indeed always existed, but have but very recently assumed this form. The particular form, character, structure, and attributes which belong to the creature denominated man are such as they are in virtue of an inexorable *necessity* involved in the nature of things; they are the result of the interaction of coincident forces, the activities of molecular aggregates, possessing just such degrees and kinds of aggregation, and thrown into just such relations to one another as were adapted to the development of just such a being. The necessity of his existence is, therefore, just equal to the impossibility of his non-existence. Both are absolute. Nature, therefore, occupies the relation to man of cause to effect, of antecedent to consequent.'*

The material processes of nature have brought man into being; they are necessary for a *causal account* of the emergent nature of man. But Ward insisted upon other aspects of this perspective which were of vital importance for the proper appreciation of the relation of the human *mind* to nature. His emphasis was that, until the emergence of man, the entirety of material nature was devoid of consciousness.

'Nature', he wrote, 'must be regarded as *unconscious*. Throughout all the changes which have resulted in the evolution of man, the process has been purely automatic. No thought, no ideas, no plan, no purpose has entered into the great cosmic movement . . . all the great processes of nature, including the development of organic forms and of man, have been impelled by blind and mindless energies guided by no intelligence or conscious power either from within or from without.'†

This entire process was an unconscious coherence of material units into aggregations of varying orders; and the 'forms' which emerged were an outcome of continuous *adaptive interaction*. This conception of the 'form' of anything in nature being essentially related to its surrounding 'milieu', or 'environment', or 'circumstances', in terms of a continuous play of *adaptive* adjustments, was absolutely central, Ward insisted, for the explanation of it; and the entirety of nature, up to and including the *emergence* of man, was a vast, ordered complexity of such adaptive interactions.

'The directive law (i.e., in the emergence of forms in nature),' he wrote, 'is that of *adaptation*. Things *are* adapted because they *have adapted them-*

* *Dynamic Sociology*, Vol. II, 2nd Edn., pp. 3–4.   † *Ibid.*, p. 5.

465

selves. What we see exists of necessity. It might have been other than it is, had the conditions been other than they were. The conditions being what they were, the results could be no other than they are. A certain degree of adaptation is necessary to the existence of a form. For forms to exist at all, they must be to a certain extent adapted.'*

We shall see in a moment that Ward did *not* mean to insist here that everything in nature was *tightly* or *well*-adapted to its circumstances; but, for now, the essential point is that the entire nature of the universe was viewed as an *unconscious* process of cohering aggregates and energies in continuous, adaptive interaction with each other.

Now the essential point which Ward then made and stressed was that this vast process of nature could not be explained in terms of mind and purpose, but, on the contrary, that mind and purpose had emerged *out of it*, as a very limited and *very recent* (as far as we are aware) occurrence, and that the emergence of mind could only be explained (up to the emergence of man) in terms of it.

'Mind', wrote Ward, 'is found only at the end of the series, and not at the beginning. It is the distinctive attribute of the creature, and not of the creator. It resides in man, and not in nature.'†

Mind and purpose gradually come into being as aspects of certain kinds of 'organization of matter'.

'The tendency to organization which has existed on this planet for a vast period, in connection with the increasing adaptation of the conditions now found upon its surface from the time when it assumed a cooled exterior to the present time, has gradually evolved a class of forms called animals, in which the remarkable quality denominated consciousness is manifested. This quality exhibits all conceivable degrees, from that seen in the monad to that found in enlightened man, and throughout this series the capacity for teleological action has steadily and uniformly kept pace with the degree of intelligence. We are therefore forced to conclude that consciousness and intelligence are products of organization; that organized beings are, as it were, devices for the concentration and intensification of molecular activities; and that mind and thought are among the necessary products of such concentrated and intensified activities—the properties of matter thus organized. The "soul of truth," therefore, in the belief that the universe possesses consciousness, intelligence, and mind, consists in the fact that the primary activities of diffused matter—activities which are never divorced from it—constitute the sole element out of which, by simple focalization, these qualities are produced.'‡

The following passage is perhaps one of Ward's best statements of this 'materialist' position.

* *Dynamic Sociology*, Vol. II, 2nd Edn., p. 8.
† *Ibid.*, p. 10. ‡ *Ibid.*, p. 10.

'Intelligence appears rather as a product than as a quality of nature. In vain we look for an intelligent recognition of our human emotions in the galaxies of incandescent worlds above us. In vain we look for an appreciating voice from within the penetralia of the earth. True, it is not the silence of eternal rest; the stars glow and the planets roll, the crystal sparkles and the flower blooms, but not until we reach the animal world is there one token of sympathy, one evidence of joy, one ray of intelligence. Poets may tell of the smiling landscape, the modest flower, the angry ocean, or the pensive stream; these are but figures of speech, and serve only as associations for the mind. There is beauty, there is grandeur, there is activity, there is even life, but mind there is none. Thought and feeling are not there. The universe is insensible. Nature has no soul, although within her are all the elements of sensibility and all the materials of intelligence. For mind is merely a relation. Thought is a mode of material activity. Intellect is a brain-wave. To secure it only requires an appropriate form. One revolution of the wheel of organization evolved the living vegetable world; another culminated in the creation of sentient beings. Higher and higher has arisen the type, finer and finer has grown the product, till brain has become the ruling force, and man has emerged from that darkness which hitherto had never permitted Nature to contemplate herself. This highest product of evolution, and which may properly be called spirit, has been described as that which "sleeps in the stone, dreams in the animal, awakes in man".'†

Having made his conception of the relation of mind to nature perfectly clear, Ward then made equally clear the implications of this for 'scientific explanation' at different levels—and it is in this, and his elaboration of it in 'sociological explanation', that he made a marked advance in clarity.

As far as the study of *nature* was concerned, scientific explanation must be in terms of *efficient causes*; the outcome of the analysis of the interdependent processes of nature which were *genetic*. In all explanations of nature, 'final causes' or 'purposes' were completely misplaced and in error.

'Nature's processes are *genetic*. The cause not only always precedes the effect, but it immediately precedes it. The effect is in immediate proximity to the cause . . . The word *genetic* combines better than any other the idea of causation in all its delicate forms with that of continuance, without suggesting either an *origin* or a *purpose*. . . . Genesis is only another name for causation, and causation is the production of change through impact. A *causa efficiens*, which is the essence of the genetic process, is simply a direct and immediate cause—one in which there is neither interval nor indirection between the cause and the effect.'

So much for the *unconscious* realms of material nature. With the emergence of *mind* and *consciousness*, however, a completely different principle of 'explanation' was introduced. Mind was con-

* *Dynamic Sociology*, Vol. II, 2nd Edn., pp. 74–5.

sciously aware of certain *ends* of *action* and therefore any satisfactory explanation must now take into account the understanding of *purpose*. The explanation of *psychical* as distinct from *physical* facts must be *teleological* as well as being, in part, genetic. And the conscious control of action in terms of purpose meant that there might well be delay and complexities of deliberation in the relationships between cause and effect; ends sought and means employed, etc.

'The wholly unconscious and unintelligent character of *nature's* processes may be safely concluded from their genetic stamp. *Intelligence* works quite otherwise. *The inseparable characteristic of conscious action is that it is teleological.* Cause and effect are remote from each other. Means are adapted to distant ends. The chain of causal impulses connecting antecedents with consequents is not direct.'*

The great importance of Ward's distinction between genetic and teleological explanation will be seen especially when we come to his system of sociology, but, for the moment, we have seen very clearly the way in which he shared a 'materialist' position with Marx and Spencer and how this conception led him to important distinctions of scientific procedure and 'explanation'. Above all, however, we have seen clearly that, though maintaining this 'materialist perspective', he did *not* fall into the metaphysical error of thinking that because mind had emerged out of matter it could be satisfactorily explained *in the same terms*. His sharp distinction here was a very considerable improvement on the 'dialectical materialism' of Marx, and even (though this was not so unqualified) on the materialism of Spencer. Like both these men, however, Ward insisted on an *evolutionary* as well as a *materialist* perspective.

(c) Evolution

Ward maintained not only that there was a coherence among all the aggregates and forms of nature as a result of 'adaptation', but also that certain *sequences* and *patterns* of transformation were demonstrable.

'So far as the history of our globe is known, the phenomena taking place upon it have presented a decided preponderance of ascending series from the remotest periods of which science furnishes any account, and such would also seem to be the case throughout the solar system at large, with exceptions only in some of the smallest bodies, as the earth's satellite. There has thus taken place a sort of *development*, or *evolution*, which in the inorganic world proceeds from a more homogeneous and less differentiated state towards a more heterogeneous state with greater concentration of parts. In organic nature organization increases, structure is complicated, and the physiological division of functional labour is combined with the

* *Dynamic Sociology*, Vol. II, 2nd Edn., p. 9.

integration of differentiated organs and their subordination to large complex organisms.'*

'As, in passing from cosmic to organic evolution, we see the continued operation of the same uniform law, so, in crossing the boundary which divides organic from super-organic phenomena—the animal from the social world—we are able to trace the same unbroken process.'†

This was exactly Spencer's conception, and no more need be said about it. We should note a few central points, however, in passing. Like Spencer, for example, Ward did not insist upon a strictly *unilinear* pattern of evolution; he spoke of 'descending' as well as 'ascending' orders of complexity. Secondly, it is clear that he also analysed the 'transformations' of evolution in the same terms as Spencer—in terms of structural-functional differentiation, integration, heterogeneity and coherence of organization, and the like. And thirdly, we might note that Ward also thought that evolution was a pattern of change found in *all* phenomena, and that this was therefore a certain unifying element among *all* the sciences. He wrote, for example:

'We not only discover one great law of evolution applicable to all the fields covered by the several sciences of the series, but we can learn something more about the true method of evolution by observing how it takes place in each of these fields. Even some of the subordinate sciences falling under the great groups that we have been considering, are capable of shedding light upon the method of evolution, and probably any specialist in science, if he would look carefully for such indications, could supplement the knowledge we have relative to the essential nature of evolutionary processes.'‡

Though it need not be elaborated here, it is clear that Ward conceived of a unity among the sciences, a kind of 'hierarchy' of sciences, essentially the same as that proposed by Spencer and Comte —though he disliked the term 'hierarchy' in this connection.

It is important to note too, that Ward agreed with Spencer in accounting for the 'directions of change' in evolution in terms of the following of the line of least resistance; of adaptation to environmental circumstances; of an equilibrium—disequilibrium balance of forces, and the like. There was a complete agreement here.

The material universe therefore manifested a pattern of *developmental, evolutionary* change which had moved from the *physical to* the emergence of the *psychical*, and then, with the increasing teleological powers of mind, to the complex development of the *social*—of the 'super-organic'.

---

* *Dynamic Sociology*, Vol. II, 2nd Edn., pp. 82–3   † *Ibid.*, p. 85.
‡ *Pure Sociology*, 2nd Edn., 1907, p. 71.

Perhaps we can leave this matter with an emphasis upon one point; a point which is as relevant now as it was in Ward's time. He realized well enough that the materialist-evolutionary perspective that he was advocating, with its enormous scale of time, and its enormous range of complex explanation of those things in nature and society which most people simply took for granted, was one which would seem too vast, too remote, perhaps beyond the grasp and beyond the patience of many. But in his view, such a resistance to this perspective was quite mistaken and unfortunate, and any sound judgment concerning the human situation and any sound employment of science positively *necessitated* the adoption of it.

'The human mind', he wrote, 'must learn to accustom itself to contemplate nature in its true relations and magnitude, and the human race can never rise to a just conception of nature or of the reciprocal relations of man and nature until the notion of infinitude, both in time and space as well as in power, has been definitely formed. It is narrow, finite, anthropomorphic conceptions of the universe which have dwarfed the labours of otherwise great minds and kept back the truths which the world now chiefly values, and it is due to the enlargement of men's views respecting the vastness of nature's periods and spaces that all true progress in our acquaintance with the universe has been achieved.'*

This is a salutary statement for those in our own time who think that anything that was published more than a fortnight ago is 'out-of-date'!

(d) Progress: the efficient control of mind, and the application of knowledge to Man's practical advantage

We come now to one of the most central features of Ward's system: the nature of *progress*.

It would be putting the matter altogether minimally, and therefore misleadingly, simply to say that, as with earlier writers (such as Spencer and Marx), Ward's ideas of material change, development, and evolution *implied* the notion of progress. Ward was far more forthright than this. He positively *insisted* that, in clearly defined ways, the emergence of mind in nature *was* attended by progress, and, furthermore, that the conscious and extended control which the *human* mind could exercise over nature by the accumulation of knowledge and techniques was a central fact of progress in the context of evolution. Ward was as forthright as Comte about this, and this point enables us to draw a few threads together. In it, we return to the point mentioned at the outset—that one essential aspect of the scientific attitude towards nature should be that of *control*,

---

* *Dynamic Sociology*, Vol. II, 2nd Edition, p. 6.

of *mastery over nature*, as well as that of careful study of it. In it also we can see strong agreements with the earlier thinkers we have mentioned—especially with Comte and Mill in their emphasis upon the centrality of mind and knowledge in society. But—and this is one of the most interesting facts—we can also see in it a very strong agreement with the *emphasis* of Marx upon the basic importance of men's *practical activities* in nature and society and the application of knowledge in *technology*. But it is here too that we can see Ward's superiority to Marx—in that the metaphysical obscurantism is done away with; the false metaphysically dogmatic 'materialism' is done away with; and the emphasis upon the accumulation and transmission of knowledge in relation to men's practical activities is stated with luminous clarity. And, as we shall see, other important principles of analysis and policy are built upon it, and the social evils which Marx raged about are attacked in quite a different way.

There were several distinct and important strands in Ward's conception of progress in nature and society.

Perhaps the best with which to begin is what he referred to as the wastefulness, the unconsidered extravagance of energies and resources, the sheer inefficiency of nature (of the *genetic* processes of the world); and, by contrast, the superior efficiency of mind—which by a clear awareness of the end desired, and a knowledge of how to attain it, can accomplish that end with a far greater economy of means. The *teleological* (consciously and purposefully directed) powers of mind are far superior to the *genetic* processes of nature. It was here that Ward made it very clear that although he conceived of all the elements of nature as being interrelated in 'genetic' processes of adaptation, he was far from thinking that this 'adaptation' of nature was characterized by *perfection*. On the contrary, he thought that nature was *profligate*; expending almost countless resources in producing particular results. Nature manifested a kind of rough-and-ready interconnection of things—by no means a perfectly well-adjusted, perfectly articulated order. Man should not be in *awe* of nature, in the sense of bowing to the superiority of nature. On the contrary, man should realize the *inefficiencies* of nature, the *superiority* of the powers of mind and knowledge, and replace his enslavement to nature by his control over her.

'Nature acts', wrote Ward, 'on the assumption that her resources are inexhaustible, and, while she never buys a wholly worthless article, she usually pays an extravagant price.'

He gave many examples of this: that 'the octopus, in order to hold its own, must lay 50,000 eggs'; that 'the codfish produces

1,000,000 young fish each year that two may survive and the species not become extinct'—and many others of a similar and well-known kind. For our purposes, however, it is more instructive to see that Ward thinks in exactly the same way about the inefficiency of 'genetic' processes even in the development of human societies.

'That the same laws have operated', he wrote, 'in the super-organic as in the organic world is quite obvious. Not only the progress out of barbarism into civilization, but the march of civilization itself, has been attended with the same incidents that characterize the development of a species or of an individual. The archaeologist digs the remains of extinct civilizations out of the earth in much the same manner as the paleontologist does those of extinct animals and plants. Besides his wars with the elements and with wild beasts, man has been perpetually afflicted by wars with his own kind; and yet this warfare of men with their surroundings, with other species, and with one another, is the strict analogue of that of the lower forms of organized beings. Even the silent battle for subsistence has its counterpart in the competitive struggles of industry. The same wasteful methods prevail in society as in the animal and vegetable kingdoms. The natural resources of the earth are squandered with a wanton disregard of the future. The forests are cut down to supply temporary wants, or purposely cleared for tillage, until the habitable portions of the earth are transformed into life-less deserts. The soil is rapidly exhausted by the first occupants, who know only the immediate present. The wild animals useful to man are soon extinguished by the heartless destruction of the fertile females and helpless young. Population distributes itself to great disadvantage. Cities grow up with narrow crooked streets, which must, from time to time, be widened and straightened at large absolute cost. Filth and disease-germs, due to dense, unregulated population, bring pestilence, and sweep away at rhythmic intervals the excess. Famines come to scale down the ranks of such as have forced their way in during years of plenty. Bitter partisanship prevails everywhere throughout society, the nearly successful effort of each party being to undo what the other has done. Labour and capital, whose dependence upon each other is absolute, are constantly found in open hostility, which greatly reduces the productiveness of both. Exchange of products is largely carried on by redundant third parties, who, through no fault of their own, are allowed to absorb the largest share of the wealth produced. Trade consists to a large extent of unnecessary and duplicated transportation. Wealth is not only unequally but inequitably distributed. In short, all the functions of society are performed in a sort of chance way, which is precisely the reverse of economical, but wholly analogous to the natural processes of the lower organic world. Great results, it is true, are accomplished, even in society, by these unregulated forces, but they fall far short of what may be easily seen to be attainable; they are not the best.

All true progress springs from that restless skepticism which dares to question the methods of nature.'*

* *Dynamic Sociology*, Vol. II, 2nd Edn., pp. 88–9.

The unconsciously connected processes of nature and society do result in a certain order, but this is not by any means such that it cannot be improved upon by the directing powers of mind, resting upon carefully established knowledge. One very important point we might simply note here is that it is perfectly possible to have a structural-functional analysis of the nature of societies and the ways in which their parts adjust themselves to circumstances of various kinds, without in any sense holding that societies do not experience *conflict*, and without in any sense holding that societies achieve something called 'functional *harmony*' or 'functional *unity*'. As far as Ward was concerned—societies manifested a certain order in their adaptive arrangements, but this not only *could* be improved upon but *ought* to be improved, and could *only* be improved, by the deliberate design and activity of mind in exercising purposeful control. Progress was achieved, then, when the *genetic* processes of nature and society were increasingly brought under the control of the *teleological* direction of mind.

'Man', Ward wrote, 'has been the servant of Nature too long. All true progress has been measured by his growing mastery over her, which has in turn been strictly proportional to his knowledge of her truths.'

Certain other specific points were rooted in this idea, and were separately emphasized by Ward.

One basic consideration was the fact that since the 'genetic' processes of nature were 'blind' regularities, they could be controlled to man's advantage with relative ease. Knowing the various forces of nature, man could engineer certain alterations of circumstance in such ways as to divert these energies to accomplish desired ends. *Control* over nature was, in fact, not a mastery over the *laws* of nature (i.e., in the sense of a power to change *them*), but—with a knowledge *of* these—a supervisory *manipulation* of them in such ways as to *utilize* their resources and energies.

'We must learn', said Ward: '. . . the important lesson that nature is really easily controlled. A very little acquaintance with natural laws is sufficient to enable us to achieve stupendous effects.'*

In exactly the same way, Ward believed that *society* could be improved, on the basis of a detailed knowledge of its nature, by the manipulation of its existing energies, institutions, and resources. Such *control*, Ward called 'attractive legislation', and it must be emphasized that he did not regard this as an 'authoritarian' business of government, but the bringing into proximity of certain improve-

* *Dynamic Sociology*, Vol. II, 2nd Edition, p. 14.

ments with clearly seen individual and group interests by the widest extension of knowledge and deliberation in a democratic society.

'If,' he argued, 'in the framing of human laws this principle were always carefully studied it would soon be discovered that man is as easily managed by intelligence as, (earlier) nature was shown to be.'*

Two other central elements in Ward's notions are immediately apparent. The first, of course, and this was the most dominant element of all, was that *KNOWLEDGE*—the *attainment, accumulation, advancement*, and *transmission* of *KNOWLEDGE*—was the necessary basis of all control, and therefore all progress.

'Knowledge is the chief element of power in enabling the mind to exercise a control over the materials and forces of nature, and a settled conviction that effects must of necessity follow and correspond to causes, renders all efforts to acquire knowledge profitable, and the possession of any knowledge possible.'†

It is because of this central importance of knowledge for *control* that *science*, of course, was so important: since the methods of science were the most effective ways of achieving and advancing knowledge. But the importance of knowledge was so dominant a component in Ward's system that we must look at it specially in a moment.

The second element which, in Ward's mind, was essentially connected with this, and with the idea of progress, was that, in most men, it was in fact *the desire to control nature and society* which formed the chief motive in *seeking* knowledge. And the reason why they sought to *know* and to *control* nature and society was—the desire for *practical advantage*.

'The primary end of knowledge is to secure practical advantage', Ward wrote.

And it was in this that his position came very close indeed to that of Marx, because it was, he maintained, in the continual *practical activities* of men to control nature in pursuit of their ends that the advancement of knowledge and therefore the achievement of progress took place. This we shall see more fully soon; but perhaps it is important to stress here, too, that by 'practical activities', Ward did *not* mean only something called 'material' activities. He did not only think of 'practical advantage' in purely material terms. He did not think of progress as 'technical' progress in a limited material sense. Man's control over nature—practical and technical and ad-

---

* *Pure Sociology*, 2nd Edition, p. 570.
† *Dynamic Sociology*, Vol. II, 2nd Edition, p. 38.

vantageous—also involved *moral* principle, *moral* judgment, and *moral* direction. In this again, Ward was in agreement with Comte in placing much emphasis upon the extension of 'altruism' in human society. All too often the 'moral' is, for some reason, abstracted from the 'practical' and the 'technical', and Ward's insistence *against* this was of very real importance.

Men have suffered in countless ways within the blind forces of nature and society—from disease, poverty, warfare, untimely death in innumerable ways; from degradation, humiliation, tragedy in the clutch of brutal and enigmatic circumstances—and progress, claimed Ward, was a completely clear matter of eliminating these elements of experience as far as possible; of maximizing practical advantage by exercising control in the light of secure knowledge.

'Men are still continually dashing blindly against the barriers which the environment presents to their free activities.'

But with greater knowledge and greater control, man's enslavement to the power of circumstances could be diminished, and his freedom extended.

This was a luminously clear idea, and, in it, man's moral aims were rightly seen as being closely enmeshed in his 'practical' ones. In order to see Ward's conjunction of the ideas of evolution and progress more fully, however, it is necessary to look more closely at some of the specific points we have introduced.

(e) The teleological attributes of mind and their crucial significance: action, purpose, systematic knowledge, invention.

We have seen that Ward's picture of evolution was one moving from the physical to the psychical, and then to the psycho-social; and we have seen quite clearly, too, the significant distinction which he drew between the *'genetic'* processes of the physical (continuing into the psychical and the social) and the quite different *'teleological'* abilities of mind. We must now clarify certain other distinctions which he made in this connection.

First of all, Ward took great pains to make it clear that with the emergence of mind, with its distinctive teleological capacities and modes of operation, it was quite imperative to distinguish *action* from *interdependence of fact*. These, he insisted were two quite distinguishable categories of empirical occurrences; and they made necessary two quite distinguishable kinds of 'explanation'.

The specific interdependencies of, say, oxygen and hydrogen in producing water, or of the power of exploding dynamite in shattering the rock-face of a quarry, are interconnections of *substances* in *motion,* and can be explained in terms of known regularities and 'efficient causation'.

The sequence of experience, behaviour, and events, however, when men, say, take one trade route to India (through the Suez Canal) rather than another (round the Cape)—is a qualitatively quite different phenomenon. It is a sequence of *action;* and though physical regularities certainly underlie it, it cannot be explained in these terms alone; it requires also an explanation in terms of the *ends* the men were seeking, the *motives* and *desires* that impelled them to seek these ends, the ways in which they had *calculated various means,* and had *decided* to *adopt* these, rather than others. Here, explanation would rest not only upon sensory (or perceptual) observations, but also upon *conceptual* and *experiential understanding.*

A full explanation of the entirety of nature, including the existence and operation of mind, and especially the human mind, within it, must therefore necessarily include *both* genetic *and* teleological kinds of explanation. *One* or *other* of these kinds of explanation was necessarily insufficient in itself. This was a most important distinction which Ward made perfectly clearly; which is wholly correct; and which is of fundamental importance for any explanation of man and society.

But it is not only the two categories of *explanation* which Ward was concerned to distinguish, but, more basically, the two categories of fact, or *phenomena,* or *events* in the world. And it was the distinction between the two categories of *fact* which was central to his account of evolution and progress.

The first category, as we have seen, was that of all the material or physical processes of nature, and here 'forms' came into being through 'blind' regularities of adaptation. The second category of events was that appropriate to life and mind, to 'psychical' phenomena, and such events were quite different. These events were *actions* as well as involving attendant material processes, and Ward analysed the elements of actions as distinct from other events.

Actions, he held, had the following attributes:

(1) They stemmed from *desires* within the organism. (2) These desires were promptings towards certain sequences of behaviour which would lead to the satisfying attainment of certain *ends.* (3) Such sequences of behaviour involved an employment (whether well-calculated or not) of certain *means.* (4) Such actions were therefore *volitional* and *motivated.* (5) They were marked by consciousness: consciousness in the experience of the desire; consciousness of the end; consciousness in the employment of the means and the appropriateness or inappropriateness of them); and consciousness of satisfaction in the attainment of the end, or of frustration in

failure to attain it. (6) Actions therefore involved *purpose*. (7) The *end*, and the *apprehension* of the end, was therefore a necessary component among the '*causes*' of actions. (8) Finally, actions were therefore characterized by the making of *efforts*; they were, said Ward, *conative*; they involved the element of *striving* for the ends apprehended, and the satisfaction of desire.

The kind of 'adaptation to their circumstances' in which all forms of organic life, including human beings, were involved was therefore quite different from the 'blind' adaptation of purely physical events; it was an adaptation which necessarily involved all these components of experience and behaviour. It will be readily seen that within this entire 'class' of 'Conative Actions', Ward was able to conceive of a whole 'series' of 'levels' of mind among all organic species: from very simple organisms in which 'action' was very little distinguished from the automatic adaptation of physical processes; through the series of more complex species of organism in which a consciousness of ends and desires and a purposeful direction of behaviour seemed to be more marked; to man—in whose conduct conscious and purposeful action was patently apparent. In all this, Ward's discussion was of great interest, and he wrote of 'instinct', for example, among animals and in man, as being a kind of 'link' of conative action—between relatively automatic responses at the level of the most simple organisms and the more conscious 'intelligent' direction of purposeful behaviour in the higher animals, and man. However, given this distinction of '*conative actions*' as a class of events quite different from those of purely material interconnection, there were really only *two* further distinctions which Ward made which are essential for our understanding of his system.

Among *all* conative actions, he thought that two chief kinds could be clearly distinguished. These were *direct* and *indirect* methods of conation; and the terms speak for themselves. *Direct* conative action was immediate impulsive action, using immediate muscular activity to secure the end desired. But it was *indirect* conative action which was distinctively *human*, and this was conscious and deliberately planned action which rested upon the acquisition and retention of systematic knowledge. This, Ward insisted, involved an entirely new principle and produced wholly new, extensive, and effective results. Its crucial characteristic was the development and use of the *intellectual* capacity of man.

'Henceforth,' wrote Ward, 'the possibilities of vital existence are to be multiplied, and the rate of organic progress enormously accelerated. For success in the sentient world is the ability to attain its ends, and the intellectual element is especially adapted to augmenting that power. By the direct method, action in this direction is restricted to cases which are within the muscular strength of the organism, and easily accessible without the intervention of obstacles. The utmost possible to be accomplished by it was measured by the energy actually expended. The least obstruction beyond the power of the individual to clear away by muscular force is an effectual bar to its access to the object of desire. By the aid of the new element all this is changed. Interposed barriers are evaded by circuitous routes of approach. Powerful natural forces are by appropriate adjustments made to do the work of overcoming resistance, and what is wholly unattainable in the present, is by the necessary adaptation, secured in the future.'*

The *intellect*, according to Ward, was not similar to the other sources of conative energy in human nature (e.g., the desires, and motives springing from feeling); it was not a 'force' of energy in itself; but rather a mental capacity for knowing and systematically ordering all the elements of experience in such a way as to *serve* and *guide* the desires in the use of *means* to attain their *ends*.

And it is here that we come to the second important aspect of this distinction which brings us back to a full understanding of Ward's emphasis upon the 'practical activities' of men in achieving progress. For, he claimed, the fundamental way in which the intellect does enable man to harness and utilize natural forces for the better satisfaction of his ends is that of *invention*. On the basis of his knowledge, man *makes artefacts*, and learns to *practise arts*, which enable him to canalize the forces of nature in such a way as to have them work more effectively for him. And this invention rests upon certain principles. For example, man learns that he can affect both the *amount* and the *direction* of natural energies. He can *intensify* the amount of force in its application (as in the lever and the fulcrum) He can *direct* forces more usefully (as in irrigation). And he can achieve a *commutation* of forces in various ways.

The central fact in all this, however, on which Ward places his strongest emphasis, is that *progress* within the context of *evolution* rests upon the control of the *natural* by the *artificial*, achieved by the *intellect* as it establishes ever more extensive, systematic, and reliable *knowledge.*. And this progress of both knowledge and control is manifested crucially in *inventions* in relation to man's desire for 'practical advantage'.

Ward gave an excellent summary statement of these distinct sequences in evolution and progress.

'We are able to perceive the several stages of progress,' he wrote, 'in the direction of economy of results. The lowest stage is that of genetic phenomena, in which we saw how great was the waste and how exceedingly small the degree of progress as compared with the amount of energy expended. This is nature's method, pure and simple.

* *Dynamic Sociology*, Vol. II, p. 100.

'The next stage is that of the direct method of conation. Here the phenomena are teleological, and hence far more productive of results in proportion to the force exerted. The immense element of waste is eliminated. Action that is not equilibrated by attempting what is beyond the power of the agent results in accomplishing the same amount of work as is represented by the energy put forth, but no more. As in genetic phenomena we were dealing with true natural forces, so in those teleological phenomena which are accomplished by the direct method we are still dealing with true natural forces. The difference is, that while the genetic forces are physical the teleological forces are psychical.

'Finally, we have as a third stage that in which the indirect method is applied, and here we see the maximum economy and the maximum efficiency in the accomplishment of results. With the development of this mode of action, great and increasing disproportion is secured between the energy expended and the work accomplished; space, time, and intervening obstacles are overcome, and the conditions are at length established for social evolution.'*

It will be clearly seen from the end of this statement that Ward thought of sociology as the scientific study of men's collective '*achievements*', as societies developed cumulative traditions of knowledge, inventions, and skills, based upon this capacity for 'indirect conative action'. But, in this place, it is enough to have seen very clearly Ward's entire scheme of analysis concerning the nature of evolution and progress; the place of the human mind, knowledge, practical activities, invention, and control over nature, within this entire perspective; and the different *levels and kinds of 'explanation'* on which he insisted.

(*f*) *The superiority of the teleological; the efficiency of scientific knowledge and control; its difficulties but its necessity*

Before moving on to outline Ward's construction of Sociology within, and as a necessary part of, this context, a remaining handful of points are worth making.

It is worthwhile to emphasize a little more than we have done so far, that Ward stressed the *efficiency* of the *teleological* processes of mind as against the *genetic* processes of nature. The purposive action of mind, resting upon carefully elaborated knowledge, could achieve its ends with a far greater economy of means by its *artificial* (i.e., by the practice of *arts* and *inventions*) control, than could profligate nature teeming with its blind, if luxurious, forces and resources. This was to become a very important basis of his attitude towards the role of government in society. But there is another aspect of Ward's thinking, connected with this, which must also be noted.

It is—that though he made the very clear distinction between

* *Dynamic Sociology*, Vol. II, p. 102.

genetic and *teleological* processes and modes of explanation, insisting that teleological processes were most highly significant in man, even so, he did *not* believe (*a*) that *only* teleological processes and modes of explanation were characteristic of man *or* (*b*) that the achievement of the satisfactory blend of genetic and teleological explanation which was necessary for the understanding and knowledge of human society was *easy* to achieve.

Ward was well aware, and made it very clear, that genetic processes underlay human nature and human society and *continued into them*, so to speak, even though teleological processes increased in their dominance. Man as a species had, of course, emerged out of the creativity of genetic processes. And these had therefore always to be taken into account. Many basic biological and psychological attributes of man were firmly laid down by nature, were a matter of genetic endowment, and *social* relationships, arrangements, organization, rested upon them and sprang from desires and needs rooted in them. And secondly—genetic processes of adaptation continued in the change and development of *societies*, even though the teleological activities of mind were involved in many specific directions of social organization. It was only gradually that man could gain knowledge and foresight of the *entirety* of society, and gain purposeful control at that high level. But this must arise in the context of massive 'genetic' adjustments; the massive creation of certain interdependencies of institutions in 'social systems'; which had already taken shape. Systematic knowledge and intelligent social control would therefore be very difficult to achieve. It would require tremendous efforts of both thought, study, research, and social *reform*. And it was here, of course, that the need for sociology —a systematic science of society—could be clearly seen.

Ward also saw, with great clarity, another major obstacle. Science and its extension into the study of man and society would be a struggle against traditionally founded, and deeply rooted (dogmatic) ideology. Men believed they already *knew* about man and society in terms of their religious beliefs, their political creeds, their metaphysical dogmas. They had for long governed society (or, at least, certain *élites* had) on certain accepted assumptions. To introduce unfamiliar perspectives of science into the knowing and making of society would be to place a cat among pigeons indeed: and the pigeons would flurry and squawk no matter how docile the cat appeared. Of course, Ward was perfectly right—and the birds are squawking still. But Ward had an interesting point of view about this. He was concerned to show that, properly understood, it was the attempt to retain dogmatic ideologies that was likely to be the greater source of social restlessness, discontent and conflict, without in any way constructively resolving social problems, whereas the extension of knowledge to as many people as possible, though it could not automatically dissipate problems, would at least provide the only sound basis for their firm solution. Ward wrote:

'Criticism of received beliefs is always sweet to a considerable number who rejoice at the overthrow of the leaders of opinion or the fall of paragons of morality. And this it is which often renders the peace of society insecure. The established code of morals is dimly felt by the lower classes to be, in some respects, radically unsound. The broad contrast between men's nominal beliefs, as spoken, and their beliefs, as acted, is apparent even to children. The standard of conduct is so much higher than that which the controllers of conduct can themselves live up to, resulting always in the punishment of the weak and the poor for the same transgressions as are daily committed with impunity by the rich and influential, that the lowest miscreant feels that there is some fundamental wrong underlying the entire social fabric, although he cannot tell what it is. All this must be regarded as the legitimate consequence of the undue supremacy of dogmatic ideas in society. So far from favouring morality, they are the direct cause of the most dangerous form of immorality, viz., a mutinous revolt against too severe and unnatural moral restraints. Rules of conduct based on these conceptions are necessarily arbitrary, while the normal intellect naturally asks a reason for its obedience.'*

In this again, Ward had clear similarities with Marx's and Engels' notion that 'ideologies' were in a sense 'false' systems of doctrines, rituals, etc., rooted in social groupings and their interests, which had to be fought and dispelled by scientific knowledge. But Ward had, which Marx and Engels had not, a clear set of criteria in terms of which knowledge could claim to be knowledge as distinct from ideology. His system was not vitiated by an unbounded 'relativism'; nor, as we shall see, were his social proposals themselves (as *was* the case with Marx and Engels) confined by any metaphysical marriage to one socio-economic-political group rather than others. Ward wanted a radical change of industrial society as passionately as anyone: but he did not relish the idea of any 'advance-guard' telling the rest of the citizens of society what their 'real interests' were. Ward was a genuine democrat, not a metaphysically castrated one.

And the final point we might emphasize here, is that—like all the men we have considered earlier—Ward wanted a sociology because he saw clearly, or believed, that the explosive expansion and complexities of modern industrial society were in great danger of outstripping man's knowledge, foresight, and control. Sociology was the science *needed* in the modern world of science, technology, and attendant social transformations. And again, Ward—though

---

* *Dynamic Sociology*, Vol. II, pp. 24–5.

confident in proposing the scientific and reforming effort that was necessary—was by no means untroubled by the difficulties.

'The future of the human race,' he wrote, 'must not be too confidently inferred from the past. The difficulties increase at a much greater rate than the density of population. The complexity of civilization augments at a rate altogether out of proportion to the advance of intelligence. Moreover, in the present state of enlightened societies, the progress being made by the *élite* of the world in scientific discovery and mechanical application is far beyond the possible power of the masses, under existing methods of instruction, to comprehend it. This tends rapidly to increase the disproportion and confusion in society, and threatens to precipitate the grand crisis which wise men cannot but foresee approaching unless a radical change is soon inaugurated in the social constitution of the civilized world. Science must supplant empiricism, and fundamental knowledge be universally diffused.'*

Despite the difficulties and obstacles in the way, however, the making of sociology was a *necessary* task. Ward's faith, if that is the right word to use, was that in sociology, as in the history of other fields of human opinion and knowledge, the most obdurate ideologies would have to yield before the 'march of established facts'.

The Nature and Elements of Sociology

We are now in a position to give a clear outline of the nature of sociology as Ward constructed it—borrowing, as he did, from earlier thinkers and other contemporaries, and couched within the scientific perspective which he had clarified.

(*a*) *Sociology: the Science of Society: the Study of Social Achievement*
In the context of nature and the evolution of mind which he had elaborated, Ward went on to define Sociology as the scientific study of the interdependent functioning, within and among societies, of cumulative human *achievements*. Many social sciences provided knowledge of human achievements in specific fields, but these were all brought together by sociology—which was the study of the *interdependent functioning of institutional achievements in societies as wholes.*

Ward wrote:

'My thesis is that the subject-matter of sociology is human *achievement*. It is not what men are, but what they do. It is not the structure, but the function. Sociologists are nearly all working in the department of social

* *Dynamic Sociology*, Vol. II, pp. 14–15.

anatomy, when they should turn their attention to social physiology. Most of them have imbibed the false notion that physiology is dynamic, and is in some way connected with social progress. They scarcely dare inquire what social physiology is, for fear that it may involve them in questions of social reform. But physiology is merely function. It is what structures and organs do, what they were made to do, the only purpose they have. Structures and organs are only means. Function is the end. It is therefore easy to see how much more important physiology is than anatomy. The latter is, of course, a necessary study, since functions cannot be performed without organs; but it is in the nature of preparation, and can be relegated to one or other of the special social sciences, which, as I have shown, supply the data for the study of sociology. The principal sources of such data are history, demography, anthropology, psychology, biology, civics, and economics; but all the sciences contribute to that highest science, social physiology.'*

And because of this, of course, sociology was essentially a historical and developmental subject because social achievement was an *active* and *changing* process, and social *development* (i.e. *cumulative achievement*) was a demonstrable *fact*.

'Sociology,' Ward stated again, 'is concerned with social *activities*. It is a study of action. It is not a descriptive science that describes objects looked upon as finished products. It is rather a study of how the various social products have been created. These products once formed become permanent. They may be slowly modified and perfected, but they constitute the basis for new products, and so on indefinitely. Viewed from the evolutionary standpoint, the highest types of men stand on an elevated platform which man and nature working together have erected in the long course of ages.'†

The 'human polyp', he wrote, trying to give a colourful illustration:

'. . . is perpetually building a coral reef, on the upper surface of which the last generation lives and builds. The generations live and die, but they leave behind them the result of all that they accomplished when living. This result is a permanent part of the great ocean bed of human achievement. As time goes on these successive additions, superimposed the one upon the other, form the bed-rock of civilization. They become lithified, as it were, and constitute the strata of the psychozoic age of the world, through which the true historian, like the geologist, cuts his sections and lays bare in profile the successive stages of human culture.'‡

And the crucial distinction which differentiated sociology as a science of human *achievements* from other sciences of nature, and especially from the scientific study of other animals was that '*whereas the environment transforms the animal*', in the case of man '*it is man who transforms the environment.*'

* *Pure Sociology*, p. 15.　　　† *Ibid.*, p. 16.　　　‡ *Ibid.*, p. 16.

Sociology, then, analysed the structural organization and inter-dependent functioning of·human achievement in societies as wholes (in relation to their environments), and studied the historical, evolutionary and developmental patterns of change which they had manifested; in all this taking fully into account, as a distinguishing feature of its subject-matter, the transforming power of mind, resting on acquired knowledge and seeking improvements of practical advantage.

It is important again to see how close Ward was to Marx here, but how clearly he was an improvement upon him.

He insisted that men's achievements were cumulative alterations of their *material* civilization; closely attendant upon their practical activities, and their practical advantage, and he also readily and clearly claimed that the cultural and spiritual life of men was so enmeshed with their material civilization as to make it a meaningless and unnecessary abstraction to try to separate the two. The direct-ness of the following passage illustrates this very well.

'*Material civilization consists in the utilization of the materials and forces of nature.* It is, however, becoming more and more apparent that the spiritual part of civilization is at least conditioned upon material civiliza-tion. It does not derogate from its worth to admit that without a material basis it cannot exist. But it is also true that the moment such a basis is supplied, it comes forth in all ages and races of men. It may therefore be regarded as innate in man and potential everywhere, but a flower so delicate that it can only bloom in the rich soil of material prosperity. As such it does not need to be specially fostered. No amount of care devoted to it alone could make it flourish in the absence of suitable conditions, and with such conditions it requires no special attention. It may therefore be dismissed from our considerations, and our interest may be centered in the question of material civilization, and this will be understood without the use of the adjective.'*

But—Ward did *not* make the error of thinking that, given all this, the basic activities and continued achievements of men were *material*. Indeed he was superbly clear that these achievements were the institutionalization of *knowledge* and *ways of doing things*. He wrote:

'Achievement does not consist in wealth. Wealth is fleeting and ephemeral. Achievement is permanent and eternal. And mark the paradox, Wealth, the transient, is material; achievement, the enduring, is immaterial. *The products of achievement are not material things at all.* They are not ends but *means. They are methods, ways, principles, devices, arts, systems, institu-tions.* In a word, they are *inventions*. It is anything and everything that rises above mere imitation or repetition. Every such increment to civilization is

* *Pure Sociology*, p. 18.

a permanent gain, because it is imitated, repeated, perpetuated, and never lost. It is chiefly mental or psychical, but it may be physical in the sense of skill.'*

He also went further, and made it clear that to speak of the most simple, direct, manual labour as being something denuded of mental and moral effort and direction was an error. Quoting Professor John Clark (a contemporary), he wrote:

'In view of the constant presence of these three elements in labour, the physical, the mental, and the moral, any effort, in the supposed interest of the working classes, to depreciate mental labour in comparison with physical is unintelligent. All labour is mental. To a large and controlling extent the mental element is present in the simplest operations. With the labourer who shovels in the gravel pit the directing and controlling influence of the mind predominates, to an indefinite extent, over the simple foot-pounds of mechanical force which he exerts.'†

And it was on exactly this kind of ground, Ward argued, that *human labour* and *animal activity* were *generically distinct* and therefore required different kinds and levels of explanation. *Inventions* with their appropriate and attendant *arts* were the basic elements in the advancement of human control on the basis of knowledge.

'In fact,' he said, 'in most of them there is scarcely any line of demarcation between them. They are pre-eminently "teleological", and it is the *function* that is primarily in the inventor's mind. He knows what he wants done, and merely devises the means of doing it. It is thus that the arts grow up. What the inventor does is to discover the principle by which he can cause the forces of nature, including the properties of the substances that he is acquainted with, to do the work that he wishes to have done and cannot do with his unaided hands. The discovery of this principle and the mode of applying it is what constitutes the achievement. This *discovery*, and not the resulting *material product*, is the lasting element in the operation. It can be used thenceforth for all time.'‡

But then Ward extended his notion of 'inventions' and 'arts' from specific tasks in nature and society to the *achievement* of *forms of social organization*. Men's practical activities and practical advantage involved also the making and improvement of political, judicial, military, industrial *institutions*, and their over-all organization in the entire community. It will be seen again how this conception immediately lifted Ward from the Marxian kind of dilemma of having to '*weight*' one institutional field against others as being more 'objectively real' or more 'basic' than others. For Ward, man's mental capacities for invention and purposive action were applicable

* *Pure Sociology*, p. 25. † *ibid.*, p. 29. ‡ *Ibid.*, p. 29.

to *all* institutions. And it was this which led Ward to a beautifully clear, simple and succinct definition of sociology and its distinctive subject-matter. For *all* cumulative achievements, he argued, could be termed 'institutions'.

'The term *institution*,' he wrote, 'is capable of such expansion as to embrace all human achievement, and in this enlarged sense *institutions become the chief study of the sociologist*. All achievements are institutions, and there is a decided gain to the mind in seeking to determine the true subject-matter of sociology, to regard human institutions and human achievements as synonymous terms, and as constituting, in the broadest sense of both, the field of research of a great science.'*

This, it seems to me, was a marvellously clear statement. Sociology is the attempt to study as scientifically as possible all human social institutions: their nature, functions, interconnections and patterns of change in all societies known to us. There is not much that is wrong, it seems to me, in this definition, and there is certainly no lack of clarity whatever.

Ward elaborated this in much more detail, speaking of the institutions of society, the 'social structure', as the 'social heritage' whereby achievements were transmitted from generation to generation and so 'continued' to form a basis for further cumulative development. But all this, I think, is already clear enough.

(b) Sociology: pure and applied

Consistently with his view that the attitude and perspective of science contained the two elements of *study* and *control*, and consistently too with his view that human *achievement* consisted of the application of knowledge in inventions which furthered human advantage, Ward divided Sociology into the 'Pure' and the 'Applied'. This we can simply note, and it need not detain us because it is so clear. Ward believed that, having established knowledge of society by exact methods of study, it was then a legitimate task of sociology to advise on the practical means, the various kinds of 'attractive legislation', whereby the details of social organization could be improved. As we have seen, this concern for the making of sociology as a basis for guiding the making of society in its modern period of industrial change, has been a perennial preoccupation.

(c) Sociology: Statics and Dynamics

Ward also showed his total agreement with Comte, Mill and Spencer, in dividing Sociology into 'Statics' and 'Dynamics', as two aspects of the study of society meriting methodological distinction. In

* *Pure Sociology*, p. 31.

486

his mind too, this distinction was exactly the same as that proposed by Comte: that is to say, it was *not* a distinction between the '*stationary*' and the '*moving and changing*' as many people now think of it; but a distinction between the *analytical clarification of the nature and components of society as a subject of study*, on the one hand (Statics), and the application of this analysis in *detailed empirical studies of the varieties of actual, changing societies* (*in seeking to establish* '*theories*' *or theoretical* '*laws*' *about them*) on the other (Dynamics).

Ward was not only perfectly clear about this distinction, but he took to task those contemporary scholars who had misunderstood it. And this is worth noting very emphatically, because the error Ward castigated has come to be writ large in twentieth century sociology. And it is here too that we can begin to see the intellectual problems of the educational 'professionalization' of the subject creeping in. The planning of 'courses' in sociology in colleges was already being well established in the last two decades of the nineteenth century in America. And within this context, there was already a tendency for the several *aspects* of the subject to become 'compartmentalized'. One such tendency was to regard 'Statics', quite literally as a '*stationary*' analysis of *structures*, and to think of the '*functioning*' of these stationary structures as the subject-matter of 'Dynamics'. The utter absurdity of this—bearing in mind all we have seen in the making of nineteenth century sociology—makes one gasp; but it is the case, hard though it is to believe, that some people involved in sociology as 'educational professionals' have interpreted the words 'Static' and 'Dynamic' in a completely literal way—with the profundity of discernment to be found in the nursery-cot. Ward hammered at this misconception.

We have already seen how, in his definition of the subject-matter of sociology, Ward made it clear that social institutions were *achievements*, the outcome of vital human energies and *actions*, and an interdependent patterning of these.

'It is not what men are, but what they *do*. It is not the structure, but the function. Sociologists are nearly all working in the department of social anatomy, when they should turn their attention to social physiology. Most of them have imbibed the false notion that physiology is dynamic, and is in some way connected with social progress. They scarcely dare inquire what social physiology is, for fear it may involve them in questions of social reform. But physiology is merely function. It is what structures and organs do, what they were made to do, the only purpose they have . . .'

. . . and so on. But he went on to make this emphasis even more clear.

'Social structures are the products of the interactions of different social forces, all of which, in and of themselves, are destructive, but whose com-

R

bined effect, mutually checking, constraining, and equilibrating one another, is to produce structures . . .

It must not be supposed that social statics deals with *stagnant* societies. A static condition is to be sharply distinguished from a *stationary* condition. Failure to make this distinction is due to what I have called *the fallacy of the stationary*. Social structures are *genetic mechanisms* for the production of *results*, and the results cannot be secured without them. They are reservoirs of *power*.'*

Ward's conception is completely clear in the following passage:

'Social structures are all the result of some form of struggle among the social forces whereby the centrifugal and destructive character of each force acting alone is neutralized and each is made to contribute to the constructive work of society. In forming these structures the various forces are equilibrated, conserved, commuted, and converted into energy and power. The structures once created become reservoirs of power, and it is through them alone that all the work of society is performed. All these structures are interrelated and the performance of their functions brings them into contact or even conflict with one another. This mild struggle among social structures has the same effect as other struggles, and leads to general social organization. The final result is the social order, or society itself as an organized whole—a vast magazine of social energy stored for use by human institutions.'†

(I) SOCIAL STATICS: THE ANALYSIS OF THE NATURE OF SOCIETY

'Social Statics,' wrote Ward, 'is that subdivision of sociology which deals with the social order. The social order is made up of social structures, and is complete in proportion as those structures are integrated, while it is high in proportion as those structures are differentiated and multiplied and still perfectly integrated, or reduced to a completely subordinated and coordinated system. This branch of sociology will therefore deal chiefly with social structures and their functions, with their origin and nature, their relations of subordination and coordination, and with the final product of the entire process which is society itself.'‡

It is obvious, from what we have said, that, for Ward, the 'order' of institutions found in any society at any time was a structuring of vital energies. A *structural-functional* analysis of this network of institutions was therefore clearly necessary, but this by no means implied the existence of something called social or functional 'harmony'. The 'order' which prevailed was an intricate accommodation of conflicting and co-operating forces, actions, achievements, pursuits of specific ends, with each other; and it was an order which canalized and directed the collective energies of men in certain determinate ways. *Change* was therefore of the essence of

---

* *Pure Sociology*, p. 183.   † *ibid.*, p. 193.   ‡ *Ibid.*, p. 184.

WARD'S SYSTEM OF ANALYSIS

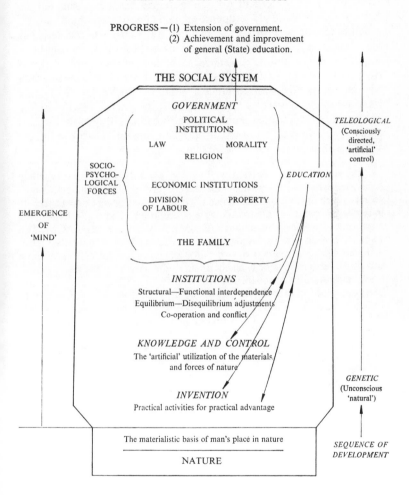

PROGRESS — (1) Extension of government.
(2) Achievement and improvement
of general (State) education.

THE SOCIAL SYSTEM

GOVERNMENT
POLITICAL
INSTITUTIONS

LAW   MORALITY
RELIGION

SOCIO-
PSYCHO-
LOGICAL
FORCES

ECONOMIC INSTITUTIONS

DIVISION   PROPERTY
OF LABOUR

THE FAMILY

INSTITUTIONS
Structural—Functional interdependence
Equilibrium—Disequilibrium adjustments
Co-operation and conflict

KNOWLEDGE AND CONTROL
The 'artificial' utilization of the materials
and forces of nature

INVENTION
Practical activities for practical advantage

The materialistic basis of man's place in nature

NATURE

TELEOLOGICAL
(Consciously
directed,
'artificial'
control)

EDUCATION

EMERGENCE
OF
'MIND'

GENETIC
(Unconscious
'natural')

SEQUENCE OF
DEVELOPMENT

society. *Conflict*, as well as *co-operative accommodation*, was of the essence of society. A vigorous play of energies, knowledge, inventiveness, pursuit of practical advantage in men's *actions* within the context of institutions was of the essence of society. A continuous surge of disequilibrium–equilibrium forces was of the essence of society.

Without elaborating this at all further, it is clear that the analysis

489

of the nature of society involved at least (*a*) a structural-functional analysis of institutions, (*b*) an analysis of the sequences of social action pursued within them, (*c*) a disequilibrium–equilibrium analysis of the forces of conflict, co-operation, and adaptive accommodation, which made for both order and change. But Ward also insisted that the clear analysis of the *regularities* of institutional interrelationships in society required a *historical and comparative* perspective of study. And in emphasizing this he showed his full awareness of all who had declared the importance of it before. Sociology, he claimed was essentially a *generalizing* science; it sought to clarify, refine upon, and extend, those regularities which all knowledgeable scholars perceived among all societies of past and present. The clear understanding of the nature of society *required*, he wrote:

'. . . the *historical perspective*. It is the discovery of law in history, whether it be the history of the past or the present, and including under history, social as well as political phenomena. There is nothing very new in this. It is really the oldest of all sociological conceptions. The earliest gropings after a social science consisted in a recognition of law in human affairs. The so-called precursors of sociology have been those who have perceived more or less distinctly a method or order in human events. All who have done this, however dimly, have been set down as the heralds of the new science. Such adumbrations of the idea of law in society were frequent in antiquity. They are to be found in the sayings of Socrates and the writings of Aristotle. Lucretius sparkles with them. In medieval times they were more rare, but Ibn Khaldun, a Saracen of Tunis, in the fourteenth century gave clear expression to this conception. His work, however, was lost sight of until recently, and Vico, who wrote at the close of the seventeenth and beginning of the eighteenth century, was long regarded as the true forerunner of Montesquieu. Still, there were many others both before and after Vico, and passages have been found reflecting this general truth in the writings of Machiavelli, Bruno, Campanella, Bacon, Hobbes, Locke, Hume, Adam Smith, Ferguson, Fontenelle, Buffon, Turgot, Condorcet, Leibnitz, Kant, Oken, etc.'*

Ward mentioned others too—Saint-Simon and John Stuart Mill for example—who emphasized this about the time when Comte gave 'the name and form' to sociology.

The conception which Ward had of the specific institutions which, in fact, comprised the 'social order' was also the same as that of earlier thinkers. He discussed, for example, marriage and the family, religion, law, morality, the state and political institutions, and—among economic elements of organization—such elements as the division of labour and property. He also agreed with Spencer that,

* *Pure Sociology*, p. 56.

for particular purposes of analysis (in both Statics and Dynamics) these many institutions could be usefully grouped in certain ways. He accepted Spencer's grouping of 'Regulative' and 'Sustaining' institutions, for example, as being 'fundamental'.

There was, however, one quite new dimension in Ward's 'social statics' which came to be specially developed in American sociology, and which had not received any extensive treatment at the hands of Comte, Mill, Spencer, Marx. This was his consideration of the *psychological* aspects of society, and the compounding, the concentrating, the direction, of psychic energies, which went on in the process of institutionalization: what Ward called—'*Synergy*'. These elements require special mention.

(II) THE SOCIAL FORCES AND SYNERGY

It will be remembered that Ward distinguished mind from material processes by its 'teleological' capacities. The conscious operations of mind could issue in *actions* which deliberately employed certain means to attain certain ends and in order to satisfy *desires*. Such purposive actions were to be distinguished from blind genetic processes in that they were *conative*; they were marked by a *striving* for ends and the intellectual capacities of man were able to guide them by knowledge and control. For Ward, then, the basic springs of human action in the life of a community were the many *desires* which motivated men in seeking their 'practical advantage', and this led him to offer a certain systematic way of regarding them and taking them into account in sociological analysis. Comte, of course, had written of 'social psychology' as distinct from the bio-psychological needs with which human nature was endowed; Mill had insisted strongly on the place of psychology and social psychology in a general science of society; Marx had claimed that the material conditions of society determined 'man's consciousness'; but no-one had made any steps at all in the direction of attempting any systematic analysis of what these 'basic' and 'social' psychological elements were.

Ward distinguished between (1) those 'desires' which sprang directly from the physiological needs of the body—hunger, thirst sex, and the like (and, coupled with these, the 'desires' which were 'indirectly' connected with them—such as the preference for pleasure and the avoidance of pain, and, in connection with sex, subsequent consanguineal feelings), and (2) those 'desires' which seemed distinctive of the human psyche ('spiritual desires')—such as moral and intellectual desires. The scheme which he proposed was as follows:*

* *Pure Sociology*, p. 261.

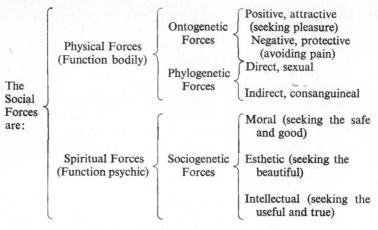

The Social Forces are:

- Physical Forces (Function bodily)
  - Ontogenetic Forces
    - Positive, attractive (seeking pleasure)
    - Negative, protective (avoiding pain)
  - Phylogenetic Forces
    - Direct, sexual
    - Indirect, consanguineal
- Spiritual Forces (Function psychic)
  - Sociogenetic Forces
    - Moral (seeking the safe and good)
    - Esthetic (seeking the beautiful)
    - Intellectual (seeking the useful and true)

But though men, in their actions, sought the satisfaction of specific desires of all these kinds, the satisfaction of *all* of them in some sort of *total* patterning of experience was also an end of human desire.

'. . . psychologically,' Ward wrote, 'all motives whatever are desires, and their satisfaction becomes an end of conation. In man, too, the satisfaction of desire in general, which in each particular case is attended with, or rather consists in, pleasure, acquires, in consequence of the highly derivative and greatly varied character of his desires, a distinctive name, not applicable to animals, and is called *happiness*. So far as the direct purposes of the sociologist are concerned, therefore, the ultimate end of conation is happiness.'*

The driving forces of human actions in society, then, were these 'desires'. But Ward then went on to try to conceptualize the way in which all these many conflicting psychic energies in society came, through their very conflict, to necessitate a 'structuring', a kind of balanced accommodation with each other, which provided a stable context—a complex of reciprocal degrees of latitude and constraint —for their action and satisfaction. Each and any one of these human strivings, pursued with total disregard to others, could lead to disruption, chaos, destruction. Some accommodation of reciprocal adaptation and constraining order there must be.

'We may qualify Darwin's severe formula of the struggle for existence,' Ward wrote, 'and look upon the whole panorama rather as a *struggle for structure.*'

But the further important emphasis of Ward here was that 'institutions' in society are not just administrative frameworks;

* *Dynamic Sociology*, Vol. II, p. 94.

they are, in fact, living modes of the constrained but also creative canalizations of psychic energy. And as such, they are genuinely *social* psychological phenomena. They are *not*, that is to say, just 'raw' impulses or desires or motives as such; neither are they just *additive summations* of these; they are qualitatively new forms and actualities of psychological experience and behaviour which rest upon the necessitous constraining creativity peculiar to *association* and its demands; peculiar, that is, to *society*. Now this idea of the *psychological creativity of social processes* was one which Ward emphasized very plainly, but which was not to receive its fullest and most controversial statement until the work of Emile Durkheim; and there are many who cannot see the nature and importance of this *social* dimension of the creation of the experience and action of individuals to this day.

It is enough for now, however, to see that Ward introduced this important dimension of the psychological aspects of society, and built it into the 'statical' analysis of the nature of society in a very clear way. This was undoubtedly one enrichment of the making of sociology for which Ward was chiefly responsible. It will be readily seen how this analysis of these 'social forces' and the nature of 'synergy' fitted into the other components—structural-functional analysis, the analysis of social action, disequilibrium–equilibrium analysis, etc.—which Ward outlined.

(III) SOCIAL DYNAMICS

Social Dynamics was then, of course, the application of this analysis together with the classification of 'types' of society, to the empirical study of actual societies and the changes which took place within and among them. It is enough to say, on this, that Ward incorporated most of the aspects of change, and factors of change, already used by earlier writers. He discussed social growth, differentiation, and integration; the division of labour, property, and class exploitation; cultural contact and interchange between societies—including conquest and assimilation; invention and innovation; and many other notions which we have already seen in the schemes of other writers. And all this was couched within an overall framework of 'evolutionary' analysis.

Using the analytical methods of 'Statics' and undertaking the empirical studies of 'Dynamics', sociology could therefore deal manageably and systematically with its vast and complex subject-matter, and become an exact science.

'It is the function of methodology in social science,' Ward wrote, 'to classify social phenomena in such a manner that the groups may be brought under uniform laws and treated by exact methods. Sociology then becomes an exact science. In doing this, too, it will be found that we have passed from chaos to cosmos. Human history presents a chaos. The only science that can convert the milky way of history into a definite social universe is sociology, and this can only be done by the use of appropriate methods . . . using the data furnished by all the special social sciences, including the great scientific trunks of psychology, biology, and cosmology, and generalizing and coordinating the facts and groups of facts until unity is attained.'*

(*d*) *Teleology: purposive action: the superiority of the 'artificial', of 'indirect' control.*

It is necessary, briefly, to reiterate some of our earlier points, in order to see how in sociology in particular, Ward came to his final and most central emphasis. Here we may simply remind ourselves that Ward maintained that the actions of men in the institutional fabric of society were teleological, and that, utilizing indirect (artificial) control resting upon systematic knowledge, men could improve their conditions. Perhaps the one thing we might note here is that to think of man in 'teleological' terms did not send shudders of philosophical horror down Ward's spine. He was quite outrightly of the opinion that mind was, at least in large part, purposive. Later, we shall argue that he was completely right.

(*e*) *But Society includes* BOTH *genetic* AND *teleological processes combined. The analysis of intended and unintended consequences.*

We also said earlier, however, that Ward recognized that human nature and society involved *genetic* as well as teleological causes, and that both had to be taken into account. And it is timely now to make this point again, and in such a way as to show that Ward's analysis, again, came close to that of Marx, but without lapsing into any ambiguity whatever.

Ward saw that there was a *genetic* process of adaptation and efficient causation in society as a whole, even though the many particular actions of men, within particular institutions, were purposive. This was a matter of *unforeseen consequences*; or reciprocal adaptation between institutional elements of which men were not conscious. Men acted purposively to achieve practical advantage in particular respects, but that might well be where their interest ceased. But institutional adaptations might take place beyond this. To take technological and economic actions as an example, Ward said:

'In transforming the physical environment the entire social system is profoundly affected and society itself is transformed. Although this is

* *Pure Sociology*, p. 62.

accomplished wholly through teleological activity, still there is a sense in which social evolution thus brought about may be regarded as genetic. What the economists call the law of supply and demand is a natural law ... This sociologic law is not affected by the fact that social demands are in large part supplied through the sagacious foresight of shrewd business men in a manner that is preeminently teleological, although strictly individualistic.

For example, as a modern city grows street railway lines are gradually extended farther and farther out into the suburbs to anticipate the increasing demands, and this will take place although the citizens of those sections make no special demand and take no steps to secure it. The corporations controlling the urban lines are ever on the alert to increase the volume of their business, and by the exercise of a strictly teleological method forestall any such demand on the part of the citizens, who from inherent inertia, natural conservatism, personal indifference, and especially defective organization, would be extremely slow to move in such matters, and could scarcely be brought to the point of raising the funds necessary to construct such lines. Now although every step in social development of this is teleological, still the development itself is genetic, and only goes on as fast as or a trifle faster than is necessary fully to supply the demand ... Thus is social genesis secured through individual telesis.

If we look over the whole field of human achievement and social evolution we shall see that by far the greater part of it belongs to the class just described. The initiative is almost exclusively individual and the ends sought are egocentric in the widest sense, which must include the satisfaction of intellectual, moral, and even transcendental interests as well as those so-called physical wants that have to do with the functions of nutrition and reproduction. The social consequences ... are unintended, and social evolution, however large the teleological factor in it may be, is to all intents and purposes unconscious.' *

In sociological analysis *both* genetic *and* teleological processes had to be taken into account.

(f) Progress: knowledge, control, 'socialization'
Consistently, however, Ward maintained that with the advancement in our knowledge of the processes of society, the unconscious and unforeseen 'genetic' aspects could be brought ever more consciously, clearly, and effectively into control. With knowledge, and the conscious creation of improved institutions, the conditions of men's life could be brought more closely into accord with their practical advantage and happiness. And to provide the way of doing this was the task of applied sociology. The one central point we need to make here is that Ward was quite insistent that this meant an extension of what he called 'socialization', For Ward, however, this word simply meant the extension of the role of the State in purposefully

* *Pure Sociology*, pp. 544–5.

controlling (improving) the institutions of society. Two aspects of this point are important.

The first is that Ward poured scorn upon the idea of 'Laissez-Faire' in government. All the evidence we had, he insisted, of the 'natural' processes of adaptation in nature and society was to the effect that, though arriving at a rough-and-ready equilibrium, these processes were profligate, wasteful, inefficient, and no respecters of persons or of human values. 'Laissez-Faire' notions of government were no less than a misguided leaving of the adaptations of society to processes which were insufficient and which could be improved on in many ways. *Knowledge* made possible *control* and *improvement*, and this could only be accomplished in society by extending the supervisory power of government. Of 'Laissez-Faire' notions, Ward wrote:

'Nothing could be more false or more pernicious. Scientists of this school, from the weight which their opinions must have, are really doing more to counteract the true tendencies of social progress than those who openly oppose them. All social progress is artificial. It is the consequence of teleological foresight, design, and intellectual labour, which are processes diametrically opposed in principle to the processes of nature. If in learning the law of evolution we must apply it to society, it would have been better to have remained ignorant of that law. In passing from the policy of inaction due to the belief that Providence is alone able to act, to the policy of inaction due to the belief that Nature is alone able to act, we have gained nothing. As well worship the old god as the new one. But, rightly interpreted, science teaches no such thing. It teaches the universal dependence of all phenomena upon antecedents, and it is this law that forms the basis of all successful action in transforming rude nature into useful shapes and guiding wild forces into advantageous channels.'*

The second aspect of this point was that Ward's treatment of the nature and development of institutions has led him to a much better, and much less negative, account of the functions of the 'State' in society than that which had been provided by Marx. Reinforcing his own conclusions by reference to the views of Comte, and also of contemporaries such as Simmel, Gumplowicz, and Ratzenhofer, Ward outlined the functions of the State as, amongst other things, those of resolving the conflicting interests of factions in society by accomplishing a 'mutual process of constraint and liberation'.

We see, he said:

'that the state, though genetic in its origin, is teleological in its method; that it has but one purpose, function, or mission, that of securing the welfare of society; that its mode of operation is that of preventing the anti-

* *Dynamic Sociology*, Vol. II, p. 628.

social actions of individuals; that in doing this it increases the freedom of human action so long as it is not anti-social; that the state is therefore essentially moral or ethical; that its own acts must necessarily be ethical; that being a natural product it must in a large sense be representative; that in point of fact it always is as good as society will permit it to be; that while thus far in the history of society the state has rarely performed acts that tend to advance mankind, it has been the condition to all achievement, making possible all the social, industrial, artistic, literary, and scientific activities that go on within the state and under its protection. There is no other human institution with which the state can be compared, and yet, in view of all this, it is the most important of all human institutions.'*

The state itself, then, could be improved as a vehicle for extending knowledge and effective control in society. 'Progress' could become an increasingly conscious and deliberate matter in human society.

(g) The supreme importance of EDUCATION

It was in this way that Ward came to the central upshot of his sociological analysis and his teaching; namely the absolutely central and crucial importance of Education in society for the fullest accomplishment of progress. And this was a persuasion arising from his sociology both 'pure' and 'applied'. In all societies it was the system (institution) of instruction and education which secured the continuity of the 'achievements' of society from one generation to the next, and which thus provided the basis for further cumulative advancements in knowledge and inventions. But also, the fullest progress in the extension of accurate knowledge about nature and society, and its best applications to human advantage, could only be accomplished if education was improved. And Ward argued strongly that education should be compulsory, and provided for all citizens by the State. Ward was so concerned to press home the importance of this, that he set his conclusions out almost in the form of a formula, or, as he put it, as a 'set of theorems'.* First, he gave a clear list of six definitions.

'A. Happiness. Excess of pleasure, or enjoyment, over pain, or discomfort.
B. Progress. Success in harmonizing natural phenomena with human advantage.
C. Dynamic Action. Employment of the intellectual, inventive, or indirect method of conation.
D. Dynamic Opinion. Correct views of the relations of man to the universe.
E. Knowledge. Acquaintance with the environment.
F. Education. Universal distribution of extant knowledge.'

* *Dynamic Sociology*, Vol. II, pp. 108–9.

And then he stated six corresponding 'theorems of dynamic sociology' as follows:

'A. Happiness is the ultimate end of conation.
B. Progress is the direct means to Happiness; it is, therefore, the first proximate end of conation, or primary means to the ultimate end.
C. Dynamic Action is the direct means to Progress; it is, therefore, the second proximate end of conation, or secondary means to the ultimate end.
D. Dynamic Opinion is the direct means to Dynamic Action; it is, therefore, the third proximate end of conation, or tertiary means to the ultimate end.
E. Knowledge is the direct means to Dynamic Opinion; it is, therefore, the fourth proximate end of conation, or fourth means to the ultimate end.
F. Education is the direct means to Knowledge; it is, therefore, the fifth proximate end of conation, and is the fifth and initial means to the ultimate end.'

Using the mathematical sign of equivalence ($\leftrightharpoons$), which, he said, should be read as—'will result in'—his formula was then:

$$F \leftrightharpoons E \leftrightharpoons D \leftrightharpoons C \leftrightharpoons B \leftrightharpoons A$$

And this scheme, Ward argued, simple though it seemed, could be elaborately defended, and was complete. The first term —A— was the *ultimate end* of society, he claimed, and the final term —F— was the *initial means* of moving towards its attainment.

Ward's analysis of education in society, and especially his proposals for the reform of education, were perhaps the most impressive part of his entire system, and it is highly significant that State education—since his time—has, in almost all modern countries, approximated to the characteristics of education which he claimed to be necessary.

Having distinguished between five chief kinds of education: education by experience, discipline, culture, research, and information, it was the last which he supported most strongly. Education should chiefly be, he argued:

'. . . a system for extending to *all* the members of society such of the extant knowledge of the world as may be deemed most important.'

It should devote itself to the *contents* of the mind rather than its *capacity*; it should be provided by the State; it should be compulsory; and it should be universal. Only if *all* the members of a society had the opportunity of acquiring the stock of knowledge available, could there be the best possible basis of the fullest application of knowledge in all activities; the best basis for research and the advancement of knowledge; and the best basis for the formation of opinion, for deliberation and judgment; and, following from this, the best basis for government itself.

'Education,' wrote Ward, 'is not only the science of sciences, but the art of the arts.'

Ward put forward the most detailed and persuasive arguments in support of these ideas, and lest it should be thought that his proposals were 'light-weight' reformist ideas when compared with the 'revolutionary' proposals of a Marx or an Engels, let it be noticed that his insistence throughout was the effective removal of inequalities of opportunity and unwarranted *class* difference.

'The knowledge,' he wrote, 'which enables one class of men to enslave another class brings misery to thousands and enjoyment to but few. The greater part of the evils of society, which are usually and correctly ascribed to ignorance, might with almost equal propriety be ascribed to intelligence. The ignorance which causes them is only *relative* ignorance. The power that enacts them is the power of relatively greater intelligence . . .

Some will wonder why so little is said in this work of the great social economic problems; why the distribution of wealth, rather than of education, is not insisted upon, since happiness depends greatly upon the possession of the objects of desire; why the contrast between civilization and barbarism, intelligence and ignorance, has been so strongly drawn, while that between wealth and indigence, "progress and poverty," has been neglected. The answer must be that the sole object of this treatise is to arrive at the *initial means* . . . And it is high time for socialists to perceive that, as a rule, they are working at the roof instead of at the foundation of the structure which they desire to erect.'*

'The distribution of knowledge,' he went on, 'underlies all social reform. So long as capital and labour are the respective symbols of intelligence and ignorance, the present inequity in the distribution of wealth must continue . . .

The differences in native capacity, though admittedly great, are small compared to the differences of information. The supposed intellectual inequality is greatly exaggerated. The large fund of good sense which is always found among the lower, uneducated classes is an obtrusive fact to every observing mind. The ability with which ignorant people employ their small fund of knowledge has surprised many learned men. While there may doubtless be found all grades of intellect, from the highest philosophic to the lowest idiotic, the number who fall below a certain average standard is insignificant, and so, too, is the number who rise above it. The great bulk of humanity are fully witted, and amply capable of taking care of themselves if afforded an opportunity.'†

Ward's passionate condemnation of the iniquity of the 'unequal

---

* *Dynamic Sociology*, Vol. II, p. 597. † *ibid.*, p. 598.

distribution of knowledge' among classes in society may be seen, finally, in the following passage.

'The present enormous chasm between the ignorant and the intelligent, caused by the unequal distribution of knowledge, is the worst evil under which society labours. This is because it places it in the power of a small number, having no greater natural capacity, and no natural right or title, to seek their happiness at the expense of a large number. The large number, deprived of the *means* of intelligence, though born with the capacity for it, are really compelled by the small number, through the exercise of a superior intelligence, to serve them without compensation. This is the result of the ultimate analysis of the problem of the present unequal distribution of wealth. For it is not the idler, but the toiler, the real producer of wealth, who has none; while the man who has wealth is usually a man of leisure— at least he has rarely or never acquired it through labour in creating it. The former occupies his position solely in consequence of his *relative* ignorance, the latter occupies his solely in consequence of his relative intelligence. Knowledge is power, and power has ever been wielded for self-aggrandizement, and must ever be so wielded. To prevent inequality of advantages there must be equality of power, i.e., equality of knowledge.'*
'A system of education,' he concluded, 'to be worthy the name, must be framed for the great proletariat. Most systems of education seem designed exclusively for the sons of wealthy gentry, who are supposed to have nothing else to do in life but seek the highest culture in the most approved and fashionable ways. But the great mass, too, need educating.'

It can only be emphasized, in leaving this point, that Ward's case for making education the crucial lever for social reform and social progress was far more strongly argued, and in far more detail, than can possibly be stated in an exposition of this kind. To my mind, his arguments are convincing and of the utmost importance for our problems even now, and the last section (Ch. XIV) of his book on *Dynamic Sociology*, in particular, well repays detailed study.

'The problem of education is,' he insisted, 'reduced to this: . . . whether the social system shall always be left to nature, always be genetic and spontaneous, and be allowed to drift listlessly on, intrusted to the by no means always progressive influences which have developed it and brought it to its present condition, or whether it shall be regarded as a proper subject of art, treated as other natural products have been treated by human intelligence, and made as much superior to nature, in this only proper sense of the word, as other artificial productions are superior to natural ones.'†

This, then, in outline, was Lester Ward's contribution to the making of sociology. Many other elements of his system have not

* *Dynamic Sociology*, p. 602.　　　　　† *Ibid.*, p. 632.

been mentioned:—the important place he attributed to the creation of moral and social 'ideals' in the pursuit of social purpose; the distinction he drew between anthropology and sociology; his rejection of many aspects of social administration and social work as spurious pretenders to sociology; his rejection of 'mathematical' sociology; and others of considerable interest. But the main components of the nature of sociology as the new and necessary science of society as he conceived it have been touched upon, and we have seen with sufficient clarity for our purposes, the important similarities and the interesting and worthwhile differences between his work and the work of Comte, Mill, Spencer and Marx.

B *WILLIAM GRAHAM SUMNER*

Somewhere, I remember reading that G. K. Chesterton, exasperated at being unable to find a fitting description, referred to Walt Whitman as a 'great big something or other'. This seems a peculiarly apt description of William Graham Sumner. He seems to have been a large, dogmatic, challenging, many-sided man. He was once a clergyman: a fiery, militant preacher by all accounts. His wide studies (some of them undertaken in Europe) covered theology and philosophy as well as anthropology and economics (which he taught). He came to despise theology and philosophy especially. 'Philosophy,' he is reported to have said at a college meeting, 'is in every way as bad as astrology. It is a complete fake!' It is obvious at once, then, that he was fully agreed with all the men we have studied, that science should replace these more speculative subjects in any attempt to establish a *knowledge* of man and society. On the strength of this persuasion, he moved quite boldly into the making of sociology; he saw the need for a science of society; but—even here (bearing in mind what we have already said about the tendencies towards the rapid, the superficial, and the contrived, in the academic 'professionalization' of the subject)—it is said that he 'detested with fury most of the work done under the name of Sociology, most of its tendencies, and nearly all those who taught it'. He must have been a forceful and impressive teacher, and was undoubtedly one of the most important American scholars contributing to the making of sociology towards the end of the nineteenth century.

His most influential book—*Folkways*—was, in fact, published in 1906, but it is correct to include him as a late nineteenth century figure since he was formulating his conceptions of society and the scientific study of it at the same time as Lester Ward. And, indeed, it is fitting that we should consider him now because he has come to be placed, in much current judgment, at the opposite end of the spectrum from Ward. Greatly influenced by Spencer's analysis of social systems and the part played by 'custom' in the 'simple societies', Sumner was also close to Spencer's 'laissez-faire' convictions concerning the role of government and legislation in society. So that whereas Ward advocated the extension of 'collectivism' and the supervision by the State of the acquisition, transmission, and application of knowledge, Sumner was much more chary of rationally based 'enactments'. Also, whereas Ward believed in the reality of 'progress', Sumner has been judged a 'relativist'. He has therefore seemed to stand in complete opposition to Ward. In what follows, however, we shall see that this is too strong, too sharp, a distinction. Sumner was, in fact, not sufficiently exacting in the philosophical clarification of his points and his distinctions, and the ambiguities which result tend to cloud his position. When these are removed, it can be seen that his differences with the 'progressive' position put forward by Ward were really differences of degree and emphasis, not at all basic differences of kind.

In general, Sumner was never specific, clear, and detailed about methodological matters, and there is not a lot to be gained from him in this direction. However, in his study of *Folkways* he offered a very clear analysis of the nature, processes and components of society, and of certain tendencies of social change. To use our earlier terms: he put forward a very clear 'social statics' and 'social dynamics', and brought together an enormous range of comparative and historical data to substantiate the analysis he proposed. *Folkways* is in fact, a work of massive scholarship, and has been, and is, one of the most 'seminal' books in sociology.

In this account of his 'system', I want, above all, to show clearly his agreement with the thinkers we have considered so far as to the nature and elements of a science of society. This is our major concern. But there were distinctive elements in Sumner's work, which were both developments of dimensions stressed by earlier thinkers and introductions of new components of analysis and theory which were going to receive considerable emphasis and development at the hands of others. Sumner is a kind of 'bridge' figure in certain ways, between the conspectus of the science as it was established by the end of the nineteenth century, and the development of specific elements of analysis *within* this conspectus which has taken place during the twentieth. It is worthwhile to indicate some of these points at the outset.

One central emphasis in Sumner's study was upon the *psychological* aspects of *society*; upon the ways in which the experience and actions of men come to give rise to a 'societal' network of usages, rituals, values, beliefs, regulations which go beyond individuals but are, at the same time, creative of individual qualities; a network which is distinctively a societal process and which is, at one and the same time, both constraining and creative. In this, he developed very considerably that element of sociological analysis which Mill called 'Ethology'. But this was also the special emphasis of the work of Durkheim, which we shall consider later, and certain American scholars too, especially Mead and Cooley, were to develop the study of this 'middle-range' element of sociological analysis—the psychological aspects of social processes—particularly. As a part of this emphasis, Sumner also introduced the distinction between

'In-Groups' and 'Out-Groups', and this, too, has led to the whole development of group analysis for the understanding of attitude and sentiment formation. Similarly, in his analysis of the way in which the 'folkways and mores' in simpler societies give way to the more rationally based 'institutions and laws' of more complex societies, Sumner provided one of the earliest formulations of what has become perhaps the most central theory of social change in the whole of sociology—one which, as we shall see, has come to be attributed particularly to Ferdinand Tönnies. In the work of Sumner, then, we are coming not only to the point of seeing the agreed formulation of the subject at the end of the nineteenth century, but also the strong germinal force of new ideas which were like seeds planted implicitly within it. But we must restrain ourselves, and deal here, still, with a clear outline of the *foundations* themselves.

Society

Sumner put forward a very clear 'model' of society: of its chief components and processes; and here we will outline each element systematically in order to bring out the similarities between these and the ideas of Comte, Mill, Spencer, Marx and Ward.

(a) Necessity, action, and the struggle for existence

As the basis of his conception of society, Sumner adopted a materialist standpoint just as emphatically as did Spencer or Marx.

'The first task of life,' he wrote, 'is to live. Men begin with acts, not with thoughts. Every moment brings necessities which must be satisfied at once.'

Men have basic needs which must, of necessity, be satisfied if they are to survive, and in this, action, not contemplation, is of primary urgency. This, inescapably, gives rise to a struggle for sheer existence, and this is intensified by the fact that, in large part, it must be competitive, and must take place in relation to the available conditions and resources of the environment: what Sumner called the 'life conditions'.

'The struggle for existence must be carried on under life conditions and in connection with the competition of life. The life conditions consist in variable elements of the environment, the supply of materials necessary to support life, the difficulty of exploiting them, the state of the arts, and the circumstances of physiography, climate, meteorology, etc., which favour life or the contrary. The struggle for existence is a process in which an individual and nature are the parties. The individual is engaged in a process by which he wins from his environment what he needs to support his existence. In the competition of life the parties are men and other organisms. The men strive with each other, or with the flora and fauna with which they are associated. The competition of life is the rivalry, antagonism, and mutual displacement in which the individual is involved with other organisms by his efforts to carry on the struggle for existence for himself. It is, therefore, the competition of life which is the societal element, and which produces societal organization.'*

Society is grounded in this basic material and human struggle.†

(i) SIZE OF POPULATION: AN IMPORTANT FACTOR

One factor of central importance in the struggle for existence and for the determination of the kind of social life which springs from it, is, claimed Sumner, the *size* of the population who share the struggle.

'The number present and in competition is another of the life conditions. At a time and place the life conditions are the same for a number of human beings who are present, and the problems of life policy are the same. This is another reason why the attempts to satisfy interest become mass pheno-

---

* *Folkways*, Mentor Paperback Edition, p. 30. (All my references are to this edition since it is the cheapest now available to students; but another paperback edition is that by 'Dover Publications' and Constable & Co.)

† It is interesting to notice that Sumner expressed his opposition to an 'Idealist' interpretation of society and history in almost exactly the same way as Marx. One can almost see him 'turning Hegel on his feet again'. Note the following passage:

'The view which has been stated is antagonistic to the view that philosophy and ethics furnish creative and determining forces in society and history. That view comes down to us from the Greek philosophy and it has now prevailed so long that all current discussion conforms to it. Philosophy and ethics are pursued as independent disciplines, and the results are brought to the science of society and to statesmanship and legislation as authoritative dicta. We also have *Volkerpsychologie*, *Sozialpolitik*, and other intermediate forms which show the struggle of metaphysics to retain control of the science of society. The "historic sense", the *Zeitgeist*, and other terms of similar import are partial recognitions of the mores and their importance in the science of society. It can be seen also that philosophy and ethics are products of the folkways. They are taken out of the mores, but are never original and creative; they are secondary and derived. They often interfere in the second stage of the sequence,—act, thought, act. . . .

'The real process in great bodies of men is not one of deduction from any great principle of philosophy or ethics. It is one of minute efforts to live well under existing conditions, which efforts are repeated indefinitely by great numbers, getting strength from habit and from the fellowship of united action. The resultant folkways become coercive. All are forced to conform, and the folkways dominate the societal life. Then they seem true and right, and arise into mores as the norm of welfare. Thence are produced faiths, ideas, doctrines, religions, and philosophies, according to the stage of civilization and the fashions of reflection and generalization.'‡

‡ *Folkways*, p. 49.

mena and result in folkways. The individual and social elements are always in interplay with each other if there are a number present. If one is trying to carry on the struggle for existence with nature, the fact that others are doing the same in the same environment is an essential condition for him.'*

This point is worth noting separately as it was also made by Spencer, and came to be emphasized by Durkheim as one of the most important factors underlying the division of labour in society.

(II) CONFLICT AND CO-OPERATION

In this struggle for existence, men are confronted with two alternatives. They can compete individually, and risk failure, or:

'. . . they may combine, and by co-operation raise their efforts against nature to a higher power. This latter method is industrial organization. The crisis which produces it is constantly renewed, and men are forced to raise the organization to greater complexity and more comprehensive power, without limit. Interests are the relations of action and reaction between the individual and the life conditions, through which relations the evolution of the individual is produced. That evolution, so long as it goes on prosperously, is well living, and it results in the self-realization of the individual, for we may think of each one as capable of fulfilling some career and attaining to some character and state of power by the developing of predispositions which he possesses. It would be an error, however, to suppose that all nature is a chaos of warfare and competition. Combination and co-operation are fundamentally necessary.'†

As a matter of fact, Sumner argued, there is always a tension of competition *and* co-operation between the members of a society; a condition of what he called '*antagonistic co-operation*'. A society is always a kind of tensile order, binding together both similar and divergent, both harmonious and conflicting, interests.

It will be seen, in this basic materialist position, how close Sumner was to Marx; and it is also worthwhile to notice that—as with Marx and others—Sumner held that though this was a competitive-co-operative struggle among men; a matter of necessity and constraint; it was also *creative* of the conditions for the *self-realization of the individual*.

(b) *Basic motives, instincts, and interests*
The struggle for existence is not, however, without shape or direction: or, indeed (among human groups) without uniformity. Though the desires of men may become very complex, there are, Sumner maintained '*four great motives of human action*' which are universal in human nature and human society. These are hunger, sexual

* *Folkways*, p. 31.   † *Ibid.*, p. 31.

passion, vanity, and fear. And under the heading of 'fear' Sumner included the fear of ghosts, spirits, and the dead, as well as of more ordinary dangers. These four basic *motives* gave rise to powerful *interests* which always drove men to action. But, though he did not wish to be precise about this, Sumner also thought it probable that man possessed a certain set of '*instinctual*' responses connected with these four basic motives. He wrote, for example:

'It is generally taken for granted that men inherited some guiding instincts from their beast ancestry, and it may be true, although it has never been proved. If there were such inheritances, they controlled and aided the first efforts to satisfy needs.'*

And also:

'It is now the accepted opinion, and it may be correct, that men inherited from their beast ancestors psychophysical traits, instincts, and dexterities, or at least predispositions, which give them aid in solving the problems of food supply, sex commerce, and vanity. The result is mass phenomena; currents of similarity, concurrence, and mutual contribution; and these produce folkways. The folkways are unconscious, spontaneous, unco-ordinated. It is never known who led in devising them . . .'†

Sumner never explored this 'instinctual' element, and did not make it an essential part of his system, but it is important to see that he did think that any such pattern of experience and behaviour that might have a hereditary basis in man could provide an element in explaining the *universality* of the folkways in human societies; the basic pattern of motives which lay at the roots of them in all communities.

At any rate, we can see that Sumner's initial steps of analysis rested upon the systematically related conception of four basic *needs* and *motives*, with a possible basis of *instinct*, which give rise to specific *interests*, which underlie men's *competitive* and *co-operative action* in the *struggle for existence*.

Bearing in mind Ward, Marx, and others, we can also see here the element of *purpose* in men's material and social activities; and, indeed, Sumner held that, in all such activity:

'However great the errors and misconceptions may be which are included in the *efforts*, the *purpose* always is *advantage* and *expediency*.'

We shall see later that Sumner tempered the word 'expediency' in certain ways.

This collective, competitive and co-operative activity of the members of a population who share the struggle for existence in

---

* *Folkways*, p. 18.   † *ibid.*, p. 33.

certain life conditions, gives rise to the 'folkways'. And first of all we must concern ourselves with definitions.

(c) *The Folkways: a socio-psychological process of creativity: a societal environment*

As primitive groups of men first came to grips with their many-sided struggle for survival, they were in a condition of ignorance; or, as Sumner put it, of 'primeval stupidity'. He put the matter as strongly as this in order to stress that men were not only *without knowledge*, but also that they made great *errors* in the formulation of their folkways owing to irrational fears and superstitions. Men's early efforts in material and social activities must have been of a 'trial-and-error' nature; they must have been attended by error, accident, and luck. There was nothing necessarily well guided about them. However, in terms of seen advantage, and balance of pleasure over pain with regard to individual and group welfare, some *ways of doing things* were preferred to others, and came to be adopted and established.

'. . . ways of doing things were selected which were expedient. They answered the purpose better than other ways, or with less toil and pain. Along the course on which efforts were compelled to go, *habit*, *routine*, and *skill* were developed . . .

Each profited by the other's experience; hence there was concurrence towards that which proved to be most expedient. All at last adopted the same way for the same purpose; hence the *ways* turned into *customs* and became *mass phenomena*.

In this way folkways arise.'

Those activities which most satisfactorily fulfilled interests became *habitual* among individuals and customs throughout the group. And Sumner conceived of the folkways as the very gradual creation of an entire network of customary practices which regulated every important activity in the community. At any given time, in a community, the folkways: 'provide for all the needs of life then and there.' But let us look more closely at the attributes which, according to Sumner, they possess.

Though, in their emergence they are '*unconscious, spontaneous, unco-ordinated*,' they come to be, he argued, '*uniform, universal* in the group, *imperative*, and *invariable*.'

All these qualities are important, but perhaps the chief one to emphasize here is that the folkways are not only usages, but *sanctioned* and *obligatory* usages throughout the community, *binding* upon its members. In this sense, the folkways, when they have assumed this force of custom, have become a *societal* force, going beyond individuals, and imposing upon individuals the regulatory framework within which all their energies and experience can be expressed.

'The body of the folkways,' Sumner wrote, '*constitutes a societal environment*. Every one born into it must enter into relations of give and take with it. He is subjected to influences from it, and it is one of the life conditions under which he must work out his career of self-realization.'*

'By habit and custom it exerts a strain on every individual within its range; therefore it rises to a *societal force* to which *great classes of societal phenomena* are due . . . We have to recognize it as one of the chief forces by which a society is made to be what it is.'

What Sumner claimed, then, was not simply that a network of folkways emerged and took definite shape out of the shared communal activities of a people, but that this close mesh of constraining and authoritative tradition was creative of the later formal structures of society as, or if, it developed. Custom was a creative social-psychological force of the most fundamental importance in the making of societies.

Before we see the process of social development which Sumner traced, however, certain other points need separate statement and emphasis.

(I) THE AUTHORITY OF THE FOLKWAYS

Sumner stressed very powerfully the strength and peculiarity of the *authority* possessed by the folkways, and his position on this point must be noticed very carefully, because it is an insight which, later on, I wish to consider as one possessing the most central importance for sociological analysis; one at the very root of all the major statements of sociological theory.

The folkways are both 'true' and 'right' within the community, Sumner showed, and yet the authority which they possess is of a very specific kind. They tend to be 'true', by and large, in that they accord with common-sense experience, expediency, and common advantage—so that, in a sense, they may be said to be borne out by experience. But firstly—this is not always so. Sometimes the folkways have been founded upon erroneous superstition, or accidental coincidence, and can be positively disadvantageous to the community—at least in some respects. So that they are not always 'true' in this sense. And secondly—even when they *are* 'true', it is not their truth which vests them with authority. Their authority resides in their 'rightness', and they are 'right' by the simple fact of

* *Folkways*, p. 73.

their existence as *sanctified immemorial usage*. Custom carries a basic authority in its own irreducible right.

'The folkways are the "right" ways to satisfy all interests, because they are traditional, and exist in fact. They extend over the whole of life. There is a right way to catch game, to win a wife, to make one's self appear, to cure disease, to honour ghosts, to treat comrades or strangers, to behave when a child is born, on the warpath, in council, and so on in all cases which can arise. The ways are defined on the negative side, that is, by taboos. The "right" way is the way which the ancestors used and which has been handed down. The tradition is its own warrant. It is not held subject to verification by experience. The notion of right is in the folkways. It is not outside of them, of independent origin, and brought to them to test them. In the folkways, whatever is, is right. This is because they are traditional, and therefore contain in themselves the authority of the ancestral ghosts. When we come to the folkways we are at the end of our analysis.'*

It will be seen in this passage that the sanctity of the folkways is supported by the feeling that they have been the ways of the ancestors; they are the ancestral traditions of the community; and it is in this sense that Sumner argued that they tended, universally in human societies, to be supported by 'ghost fear'; by the sense of awe surrounding the dead; by religion.

The further point here is that the authority does not reside in the *known origins* of the folkways, because no-one knows what these origins were. 'They arise no-one knows whence or how.' Indeed, said Sumner: 'It is only by analysis and inference that we can form any conception of the "beginning" which we are always so eager to find.'

The point which is of the greatest importance here, however, is this. The basic regulatory order of a society, beyond which *societal* analysis can scarcely probe (indeed, beyond which it can only probe by conjecture); which embraces the material, technical, organizational structuring of men's relationships; is *essentially* a *moral order*. There is *no* societal fabric of technical and social procedures and relationships which is not at once an order interpenetrated by *morality*. The importance of this point cannot here be sufficiently brought out, but it is enough just to note and to insist upon Sumner's teaching—that morality is not, and is never, an abstract, intuitive thing of philosophical ethics *alone*, but is a part and parcel of men's *practical efforts to live well*, to accomplish *welfare in society*, and—what is crucial—is not *one aspect of society*, but an all-pervading, interpenetrating core of *all* social relationships.

'The morality of a group at a time', wrote Sumner, 'is the sum of the taboos

* *Folkways*, p. 41.

and prescriptions in the folkways by which right conduct is defined. There-fore morals can never be intuitive. They are historical, institutional, and empirical.

World philosophy, life policy, right, rights, and morality are all products of the folkways. They are reflections on, and generalizations from, the experience of pleasure and pain which is won in efforts to carry on the struggle for existence under actual life conditions. The generalizations are very crude and vague in their germinal forms. They are all embodied in folklore, and all our philosophy and science have been developed out of them.'*

This point must be left now, for the moment (reluctantly!), but its importance cannot be over-emphasized.

(II) THE FOLKWAYS: A LONG HISTORICAL TRADITION

It follows, of course, that the established folkways of a community, in Sumner's view, were always the outcome of an extremely long historical past, and embodied the cumulative experience of count-less generations of men, and countless accommodations to par-ticular, and perhaps changing, life conditions. It was in this sense—almost in the sense of an Edmund Burke—that Sumner could be said to be 'relativist.' His point was only that the system of folkways in any community was valid for the life conditions of that com-munity—no matter how strange they might appear to others. But we have already seen that because of the basic motives, needs, and interests in all societies, Sumner's position was not entirely 'rela-tivist', in the sense that there was, for him, a core of uniformity, of similarity, of universality, at the roots of the folkways of all societies no matter how widely their specific forms varied. And we shall come to other elements of Sumner's analysis, too, which will demonstrate the error of regarding him as being committed to an extreme 'rela-tivity' of values.

(III) THE FOLKWAYS: A CONTINUOUS CREATION

It is also important to note, however, that—though they stemmed from a long ancestral past—the folkways were never *final* in Sumner's conception. They possessed flexibility and could be changed as 'life-conditions' changed. Their essence was that they were a con-tinuous process of *creative accommodation to conditions*. In this sense, Sumner gave illustrations of contemporary folkways that were taking shape in relation to new techniques and instruments—such as the telephone, and mass-communications, for example.

* *Folkways*, p. 41.

(IV) THE FOLKWAYS: THE OUTCOME OF UNINTENDED CONSEQUENCES: THE UNCONSCIOUS, CUMULATIVE LAYING DOWN OF A SOCIAL ORDER

One other essential aspect of Sumner's conception was that although he believed that men acted purposely—as individuals—with motives pressing them, with interests in mind, seeking their own advantage, he did *not* believe that the creation of the folkways was a conscious purposeful process. We have already seen that he thought of the emergence of the folkways as being 'unconscious, spontaneous, unco-ordinated'. He wrote very clearly and definitely in this way:

'It is of the first importance to notice that, from the first acts by which men try to satisfy needs, each act stands by itself, and looks no further than the immediate satisfaction. From recurrent needs arise habits for the individual and customs for the group, but these results are consequences which were never conscious, and never foreseen or intended. They are not noticed until they have long existed, and it is still longer before they are appreciated. Another long time must pass, and a higher stage of mental development must be reached, before they can be used as a basis from which to deduce rules for meeting, in the future, problems whose pressure can be foreseen. The folkways, therefore, are not creations of human purpose and wit. They are like products of natural forces which men unconsciously set in operation, which are developed out of experience, which reach a final form of maximum adaptation to an interest, which are handed down by tradition and admit of no exception or variation, yet change to meet new conditions, still within the same limited methods, and without rational reflection or purpose. From this it results that all the life of human beings, in all ages and stages of culture, is primarily controlled by a vast mass of folkways handed down from the earliest existence of the race, only the topmost layers of which are subject to change and control, and have been somewhat modified by human philosophy, ethics, and religion, or by other acts of intelligent reflection.'*

Here, yet again, we have the emphasis upon the importance of 'unintended consequences' in the creation of societies; but perhaps the chief point to isolate for clarity here is that, in this way, *an interconnected social order, integrated to some degree, fitted to the environmental and social conditions of the community, is laid down without over-all conscious and rational planning, and before men become aware of it, let alone desirous of reforming it.* And it is *out* of this order, that later and more formal differentiations of structure may arise, and that conscious control (to some extent) may take place. But the order is laid down before this, and, indeed, it is always the case that no man can ever possibly see, grasp, or understand the entirety of it. This, again, is a point of the most basic importance.

* *Folkways*, p. 19.

Before leaving this, we might pause to note that, on the face of his treatment, Sumner seemed to lay much greater weight than did Ward upon what Ward called the *genetic* rather than the *teleological* aspects of the making of society; and we shall see later that this impression seems to be reinforced by Sumner's apparently greater reluctance to concede a role of any great extent to social legislation and reform. It might be said that Sumner placed more emphasis upon the worth and wisdom of the *genetic* processes of society than did Ward. But such a judgment would be, it seems to me, a mistake. We have already seen that Sumner thought the folkways could rest upon error, accident, and superstition, and we shall see, increasingly, that, in fact, he was quite as definite and committed as Ward on the matter of reform and progress—it is only that he was clouded by ambiguities, or perhaps one should say an insufficiency of care in making himself clear. We can see some of the evidence for this point of view in the next point.

(v) THE FOLKWAYS: THE STRAIN TOWARDS IMPROVEMENT AND CONSISTENCY

The picture given by the emphasis upon the 'unconscious' and 'unintended' growth of the folkways was qualified by Sumner's insistence that there was a strain towards *improvement*, and a strain towards *consistency* among them. Sumner made these points as an outcome of the fact that the folkways came into being to satisfy needs, to serve powerful motives, and were adopted because of a balance of pleasure over pain, and of practical advantage. If this was so, then if they were only imperfectly adapted to the 'life conditions' of the community, there must always be a strain towards the *improvement* of them; and, since they would be more efficient if well articulated with each other, there must always also be a strain towards *consistency* among all of them. In short, there was a tendency towards *progress* in the light of extended knowledge and experience, and a tendency towards the making of a *coherent system* of all the elements of custom.

'The folkways', Sumner wrote, 'are, therefore, (1) subject to a strain of improvement towards better adaptation of means to ends, as long as the adaptation is so imperfect that pain is produced. They are also (2) subject to a strain of consistency with each other, because they all answer their several purposes with less friction and antagonism when they co-operate and support each other. The forms of industry, the forms of the family, the notions of property, the constructions of rights, and the types of religion show the strain of consistency with each other through the whole history of civilization.'*

* *Folkways*, p. 21.

513

Furthermore, the extent to which conscious reason and reflection could, and should, enter into men's judgments about the nature and quality of the folkways can be seen in what Sumner had to say about 'suggestion' and 'suggestibility' which, together with constraining pressures and imitation, he thought were the psychological processes whereby the folkways were communally established. *Criticism*, he maintained, was the only way in which individuals could protect themselves against credulity, emotional bias, and fallacy.

'The power of criticism', he wrote, 'is the one which education should chiefly train . . . Our judicial institutions are devised to hold suggestion aloof until the evidence is examined. An educated man ought to be beyond the reach of suggestions from advertisements, newspapers, speeches, and stories. If he is wise, just when a crowd is filled with enthusiasm and emotion, he will leave it and will go off by himself to form his judgment. In short, individuality and personality of character are the opposites of suggestibility . . . A highly trained judgment is required to correct or select one's own ideas and to resist fixed ideas. The supreme criticism is criticism of one's self.'*

It is quite clear that, if this argument was to be followed, critical reason could enter into the reform of the folkways in good measure; and we shall see later that Sumner really did advocate this. It was only—again like Burke—that he threw all his weight in the scales against *brash, careless, uninformed, and irresponsible* efforts of reform, of which, of course, there are plenty in this world.

So much, however, for the nature of the primary folkways in Sumner's system: the first, basic societal order.

(d) Mystical Regulatory Doctrines

The next major element in Sumner's 'model' of society was the 'Mores' which grew distinctively out of the primary stuff of the 'Folkways', but this growth was mediated, he claimed, by the development of 'mystical doctrines'—myths—which provided a kind of over-all 'rationale' for the folkways. It was here that Sumner stressed the element of 'ghost fear' and religion as an important support of the folkways. There was a kind of blending of the fear of the dead ancestors and the awe in which they were held, and the practical provisions both for them and the needs of the living.

'With great unanimity', Sumner wrote, 'all over the globe primitive men followed the same line of thought. The dead were believed to live on as ghosts in another world just like this one. The ghosts had just the same needs, tastes, passions, etc., as the living men had had. These transcendental

* *Folkways*, pp. 37–8.

notions were the beginning of the mental outfit of mankind. They are articles of faith, not rational convictions. The living had duties to the ghosts, and the ghosts had rights; they also had power to enforce their rights. It behoved the living therefore to learn how to deal with ghosts. Here we have a complete world philosophy and a life policy deduced from it. When pain, loss, and ill were experienced, and the question was provoked, Who did this to us? the world philosophy furnished the answer. When the painful experience forced the question, Why are the ghosts angry and what must we do to appease them? the "right" answer was the one which fitted into the philosophy of ghost fear. All acts were therefore constrained and trained into the forms of the world philosophy by ghost fear, ancestral authority, taboos, and habit. The habits and customs created a practical philosophy of welfare, and they confirmed and developed the religious theories . . .'*

These 'myths' were therefore theoretical and regulatory justifications of the folkways, but their important characteristic was that they introduced new, and general, ideas and concerns for *welfare*. They included judgments about welfare, and this, Sumner held, lifted some of the folkways to a new and qualitatively distinct level: it gave rise to the 'Mores'. Here again, we must be very careful about definitions.

(e) The Mores
Sumner defined the 'mores' in this way:

'When the elements of truth and right are developed into doctrines of welfare, the folkways are raised to another plane. They then become capable of producing inferences, developing into new forms, and extending their constructive influence over men and society. Then we call them the mores. The mores are the folkways, *including the philosophical and ethical generalizations* as to societal *welfare* which are suggested by them, and inherent in them, as they grow.'†

Now it is very clear from this that the folkways and the mores, in Sumner's analysis, are not different *entities;* they are qualitatively different *levels* of *development* of the same social-psychological processes. The mores *are* the folkways—but *now* with the additionally developed qualities of more *explicit, general, ethical* conceptions and *judgments* of *welfare*. It is most important to see that this very conception is a *theory of social development*; and it *cannot be understood otherwise*. Sumner's model of society was therefore, clearly, a *developmental* model. Let us look again at a very careful definition of the 'mores' which Sumner gave:

'They are the ways of doing things which are current in a society to satisfy human needs and desires, together with the faiths, notions, codes, and

* *Folkways*, p. 42.   † *ibid.*, pp. 42–3.

standards of well living which inhere in those ways, having a genetic connection with them. By virtue of the latter element the mores are traits in the specific character (ethos) of a society or a period. They pervade and control the ways of thinking in all the exigencies of life, returning from the world of abstractions to the world of action, to give guidance and to win revivification.'*

(I) TABOOS AND MYTHS

The mores consisted in large part, Sumner held, of behavioural 'taboos' which directly regulated conduct, and the 'myths' which provided colourful, dramatic and symbolic notions of destiny and welfare. They were not 'rational philosophies', but they encapsulated ideas and judgments in their imagery.

'The myths, fables, proverbs and maxims of primitive men,' Sumner wrote, 'show that the subtler relations of things did not escape them, and that reflection was not wanting, but the method of it was very different from ours. The notion of societal welfare was not wanting, although it was never consciously put before themselves as their purpose . . .'

(II) RITUAL

One other vital process in the development, establishment and continuity of the 'mores' which Sumner emphasized was that of *ritual*. Ritual is a repetitive regularity of observance consisting of elements, such as words, gestures, symbols, signs, and is very much more powerful in the sustaining and transmission of values and ideas than the apprehension of the ideas themselves.

'In primitive society', wrote Sumner, 'it is the prevailing method of activity and primitive religion is entirely a matter of ritual . . . Primitive religion is ritualistic not because religion makes ritual, but because ritual makes religion . . .

Ritual is not easy compliance with usage; it is strict compliance with detailed and punctilious rule. It admits of no exception or deviation.

Ritual may *embody* an idea . . . but it always tends to become perfunctory, and the idea is only subconscious . . .

Ritual operates a constant suggestion, and the suggestion is at once put in operation in *acts*. Ritual therefore suggests *sentiments*, but it never inculcates *doctrines*.'

The power of ritual in impressing and upholding the continuous 'suggestion' which perpetuates the 'mores' in society was made a matter of the utmost emphasis by Sumner, and it must be understood that he was not *only* referring to the markedly conspicuous ritual attending religious ceremonial and the like, but also to every element and facet of established regularity of practice in *all* the ways of

* *Folkways*, p. 66.

behaviour of a people—in their eating, drinking, family life, recreation, work, and in the entire fabric of their conduct. Sumner wrote, for example:

'The mores are social ritual in which we all participate unconsciously. The current habits as to hours of labour, meal hours, family life, the social intercourse of the sexes, propriety, amusements, travel, holidays, education, the use of periodicals and libraries, and innumerable other details of life fall under this ritual. Each does as everybody does. For the great mass of mankind as to all things, and for all of us for a great many things, the rule to do as all do suffices. We are led by suggestion and association to believe that there must be wisdom and utility in what all do. The great mass of the folkways give us discipline and the support of routine and habit.'*

In this sense, the entire patterning of life in a community is sustained and transmitted by a vast and intricate play of ritual of which the members of the community may be scarcely aware.

(III) STATUS

One other important aspect of the entire network of the mores in a society upon which Sumner placed great emphasis, was that this, in fact, was a vast system of conferring *statuses* upon all the members of society in relation to their membership of groups, their tasks, their relationships with each other. And this vast network of statuses held and 'grasped' people; was a determinate patterning influence upon their nature and conduct; and could not easily be altered. From the apparently inter-personal relationships of marriage and the membership of the family, through the whole gamut of ordered relationships, to the most massive authorities of the state, people were vested with appropriate statuses; all the intricacies of human relationships were governed by their appropriate context of rights, duties, expectations. Later, we shall see that Sumner was disturbed by the extent to which this fabric of 'status' in society was upset, disrupted, and indeed not even understood, in the great expansion of 'contract' and legislation in more complex societies. Here again, we can see more than the germ of another central generalization which has emerged in sociology, and which has been specifically attributed to Sir Henry Maine—namely the movement from 'Status' to 'Contract' in the development of society.

(IV) GROUPS, GROUP INTERESTS, AND FORCE IN THE MORES

It is necessary to mention too, but only briefly for the sake of completeness, that Sumner did not by any means give a picture of a smooth development of the mores from the folkways accomplished

* *Folkways*, p. 68.

517

by the communiity as a whole. He especially noted that particular groups and classes in society pursued their own interests as against the interests of others and used all kinds of force in doing so. These specific elements of interests and force were often woven into the pattern of the folkways and mores, and characterized the 'ethics' of a society; and they, too, came to be built into the taboos, myths, rituals and network of statuses. The mores included accommodation to the conflicts of specific factions in society as well as embodying many interests and practices of the people 'as a whole'.

(V) IMAGINATION AND KNOWLEDGE

It also deserves to be mentioned that Sumner discussed the ways in which imagination and the growth of increasingly accurate knowledge entered into the 'myths' and the 'world philosophies' which they presented. And this will serve to illustrate very well the kind of ambiguity in which his writing appears to result. That imagination and knowledge *did* enter actively into the shaping of the mores, Sumner had no doubts.

'The correct apprehension of facts and events by the mind', he wrote, 'and the correct inferences as to the relations between them, constitute knowledge, and it is chiefly by knowledge that men have become better able to live well on earth. Therefore the alternation between experience or observation and the intellectual processes by which the sense, sequence, interdependence, and rational consequences of facts are ascertained, is undoubtedly the most important process of winning increased power to live well.'*

It is obvious that if this point was pursued to its logical conclusion (which Sumner did indicate elsewhere), it would give a clear basis for the analysis, critical assessment, judgment, and conscious reform of the mores; and Sumner did believe that this was possible. Yet—having clarified the worth of knowledge, he wrote:

'Yet we find that this process has been liable to the most pernicious errors . . .'

and he went on to show how the 'knowledge' of particular societies in particular periods had been woven, in the form of great errors and fallacies, into mores and myths, and in such a way as to accommodate themselves to the 'life-conditions' prevailing. And it was this that led him to insist upon a 'cultural relativism'.

'The logic of one age', he wrote, 'is not that of another. It is one of the chief useful purposes of a study of the mores to learn to discern in them the operation of traditional error, prevailing dogmas, logical fallacy, delusion, and current false estimates of goods worth striving for.'†

* Folkways, p. 44.   † ibid., p. 45.

Actually there is no necessary connection between the *diversity* of cultures (and the difference of 'truths', 'values', 'logics', relative to them) and *relativity* in epistemology or ethics. This we shall come to much later; but it is worth noting that even Sumner himself believed this—even though his writing *appears* to suggest the contrary.

(VI) THE 'ETHOS' OF A SOCIETY

A final particular emphasis which Sumner made was this. The folkways and mores are not a set of societal 'entities' totally distinct from the people who live within them—like a set of clothes they can wear or discard as they wish. They are, in fact, the collective *character* of the people; they are the *ways* of *feeling, thinking, acting, doing, organizing, deciding, speaking, dressing, gesturing* . . . and so on almost indefinitely, of *the people in that community*. The folkways and mores constitute a distinctive 'ethos' of that people, and Sumner made it clear that he would, indeed, have much liked to use a word derived from the Greek word 'ethos' to indicate very specifically what he had in mind. He considered the words 'Ethica' and 'Ethology', but felt that these had been spoiled. Especially, he thought that the term 'Ethics' had come to be so attached to the philosophical study of the presuppositions of moral assumptions, and so divorced from the study of *morals* as they existed among men in societies, that he did not wish to entertain the possibility of confusion.

'These methods of discussion', he wrote, (i.e. of philosophical ethics), 'are most employed in treating of social topics, and they are disastrous to sound study of facts. They help to hold the social sciences under the dominion of metaphysics.'*

Sumner therefore abandoned such terminology and used the Romans' word—'mores'—instead. It is important for our purposes, however, to see that Sumner had in mind this conception of a *societal* se of tregulated usages which were *simultaneously* (in terms of both *social* and *individual psychology*) the *character* of a people. This, it will be seen, is completely in keeping with Comte's 'social psychology' notions, Mill's 'Ethology', Marx's 'social consciousness', and other ideas we have considered.

So much, then, for the nature of the 'mores' as a major element in Sumner's 'model' of society. Before we leave this, however, let us note again the all-embracing role that he gave them, the all-embracing nature which, in his conception, they had.

* Sumner's impatience can be readily understood, but the distinction he made was much easier to raise than to resolve. The distinction between a philosophical study of 'ethics' and a sociological study of 'morals' can be made with *apparent* clarity; but the relations between the two are more complex than it seems.

'We must conceive of the mores as a vast system of usages, covering the whole of life, and serving all its interests; also containing in themselves their own justification by tradition and use and wont, and approved by mystic sanctions until, by rational reflection, they develop their own philosophical and ethical generalizations, which are elevated into "principles" of truth and right.*

The mores come down to us from the past. Each individual is born into them as he is born into the atmosphere, and he does not reflect on them, or criticize them any more than a baby analyses the atmosphere before he begins to breathe it. Each one is subjected to the influence of the mores, and formed by them, before he is capable of reasoning about them.†

We learn the mores as unconsciously as we learn to walk and eat and breathe. The masses never learn how we walk, and eat, and breathe, and they never know any reason why the mores are what they are. The justification of them is that when we wake to consciousness of life we find them facts which already hold us in the bonds of tradition, custom, and habit.'‡

(f) The Folkways and the Science of Society: a summary
Of all the components we have dealt with so far, Sumner himself gave an excellent summary, and it is of importance that we should note this as it states with great clarity the relations between the folkways and the structuring of groups, the nature of the entire 'societal process' as he conceived it, and the way in which Sumner conceived the science of society as a study of them.

'Men in groups,' he wrote, 'are under life conditions; they have needs which are similar under the state of the life conditions; the relations of the needs to the conditions are interests under the heads of hunger, love, vanity, and fear; efforts of numbers at the same time to satisfy interests produce mass phenomena which are folkways by virtue of uniformity, repetition, and wide concurrence. The folkways are attended by pleasure or pain according as they are well fitted for the purpose. Pain forces reflection and observation of some relation between acts and welfare. At this point the prevailing world philosophy (beginning with goblinism) suggests explanations and inferences, which become entangled with judgments of expediency. However, the folkways take on a philosophy of right living and a life policy for welfare. Then they become mores, and they may be developed by inferences from the philosophy or the rules in the endeavour to satisfy needs without pain. Hence they undergo improvement and are made consistent with each other.'§

Then: on the emergence of groups and social organization in the struggle for existence:

'The relations of men to each other, when they are carrying on the struggle for existence near each other, consist in mutual reactions (antagonisms, rivalries, alliances, coercions, and co-operations), from which result

---

* *Folkways*, p. 82.   † *Ibid.*, p. 80.   ‡ *Ibid.*, p. 81.   § *Ibid.*, p. 45.

societal concatenations and concretions, that is, more or less fixed positions of individuals and subgroups towards each other, and more or less established sequences and methods of interaction between them, by which the interests of all members of the group are served.'*

On the relations between these elements of grouping and social organization and the folkways:

'The societal concretions are due to the folkways in this way—that the men, each struggling to carry on existence, unconsciously co-operate to build up associations, organization, customs, and institutions which, after a time, appear full grown and actual, although no one intended, or planned, or understood them in advance. They stand there as produced by "ancestors". These concretions of relation and act in war, labour, religion, amusement, family life, and civil institutions are attended by faiths, doctrines of philosophy (myths, folklore), and by precepts of right conduct and duty (taboos).'†

And on the part of individuals in the folkways and their unique 'societal' nature:

'Every act of each man fixes an atom in a structure, both fulfilling a duty derived from what preceded and conditioning what is to come afterwards by the authority of traditional custom. The structure thus built up is not physical, but societal and institutional, that is to say, it belongs to a category which must be defined and studied by itself. It is a category in which custom produces continuity, coherence, and consistency, so that the word "structure" may properly be applied to the fabric of relations and prescribed positions with which societal functions are permanently connected. The process of making folkways is never superseded or changed. It goes on now just as it did at the beginning of civilization. "Use and wont" exert their force on all men always.'‡

Elsewhere, too, Sumner insisted that the nature of 'societal' phenomena formed a category of facts distinct from material and organic facts, and, as such, required a new science.

The folkways, he wrote: '. . . are not organic or material. They belong to a super-organic system of relations, conventions, and institutional arrangements. The study of them is called for by their *social* character, by virtue of which they are leading factors in the science of society.'

'The life of society consists in making folkways and applying them. The science of society might be construed as the study of them.'

Sumner's systematic exploration of the nature of society was admirably clear. On this basis, he then went on to consider and analyse the ways in which the established order of folkways and mores in a society *changed*, giving rise to more formal elements of

---

* *Folkways*, p. 46.   † *Ibid.*, p. 45   ‡ *Ibid.*, p. 45

social structure. It is these ideas of change and development which round out and complete Sumner's system.

(g) Social change and 'types' of society

From what has been said about Sumner's conception of the folk-ways and mores as a process of creative accommodation to 'life conditions' it is obvious that, though he emphasized their controlling, constraining, conserving power, he did not think of them as being 'static' in any sense. He thought, as we have seen, that they were *developments* over a historical period so long as to be unrecorded in its early beginnings, and the 'strain' towards improvement and consistency clearly provided grounds for analysing the *directions* of change. But Sumner's *basic* teaching here was that since the folkways are accommodations to 'life conditions', the primary reasons why they change must be *changes in the 'life conditions'*. It is here that the *causes* of societal change must be sought. This, again, will be seen to be a position completely in accord with the ideas of Marx and Ward, but without entailing any metaphysic of 'deter-minism'.

'Changes in history,' wrote Sumner, 'are primarily due to changes in life conditions. Then the folkways change. Then new philosophies and ethical rules are invented to try to justify the new ways. The whole vast body of modern mores has thus been developed out of the philosophy and ethics of the Middle Ages. So the mores which have been developed to suit the system of great secular states, world commerce, credit institutions, contract wages and rent, emigration to outlying continents, etc., have become the norm for the whole body of usages, manners, ideas, faiths, customs, and institutions which embrace the whole life of a society and characterize an historical epoch.'*

It will be noted that the mores are not thought to 'reflect' the 'life conditions' and the social regularities of a period, they are thought *to be part of* the social activity of men which '*suits*' their grappling with their new problems: they are an essential part of the creative societal activity itself. Though there is no 'metaphysic' of 'material determinism' here, therefore, there is nonetheless a view about the close interdependency of all social phenomena in relation to the changing life conditions which points to a very systematic method of analysing and explaining social change. Sumner's con-ception of this is worth noting both because of its accordance with earlier thinkers and because of its similarity to the ideas of important theorists—such as Durkheim—which we shall come to consider later.

* *Folkways*, p. 47.

When seeking an understanding of the reasons for the existence and form of *any particular element of social structure*, it must be looked for by tracing its relation to the mores of the society in that period. 'The real reason' for the existence and nature of any element of social structure, said Sumner, 'is that it conforms to the mores of the time and place.'

When seeking an understanding of the reasons for *changes* in the structures of societies, it must be sought by: 'showing their connection with changes in the life conditions, or with the readjustments of the mores to changes in those conditions.'

What is more, Sumner argued that this perspective of the interdependency of institutions with each other and with relation to the life conditions was the *only* perspective within which social change *could* be understood.

'Historians,' he wrote, 'have always recognized incidentally the operation of such a determining force. What is now maintained is that it is not incidental or subordinate. It is supreme and controlling.'

Nothing can be understood excepting in this context of social interdependency in coming to terms with changing life conditions.

Bearing in mind Sumner's conception of the validity of a particular system of folkways for a particular people in coming to terms with their own particular life conditions, and thus creating an 'ethos' distinctively their own, it follows that Sumner also thought that historical change and development gave rise to '*types*' of society. Social systems were *entireties* with distinctive total characteristics. 'A society is a whole made up of parts. All the parts have a share in the acts and sufferings of the society. All the parts contribute to the life and work of the society.' And 'types' of society arose in so far as their life conditions were similar. (It may be noted, by the way, that to think of 'types' of society in no way denies the *uniqueness* of each society: it only postulates significant similarities among some of them which makes it worthwhile to group them together for study.)

'India, Chaldea, Assyria, Egypt, Greece, Rome, the Middle Ages, Modern Times,' wrote Sumner, 'are cases in which the integration of the mores upon different life conditions produced societal states of complete and distinct individuality (ethos).'*

It is clear from this that Sumner's position is very similar to that of Marx: in classifying societies according to the basic characteristics of the 'life conditions' with which they are having to deal.

* *Folkways*, p. 47.

(h) Social change: complexity, élites, hierarchical organization and institutions

So far, we have seen how Sumner's 'model' of society depicted the activities of men, based upon motives and interests in relation to life conditions, giving rise to the folkways and mores with their collective 'sentiments' and their over-all 'ethos'. With the consideration of the factors involved in social change, and the growth of types of society from simple communities governed by the folkways to large complex civilizations with massive structures of social organization, Sumner introduced additional elements in his 'model' of a very interesting kind. Though we can deal with these elements only briefly, it is essential to see them clearly because they are all ideas of importance.

(i) 'IN-GROUPS' AND 'OUT-GROUPS'

First of all, Sumner tried to give a clear analysis of the processes which led to the formation and intensification of the folkways and mores in the simplest groups and most simple (primitive) societies. This was important for itself, but also to explain the great dominance which the folkways and their attendant myths had upon the minds of men in societies, and the ways in which they frequently stood in the way (as powerful obstacles) of any wider co-operation between groups and societies; of the ways, in short, in which they operated to cement human differences and distinctions. Sumner put the matter very clearly like this:

'The conception of "primitive society" which we ought to form is that of small groups scattered over a territory. The size of the groups is determined by the conditions of the struggle for existence. The internal organization of each group corresponds to its size. A group of groups may have some relation to each other (kin, neighbourhood, alliance, connubium and commercium) which draws them together and differentiates them from others. Thus a differentiation arises between ourselves, the we-group, or in-group, and everybody else, or the others-groups, out-groups. The insiders in a we-group are in a relation of peace, order, law, government, and industry, to each other. Their relation to all outsiders, or others-groups, is one of war and plunder, except so far as agreements have modified it.'*

Beyond this, however, said Sumner, the intensification of the sentiments among the members of the 'In-Group' is directly connected with the sentiments of hostility which they share towards the 'Out-Group'.

'The relation of comradeship and peace in the we-group and that of hostility and war towards others-groups are correlative to each other. The

* *Folkways*, p. 27.

524

exigencies of war with outsiders are what make peace inside, lest internal discord should weaken the we-group for war. These exigencies also make government and law in the in-group, in order to prevent quarrels and enforce discipline. Thus war and peace have reacted on each other and developed each other, one within the group, the other in the intergroup relation. The closer the neighbours, and the stronger they are, the intenser is the warfare, and then the intenser is the internal organization and discipline of each. Sentiments are produced to correspond. Loyalty to the group, sacrifice for it, hatred and contempt for outsiders, brotherhood within, warlikeness without—all grow together, common products of the same situation. These relations and sentiments constitute a social philosophy. It is sanctified by connection with religion. Men of an others-group are outsiders with whose ancestors the ancestors of the we-group waged war. The ghosts of the latter will see with pleasure their descendants keep up the fight, and will help them. Virtue consists in killing, plundering, and enslaving outsiders.'*

This process of reciprocal intensification gives rise, Sumner claimed, to 'Ethnocentrism'.

'Each group nourishes its own pride and vanity, boasts itself superior, exalts its own divinities, and looks with contempt on outsiders. Each group thinks its own folkways the only right ones, and if it observes that other groups have other folkways, these excite its scorn. Opprobrious epithets are derived from these differences. "Pig-eater", "cow-eater", "uncircumcized", "jabberers", are epithets of contempt and abomination. Ethnocentrism leads a people to exaggerate and intensify everything in their own folkways which is peculiar and which differentiates them from others. It strengthens the folkways.'†

It will readily be seen that this analysis of sentiment formation in the context of group-relations can be extended to the study of groups, both large and small, *within* communities as well as *between* them, and this has in fact become one of the basic components of sociological analysis—commonly referred to now as 'Reference Group Theory'. But it is enough for us to see that, by this means, Sumner explained the cohesion of simpler societies in history; the laying down of the systems of folkways in the world; which really were the foundation of all subsequent patterns of conflict and co-operation as culture-contact between the peoples of the world came to be extended.

(II) SOME GROUNDS OF SOCIAL CHANGE

This early and relatively simple and intense cohesion between relatively unified communities obviously came to be changed, splintered, disrupted, made more complex, brought into various kinds of international connection, and it is only necessary here to note that Sumner did offer a discussion of the many factors involved. He

* *Folkways*, p. 27.   † *Ibid.*, p. 28.

discussed for example, the kinds of 'criticism' and change of the folkways brought about by the differing experience of 'generations'— even within the same society; by 'social mobility' (of movement of individuals between social classes), and 'travel', which leads people to consider their folkways more objectively and to reflect upon them; by 'missionary' activity of various kinds between societies; and by 'agitation' of various kinds resulting from changes of fortune of particular sections of a community. Most important, perhaps, was his discussion of kinds of contact *between* groups and societies, and what he called 'syncretism'. Sumner wrote in this way:

'When groups are compounded by intermarriage, intercourse, conquest, immigration, or slavery, *syncretism* of the folkways takes place. One of the component groups takes precedence and sets the standards. The inferior groups or classes imitate the ways of the dominant group, and eradicate from their children the traditions of their own ancestors . . .

'Contiguity, neighborhood, or even literature may suffice to bring about syncretism of the mores. One group learns that the people of another group regard some one of its ways or notions as base. This knowledge may produce shame and an effort to breed out the custom. Thus whenever two groups are brought into contact and contagion, there is, by syncretism, a selection of the folkways which is destructive to some of them. This is the process by which folkways are rendered obsolete.'*

As a result of these, and other factors, then, societies become larger, interrelated with other societies, and more complex in their organization. There was one other fact about society, however, on which Sumner placed special stress in his analysis of change: this was the existence in any total population of certain *classes*; but his treatment of this was extremely interesting and quite different from that of Marx.

(iii) CLASSES IN A SOCIETY'S POPULATION

By the 'classes' of a population, Sumner did not mean at all what almost every other sociologist has meant: some form of 'stratification' according to socio-economic position. He based his analysis on the work of Galton, and argued that each population consisted of classes of people of differing ranges of *ability*. To put the matter simply here, Sumner argued that there was always a small proportion of the population possessing very high ability; an equally small proportion possessing very low ability; and a very large middle range possessing mediocre ability (graded between low and high). Though we shall not consider this in detail, it might be clearest to give the diagram which he used—drawn from Ammon's development of Galton's ideas. It was as follows.†

* *Folkways*, p. 112.   † *Ibid.*, p. 51.

It is enough for us to see that one essential component of Sumner's 'model' of society, and a component continuously employed in the analysis of changing folkways and changing social structures, was this conception of 'élitism'. In many ways—large and small and variously effective—there was a continuous interplay of influence between the able and active élite in society and the less able and more conservative 'masses'; and the changing folkways included accom-

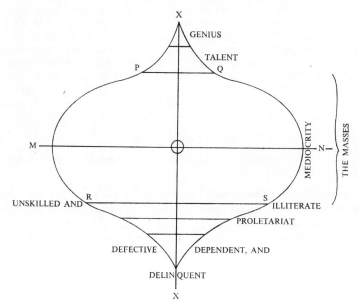

modations between 'classes' of this kind. It is interesting to notice that, in Sumner's conception, it was always 'the masses' who were the most conservative element (and thus a massive constraint in another sense) as far as the persistence of the folkways was concerned. It is also worth noting that Sumner thought that every society had to carry a 'lower' proportion which was always a 'weight' of sub-normal and defective ability prone to delinquency and social 'diseconomies' of various kinds.

The major point which Sumner drew from this analysis of 'classes', however, was the necessity for 'hierarchical organization' in society.

(IV) HIERARCHICAL ORGANIZATION AND ITS SOCIAL BENEFITS

Sumner was refreshingly forthright on this subject.

'Masses of men,' he wrote, 'who are on a substantial equality with each other never can be anything but hopeless savages. The eighteenth-century notion that men in a state of nature were all equal is wrong-side up. Men who were equal would be in a state of nature such as was imagined. They could not form a society. They would be forced to scatter and wander, at most two or three together. They never could advance in the arts of civilization. The popular belief that out of some such horde there has come by the spontaneous development of innate forces all the civilization which we possess is entirely unfounded . . .

'Masses of men who are approximately equal are in time exterminated or enslaved. Only when enslaved or subjugated are some of them carried up with their conquerors by organization and discipline . . . A horde in which the only differences are those of age and sex is not capable of maintaining existence . . . When it is subjugated and disciplined it consists of workers to belabour the ground for others, or tax payers to fill a treasury from which others may spend, or food for gunpowder, or voting material for demagogues. It is an object of exploitation. At one moment, in spite of its aggregate muscle, it is helpless and imbecile; the next moment it is swept away into folly and mischief by a suggestion or an impulse.'*

Very definitely, Sumner concluded:

'Organization, leadership, and discipline are *indispensable* to any beneficial action by masses of men.'

Furthermore, Sumner was very positive in his view that this kind of organization required the creation of regulating *institutions*, and that these were produced never by the masses, but by those leading men and 'classes' who gained control over the collective power and resources of society and, out of the mores, created the kinds of arrangement they judged important in dealing with societies' problems. This, in short, was a process of 'élitist' creation of institutions within the context of the folkways and mores—again a very clear and firm plank of analysis. For the creation of these institutions, Sumner wrote:

'The increase of *power* is the primary condition. The classes strive with each other for the new power. Peace is necessary, for without peace none of them can enjoy power. Compromise, adjustment of interest, antagonistic co-operation, harmony, are produced, and institutions are the regulative processes and apparatus by which warfare is replaced by system.'†

Sumner was therefore quite definite in his 'élitism' in this growth of institutional organization. Indeed, he went so far as to deny the efficacy of 'educating' the masses with regard to accomplishing their 'enlightened' participation in the making of institutions. This, he thought, was absurdly unrealistic.

'Every impulse given to the masses', he wrote, 'is, in its nature, spasmodic and transitory. No systematic enterprise to enlighten the masses ever can

* *Folkways*, p. 57.   † *Ibid.*, p. 58.

be carried out. Campaigns of education contain a fallacy. Education takes time. It cannot be treated as subsidiary for a lifetime and then be made the chief business for six months with the desired result.'*

This, however, did not mean, as we shall see, a lack of concern for education in a general sense—only an impatience with the idea of a kind of 'égalitarian participation' in the making of institutions produced by an appropriate 'education of the masses'. This, he thought, was a pipe-dream.

(v) INSTITUTIONS AND LAWS

It is here that we come to the final component in Sumner's 'model' of society. We have seen how he portrayed the two distinctive societal levels of the folkways and—developing out of these—the mores. Now we can see how, within this same context, he distinguished the third level: the development of *institutions*. And again, we must be very clear about Sumner's definitions.

'Institutions and laws', he wrote, 'are produced out of mores.

'An *institution* consists of a *concept* (idea, notion, doctrine, interest) and a *structure*. The structure is a *framework*, or *apparatus*, or perhaps only a number of *functionaries* set to co-operate in prescribed ways at a certain conjuncture. The structure holds the concept and furnishes *instrumentalities* for bringing it into the world of facts and action in a way to serve the *interests* of men in society.'†

Let us notice very clearly, here, the components of 'institutions' as distinct from the nature of the folkways and mores. They are specific *structures* of procedure, embodying specific *concepts*, a specific *apparatus*, specific *functionaries* and *instrumentalities* to pursue specific *interests*. Later, we shall see how similar this conception is to that of Malinowski, for example. Institutions, then, are specific differentiations of structure and function crystallizing (whether by conscious device or not) out of the folkways and mores. But Sumner then thought it important to distinguish between two *kinds* of institutions.

'Institutions', he wrote, 'are either *crescive* or *enacted*.

'They are crescive when they take shape in the mores, growing by the instinctive efforts by which the mores are produced. Then the efforts, through long use, become definite and specific. Property, marriage, and religion are the most primary institutions. They began in folkways. They became customs. They developed into mores by the addition of some philosophy of welfare, however crude. Then they were made more definite

---

* *Folkways*, p. 60.
† *Folkways*, p. 61. Compare with Malinowski's analysis of an 'institution': *The Making of Sociology*, Vol. 2, Part Four, Ch. 1.

and specific as regards the rules, the prescribed acts, and the apparatus to be employed. This produced a structure and the institution was complete.'*

They are *enacted* when they are:

'. . . products of rational invention and intention. They belong to high civilization. Banks are institutions of credit founded on usages which can be traced back to barbarism. There came a time when, guided by rational reflection on experience, men systematized and regulated the usages which had become current, and thus created positive institutions of credit, defined by law and sanctioned by the force of the state. Pure enacted institutions which are strong and prosperous are hard to find. It is too difficult to invent and create an institution, for a purpose, out of nothing. All institutions have come out of mores, although the rational element in them is sometimes so large that their origin in the mores is not to be ascertained, except by an historical investigation (legislatures, courts, juries, joint stock companies, the stock exchange).'†

Enacted institutions, of course, are closely connected with legislation, and in this, too, Sumner gave a clear picture of the growth of rationally directed law from the earlier 'custom' and 'common law' of the folkways. Enactments and the institutions they created were specific, and were provided with specific sanctions, and thus were rather more rigid than the process of the folkways; they entailed a certain measure of 'sacrifice of the elasticity and automatic self-adaptation of custom', but their creation could be understood when 'conscious purposes' were formed. Again, we see the emergence of the 'teleological' out of the 'genetic' which Ward had described.

Sumner emphasized especially the differences of 'sentiment' and 'reason', the differences of diffuseness and specificity, which distinguished 'institutions and laws' from the folkways and mores. For example:

'The element of sentiment and faith inheres in the mores. Laws and institutions have a rational and practical character, and are more mechanical and utilitarian. The great difference is that institutions and laws have a positive character, while mores are unformulated and undefined . . . Acts under the laws and institutions are conscious and voluntary; under the folkways they are always unconscious and involuntary, so that they have the character of natural necessity . . . The laws, being positive prescriptions, supersede the mores so far as they are adopted. It follows that the mores come into operation where laws and tribunals fail. The mores cover the great field of common life where there are no laws . . . They cover an immense and undefined domain, and they break the way in new domains, not yet controlled at all. The mores, therefore, build up new laws . . . in time.'‡

It will be seen in this 'model' of society and this analysis of change,

* *Folkways*, p. 62.   † *Ibid.*, p. 62.   ‡ *Ibid.*, p. 64.

SUMNER'S SYSTEM OF ANALYSIS

THE SOCIAL SYSTEM

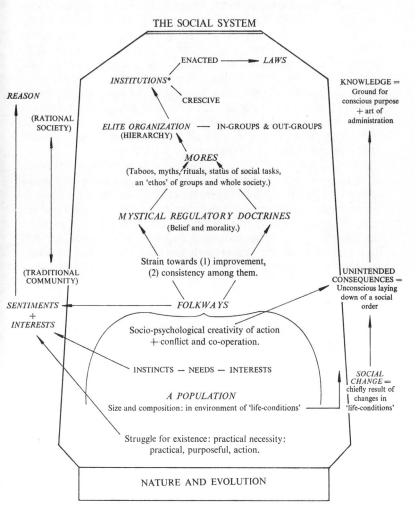

ENACTED ⟶ *LAWS*

*INSTITUTIONS**

CRESCIVE

REASON

(RATIONAL
SOCIETY)

KNOWLEDGE =
Ground for
conscious purpose
+ art of
administration

ELITE ORGANIZATION —— IN-GROUPS & OUT-GROUPS
(HIERARCHY)

MORES
(Taboos, myths, rituals, status of social tasks,
an 'ethos' of groups and whole society.)

MYSTICAL REGULATORY DOCTRINES
(Belief and morality.)

Strain towards (1) improvement,
(2) consistency among them.

(TRADITIONAL
COMMUNITY)

UNINTENDED
CONSEQUENCES =
Unconscious laying
down of a social
order

SENTIMENTS
+
INTERESTS

FOLKWAYS

Socio-psychological creativity of action
+ conflict and co-operation.

INSTINCTS — NEEDS — INTERESTS

A POPULATION
Size and composition: in environment of 'life-conditions'

*SOCIAL
CHANGE* =
chiefly result of
changes in
'life-conditions'

Struggle for existence: practical necessity:
practical, purposeful, action.

NATURE AND EVOLUTION

* The diagram would be too complicated if we were to include the actual institutions in the total social system which Sumner dealt with, but they were: Marriage, family, and kinship; economic institutions; religion; sport, art, and drama; education; law; morality; etc.

531

that Sumner was stating a very large-scale theory of social development: that human societies, in coming to terms with their life conditions, developed from a relatively simple condition in which the societal order consisted of the folkways, through a rather more complex and reflective creation of the mores, to conditions of considerable complexity in which there was a differentiation of specific institutions and laws consciously articulated for specific purposes. The earlier condition was characterized by 'sentiment' and sanctioned usage, the later condition by conscious reflection and purpose and 'rational' calculation. As we shall see, this generalization was to become one of the most centrally agreed ideas in sociological analysis, and one of central (theoretical) utility for the understanding of the changes in society brought about by science and its application in industrial technology. But its similarity to all that had been said by Comte, Mill, Spencer, Marx and Ward is also patently clear.

This component of the 'institutions and laws' of society rounded off Sumner's 'model' for the analysis of social order and social change. All that remains is that we should be clear about his apparent 'ambiguities' with regard to 'relativity' and 'progressive reform' and that we should see, too, the particular nature of his concern about the dilemmas of modern industrial society: for here, too, we shall find him in close agreement with the major scholars who both preceded and followed him.

(i) *The limitations of reform; Progress; Social Science and the Art of Administration; the problems of modern industrial society*

There is no doubt that Sumner not only *appeared* ambiguous, but *was* ambiguous, in many of his statements about the 'rightness' and 'sufficiency' of the folkways and mores for a society at any one time; about their validity for particular societies relative to their life-conditions; and about the extent to which 'reflection, reason, and conscious purpose' was disruptive of them, and of no avail with regard to them. It would be too long a task to document every aspect of this; but a few examples will be enough.

In some of his statements, Sumner was emphatic about the definiteness, the all-sufficiency, the rightness, of the mores. He wrote, for example:

'*Everything* in the mores of a time and place must be regarded as justified with regard to that time and place . . . For the men of the time there are no "bad" mores.'

Indeed, he went on:

'What is traditional and current is the standard of what ought to be. The masses never raise any questions about such things . . .

'The reason is that the standards of good and right are *in* the mores.'

And yet, at other times, as we have seen, he argued that the mores were questioned by new generations, as a result of social mobility, as a result of group conflict and group agitation (within the society) as well as of conflicts stemming from culture-contact from without. And he was insistent always, on the 'strain to improvement and consistency' among the mores. Sometimes then, he emphasized the conservative dominion of the force of 'sentiment' of the folkways over 'rational' calculation; but at other times he emphasized the elements of reason and reflection *implicit in them* which simply became more explicit and articulate with changing conditions.

It will have been noticed, too, that he spoke of the '*advance*' and the '*degeneration*' of the folkways—but it is difficult to see what precise meaning such terms could have if the folkways are held *always to be suited to the life conditions of society*. He also frequently spoke of the 'corruption' of the folkways by the development of 'rationality', and other factors, and we shall come to this again in a moment. But again, it is enough to see that one cannot speak of folkways becoming '*corrupted*' if they are *always relative* to the conditions to which they are adapted.

Another example may be mentioned with regard to education. We have seen that Sumner brushed aside the possibility of 'educating' the masses for participation in the making of institutions. Elsewhere, also, he claimed that 'educative reflection and skepticism' could 'disturb' the spontaneous, unconscious, involuntary operation of the folkways. And yet—in his discussion of 'Ethnocentrism'—we find that he distinguished between genuine and false '*patriotism*', and insisted that education should be a guide enabling men to judge soundly between them. Patriotism, he argued, may degenerate into a vice, as:

'. . . is shown by the invention of a name for the vice: chauvinism. It is a name for boastful and truculent group self-assertion. It overrules personal judgment and character, and puts the whole group at the mercy of the clique which is ruling at the moment. It produces the dominance of watchwords and phrases which take the place of reason and conscience in determining conduct. The patriotic bias is a recognized perversion of thought and judgment against which our education should guard us.'*

Not only were there distinctions, then, between genuine folkways and 'degenerations' or 'vices'—but only reason could clarify the criteria by which we should judge, and only education could secure the persistence of sound judgment. There are obviously quite definite elements of ambiguity here.

* *Folkways*, p. 30.

Furthermore, Sumner positively advocated free and rational criticism for the 'health' of the mores.

'Since it appears', he wrote, 'that the old mores are mischievous if they last beyond the duration of the conditions and needs to which they were adapted, and that constant, gradual, smooth, and easy readjustment is the course of things which is conducive to healthful life, it follows that free and rational criticism of traditional mores is essential to societal welfare. We have seen that the inherited mores exert a coercion on every one born in the group. It follows that only greatest and best can react against the mores so as to modify them . . . The trained reason and conscience never have heavier tasks laid upon them than where questions of conformity to, or dissent from, the mores are raised. It is by the dissent and free judgment of the best reason and conscience that the mores win flexibility and automatic readjustment.'*

One other example (an important one) will be enough.

In some of his emphases, Sumner was very far-reaching in the claim that he made for the dominion of the mores over man's thought. Indeed, he argued, men *could not* liberate themselves from this domination.

'It is vain', he insisted, 'to imagine that any man can lift himself out of these characteristic features in the mores of the group to which he belongs . . . It is vain to imagine that a "scientific man" can divest himself of prejudice or previous opinion, and put himself in an attitude of neutral independence towards the mores. He might as well try to get out of gravity or the pressure of the atmosphere. The most learned scholar reveals all the philistinism and prejudice of the man-on-the-curbstone when mores are in discussion. The most elaborate discussion only consists in revolving on one's own axis. One only finds again the prepossessions which he brought to the consideration of the subject, returned to him with a little more intense faith.'†

And it is upon this kind of ground, as well as upon his persuasion concerning the dominating force and conservatism of the mores, that he argued strongly that the possibilities of legislative reform in society were so limited. And yet,—knowing how *mistaken* the mores can be—we find him writing like this:

'Stoll boldly declares that if one of us had been a judge in the times of the witch trials he would have reasoned as the witch judges did, and would have tortured like them. If that is so, then it behooves us by education and will, with intelligent purpose, to criticize and judge even the most established ways of our time, and to put courage and labour into resistance to the current mores where we judge them wrong.'‡

But if this is so—then we must have confidence that, in our

* *Folkways*, pp. 95–6.   † *Ibid.*, p. 98.   ‡ *Ibid.*, p. 114.

thinking, we can indeed *liberate* ourselves from the mores which are so constraining upon us; go *beyond* them; and—what is more—find *criteria of truth* which are not 'relative' with regard to them, and provide procedures of education which instil *these* criteria, and *these* qualities of mind, as a basis of critical judgment *against* the folkways. In a way which was genuinely inconsistent and ambiguous, Sumner seemed to see a close relation between reason and feeling when speaking of their interconnections in the folkways themselves, but to insist on a flat conflict between them when the folkways came to be subjected to rational criticism. And—hating philosophy as he did—he seems not to have made sufficient use of the clarification which it can offer!

However, having noted (and given due weight to) these elements of ambiguity in Sumner's system, we can resolve them quite satisfactorily for our own purposes. For a completely fair statement of Sumner's position is this. He was *not*, in any fundamental sense, *opposed* to the conscious application of reason, critical reflection, legislative reform, and education in efforts to *improve* the social order. Indeed, as we have seen, his entire theory is one in which the folkways, mores, and created institutions, 'strain towards' improvement. What he *was* opposed to—and very powerfully—was the *brash, uninformed, superficial, irresponsible* attitudes of mind of those politicians and others who thought they could create institutions anew *without any knowledge of the deeply-rooted fabric of the folkways*, and without taking them fully into account. And he was opposed to this not only because it could fail disastrously as such, but also that it could spill over—beyond all wise bounds—into areas of social life in which it was misplaced, and in so doing, it could indeed despoil and wreck the folkways—putting nothing in their place but emptiness and confusion. Legislation, too irresponsibly expanded, could *destroy* the communal ways of a people, and leave only a tragic and dangerous vacuum in their place.

Once this *emphasis* is clearly understood, it can be seen that no fundamental gulf or difference separates Sumner from Ward or any of the other theorists we have studied. He is as much concerned with the reasonable improvement of the life of society as they; it is only that he wants the *nature of society to be fully appreciated* by those responsible for legislative reform, and he wants to see legislation *very carefully done*. He was, of course, quite right in this emphasis, and we can see how reminiscent his whole stand was of that of earlier men such as Montesquieu and Burke.

That this is a correct, and not just a personal interpretation of his standpoint may be seen from his own words, and we can see here again the perennial and all-pervading desire of all the men concerned

535

with the making of sociology—namely, that such a science should be the basis for a wise and satisfactory *art* of achieving a new, enriched order of human society out of the chaos of modern industrial change.

Having emphasized in many ways the *difficulties* of changing the folkways, and the *care* which should be exercised in trying to improve them, Sumner wrote:

'It is not to be inferred that reform and correction are hopeless . . .

'The statesman and social philosopher can act with such influences, sum up the forces which make them, and greatly help the result. The inference is that intelligent art can be introduced here as elsewhere, but that it is necessary to understand the mores and to be able to discern the elements in them, just as it is always necessary for good art to understand the facts of nature with which it will have to deal. It belongs to the work of publicists and statesmen to gauge the forces in the mores and to perceive their tendencies . . .

'Great crises come when great new forces are at work changing fundamental conditions, while powerful institutions and traditions still hold old systems intact . . . It is in such crises that great men find their opportunity. The man and the age react on each other . . .

'The interaction defies our analysis, but it does not discourage our reason and conscience from their play on the situation, if we are content to know that their function must be humble . . .'*

This, surely, was a very wise statement of conclusion.

'It would be a mighty achievement of the science of society', Sumner said, 'if it could lead up to an art of societal administration which should be intelligent, effective, and scientific.'

Clearly, there was no divergence between Ward and Sumner here. They were spokesmen of the same excellent and humane objectives: of the achievement of the most reliable knowledge, and the attempt at the most responsible control: the objectives which underlay the aspirations not only of the early Americans, but united *all* the sociologists of Europe and America from Comte onwards.

It is worth our while, in bringing our study of Sumner to a close, to see clearly how similar his worries were about the nature and dangers of nineteenth-century industrial capitalism to those of the other men we have considered.

'The history of the nineteenth century', he wrote, 'plainly showed the power of capital in the modern state. Special legislation, charters, and franchises proved to be easy legislative means of using the powers of the state for the pecuniary benefit of the few . . . The history is disgraceful, and it is a permanent degradation of popular government that power could not be found, or did not exist, in the system to subjugate this abuse and repress

* *Folkways*, pp. 113–14.

536

this corruption of state power . . . The corrupt use of legislation and political power has affected the mores. Every one must have his little sphere of plunder and especial advantage. This conviction and taste becomes so current that it affects all new legislation. The legislators do not doubt that it is reasonable and right to enact laws which provide favour for special interests . . . They laugh at remonstrance as out of date and "unpractical". They think that that is only common sense. "What else are we here for?" . . .'*

And in his judgment of this rapid and savage development of industrial capitalism, we can see that Sumner believed that this actually and actively led to a *moral deterioration*, a *moral* vacuum in society. Later, we shall see how completely this is in agreement with almost all the major sociologists and especially with Emile Durkheim's notion of the development of 'Anomie' (normlessness) in the complexities of modern industrial society.

'It is the supreme test of a system of government', Sumner wrote, 'whether its machinery is adequate for repressing the selfish undertakings of cliques formed on special interests and saving the public from raids of plunderers. The modern democratic states fail under this test. There is not a great state in the world which was not democratized in the nineteenth century. There is not one of them which did not have great financial scandals before the century closed. Financial scandal is the curse of all the modern parliamentary states with a wide suffrage. They give liberty and security, with open chances for individual enterprise, from which results great individual satisfaction and happiness, but the political machinery offers opportunities for manipulation and corrupt abuse. They educate their citizens to seek advantages in the industrial organization by legislative devices, and to use them to the uttermost. The effect is seen in the mores. We hear of plutocracy and tainted money, of the power of wealth, and the wickedness of corporations. The disease is less specific. It is constitutional. The critics are as subject to it as the criticized. A disease of the mores is a disease of public opinion as to standards, codes, ideas of truth and right, and of things worth working for and means of success. Such a disease affects everybody. It penetrates and spoils every institution. It spreads from generation to generation, and at last it destroys in the masses the power of ethical judgment.'†

For Sumner then, as for all the others, the pressing need for the making of sociology was the same: to provide reliable knowledge of society so that such matters could be put right.

* *Folkways*, p. 154.   † *Ibid.*, p. 156.

c FRANKLIN H. GIDDINGS

A third scholar who contributed much to the making of sociology in America was Franklin Giddings. It might be argued by some that Giddings made no contribution of note distinctively beyond the work of Ward and Sumner, but accomplished, rather, a more systematic statement than they of all that was already agreed and accepted. To some extent this was true. Giddings devoted a good deal of effort to clear teaching. He was convinced (like Ward) of the importance of education as such; but he was also convinced of the great importance of sociology as a subject for education in the modern world. By 1898, he had not only written a large-scale *Principles of Sociology* and a book on *The Theory of Socialization*, but also a text-book for colleges and schools on *The Elements of Sociology*.

This sheer effort at clear statement for educational purposes was itself worthwhile from our own point of view. It showed, with perfect clarity, how the contributions of Comte and Spencer had been accepted (to a very large extent) by the Americans, and used to form the foundations for an entire scheme of sociological analysis. It displayed the clear and systematic method which sociological analysis could bring to the study of man and society, and demonstrated the utility of such studies for educating young people in the tasks and duties of citizenship. It was a good example of how, by the end of the nineteenth century, sociology had not only been founded as a science, but had also come to be conceived as a subject which could and should play an important part in higher education. Giddings' text-book gave a clear picture of how the subject was then designed for teaching purposes. There is no doubt, then, of the truth of the statement that Giddings' contribution was in large part that of a 'teacher'; a 'systematizer'—if that is not too ugly a word. But to leave the judgment there would be an error. There are several reasons why we should take the work of Giddings into account—in addition to that of Ward and Sumner—if we are to provide ourselves with a reasonably complete picture of the foundation of sociology as it was conceived by the early Americans.

Giddings, like Ward and Sumner, was a man of very considerable breadth of learning who brought together many other subjects in his formulation of sociology. He was not simply a kind of systematic regurgitation of Comte, Spencer, etc. He drew on men as diverse as Aristotle, Tacitus, Burke, Lecky, Bagehot, Buckle in discussing aspects of the development of institutions. He considered the views of Blackstone, Wundt, and Maine in his discussion of the nature of 'custom', its relation to law, and its place in various kinds of societies. He was well aware of the analyses of Adam Smith and Gabriel Tarde when discussing the growth of group sentiments and social values. But besides being well informed in this general scholarly sense, Giddings was acutely aware of the developments of his own time. Like Sumner, for example, he knew the work of Galton, and tried to incorporate it into his analysis of populations. He knew Sidney Webb's *History of Trade Unions* and took it into account in discussing the complexities of 'conflict and co-operation' in modern industrial societies. Two things, however, are perhaps particularly important.

The first was that Giddings did not only draw together, in systematic form, the earlier contributions of Comte and Spencer. He drew these together in relation, also, to the contemporary work of Ward and other American influences. Giddings, in short, accomplished a contemporaneous systematization; a bringing together of many of the *current* contributions towards the end of the nineteenth century. And the second fact of considerable importance was really a part of this, but deserves special emphasis.

This was that Giddings, like Ward, was very clearly aware of the intimate relationship between psychology and sociology, and, in pursuing his study of this, brought the work of men like William James, Titchener, and Wundt into the context of his analysis of social processes. In his conception of a science of man and society (as had been the case with Mill), psychology and sociology were closely conjoined.

In matters concerning the analysis of the nature and components of societies (i.e., in terms of elements of social structure or organization); in the classification and comparative study of types of society; and in theories of social change, development, evolution and progress; Giddings was almost entirely in agreement with Comte and Spencer and had little to add to them. On all these elements of analysis— important though they are—our discussion can only be relatively brief and confined chiefly to seeing clearly the nature of Giddings' agreement about them. Even here, however, we shall see that Giddings had something very interesting to say about the study of 'social action' and the way in which this was related to 'social structures' and 'types' of society.

It was in the systematic analysis of the *psychological processes accompanying association*, however, (the 'middle' field which Mill had called 'Ethology') that Giddings, like Ward, went beyond these European thinkers. Too much must not be claimed even here; but some aspects of Giddings' treatment do deserve special note. Ward had made much of the psychological aspects of social processes, but

Giddings, though not, perhaps, more profound than Ward, might be said to have been more systematic in laying out an analysis of all the components involved in the relations between the '*self*' and '*society*', and this, though far from being definitive, was a foundation of what was to be perhaps the most distinctive contribution of the Americans: the development of 'social psychology'. We have seen that, apart from John Stuart Mill's methodological discussion of the importance of these 'middle principles' of personality and social psychology, the European scholars had so far left this area relatively unexplored. Ward had made much of it. Sumner was emphasizing its importance in analysing the formation of the 'folkways'. But Giddings set the entire matter out with great conceptual clarity and with a clear system of analysis, and it was within this kind of context that the work of C. H. Cooley and G. H. Mead was to develop. When we come to twentieth-century developments I shall argue that this has been probably the major distinctive contribution of American sociology, and has culminated in much of what has come to be called 'role theory', and some of the most central work of Robert Merton, for example, in his considerable emphasis upon 'Reference Group Theory'.

What this amounts to, then, is that Giddings, as one of those who contributed to the making of sociology in America was another scholar who not only drew together existing contributions in a critically digested and systematic form, but also contributed a conceptual and analytical formulation which possessed originality and was a basis for much future development.

There are one or two other points which I will bring in at this stage—though I want to make them much more forcefully later. They are very important. We have already seen that, among all the thinkers we have discussed so far, but perhaps most explicitly and articulately in Ward, the study of 'social action' in terms of the ends which men seek and the means which they employ, was clearly thought to be a necessary element in any satisfactory 'causal' account of society and its processes. It was quite clearly conceived as a kind of 'teleological' causality, different from 'efficient' or 'genetic' causality, which distinguished the subject-matter of sociology from all other fields of 'phenomena' in nature. There was not the slightest lack of clarity about this. And yet it has come to be a firm persuasion among present-day scholars (even Americans) that this dimension of sociological analysis and theory-construction was absent from sociology until it was stated with a flash of originality out of the depths of a philosophical fog in continental Europe (in this case—Germany*). Here I want only to note this, and to point out (and this

* i.e. In the work of Max Weber.

will be much more clear very soon) that Giddings too had very significant things to say in this direction. But—and it is this consideration which leads me to introduce these points here—it is also thought that the introduction of the conception of '*social*' psychological facts; of psychological facts which were the outcome of processes of *association*, of *collective* processes; the introduction of the 'perspective' that the understanding of *individual personality* required the analysis of *social* processes; was an original contribution stemming from France.* And again, I want only to note that this is not true. Ward and Giddings (and other Americans we shall consider later) had already built this with complete conceptual clarity into the entire nature of sociological analysis by the end of the nineteenth century.

Though I do not wish to develop these points here, I think it is important to make it clear that they are raised *not at all* simply as a matter of claiming 'who said what first'. My much more important underlying concern is this. It seems to me that many of the elements and dimensions of analysis developed by Max Weber and Emile Durkheim—Durkheim especially—have brought with them a kind of 'philosophical mystique' (different in each case) which is altogether avoided in the formulations of the early Americans. In short, that in some ways, the distinctive 'teleological' dimensions of human society and sociology were *better* formulated by the Americans than by Max Weber. (They were not weighed down by having to struggle out of the same philosophical fog.) And the relations between 'individual' and 'social' psychological facts were in some ways *better* formulated by Ward, Giddings, Cooley and Mead than by Emile Durkheim. This must not, by any means, be taken to be a *derogatory* statement about the contributions of Weber and Durkheim. Later, we shall, in fact, come to consider their very great importance. It is only (*a*) to note that the elements of analysis on which they placed much emphasis were already taken into account in American sociology, and (*b*) that in some respects the formulation of the American scholars was, by contrast with some later formulations, to be upheld for its care and lucidity. However, these points will be fully pursued later.

For the moment, and bearing these issues in mind, let us complete our picture of the 'early Americans' by a brief outline of Giddings' 'system'. Perhaps it should be noted that here we shall deal only with the work Giddings had produced before the end of the nineteenth century. Later, for example, he contributed much in exploring and emphasizing the employment of statistics in sociological investigation; but this will not enter into our consideration here.

* i.e. In the work of Emile Durkheim.

541

Science and knowledge

Like all the other men we have considered, Giddings agreed that only the methods of science produced testable knowledge, and that if we desired reliable knowledge about man and society these were the methods which we should employ—to such degree of exactitude as was possible. To a large extent, Giddings wrote of 'science' as a process of meticulous and accurate 'description'. Each science clarified its 'unit of investigation', its distinctive subject-matter, and then tried to achieve a thorough 'description' of its nature, its components and the relations between them, and the 'processes' of order and change which were peculiar to it. Giddings used the term 'description' to emphasize the empirical, factual, testable grounding of scientific methods, but he included within this 'causal' theories and the statement of 'laws', which were: 'certain uniformities of order, sequence, proportion, and so on, among the facts that have been described'.

Indeed, this matter of the discovery and clear statement of 'uniformities' was quite a central emphasis in Giddings' treatment. Quite fundamentally, science followed upon our perception of 'resemblances' among all the elements of our experience. It was, initially, a *grouping* of things together in terms of the *resemblances* and *differences* which we felt to be significant among them; it was a formation of 'classes' or 'categories'.

'Endless progress in knowledge is possible only because we observe resemblances as well as differences. As rapidly as we discover that things are alike, we put them together in our thought as a group, or class, or kind . . .

'Classification, then, is the foundation of all scientific knowledge; and classification consists simply in putting together in our thought those things that are truly and essentially alike.'

This was then followed by careful analysis and the formulation of 'causal' theories which were subjected to test. All this, then, was simple and clear. Like Comte and Spencer, Giddings was also quite clear about the *limitations* of science, and kept well away from the 'metaphysical' dimensions which crept into the implicit assumptions of a man like Marx. Disclaiming any kind of ultimate 'monistic materialism' or 'idealism', Giddings wrote quite clearly:

'It is not any part of the business of science to deal with these ultimate problems of philosophy. Science stops short at the point where the possibility of verification ends and knowledge passes into speculation.

Verification is a confirmation by the senses of conclusions reached by reasoning.'

Science, in short, was confined by the testability of hypotheses.

The concept of Evolution and the relations between the sciences

Giddings also accepted the new perspective provided by the concept of 'evolution'. Like all the men we have mentioned, he saw nature as a complex process of interrelated and interdependent 'forms' which existed always in an environmental context, and were continually undergoing processes of 'transformation'—both in *persisting* in a certain order, and being *modified* by patterns and sequences of change. The scientific study of all aspects of nature must therefore essentially take account of this continuous interrelated process of order and change, and each science had its defined place in that it concerned itself with the study of one distinctive and determinate aspect of it. In this way, Giddings had the same conception of the interconnected order of the sciences, and the relations between the sciences, as had Comte, Spencer, Ward and others, and he did not feel it necessary to comment on this further. He simply accepted it. Like the others, too, whilst holding that all the sciences should be seen in relation to each other, he did *not* hold that the 'laws' or 'hypotheses' of any one science could be '*reduced*' to the concepts and hypotheses of another.

For Giddings then, as for others, the 'evolutionary perspective' was one in which all aspects of nature could be consistently seen for the systematic exploration of science. Human societies, as well as biological organisms and purely physical systems, were a part of this vast process of order and transformation, and all could be analysed usefully in the similar terms of growth, differentiation of parts and functions, segregation, integration, adaptation to changing circumtances of the environment, and the like. It can be seen from this how solidly Giddings accepted Spencer's perspective and system of analysis.

The study of society: populations in their environments

Before moving to Giddings' clear definition of the distinctive subject-matter of sociology, it is interesting to note two relatively preliminary points which followed from his conception of science and evolution, and which remained permanent elements and emphases in his system.

Obviously, in some sense or other, sociology was concerned with aggregations of human beings; with human populations. And obviously, in keeping with the classificatory procedure of science, it must 'distinguish' populations, and 'group' them together in some way according to the 'resemblances' to be observed among them. But here, at once, Giddings argued, we come to some qualitative distinctions between sociology and its subject-matter and other sciences which are of quite a fundamental nature; and there were two considerations especially which Giddings emphasized. The first was that in 'distinguishing', 'grouping', or 'classifying' human populations for purposes of study, sociologists were not in the ordinary position of scientists who could rest their criteria upon the 'resemblances' which they themselves perceived in their subject-matter. A botanist, for example, could 'group' certain trees in accordance with whether or not they shed their leaves with certain seasonal changes; or certain plants in accordance with whether they were characterized by 'bulbs' or 'corms' or 'roots', etc. The sociologist, however, found that *some* of the criteria of 'resemblance' and 'difference' which he had to take into account in classifying and describing populations, were *conceptions* of 'resemblance' or 'difference' which the members of the populations *themselves subjectively perceived and adopted in their own selective associations.* Among human populations there always existed some *subjectively held 'consciousness of kind'* in relation to which, alone, certain groupings and conflicts and· regulations could be understood and explained. So that some of the 'objective' criteria of the procedures of description and classification of the sociologist were the 'subjective' criteria of 'resemblance' held by the populations themselves. This was, immediately, a qualitative difference of methodology which distinguished sociology from other 'natural' sciences, and it involved clearly a dimension of 'subjective understanding' in 'objective procedures' from which other sciences were free.

The second important aspect of this point, however, which was a fundamental consideration at the very roots of Giddings' systematic development of the 'social psychological' aspects of social processes, was *the actual existence* of this 'consciousness of kind' in all populations as a basic principle of (or concomitant of) human grouping. Clearly the 'resemblances' which men saw between themselves and others, and which led them to associate with *these* men rather than *those,* varied very considerably. Men might sympathetically identify themselves with each other as a result of the similar colour of their skins, their membership of the same kinship grouping, the fact that they were born in the same locality, spoke the same language, shared the same occupation, and so on. But the *fact* was that *all* forms of association entailed *some* kind of 'consciousness of kind'; indeed the process of association established, cultivated, and consolidated it; this was an *objective characteristic* of human populations; and therefore the study of it (and of its various kinds and sources) must form a basic part of sociological analysis. The study of 'forms of association' must necessarily include study of those distinctive varieties of 'consciousness of kind' in relation to which these associations persisted. The very ground of sociological understanding was therefore, in large part, a *social psychological* ground.

The grouping of human populations on the basis of some 'resemblances' which were significant for classification, analysis, description, and the exploration of theories, therefore led Giddings to this very fundamental starting-point; the recognition of subjectively held 'consciousnesses of kind' among people (*a*) as *objective facts* interpenetrating the observable 'forms' of association and 'society', and (*b*) as necessary components of investigation, method, and theory-construction in sociology.

Bearing this in mind Giddings then simply noted that, no matter how complicated the analysis of 'societies' might become, sociology was still basically concerned with the study of aggregate populations which were living in the context of the characteristics and resources of determinate physical environments.

In sociology, then, *ecological* studies (of the life of populations in relation to their environments) and studies of the size and composition of *populations* must always be important. It is not necessary to elaborate on these two points, excepting to note that Giddings did propose a systematic method of studying populations—distinguishing changes in size due to 'Genetic Aggregation' (natural balance of births against deaths) from those due to various kinds of 'Congregation' (internal and external migration, etc.), and establishing clear knowledge of the 'composition' of populations (the numbers and distribution of ethnic groups, national groups, immigrants, etc.). Though we shall not dwell upon them here, ecological and demographic studies were therefore seen as being of basic importance by Giddings, and his studies of 'consciousness of kind' were always in relation to the understanding of varying degrees of cohesion, unity, variation, conflict, and change among the various groupings within a population.

Society and the Science of Society

It is significant, bearing in mind this 'psychological' emphasis that underlay Giddings' whole approach, that, when he came to define

545

'society', he began with the 'verbal' sense of the word: treating it as an *activity* of association, and only finally concluded with the word as a 'noun': referring to some kind of collectivity of associational forms. It is significant, too, that his basic and distinctive 'unit of investigation' for sociology was the *individual* as a 'socius' (i.e., as an associating person); the *individual* in his *associational* aspects.

'The word "society"', he wrote, 'is derived from the Latin word *socius*, meaning a companion or associate . . .
    'Society, then, *as a mode of activity* of intelligent individuals is the cultivation of both acquaintance and like-mindedness.
    'Its product is a group of like-minded persons who enjoy and keep up this mode of activity. Such a group or product is called a society.'

The passage from 'verb' to 'noun' is very clear here. He rounded out his definition with one more element—the working for common ends.

'A society is a group of like-minded individuals ("socii") who know and enjoy their like-mindedness, and are therefore able to work together for common ends.'

This, however, was only the most general of definitions, and Giddings extended and elaborated it by describing different '*kinds*' of society. He distinguished, for example, a '*Natural Society*' which was a population sharing a mode of life in a particular area and working together for common ends. An '*Integral Society*' was a natural society large enough to carry on all the known kinds of associational activity, and which was able, independently, to govern its own destiny within the area it occupied. It was a *total* society—incorporating all the major forms of social structure: family, economic system, government, law, religion, education, etc. Within the Integral (total) Society, two further kinds of society were distinguished: '*Component Societies*'—which were smaller communal groups which were capable, if necessary, of maintaining a complete social life of their own (for example—'states' within federal totalities; village and town communities; or even neighbourhood communities of family groups), and '*Constituent Societies*' which were purposefully and rationally devised associations, with definite forms of organization, established for the pursuit of specific ends. These were, in fact, specific associational groups, but, Giddings argued, they were always interrelated and interconnected in any total society, so that, taken together, they constituted the 'complete social organization of the integral society'.

From the 'unit of investigation' as the '*associating* individual', Giddings thus moved from the *activity* of society to the clear analysis

546

of various *kinds* of societies: and his analysis of any total social system—of any 'Integral Society'—into its organizational structure of 'constitutent societies' (specific associations); and its composition of 'component societies' (communities) and 'natural societies' (populations sharing the particular environmental conditions of a territory), was perfectly clear.

It must be emphasized, too, that Giddings was very meticulous when defining the 'unit of investigation' of sociology in terms of the 'individual'. He was well aware that the individual *as such*; as an organic and psychic totality; was not the distinctive focus of sociology. Biology included within its province the study of the organic attributes of the human individual, and psychology properly focused upon the psychic attributes of the individual. It was all those attributes of the individual which were relevant to the study of his *associational* activities and experiences that Giddings marked out as the distinctive province of sociology. This, he claimed was a clear and distinct field of study; a field which it was *necessary* to distinguish if we were to achieve reliable and testable knowledge about it; and a field which contained elements *other than* those of biology and psychology. Furthermore, Giddings argued, the associational and cultural fabric of human relationships is a cumulative societal context which has its continuous influence *upon* psychological and biological elements of human nature. The understanding of man the individual personality could therefore only be accomplished by establishing knowledge about the *associational* context of his life— and for this, the distinctive science of sociology was necessary.

Here again, we can see how perfectly clear and valid Giddings' position was, and how completely in keeping it was with that of Comte and others. Later, we shall see that this was the position also elaborated by Durkheim, so that, far from being an innovation of twentieth-century thought, a clear continuity of this distinguishing feature of sociology can be traced from the earliest statement of the subject to the present day.

However, it is enough for the present to see that, following upon these considerations of the 'distinctive subject-matter', Giddings' definition of sociology was also perfectly clear.

'The facts that we have been describing', he wrote, 'are *social facts* or *facts of society*.

'Scientific description results in the discovery of . . . causes and laws, which are . . . certain uniformities of order, sequence, proportion, and so on, among the facts that have been described.

'Using the word "description" in this sense, we may say that Sociology is the scientific description of society.'

The practical activities of men in society

Giddings' agreement with the other thinkers we have considered was also shown clearly by the emphasis which he placed upon the 'practical activities' of men in working upon, and accommodating themselves to, their environment, as the basis for all the forms of association, of social structure, which developed among them. His direct similarity to Spencer, Marx, Ward, Sumner, was quite evident. Even so, with his social psychological emphasis, he outlined the elements of these 'practical activities' in the form of a systematic analysis based upon the ways in which all individuals had to come to terms with the physical and social environment with which they were confronted.

There were, Giddings claimed, *four* necessary components in all forms of human social action, and these he called the *Simple Modes of Activity*. First of all, there was the activity of *Appreciation*. Individuals had to learn effectively about all the characteristics of the environment with which they had to come to terms. Secondly, there was the activity of *Utilization*. Individuals, having established effective knowledge about the elements of their environment, had to learn how to manipulate and utilize these elements in the satisfaction of their wants and the pursuit of their interests. Thirdly, in this complex process of learning about the environment and learning how to act in relation to it in order to use it, individuals were forced to the realization that effective and successful action rested upon the achievement, in themselves, of certain qualities of character. There was the activity of *Characterization*. Courage, persistence, endurance, initiative, independence, and many other qualities were called for, and, of course, the relative weighting of these, and the emphasis placed upon all kinds of secondary qualities would vary in accordance with the nature of the society of which the individuals were members. 'Character-Formation' would therefore have variations from society to society. And fourthly, there was the activity of *'Socialization'*. In knowing and using elements of their environment in accordance with certain required qualities of personality and character, individuals found that they were involved in relationships of conflict and co-operation with other individuals, and therefore had to come to terms with the institutions and associational groupings of society. They had to develop effective behaviour in the context of social relationships, and, indeed, learn how to initiate and cultivate social relationships in relation to their interests.

Before leaving this analysis of 'simple practical activities' which Giddings thought necessary and fundamental in all forms of human

548

action, we must note that Giddings also outlined these activities as a *sequential order* which was followed by the *child* in growing up to become an effective adult member of a society. It was, in fact, an *order and process of individual maturation* in society, as well as merely a *set* of activities. And this must be borne in mind because Giddings' whole conception of the relationship between 'society' and the formation of the 'self' can be seen in it.

Giddings also systematically analysed the 'motives' and the 'methods' which were appropriate to each of these four basic activities. These need not be elaborated here, but it is important to notice that Giddings did in fact provide an entire and systematic analysis of the whole process of the growth of the individual to adulthood in society. This was an analysis which connected, in the most detailed and systematic way, the knowledge of the entire structure of a society on the one hand with the components of social action and the growth of the individual personality within this context, on the other. It was an *entire* fabric of sociological and social-psychological analysis.

Following this, however, Giddings then went on to clarify the various '*forms*' of social action in which these four 'simple activities' came to be embodied by an analysis of '*complex*' activities, and by these he meant the major forms of institutionalization which took shape in all societies; the chief elements of social structure. Those on which he placed most emphasis were Economic Activity, Legal Activity, and Political Activity, and he dealt with the development of attendant and additional values, beliefs, ideals, etc., under the heading of Cultural Activity—in which artistic, religious, and educational institutions were included. Again, we need not elaborate this: it was an account of those elements of social structure which comprise a total society such as the other theorists had made clear; but again, it is worthwhile to note that Giddings was very systematic in this: showing, in each case, how the 'simple' modes of human action— appreciation, utilization, characterization, and socialization—were characteristically embodied in economic, legal, political, religious, educational (etc.) institutions in turn. The methodical elaboration of a complete system of analysis was very impressively carried out in all Giddings' work.

For our own purposes, however, it is clear enough how, on the basis of the analysis of 'practical activities', Giddings moved towards a systematic account of all the elements of social structure in a society as a whole. It was, in short, a 'structural-functional' model of the entire organizational framework of society, within which all the activities and experiences of men and the formation of their individual personalities could be systematically studied.

Perhaps the one remaining point which deserves emphasis before

549

leaving this aspect of Giddings' work is that, in this whole analysis, the element on which he placed most stress was that of 'socialization'. He did not stress this unduly, or conspicuously, but he did deal with it at rather greater length and with more elaboration than with the other components of his system. He analysed the kinds of resemblance which led men into various concerns with 'socialization', and emphasized, for example, the importance of *family and kinship ties*, the *mental and moral resemblances* which led men into activity resting upon common values, beliefs and purposes, and the *perception of 'potentialities'* of similarities between individuals and groups which led men to seek to cultivate certain kinds of activity and association rather than others. He also analysed the psychological factors involved in this 'consciousness' of the various kinds of resemblance: various kinds of reflective sympathy, affection and affinity, desire for recognition, and so on. And he discussed too the important aspects of the processes of *association* and *communication* (as objective factors) which led to the consolidation, extension, and cultivation of these subjectively-felt ties of resemblance. This emphasis upon the central importance of the characteristics of the system of *communications* in a society for the establishment of a sense of *community* and the closely related formation of *individual character*, was an especially important insight of Giddings, and we shall see later how this was also made a central consideration in the work of C. H. Cooley.

'Socialization', then, was one of the most important strands in Giddings' analysis of the entire social system, and it is clear that this stemmed from his central persuasion that varieties of 'consciousness of kind' lay at the heart of the forms of association in a society and his concern to understand the factors that gave rise to these and sustained them.

The continuous interplay of Conflict and Co-operation

In clarifying his 'structural-functional' analysis of the nature of a society and its parts: of a fabric of associations which was the persisting resultant of the accommodation to each other of many social activities—and all in relation to an environment and its resources, Giddings did not think of this for a moment as a process of accomplished harmony. On the contrary, he argued that in all societies, the manifold practical activities of men must always give rise to *both* conflict and co-operation. The very accommodation of groups and organizations and individuals to each other; the very business of modifying and restraining and compromising and deliberating upon, *different* interests, *different* policies, *different* purposes, but often with *common* concerns, principles, and widely agreed objectives; was evidence of the continuous give-and-take, stress-and-strain, of conflict and co-operation. And, indeed—Giddings held—one of the important ingredients of social progress was the growing recognition by men of the *benefits* of *diversity* in society; of the tolerance of differences as well as the enjoyment of resemblances.

The important thing, again, for us to notice is only that a 'structural-functional' way of analysing the nature of a society was *not* by any means identical with a *static* or *harmonious* conception of society. On the contrary, the *structure* of society was conceived as an order of institutions which persistently accommodated *both* conflict *and* co-operation and made possible the *tolerance* of conflict and the acceptance of *change*. Here again, Giddings was completely in agreement with all the other thinkers we have considered. Like them he thought that societies were essentially *historical* processes, in which *order* was commensurate with *conflict* and *change*. And indeed, like Spencer, Marx, Ward and Sumner, he saw this as an inescapable aspect of the continuous transforming processes of the *material universe*; it was an enduring characteristic of *nature*. Conflict and change were the very stuff of the 'forms' produced in the evolution of societies, just as they were in the evolution of other forms of nature.

Furthermore, Giddings believed that—no matter what the 'equilibrium' of institutional structure a society had developed—there were always factors which made for radical conflict, and potential disruption. These were, he wrote:

'. . . the instincts of conquest which are kept alive by the necessity of destroying life to maintain life, and the instincts of aggression that are kept alive by the opposition always met with by those individuals and populations that develop more rapidly than others. Wherever civilization finds itself face to face with savagery, or a young and growing civilization finds itself opposed to one old and decaying, the antagonism is too serious to expend itself in the lesser forms of secondary conflict.'

There were also radical differences between new sections of populations (e.g., immigrants) which were insufficiently 'assimilated' in the larger society; and occasional disruptions caused by disasters of natural fortune: such as a massive failure of crops, the unexpected spread of a plague, the destructiveness of floods, and the like.

There was then—once again—nothing approaching a 'static' conception of society, or a conception of 'functional harmony', in Giddings' 'structural-functional' system of analysis. This conception of the interdependent fabric of institutions *especially rested upon* a basic conception of a continuous interplay of conflict and co-operation, of *order* as an accommodation to elements of *difference* and

T

change. The network of institutions in a society was in part an embodiment of the *toleration* of diversity; which could be attended, in more complex societies, by a *subjective appreciation* (among their members) of the *positive value* of tolerance in society.

The one other aspect of this recognition of continuous conflict and co-operation in the conception of Giddings which we can simply note, was the element, in his system, of 'equilibrium-dis-equilibrium' analysis: another point of clear agreement with the earlier writers.

The psychological aspects of 'society'

It was in his careful analysis of the psychological aspects of all the processes of 'society', or 'association', that Giddings went distinctively beyond the earlier writers (with the possible exception of Ward). We have already seen the elements of the systematic way in which he examined the growth of the 'self' in the context of 'society', and it would be too elaborate a task to undertake a detailed exposition of his system here. It will be enough, however, if we see very carefully the way in which Giddings' 'sociological' perspective led him to understand the 'psychology' of the individual personality—for this is a fundamental position of sociology which must be made clear; and if we then go on to see clearly what Giddings had to say about the basic 'modes' of the 'social mind' and 'social nature' which had developed in different types of society.

(a) The insufficiency of a purely individual psychology for the under-standing of the individual
This is a point of the most fundamental importance. It is very simple; yet few people seem able clearly to comprehend it. It is as though people have a kind of mental 'blockage' against conceiving the 'individual' as being anything other than an entity bounded by his skin. By contrast, 'society' seems to them something vague and nebulous. It therefore goes without saying, for them, that 'society' can be explained in terms of 'individuals'; but that 'individual psychology' cannot possibly be derived from 'society'. Such a conception is an absolutely fundamental error, and one of the great merits of Giddings' writing was that it made this matter perfectly clear.

The qualities and characteristics which distinguish an individual human person from individual animals of other species are the elements of a *social nature,* and the qualities of mind resulting from *social* influence and *social* experiences, which he, or she, has come to possess. The very conception of 'self' and of his *own* 'self' which a person comes to have is an outcome of communication with others, and results from the observations and judgments which they make and which the person experiences from earliest childhood. The very *awareness of self* is a concomitant of social intercourse. But also all the elements of *judgment, value, belief, qualities of character, truth, taste,* and the awareness of the *language, symbols, gestures* and *art* in which these are all expressed are elements established in the individual's mind and feelings as a result of his *social experiences*. A large part of an individual's *personal* nature is *socially engendered*.

It follows from this that *society* is a collective associational process possessing psychological aspects within the context of which individual persons come to be what they are. And it also follows from this that to study the *individual* alone, in terms of something called *'individual psychology'* alone, cannot possibly provide a satisfactory knowledge of the individual. It must leave out all those dimensions of the person's nature which are attendant upon *social* processes. An analysis of *society*, a *social psychology*, is the only possible way in which we can come to an understanding of the nature of the individual.

Giddings wrote like this:

'There was a time when the human mind was studied as if it were an independent thing. The various states of mind were analysed and classified. No one thought of asking whether they had been produced by the interplay of the mind with other minds and with physical nature. In short, the mind was studied as if it had either existed from all time without change, or had instantly come into existence complete and fully prepared for the experiences of life.'*

However, he continued, the study of the individual mind could now be undertaken within the context of the changing, historical society in which it existed, and:

'In studying the mind from this evolutionary or genetic point of view, it is discovered that in almost every experience and in every stage of growth, the social intercourse of an individual with his fellow-beings is one of the chief influences at work upon his own processes of thought, affection, and will.'†

The sociological perspective is therefore necessary for a full understanding of the nature of the individual. Giddings, of course, went on to provide an analysis of this socio-psychological process, but it is enough for our purposes to have noted clearly this emphasis.

* *The Elements of Sociology*, Columbia University Press, Macmillan Co., New York, 1898, p. 95.
† *Ibid.*, p. 96.

In exactly the same way, Giddings was perfectly clear in guarding against possible misconceptions of this point, and it is here that his position, or rather his statement of this position, may be favourably compared with that of Durkheim—to whom we shall come later.

One of the commonest misconceptions of this position, and indeed one of the commonest dangers to which it is prone, is the idea that it is claiming that there exists in society a 'consciousness' or a 'collective psychology' *additional* to all the conscious individual minds and *independent* of them: hanging like some great metaphysical ceiling over their heads, and *determining* them. But of course this conception suggests nothing of the kind. It merely insists that human minds *in association with each other* have a collective, creative outcome which is different from what each individual mind could possibly be in isolation. The *association* of minds is a *creative* process. It brings into being an accumulative fabric of institutions, symbols, languages, regulated modes of conduct, stocks of knowledge, proverbs, customs, shared judgments, all of which persist as a traditional heritage which influences subsequent minds, and *none* of which could be said to exist in any one individual mind *before* it experienced *association with others*. There exists in society no 'conscious mind' independent of individual minds, but yet the 'associational activity of intercommunicating minds' is a *level* of creative psychological experience on which these individual minds could not, and would not operate, excepting in this associational activity. This is such an important matter that we should note exactly how Giddings expressed it.

'There is no reason', he wrote, 'to suppose that society is a great being which is conscious of itself through some mysterious process of thinking, separate and distinct from the thinking that goes on in the brains of individual men. At any rate, there is no possible way yet known to man of proving that there is any such supreme social consciousness.

'Nevertheless, there is a group of facts of great interest to the sociologist and to the man of affairs for which the name "the social mind" can, with entire propriety and with great convenience, be used . . . We have shown that the most essential fact in society is like-mindedness, meaning by this term a close resemblance between the ideas, emotions, and preferences of any given individual and those of other individuals who live in the same social group with him. It has been shown also that such like-minded individuals usually discover their mental and moral resemblances, think about them, take pleasure in them, and turn them to good account in many useful ways.

'When, then, two or more individuals at the same moment are receiving like sensations, perceiving the same relations, experiencing the same kind of emotion, thinking the same thoughts, arriving in their judgments at the same conclusion—a state of facts exists in the population which evidently must be classed among facts of mind, and yet must be distinguished from the mental activity of an individual who, absolutely alone, completely cut off from communication with his fellow-men, thinks solely about himself and his immediate material surroundings. In the one case there exists a *concert* of the emotions and thoughts of two or more individuals; in the other case, the thought of the individual is peculiar to himself and his isolated condition.

'To the group of facts that may be described as the simultaneous like-mental-activity of two or more individuals in communication with one another, or as a concert of the emotion, thought, and will of two or more communicating individuals, we give the name, the social mind. This name, accordingly, should be regarded as meaning just this group of facts *and nothing more*. It does not mean that there is any other consciousness than that of individual minds. It *does mean that individual minds act simultaneously in like ways and continually influence one another; and that certain mental products result from such combined mental action which could not result from the thinking of an individual who had no communication with fellow-beings.*'*

If that is not perfectly clear, then heaven help us all!

Giddings then went on to analyse the nature of these 'social-mental' processes. At the simplest level of all, he described the awareness among people of a sheer *simultaneous similarity of response* which, with the awareness, came to have a 'concerted' power: as, for example, when people became suddenly aware of a common terror and panicked into an explosion of blind action. Secondly he discussed the consolidation of social feelings, conceptions and ties which came as a *reciprocal consciousness of kind* developed among a people. Thirdly, he analysed the way in which '*symbols*' came to be created as part of the collective culture of a people and served to focus and canalize their feelings, conceptions and energies. That Giddings did not think that these were necessarily wisely based was reflected in the fact that he referred to them as 'Shibboleths' as well as 'Emblems'. Fourthly, he described the integration and consolidation of a people's shared values, judgments and orientations of ideas and actions which came about with the developed consciousness of a shared *historical tradition*: when the collective culture of a people linked the living with the past, and possessed a powerful authority over new generations. And finally, he distinguished the formation of shared *public opinion* which came with the opportunity and practice of critical, rational deliberation and the dissemination of knowledge in society. This again was all redolent of the ways in which Ward and Sumner were thinking, but the aspects of Giddings' analysis here which it is most important to select for special emphasis is what he called the 'Modes of Social Action'.

* *The Elements of Sociology*, pp. 119–21.

(b) *The Modes of Social Action*

The entire analysis of the elements and processes at work in the emergence of various types of 'consciousness of kind', and the development of 'social aspects of mind' was of basic importance in Giddings' mind for one central reason: because it provided the necessary basis for understanding the *social action* which men pursued. These elements of 'social mind' resulted, he argued, in 'common purposes and concerted acts', and one important and necessary part of sociology was the *explanation of social action*. Here, the 'teleological' emphasis of Ward was clearly evident, and agreed upon, but Giddings provided an excellent analysis of *'types of social action'* which possessed originality and, to my mind, is of the greatest interest for us because of its important prospective reference to the later work of Max Weber.

Giddings distinguished three types of social action: Impulsive, Traditional, and Rational, and each of these rested upon a distinctively different kind of 'Like-Mindedness'. The similarity between Giddings' treatment and the later notions of Weber is so staggering (it is almost an *identical* typology) that we simply must see in more than cursory fashion what he said about each 'type'.

(I) SYMPATHETIC LIKE-MINDEDNESS AND IMPULSIVE SOCIAL ACTION

Impulsive social action was that which sprang from immediate impulse and the simplest kind of 'contagious' sympathetic feeling of which men were aware. It issued in action without intervening reasons or deliberation, and tended to be, therefore, a 'blind' response to feeling. The simplest examples of this were those rooted in 'panic' conditions or 'crowd' situations, but Giddings also saw this kind of social action as playing a very important part in the ongoing events and affairs of historical societies, since it could spring from conditions of ignorance, and could therefore be played upon by leaders and *élites*, as well as being aggravated by unexpected social conditions—such as chronic unemployment, poverty, mass-deprivation, and the like.

'The simplest combination of the feelings and ideas of a number of individuals', Giddings wrote, 'is that which occurs sympathetically and imitatively without the intervention of any process of critical thinking. The panic of a terrified crowd was mentioned as one of the lamentable forms that sympathetic mental activity may assume. That the like-mindedness which is purely sympathetic, imitative, or emotional should be impulsive and hasty in action, is inevitable . . . This action takes place without any thought process or critical reasoning . . .

'A good chess player does not move his piece until he has thought out all the possible moves that he can make, and has decided which one is, all things considered, the best. A poor player sees, at the most, only two or three of the possible moves; and seeing so little to think about, he moves much sooner than a superior antagonist. These conditions are not changed when men act together in large numbers. On the contrary, if they have natures that are sensitive to every impression that is made upon their senses, if they are sympathetic and quick to imitate, if they have but little power of patient deliberation—they are quick to act, and their action is impulsive, emotional, lacking in coolness of judgment, and perhaps disastrous to themselves and others. Especially is this true if they are by nature or circumstance subject to . . . suggestion; if they respond unconsciously to an idea.'*

This 'suggestibility' made possible the influencing of some men by others to 'impulsive action'. In the most subtle ways, Giddings wrote:

'. . . thoughts and courses of action are often suggested to men in crowds. A skilful public speaker can work a crowd to a great pitch of excitement by artfully insinuating the truth of that which he wishes them to believe, or the wisdom of that which he wishes them to do, while apparently directing his argument upon some quite different question.'†

Giddings' conception of the extensiveness of this kind of social action in society may be seen in the following passage.

'A large part of all the social action in which many individuals take a concerted part is impulsive rather than deliberate; and therefore many of the dramatic events of history have been impulsive social actions . . .

'Sometimes these events are violent in character, taking the form of riots, lynchings, and turbulent conduct in connection with strikes or lockouts. Sometimes they are entirely peaceful and lawful, but none the less hasty and inconsiderate—as when a legislative body, moved by a wave of popular feeling, enacts a law without deliberation, simply assuming that the popular belief or demand is to be accepted at its face value without opposition or criticism. Sometimes an entire nation is thus wrought up to impulsive action which carries it onward to frightful disaster.'‡

Giddings then went on to analyse the conditions which gave rise to impulsive social action: discussing in turn the physical, geographical and climatic conditions of a people; their 'mental conditions'—as, for example, the conditions of fear, ignorance, and subjection in which they might be held in a society; 'crowd' conditions; and the like. Following upon this, he stated certain 'laws' of the relationship between the incidence of impulsive social action and these conditions: laws which, he thought, could be useful in controlling such action. We have seen clearly, however, how Giddings characterized this 'type' of social action and the part it played in society.

* *The Elements of Sociology*, pp. 129–31.   † *Ibid.*, p. 132.   ‡ *Ibid.*, p. 132.

(II) FORMAL LIKE-MINDEDNESS: TRADITIONAL SOCIAL ACTION

Traditional social action was still chiefly based upon the 'sympathetic emotional, imitative' modes of mental activity—as distinct from rational and deliberative thought; but, unlike impulsive social action, it did not spring from ungoverned impulse, but from feeling governed by the acceptance of the traditional, customary beliefs, values, ideas of the community. Traditional social action was action in conformity with the 'authority' of customary usage, and it rested upon the 'formal like-mindedness' of the people of the community whose feelings were all similarly governed; whose traditional values and beliefs were shared. It will be seen that this kind of social action rested distinctively upon *'belief'*, and the *'authority* of traditional belief', as against critically assessed, rationally demonstrable *knowledge.*

The great body of ideas, values, precepts inherited by a community could be collectively called its 'Tradition'. And, Giddings wrote:

'The popular acceptance of tradition—of beliefs that have been handed down from past generations—and obedience to the rules and precepts that are embodied in the various traditions, are modes of like-mindedness. But, unlike those described in the preceding chapter, they are not spontaneous or impulsive; they are rather to be described as formal like-mindedness. They are analogous to habit in the individual mind.'*

This 'formal like-mindedness', and its strength and authority, was produced, Giddings held, by two factors in particular: firstly, the *reinforcing* power of the knowledge that beliefs were shared by others—in both the present and the past—in whom people have confidence, and secondly, the power of education, including habitual discipline.

On the first of these, Giddings wrote:

'The tendency of the mind to accept as true whatever is vividly imagined or ardently desired, if no critical activity of the reason intervenes, is enormously strengthened when the thing believed . . . is already believed by other persons in whom the individual has personal confidence . . . In short the consciousness of kind is a powerful element in the growth of popular belief.

'Yet further is the tendency to believe strengthened by the knowledge that not only one's contemporaries believe, but that preceding generations for ages past also have believed. The presumption in favour of the truth of the belief has become enormous, not only because its antiquity is an impressive fact appealing to imagination, but because, if the critical intelligence begins to question, it is likely to be easily satisfied by the reflection that if the belief were untrue, its falsity must long ago have been discovered and exposed.

* *The Elements of Sociology,* p. 152.

'Tradition thus acquired in human society all the tremendous force of authority. Authority is a moral power that constrains man's will without his knowing or being able to find out why. It is born of emotion and belief rather than of reason, which is ever asking the wherefore and the why. Nevertheless, since reason and rational self-control are of slow growth, the authority of tradition serves a useful end in helping to maintain social order.'*

And on the second—the factor of direct teaching, discipline, and habituation—he wrote as follows:

'Tradition is imposed upon the child by his parents and elder acquaintances. He is directly taught that the traditional beliefs are true, and that it is even wrong to doubt their truth and authority. Disbelief is often punished; and disobedience of traditional precept is punished usually. Not only so, but through the intimate association between tradition and the everyday activities of life, the child insensibly associates the practical activity with its traditional background. In his economic life, in his legal relations and political activities, he can take no single step without practically accepting most of the traditional system. Daily life thus becomes a ceaseless discipline and drill in activities which openly or tacitly assume the truth and sufficiency of tradition . . .

'The routine of habitual activity, the teaching and the discipline of life, continually tend to produce formal like-mindedness, including conformity to established customs.'†

As we might suppose, Giddings believed that 'traditional' social action played a very large part indeed in the ordered patterns of action in all societies. We can see how similar his conception was to Sumner's analysis of the formation of the 'folkways and mores' and Ward's analysis of the 'genetic' building up of a social order. In his discussion of the *kinds* and *sequences* of traditional social action, however, his great similarity to all the other men we have considered was clearly apparent.

Basing his analysis upon his earlier account of men's 'simple' and 'complex' kinds of 'practical activities', Giddings distinguished three orders of tradition: primary, secondary, and tertiary. The *primary* tradition in any society was the accumulated body of ideas, values, symbols, precepts, and procedures which had become the embodiment of its economic, legal, and political activities. These three were directly and intimately related to each other; indeed, in his conception of the *sequence* of these, Giddings was very close to the teaching of Marx. The economic tradition, he claimed, was 'probably the first to grow out of human experience'. The juristic tradition '. . . grows out of the relations of antagonistic equals', and was second in importance, and: 'the political tradition is developed

* *The Elements of Sociology*, p. 152.   † *Ibid.*, p. 153.

out of the economic and juridical traditions, and in its evolution is closely interwoven with them.' This similarity is also clearly seen in the fact that Giddings classified the 'ideological' traditions of men—their religions, poetry, art, etc.,—as the *'secondary'* order of traditions.

However, too close a parallel must not be drawn. Giddings' point of distinction was really that the *primary* order of traditions dealt with human experience of, and relations with, the *tangible* world, whereas the *secondary* order of traditions dealt with men's impressions of the intangible elements of their experience of the world.

The third order was that of *'tertiary'* traditions, and these were the traditions forming and governing systems of *conceptual thought*. These constituted a record of 'reasoning and speculative thinking rather than of mere impression and belief', said Giddings, and he then went on to describe the *three* chief tertiary traditions (systems of conceptual thought) which were distinguishable in a comparative and historical study of societies. And here again, we must look at his own words, because in them we can see how completely he drew into his system the generalizations of Comte. Here—quite plainly and deliberately—Giddings utilized Comte's law 'of the three stages'; his conception of the three 'types of social order' resting on three distinctive systems of 'knowledge'.

'The oldest of the tertiary traditions', wrote Giddings, 'is the *theological tradition*, which was created by an elaborate process of reasoning and speculation upon the materials furnished by popular religious beliefs. It is the sum and record of attempts to demonstrate by reason the existence of a personal God, to explain his nature and purposes, and to prove that he created and providentially governs the world and man.

'The second of the tertiary traditions is the *metaphysical*. It has been derived from the theological. It refines the theological explanation of the universe by interposing "secondary causes", laws, and principles between phenomena and their ultimate cause—the fiat of God.

'The third of the tertiary traditions is the *scientific*. The scientific tradition is the sum of our actual knowledge of the world and of man as distinguished from our conjectures about them. It is the sifted record of observations, experiments, and classifications. Making no attempt to penetrate the final mystery of existence, the scientific tradition explains the constitution of the world only to the extent of showing how one thing is related to other things in sequence and in coexistence.'*

It is abundantly clear in Giddings' treatment of the types of social action how practically all the conceptions we have considered earlier were brought together, and found their place, within a systematic whole. The making of sociology was clearly being undertaken as a critically creative, a systematizing process of knitting together the

* *The Elements of Sociology*, p. 151.

various contributions as they arose. But it was not being done conspicuously or dramatically: it was assumed to be part and parcel of the continuous, deliberative effort which was directed to the satisfactory creation of the new science. In the work of Giddings this was very marked, and it is worthwhile to notice, too, that he made no attempt whatever to *appear original* in all this. On the contrary, he openly utilized the contributions and conceptions of others as the 'building blocks' of the science which all scholars concerned were trying to fit together. It was assumed to be an argumentative co-operative, creative inter-communication of scholarship throughout.

So much, however, for Giddings' clarification of 'traditional' social action.

(III) RATIONAL SOCIAL ACTION: THE FORMATION OF PUBLIC OPINION AND SOCIAL VALUES

The third 'type' of social action was that characterized by 'rationality' and resting crucially on critical judgment and knowledge. Giddings distinguished sharply between 'public belief' (still resting upon emotion and traditional authority) and 'public opinion'—which was the formation of considered judgments following a process of critical reflection and involving, therefore, clearly defined *rational* criteria.

'Public opinion', he wrote, 'comes into existence only when a sympathetic like-mindedness or an agreement in belief is subjected to criticism, started by some sceptical individual who doubts the truth of the belief or the wisdom of the agreement; and an opinion is then thought out to which many communicating minds can yield their rational assent.'*

The very *possibility* of rational deliberation and rational social action necessitated certain conditions. Public opinion developed in any community, Giddings maintained:

'... just to the extent that men are in the habit of asking searching questions and compelling one another to prove their assertions.

'Public opinion, therefore, can exist only where men are in continual communication, and where they are free to express their real minds, without fear or restraint. Wherever men are forbidden by governmental or other authority to assemble, to hold meetings, to speak or write freely, or wherever they stand in fear of losing social position, or employment, or property, if they freely speak their minds, there is no true public opinion; there is only a mass of traditional beliefs or outbursts of popular feeling.†

'The *essential condition* of deliberate social decision is the alternation of meeting and discussion with separation.'

Rational social action always grew out of critical reflection upon impulsive and traditional social action, and Giddings went on to

* *The Elements of Sociology*, p. 155.   † *Ibid.*, p. 156.

show how—in each sphere of practical and social activity—new rational elements came to be blended with earlier traditional elements. Thus traditional economic methods of technique and exchange came to be modified by rational calculation of production for complex market situations. Custom came to be amended and replaced by legal reforms and legal codes. Traditional political authority came to be changed by new rationally devised political constitutions and public 'policies' of all kinds. And in the same way, science itself grew out of the questioning and challenging of previously uncritically accepted beliefs.

Rationality also brought with it the considered clarification of new personal and social *values*, and these—related to every aspect of personal and social life in more complex societies—were different from earlier *traditional* values in that their basis of *authority* no longer lay simply in the fact of immemorial usage and emotional acceptance, but in the *reasons that could be given for holding them*. This was an extremely important change, because, with the emergence, development and extension of rationality, the clarification of the rational values on which the entire process of rational deliberation and rational social action rested became supremely necessary. Without this clarification, the disruption of traditional values by rational criticism might leave—only a vacuum! Here again, we see in the American writers this strong awareness of the central importance of *values in society*; this vision of values as the *very mesh of social institutions*—as the thread of regulation that fastens together the entire fabric of the social order; and this is a central insight which we shall come to focus on with very powerful insistence a little later.

Giddings, like Ward, emphasized the growing importance of rational, self-direction in society and wished to point to the *continuous efforts* which it entailed. He was well aware that many denied and decried the efforts of reason in society; but this was his answer:

'Social values are the grounds of rational social choice, and of all action of the social will that is deliberate rather than impulsive.

'There have been writers on Sociology who have denied that masses of men ever act rationally. They have argued that as men differ less in feeling than in intelligence, and as men in crowds are peculiarly susceptible to emotion and suggestion, the intellectual processes have, under such circumstances, very little opportunity to manifest themselves.

'Nevertheless, there is abundant historical proof that communities do oftentimes arrive at rational decisions, after many years of persistent discussion of the merits of the question. Among excellent examples have been most of the amendments to the constitution of the United States, and to the constitutions of the several commonwealths.'*

* *The Elements of Sociology*, p. 167.

Giddings did however, as we have seen before, think that some (more able) men could influence others of lesser ability and greater ignorance, and it is necessary just to note that he undoubtedly adopted an 'élitist' view in this matter.

The 'classes' of society

In almost exactly the same way as Sumner, Giddings drew upon the work of Galton and conceived of every total population (in an entire society) as consisting of various proportions of people possessing differing ranges of intelligence and ability. His notion of 'classes' in society was therefore of this kind, rather than of the nature of 'socio-economic strata' as we now tend to think of them. We need not here elaborate Giddings' treatment of this aspect of his analysis —it was so similar to that of Sumner; but it is worthwhile to note how strongly he conceived the role of the intellectual, moral, social *élite* to be. It was this proportion of any society, in his view, which was responsible for the extent and effectiveness of such rational progress as it achieved; and—in our very egalitarian age—Giddings seemed uncomfortably definite and direct about this.

'Men and women', he wrote, 'who have health, originality, and that unselfish love of mankind which moves them to devote their efforts to promoting the social welfare, certainly deserve to be recognized as, in the truest sense of the word, superior to their fellow-beings.

'This superior section of the social class is the most efficient class in the community. Small as it is in numbers, it accomplishes the greater part of those undertakings which, in their totality, we call progress. It gives to society the new inventions, the improvements in law, industry, art, religion, and morals which make life richer in its achievements and larger in its possibilities. It is this class alone that deserves to be called an *élite* or an aristocracy.'*

This pre-eminent social class, Giddings maintained, 'does most of the original thinking for society'; it 'does most of the leading, directing, and organizing'; and, in the long run, 'the unwritten laws of society' are made by it.

All we need notice here, however, is that in the changing nature of the 'consciousness of kind' in the various associations of society; in the changing, cumulative social systems of traditions, symbols, and rational procedures; and in the sequences of change from one 'mode' of social action to another; Giddings takes into account the differential part played by various sections of the population—from the few

* *The Elements of Sociology*, pp. 113–14.

of markedly high ability to the masses whose ability and condition of knowledge is relatively low.

In these ways, then, Giddings gave a systematic account of the 'psychological aspects of society' and the several 'types of social action' and it will have been seen that this account included, quite clearly, both the 'genetic' and the 'teleological' components distinguished and insisted upon by Ward. All this, however, Giddings framed within the context of a strictly organizational analysis of the structure of society, and a theory of the evolution and progress of 'types' of society, and to round out his entire system we must glance quickly at this 'societal' account.

Before doing this, however, let us pause again just to reiterate deliberately and emphatically this central and continuing point. We have seen—clearly, and with not a vestige of doubt—that in the system of sociological analysis offered by Giddings *all* the following components: a structural-functional account of the nature of societies; an essentially historical account of social change involving *both* conflict *and* co-operation; a psychological account of the relations between individual and society and of the 'psychological aspects' of all the elements of social structure and forms of association; a subjective understanding of several 'types' of social action; an analysis of populations in the contexts of their environments; and a theory of social evolution and progress—*were combined*, and seen as being *essential parts and dimensions* of a satisfactory way of conceiving, studying, and producing testable knowledge about societies as whole social systems. *All these elements were interrelated parts of Giddings' system*—just as they had been in the work of all the other men we have studied. Here we will simply note this—with a kind of dogged insistence, and later its full significance will be seen.

To conclude our study of Giddings, however, let us look briefly at his analysis of 'social organization' and his picture of 'social evolution' because it is important to see how the 'types of social action' were seen to be correlated with, and seen in the context of, specific changes of social organization and 'types of society'.

Elements of social organization

Giddings' analysis of the components of the organizational structure of society has already been indicated briefly in section (iv) above, but it is worthwhile to note this a little more fully now. Very much like Ward and Sumner, Giddings thought of the formation of the established structure of society as being the outcome of a two-fold process. In the thronging practical activities of men, in the context of conflict and co-operation, certain spontaneous ways of doing things and regulating relationships emerged, and those which were most advantageous in shared experience came to be supported and became habitual and 'customary'. These came also to be connected in unforeseen and unintended ways (i.e., had unintended consequences) so that they came to assume, to some degree, the nature of an interconnected 'system'. This was Ward's 'genetic' order and Sumner's network of 'folkways'. At some point, however, and for some reasons, men came to be consciously aware of these established elements of order and came to reflect upon them, to challenge them, to deliberate about them and to change them or reinforce them. In short, a formal conscious, purposeful 're-making' of the social order took place and a conscious furthering or creation of new forms of social organization was undertaken in the light of new knowledge and new purposes. This was Ward's 'teleological' development, and Sumner's development of the 'mores' and subsequent 'law-making' which grew out of reflection upon the 'folkways'. The conception was the same; but the *elements* of social structure which Giddings specified were these.

First of all he distinguished '*institutions*' from the less formal and reflective relationships in society.

'An institution', he wrote, 'is a *social relation that is established by adequate and rightful authority*. The ultimate source of authority in society is the social mind. Consequently, those forms of organization, those relations and arrangements which the social mind has reflected upon, which it has accepted, allowed, or commanded—and those only—are institutions.'*

Secondly, the structure of society could in part be analysed in terms of its '*Social Composition*' which consisted of various '*component societies*' (each with its own particular 'consciousness of kind'). And thirdly, in part it could be analysed in terms of its '*Social Constitution*' which was the entire network of social organization formed by its '*constituent societies*' (again, each with its own appropriate 'consciousness of kind').

The component societies which made up the entire composition of society were wholly or partly aggregations of kindred: wholly, for example, in the case of families, and perhaps some villages; partly, in the case of cities and distinctive territorial regional communities. In the latter cases, various factors making for kinds of 'congregation' existed in addition to the purely 'genetic' (i.e., in this sense—blood-kinship) social bond. Under this heading of 'component societies', Giddings discussed families, tribal societies, ethnic groups, and groupings of a non-kinship nature. As 'ethnic societies', he analysed

* *The Elements of Sociology*, p. 175.

hordes, tribes, confederations of tribes, and distinguished groups based upon matriarchal and patriarchal principles.

Under the heading of constituent societies, Giddings dealt with all *organized forms of association*—from those which were actually a part of the simpler 'component societies': such as the 'household', the 'clan', and other 'tribal' associations, to those large-scale associations of complex societies such as the highly organized components in the constitutions of 'civil societies' up to the organization of the 'State' itself. Here, his picture was one of an increasing differentiation of specialized *associations* as society became larger and more complicated, and as rational social action increased over earlier traditional forms. Here, it is worthwhile to note in detail his own conception of such a specialized 'association' because it is useful to compare it with the picture of institutional development put forward by Ward and Sumner.

'Every purposive association', Giddings wrote, 'has not only a function but also a composition and a constitution which are adapted to the performance of the function.

'In the composition of purposive association, individuals are combined as persons and by categories; for example, the categories of employer and employee, in the composition of an industrial group. The composition of associations must be studied with reference to the common trait or interest that unites their members.

'The constitution of a purposive association is the plan of organization of its membership. The categories of individuals which compose it are combined in accordance with some principle of subordination or coordination; and the entire membership may be divided into sub-societies, bureaus, or committees.'*

Later, this may also be compared with Malinowski's conception of an 'institution', but we might note here the several important elements into which an 'association' can be broken down by analysis. It has a 'composition' and a 'constitution' specifically related to the pursuit or performance of a 'function'. It has also a definite 'personnel', the members of which are organized in certain 'categories' or roles and in certain relationships of authority, and certain operational 'groups' (such as committees). The members are also related to each other in terms of *some* 'consciousness of kind'; some 'traits' or 'interests' which unite them.

It will be seen at once that Giddings' analysis of the entire organization of a society dissected every element of association—from the most massive structure of the 'state', through all the large-scale elements of the 'legal system', the 'economic system', the 'religious

* *The Elements of Sociology*, p. 200. Compare with Sumner, p. 529, and Malinowski: *The Making of Sociology*, Vol. 2, Part Four. Ch. 1.

system', the 'educational system', right down to the specific specialist association, even the 'household'; and, furthermore, that his analysis of association dissected social structure right down to the specific roles which individual persons fulfilled. This was therefore a satisfactory 'schema' of analysis—embracing every detail from social structure at the most large-scale and general level, to the formal tasks of individuals, the complexes of roles which they had to fulfil.

Giddings also elaborated his analysis further to take into account public and private organizations, incorporated and unincorporated organizations, and voluntary organizations in all fields of social activity: political, legal, economic, cultural, etc.;* but these we need only mention. Here again, there was a strong similarity between Giddings' treatment and the distinction which Sumner made between 'crescive' and 'enacted' institutions.

One final aspect of Giddings' account of the elements of social organization which must be stressed, is the fact that he saw all these elements as being *interrelated* in a close way—in the sense of interdependence and interaction—in the 'system' of society as a whole. His way of formulating this conception made it clear that there was an 'order' of authority and subordination *among* them as well as *within* each of them, and also that he did *not*—despite his emphasis upon 'practical activities' and their primacy—hold any kind of 'material determinism', but agreed closely with Ward that men, in furthering their knowledge and deliberation, acted purposively to shape the structure of society towards the attainment of their ends. It is clear, too, that Giddings saw the proliferation of 'associations' of 'constituent societies', as part and parcel *not* of social *disorder*, but the gradual achievement of a more *flexible* social order in which rational action and the pursuit of a diversity of purposes was both possible and tolerated. It was, in short, a process of enriching society and the creation of a kind of order which made continuous progress possible. Again, we see Comte's dictum of 'order' and 'progress' writ large. Giddings put the matter simply like this:

'The various organizations of society are not only correlated, but are also subordinated, some to other organizations, and all to a general end. The supreme end of society in general is the protection and perfecting of sentient life. The end of human society is the development of the rational and spiritual personality of its members. Only the cultural associations are immediately concerned in this function. Educational institutions, religious,

* For example: political parties, associations for political reform, voluntary boards of arbitration, societies for preventing cruelty to children and animals, or for enforcing sanitary laws or temperance laws, industrial firms, partnerships, corporations, associations of employers and workmen, churches, sects, charity organizations, etc.

GIDDINGS' SYSTEM OF ANALYSIS

THE SOCIAL SYSTEM

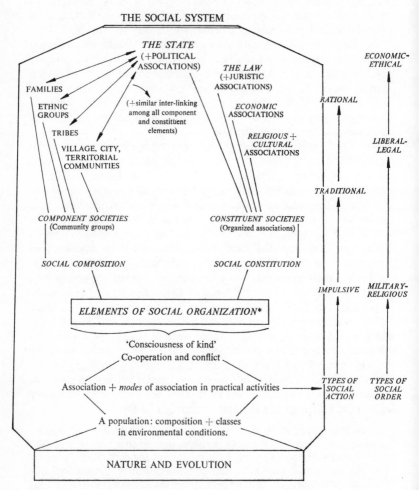

* Again, it would be too complicated to depict *all* the elements of social organization Giddings included, and the complex interlinkings between all component and constituent elements. These diagrams can only be indicative.

scientific, ethical, and aesthetic organizations, and polite society act for good or ill directly upon the individual. To these the economic, the legal, and the political organization are, in a functional sense, subordinate. In a functional sense, they exist for the sake of cultural organization and activity. The social mind has always perceived this truth, and by means of its sanctions has endeavoured to mould the social constitution into accordance with it. Associations and relationships are fostered or abolished with a view to cultural no less than to protective ends.

'For both ends specialization and a division of labour are necessary. Therefore, while society maintains the homogeneity of its composition, it is obliged to tolerate and to promote differentiation in its constitution. Psychologically, therefore, the social constitution is the precise opposite of the social composition. It is an alliance, in each simple association, of individuals who, in respect to the purpose of the association, must be mentally and morally alike, but who in all other respects may be unlike; supplemented in the relations of associations to one another and to integral society by toleration and coordination of the unlike . . .

'We may state the law of development of the social constitution as follows: *The development of the social constitution depends upon the growth of an appreciation of the value of variety or unlikeness in society.*

'The social constitution, therefore, is the result of a desire to combine variety with homogeneity in a complex unity.'*

Having clarified his conception of the composition and constitution of society as a whole (i.e., having clarified his 'social statics'), Giddings then described the various types of society, and the actual process of change, growth, evolution, development, and progress of which historical and comparative studies provided knowledge. (i.e. He then undertook his 'social dynamics': using his analysis of the nature of society in the empirical study of the concrete varieties of society which had existed, and did exist, in the world.)

Social Evolution and Social Progress

In his account of the evolution and progress of societies, Giddings accepted and adopted Spencer almost exactly. We need not, therefore, study this very elaborately. Our chief concern is to *see* that this similarity was there, and accepted, and, in particular, to see clearly how—in this picture of evolution and progress—Giddings drew together, in a completely systematic way, all the strands of analysis we have mentioned so far.

The first thing to emphasize is that, in addition to the components of analysis he had so far clarified—his structural-functional model, his study of the psychological aspects of society, his study of types of

* *The Elements of Sociology*, pp. 214–15.

social action, and the like—he now insisted that the *historical* and *comparative* methods of study were essential parts of sociology. Society was a *historical* process, and historical study was necessary for the understanding of it. Also, it was impossible to judge and test the generalizations arising from sociological analysis without empirical, comparative studies. Historical and comparative studies were necessary for the straightforward descriptive awareness of the nature of diverse societies, and for the sharper testing of theories.

Giddings' account of social evolution, and his description of 'types of society', followed Spencer even in using the two methods of classification: the clarification of the nature of societies in accordance with their 'degree of composition' or 'aggregation', and by the method of constructing 'types' which selectively emphasized the main characteristics in which one was hypothetically interested—i.e., the construction of models.

On the basis of the 'degree of composition', Giddings traced the development of societies in a large-scale manner. He discussed the 'sub-human', 'sub-social' animal ancestry of man and analysed what, in terms of our knowledge, appeared to be the earliest growths of social traditions. Then, from a description of various kinds of 'Tribal Society', he traced the several factors of amalgamation, growth, conquest, which led to 'Tribal Feudalism' and the emergence of the 'Ethnic Nation'. From this, he described the processes of trading and migration which, again, had led to the extension of civilization over greater areas, and had given rise to 'Developed Feudalism', and, with commercial complexity especially and the growth of towns and great cities, the 'Civic Nation', and the larger civilizations which had resulted from the various kinds of inter-connection between these. In all this, whilst accepting Spencer, Giddings did not simply *reiterate* Spencer. This picture of the various forms of societies and the pattern of social evolution which could be discerned among them was put forward on the basis of a very rich historical knowledge. Much detail was produced in its clear elaboration.

It is also important to note that—like Spencer—Giddings did *not* maintain that *all* societies experienced *all* these 'stages'; or that the process of evolution, once begun, was *inevitable*. He discussed societies in the contexts of their environmental situations, and readily saw that some societies remained relatively unchanged over long periods, whilst the environmental conditions remained unchanged. But also, and more important, he analysed the several components of social organization involved in the nature of a society in changing from one 'type' to another, and claimed, quite clearly, that some societies remained in a certain condition as an outcome of deliberate policy. He analysed, for example, the role of military organization, religious and ecclesiastical hierarchies, detailed administrative bureaucracies, and—to give but one example—he argued that, when a certain large-scale power and sufficiency had been reached, some societies deliberately 'isolated' themselves from others: with a resulting traditional continuity lasting for millennia. He wrote, for example:

'When national unity and power have fairly been achieved and the nation is in no immediate danger of overthrow by more powerful enemies, a further policy often carried out is that of isolation. Feeling the superiority of its culture and institutions to those of other peoples, the nation endeavours in a measure to cut itself off from intercourse with them, lest foreign laws and manners shall corrupt, contaminate, and disintegrate the national life. This policy may perhaps have its justification under exceptional circumstances; but usually it has been a step towards national decay. It has been a chief factor in producing what are called "arrested civilizations", like those of China and Persia.'*

There was, therefore, nothing 'inevitable' or 'unilinear' about Giddings' account of social evolution. It was a portrayal of the kinds of amalgamation, confederation, assimilation, growth, increasing complexity of social organization which *had* taken place in many societies; a 'schema' of 'degrees of composition' which could be clarified by bringing together such knowledge as we possessed of all societies; but it was a *causal* analysis within this schema which could explain how societies became *unstable* as well as *stable*; how they *diminished* as well as *grew*; *declined* and *dissolved* as well as *developed* into greater *complexities*; or even became relatively '*arrested*' in continuing conditions. As we saw with Spencer, it made possible a kind of 'If . . . then . . .' analysis which was perfectly clear and could examine any kinds or directions of change.

In order to be exactly clear about the framework of Giddings' description of the emergence of 'Civilization'—i.e., the social and cultural system of the 'Civic Nations'—and to see perfectly clearly its complete agreement with Ward, let us see how he summarized this. It is necessary to note, in the following passage, that Giddings used the word 'demogenic' to mean social processes stemming from a 'people', a 'demos', with a shared awareness of each other, and of their social unity, going *beyond* 'kinship' membership (which is termed 'ethnogenic' association).

'Civilization', wrote Giddings, 'is the first stage of demogenic association. As zoogenic association was that earliest social intercourse which developed the forms of animal life; as anthropogenic association was that more varied

* *The Elements of Sociology*, p. 285.

intercourse which created the human mind; as ethnogenic association was that organized intercourse which created a folk; so demogenic association is that intercourse, both varied and organized, which develops great civic peoples, ever increasing in wealth and in population, and ever growing more democratic in mind.

'Civilization cannot be defined in a phrase, because it includes many things, all of which are essential. It consists in the adoption of a permanent territorial home and of habits of settled life; in the supremacy of the state and, therefore, of the social constitution over the entire social composition; in the substitution of mental and moral resemblance for kinship, as a basis of social organization;· in the assimilation of various population elements in a new and larger ethnic unity; in an integration of the social composition; and in an increasing homogeneity in politics, religion, manners, and habits. Chief among these elements of civilization, however, is that sympathetic and traditional like-mindedness which is unlimited by ties of kinship and which, manifesting itself in a passion for homogeneity in the nation, creates those policies of military discipline, religious conformity, and moral requirement that result in national and social unity.

'The homogeneity of the civic nation has had two consequences without which those further developments of society and of human life to be described under the head of Progress could not have appeared . . . Liberty depends upon homogeneity in the population. In its earliest stages, civilization allowed little freedom to the individual. It permitted no growth of the voluntary forms of organization in the social constitution. But by hastening the processes of assimilation, by eliminating irreconcilable differences from the social population, by creating homogeneity, sympathetic and traditional like-mindedness, it did prepare populations for liberty later on. It made men fit for the self-government and the voluntary enterprise of a second stage of demogenic association.'*

This passage is particularly useful for our understanding of Giddings, because it is in considering this 'second stage of demogenic association' that he developed Spencer's second method of classification—the construction of 'types' to highlight certain major considerations, and also linked his conception of *progress* to the ideas of *development* and *evolution*. There is also a striking accordance here, though it is expressed in very different terms, with Marx's idea that the entire development of human society so far has been the 'pre-history' of man, and that only with the emergence of reason, and technological control, and the creation of a *humane* society can man commence his conscious making of history, free from earlier bonds of subjection, alienation, and the constraining tyranny of dogmatic traditions and ideas.

The facts already set out in this schema of social evolution, Giddings wrote:

* *The Elements of Sociology,* p. 288.

'. . . whether they appeared in the history of the world before the Christian era, or whether they appear now, are facts of the first stage only of civic national life.

'A second stage of demogenic evolution begins whenever the nation learns to appreciate the value of unlike-mindedness in the population; the value of doubt, scepticism, and denial in the social mind; the value of individual initiative and voluntary organization; the value, in short, of variation and criticism, as causes of progress. In other words, while civilization is established by sympathetic and traditional like-mindedness, a social organization that is no longer fixed, unyielding, hardening into a rigid system that must presently decay, but is becoming ever more variable, flexible, adaptable, in a word, progressive, is a product of unlike-mindedness, discussion, and agreement, and of the resulting rational like-mindedness.

'On the side of the social mind, then, the second stage of civic evolution is the gradual subordination of traditional to rational like-mindedness. On the side of social organization, it is the growth of the free or voluntary forms of purposive association, replacing the arbitrary coercive forms of a military system; and in the relation of the individual to social organization, it is the substitution of liberty for authority and coercion.'*

Giddings then arranged the 'evolutionary scheme' of societies in a new way, by constructing 'types' of social order, or 'stages', which threw the clearest light upon the nature and possibility of social progress.

Types of Social Order and 'Character-types'

The first massive stage of the building up of the 'traditional' societies of the world, he termed the 'Military-Religious' type of social order, and that which was growing out of these traditional societies in the modern world of scientific knowledge and industrial technology, he termed the 'Liberal–Legal' type of social order. Again we may note the complete identity of this typology with the later formulation of Max Weber of the two basic types of social authority: the 'Traditional' type and the 'Rational–Legal' type. For Giddings, the 'Liberal–Legal' type was that form of civilization in which: 'the forms of constitutional law and of free contract have replaced those of despotic authority and of "divine right" '. The great and distinctive difference between the 'Liberal–Legal' and the 'Military–Religious' types, as Giddings described them, can be seen in the following passage, and again this might be noted very carefully with our later study of Max Weber in mind.

'When a people has consciously entered upon the progressive stage of

* *The Elements of Sociology*, p. 290.

civic evolution, it usually attempts to perfect its liberal-legal civilization by a conscious policy, as people in the military-religious civilization endeavour by definite policies to perfect and maintain that.

'The policies by which the liberal-legal civilization is perfected are naturally quite the opposite of those by which a military-religious civilization is established. In many respects rational like-mindedness is different from the traditional like-mindedness whose chief component is belief, rather than the opinion that is created by free discussion.

'*World Intercourse*.—First, then, among the policies by which the liberal-legal civilization is perfected is the encouragement of the widest and freest world intercourse. The contact with other peoples, customs, manners, and thought is recognized as the indispensable condition for catholicity of view and alertness of mind. Progressive peoples invariably distrust any policy that tends towards isolation.

'*Free Thought*.—Secondly, progress is assured by encouraging the fullest investigation and the freest discussion of every subject. Instead of trying to compel all men to accept the same beliefs taught by authority, the progressive nation encourages every man to think for himself, to develop his own mental powers, to take an independent position upon every question and interest, knowing full well that reason is not a chaotic or lawless power, but is one that invariably brings men to agreement upon the basis of real knowledge and demonstrated truth.

'*Legality*—Thirdly, the progressive nation tries to perfect its liberal-legal civilization by a continued study of law and development of legality, which it is ever striving to substitute for arbitrary authority, not only in government, but in all social relations. Only that nation which succeeds in perfecting the constitutional, that is to say the legal and rational, method of government and procedure, can preserve both individual liberty and public order.'*

Again we must note that Giddings did not think there was anything *inevitable* about this progress. Many nations, he said, which have entered upon the 'Liberal–Legal' stage of social evolution 'have been unable to complete it'. But we can also notice, again, that the movement towards the 'Liberal–Legal' type of society *necessarily involves* a change of *social values*, and *necessarily entails* a *rational clarification of these values*. Again, we have this clear sight of the *centrality of values* in the social system, and for the distinctive differences between social systems. *Values actually are the fabric of society*. At the end of our entire study we shall see what a fundamental insight this is.

Growing out of the 'Liberal–Legal' type of social order, however, there was, Giddings maintained, a third 'type' of society, and it was in the throes of this that we found ourselves in the contemporary world.

* *The Elements of Sociology*, p. 298.

'There is a third stage of civic evolution', he wrote, 'upon which nations enter when they have so far perfected the liberal-legal civilization that they have a strong constitutional government to maintain social order and, at the same time, practically unlimited freedom of individual enterprise and voluntary organization.

'When, in such a nation, the most urgent problems of constitutional government have been solved, men turn their attention seriously to the task of improving their material condition, and give themselves earnestly to industrial affairs. Then is witnessed a marvellous development of invention, of mechanical progress and industrial organization, and an enormously rapid growth of wealth. Consequent upon this economic progress, there is an astonishing growth of population, which brings with it new and complicated social problems, especially those that grow out of the relations of employers and employed and the aspirations of the working classes. The final outcome is a development of democracy, and coincident with it a marked development of ethical interest. This third stage of civic evolution may, therefore, be called an "*economic-ethical*" civilization, or it may, with equal propriety, be called a democratic civilization.'*

It will be seen how closely Giddings' three 'types' of social order approximated to the 'Militant', 'Industrial,' and 'Ethical' types of Spencer. In the rest of his discussion, Giddings analysed the problems of the 'Economic–Ethical' type of society (i.e., in our terms: the 'Welfare State') and exposed the 'perils' as well as the benefits of democracy; and some of his judgments have a remarkable aptness for the problems we are perplexed about in the twentieth century. He also deployed the Spencerian 'explanations' of evolution in systematically analysing this entire schema of evolution and progress. For us, however, it is enough to concentrate on two further points: the first, a note on one aspect of Giddings' 'social psychology' in the context of this elaborate sociological analysis, and second, a clear indication of how the several strands of his system were related to each other.

We have noted throughout that Giddings emphasized the close relation between 'self' and 'society', between individual character and the characteristics and values of the 'associations' in which he was behaviourally involved. Almost as though he was following Mill's emphasis on the importance of 'Ethology' to the letter, Giddings was always careful to examine the psychological attributes correlated with the requirements and constraining influences of 'association'. This was well marked (as in other dimensions of his system) in his attempt to clarify the relationships between 'character and social-structure', and this is important to note because here again we see the preoccupation with an area of analysis in which American

* *The Elements of Sociology*, p. 302.

scholars have made special contributions, and in which there has been a strong continuity of interest.* Giddings gave clear descriptions of the 'character-types' which were correlated with the different kinds of social control and authority which he outlined, and these, it must be agreed, provided a remarkably systematic account in relation to his entire picture of 'social evolution'. The chief types he specified were these:

(i) *The Sympathetic Type:* developed in a community of kinsfolk where the chief social bond was that of sympathy.

(ii) *The Congenial Type:* developed in a community which was based upon the affinity of ideas and interests; for example—amongst groups which shared particular political persuasions or religious beliefs and ideals.

(iii) *The Approbational Type:* developed where the social bond rested simply upon the approbation of particular qualities or modes of conduct; as for example, in groups of warrior-companions, or in gangs.

(iv) *The Despotic Type:* developed in communities where the social bond was that of tyrannical power, together with a demand for obedience based completely upon fear.

(v) *The Authoritative Type:* developed in a community where the pattern of authority had become powerfully established in *tradition* and where the social bond rested upon a *reverence* for this authority.

(vi) *The Conspiratorial Type:* developed in situations where the bond of association, and the 'like-mindedness', rested upon intrigue.

(vii) *The Contractual Type:* developed where the social bond was based upon mutually undertaken covenant or contract, and an acceptance of reciprocal responsibility.

(viii) *The Idealistic Type:* developed where all the members of the community were consciously concerned for social values and responded to the appeal of great ideals; where the social bond was that of mutual faithfulness to these ideals and qualities; where a powerfully shared altruism and idealism was felt and where the members of the community had full confidence in the commitment and the shared qualities of others.

We are now in a position to see how some of the chief strands of Giddings' system were correlated with each other. Nothing elaborate is required, and I think the relationships can be made clear enough in a simple table.

---

* Earlier, we mentioned the significance of this in relation to the subsequent work of Cooley and Mead, and the 'role' and 'reference-group' analysis of Merton. Later, we shall see that this is writ large in recent American sociology—in systematic books like that of Gerth and Mills on 'Character and Social Structure' and in specific essays like that of Riesman: 'The Lonely Crowd'.

SOCIAL EVOLUTION AND PROGRESS

(1) SOCIAL EVOLUTION	(2) TYPES OF SOCIAL ACTION	(3) TYPES OF CONCEPTUAL THOUGHT	(4) TYPES OF CHARACTER	(5) TYPES OF SOCIAL ORDER & PROGRESS
SIMPLE TRADITIONS		SIMPLE TRADITIONAL BELIEFS (NOT CONCEPTUAL)	SYMPATHETIC	
TRIBAL SOCIETIES	IMPULSIVE SOCIAL ACTION			MILITARY–RELIGIOUS TYPE
TRIBAL FEUDALISM	→ TRADITIONAL SOCIAL ACTION	→ THEOLOGICAL	CONGENIAL APPROBATIONAL DESPOTIC AUTHORITATIVE	
ETHNIC NATIONS		→ METAPHYSICAL		
DEVELOPED FEUDALISM			CONSPIRATORIAL	LIBERAL–LEGAL TYPE
CIVIC NATIONS	→ RATIONAL SOCIAL ACTION	→ SCIENTIFIC	CONTRACTUAL	
COMPLEX FEDERATIONS & CIVILIZATIONS			IDEALISTIC	ECONOMIC-ETHICAL TYPE

577

Of course, the 'Character-Types' especially do not link up in the kind of exact order which such a diagrammatic presentation portrays; but I have included them to try to indicate the way in which all the elements of Giddings' analysis did form part of a very impressively worked out system. Here, at least, we can see the relatedness in Giddings' mind between his analysis of the *organizational* nature of societies, the systems of *conceptual thought* in them, the systems of *social action* appropriate to them, the overall *'types'* of *social order* into which they could be grouped, and the *'social-psychological'* correlations between kinds of associational relationship and kinds of individual personality and character which could be uncovered within them.

It is perfectly clear, too, in this presentation, how Giddings conceived the distinctive changes and qualities which characterized the nature and problems of human society in the modern world. His aim was to throw the rapid changes of modern industrial society into clear perspective; to produce an awareness of the juncture of civilization at which men had arrived; and—by the making of sociology—to provide a body of knowledge on the basis of which sound judgments could be made and enlightened policies and efforts could be sustained in grappling with these dilemmas. It was in this sense that Giddings thought of sociology not as a 'professional academic expertise', but as a fundamentally important educative subject which could provide a necessary and excellent basis for citizenship: for the wisest approach to both social commitments and personal fulfilment. He was, of course, perfectly right: and again, in his work, we can see the humane commitment and the anxiety to become clear about the plight of mankind in the modern scientific and industrial age, which lay at the heart and the intellectual effort of all the men we have considered. Indeed, the wisdom and profundity of Giddings' commitment both to the making of sociology for the sake of education, and to the clarification of the political perspectives and tasks of our time can be seen in the preface to his textbook. He foresaw very clearly the *intensification* of these dilemmas that lay ahead for America and for all societies as the social changes which were then afoot extended throughout the world during the twentieth century.

In 1898 he wrote, with regard to Sociological Theory as a subject, as follows:

'No other subject calls for such serious attention from teachers and students of educational philosophy at the present time as that of the best preparation for an intelligent and responsible citizenship. Marvellous as the development of the United States has been during the century that is now closing, greater destinies are yet to be realized. Our task in furthering the civilization of the world is to be a large and responsible one; no other

nation can assume it for us or perform it if we fail. Delicate as our international relations have been during our attempt to establish a secure
republic in a world of monarchies, they are to be more delicate and more
difficult in the near future when the European powers attempt to rectify
their colonial boundaries. Complicated as our financial problems have
already been, they will hereafter call for greater wisdom than has been
bestowed upon them hitherto. Difficult as has been the attempt to organize
efficient, economical, and honest municipal government for cities number-
ing millions of inhabitants, the difficulties will continue to increase as
population grows and wealth accumulates. Neither good luck nor any
mere intuition of common sense will enable us to maintain the reality of
republican freedom unless we have other resources to draw upon. Besides
common sense and energy, we must have knowledge, training, and an
unselfish devotion to the cause of human progress.

'It is certain, however, that schools and colleges cannot furnish detailed
courses in all branches of economic, legal, and political science. The field is
too vast and the years of study are too brief. To a majority of teachers the
alternative seems to be to give either a thorough course in some one subject
—Political Economy, for example—or a superficial course in many subjects, including "Civics" (or Elementary Constitutional Law), International
Law, and Political Ethics.

'In the judgment of the present writer, it would be wise to devote a large
part of the time available for such disciplines to a careful study of the nature
and laws of human society. This study would familiarize the pupil with the
principal forms of social organization; with the thoughts, the sympathies,
the purposes, and the virtues that make society possible; with the benefits
that society confers; and with the conduct that worthy membership of
society requires. These are the facts and principles that underlie all details
of law and politics, all sound political economy, and all public morality.
Well instructed in these matters, the student is fitted to continue his study
of society and public policy throughout life. Without this foundation, no
acquaintance with legal or historical detail can give him a comprehensive
grasp of social relations.'*

This view seems to me, still in 1970, totally correct, and it will be a
marvellous day when 'progressive' educationalists not only catch up
with this seventy-years-old opinion, but also take the trouble to
acquaint themselves with the sociological perspectives on which it
was based.

Giddings, then, was one of the early Americans who contributed
clearly and substantially to the making of sociology. In his work
could be clearly seen the critical digestion of the ideas of the European
scholars in the ongoing effort to lay the firm foundations of the
subject. And in his work could be clearly seen, also, the strong,
consistent, and very clearly stated perspective of 'Evolution, Knowledge and Conscious Control' which was basic in, and common to,

* *Elements of Sociology*, Preface, pp. v-vii.

other American writers. Our discussion of the work of Ward, Sumner, and Giddings has, I believe, been sufficient to make this shared position clear beyond any kind of doubt or ambiguity. We have seen, too, the firm beginnings of the concern for the study of the psychological aspects of society which was to be continued by American scholars, and developed more exactingly later; and we have seen too, the clear insight as to the central importance of *values* in society: a theme which I shall press again and again. A final point we might note is the supreme *clarity* of the American writers. They escaped all the befogged ambiguities of writers like Marx and Engels; they eschewed all metaphysical assertiveness; but they were no less forthright in stating their intellectual persuasions and humane commitments. We shall see later that this was a quality in which they compared very favourably with some European scholars; but, alas, it is almost as though some recent American sociologists have made their chief objective the transportation of European fogs back into America. The light has been obscured—to say the least.

SUMMARY OF THE EARLY AMERICANS

Despite their independence of mind, their differential treatment of certain aspects of the subject, their introduction of different concepts and terms, the great unity of conception of the early American sociologists has become convincingly clear in these brief studies of them. This is especially so when it is borne in mind that we have considered both the 'right' and the 'left' wing of the subject, so to speak. Lester Ward was forthright in his advocacy of 'collectivization'; the improvement of the administrative processes of the modern state, and, supremely, the state provision of education as the basic means of democratic progress. Sumner was very much, by contrast, of a 'laissez faire' persuasion. However, we have seen that common conceptions and a common concern underlay these apparent differences. On all fundamentals of both sociological analysis and the criteria of 'progress', they were agreed. We have seen, too, how these American scholars drew upon the work of the Europeans, critically assessing these basic contributions, and building them constructively into their own systems of thought and analysis. The cumulative, co-operative task of the making of sociology was well exemplified in their work.

It has also become quite apparent how, within the context of their agreement with the over-all perspectives of the Europeans, the Americans made quite distinctive contributions. Their perfect clarity concerning distinctions which men like Marx left clouded in ambiguity—such as that between 'genetic' and 'teleological' kinds of causation; their detailed and systematic analysis of the nature and types of 'social action' and of the 'psychological aspects of society'; their fundamental clarity of understanding that the 'social order' of men's practical activities and social relationships was essentially a *moral* order, an order of *values;* and their efforts to organize and present sociology as a 'subject' of crucial importance in education: all these have been seen quite clearly. And we may perhaps remark, too, that it has become quite plain how, with this great clarity of important distinctions, the Americans were able to adopt just as radical a position as any of the European scholars with regard to social reform and social action whilst avoiding the *extremes* into which some of these fell, and which held so much of intellectual and social error and danger. The early Americans embraced the earlier and contemporary nineteenth-century contributions to the making of sociology, and then took the subject distinctively further—both in rounding it out as a whole system of analysis, and in deepening it by adding more detailed explorations of particular dimensions within it.

Again, for our own particular purposes of clarifying the foundations of the subject, and seeing the wide and cumulative agreement of all these nineteenth-century scholars, let us attempt a clear summary statement of the ideas of the Americans which we have traced.

Scientific knowledge: a clear delimitation

Ward, Sumner and Giddings obviously agreed completely, both with each other and with the Europeans we have mentioned, that theological and metaphysical speculation had had their day in the pursuit of testable knowledge about our experience of the world, and that only the methods of *science* were productive of such knowledge. Again, this was not a claim of arrogance, but a claim of modesty: that we could only lay claim to *knowledge* within clearly *delimited* bounds. They were just as definite as the varying kinds of European 'positivism' in this; insisting, indeed, that science required a fundamental reorientation in men's attitudes of mind towards acquiring knowledge about nature and society, and considerable *effort* in coming to the adoption of new and unfamiliar perspectives (e.g., as in the enormous time-scale of evolution). They agreed, too, that the adoption of scientific method was a matter of *necessity* as well as of intellectual interest, in that science alone could provide a reliable basis for prediction and action. The following were some of the characteristics of science on which their agreement was unquestionably clear and firm.

(a) The detailed study of FACTS
Science was, first of all, essentially *empirical*. It required a detailed and painstaking description and analysis of the *facts*. Knowledge was not to be had easily, in 'a priori' fashion, but had to be gained by careful empirical *study*.

(b) The elucidation of LAWS
Science was not confined to a bit-and-piece amassing of facts, however. It focused upon the resemblances and differences among things, and sought to establish *generalizations*, or *laws*: which were uniformities or regularities of contiguity, order, sequence, in the relations among things.

(c) The delimitation of theories: verification
Science also proposed theories to 'explain' these regularities;

but these theories differed from other philosophical speculations in that they were deliberately submitted to procedures and criteria of *testability*. This was their one ground of reliability. They did not seek to go beyond it.

(*d*) *Each science: a distinctive subject-matter*
Each particular science was defined by its distinctive subject-matter: its 'unit of investigation' which was distinguished from the concerns of other sciences. Having clarified its unit of investigation, each science sought to describe and analyse its appropriate field of 'facts', and to state and explain generalizations about them.

(*e*) *Prediction and control*
Theories about generalizations about facts, of this kind, formed the most reliable basis of *prediction* which could be achieved, and therefore the most reliable basis of *guidance for action*. And, as we have seen, the Americans made much of the *control* of the *natural* by the *artificial* which knowledge made possible. Any science, then, had its pure and applied aspects.

(*f*) *A science of man and society*
With all these points in mind, the Americans were agreed that anything that could be called a reliable *knowledge* of the nature of man and society could only be achieved by applying these methods in the study of man and society to as exacting a degree as was possible. They were all agreed therefore on the necessity and value of trying to create a reliable science of society: Sociology.

It will be readily seen that all these points were in agreement in every respect with those outlined and adopted by the Europeans.

Nature, Man, Society: Evolution and Progress: over-all perspectives

The early Americans were also agreed in accepting the over-all perspective of 'evolution' as the correct context in which to couch all scientific studies. Again, it is important to see that this was far from being just an acceptance of the *biological* theory of evolution. It was, exactly as with Spencer, a much broader cosmological view of the emergence and transformation of *all* the 'forms' of nature. It saw all 'forms' as particular patterns of growth, adaptation, transformation within specific environmental contexts: so that it was, at once, a way of comprehending and explaining both 'order'

U

and 'change': indeed, kinds of order *were* kinds of change, which could themselves change in accordance with changes in internal or external conditions. All so-called 'objects' or 'entities' in nature were thus seen essentially as *processes*. Again, the similarity with Marx's 'Dialectical Materialism' is readily apparent. The following were important aspects of this over-all perspective accepted by the Americans.

(a) The context of evolution: nature and man

Man was essentially seen as a being who had emerged out of the complexities of an earlier and almost immeasurably long process of physical and biological evolution. A 'causal explanation' of the emergence of man had, therefore, to be sought in these earlier processes of evolution. Such an account was necessary for any accurate understanding of those biological and psychological characteristics of man which underlay, and necessitated, his own particular kinds of *social* activity. The *origins of society* were therefore also seen within this evolutionary context, and, furthermore, the *ongoing nature* of society was thought to be essentially historical and developmental: a process of cumulative achievement, of adaptation and transformation in meeting changing conditions. The time-scale of human and social development was therefore seen to be very large, involving far greater periods of groping, trial-and-error attempts to deal with the world, and far greater details and complexities of social development, than had been assumed in earlier doctrines of human nature. Man and society could only properly be understood within this larger context of 'nature'—which was, itself, a vast interwoven fabric of order, change, and transformation. This was the new and true perspective.

(b) Evolution: The relations between the sciences

As with the earlier thinkers, so the Americans held that all the sciences could be classified, or be seen to fall into a systematic arrangement, in that each of them was devoted to one defined area of subject-matter within the entirety of evolution. The sciences were therefore not *arbitrary*, but each came into existence to study a distinctive range of facts within this entirety, so that all of them together provided an entire schema of knowledge.

(c) The material basis of human society: men's practical activities

The Americans also accepted in a very real and down-to-earth sense, that man—emerging as one species among others in the physical context of nature—had to make his society by working upon the material resources of the world. Everything that man had to do—

from winning his bare livelihood to organizing armies and governments and religions—necessitated *practical activities* in relation to other men and to nature. Furthermore, all these activities were undertaken for *practical advantage*. The evolutionary perspective therefore entailed a materialist basis for the social activities of man, and this was a continuous accompaniment of all social evolution, development, and progress.

(*d*) *The distinction between nature and man: the Genetic and the Teleological: the implications for kinds of 'causal explanation'*
Even so, the American sociologists escaped the 'reductionist' error of a 'materialist' explanation of human society (of a metaphysical kind) such as Engels and Marx had put forward. The distinction was clearly drawn between 'genetic' or 'efficient' causation among factors which were blindly involved in material processes (and which interacted unconsciously with each other), and 'teleological' causation—when men consciously apprehended certain ends, and, in the light of many considerations, deliberately employed a certain set of means to achieve them. Human activity (*actions* as distinct from the *occurrences of events*) was predominantly 'teleological'—and therefore 'causal explanations' of human society were different from those of 'nature'. A science of man and society had to incorporate conception, elements, methods, criteria of observation, interpretation, etc., which were different from those of the 'natural' sciences.

Within the over-all evolutionary perspective, therefore, important distinctions of *level* (of both *fact* and *methods of study and explanation*) were clearly and carefully made.

Sociology: the science of society

The Americans' conception of the nature and elements of Sociology can, perhaps, best be summarized by tracing them from the way in which they saw human activities as being rooted in this larger evolutionary order of the nature of things.

(*a*) *Necessity: practical activities and practical advantage*
Men's activities were, primarily, *necessitous* in the sense of having to grapple with the life-conditions which nature set in such a way as to ensure *survival*. A rigorous necessity lay at the heart of the origins of human society. The needs which men had as well as the conditions which they confronted were implanted by nature; and the drive of necessity made the success of *practical activities* imperative.

585

These activities aimed essentially at *practical advantage*, and included men's accommodation to each other, as well as to the forces and resources of nature. Material necessity and practical activity therefore lay at the basis of human society. Even at this very basic level, however, the Americans saw that this was a new level of *mental* and *purposive* activity in nature, and that, in pursuing *advantage*, it contained, essentially and implicitly, right at the outset, the drive towards *'progress'*.

(b) Populations in their environments: ecology
Human activities were never those of individuals *isolated* in nature: they were always activities of groups or populations, the members of which, experiencing conflict and co-operation, were unified with a certain 'consciousness of kind', and were thus involved in an interconnected 'whole' of relationships in meeting their collective destiny. Two basic *facts* which underlay any human society, therefore, were the *population* and the *environment* in relation to which it had to build its life. The scientific study of society necessarily involved *demographic* and *ecological* aspects. Societies should always be seen within their environmental conditions.

(c) Population: size and quality
The study of a population should include both its *quantitative* and *qualitative* characteristics. The *size* of a population in relation to its environmental resources had important bearings upon its division of labour and other institutional arrangements. But also, a total population might be 'composed' of groups possessing qualitative differences. This qualitative 'composition' should be studied. And, over-all, the population would contain different 'classes'—in terms of ability and potential capacities of different kinds—which had relevance to the emergence of *élites* and many other aspects of social organization.

In *all* societies, questions of population and ecology were of fundamental importance, and the study of them was therefore a basic part of sociological analysis.

(d) The 'GENETIC' *development of social systems: the laying down of a social order*
Although human activities were distinctively purposive, the American sociologists were far from believing that the making of human societies was a matter of purely rational construction. They held that over the greater part of human history, the knowledge of men was slight, erroneous, fragmentary, clouded with many kinds of ideological misconception, and that human activities were necessarily

586

of a slow, groping, trial-and-error kind. Nonetheless, the many practical activities of men, resting on their rudimentary knowledge, gave rise to interdependent systems of 'folkways' and 'mores' which possessed credence and authority. In this process of social accommodation, it was also the case that though the many activities of men—each in its own way—were 'teleological', aiming at practical advantage, the interests of men terminated in their attainment of particular advantages, whereas their many achievements would have *unintended consequences* upon others, on themselves, and on the nature of social relationships, going beyond this. Because of the necessary degrees of interdependence of social relationships, there would also be—in the adjustments of these unintended consequences—a *strain towards consistency*; so that an over-all *system* of relationships, a social *order* as a whole, with its own '*ethos*', would arise. In this way there had been, and there was always likely to be, a complex process of *genetic* development, and *genetic* causation, in the laying down of the order of social systems, even though human activity was distinctively *teleological*.

In the study of this changing order (the factors making for innovation, change, conflict, and the factors making for accommodation, interdependency, and social consistency) an '*equilibrium-disequilibrium*' analysis was necessary. And it was important to bear in mind that, permeating this entire *genetic* development, there was this strain towards practical advantage; the 'strain towards improvement'. In short, there was still a progressive, teleological strand within the many-dimensioned genetic process.

(e) *Teleological developments within the genetic social order: reconstruction and progress in the light of knowledge and criticism*
Within the ongoing complexity of any social order, the Americans held that 'teleological' direction, always implicit, could become increasingly explicit, effective, and dominant as knowledge grew and the criticism of traditional ways of doing things developed accordingly. In the light of more exact knowledge, nature could be more successfully controlled by *artifice*, and greater practical advantage could be achieved. Progress could be deliberately planned and made.

Out of an earlier genetically created social order in which *adaptation* to necessitous conditions was predominant, grew an increasingly teleological social order, consciously directed, in which the active *transformation* of both the natural and social environment was predominant. The evolution of society grew from a predominantly genetic to an increasingly teleological condition—and the acquisition and dissemination of *knowledge* was the central factor in this process,

587

coupled with the application of this knowledge in the form of *inventions*. This embraced not only the purely technical activities of men, but also their improvement of social institutions, so that this continued improvement by the artificial control of the natural, was an activity of re-making the whole social order. Throughout, then, sociology was a study of the interdependent *achievements* of human activity. Social evolution was essentially a process of interconnected *development* (i.e., a cumulative advance upon earlier achievements) and it rested upon a *progressive* drive and intention.

(f) *Social Statics: The analysis of society*

In addition to the study of population and their environments, and this conception of the evolution of society in this entire evolutionary context, the Americans provided a very clear analysis of the nature and elements of *Social Systems*. Societies were seen as entire systems of interconnected activities, relationships, values, ideas, etc., and the following components were thought to be essential for a full description and analysis of them, and as a basis for possible theories about them.

(I) A STRUCTURAL–FUNCTIONAL ANALYSIS

The patterned relationships to be observed in a society could be analysed in terms of their *structure* (i.e., the form, regularity, or pattern of organization which they assumed) and the *functions* which they performed (i.e., in seeking to fulfil certain purposes, satisfy certain needs, operate interdependently with other institutions, etc.). The entire network of society could thus be analysed in terms of family and kinship groups, the division of labour and property relations, law, government, religion, education, and the like. Again, we might remind ourselves of Ward's castigation of the 'error of the stationary'. This analysis did *not at all* imply a *static* view of society; it was simply a way of analysing the *order* of society which was essentially a *process* of activities.

(II) ORDER AND CHANGE

Social institutions were developed *achievements*, and therefore *continuity* and *change* were essential characteristics of them. The study of order and of change were therefore parts of the same study, and the structural-functional analysis of institutions was part of a *historical* analysis. This perspective of process, order, change, development was a necessary accompaniment of structural-functional analysis. There was not, in the slightest degree, any opposition between them.

(III) CONFLICT AND CO-OPERATION

Similarly the *order* of society, though manifesting systematic inter-connection, interdependency, and even possessing an over-all 'ethos', did not at all imply a *satisfactory* order, or a *harmonious* order in the sense of possessing no characteristics of *conflict* and pressure for *change*. On the contrary, the *order* of a whole society was the outcome of a necessary blend of continuing elements of *both* conflict *and* co-operation. In all their many-sided activities and diverse interests, men were bound to experience *both*; and the *order* of society was an outcome of reciprocal accommodation among many groups, élites, and masses, and many conflicting interests. The structural-functional analysis, and the historical analysis of order and change, *assumed*, therefore, a continuous experience in societies of conflict and co-operation, and were designed to provide a description and possible explanation of them. Like order and change, conflict and co-operation, properly understood, were two sides of the same coin.

(IV) FROM 'FOLKWAYS' AND 'MORES' TO INSTITUTIONS, ASSOCIATIONS AND LAW

This analysis of structure-function, order-change, conflict-co-opera-tion, was able to encompass and fully take into account the complex 'genetic' development of social regularities (the systems of 'folkways' and 'mores'), and the more deliberately 'teleological' forms of social regularity (specific institutions and the consciously contrived con-stitutions and laws that accompanied them). We need not elaborate on this but might only note that this had its importance *both* for fullness of analysis of any particular society (i.e., in ensuring that all kinds and levels of social regularity were taken into account), *and* for developmental perspective (i.e., in that 'teleological' institutions could be seen within their earlier 'genetic' contexts, etc.). We may note, too, that this distinction was, of course, not so starkly simple as this summary form of statement implies. Distinctions were also drawn even among institutions—e.g., the 'crescive' and 'enacted' institu-tions of Sumner, which took the same emphasis of analysis further.

(V) THE ORGANIZATIONAL ANALYSIS OF INSTITUTIONS

In connection with the emergence of more formal 'institutions' or 'associations' it is worth our while to note that the Americans deepened, and made more specific, their 'structural-functional' analysis by making very clear indeed how they would analyse these more complicated forms of social organization. Sumner, for example, analysed institutions in terms of their *concepts* (purposes, doctrines, etc.), their structural *apparatus*, their defined set of *function-aries*,* their prescribed *rules*, and their organized *instrumentalities* for achieving the *interests* of their members.† Giddings analysed them in terms of their *purposes* or *functions*, their *constitutions* (for the performance of the functions), their *compositions* of members in terms of *categories*‡ and appropriate *qualities*, the *plan of organization* and *authority*, including any *sub-groups*, *committees*, etc.

This was an agreed system of analysis, completely clear, and we shall later see how it cropped up in the literature of the twentieth century.

(VI) SOCIAL ACTION AND TYPES OF SOCIAL ACTION

Since 'action' was of a teleological nature, and quite different from a simple 'occurrence of events', it was necessary, however, to go beyond the structural-functional and historical description of social regularities, and to seek a causal explanation in terms of the *understanding* of the *ends* which men sought and the *means* which they employed to attain them. In short Sociology had to include the *understanding and explanation of social action* as a special and distinctive component of analysis if it was to achieve a full and satisfactory account of its distinctive subject-matter. Distinctive—in that this 'teleological' level of mind in deliberate action which was characteristic of man, did not apply to any other 'phenomena' of nature.

The study of social action was therefore, according to the Americans, an essential and distinctive component of sociology additional to the structural-functional and historical analysis of institutions. As we know, they elaborated this in much detail and clarified certain 'types' of social action—the Impulsive, the Traditional, the Rational—which, again, were 'models' for the interpretation of observed historical changes and tendencies.

(VII) THE PSYCHOLOGICAL ASPECTS OF SOCIETY

Closely related to this concern for the understanding of purposive social action was also, of course, the importance which the Americans attached to the study of the *psychological* dimensions of society, and here they laid the foundations for several clear and interesting directions of enquiry. Here, we need only note what these were, but again it is worth while to remind ourselves that the early Americans saw *no gulf whatever between psychology and sociology;* between

---

* What everybody now calls, with great originality, 'roles'.
† Compare with B. Malinowski in *A Scientific Theory of Culture*.
‡ Again, aspects of defined 'roles'.

the study of the *individual* and the study of *society*. On the contrary, they saw the study of man and society as a science which necessarily embraced both psychological and societal elements; and, furthermore, they saw perfectly plainly, as the theorists from Comte to Marx had done, that it was impossible to study *man the individual* excepting in the context of his *social* influences: or, to put it differently, that the very dichotomy between *individual* and *society* was highly dubious. For the moment, however, we can simply note that the Americans distinguished at least five clear ways in which psychological considerations should form a part of sociological analysis.

PSYCHOLOGICAL FORCES: FROM INDIVIDUAL MOTIVES TO SOCIAL 'CONATION'

Firstly, they saw clearly that psychology was necessary for a knowledge of some of the basic motives which were characteristic of human nature and which underlay much social action. Sumner had spoken, for example, of certain instincts and basic motives of hunger, sex, vanity, and fear, and Ward and Giddings held similar positions. But also, they were aware that, in the many collective influences of social life, conative 'drives', public urges, demands and currents of feeling could be engendered which might, or might not, be connected with basic individual motives, but which certainly possessed powers and qualities going beyond them. Society, in short, was creative of *group* psychological qualities and purposes which required study.

PSYCHOLOGY AND SOCIAL ACTION

The Americans were also very clear that human *psychology*, just as human *sociology*, could never satisfactorily be framed in terms of 'genetic' or 'efficient' causation. Human beings *acted* (deliberately, exercising choices with ends in mind) and therefore the psychological as well as the societal dimensions of human activities needed to be couched in terms of 'teleological' understanding. For the Americans, then, the understanding of social action and psychological explanations were very closely allied.

THE PSYCHOLOGICAL ASPECTS OF INSTITUTIONAL MEMBERSHIP AND SOCIAL RELATIONSHIPS

The Americans also saw clearly that some psychological qualities (of experience and conduct) among individuals, which were of importance for the understanding of their social action, were actually brought about by the structures of group relationships and the

591

requirements of the membership and tasks* of institutions. Giddings, for example, showed how different groups and institutions actually engendered, as well as drew upon, differing kinds of 'like-mindedness' or 'consciousness of kind'; and showed also how important these were for explaining the nature and solidarity and boundaries of groups. Sumner, too, in his analysis of 'In-Group' and 'Out-Group' tendencies, showed how group conditions could create collective (and thus individual) psychological qualities. Indeed, Sumner discussed the ways in which a collective 'Ethos' arose in a society as a whole, and which then formed a part of every individual person's private experience.

SOCIETY AND 'SELF'

This leads us directly to the fourth point: that the Americans (and especially, here, in the work of Giddings) saw and explored more clearly and deeply than those before them, the intricate relations between *social* (or *associational*) influences and the actual formation of the individual *personality* and *character*.

CHARACTER AND SOCIAL STRUCTURE

Similarly, the Americans produced a more detailed analysis than others of the relationships between character and exposure to particular kinds of social structure that John Stuart Mill had in mind in his insistence upon the importance of 'Ethology'.

All these 'psychological aspects' of society, of course, were closely connected in the thinking of the American sociologists, but they are sufficiently important to distinguish, and it is at least sufficiently clear for our purpose that the Americans did much to emphasize, elaborate, and show the worth of these psychological dimensions of sociological analysis, and began a direction of work for which American sociology has been distinguished ever since.

(VIII) 'CLASSES' AND ÉLITES

We should note briefly, too, that in their analysis of social systems as wholes, the Americans not only did not neglect to take into account conflict as well as co-operation, they also did not fail to take into account the analysis of 'classes' of ability in the population of a society and the attendant analysis of élites. This included the more ordinary examination of hierarchical organization in society, the formation of 'socio-economic classes', etc.; but it also dealt with the difficult questions of ranges of ability in society and what this entailed for issues of government, democracy, education. The im-

* I am purposely avoiding the term 'roles'.

passioned concern of all of them for education—especially of Ward and Giddings—is enough to show that this concern for 'differentials' of ability by no means entailed any 'reactionary' attitudes of mind towards social inequalities.

(IX) THE CENTRAL IMPORTANCE OF 'VALUES' IN SOCIETY: THE SOCIAL ORDER ESSENTIALLY A MORAL ORDER

A final component of sociological analysis on which all laid emphasis was this insistence that *values* lay at the heart of the institutional fabric of society. Though insisting quite firmly upon the basic importance of *practical* activities for *practical* advantage in society, the Americans never lost sight of the fact that these activities were nonetheless *purposive*, that they gave rise to reciprocal accommodations of interest and the accompanying development of obligations in the regulation of relationships, and, furthermore, that they carried with them certain standards and qualities of human character. The fabric of society was in large part a fabric of material and practical activity, but, at one and the same time, it was a *moral* order. In this realm of the values at the heart of the folkways and institutions, as in all other kinds of activity, the Americans saw a rationally clarified, and consciously sought, moral order of society arising out of the 'genetic', rule-of-thumb values which had been established earlier. Moral progress as well as technical progress found its clear place in their analysis of social systems.

These, then, were the major components in their analysis of the nature of society.

(g) *Social Dynamics: Evolution, Development, Progress*

We have said enough of the way in which, using this system of analysis, the American sociologists went about their comparative and historical study of actual societies and attempted to frame theories and interpretations of social change. For the sake of summary completeness, however, the following clear points ought to be noted.

(I) EVOLUTION: A CAUSAL, HISTORICAL ANALYSIS

Firstly, like Spencer, the Americans did not employ the concept of 'evolution' as a naive, all-embracing descriptive term which was vacuous as far as explanatory worth was concerned; or simple-minded in postulating anything like 'unilinear', 'inevitable' sequences and the like. They *analysed* the processes of evolutionary change in terms of the factors which came into play when societies met the changing challenge of their environments. They gave causal accounts of kinds and directions of growth; processes of differentiation and integration; specific developments in the division of labour, property, class exploitation, education, etc.; processes of invention and innovation; and kinds of influences operating between societies—conquest, trade, assimilation, syncretism, and so on. Evolution was not a simple-minded 'blanket-term' by any means, but a conception of a complex process which yielded a detailed causal and historical analysis.

(II) CLASSIFICATION AND COMPARATIVE STUDIES

As with the European scholars, the American sociologists saw clearly, and employed fully, the necessary method—in generalizing about social change—of classifying 'types' of society in accordance with certain criteria, and undertaking, in the light of such a classification, detailed comparative and historical studies.

(III) TYPOLOGIES: OF SOCIAL ACTION; OF SOCIAL ORDERS

Similarly, we have seen how the Americans constructed 'models' or 'types' of society in the light of which they were able to interpret and understand observed regularities of change. The 'Impulsive, Traditional, and Rational' types of social action were, as we shall see, almost exactly those later constructed by Max Weber. The 'Theological, Metaphysical, and Scientific' types of tradition were clearly the three types ('stages') of social order proposed by Comte. The 'Military–Religious', the 'Liberal–Legal' and the 'Economic–Ethical' types of society were almost exactly the same as Spencer's 'Militant, Industrial, and Ethical' types. And these 'typologies' were used in exactly the same interpretive way in illuminating sequences of change in 'Social Dynamics'.

(IV) A PERSPECTIVE FOR ACTION

Finally, it is perfectly clear how the Americans found, in classifying these sociological perspectives, a clear perspective for judgment and action in their own time, in relation to their own problems. But this leads to a concluding emphasis.

(h) Sociology for USE

The early Americans, just as directly and forthrightly as their European counterparts, had crucially in mind the perspective of the modern world which we emphasized at the outset and from which the work of Comte sprang at the beginning. They too were clear-sightedly concerned with the modern disruption of all the traditional orders of societies of the past, and the complex problems born of rapid scientific, technological, industrial and urban change.

594

They were equally aware that these problems would not be resolved without political effort, and without the achievement of a reliable body of *knowledge* on which the making of social policies could rest. Again, then, we see the making of sociology at the heart of a concern for the re-making of society. The making of sociology was for human *use*.

In this, the Americans pressed, if anything, further than the Europeans who had influenced them, though their effort was exactly of the same kind. They advocated a new approach to the provision of an informed art of administration, resting on the scientific study of society. They advocated a positive approach to the provision of education for all by the State. And they were foremost in trying to introduce sociology as a subject at various levels of education, and in trying to 'organize' it effectively and persuasively for these teaching purposes.

The early Americans, then, of great stature and interest in their own right, stood four-square with the European scholars in laying the foundations of sociology, and our study of them demonstrates to the hilt the great cumulative agreement which characterized the efforts to create the subject during the nineteenth century. Their work demonstrated that, by the end of the century, the clear construction of an entire conspectus of the subject had indeed been successfully accomplished.

E THE PERSPECTIVE OF PROGRESS: A FINAL NOTE

Before leaving this study of the early Americans, there is one further comment I would like to make, which, to me, is of considerable interest and possibly of the very greatest importance in connection with their quite central insistence on the idea of 'progress'. We have already noted their rejection of the *'error of the stationary'* when insisting on the necessity of 'structural-functional' analysis; and we have seen, too, that their awareness of the 'teleological' characteristics of human 'action' led them wisely to avoid what we might call the *'error of psychology'**: the error of assuming that human experience and behaviour in society could be exhaustively explained in terms of 'efficient' causation. Though concerning themselves very much with the psychological aspects of men's individual and social behaviour, they clearly and carefully introduced, in addition, the teleological *'understanding* of social *action'*. But as well as all this, I would like to suggest that they also exposed with great clarity what I want to call later, the *'error of social anthropology'*.

This is what I have in mind, though here I will make the point only briefly.

We have seen that *all* the nineteenth-century sociologists we have considered—from Comte to Giddings—adopted the *evolutionary* context for understanding the emergence and development of societies, and, more than this, that they insisted upon the centrality, within this context, of the drive towards *progress*. Of them all, the American writers, with their distinction between the 'genetic' and the 'teleological', were perhaps most clear. And certain aspects of the central place attributed to 'progress' within sociological analysis deserve to be made absolutely clear; indeed *must* be made clear if we are going to have correct perspectives later.

This idea of 'progress' went *far beyond* the simple notion of *evaluating certain social changes in the light of adopted ethical principles*—in the sense that Spencer, for example, held that a 'laissez-faire' or 'liberal' industrial society was 'better' than a militant society, or that Marx held that a 'collectivized' society was an 'improvement' upon industrial capitalism. It was far more than this. It really stemmed from the insistence that, even in the most simple social conditions known to us, human action was *'purposive'*; deliberately undertaking consciously directed *actions* to achieve

* This is more fully discussed in Vol. 2.

clearly apprehended *ends*; and that, as such, it was a category quite distinct from other events of nature, and even other animal behaviour. This meant that all the practical activities of men aimed at practical *advantage*, and that, therefore, even in the earliest groping through experience towards more accurate knowledge, the selection of those activities which yielded the greater advantage, clearly implied a drive towards *progress* (a 'strain towards improvement' as Sumner put it).

The 'functions' of the inventions, folkways, mores, institutions which men developed were therefore nothing mysterious. They were the fulfilments of human intentions and purposes. Now the Americans (and all others) certainly held that a great part of the development of human societies, a very long period of the laying down of established social order, had its *genetic* aspects; but, even here, there was nothing mysterious (or *hidden*, in any obscure way) in mind. The fundamental conception here was—among *all* the theorists— that of *unintended consequences*. Men sought their own interests teleologically; but (*a*) their interests frequently only went as far as the successful attainment of their own purposes (they were not necessarily concerned with all the effects of their activities upon others) and (*b*) they did not foresee all the consequences of their actions—whether upon others, upon themselves, or upon existing relationships and institutions. In short, even the 'genetic' processes of society were pervaded by 'teleological' activities—conscious, purposive, social creativity; it was only that *knowledge, foresight*, and degrees of conscious *control* over nature and society were *limited*.

Sociology, as all these nineteenth century scholars conceived it, took the 'simpler' or 'primitive' societies into account, as we have seen, but saw them as 'limited' terms of knowledge and its application; in terms of the control over the natural by the artificial. The 'historical' civilizations, in which literacy, numeracy, the systematic acquisition, dissemination, and application of knowledge, enormously improved men's control over nature and their practical advantage, were seen as developments *from* the primitive, *over* the primitive, and as 'progressive' in their successful extension of control. The extension of knowledge and reason were thus central in achieving a progress which had always been implicit in the purposive activity and endeavour of men from the beginning. This perspective was perfectly plain.

Now what I wish to argue here is this. Throughout its creation during the nineteenth century, Sociology was conceived as the scientific study of social systems, among which were included the 'simpler' or 'primitive' societies. These societies, as all others, were seen as manifestations of the purposive activities of populations

597

in seeking practical advantages within their environments. They were held to be 'primitive' or 'limited', *not* in that their social and psychological processes were entirely different in kind from those of other societies, but only in that their knowledge was such as to give them such limited control over nature by artifice and invention that they were relatively 'arrested' in a certain condition of adaptation to their environments, and did not manifest the more complex patterns of growth, change, development, differentiation such as were manifested in the cumulative historical societies. In this sense, they remained predominantly in the 'genetic' condition, and all the more complex patterns of increasingly exercised 'teleological' social change and development were to be found in the historical civilizations. The 'simpler' societies therefore formed a limited part of sociology, and exemplified these simpler 'genetic' levels of adaptation. The greater part of sociology was concerned with the more complex patterns of society once mind, knowledge and its purposive power had risen above, and grown beyond, these simpler levels.

In this sense, Ward—especially—saw the simpler societies as being a very limited part of Sociology; thinking indeed, that they really formed a part of 'Anthropology' (i.e., *then—physical* and *cultural* anthropology; *not—social* anthropology) as constituting examples of human groups who had grappled with the task of establishing their 'place in nature' only to a limited extent. They constituted social systems resting upon limited achievements of knowledge and technical and institutional kinds of control. The study of them could not be expected to contribute beyond a certain point to the understanding and explanation of the more complex, historical societies, in which the 'teleological' powers of men were so greatly extended. Sociology was predominantly faced, then, with the study of this far larger and more complex fabric of men's societal *achievements*.

One other point needs great emphasis. All these founders of sociology—seeing the study of the simpler societies within their entire conspectus; readily insisting upon the great importance of the long 'genetic' periods in the gradual making of societies and social traditions; readily seeing that social systems came to assume a shape appropriate to functional adaptation by means of 'hidden consequences' and institutional adjustments as well as by conscious intention—nonetheless *not only* insisted that the activities of men in the simpler societies were pervaded by *teleological* dimensions, but *also* that the *patterns of social custom* which had come to exist in them could certainly *not* be taken to be *harmonious* social patterns (possessing no sources or kinds of conflict); *functionally satisfactory* social patterns; or even *correct* social patterns (possessing no possible grounds for social change). On the contrary, these social patterns were seen as the continuing fabric of traditional *ways* of dealing with conflict as well as co-operation, and as seeking practical advantage—prone to change continuously as 'life conditions' changed. In short, then, the 'simpler' societies were a process of *development* at their own level. It was simply a *limited level*. But the fact that they accomplished a certain adaptation to any given life-conditions did not at all mean that they were completely articulated, functionally integrated, systems containing no inadequacies, no conflicts, no rough edges or loose ends, no room for or potentialities for change.

I hope my insistence on this one point will be forgiven; but my concern is this. I want to insist upon the argument as fully and consistently as I can: (*a*) that the evolutionary and 'progressive' perspective of the founders of sociology was perfectly clear, (*b*) that it was correct, and did not suffer the supposed errors of false ethical evaluation with which it has been charged, and (*c*) that the introduction of a supposedly new subject—'*Social* Anthropology' in the early twentieth century has been such as to create grave error and to intrude (or *re*-intrude) false conceptions, false perspectives, and new mystifications—both philosophical and factual, which have filled the study of society with unnecessary and misleading confusions. Later, I shall argue that '*Social* Anthropology' was no more than the discovery and use by physical and cultural anthropologists of *Sociology*; but that, in applying sociological analysis to the study of the simpler, non-literate societies, the earlier well worked out perspective of sociology was lost sight of; the distinction between 'genetic' and 'teleological' was ignored; the limited degree of application of 'structural-functional' analysis was ignored (indeed its assumptions became absurdly inflated); the *fact* that societies were essentially processes of development was to an astonishing degree overlooked; and the proper perspective of the study of these societies within the wider comparative studies of other types of society was simply not considered or taken into account. The distinctive kinds of explanation and understanding in terms of men's *conscious purposes*, which the Americans especially (but others also) had made so scrupulously clear, were abandoned in a new fog of purely 'genetic' explanations in terms of 'efficient' causes, and something called 'functional' explanation—which, fantastic though it seems—was thought to be *new*. What I am saying is that the supposed novelty of Social Anthropology in the early twentieth century was bogus. And it was not only bogus, but misleading in its errors of omission (in *not* seeing certain fundamental philosophical distinctions which had already been made clear) and of over-emphasis (i.e., on 'genetic' rather than 'teleological' explanations.) Rather like some psycho-analysts who, burrowing into the dark night of unconscious motives, derogated altogether the rational deliberations and conscious choices of men; so *some* Social Anthropologists burrowed into a dark night of hidden functions, latent functions, underlying functions, derogating almost entirely the conscious pursuit of ends. A new, retrogressive, 'genetic' metaphysics fell upon us, resting upon a revived notion of 'determinism'—long ago exploded by John Stuart Mill.

With one isolated bit of sociological analysis in their pockets (i.e., structural-functional analysis), made up into a little guidebook for research by Malinowski, the Social Anthropologists ceased to *read*—whether in the British Museum or at the London School of Economics—and, instead, rode out on bicycles in their white duck suits, to look at men in huts. Now looking at men in huts can certainly be exciting, and it can certainly provide testable knowledge about men in huts; but the persuasion that, excepting within the context of comparative and historical sociology, it can provide more than a limited knowledge of the nature of societies and social processes is an illusion. This fog of error has become so thick that, nowadays, people have come to speak about the *distinction between* the 'anthropological' approach and the 'sociological' approach, and about the 'relations between' social anthropology and sociology, whereas, in fact, there is nothing to talk about here at all—except confusion: a confusion inflated by professionals, and misunderstood by ill-informed editors of popular social-science journals and television producers.

I have taken this point a little further than I had intended at this stage, but I think it is right to do so. To note it clearly, forcefully, now, will help much more than now seems apparent when we come to disentangle the various 'developments' of sociology in our next section. However, for the moment, we must leave it. It is enough to have seen very clearly that—in addition to the 'consensus' of agreement among the Americans, and between them and the European scholars—there was this quite central dimension of the 'progressive' within the evolutionary and developmental perspective of the changing nature of societies; that this position was very clearly stated and there was much to be said for it; and that much interesting controversy ensued when this perspective came to be forgotten, ignored, or, too brashly, overlooked. But these fireworks of controversy—we must come back to later: and with relish!

Meanwhile, we are now able to move to our conclusions about the nineteenth century 'foundations' in the making of sociology.

7

The Foundations of Sociology:
A Summary Statement of Nineteenth
Century Agreements

We have now surveyed the major contributions to the making of
sociology during the nineteenth century. We have studied the chief
theoretical systems produced by scholars in Continental Europe,
Britain and the United States and, by this time, their wide-ranging
agreement about the nature and elements of the subject, and its
importance for both understanding and dealing with the problems
which men faced in the period of modern science and industrialization, must be clear beyond doubt.

Our practice of summarizing the work of each man, or group of
men, at the end of our study of them, must have been cumulative
evidence of this agreement, and, indeed, must have demonstrated the
large extent to which there was cumulative argument and collective
achievement among them all. From Comte to the Americans, it has
become clear that the basic elements of the new science were conceived to be the same. This is so clear that it would be unduly tedious
to go over the entire range of agreements again in an attempt to
dovetail them too closely.

At the same time, because I want the conspectus of the nature
and elements of sociology which had been clarified by the end of the
nineteenth century to be *undeniably* clear; because I want this study
to be *definitive*, and completely *firm* for an accurate assessment of
subsequent twentieth century developments; I want, at the end of
these studies, simply to collect and emphasize in a systematic way,
the agreements which had been reached: to draw up a kind of
'end-of-nineteenth-century' statement of agreements. I want to do
this, too, in such a way as to show (without reiterating all the
intricate details) that the ideas of *all* the writers we have considered
can so be drawn together. Each had his own conception; each had his
own emphasis; but the major agreements among all of them were
perfectly plain.

If I seem unduly tenacious in this task I can only ask the reader to
bear with me, and to remember (*a*) that I wish to be *clear* beyond any
degree of doubt or equivocation, (*b*) that I have in mind the condition

of knowledge of the critics of sociology, and, in view of this, want to demonstrate the nature of the subject up to the hilt. If your opponent has a skin like the hide of an elephant, and an intellectual awareness of appropriate proportions, you are strongly disposed to drive your sword in deep. Even then, I am well aware that the brute is likely to turn away in silence, giving no sign of admitting anything, but my hope is that, when he does so this time, he will be dead! And (c) I have in mind also the perspectives placed upon the subject by certain twentieth century sociologists; and for the assessment of these, too, we need now to build very firm foundations.

Let us proceed, then, methodically.

A SCIENCE AND KNOWLEDGE

As to the nature and necessity of science for the acquisition of reliable knowledge, all the thinkers we have studied were agreed:

(*a*) That only the methods of science were productive of *testable knowledge* as distinct from *conjectural opinion*.

(*b*) That science stemmed from careful reflection on common sense and common practical experience, and that, though it went beyond this, it could continue to gain help from its shrewd insights and should always meet any questions or objections which it might raise.

(*c*) That the methods of science produced *accurate* knowledge in relation to their *prescribed limitations*.

(*d*) That science prescribed a *limitation of subject-matter*: (i) in that each science studied a distinctive, clearly defined 'unit of investigation' or 'range of facts', and (ii) in that it concerned itself only with this defined range of *phenomena*: qualities, objects, and relations in the world *as we experience and observe them*. Questions concerning the 'ultimate' nature of 'reality' were *not* the province of science. On *these* questions, science had to adopt a position of carefully delineated agnosticism.

(*e*) That science also prescribed, accordingly, a *limitation of method* in that—though including *many* methods: of observation, analysis, description, generalization, classification, comparison, experimentation, etc.—its *crucial* characteristic was that of *always submitting its theories to conditions of test* in relation to the *facts* they sought to explain.

(*f*) That, accordingly, science abandoned the conjectural methods of theology and speculative (or entirely 'a priori' and deductive) metaphysics. This was not to say that these subjects were totally devoid of value; or that they could not give rise to imaginative insight and hypothesis; *only* that they overstepped the *boundaries of testability* beyond which science could not go.

(*g*) That science was not a directionless empiricism: simply collecting and amassing 'facts'; but was a systematic study of the resemblances and differences of things, and of the relations between them, and was centrally concerned to establish *laws*. Science produced *'empirical generalizations'* (descriptive statements of regularities) and *'theories'* (hypothetical explanations) about them: all of which were always subjected to conditions of test. The role of 'hypothesis' in the establishing of scientific 'theories' as carefully stated 'conjectures' couched within specified conditions of 'verification' or 'refutation'—was clearly understood and acknowledged. *Theory* was central in guiding the observation and manipulation (in classification, comparison, experimentation, etc.), of facts.*

(*h*) That science, whilst abandoning speculations about 'ultimate' reality, could nonetheless, by the pursuit of its methods, uncover 'hidden laws' which were beyond the range of common sense, and which might (i) give hitherto unsuspected explanations of familiar facts, or (ii) even reveal realms of facts which were themselves beyond the range of common perception. In such ways science extended knowledge.

(*i*) That each science concerned itself with its own distinctive subject-matter; and that all the sciences could be arranged or classified in such a way as, together, to provide a systematic compendium of knowledge of all aspects of experience. Though no man could encompass it all, knowledge could be so arranged, and could be transmitted in the many branches of education.

(*j*) That each science consisted of 'statics' and 'dynamics': the first producing 'laws (uniformities) of coexistence' (about the interdependence of parts in the distinctive 'consensus' of the subject-matter—the 'organism' in biology, the 'social system' in sociology, etc.); and the second producing 'laws of succession'—i.e., about the actual changing forms of the subject-matter existing in the world. Statics and Dynamics, however, were not two distinctive kinds of subject-matter within each science, only two (and these very intimately related) different aspects of method and theory.

(*k*) That science, resting crucially upon testability, provided the most exact basis possible for *prediction*, *action*, and *control*. Each science had, therefore, its *pure* and *applied* aspects, which could not be dissociated from each other. The two attitudes of the scientist—to *understand* and to *control*—were necessarily connected. To understand nature as a student was inescapably related to the capacity to control nature as a master. Experimentation and practice were closely connected. To control was to manipulate nature in accordance with predictable knowledge. To see was to foresee. The *degree* of control depended upon things other than knowledge—the nature and magnitude of the facts and forces concerned, the state of accomplished technology, etc.—but the *possibility* of reliable, calculated control rested upon knowledge.

(*l*) That scientific knowledge was never *final* knowledge, but—always exposed to test—was always capable of change and extension. Scientific knowledge provided, within its prescriptions, the most secure grounds for its own continuous testing and probable expansion. Scientific knowledge, furthermore, was always *relative* to the

* The exception to this would be Marx's 'sheer empiricism'.

many conditions of the human situation in which it was, at any time, being pursued; but it was not *arbitrary:* it was the most accurate knowledge possible by employing scientific method in that time and in these conditions.

(*m*) That the essential attitudes of mind required by science were those of humility before the facts; rigorous care with regard to prescribed limitations; integrity with regard to purposeful exposure to conditions of test; and readiness to change explanations in the light of evidence. This point deserves emphasis: that in claiming to set the standards of knowledge according to the limitations of human experience and the clearest procedures of the human mind— science was not *arrogating* to itself a *totality* of knowledge; it was accurately *delimiting* the claims of knowledge in accordance with a recognition of human *limitations;* and, in so doing, it had to deny these degrees of exactitude to those subjects whose conjectures went beyond these bounds.

(*n*) That, in the *application* of scientific knowledge for the attainment of certain human *ends*, the exercise of *critical judgment* (including a consideration of ethical principles) and an *assessment of practical possibilities*, and *appropriate 'arts'* had to enter—which went beyond scientific expertise as such.

(*o*) That, following upon these considerations, such *knowledge* as could be established about man and society could only be discovered by employing these methods of science to such a degree of exactitude as proved possible.

B THE SCIENCES AND THE STUDY OF NATURE, MAN AND SOCIETY: PERSPECTIVES OF KNOWLEDGE

As to their conception of nature, of the place of man and society within it, and the proper conception of the sciences in the study of this entirety of man's experience of things, all the thinkers we have studied were agreed:

(*a*) That nature consisted of a vast, interconnected multiplicity of finite living forms in a continuous process of order and transformation, and that all these forms were the manifestation of definite regularities and definite relationships with the elements of the environments in the context of which they came into existence, grew, developed, and went out of existence. Any '*order*' in nature, any perpetuated '*form*', was itself a *process*. Both order and change in all these forms was a re-ordering of elements in a process of adjustment to specific constraining and sustaining environmental conditions.

(*b*) That, accordingly, any 'forms' ('object', 'species', etc.) in nature had essentially to be understood as a *process* within *environmental conditions*, and could only satisfactorily be explained in these terms.

(*c*) That nature was not only an interdependent entirety of 'forms', but that all its processes of order and transformation assumed a certain *pattern:* the pattern of '*evolution*'. From simple elements of material substance and energy which were similar to each other, possessing relatively little definiteness of organization, emerged varieties of definite forms possessing a differentiation of internal parts which were coherently organized. The nature of these forms was intimately connected with their accommodation to their environmental conditions, and followed a definite sequence of origination, growth, development, dissolution, and sometimes reproduction. Changes in these distinctive forms were closely related to changes in their environmental conditions. Nature's vast mesh of transformations thus possessed an 'evolutionary' pattern.

(*d*) That the recognition, analysis and study of these processes of 'evolution' therefore provided grounds for the explanation of all the 'forms' of nature. For example: The initial condition of homogeneous elements was seen to be an unstable condition; once differentiation of particular forms had begun—a multiplicity of effects could be traced; factors making for the specialization and segregation of parts could be analysed; reciprocal accommodations and adjustments of parts to secure stability, equilibrium, and effectiveness in dealing with environmental circumstances could be analysed and described, as could factors making for decline, disintegration, destruction and dissolution; the ways in which quantitative processes among material substances gave rise to qualitatively new forms could be analysed and explored. The recognition of the processes of evolution provided, then, not simply a descriptive 'word' or 'concept' which—like a magic talisman—was thought to explain everything in nature; but provided a *set of concepts*, and an awareness of a *multiplicity of factors*, in accordance with which the complex processes of nature might be explained in detailed ways.

(*e*) That the 'normal' characteristics of any form in nature, the 'normal' functioning of its parts, and its relations with its environmental conditions, could sometimes be greatly illuminated by the careful study of 'pathological' conditions.

(*f*) That this conception of nature and all its interdependency of forms opened up vast perspectives—of time, of space, of complex contiguities of things—with which men had been hitherto unfamiliar; and that therefore a great effort of mind and judgment was necessary in approaching the task of knowledge anew.

(*g*) That, within this entire study of nature and its evolutionary processes, each science concerned itself with the study of one distinctive 'level' of 'forms' (one clearly defined 'level' of subject-matter). The emergence of the sciences was not arbitrary: new sciences emerged to study 'levels' of phenomena of which men were newly aware, and which could not be satisfactorily explored and explained by existing sciences. And again, all the sciences, taken and arranged together, could provide a compendium of knowledge of all 'forms' and all 'levels' of phenomena in nature.

(*h*) That, accordingly, though all the sciences employed 'scientific methods': observation, analysis, the submission of hypotheses to conditions of test, etc.—there was no such thing as *one, uniform, set of 'scientific' concepts or procedures*. The concepts, techniques, procedures, used; the degrees of controlled experiment and exactitude it was possible to achieve; would necessarily vary from science to science in accordanc with the nature and complexity of its subject-matter. The insistence upon 'positive' science was, in *no* sense, then, an insistence that all sciences should ape *one* particular kind of science (say, the 'natural' sciences).

(*i*) That the one most crucial distinction of 'levels'—both with regard to the qualitative distinction of subject-matter, and with regard to the necessity of distinctively different concepts of 'scientific explanation'—which was to be recognized and clarified within the entire perspective of 'nature' and 'evolution', was that of the emergence of man and of human society. The evolutionary context entailed a new appraisal of man's place in nature.

(i) One important element of this perspective was that man had emerged out of the material processes of nature, as one animal species among others in the process of biological evolution. A full knowledge of man's nature required, therefore, an understanding of these material and biological roots.

(ii) Human *societies* were systems of group activities which were also (like other 'forms' in nature) intricately involved in struggles of adaptation within contexts of environmental conditions. They also had origins in a distant past it was difficult to uncover; and they also seemed to assume their over-all shape in relation to factors going beyond 'individual intentions' alone. They were a qualitatively new 'level' of fact of which man had become aware—a 'super-organic level of phenomena'—which required distinctive concepts and a new, distinctive science.

(iii) The nature of '*man the individual*' was so much a correlate of the conditions and developments of his social life, that it was at least necessary to study the nature, development and cumulative achievements of *society*, in order to have a sufficient basis of knowledge for an adequate exploration and understanding of the individual as a *person*.

(iv) At the same time, men—as individuals or as groups alike—had had to make their societies, and win the basis for their livelihood and security, from practical activities in relation to the material resources and conditions of nature. This practical and material basis of human activities had therefore to be borne firmly in mind. The attainments of the human mind and spirit, and glories of culture and civilization, had been won by man's struggles in nature—not simply dropped like ready-made 'Manna' from some transcendental heaven.

(v) Even so—one absolutely important distinction between man and all else in nature had to be recognized: that the human mind was capable of knowledge, choice, and conscious, deliberate action. Even in his material and practical activities, man was 'purposive'. Human *action* was categorically distinct, therefore, from inanimate occurrences of *events*, or sequences of *animal behaviour*, and therefore required a 'teleological' as distinct from a purely 'genetic' kind of causal explanation. These 'choices' and 'deliberate pursuits of ends' were still determining *causes* of sequences of human action—but they were causes of a different kind, and they could not be couched in terms of a 'necessitarian determinism'. Knowledge, choice, deliberation, will, and character (as distinct from conditioned 'personality') entered into human individual and social life, and any science of man and society had therefore to take these qualitatively different 'levels' of facts thoroughly into account.

Here, then, was a very special case in which a qualitatively distinctive 'level' of subject-matter necessitated not only a new science, but a new science with distinctively different concepts, methods, and principles of 'explanation'.

(vi) This distinction had one other important corollary. Knowledge brought with it *control*, and therefore man was also distinctive within nature in that he was able not only to *adapt* himself to the vicissitudes of nature, but to *transform* them in accordance with his own ends. Knowledge made possible the control of nature by *artifice*. Human societies were therefore cumulative developing processes: they were the embodiment of human *achievements*, and formed a *social heritage* which transmitted these achievements to new generations.

(*j*) That the science of man and society, should therefore form one part of the scientific study of nature—and, indeed, since all the sciences were themselves social achievements, sociology should provide a new perspective for the systematic arrangement or classification of the sciences. The science of society was *like* the other sciences, in trying to pursue the same rigorous methods, but also *unlike* them (as they, among themselves, were unlike each other) in that it had to include qualitatively distinct dimensions.

(*k*) That, finally, the sciences could be systematically arranged in accordance with the degree of complexity of their subject-matter, the degree of exactitude that was possible, and the connected degree of modifiability of the subject-matter. The science of society dealt with a subject matter more complex than that of other sciences; the degree of precision it could expect to accomplish was therefore less; but, nonetheless, such knowledge as it could provide would be of very considerable importance since its subject-matter was more modifiable than that of other sciences and therefore more could be accomplished by control to achieve desired ends.

In these ways, then, the methods of science could establish appropriately exact knowledge about all the processes of transformation of nature—including the nature of man and society. And these were the *only* methods by which such knowledge could be achieved. The entire scientific enterprise on which man was embarked and which he was seeking to round out and systematize completely in the modern period, was therefore of basic importance for man's understanding and control of all aspects of his situation.

C SOCIOLOGY: THE SCIENCE OF SOCIETY

As to the nature of Sociology—the new science of society which they were at such great pains to create—all the thinkers we have studied were agreed:

Sociology: A Science

That sociology was, indeed, one science among others in accordance with all the elements of definition clarified above. It had become necessary because a specific 'level' of facts had become recognized in human experience (and in the context of pressing problems) which existing sciences could not sufficiently explore or explain.

The existence of 'Social Systems': the distinctive subject-matter of Sociology

That the groups which men formed, the institutional procedures by which their conduct and relationships were ordered—in short, all the '*associational*' aspects of human life—existed in some relationships of interdependence in *societies as wholes*, and that they could only be properly understood within this perspective. The organizational entirety of societies included elements *other* than *physical* processes, *other* than *biological* processes, and *other* than the *psychological* qualities and intentions of *individuals*. Sociology was necessary therefore, as the scientific study of 'social systems'—and this was the distinctive definition of it.

The necessity of the methods of science

That testable knowledge (as distinct from untested opinion, speculation, conjecture) about the nature of 'social systems', as about any other 'level' of facts in our experience, could only be achieved by using the methods of science. Sociology should pursue its studies with the same rigorous methods, and the same crucial insistence upon the empirical testing of theories, as the other sciences. This did *not* mean, however, that it should confine itself to the concepts, techniques and procedures of the other sciences—since every science had (necessarily) distinctive concepts in relation to its own 'level' of subject-matter, and 'social systems' certainly possessed distinctive dimensions which required special concepts. The degree of exactitude which could be achieved in the study of 'social systems' remained to be seen; but it could *only* be seen by employing the methods of science as far and as carefully as possible.

The abandonment of 'metaphysical' kinds of explanation

That, accordingly, Sociology should abandon all explanations of 'social systems' in terms of 'final ends' or 'ultimate realities or purposes', or even 'ultimate *causes*' in the sense of dogmatic reductionism to some ultimate level of fact where supposed causal efficacy was not susceptible to test. 'Causal Laws' were not to be conceived as iron bands inevitably determining the nature of society, but as statements of regularities of our experience and observation of society which were testable; about which testable theories could be stated; and which could be used to explain and predict specific events and relationships.

Especially, too, Sociology should abandon the attitude of mind that a knowledge of man and 'social systems' could be gained in 'a priori' fashion, from solely intuitive sources, and elaborated purely by procedures of deduction. It should adopt the scientific attitude of mind that any knowledge of a specific range of *facts* could only be accomplished by *observing, analysing, describing, classifying,* and *attempting theoretical explanations* of these facts which could be *tested.* It should adopt the empirical orientation of science, and proceed on the assumption that any reliable knowledge about the nature of 'social systems' could only result from a careful, searching, empirical study of them. We should study *social facts* with the same orientation towards objectivity that we employ in our study of other facts in our experience.

This did *not* mean the assumption of 'necessitarian determinism'

That this adoption of the methods of science did not mean the adoption of any new metaphysic of 'necessitarian determinism'. 'Social Systems' were *not* physical, or mechanical, or organic phenomena; they were systems of associational forms in which men exercised conscious choice, and pursued deliberate sequences of social action in accordance with interests and to accomplish ends. The nature of 'causality' among the regularities of 'social systems' was therefore complex and contained distinctive qualities. Though always within a context of delimiting constraints, 'men made their own history'. Even so, careful empirical procedures of study were necessary to provide reliable knowledge about them—but this did not at all mean treating 'social systems' and the people who lived and acted within them as if they were sticks or stones. Sociology as a science did not deny, or fail to recognize, the human capacities for calculated knowledge, deliberate choice, and conscious purpose: on the contrary, it shaped its concepts and methods to take these distinctive qualities of its subject-matter satisfactorily into account. This was so both in its recognition of *character-formation* within societies, as distinct from the conditioning influences of a cultural 'ethos' upon attributes of personality; and in its recognition of the explanation of social *action* in terms of 'teleological' causation, as a category distinct from the explanation of physical or organic *events*, or sequences of animal *behaviour*, which was possible in terms of 'genetic' or 'efficient' causation.

The delimitation of Sociology

That Sociology, by this kind of careful definition in relation to a distinctive subject-matter was properly delimited to a range of study, a 'universe of discourse', within which it could pursue appropriate kinds and degrees of exactitude. Sociology deliberately confined itself to discovering and stating regularities about the nature of 'social systems': the interconnections between their parts in whole societies; the psychological aspects of these social relationships; the sequences of social action pursued within them; and the relations between such whole societies themselves. Total 'social systems' were related to each other to some extent and in certain ways within 'human society' as a whole throughout the world, and had come to be what they were within the cumulative processes of history. Sociology was concerned to establish knowledge about the many aspects of this entire fabric of 'associational' interdependency. It goes without saying that this was the defined 'conspectus' of sociology as a distinctive field of study. No scholar was so megalomaniac as ever to propose that any one man could encompass the whole of it. *Within* this agreed conspectus, and with all its *perspectives* in mind, each scholar could pursue his own dimension of interest; his own theoretical concern and persuasion.

Sociological 'laws'

That sociology, in common with other sciences, should not pursue a 'directionless empiricism'; a mere bit-and-piece 'sociography'; an amassing of descriptive studies; but that it should be—according to the character of science properly understood—a *generalizing*, *theoretically orientated* study of the resemblances and differences of the aspects of social systems, and should seek the clear statement of testable 'laws'. These 'laws' concerning social regularities would be of at least two kinds: (*a*) 'uniformities of co-existence' (about the nature of the 'social system' as a distinctive subject-matter; the kind of 'consensus' of facts a 'social system' was; the kinds of relationship which existed between the parts of a 'social system' within the whole, etc.) and (*b*) 'uniformities of succession' (about the changing nature of the actual varieties of 'social system' in history).

Social Statics and Social Dynamics

That, in Sociology, as in other sciences, it was useful to distinguish two aspects (though closely connected aspects) of method and theory: statics and dynamics. Social Statics was the necessary conceptual analysis of the nature of 'social systems': their components, their functions, their interrelations, their psychological aspects, the patterns of social action which they comprised, etc. Social Dynamics was the application of this analysis to achieve an understanding and explanation of the varieties of social systems in the world. Statics was the analysis of the distinctive nature of social systems; Dynamics, guided by this analysis, was the detailed study of societies (empirical, comparative, historical) in relation to specific theories. Statics and Dynamics did *not* have separate subject-matters, they were two different aspects of method and theory; and, of course, they were intimately connected, in that the specific studies and theories of Dynamics could well lead to fresh formulations of the analysis of Statics—which itself could then lead to new theoretical insights and new specific studies in Dynamics.

Social Statics: The Analysis of the Distinctive Nature of Society—'The Social System'

That the nature of a 'society' or 'social system' comprised the following important components and could be analysed exhaustively in terms of them:

613

(a) A population and its environmental conditions

Any society consisted of a population sustaining itself, and creating and perpetuating its social life, by working upon and adjusting itself to a specific set of environmental conditions. The study of the population and of the environmental conditions therefore formed a necessary part of sociological analysis; and both involved quantitative and qualitative aspects. As far as the population was concerned, the qualitative composition and the quantitative size, rate and pattern of change, distribution throughout the territory, etc., were all important factors. But the unity and solidarity of populations—which bound them together as communities, sharing continued traditions—rested upon various types of 'consciousness of kind' in accordance with which men identified themseves with each other and marked themselves off from each other. These too, therefore, were necessary factors of analysis and necessitated the study of societal and psychological components.

(b) A Consensus of associational forms: Structural-Functional Analysis

In any society, the activities of the population in relation to their life-conditions and to each other were not arbitrary, but assumed certain *regularities*. In their associations in family life and kinship relationships; working life and property-relations; in their activities of instruction, training and education; in their religious observances of belief and ritual practices; in their procedures of government and law; in *all* their associations, certain *regularities* prevailed. These were specific, regular, associational *forms* of social action. Furthermore, all these specific forms were found to be interconnected and interrelated in a complex and intimate fashion. Marriage, for example, was an institution of the family, of religion, of government, of law, and had many attendant customs; so that all these associational forms were interlinked in a quite definite manner. Similarly, objective conditions and subjective identifications of 'Social Classes' arose from occupations, property-relations, family membership, relationships to law and government, etc. The *associational forms* in a society were, in short, interconnected in a certain kind of '*consensus*' which even came to possess an attendant '*ethos*'. There was a '*social system*', a *system* of interdependent institutions, within which many kinds of regular and well-defined *groups* of the population conducted their activities.

This entire, interlinked network of social relationships with all its elements of social procedure and organization could most clearly be studied by a 'Structural-Functional Analysis'. This had certain clear components.

(1) THE CLEAR ANALYSIS OF FUNCTIONAL REQUISITES AND APPROPRIATE ORGANIZATIONAL FORMS

There were certain *functional requisites*—stemming from the universal psychological characteristics of man and certain determinate problems which were necessarily encountered where men were collectively involved in working upon the same life-conditions and seeking to satisfy their many needs—which had to be provided for, in appropriate organizational forms, in every society.

Such institutions, rooted in functional requisites, were *universally necessary*. The following were specified:

DOMESTIC INSTITUTIONS AND ATTENDANT KINSHIP RELATIONSHIPS

Some form of marriage and family relationships to regulate sexual behaviour in relation to the responsible upbringing of the young were necessary; and, in relation to any specific form of marriage, there would necessarily be a determinate network of kinship relationships.

ECONOMIC INSTITUTIONS: PRODUCTION, DISTRIBUTION, AND PROPERTY

The working activities of the members of a society had to be regulated in such a way as to *produce* adequate sustenance from the material resources of the environment. This entailed some *division of labour*—some allocation of tasks to those who were thought most fitted and appropriately trained to do them. Both the material resources, and the products of collective work, had also to be *distributed* according to some principle and procedure among the population. And the principles and procedures for establishing legitimate degrees of control over material resources and products were institutions of *property* and gave rise to determinate property-relations.

REGULATORY INSTITUTIONS: CUSTOM, LAW, GOVERNMENT, RELIGION

Some institutions were also necessary to provide stable methods for resolving disputes, and for taking or interpreting these decisions which were binding upon all the members of society. Such institutions had to possess 'authority' and power, and would have to include some consensus of beliefs and values as well as regulated practices. Bodies of custom, more formal systems of law, constitutions of government, and religions with their systems of doctrines and ritual-practices were institutions of this kind.

W

MILITARY INSTITUTIONS

The members of a society needed to be protected from external threats and attacks as well as from internal disorder and insecurities, so that some form of military organization, as part and parcel of the 'regulatory institutions' was also necessary.

EDUCATIONAL INSTITUTIONS

If the security, stability and desired qualities of a society were to be preserved, the accumulated knowledge, skills, beliefs and values of the social order would have to be effectively transmitted from generation to generation, so that institutions of instruction, training and education were necessary.

RANKS, CLASSES AND ÉLITES

This institutional ordering of human relationships in all forms of association necessarily involved differentiations of function and ability; allocation of responsibility; the designation of authority and kinds of subordination; and necessarily led to the distinction of *élites*, of variously graded 'ranks', and the emergence of 'classes' of the community who experienced differing sets of conditions.

This is by no means an exhaustive statement of this component of 'functional requisites' and their appropriate organizational forms. It is simply a mention of this one basic element of structural-functional analysis: that basic *functional requisites* could be postulated which were universal in society and gave rise to *basic types of institutions*—each serving these functions and possessing attributes of form and organization appropriate to them. This was clearly stated, and the institutions we have mentioned were among those clarified by the nineteenth century thinkers. This analysis itself formed a clear basis for comparative studies, and it may be remembered that Mill was so impressed by the confirming evidence of comparative studies that he was ready to claim that these analytical propositions themselves were of the nature of 'scientific truths'.

(II) THE PROLIFERATION OF INTERESTS, FUNCTIONS, AND SPECIALIZED ASSOCIATIONAL FORMS

About these basic functional requisites, massive networks of folk-ways, mores, and then formally regulated and consciously amended institutions and laws developed, and could be analysed in the same structural-functional terms. However, in more complex societies, with considerable degrees of differentiation, freedom, and knowledge many consciously devised associations were created to seek quite specific ends. These specialized associations could also be carefully

616

analysed in terms of the purposes they sought, and the structures of organization—their 'apparatus', their arrangement of 'functionaries', their kinds of 'instrumental means', their pattern of authority, subordination, committee-arrangements, etc.—which they established to seek these ends.

Two points were important here: (*a*) no matter how complex the number and nature of associations in a society, the method of structural-functional analysis remained applicable and satisfactory, and (*b*) it was clear that *elements of social structure*—from the most massive (such as governments, armies, ecclesiastical organizations) to the most small and specialized (such as a society to prevent cruelty to animals) could, by this method, be broken down into all the specific units-of-action of 'functionaries' which were requirements of behaviour for *individuals*. In short, structural-functional analysis provided a detailed picture of the *structure of society* within which the *units of behaviour* of *individuals* could be clearly seen and understood.

(III) FUNCTIONAL INTERCONNECTION

Besides the clarification of basic functional requisites of large-scale institutions and the specific purposes of specialized associations, structural-functional analysis also clarified the *functional interdependency* of all elements of social structure in the 'consensus' of society as a whole. It clarified the ways in which institutions were *linked* in their connected operation in society as a whole.

(IV) THE PROCESS OF SOCIETY: ORDER, CHANGE, DEVELOPMENT

The structural-functional analysis of institutions was proposed and used with the insistent awareness that society was *essentially a historical process of achievements, and the transmission of achievements,* as succeeding generations of men grappled with their environmental conditions. It especially warned against the 'error of the stationary'. Structural-functional analysis was part of the study of society necessary for a satisfactory explanation of *process*: and this included the understanding of *both* order *and* change—since *both* are essentially *processes*. Indeed, these men who put forward the earliest 'structural-functional' models of social systems were the men who have provided the most impressive and influential theories of social change. It is worth remarking, in addition, that the transmission of achievements in both order and change entailed the recognition of the *fact* of social *development*: namely a process of the cumulative furtherance of achievement resting upon earlier achievement.

617

(V) CONFLICT AND CO-OPERATION IN SOCIETY: ORDER NOT NECESSARILY HARMONY

The structural-functional analysis of institutions was also proposed and used with the insistent awareness that society contained continuous sources of *conflict* as well as tendencies of co-operation. Social *order* was not at all construed as something called functional *harmony*. The *order* of institutions was a pattern of procedures which had been shaped in order to deal with conflicts of interests, conflicts of classes; its very nature was that of an institutional 'modus vivendi' within which men and groups with manifold interests could pursue these interests and resolve their differences. Sometimes conflict was radical and disruptive; sometimes it was not; but structural-functional analysis took it thoroughly into account.

(VI) FUNCTIONAL INTERCONNECTION NOT FUNCTIONAL INTEGRATION

Similarly, structural-functional analysis did not at all entail the assumption or reach the conclusion that all the institutions of society were 'integrated' in some sense of being so perfectly articulated that there was no possible source of internal social change. The institutions of a social system were interlinked, but they could be institutionalizations of power and control which might well be disrupted and overthrown, and, in any case, they were in many ways imperfect, resting on limited knowledge which was prone to change. There was always a drive to progress, to a furtherance of practical advantage, within them, as well as a 'strain to consistency' among them, and the activities and interests of men were never smoothly tamed within their bounds.

(VII) EQUILIBRIUM-DISEQUILIBRIUM ANALYSIS

Quite apart from any specific theory of social change, then, the structural-functional analysis of society rested upon a firm recognition that *the very nature* of society was that of a *process* always prone to change, alive with manifold interests and sources of conflict, and never nicely confined and controlled, so that, *as a part of itself*, it employed an '*equilibrium-disequilibrium analysis*' which could explore the transformation of society from one 'structural-functional' pattern to another.

(VIII) THE NORMAL AND THE PATHOLOGICAL

A final element, most clearly introduced by Comte, was that the understanding of the 'normal' functioning of a social institution within a certain type of social system might well be more clearly

618

illuminated by careful studies of particular 'pathological' situations in which the normal condition of the society had, for some reason, broken down.

A clear analysis of a social system could be achieved, then, by this method of 'structural-functional analysis'; the clear analysis and description of each institution, its own specific functions, and the functional interconnectedness of them all within the system as a whole. It can be seen that this kind of analysis of social systems readily lent itself to a systematic clarification of 'types' of social system and made manageable clearly conceived comparative studies.

(c) Human activities: social institutions not 'entities' self-sufficient for explanation

Though structural-functional analysis could provide a clear knowledge of all the associational forms in a society and the nature of their articulation with each other in the entire social system, and though such a picture could provide a clear basis for tracing 'cause and effect' relationships, it was nonetheless still at the level of *analysis* and *description*, and not sufficient in itself to *explain* order and change in society. The order of social institutions had come into being to regulate and serve many kinds of human *activities*, and therefore the further study of these activities was necessary for causal explanation.

The point of crucial importance emphasized here was that *social institutions were not self-subsistent 'entities' which could be held to have cause-and-effect relationships with each other*. They were associational *regularities*: but regularities of what? They were ways of ordering the *feeling, thinking, and acting of groups of men pursuing certain interests*. Comte, Mill, Spencer, and the Americans alike warned against the basic error of regarding institutions with a misplaced concreteness—as social entities in their own right.

The clear knowledge of social regularities and the interconnections (whether of continuity or change) among them was not therefore in itself sufficient, and had to be supplemented by a study of the many aspects of human *activities* for any satisfactory *causal* explanation. We need not elaborate again here the way in which all the nineteenth century thinkers emphasized men's *practical activities* and their many-sided pursuit of *practical advantages* within the entire framework of the institutions of society.

One centrally important aspect of this point is that a *causal account* of changes in society could *not* take the form of 'weighting' one institution or a group of institutions as being the *determinants* of others. Any statement that one institution *caused* changes in others was an error.

The societal level of 'associational forms' or 'regularities' about which it was so important to establish knowledge was still not to be mistaken as a level of self-subsistent entities.

(d) The Psychological Aspects of Society

Since the *activities* of men had to be studied, and since these activities were sequences of feeling, motivation, thinking, choice, deliberation and action, the study of the *psychological aspects of social regularities* formed a necessary part of sociological analysis. Again, we need not elaborate all that was contributed in clarifying this area of study, but the important points made, and the important dimensions of enquiry distinguished and quite extensively analysed, can be stated in a summary way.

(i) There was no doubt that sociology needed to draw upon biology and psychology for such knowledge as they could provide about the basic bio-psychological endowment of human nature, and that these two sciences were themselves experimental sciences. Basic questions and qualifications were made, however, about the nature of psychology—which we shall come to in a moment.

(ii) Knowledge was also necessary of the 'motives' in human nature—and the motives at all levels. Some of these were at the level of physiological needs and even 'instincts', and these underlay broad ranges of social action: the quest for food, sexual gratification, the protecting of children, security, shelter, etc. Others, however, were engendered by social experience, by tradition, by social constraints themselves: so that the study of collective kinds of 'social conation' was also required.

(iii) Membership of groups, the fulfilling of tasks as 'functionaries' of associations, the experience of the rules, values, constraints, and ideals of institutions also had their psychological aspects. Social regularities obviously had their influences upon the experience and behaviour of individuals. This had many dimensions: the existence of many kinds of 'consciousness of kind' in group identification and group demarcation; the creation of a societal 'ethos'; the institutional engendering of specific interests, habits, and characteristics in individuals, etc. And these, of course, might well form part of, or be caught up in, the thick of massive historical movements and intense conflicts, as well as in the more ordinary accommodation to patterns of social life. Groups themselves might entail psychological processes which were formative of constellations of individual perception and feeling: and the analysis of such processes was not only suggested, but substantially begun in the study of 'In-groups' and 'Out-groups'.

(iv) As part of this, but going more deeply, it was also necessary to understand the relationship between the emergent nature of the 'Self'; of the personality and character of the individual; and the cultural context of society. The very study of the 'individual' could, it seemed, only be satisfactorily undertaken within the societal context.

(v) As a corollary of this, too, it was assumed that certain kinds of 'social structure' would be likely, within the constraints and influences of their requirements, to engender appropriate kinds of 'character', and so the exploration of 'types' of 'character and social structure' was begun in comparative studies.

The field of 'social psychology' was therefore not only *indicated* but quite clearly and substantially defined, and certain very important points were involved in this which deserve clear statement and emphasis.

Firstly: no conflict was seen whatever between psychology and sociology. On the contrary, the study of man and society was seen essentially as a unified science in which the societal and the psychological aspects played their necessarily interconnected parts.

Secondly: these social-psychological dimensions were seen as necessary 'middle-principles' of sociological explanation. This, it will be clearly seen, was by no means, and in no intelligible sense, to 'reduce' sociology to psychology.* Causal explanations in terms of 'institutions' as 'entities' were an error. Clearly the 'institutional regularities' of society were also inexplicable in terms of 'individual' psychology; involving many elements which went beyond this. The study of men's 'social activities' was an additional necessity, and *part* of this was the study of the psychological aspects of life within institutions and groups. No reductionism was involved: this was simply a recognition of the *several* levels necessarily involved in an *entire* and *satisfactory* explanation of the distinctive characteristics of social systems.

The third point which can follow this is that this position clearly demonstrated (*far* from a 'reductionism' to individual psychology) the necessary *sociological perspective* of psychology. Just as the study of society was insufficient without the consideration of the psychological dimensions of it, so the study of man the individual was completely impossible. excepting by seeing the 'person' within his social context.

And the fourth point which springs out of this is that the extent to which psychology *can* be an experimental, 'natural' science, was held to be extremely dubious. The comments of Marx here were perhaps the most telling. If man *the individual*, if the *very qualities* of distinctively *human* nature, are the products of long cultural processes of cumulative social creativity, how is it *possible* to rest a science on the study of human 'experience and behaviour' *abstrac-*

* See note in Appendix (4) on Popper.

ted from all this? This, in itself, might well be a fundamental error of the most fatal kind, and of the most simple-minded kind, and might lead to a *distortion* of our views about human nature rather than to a deeper knowledge of it. At any rate, practically all the nineteenth century scholars adopted this *direction* of view: as Comte put it, that all human psychology was *social* psychology, and that a *sociological* perspective was necessary for the understanding of *man the individual*. Mill was most ready to recognize an experimental science of psychology, but, as we have seen, even he insisted fully on the 'middle principles' of social psychology in addition to this.

A fifth and final point which is of interest and importance is that this exploration of the psychological aspects of society made possible the *linking* of the study of *society* and of all the *individual members* of it. Or—to put this in a better way—it presented a clear perspective of the entirety of society in such a way as *not* to conceive only of abstract categories of social regularities ('elements of social structure', 'institutions', etc.) but *also* to see in clear and rich detail the individual 'units' of action, and the individual 'personalities' pursuing their purposes within it. Just as the very detailed way of analysing 'institutions' in such a way as to make clear all the particular tasks of 'functionaries' (put forward by Sumner and Giddings especially) made it possible to see 'individual actions' within the many forms of social structure—no matter how massive they might be; so this study of the psychological aspects of society could explore all the patterns of experience and behaviour within this entirety of social structure—from the largest level of 'collective' motives, constraints, enthusiasms, etc., when the population faced and shared 'collective' conditions, down to the most detailed level of the influence upon the individual of the requirements and performance of particular tasks (e.g., as husband, father, workman, property-owner, political citizen, member of a trade union, member of a religious community, etc.) and the development of the individual's own personality and character within the context of them.

This mention of 'character', however, as distinct from the notion of purely conditioned 'personality' leads to the next distinctive and additional component of sociological analysis.

(e) The understanding and explanation of Social Action: Teleological dimensions of facts and analysis
Because the human mind was distinguished by its capacity for the conscious apprehension of ends; the acquisition of knowledge; deliberation, judgment and choice; and the deliberate direction of action and critical employment of means to achieve these ends: *neither* the structural-functional analysis and description of the

institutions and groups within which men lived and acted, *nor* the study of the psychological aspects of experience and behaviour within this framework; *nor* the two combined—*in terms of efficient causation*—could possibly be enough. These were two necessary components of sociological analysis, but they were not in themselves enough. Men were distinctively *purposive* and capable of *choice* and conscious *calculation* in formulating and carrying out their activities, and therefore an *additional* component of analysis was necessary: the *teleological* explanation of *social action* in terms of the ends men sought, and their ways of pursuing them.

This was a very important distinction of both *fact* and *method*. It insisted that the facts studied by sociology were qualitatively different from the facts studied by other sciences, and it also insisted, accordingly, that the methods and theories of sociology must be qualitatively different in order to deal satisfactorily with them. Kinds of social action had to be understood in terms of different kinds of ends and different kinds of means employed for attaining them. These we need not elaborate again here, but we can simply note that certain *models* for this purpose were provided: Impulsive, Traditional, and Rational social action; and these were linked with the analysis of social structures and of psychological processes to provide a full analysis of all the dimensions of society.

From the 'types' of social order elaborated by Comte—the three kinds of ordering of feeling, thought and action; through Mill's insistence upon the human capacity of choice; to the teaching of Ward, Sumner and Giddings at the close of the century on the importance of recognizing these dimensions of 'purpose' and 'teleology'; there had been, in the making of sociology, this clear recognition of the need, in the science of society, for a dimension of explanation different from that existing in the so-called 'natural' sciences. And it is important to reiterate: that all these men were, at one and the same time, insistent upon the necessity of using the methods of positive science in the study of society *and* that these methods would have additional and distinctive components because of the different qualities, the different level of subject-matter with which they had to deal. Sociology was a 'positive science' which incorporated 'teleological' as well as 'genetic' explanations.

(*f*) *Society* MORE *than human purposes: Hidden Laws: Unintended Consequences*

A systematic and testable knowledge of any society could be provided then, by:

(i) the study of the qualitative and quantitative aspects of the population within,

623

   (ii) its environmental conditions,

   (iii) the structural-functional analysis of its 'Consensus' of institutions and groups,

   (iv) the study of the psychological aspects of these associational forms and their influences upon individuals, and

   (v) the study, in 'teleological' terms, of the sequences of social action which men pursued within this framework.

Even this, however, was not sufficient without taking one other basic and perennial fact into account.

Though men were purposive, the order of society resulted from *more* than their purposes. Though they pursued activities in the service of interests and to attain ends; the detailed interconnections of social events and actions *always went beyond these conscious purposes, in ways, whether advantageous or not, which were unforeseen.* For example, though acting consciously to achieve ends, men may be conscious of these ends in varying degrees, not necessarily *fully*; nor did it follow that *other* ends may not be pulling them of which they were *not* conscious. Also, though acting consciously to satisfy interests and achieve ends, men's interests and purposes were limited, terminating at certain points. The *consequences* of their actions, however, might always go far beyond their intentions—and in many ways. They might have effects upon other people, other institutions, and even upon themselves, in ways which were not looked for, and were not even a matter of conscious interest. There might, in short, be influences working upon their minds, shaping the 'ends' for which they struggled, of which they were unaware, or only partially aware. The results of their actions might be altogether or partially different from what they had intended, and might have consequences going far beyond their awareness. And also, *institutional adjustments,* kinds of reciprocal articulation between associational forms, might well take place as an outcome of the entirety of complex social activity in the community *without being consciously sought, or planned, as an over-all pattern of organization at all, or by anyone.*

This recognition of the complex interconnections of social processes—insisted upon repeatedly by all the men we have studied—emphasized, in yet another way, quite basic and important points. It emphasized especially that though *components* of sociological analysis could be methodologically distinguished and clarified, *no one of them* was sufficient for satisfactory analysis, description and explanation. Men were purposive, and the teleological understanding of their purposive action was necessary—but *it was not of itself, enough.* The psychological aspects of men's social activities and their complex 'membership' of institutions and groups, formed a necessary element in any satisfactory knowledge of social processes—but *in itself it was not enough.* The entire framework of associational forms in which men lived and acted could be clarified by a structural-functional analysis which was necessary—but *not of itself, enough.* *All* these elements of *fact* and components of *method* were necessary *in close conjunction with each other* for a satisfactory analysis of the vast 'consensus' of facts which comprised *'the social system'*: the distinctive subject-matter of sociology. Sociological analysis was *not,* therefore, one or other of these components, or *separate* components used here and there, but was distinctly and distinctively *all these components together in one entire system of analysis.*

This point re-emphasized, and made perfectly clear, too, the way in which sociology—whilst properly rejecting the metaphysical notions of 'ultimates' *behind* phenomena (whether 'ideal' or 'material'), could, nonetheless, still properly investigate elements and dimensions of the actuality of social and psychological processes which might not be evident in the overt expressions of men's conduct, and might not even exist in their consciousness. And this was nothing mysterious. It was not replacing a 'metaphysical' with a 'scientific' mystique. It was simply a recognition that men's consciousness in society did not, and could not, embrace everything; and that elements of society *not evident, not intended, not foreseen,* could be brought to light by careful study. This was a careful insistence, again, that sociology embraced, necessarily, *both* genetic (in terms of 'efficient' causes of *events*) *and* teleological (in terms of 'ends' deliberately sought in *action*) components and principles of explanation.

And this point re-emphasized, too, the fundamental persuasion of sociology, that social systems *existed* as *complex interdependencies of associational facts.* The *actual nature* of society, though containing individuals and their purposes, was an empirically found interconnectedness of associational facts possessing qualities and including processes which were *other* than them, and went *beyond* them.

All the nineteenth century founders of the subject were agreed, then, on this final component in the analysis of the nature of society: the inclusion of the study of the *unintended consequences* of men's social activities.

To summarize, then:

It was held that a satisfactory analysis of the nature of society, of the 'social system'—which was the distinctive subject-matter of sociology—necessarily included:

    (i) the study of the qualitative and quantitative aspects of the population,

   (ii) its environmental conditions,
  (iii) the structural-functional analysis of its 'consensus'* of institutions and groups,
  (iv) the study of the psychological aspects of these associational forms and their influences upon individuals,
   (v) the study, in 'teleological' terms, of the sequences of social action which men pursued within this framework, and of their 'character' as well as 'personality' formation, and
  (vi) the study of the unintended consequences of men's social activities.

Sociological analysis was not one or other of these components, but (though they could be distinguished for purposes of clarity and accuracy of understanding), the incorporation of *all* of them in a *system* of analysis which sufficiently took into account the *empirical existence* of *social systems* which were *actual societal interdependencies of facts* of which all these components and dimensions were *aspects* closely interwoven and conjoint. Any persuasion that *part* of this societal interdependency of facts could be sufficiently explained *in isolation* from its context; *without* being seen within this perspective of interconnection; was, it was insisted, an error.

Social Dynamics: The Application of this Analysis to the Study of Actual Societies in History: Theories of Order and Change, Similarity and Diversity

That this analysis of social systems—derived from the clarification of the distinctive qualities of which we were aware in our existing experience and observation of them—could then be systematically applied to the empirical study of actual societies, of both the past and the present, in an attempt to establish testable knowledge about them; to discover and state generalizations about them; and to achieve theories about the kinds of 'consensus' found among them: theories about their similarities and diversities; about their processes of both order and change.

   Social Statics was a systematic analysis of the distinctive subject-matter of sociology: the nature of the 'social system'. Social Dynamics was the application of this analysis in the empirical study of actual societies and the careful elaboration of specific theories about them.

* We must still be careful to note that this term 'consensus' did not mean 'harmony'—but only a 'kind of interdependence'—which dealt with conflict as well as co-operation.

The subject-matter of 'Statics' and 'Dynamics' was the same: the scientific study of social systems; they were only useful distinctions of method and theory—and, as such, they were, clearly, in the closest relationship with each other. The formulation of 'Statics' was derived from our *existing* experience and observation of the nature of society; and, once clearly formulated, it guided our empirical studies and underlay the hypothetical assumptions of our 'theories' in 'Dynamics'. But also, conversely, our systematic empirical studies and the detailed consideration of 'theories' might well lead us to alter—perhaps slightly, perhaps considerably—our formulations in 'Static' analysis, to take into account dimensions of fact, or kinds of interconnection, of which we had been unaware and which our empirical studies had revealed. There was, therefore, continuous interchange between the two; they were both parts of the ongoing enterprise of achieving the greatest scientific accuracy possible.

The application of the system of analysis, as outlined, to the empirical study of actual societies and the construction of specific theories, necessitated the recognition, clarification, and employment of the following additional components of fact and method:

(a) The Classification and Comparative Study of Societies

The attempt to establish generalizations about social systems necessitated (indeed entailed!) the gathering together and arrangement of knowledge about them in some systematic and manageable form. To *generalize* at once meant the clarification of resemblances and differences between societies: it immediately entailed a *classification* of facts. To *generalize* also meant, at once, not an *arbitrary* selection and comparison of facts, but a *systematic comparative study* so that their empirical truth (the fact that they really *were* descriptive generalizations) could be demonstrated and checked. *Generalization, classification, systematic comparison*, were *all of a piece*: none could exist without the other. There was, then, no *one kind* of sociology called 'comparative sociology': sociology was *essentially* comparative as a *scientific* study of societies, attempting to establish testable generalizations about them.

But a further point was important here: namely, that generalization, classification, and systematic comparison were inseparable from (were, strictly speaking, part and parcel of) the statement of specific theories. The *criteria* adopted for the classification of societies (e.g., Property-Relations in the case of Marx, States of Knowledge in the case of Comte, etc.) would themselves be indicative of a hypothetical persuasion that *these* were the factors most significant for understanding and explaining the various kinds of society and their processes of order and change. This can be put simply in this way: that the *procedures* of generalization, classification, and systematic comparison were intimately connected with the formulation and satisfactory statement of *specific theories*; they were the procedural embodiment of hypothetical persuasions—whether implicit or explicit. Bearing this in mind, it can further be said that the *procedures* of generalization, classification, and systematic comparison were necessary: (*a*) for the systematic arrangement of descriptive knowledge—which might yield hypothetical persuasions previously unlooked for, even though it might rest on certain hypothetical persuasions already implicitly held, and (*b*) for the *testing* of *theoretical generalizations* at various levels when they were *explicitly* made.*

The theorists we have studied took these matters into account in both implicit and explicit ways, and it is here that we can see very clearly the theoretical point of 'weighting' some component of the analysis of 'statics' more than others for the construction of theoretical models which embody hypothetical persuasions. It is impossible to be exhaustive on this—but it is sufficient to note clearly that the *classification* of societies was proposed, and accomplished, in *two* ways.

On the one hand, societies were classified in accordance with some kind of *observable regularity*, some *empirical fact*, which was distinctive. Thus, though some were more specific than others, all the theorists accepted that human societies could be classified in accordance with what Spencer called their 'degree of aggregation': whether they were groups of families, clans, tribes, confederations of tribes, civic nations, empires, confederations of nations. This was one procedure of classification and comparison which made possible much more elaborate study of the kinds of 'consensus' which characterized each 'level of composition', each distinctive 'type' of society; and it could be expected to provide a useful basis for further theories and the advancement of knowledge. Even here, it must be said that this classification entailed the implicit hypothesis of a process of 'social evolution', but, as we have seen, this was not a blanket-like concept of inevitability, as commonly supposed, but provided for a causal analysis of the *many factors* involved in

* This has been much discussed as the 'problem of inductive logic' by contemporary scholars such as Karl Popper and Peter Medawar, but I shall not discuss it further here because in my opinion it has been done to death. It may well be that there is no '*logic*' of induction, but what were called the inductive *procedures* were undoubtedly necessary in relation to theory-formulation, and were very likely to *yield* fruitful theories simply as an outcome of detailed acquaintance with a particular 'universe' of facts. However, once the implicit nature of hypothesis in these procedures is recognized, there is no further problem.

628

evolution (and dissolution!) But here it is enough to say that the *distinctive degrees of aggregation* were empirically *there*, whatever the details of the evolutionary hypothesis. A 'tribe' was clearly distinguishable from a 'City-State' founded by the union of a number of tribes, and both were distinguishable from, say, the modern 'Nation'. This was a firm empirical basis for classification which stood firm whatever the hypothesis that might be entertained to *explain* this variety of forms.

However, in addition to this, a second method of classifying societies was also proposed *explicitly for* a parallel theoretical interpretation of these various forms and 'levels' of social organization. Thus Comte's 'Law of the Three Stages' was a construction of three models of social order which also embodied a theoretical understanding of the chief historical changes which were observable among all the societies in the world. They were models of society, incorporating all the components upon which the analysis of 'Statics' insisted, but 'weighting' the component of mind and knowledge, and specific cumulative developments in them and in their powers of control, as being especially significant in bringing about social changes. Similarly, Spencer's classification of three 'types' of society—the Militant, Industrial, and Ethical, parallel to the classification in terms of 'degrees of aggregation'—was a construction of three 'models' for analysing, interpreting, and explaining the patterns of change which the first classification described. And these models—again, including all the components insisted upon by the analysis of 'statics'—were constructed by the significant 'grouping' of institutions (the Regulatory, the Sustaining, the Distributive), and the 'weighting' of one or other of these to explain particular kinds of social change. Marx's classification—though his models were not so clearly worked out—rested similarly upon 'weighting' the economic and property relations, which, in his view, were hypothetically significant. And we have seen how Ward, Sumner and Giddings, too, employed the same practices of classification and comparison: Giddings, especially, managing to incorporate practically all the earlier ideas.

Classification, then, rested upon (1) the designation of observable degrees of *social aggregation* or *social composition*: which arranged knowledge systematically for further detailed study, and (2) the construction of 'types' or 'models' which, much more explicitly, incorporated a 'theory'.

A final aspect of this was that the *Comparative Method* in sociology was accordingly seen in two (though clearly connected) ways: (1) as the systematic descriptive study of societies, accomplishing an arrangement of knowledge resting upon generalizations, but making the exploration for further, and more detailed, generalizations possible, and (2) as the only alternative which sociology had to the method of artificially controlled *experiment*. In this sense, the careful employment of comparative studies was the only way of *testing theories*.

(b) *The Construction of Theoretical Models*

Enough has been said on the construction of 'models', appropriately 'weighted', for the careful elaboration of theories, but one or two specific aspects of this method need to be stated clearly. The first is that this method was of more detailed application than that we have mentioned—the construction of 'types of society'. In Giddings most clearly, it was also employed to construct 'models' or 'types' of *social action* which were used to explain 'teleologically' various kinds of social process—whether large-scale or small. The three types he elucidated: the Impulsive, Traditional, and Rational types of social action were applicable to small groups and various institutions as well as to the types of action which parallelled changes in society as a whole (i.e., which involved large-scale historical movements.)

And this leads to the connected point that, because of the distinctive qualities of human societies, *theories* could not simply be statements of interconnection (whether of institutions or of their psychological aspects) in terms of *efficient causation*, but had also to incorporate the necessary elements of conscious, deliberate 'teleology'. The *interdependencies of institutions* and of the *psychological aspects of social relationships—all* such regularities or uniformities—had also to be accompanied by a teleological explanation in terms of the understanding of social action. What this amounts to is that *theories* in sociology seemed only possible (seemed only adequate in taking all these interdependencies into account) *by the construction of such models*.

This, it must be clearly seen, was not in any sense a denial of the methods of empirical science, it was, on the contrary, the proper construction of concepts and methods to make the science of society *sufficient* for engaging accurately with the actual distinctive complexities of its subject-matter.

(c) *Historical Study: conceptions of persistence and change. Change, Evolution, Development and Progress.*

The attempt to achieve testable description, generalization, and explanation, requiring the necessary procedures of classification, comparative study, and the interpretive understanding of social action, was conducted on the completely firm and agreed recognition that societies were *essentially* cumulative *historical* phenomena. Certain aspects of this require clear statement.

Social systems—even the most simple societies of all—were *essentially* accumulations and transmissions of the *achievements* of men in their many social activities. To adopt a non-historical, or a-historical view of any society (no matter how simple) was therefore an *error*. Even a simple society which manifested no change *now*, was, in fact, the outcome of an untold period of accommodation to the life-conditions of the group; so that to regard it as a *non*-historical system was no more than to lose sight of the true evolutionary perspective of human and social development.

The study of *persisting order* and of *change* were therefore *both* aspects of the recognition that societies were *processes* of cumulative transmission. It is important to see here that *persisting order* was as much a *historical* matter, requiring understanding and explanation, as was *change*. But both order and change came to be studied within the context of other conceptions.

CHANGE

Firstly, it is worth emphasizing that all earlier theories of an *eternal order* of things, and all '*cyclical*' theories of change, were abandoned. *Change* was simply thought of as something *different* from that which had existed previously; and it was agreed that human society had undergone ongoing change in this sense.

EVOLUTION

Secondly, however, the *changes* of societies were held to be not arbitrary, but explicable in terms of the activities of men in meeting their environmental conditions—first in adapting successfully to them, then, increasingly, in achieving the knowledge and power to transform them. But unintended consequences, as well as conscious purposes, entered into the shaping of societies, so that the analysis and explanation of social systems in the contexts of their environments was required, and this was provided by the concept of *evolution*. Again, this need not be elaborated, but we must note for completeness of statement that this was *not* a blanket-term description, but the provision of a *set* of explanatory components. Without being exhaustive, these included at least:

(i) the grounds of the instability of the homogeneous,
(ii) the reasons for the multiplication of effects once differentiation has begun,
(iii) the factors making for the specialization and segregation of parts,
(iv) the 'equilibrium-disequilibrium' adjustments to changing conditions,

631

    (v) the factors making for disintegration and dissolution, and,

    (vi) (to bring in Marx) the possibility that changing quantitative conditions may produce *qualitatively* different modes of social life, etc.

It was clear, in all this, that *evolution* was *not* one theory of change, or a *'mono-causal'* theory, but provided within its perspective for *many* patterns of causal explanation; and it is clear, too, that it entailed an 'equilibrium-disequilibrium' analysis of accommodations to the stresses of changing conditions—which could, of course, result in *dis*equilibrium as well as equilibrium, and which, if extreme, could lead to *dissolution* as well as integrated development.

DEVELOPMENT

A third essential concept was that of *Development*. Societies did not simply become *different*, nor did they only manifest certain patterns of 'adaptation' to their environments. They were characterized by *cumulative development*. Men achieved certain skills, techniques, bodies of knowledge, judgments of value, in their activities. These were transmitted as the 'heritage' of the society and new achievements were possible on the basis of them. *Social development*—in the changing nature of technical skills and of social institutions—was recognized as an essential *fact* of human society and was therefore a necessary element to take into account in theories of social change.

PROGRESS

It is impossible to conceive of *development*, however (as cumulative achievement), without acknowledging an element of *improvement*; and this leads to the fourth important element in considering theories of social change: the concept of *progress*. For the moment, we need not enter into the ethical questions surrounding the idea of 'progress', because the central agreements of the nineteenth century theorists can be made clear without them. Their contention was simply this: that men in their practical activities sought practical advantage; that the folkways, mores, institutions and laws of all societies embodied the ways of doing things which had been selected, largely on a basis of trial and error, over long periods of social development; that men established ever more accurate knowledge that gave them better powers of control over nature and improved their capacities to act purposively in *transforming* their environments (rather than being a prey to them); so that there was certainly a *drive towards progress* in society. There was a 'strain towards improvement' in skills and institutions even in their simplest forms in the most traditional societies, and this was consciously and purposively pursued as greater knowledge and control was achieved. The nineteenth century theorists also believed, of course, that *moral* progress was a possible concomitant of these changes, but none of them held that such progress was *inevitable*; on the contrary, their very effort in the making of sociology was based upon their conviction as to the conscious and deliberate *effort* which men would have to make if the massive problems of industrial society were to be satisfactorily met and overcome. The essential point, however, was that— for them—the very nature of society was such as to include a drive for *progress*, as well as elements of evolutionary adaptation, cumulative development, and ongoing difference. The concepts of change, evolution, development, and progress were therefore all necessary concepts in the study of the *historical* dimensions of societies.

(d) *The centrality of Mind and Knowledge in the 'Models' of society and the Theories of Social Change*

A quite basic point of agreement among all the nineteenth century theorists we have studied was their conviction that it was the capacity of the human mind to establish knowledge and control over both nature and society, which was of central importance in explaining the major sequences of social change, evolution, and development in history. The only theorist who might, at first glance, seem to be an exception to this was Marx, but we have seen that once his 'materialism' is thoroughly examined, it, too, is a theory resting upon the extension of knowledge and control in men's practical activities, and the hidden adjustments of society are no more than the 'unintended consequences' which we have seen plainly in all the other theorists. All of them, without exception then, emphasize the central importance of the purposive powers of mind and the cumulative achievement of ever more accurate knowledge on the basis of which prediction could be more reliable and social action more effective in attaining its ends.

Two particular points are worth clear emphasis here.

The first is that it was this persuasion concerning the powers of the human mind and the crucial importance of the acquisition, dissemination, and transmission of knowledge in society which underlay the importance which all these men attributed to 'progress' in social change. These powers of mind, these accumulations of knowledge and control, were the central distinguishing *facts* in the nature of societies and their processes of change; and no theory of order and change could properly ignore them. This persuasion too, of course, underlay the concern felt by these men for *education* and *democracy* in society.

The second point, however, is of even greater interest, and is that—though expressed in various ways—all these men agreed that the entire processes of natural and social change, evolution, development, and progress in the entirety of the history of the world before the emergence of the modern scientific epoch was no more than the *pre-history* of man. Hitherto, through all the long ages of history, through all the complex processes of man's struggle in the world and in society, *genetic* constraints and limitations had been predominant. Men had groped their way through their many struggles aiming at immediate and necessitous objectives; a social order, culminating from many unintended and unforeseen consequences, had come to be laid down. But only now—with modern science and much improved technological control was man able to comprehend this entire situation, to see and assess it clearly, and, with conscious responsibility, to begin the period of his own purposive creation: to make his own history; to make himself. Again, we see the centrality of sociology (in the minds of these men) in this awareness of the crucial situation of human action. For better, for worse: men now had to be responsible for their own nature and destiny; and for this, a firm knowledge of society, as of nature, was indispensable.

It is, to my mind, of convincing importance that, coming from so many *apparently* different roots and persuasions, the theories of social change, offered by all these men focused upon this central feature of the modern human situation: *man's self-responsibility in knowledge, morality, and creative social action.*

This it was which had been at the roots of the insufficiency of earlier social theories, and the awareness of the need for a science of society, at the beginning of the nineteenth century. This it was which provided the central focus, the central agreement, of all these theoretical studies which had, by the end of the century, laid the foundations of this science.

An entire conspectus of sociology had therefore been achieved in both 'Statics' and 'Dynamics'. Agreement had been clearly found in the necessary components for the analysis of the distinctive nature of society, of the 'social system'; and agreement had also been found in the necessary components for specific theories in applying this analysis to the study of particular kinds of societies, kinds of social change, etc. And agreement was still clear about the central focus: of the necessity of the science of society for grappling with the qualitatively new and challenging situation in which man found himself.

A simple indication of these similarities of conclusion, despite apparently different concepts and starting-points, may be seen in the accompanying diagram.

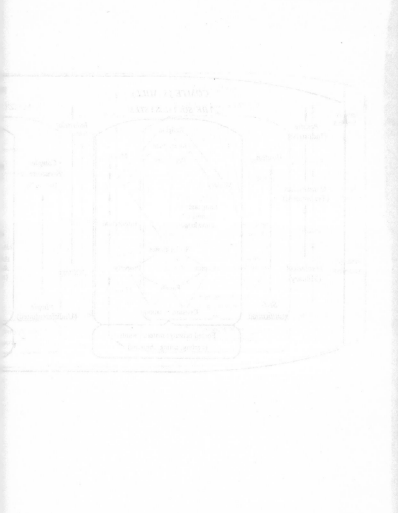

Some Distinctive Methods of Sociology

It was agreed, too, that sociology required certain distinctive methods, as a science, in accordance with its distinctive subject-matter.

Many of the methods of sociology were, of course, exactly the same as those of other sciences. There was the same insistence upon careful observation, description, analysis, classification, comparative study, in order to arrive at testable generalizations and theories. Where appropriate, there was the same concern for both qualitative and quantitative (i.e. measurable, statistical) methods. We have seen, too, the many specific methods outlined for the study of 'social systems': structural-functional analysis, equilibrium-disequilibrium analysis, the analysis of group processes—including their psychological aspects, and so on—and there is no point in reiterating these. It is worthwhile, however, simply to note clearly those methods which, according to the nineteenth century theorists, were distinctive of sociology, and we might note the agreements about the *rejection* as well as the acceptance of certain methods.

(a) The Historical Method

Social systems were essentially historical processes, and therefore the historical method was essential to sociology. We have seen what went into this, but we may just emphasize again that this was distinctive from anything found in the sciences of 'nature' because social systems were essentially cumulative traditions compounded of human *achievements*, and *these* historical processes were different from anything else found in nature.

(b) The Comparative Method

Distinctive emphasis was placed upon the Comparative Method not because it was not important in other sciences, but because it was of *crucial* importance in sociology as the only alternative to artificial experimentation. Only by careful comparative studies could generalizations and theories be subjected to conditions of test.

(c) The Inverse-Deductive Method

Since the greater number of the social events which have impressed us, about which we have knowledge, and which lead us to desire theories about them are *already of the past*, and cannot be artificially re-created for prospective experimental tests, the employment of the historical and comparative methods must entail a certain large measure of 'inverse-deductive' procedure. We are, more often than not, trying to find adequate explanations of empirical generalizations and concrete instances which we already know. This does not preclude all possibility of prediction of existing or forthcoming events for the purpose of submitting a theory to conditions of test; but it does mean that, at any given time, the bulk of our knowledge is of the past; in any ordinary sense* unrepeatable; and we are necessarily in the position of seeking, retrospectively, adequate explanations, and can only manipulate the available data to the best advantage possible.

It is a point worth making here, that the greater part of the *empirical data* of sociology must be of a *documentary* kind. Much hangs on this. It could be said with much truth that many sociologists have neglected the importance of this. On the other hand men like Comte, Marx, Spencer did not find a lot of worthwhile history to hand when they looked for it. The truth is that sociology and historiography are intimately connected, and the theoretical preoccupations of both have been very similar, if not identical, from the early nineteenth century to now.

(*d*) *The Multiplicity of Factors and the Compounding of Causes and Effects*

The study of society necessitated the consideration of several essential aspects, always closely related in any social actuality: as, for example, the structure of social organization, the analysis of functions, the analysis of groups, the study of the psychological aspects of the situation, and the study of the 'teleological' elements of the sequences of social action. Also, the actuality of society was always very complex, so that any simple-minded postulation of one cause explaining one event was of very dubious value, if it was not always doomed to failure. The essential thing in satisfactory sociological analysis was that *all* these components should be taken into account in relation to each other, and that care should be taken to try to trace the many kinds of cause-and-effect relationship and compound them into a satisfactory explanation.

(*e*) *Teleological explanation and the construction of 'Types' of 'Action'*

The most distinctive method of sociology, however, was attendant upon the persuasion that human *action* was different from all other events and elements of behaviour in nature, and necessitated a qualitatively different kind of causal explanation in terms of the understanding of the ends which men pursued and the choices, deliberation, calculation, and use of means which went into their conscious activities. All these theorists employed this conception

* i.e. in any sense of repetition as a controlled experiment.

of *action*: from Comte to Ward and Giddings; and, again, even in Marx there was a forthright recognition of it. This 'teleological' kind of explanation was, then, quite distinctive, and it led to the construction of 'types' or 'models' of societies and of sequences of social action which attempted interpretive explanations in addition to (and parallel to) the 'genetic' kinds of explanation of social and psychological regularities.

(f) Agreed REJECTIONS *of method*
It almost goes without saying that all these theorists were agreed in *rejecting*, as *not* being distinctive of sociology, (*a*) the idea of scientific empiricism as a bit-and-piece collection of 'facts' quite unguided by theory, and (*b*) pure deduction from 'a priori' premises.

The Limitations of Sociology: But its Use for the Central Perspective of Social Action

On the relations between sociology and philosophical ethics there was a good deal of confusion among the nineteenth century theorists, but two or three points were fairly widely and firmly agreed, and all were important. These were:

(a) Sociological knowledge never final: RELATIVE *but not* ARBITRARY
That, in addition to being unable to reach any 'ultimates' in explanation, sociology could never claim to reach *final* knowledge. The knowledge of sociology; the theories which it proposed and tested; would always, necessarily, be limited to the mental and perceptual equipment of man and relative to the many details of his social situation. At the same time, such knowledge was not *arbitrary*. It would be the most accurate knowledge possible from the use of the scientific method at the time and in these conditions. But the 'truths' and 'laws' of sociology would always be 'theories' open to test.

(b) The most reliable basis for Prediction and Social Practice
That, if the methods of sociology were carefully pursued, the knowledge provided would be—if not exact (since it could not hope for the degree of exactitude of other sciences)—at least the most exact that was humanly possible. As such, it could provide the best basis for prediction and social action. Even here, however, care had to be exercised. For sociological knowledge (or the knowledge of any other social science) was not in itself enough. Ideally, it was best considered in relation to ethical principles as clarified by the moral philosopher, and the practical assessments and judgments of men

who had had much experience in the 'arts' of society: the judge, the, lawyer, the doctor, the statesman, etc. With all these three combined that basis for action could be arrived at which would be the most reliable that was possible.

The other aspect of this point which was most important was the recognition that the subject-matter which yielded a lesser degree of exactitude of knowledge, was also the subject-matter which was most *modifiable* by deliberate action. Mill's insistence, then, that: 'a degree of knowledge altogether insufficient for prediction, is nonetheless of the utmost value for guidance . . .' was of very considerable importance. Indeed, when all the theories of the nineteenth century are drawn together, it is the composed, balanced wisdom of Mill which seems of greatest worth in qualifying extremes and leading to properly modest and satisfactory conclusions.

(c) The Sociological Perspective the Only Perspective for Social Study and Social Action

The final point on which all were agreed was the conviction that— whatever the difficulties attending the subject—the sociological perspective: the study of societal facts and sequences of social action as parts and aspects of *social systems* undergoing historical processes of order and change, was the *only* correct perspective. Any other approach had been shown to be superficial, insufficient and discredited. For better, for worse—sociology was the only valid approach in the quest for testable knowledge about the complex institutional life of men in society: all trends of intellectual thought had led to it; all urgent social needs cried out for it. To try to create such a science, as satisfactorily as possible, was all we could do. If there were those who denied and rejected it: then the onus lay upon them to produce something better.

All the theorists were completely agreed with the perspective which has guided us from the start: namely that a science of society had become *necessary* as an objective of endeavour in the modern world, because of the disruption of the old traditional order of society and the situation which now confronted mankind—qualitatively new in scale and complexity, in knowledge and power—of taking upon himself, with a full consciousness of his responsibility, the deliberate reconstruction of society; the making of his own destiny. The making of sociology was a necessary part of the making of a new society.

This, then, is a summary statement of the entire conspectus of the new science of sociology as it had been founded by the end of the nineteenth century.

Such a summary could not possibly be exhaustive in its detail; it could not possibly include all the detailed points and nuances provided by each theorist; but I hope that it is reasonably comprehensive as an *outline;* that it makes clear, at least, all the essential components of the subject; and that it can be seen how the many ideas of the various theorists could be fitted into the entire schema.

Let us now stop for a moment; remind ourselves that all this was accomplished by the end of the nineteenth century; and make one or two comments in retrospect.

It is interesting, first of all, to see that this conspectus of sociology, after all the detailed thought and study that had gone into its foundation throughout the nineteenth century, was, in its achieved form, still entirely in accordance with all the assumptions of common sense as we outlined them earlier. It is worthwhile at this stage to glance back to our summary statement of our common sense assumptions (on page 70) and to see how all the persuasions outlined there were embodied in the newly defined science of society. The foundations of sociology were, then, well laid in this respect: they clearly constituted a searching reflection upon common sense assumptions and were a clear advance upon them. They were not foreign to them in any respect.

Similarly, it is also worthwhile at this stage to note that these foundations of sociology were a clear advance upon the earlier social theories—of religion, political philosophy, the philosophy of history, etc.—which we summarized at the outset. A glance at our summary statement of the components of religious theories, for example, (page 91) will show that sociological theory dealt with the same elements—but with immeasurably improved, more searching, and more reliable methods. At the same time the central humane concern was not diminished by one iota. Indeed the struggle against earlier religious theories for the achievement of sociology and a more reliable understanding of the social predicaments of man was undertaken entirely *because* of a deep humane concern. It was part of a profound commitment on the part of these men to the struggle to create a new social order which, though rooted in massive disruptions and holding grave dangers of dehumanization, could be the basis for the achievement, throughout the world, of those high qualities of life, culture, social justice and personal character which, hitherto, had been only known as elements of 'vision'. Sociology was foreign to these early social theories only in that it sought to be an improvement upon them.

Even in these first foundations, then, sociology had accomplished a clear advance upon both common sense assumptions and earlier social theories: growing out of them, and growing beyond them. It had already produced specific theories which were rich in the detail of systematic comparative studies, provided new perspectives, and had set out clear principles of analysis and methods of study in the light of which theories could be tested and knowledge could cumulatively advance.

A third comment, worth a simple note, is that the foundations of sociology were *perfectly clear*. All the elements of the new systematic science of society were stated with *perfect clarity*. There was nothing whatever that was obscure; nothing difficult; nothing misleading by any kind of purposeful obscurantism; nothing outrageous by way of invalid or unfounded intellectual claims. The nineteenth century theorists struggled towards *clarity*, and they achieved it. If there are those who do not find these matters clear, we have no alternative but to conclude that there is something defective in their mental equipment. There are only two other possibilities: (*a*) that they have not sufficiently read and studied that which they criticize, or (*b*) that they have entrenched academic interests of their own which lead them to preserve and promulgate this endless, tedious, and silly myth about sociology's obscurantism.

The foundations of sociology provided an entire system of analysis very clearly worked out, and accomplished after very thorough argument. Obviously, it was possible to disagree with aspects of this system of analysis and the kinds of theory which it made possible, and the whole emphasis of sociology was that such continuous criticism should take place. Science *consists* of continuous criticism, and sociology explicitly provided for this in its methods. But in no sense could it be charged with a lack of clarity.

There is, of course, the third possibility that sociology has been not only misconstrued by those who have never studied it, but also attacked by those committed to other subjects which were, and are, endangered by it. At the very end of this book we can come back to this question; but here it is enough to note again the peculiarity of sociology: that it was not founded by '*academics*' and was not a '*university subject*' (or '*discipline*', as the critics like to say). The making of sociology was part of the task of making a new society, and the founding of the new science was accomplished by men who were at the heart of political thought and political action; who were *engaged* in the fullest sense with public affairs; and involved in continuous critical discussion and writing about them. All the men we have considered were men of powerful human concern; admirable in the depth of their commitment and the scale of their efforts in seeking a basis of knowledge sufficient for the task of reconstruction which they saw before them. All of them had emphasized the importance of the sociological perspective in education, from Comte onwards, but it was only among the Americans, at the end of the century, that direct steps were taken to introduce the science as a 'subject' at the several levels of schools, colleges, and universities. In Giddings especially, there was the direct concern for teaching, and the writing of a text-book setting out the elements of sociological analysis.

Here we need only note that the practical roots of the intellectual effort that went into the making of sociology; the common-sense roots, too; were also borne out by this fact: that sociology was not a creation of the universities. But the introduction of it into education was just beginning when its foundations had been firmly laid by the end of the century. From this point on, quite new issues of the educational 'professionalization' of the subject, and the struggles between its proponents and opponents in the universities, began to arise. And these we shall be able to trace when we come to the developments of the subject during our own century.

A final group of points remain.

What are we to make of those people who believe that sociology is a 'new' subject, which has been created in the universities since the last war? Surely only one thing: they are ignorant of it. They can know nothing about it.

What are we to make of those people who believe that sociology is the 'newest' of the social sciences?—having been developed only recently, and long after the consolidation of economics, political science, and the like? Surely, again, only that they are ignorant of these matters.

The foundations of sociology were already firmly and clearly laid by the end of the nineteenth century—and that, after a century of detailed argument and study. And this course of argument and study *parallelled* the development of economics and political science; being just as long-lived as they, and rooted in exactly the same nexus of intellectual ferment and social disorder.*

Such critics simply do not know what they are talking about. They are teaching a perspective which is totally false.

What also are we to say of those people who claim that sociology is a 'rag-bag' of bit-and-piece studies of social life, and a collection of theories, which appear to be quite disconnected, and in disagreement with each other? What are we to say of those who claim that the work of the founders of sociology was 'rarely cumulative'; that it was often characterized 'more by passion than by precision', by 'imagination rather than by order', and was 'sometimes not *scientific* on any definition . . .' and that these men 'did not spell out

* Just as it parallelled the fundamental re-making of historiography during the nineteenth century.

in any detailed way the precise nature either of sociological problems or of sociological analysis'? One can only gasp at the outrageous nature of such judgments.

We have seen in the most detailed way, the great consistency which existed among all the great figures of the nineteenth century—despite their differences of particular concepts and particular emphases; but, more especially, we have seen the completely demonstrable connections linking all these theorists in the ongoing argument of the century. Again, it is true that Marx appears something of an 'odd man out' here, but—even here—we have seen how similar his notions were to those of the other theorists underneath his metaphysical confusions and political polemics. But as for the rest: the thread which runs through Comte, Mill, Spencer, Ward, Sumner, and Giddings is completely and utterly clear, and Giddings in a quite indisputable way can be shown to be a critical summation, a systematization, of practically all the important elements of analysis which had been clarified before him. The cumulative nature of the work of the founders of sociology was perfectly clear, and the articulate statement of the orderly system and the related components of sociological analysis to be found in it was plain for all to read.

These and similar judgments are therefore such as completely to defeat understanding: especially when they are asserted by some of those who are *teaching* sociology, as well as others—economists, political scientists, members of the House of Lords, Vice-Chancellors, and the like—whose errors and superficialities of judgment can be more readily understood. The only conclusion there can possibly be is that people *do not read and study the things they criticize*: a fantastic and lamentable state of affairs!—especially among people who make public noises in supposed defence of standards of intellectual excellence.

However, our own concluding statement of the nature of the 'Foundations of Sociology' as accomplished by the end of the nineteenth century is clear beyond doubt. It has cost a good deal of study and effort, but the achievement of this basic clarity will be seen to have been well worth while. From this basis we can move on confidently to assess the 'Developments' of our own century; and, having done this, we shall then be in a position to clarify and throw into the wastepaper-basket a score of fallacies which are ruining the contemporary perspectives of the subject and breeding misunderstandings.

Appendices

Appendix 1
The Scottish School

Some historians of social thought would claim that the beginning of sociology proper was to be found not in the work of Comte, but in that of this closely related group of scholars in the Scottish Universities during the eighteenth century; and certainly quite a strong case could be made for this. Centrally, these men were moral philosophers, but, like others we have mentioned, they were strongly influenced by Montesquieu, and had the common persuasion of the time that morality could only be understood in the context of social institutions, and that social institutions could only be understood in the context of an analysis of society as a whole. Furthermore, they sought an understanding of the psychological (as well as the social) aspects of moral experience, and saw all this within the cumulative changes of the history of society.

These men have come to be grouped together as the 'Scottish School'; they were in many cases personal friends and colleagues; and certainly a clear intellectual (critical) development of their ideas took place during the century—from those of Francis Hutcheson, for example, on the nature of the moral sense in human nature, to those of Thomas Reid and Dugald Stewart which were the outcome of a critical study of these and similar ideas.

The chief writers in this 'School' were: Francis Hutcheson (1694–1747), David Hume (1711–76), Adam Smith (1723–90), Adam Ferguson (1723–1816), Lord Kames (1696–1782), Thomas Reid (1710–96), Dugald Stewart (1753–1828), and Lord Monboddo (1714–99). They were all professional scholars of distinction; many were men of affairs—connected with the law, agriculture, etc. (and sometimes both); and all saw the closest relations between all the social sciences; between these and philosophy; and between careful scholarship and a detailed concern for, and engagement in, practical social and political affairs. Their work covered a wide range, systematically, and with excellence; their books still repay detailed study; and there is no doubt whatever of their importance.

The reason why I have chosen not to lay emphasis upon them in this account of the 'Beginnings' and 'Foundations' of sociology—or, rather, the reason why I have not selected them to mark the initial *foundation* of the subject—is not in any sense because of a low estimation of their work, but simply because, as it seems to me, though offering a wealth of comment upon the nature of man and society, they nowhere produced *a conceptual system of sociological analysis or sociological theory* such as that produced by Comte. Their pages are full of comparative and analytical comments about human psychology and the nature and development of society which amount to substantive theoretical pronouncements—but nowhere is a clear systematic schema established whereby observation, description, classification, generalization, comparison and testing could thereafter be pursued in an agreed way. Their comments and speculations—though rooted in a comparative study of social facts—were still, as they themselves forthrightly stated, of the nature of 'conjecture' in portraying, chiefly, a history of social institutions, or a 'history of civil society'.

It was Comte, more than anyone else, who produced a clear statement of the nature of science and a clear scheme of analysis whereby man and society could be studied scientifically; who thus marked the definitive foundation of the new science of sociology; who brought earlier developments (including those of the Scottish thinkers) clearly to a head, and established the basis for a new point of departure. And this is why I have selected him, and not the Scots, for special emphasis: to mark boldly this initial statement of a new science.

But the work of these slightly earlier thinkers was, nonetheless, filled with insights, theoretical principles, and specific comments which remain of value, and some of which, indeed, are perennially true. Adam Smith in his *Theory of Moral Sentiments* had much to say on the ways in which human morality was rooted in instinct, emotion and sympathy, which was to influence many later thinkers. Indeed, Hutcheson, Hume, Kames and others had much to say about social psychology in their various discussions of man's 'moral sense'. They also saw, and indicated, but with very careful qualification, the place of animal studies in the study of man. And they emphasized many of the points which came to be stressed and elaborated by others: that society was essentially historical; that social processes could not be 'reduced' to explanations in terms of 'individual psychology'; that moral evaluations lay at the heart of 'institutionalization'; etc., etc. It is impossible therefore to indicate all the dimensions of their work, but a few brief examples might be given from *An Essay on the History of Civil Society*, by Adam Ferguson, which is unquestionably one of the great books in the making of sociology; and these will serve to illustrate, at least, the quality of the thought to be found in these writings.

In the first place, Ferguson attacked the assumption that the complex nature of man in society as he existed at *present*, could only be understood by some conjecture about a simpler nature which he had possessed *originally*. In making such an assumption, and entertaining such conjectures, he said: '... we are the dupes of a subtilty, which promises to supply every defect of our knowledge, and, by filling up a few blanks in the story of nature, pretends to conduct our apprehension nearer to the source of existence.' We should, he argues, reject such conjectures, and chiefly study man *as he is*; *as our comparative studies actually find him.*

'In every other instance, the natural historian thinks himself obliged to collect facts, not to offer conjectures. When he treats of any particular species of animals, he supposes that their present dispositions and instincts are the same which they originally had, and that their present manner of life is a continuance of their first destination. He admits, that his knowledge of the material system of the world consists in a collection of facts, or at most, in general tenets derived from particular observations and experiments. It is only in what relates to himself, and in matters the most important and the most easily known, that he substitutes hypothesis instead of reality, and confounds the provinces of imagination and reason, of poetry and science.

'... it may be safely affirmed, that the character of man, as he now exists, that the laws of his animal and intellectual system, on which his happiness now depends, deserve our principal study; and that general principles relating to this or any other subject, are useful only so far as they are founded on just observation, and lead to the knowledge of important consequences, or so far as they enable us to act with success when we would apply either the intellectual or the physical powers of nature to the purposes of human life.

'If both the earliest and the latest accounts collected from every quarter of the earth, represent mankind as assembled in troops and companies; and the individual always joined by affection to one party, while he is possibly opposed to another; employed in the exercise of recollection and foresight; inclined to communicate his own sentiments, and to be made acquainted with those of others; these facts must be admitted as the foundation of all our reasoning relative to man.'*

The many aspects of *society*, Ferguson insisted, must be taken to be *natural* to man, and he scorned the argument—so often found in modern psychology text-books—that society must be *learned* because it can be shown that a human individual brought up in total isolation from others fails to develop social attributes.

'Particular experiments which have been found so useful in establishing the principles of other sciences, could probably, on this subject, teach us nothing important, or new: we are to take the history of every active being from his conduct in the situation to which he is formed, not from his appearance in any forced or uncommon condition; a wild man therefore,

* *An Essay on the History of Civil Society*, p. 3.

x

caught in the woods, where he had always lived apart from his species, is a singular instance, not a specimen of any general character. As the anatomy of the eye which had never received the impressions of light, or that of an ear which had never felt the impulse of sounds, would probably exhibit defects in the very structure of the organs themselves, arising from their not being applied to their proper functions; so any particular case of this sort would only shew in what degree the powers of apprehension and sentiment could exist where they had not been employed, and what would be the defects and imbecilities of a heart in which the emotions that arise in society had never been felt.

'Mankind are to be taken in groups, as they have always been subsisted. The history of the individual is but a detail of the sentiments and the thoughts he has entertained in the view of his species; and every experiment relative to this subject should be made with entire societies, not with single men.'*

Similarly, he argued, though some conjectural theories as to the 'origins' of human society had led men to seek explanations of their own nature in terms of knowledge about other animal species, great care had to be exercised in such animal studies, and the *differences* between man and other species had very clearly to be remembered, as well as the similarities.

'The progress of mankind, from a supposed state of animal sensibility, to the attainment of reason, to the use of language, and to the habit of society, has been accordingly painted with a force of imagination, and its steps have been marked with a boldness of invention, that would tempt us to admit, among the materials of history, the suggestions of fancy, and to receive, perhaps, as the model of our nature in its original state, some of the animals whose shape has the greatest resemblance to ours.

'It would be ridiculous to affirm as a discovery, that the species of the horse was probably never the same with that of the lion; yet, in opposition to what has dropped from the pens of eminent writers, we are obliged to observe, that men have always appeared among animals a distinct and a superior race; that neither the possession of similar organs, nor the approximation of shape, nor the use of the hand, nor the continued inter-course with this sovereign artist, has enabled any other species to blend their nature or their inventions with his; that, in his rudest state, he is found to be above them; and in his greatest degeneracy, never descends to their level. He is, in short, a man in every condition; and we can learn nothing of his nature from the analogy of other animals. If we would know him, we must attend to himself, to the course of his life, and the tenor of his conduct. With him the society appears to be as old as the individual, and the use of the tongue as universal as that of the hand or the foot. If there was a time in which he had his acquaintance with his own species to make, and his faculties to acquire, it is a time of which we have no record, and in relation to which our opinions can serve no purpose, and are supported by no evidence.'†

* *An Essay on the History of Civil Society*, p. 5.   † *ibid.*, p. 8.

Not all modern 'Comparative Ethology' is so unguarded as to be open to this kind of criticism; but, on the other hand, some of it *is*: and Ferguson's point has strong and permanent validity.

Ferguson also emphasized very clearly some of the other points which came to be quite central in sociological theory: such as, for example, the fact that man's activities in nature and society were *essentially* purposive and *progressive*: that there was a central motive towards *progress* in man's accumulation of knowledge and the practice of his many 'arts'. Many subsequent critics have been 'duped by the subtilty' of their own sophisticated cloudiness; but Ferguson was perfectly clear. In the following passage there is a completely clear picture of the creative, and the self-creative, activity of man in nature and society.

'We speak of art as distinguished from nature; but art itself is natural to man. He is in some measure the artificer of his own frame, as well as of his fortune, and is destined, from the first age of his being, to invent and contrive. He applies the same talents to a variety of purposes, and acts nearly the same part in very different scenes. He would be always improving on his subject, and he carries this intention wherever he moves, through the streets of the populous city, or the wilds of the forest. While he appears equally fitted to every condition, he is upon this account unable to settle in any. At once obstinate and fickle, he complains of innovations, and is never sated with novelty. He is perpetually busied in reformations, and is continually wedded to his errors. If he dwell in a cave, he would improve it into a cottage; if he has already built, he would still build to a greater extent. But he does not propose to make rapid and hasty transitions; his steps are progressive and slow; and his force, like the power of a spring, silently presses on every resistance; an effect is sometimes produced before the cause is perceived; and with all his talent for projects, his work is often accomplished before the plan is devised. It appears, perhaps, equally difficult to retard or to quicken his pace: if the projector complain he is tardy, the moralist thinks him unstable; and whether his motions be rapid or slow, the scenes of human affairs perpetually change in his management: his emblem is a passing stream, not a stagnating pool. We may desire to direct his love of improvement to its proper object, we may wish for stability of conduct; but we mistake human nature, if we wish for a termination of labour, or a scene of repose.'*

This was a clear portrayal, too, of what were later called the perpetual 'dialectical processes' of man's activities in history, and Ferguson linked some very important points to it. Here, we will only note one other—namely the way in which he saw even the supposed 'Simple Societies' as being essentially engaged in the same 'progressive' creative activities. Later, our considerations of the relations.

* *An Essay on the History of Civil Society*, p. 10.

between sociology and social anthropology will be seen to have a root in this.

'If nature is only opposed to art, in what situation of the human race are the footsteps of art unknown?

'In the condition of the savage, as well as in that of the citizen, are many proofs of human invention; and in either is not in any permanent station, but a mere stage through which this travelling being is destined to pass. If the palace be unnatural, the cottage is so no less; and the highest refinements of political and moral apprehension, are not more artificial in their kind, than the first operations of sentiment and reason.

'If we admit that man is susceptible of improvement, and has in himself a principle of progression, and a desire of perfection, it appears improper to say, that he has quitted the state of his nature, when he has begun to proceed; or that he finds a station for which he was not intended, while, like other animals, he only follows the disposition, and employs the powers that nature has given.

'The latest efforts of human invention are but a continuation of certain devices which were practised in the earliest ages of the world, and in the rudest state of mankind. What the savage projects, or observes, in the forest, are the steps which led nations, more advanced, from the architecture of the cottage to that of the palace, and conducted the human mind from the perceptions of sense, to the general conclusions of science.'*

Many other insights of this kind are to be found in Ferguson, including a very sane and satisfactory view concerning the relations between the social sciences in trying to see all institutions in their 'ensemble' in society as a whole. When discussing commercial institutions, for example, he warned against the danger in economic analysis and in political practice of isolating these too much from their interdependence with other institutions. And his comments on specific aspects of social life were continuously interesting and arresting. Here, for example, is what he had to say about the distancing of the mind from a real engagement in practical affairs which could come with academic 'professionalization'.

'We may be satisfied, from the example of many ages, that liberal endowments bestowed on learned societies, and the leisure with which they were furnished for study, are not the likeliest means to excite the exertions of genius: even science itself, the supposed offspring of leisure, pined in the shade of monastic retirement. Men at a distance from the objects of useful knowledge, untouched by the motives that animate an active and a vigorous mind, could produce only the jargon of a technical language, and accumulate the impertinence of academical forms.

'To speak or to write justly from an observation of nature, it is necessary to have felt the sentiments of nature. He who is penetrating and ardent in the conduct of life, will probably exert a proportional force and ingenuity

* *An Essay on the History of Civil Society*, p. 13.

in the exercise of his literary talents: and although writing may become a trade, and require all the application and study which are bestowed on any other calling; yet the principal requisites in this calling are, the spirit and sensibility of a vigorous mind.

'In one period, the school may take its light and direction from active life; in another, it is true, the remains of an active spirit are greatly supported by literary monuments, and by the history of transactions that preserve the examples and the experience of former and of better times. But in whatever manner men are formed for great efforts of elocution or conduct, it appears the most glaring of all deceptions to look for the accomplishments of a human character in the mere attainments of speculation, whilst we neglect the qualities of fortitude and public affection, which are so necessary to render our knowledge an article of happiness or of use.'*

This, it will be agreed, is highly relevant to the problems of academic 'professionalization' which we are now facing. It was written almost exactly (1767) two hundred years ago.

A book of similar interest is '*Sketches of the History of Man*' by Lord Kames which was published a little later than Ferguson's book (1774) and which covered similar ground, though in a rather more loose and discursive way. Enough has been said, however, to indicate the great interest and importance of these thinkers, but at the same time, to make it clear why they were not given a more conspicuous, or crucial, place in this study.

* *An Essay on the History of Civil Society*, p. 299.

Appendix 2
John Stuart Mill on Comte's Extravagances

In this section on Comte, it will be appreciated that I have concentrated solely upon his sociological ideas—and have not dwelt at all upon his mental aberrations and the extraordinary lengths of the absurd to which these led him. Similarly, in the section on John Stuart Mill, I have dwelt chiefly on the kinds of agreement which Mill found with Comte after critical study. I have kept away from any consideration of Comte's mental condition, and extravagances, because they are irrelevant to the truth, or falsity, or value of his ideas.

However, critics have sometimes made much of Comte's 'manias' of one sort or another, and it is as well, therefore, to make it quite clear that we are aware of these; and, especially, to draw attention to John Stuart Mill's excellent and sensitive judgment in his book: *Auguste Comte and Positivism*. This is an extremely searching study, going to great pains to sift what is of value from what is nonsensical, not failing to be severe in adverse criticism where it is warranted, but being always careful not to dismiss intellectual ideas of worth because of extremities of mind and character which clearly possessed, to some extent, pathological roots. Here, we might note just one example of such an extremity, and Mill's judgment.

Comte's last publication on the Philosophy of Mathematics which Mill thought 'a sadder picture of intellectual degeneracy than those which preceded it', nonetheless contained many notions which were profound and suggestive. But, Mill went on:

'. . . mixed with these, what pitiable *niaiseries*! One of his great points is the importance of the "moral and intellectual properties of numbers". He cultivates a superstitious reverence for some of them. The first three are sacred, *les nombres sacrés*: One being the type of all Synthesis, Two of all Combination, which he now says *is* always binary (in his first treatise he only said that we may usefully represent it to ourselves as being so) and Three of all Progression, which not only requires three terms, but, as he now maintains, never ought to have any more. To these sacred numbers all our mental operations must be made, as far as possible, to adjust themselves. Next to them he has a great partiality for the number seven. . . .'*

* *Auguste Comte and Positivism*, p. 195.

652

. . . and so on. But Comte went much further and insisted that 'numbers' provided the 'great instrument for the regulation of the details of life' and that they should be introduced into all our conduct. He himself applied them to the correction of his literary style which had been much attacked, and produced a detailed 'plan for all compositions of importance'.

'Every volume really capable of forming a distinct treatise should consist of seven chapters, besides the introduction and the conclusion; and each of these should be composed of three parts. Each third part of a chapter should be divided into seven sections, each composed of seven groups of sentences, separated by the usual break of line. Normally formed, the section offers a central group of seven sentences, preceded and followed by three groups of five: the first section of each part reduces to three sentences three of its groups, symmetrically placed; the last section gives seven sentences to each of its extreme groups. These rules of composition make prose approach to the regularity of poetry, when combined with my previous reduction of the maximum length of a sentence to two manuscripts or five printed lines, that is, 250 letters . . .'*

The 'plan' went on to give even more precise details, but we have seen enough of them. What is of great interest is Mill's final judgment—and it must be remembered that Mill had done much to support and to publicize Comte, and had himself been much criticized for doing so. He concluded:

'Others may laugh, but we could far rather weep at this melancholy decadence of a great intellect. M. Comte used to reproach his early English admirers with maintaining the "conspiracy of silence" concerning his later performances. The reader can now judge whether such reticence is not more than sufficiently explained by tenderness for his fame, and a conscientious fear of bringing undeserved discredit on the noble speculation of his earlier career.

'M. Comte was accustomed to consider Descartes and Leibnitz as his principal precursors, and the only great philosophers (among many thinkers of high philosophic capacity) in modern·times. It was to their minds that he considered his own to bear the nearest resemblance. Though we have not so lofty an opinion of any of the three as M. Comte had, we think the assimilation just: these were, of all recorded thinkers, the two who bore most resemblance to M. Comte. They were like him in earnestness, like him, though scarcely equal to him, in confidence in themselves; they had the same extraordinary power of concatenation and co-ordination; they enriched human knowledge with great truths and great conceptions of method; they were, of all great scientific thinkers, the most consistent, and for that reason often the most absurd, because they shrank from no consequences, however contrary to common sense, to which their premises appeared to lead. Accordingly their names have come down to us associated

* *Auguste Comte and Positivism*, p. 198.

with grand thoughts, with most important discoveries, and also with some of the most extravagantly wild and ludicrously absurd conceptions and theories which ever were solemnly propounded by thoughtful men. We think M. Comte as great as either of these philosophers, and hardly more extravagant. Were we to speak our whole mind, we should call him superior to them: though not intrinsically, yet by the exertion of equal intellectual power in a more advanced state of human preparation; but also in an age less tolerant of palpable absurdities, and to which those he has committed, if not in themselves greater, at least appear more ridiculous.'*

The critical estimation of the worth of Comte's ideas in the making of sociology was clearly not undertaken without a complete awareness of, and a sympathy with regard to, the fantastic extravagances to which Comte was prone.

* *Auguste Comte and Positivism*, p. 199.

Appendix 3*
Frédéric Le Play

One other important 'system' of sociological analysis was produced in France during the nineteenth century; that of Frédéric Le Play. I have not included it in the mainstream of our argument because it did not, as it seems to me, make a distinctive contribution to the advancement of sociological theory proper. At the same time, Le Play's system was admirable, as were the wide comparative empirical studies which he accomplished on the basis of it, and it is therefore a good thing to take note of it. In some ways, too, Le Play stood opposed to some central aspects of nineteenth century sociology. He was opposed to the 'evolutionary' perspective, and thought there were great dangers in it. He was opposed to the 'rationalistic' idea that the men of one generation can 're-make' the institutional structure of a society, and thought that government which had such a grandiose undertaking in mind was a threat and a curse. He could be counted on the side of men like Montesquieu, Burke, Sumner, and—later— Emile Durkheim, who saw the growth of institutions in society as a gradual, many-dimensional accommodation of custom, morality and law to environmental problems and the social situations they pro-duced. It is worthwhile also to say that Le Play was of great worth in that he stood mid-way between analysis and theory on the one hand, and detailed empirical research on the other—and brought them together in a valid embrace. His studies seem entirely of a *sociographical* nature—of the nature of fact-finding surveys—but they were not *just* this; they were sociographic studies undertaken within a very clear analytical scheme which conceived of societies as *wholes*: as social systems of interdependent institutions. In this sense, as is quite clear, he did in fact agree with many other dimen-sions of sociology: the emphasis upon structural-functional analysis, the importance of tracing historical development, and so on. Le Play, too, had a much wider influence than is now sometimes realised. Institutes were founded to develop his work in France, and the great sociographers in Britain—Booth, Branford, Geddes, and all that grew out of the 'Institute of Sociology'—were rooted in his concep-tion. Indeed, it is hardly too much to claim that Le Play established

* The greater part of this appendix, in slightly different form, was written as an article for 'New Society', (Vol. 9, No. 226, 26th January, 1967) and then included in the Pelican book: *'The Founding Fathers of Social Science'*.

an 'environmentalist' perspective for sociological analysis and research which was every bit as influential as that which has come to be distinctively thought of as the 'Chicago School' under the influence, chiefly, of Robert Park. The following is a very brief account of his work.

Nowadays, Le Play is known chiefly, perhaps only, for his generalizations about the form of the family in society, yet his work went far beyond considerations of 'the family' alone. It offered a mode of analysing societies in their entirety, and has much to say about every aspect of modern society and its problems. It is worthwhile to note that Le Play, in his personal life, grew up with the same experience of profound distress at the rapid changes towards a predominantly industrial society which lay at the heart of Auguste Comte.

The first few years of his life were spent in a small fishing community near the port of Honfleur—poor, and made the more insecure by the blockading activities of the British fleet during Napoleon's rule. The struggle for survival of the family in a harsh environment was, for him, a close reality. When he was five his father died and he was taken to live with an aunt and uncle in Paris. Here he was miserable in a tightly disciplined school (later he voiced much criticism of 'formal' education), but he enjoyed a happy home life and was much influenced by several guests of the household who were forever discussing the disruption of the Ancien Régime and their doubts and bewilderments about the kind of society that was in the making.

In 1815 Le Play's uncle died, and during the next seven years he again lived with his mother, studying the humanity courses at the Collège in Le Havre, and developing an absorbing interest in ecological studies. These were largely botanical but they involved him in detailed and extensive surveys of the neighbourhood.

Le Play then lived briefly with a friend of the family—a civil engineer—who encouraged him to take his studies further. Here again, Le Play enjoyed a broad cultural background: reading the classics, and Montaigne in particular (he was a Roman Catholic, but this was enough, in itself, to indicate the tolerance of his Catholicism). In 1825 he entered the Ecole Polytechnique in Paris, and from then on his career was marked with high distinction. After two years he passed as the most outstanding student for the Ecole des Mines, and, after two years there, he again passed at the head of the school.

A close friendship developed between Le Play and a fellow-student, Jean Reynaud. Reynaud was an ardent advocate of Saint-Simon and all the new ideas of 'positivism', progress and social reform, and the two were involved in continual and passionate argument. Le Play was deeply sceptical about the idea of progress, and critical of what he thought were brash notions of justice, reform and the rational reconstruction of society by governmental means. The principles of social order had been long established in various forms of human community, he thought. It was absurd to think that they had remained undiscovered by mankind until the nineteenth century. There were vast changes disrupting traditional societies, which required urgent study and action, but these changes were not necessarily progressive. Le Play came to hold a cyclical theory of social change and was conservative about social reform. He believed that society, with its new industrial characteristics, could only preserve important human values and improve human life if men reached careful judgments from a knowledge of social facts and their interdependence in society as a whole. He was, as we have said, quite obviously in the tradition which runs through much of French thought from Montesquieu to Durkheim.

Le Play and Reynaud decided to undertake a detailed survey of the mining districts of north Germany. Each had to undertake a scientific journey to complete his professional training, and this choice enabled them to study not only the technical aspects of these mining communities but also their social organization and how this was related to their environment. Their aims were: to observe accurately the organization of the communities; to participate as closely as possible in their family and social life in order to understand them fully and distinguish purely local factors from those general in mining communities; and to interview those who exercised authority.

The journey undertaken by these students reads, nowadays, rather like a sociological saga. Carrying a minimum of equipment, they travelled entirely on foot for seven months and covered more than 4,000 miles. This study established a few things firmly in Le Play's mind. He saw how his professional career could be linked with the pursuit of social studies and his aims of social service and reform. He was convinced of the intimate relationship between a community's social organization and the struggle for life which the natural environment forced upon it. An understanding of human society could only come from the same painstaking study of facts, and some pursuit of scientific method as in the natural sciences. A further persuasion was that travel was essential to comparative research in sociology. 'Travel is to the science of societies', he wrote, 'what chemical analysis is to mineralogy, what fieldwork is to botany, or, in general terms, what the observation of facts is to all the natural sciences.'

For a long time, however, Le Play devoted himself chiefly to engineering, and sociology formed only his 'favourite recreation'. But his deepening distress about the social disorders of his time increasingly committed him to social study. After the revolutions of 1848, he decided to relinquish the Chair of Metallurgy, to which he had been appointed in 1840, and devote himself wholly to this. In 1855 he published *Les Ouvriers Européens*, and, on the recommendation of the Académie des Sciences, a society was founded in 1856 to pursue Le Play's methods. Some of his central ideas were these:

(I) ECOLOGY

Its *ecological context* was the most significant factor for understanding the nature of a society. Within the environment, a number of families had to struggle for survival, security and happiness. *Occupations* were the basis of social organization. A community structure of traditions, institutions, laws and morality was based on these. No matter how complex the structure of society, its reality for most people rested on their occupations and the livelihood they derived from them, and was manifested in the nature of their family life.

(II) THE FAMILY

The *family*, not the isolated individual, was the significant unit for understanding society. The institutions of society were closely related to, and were always organizationally focused upon, families and family relationships. The family was not only a focal unit for the individual's experience of the structure of society, but also for sociological investigation. Like Durkheim, Le Play took *social facts* to be the basic facts for sociological study, and thought that the nature and quality of the individual's experience could only be understood within this context.

(III) THE WORKERS

The family organization of the *workers* must be studied in order to understand society as a whole. Some *élites*—absentee landowners, speculative financiers, for example—were cut off from the roots of community life. But the family life of the workers derived from their immediate relationships with their environment and its resources; and their traditions, customs, attitudes, would all reflect this. The workers were not only the majority, the masses, but the people whose material and moral life were one. This was the bedrock of society's structure.

(IV) 'TYPES' OF FAMILY AND SOCIETY

On these assumptions, the best way into the understanding of societies was a detailed study of 'typical' families. He undertook a series of *monographs* of working class families typically found among people in particular occupations. He then grouped these families in the types of society in which they existed and showed these societies to be appropriate to specific ecological situations. Le Play wished his studies to be as testable as possible and sought some method of measurement. He took it that the most important pattern of any family's activities would be reflected in the regular budget they had worked out for their lives. The core of each monograph was a detailed budget of a 'typical' family, but it also included details of occupation, the grade within the occupation, the kind of contract existing between worker and employer. There were difficulties in this method of measurement, but Le Play always included relevant qualitative background factors: local geography, aspects of social and economic history, and the like.

Detailed Family Monographs: comparative and classificatory studies

His family monographs related to Russia, Morocco, Germany, Austria, France, Britain, Spain and eastern European countries. Simplified, his main generalization was this: in all traditional communities there were three important types of family and social tradition, rooted in three basic occupations.

On the large grasslands of the world, communities were nomadic—shepherds who followed their flocks to new pastures when necessary. The family and social organization was 'patriarchal', with a central authority, and was essentially conservative, clinging to firmly founded traditions. Women were subservient to men.

Secondly, in coastal areas, communities lived by fishing. Fishing communities had a nomadic occupation in part, sailing in search of fish, but they required a fixed home. This kind of life made for individual resourcefulness and a distribution of authority, skill and responsibility in the handling of vessels. It made too, for a division of authority between man and woman, since the woman was responsible for the continuity of the home. This gave rise to the 'stem' or 'stock' type of family, in which family property was left to a single male heir who remained responsible for the other members of the family—starting them up in life and helping them when necessary. Central security was blended with independence and flexibility. There was a blend, too, of stability (a core of conservatism) and adventurous initiative (an impulse to change and progressiveness).

The third type of family and society was found in forest areas among roaming hunting communities, and Le Play called this the 'unstable' type. The family was a union of the sexes, growing and diminishing in size as children were born and grew to maturity and left, and having little continuity between the generations. Families lived in the insecurity of the moment, and were, said Le Play, 'decadent' compared with the stable qualities of the other two types.

The malaise of modern industrial society

He then argued that the conditions of industrial society made most families approximate to the 'unstable' type. We must remember that he was writing when the working people in European societies were suffering from the early calamities of unregulated industrial and urban change. He had various factors in mind. In particular, he believed that the French law of 1793, which abolished freedom of bequest and established a compulsory division of property in every generation, caused the disruption of the 'stem' family and its security. Mechanization stripped the individual of any personal distinction in his work. Men became factors of production; were employed or not as market forces fluctuated; and became 'nomadic' in a new and disastrous way, having no secure roots in one place. Few could afford their own homes, and were migratory in this additional sense of having to move from rented house to rented house as their fortunes changed. Home life was impermanent; family life was insecure. This engendered irresponsibility. Many married young, with no provision for their future. They had large numbers of children but could not care for them. Home life tended to be non-existent; children spilled into the streets and their fathers into public houses. Despite additional legal rights, the position of women in the family and society had worsened. Driven out of the home into employment, they played a diminished part within the home.

The growing dominance of manufacturing industry and commerce meant a decline in values and morality. The criterion of profit had displaced the paternalistic obligations which gave stability and continuity in the traditional society. All this led Le Play to maintain that industrialization had brought a degeneration of family life, an instability and malaise in the whole nature of modern society.

After this diagnosis, some of Le Play's most interesting ideas came in his *La Réforme Sociale en France* (1864). On law and the family, he argued that everything should be done to increase home-ownership. Testamentary freedom should replace compulsory division of property, in order to strengthen the authority of the head of the family (in this he upheld British law as against the French). The law should not treat men and women as though they were on the same social footing.

On economic matters, he urged the rehabilitation of local agriculture and the elimination of landlord absenteeism. He thought that communistic kinds of ownership and management were doomed to failure (he quoted experiments in France after 1848). Joint-stock companies, too, might be necessary for large concentrations of capital, but these also suffered from size and impersonality. Le Play favoured small enterprises in which relations between employee and employer were personal and direct. He opposed voluntary and charitable associations because he thought they made societies' inadequacies chronic.

On education, he thought that children were subjected far too long to 'formal' education and artificially withheld from employment and engagement in social affairs. Education was not something to be handed over to schools and schoolteachers. Some work was positively good for children. Education for girls* should be different from that for boys—but not, by any means, more narrow. It should focus on homemaking—not in any kitchen-sink fashion—but in such a way as to broaden out into scientific and cultural subjects. As wives and mothers, girls would then become a rich educative influence in home and society. Woman's place was in the home, Le Play said. But the home was the most important place not only for children, but also for the personal life and happiness of adults.

Finally, on the role of the State, Le Play thought that the only good government was one that sought to render itself unnecessary. Nothing was worse than 'rational' lawmaking and bureaucracy that rested on moral principles seen separately from a detailed understanding of social processes. The French property law of compulsory division, for example, was based upon the abstract principle of equality, and its consequence, Le Play said, was to ruin the family structure of France.

Today, Le Play's work still repays careful study. It will be seen that he was much less sanguine about the possibilities of government than Comte; but still—even his *opposition* to brash government rested on a reliable knowledge of society—so that his fundamental persuasion was the same as that of Comte: namely, the necessity for a scientific study of society on which social policy could reliably rest. There is still much value in his idea of a comparative study of family monographs—though not necessarily with the same budgetary ideas that he used. If researchers in the many countries of the world

* Here, again—in his conviction of the cultural (indeed 'spiritual') importance of women in society—Le Play agreed very considerably with Comte.

carried out monographs on an agreed basis, we would at once have something better than we now possess—a broad and useful knowledge of the family in modern societies. Secondly, whether or not one agrees with Le Play's specific legal criticisms and proposals, his insistence on what amounts to the development of a sociology of custom, morality and law remains important.

He rightly insisted on rigorous scientific method, on the importance of a detailed acquaintance with social facts and on the constant reference of theories to the facts which they purport to explain. But his empirical studies did have theoretical orientation and, though specific and searching, were couched within a conceptual model of social systems as wholes, and, though differing about the notions of 'evolution' and 'progress', it can be seen that, in his structural-functional analysis, his historical, comparative, and classificatory studies, and, in all these, his employment of 'types' of social structure, he was in considerable agreement with other nineteenth century scholars as to what the major components of a reliable system of sociological analysis were.

Appendix 4
Some comments on Sir Karl Popper's criticism of Mill: of 'Holism', 'Psychologism', and 'Historicism'.

A satisfactory critique of Karl Popper's estimations of some of the writers with whom we are dealing (especially Comte, Mill and Marx), and some of the positions he has adopted in sociological theory, both requires and merits a very thorough essay in its own right; something, clearly, much more substantial than can be attempted here. At the same time, some of his judgments, and some of his portrayals of the nature of these theorists, have become so influential that they cannot be left without comment. Here, I would like simply to take issue with some of his points which, in his work, are focused upon John Stuart Mill, though—as is well known—they are also more widely treated in discussing what Popper takes to be the errors and dangers of 'holism', 'psychologism' and 'historicism'. These criticisms are not hostile—because one cannot but admire the detailed range and depth of Popper's scholarship; any serious student of his work knows that he has studied the writers he criticises very fully and always goes to great pains to make it clear what he has gained from them, even when he is taking issue with them on some points. Furthermore, I am very much in sympathy—though not in complete agreement—with the final humanistic and scientific position at which he arrives. But they are very fundamental criticisms, because I believe that, in a sense, Popper is a victim of the power of his own argument, the argumentative simplicity of his own categories and dichotomies (almost of his own 'imagery'), and that this leads him to falsify the position which some of these men adopted.

Let us take 'Holism' first. The 'holistic' (and 'Utopian') approach in sociological theory and social reform—according to Popper—is that which thinks it necessary, in analysis, to think of 'society as a whole', and, in reform, to think of re-modelling 'the whole of society' according to some definite 'plan or blue-print'. By contrast, 'piecemeal social engineering' is much more modest. The piecemeal social engineer 'knows how little he knows'; knows 'that we can only learn from our mistakes'; recognizes that 'only a minority of social institutions are consciously designed while the vast majority have just 'grown', as the 'undesigned results of human actions'; and therefore moves step by step in social experimentation and specific social reform: bit-and-piece, cautious, always on the look-out for mistakes and consequences which were unforeseen. Now it would be possible to argue that this is a false dichotomy. It may well be that 'Holists' of Popper's extreme are to be found—a Hegel, a Lenin, a Mussolini (though this would be a poor version); and 'piecemeal engineers' too —Herbert Spencer goaded into action. But this does not mean that someone else might well insist on studying 'society as a whole of inter-dependent parts'—much of which was the outcome of 'unforeseen consequences'—and even wish to frame policies with this context in mind—and *yet* be cautious, modest, specific, careful not to attempt too much, and ready to change in the light of mistakes. To conceive of society 'as a whole' is certainly not be to equated with a brash ideological 'Utopianism'. Furthermore, alternatively, a 'piecemeal' approach to theory and action can be shown to be equally vulnerable to superficial errors. The dichotomy is not a firm one. However, let us be more limited than this and confine ourselves to Popper's interpretation of Mill in relation to 'holism'.

In *The Poverty of Historicism** Popper writes:

'Mill's approach is very clearly shown to be holistic when he explains what he means by a "State of Society" (or historical period): "What is called a state of society", he writes, ". . . is the simultaneous state of all the greater social facts or phenomena." Examples of these facts are *inter alia*: "The state of industry, of wealth and its distribution"; society's "division into classes, and the relations of those classes to one another; the common beliefs which they entertain . . .; their form in government, and the more important of their laws and customs." Summing up, Mill characterizes states of society as follows: "States of society are like . . . different ages in the physical frame; they are conditions not in one or a few organs or functions, but of *the whole organism*." '

In *The Open Society and its Enemies†* he tells us, on the contrary, that:

'This remark‡ of Mill's exhibits one of the most praiseworthy aspects of psychologism, namely, its sane opposition to collectivism and holism, its refusal to be impressed by Rousseau's or Hegel's romanticism—by a general will or a national spirit, or perhaps, by a group mind. Psychologism is, I believe, correct only in so far as it insists upon what may be called "methodological individualism" as opposed to "methodological collectiv-

* Routledge & Kegan Paul, 1957, p. 72.
† Routledge & Kegan Paul, 1962, Vol. II, p. 91.
‡ Which is a remark where Mill is attacking the 'chemical compound' method, insisting that: 'Men are not, when brought together, converted into another kind of substance . . .'

ism"; it rightly insists that the "behaviour" and the "actions" of collectives, such as states or social groups, must be reduced to the behaviour and to the actions of human individuals.'

According to Popper, then, Mill is to be praised for being sanely opposed to 'holism' and castigated for being 'holistic'. I do not know whether this seems as odd to the reader as it does to me—but, even setting the oddness of such a judgment aside, surely Mill is exactly the kind of thinker who proves to the hilt that Popper's dichotomy simply does not hold good. Certainly Mill argues—as all sociologists have argued—that institutions can only be reliably known and understood if their interconnectedness in society as a whole is borne in mind; and certainly he argues that institutions are not found to exist in arbitrary 'collections'—but that they manifest certain concomitancies which characterize 'types' of society. But, even so, no-one could be more clear than Mill that 'societies' and 'social institutions' do not exist as 'entities' completely independent of the nature and activities of human beings; that there are unintended consequences in the changing nature of institutions as well as conscious choice and design; that our knowledge to the degree of precision which allows of prediction is very limited (so that we must use it only for 'guidance'); and that the utmost care must be taken—among social scientists, moral philosophers, and men of practical affairs—in the formulation of social policies. Surely, these are the very things upon which Mill insists with much persistence and tenacity.

Any 'holistic' charge against Mill—in the sense that he is guilty of those conceptual errors which Popper is attacking under this 'label'—are clearly absurd. Mill does not think that any 'whole society' is going anywhere 'like a planet'.

The same kind of insufficiency can be seen to lie in Popper's attack on Mill's (among others') supposed error of 'historicism', and his supposed error of identifying 'laws of succession' (statements of regularities of connections in the sequential change of social institutions) with 'trends'. Again, Popper distinguishes between 'Prophecy'—a kind of prediction which foretells specific future events, and 'Technological Predictions'—which 'intimate the steps open to us if we want to achieve certain results'; which provide a basis for piecemeal social engineering. The 'Historicist' is the one who attempts 'prophecy', and for whom sociological 'laws' are unalterable laws of history by means of which the future can be foretold. Now again, this could be attacked as a false dichotomy, and it could certainly be shown that the notions of 'prediction' held by sociologists from Comte onwards were never as naïve as those criticized by Popper—though, no doubt, some extreme statements and positions could be cited.* But let us, as before, confine ourselves to Popper's specific interpretation of Mill. In *The Poverty of Historicism,*† on this matter of 'laws' and 'trends', Popper writes:

'Now we have seen that there are no *laws* that determine the succession of such a "dynamic" series of events. On the other hand, there may be *trends* which are of this "dynamic" character; for example, population increase. It may therefore be suspected that Mill had such trends in mind when he spoke of "laws of succession". And this suspicion is confirmed by Mill himself when he describes his historical law of progress as a *tendency*. Discussing this "law", he expresses his "belief . . . that the general *tendency* is, and will continue to be, saving occasional and temporary exceptions, one of improvement—*a tendency towards a happier and better state*. This . . . is . . . a theorem of the science" (viz, of the social science). That Mill should seriously discuss the question whether "the phenomena of human society" revolve "in an orbit" or whether they move, progressively, in "a trajectory" is in keeping with this fundamental confusion between laws and trends, as well as with the holistic idea that society can "move" as a whole—say, like a planet.'

Now this is a quite false and misleading interpretation of Mill. Let us notice again that he is charged with a very simple-minded 'holism', but then—more important—that his opinion concerning the question as to whether social change is, in the long term, char- acterized by 'improvement' is taken as a demonstration that he thinks of a 'law' as a 'trend' or 'tendency'. But this is quite a direct misinterpretation of what Mill in fact says, and I would like to be very specific here.

Popper says quite deliberately here that Mill is describing his historical law of progress as a *tendency*; and that it is whilst 'discus- sing this law' that he expresses—and let us note these selected words carefully—his:

'. . . "belief . . . that the general *tendency* is, and will continue to be saving occasional and temporary exceptions, one of improvement—*a tendency towards a happier and better state*. This . . . is . . . a theorem of the science." (viz. of the social science.)'

And now let us note—very exactly—certain points. Firstly in this place Mill is *not* describing a 'law of progress' at all! Secondly, he is not discussing the nature of such a law at all. Thirdly, he is very definitely *not* thinking of, or describing, such a law as a *tendency*. And fourthly, he does *not* say, as the selected quotation implies, that this tendency *is* a theorem of the social science. These statements are false.

* Comte's own statements on the nature of 'prediction' may be referred to again. See p. 174.
† Routledge & Kegan Paul, 1957, p. 118.

The fact is that in this place Mill is pointing out that the earlier ideas of men like Vico that 'the phenomena of human society revolve as in an orbit'; that the changes of societies are cyclical; have been replaced by the idea that historical change is progressive—*in the strict sense only* that the phenomena of society, in changing, become *different* from what they were before: that historical change is *not* cyclical, but an ongoing emergence of *differences*. This is what Mill is insisting. And, in doing so, he wishes to make it plain that this is *all* he is meaning, and that he is *not* meaning that historical change is progressive in the sense of being necessarily a matter of improvement. When he writes the words which Popper selectively quotes, he is only clarifying his use of the word 'progressive', and giving his *opinion* about the possible facts of improvement. His actual words are these:

'The words Progress and Progressiveness are not here to be understood as synonymous with improvement and tendency to improvement. It is conceivable that the laws of human nature might determine, and even necessitate, a certain series of changes in man and society, which might not in every case, or which might not on the whole, be improvements. It is my belief indeed that the general tendency is, and will continue to be, saving occasional and temporary exceptions, one of improvement—a tendency towards a better and happier state. This, however, is not a question of the method of the social science, but a theorem of the science itself. For our purpose it is sufficient that there is a progressive change, both in the character of the human race and in their outward circumstances so far as moulded by themselves; that in each successive age the principal phenomena of society are *different* from what they were in the age preceding, and still more different from any previous age: the periods which most distinctly mark these successive changes being intervals of one generation, during which a new set of human beings have been educated; have grown up from childhood, and taken possession of society.'*

It will clearly be seen in this statement that Mill is distinctly *not* putting forward the 'tendency' as a 'law' as Popper claims; he is *not* saying that the tendency *is* a theorem of the social science—on the contrary, he is saying that this is not a matter of the *method* of social science at all, but one of the facts or tendencies that *remains to be discovered*. This, then, is a complete misconception and misinterpretation of Mill. When Popper follows this by saying: 'That Mill should seriously discuss the question whether "the phenomena of human society" revolve "in an orbit" or whether they move progressively, in "a trajectory" is in keeping with this fundamental confusion between laws and trends, as well as with the holistic idea that society can "move" as a whole—say, like a planet'—this is being little short of

* *A System of Logic*, 1884 Edn. p. 596.

facetious. For Mill, as is plain, was doing no more than point out that 'cyclical' notions of social change had given way to 'progressive' ones. There was no confusion between 'laws' and 'trends' at all; and nothing approaching a planet had swum into anyone's view other than Popper's own. But let us take the matter further.

Mill does go on to say that this historical perspective has been used by thinkers on the continent:

'. . . by a study and analysis of the general facts of history to discover (what these philosophers term) the law of progress; which law, once ascertained, must according to them enable us to predict future events, just as after a few terms of an infinite series in algebra we are able to detect the principle of regularity in their formation, and to predict the rest of the series to any number of terms we please. The principal aim of historical speculation in France, of late years, has been to ascertain this law.'*

But what does Mill think of such a 'law' and such a basis for a 'prophetic prediction'? Does he mistake a 'law' for a 'trend'? This is what he says.†

'But while I gladly acknowledge the great services which have been rendered to historical knowledge by this school, I cannot but deem them to be mostly chargeable with a fundamental misconception of the true method of social philosophy. The misconception consists in supposing that the order of succession which we may be able to trace among the different states of society and civilization which history presents to us, even if that order were more rigidly uniform than it has yet been proved to be, could ever amount to a law of nature. It can only be an empirical law. The succession of states of the human mind and of human society cannot have an independent law of its own; it must depend on the psychological and ethological laws which govern the action of circumstances on men and of men on circumstances. It is conceivable that those laws might be such, and the general circumstances of the human race such, as to determine the successive transformations of man and society to one given and unvarying order. But even if the case were so, it cannot be the ultimate aim of science to discover an empirical law. Until that law could be connected with the psychological and ethological laws on which it must depend, and, by the consilience of deduction *a priori* with historical evidence, could be converted from an empirical law into a scientific one, it could not be relied on for the prediction of future events, beyond at most, strictly adjacent cases.'

Now this is surely plain enough. One may take issue with Mill on the part he allots to psychological and 'ethological' factors in this process, but what is absolutely certain is that he does not take a historical tendency (even if it is established as a uniform fact!) to be a law; nor does he think it offers a ground for 'prophecy'.

The simple truth is that Popper offers a complete misinterpretation

* *A System of Logic*, 1884 Edn. p. 596.   † *ibid.*, pp. 596–7.

of Mill. His supposed Historicism is as much a fancy as his supposed 'Holism'. And very much the same can be said about his supposed 'psychologism'.

By 'psychologism', Popper means the theory (or position) that 'sociology must in principle be *reducible* to social psychology', and he maintains that Mill is an exponent of this error and that Marx, especially, is correct in avoiding it and arguing for an 'autonomous sociology'. Now it seems perfectly plain to me that the error in Popper's interpretation here lies in his use and repeated insistence on the word '*reducible*'—for nowhere does Mill ever insist on it and, indeed, the whole of his (and of Comte's) emphasis is *opposed* to reductionism of any sort between the sciences. It is true that Mill insists that Psychology is a basic component of a science of man and society. It is true that he insists that social institutions cannot have a cause-and-effect relationship between each other as 'entities', independent of the activities, dispositions and qualities of character of the people who are members of society. And it is true that he insists on social psychology as the study of the way in which the institutional framework and 'ethos' of society acts on psychological endowment to produce 'settled dispositions, sentiments' and the like in individuals and groups. But where is the 'reductionism' in all this? It does not exist. Mill is not arguing that explanations of man in society, and of the changing nature of institutions should be *reduced* to psychological components. He is only insisting that *all* these components: empirical generalizations about institutions, empirical generalizations about psychological endowment, and generalizations of a social psychological nature, are necessary for any full and satisfactory explanation. And we may note, too, that he is insistent that the influence of institutions and environmental circumstances (family, education, class, nation, etc.) *upon* psychological components is as of great an importance as anything else. His only insistence against something called an 'autonomous sociology' is that causal laws cannot be propounded about the interconnections of institutions as 'entities' in themselves.

Popper's arguments against Mill on this count are very strange. On the one hand he seems to suggest that Mill is insisting that every regularity in human society can be explained in terms of some 'original human nature' and that this forces him into the position of arguing that there was some 'beginning of society' before which there were only the psychological components of human nature, and that, therefore, the many institutions of society could be explained entirely in terms of instincts, needs, purposes, and conscious designs. All one can say is that Mill says none of these things. Popper then goes on to insist that *institutions* must be taken into account;

that *unintended consequences* go into their changing historical nature; that men act in *social situations* and must be understood within such contexts; and that sociology must seek explanations of these, and not only psychological and purposive components. But of course Mill quite agrees with all this. What he would ask—with some astonishment after all these criticisms—is: 'But is that all you mean by an autonomous sociology?' And, incredibly, the answer would have to be: yes! In Chapter 14 of *The Open Society and its Enemies* Popper does not set up anything that could be called an 'autonomous sociology' to which Mill would want to raise more than a faint eyebrow!

Again, I think it is worthwhile to be quite specific about the use of quotations. On page 88 of *The Open Society*, Popper argues that Mill believes that the study of society must be reducible to psychology:

'. . . that the laws of historical development must be explicable in terms of *human nature*, of the "laws of the mind", and in particular, of its progressiveness'.

—and he then follows this statement with the quotation:

'The progressiveness of the human race', says Mill, 'is the foundation on which a method of . . . social science has been . . . erected, far superior to . . . the modes . . . previously . . . prevalent. . . .'

The dots and dashes are almost like a Morse Code. But in fact, in this passage, Mill is *not* writing about the 'laws of the mind' or even of 'human nature' *at all*. He is writing about the '*progressive*' changes in *history* of the 'phenomena of human society'. This is drawn from the same passage in which he is stressing the historical perspective which rests on the assumption that ongoing social changes are simply *different* from what they had been before, *not* that they followed a *cyclical* pattern. *This* is what is meant by *progressiveness* here: *ongoing difference in social change*; and the full sentence reads:

'The progressiveness of the human race is the foundation on which a method of philosophizing in the social science has been of late years erected, far superior to either of the two modes which had previously been prevalent, the chemical or experimental, and the geometrical modes.'*

Popper's criticisms of Mill's 'holism', 'historicism', and 'psychologism' fall to the ground. Much more could be said on other, similar issues: on Comte's and Mill's supposed errors of 'inductive logic' and the use of hypothesis, for example; and of the nature of 'statics' and 'dynamics', about which I think Popper is ambiguous,

---

* *System of Logic*, p. 596.

indeed incorrect. But we have looked sufficiently at the points which, here, chiefly concern us.

As a matter of interest it might be noted that many of the statements about the nature of scientific method and its philosophical assumptions which Popper makes in *The Open Society* as being modern, indeed of almost contemporary validity—as, for example, these:*

(1) '. . . the belief that the terms "scientific" and "determinist" are, if not synonymous, at least inseparably connected, can now be said to be one of the superstitions of a time that has not yet entirely passed away.'

(2) '. . . No kind of determinism, whether it be expressed as the principle of the uniformity of nature or as the law of universal causation, can be considered any longer a necessary assumption of scientific method. . . .'

(3) '. . . Determinism is not a necessary pre-requisite of a science which can make predictions.'

(4) '. . . Science can be rigidly scientific without this assumption.'

—were all insisted upon quite clearly and specifically by Mill in his discussion of 'determinism'.

* See *The Open Society and its Enemies*, p. 85.

Appendix 5
Tylor and Frazer: Evolution in Anthropology

It is worth while to note, though briefly, that the formulation of Anthropology during the nineteenth century was also based on the concept of evolution.* Tylor (1832–1917) lived into the present century, but all his important work was completed in the nineteenth century, and Emile Durkheim, for example, was already referring to him as a scholar of authority. Frazer lived until 1941 (b. 1854), and produced much work in the present century, but *The Golden Bough* was published in 1890, and rested upon the same evolutionary conception as that laid down by Tylor. Perhaps the basic fact to notice, however, is that their evolutionary perspective was one of transformations of *culture* (the complex of arts and artefacts of society) rather than of *social systems*, as was the case with Spencer; but their effort, like his, was to define a clear field of social phenomena which could be studied scientifically, and about which generalizations could be *tested*.

Tylor defined Anthropology—the 'science of Man and Civilization'—as the Science of Culture:

'Culture or Civilization is that complex whole which includes knowledge, belief, art, morals, law, custom, and any other capabilities and habits acquired by man as a member of society. The condition of culture among the various societies of mankind, in so far as it is capable of being investigated on general principles, is a subject apt for the study of laws of human thought and action. On the one hand, the uniformity which so largely pervades civilization may be ascribed, in great measure, to the uniform action of uniform causes; while on the other hand its various grades may be regarded as stages of development or evolution, each the outcome of previous history, and about to do its proper part in shaping the history of the future.'†

Then, as now, he had to struggle against those who dogmatically objected to a 'scientific' study of human culture, but he set aside

---

* This, of course, was rooted in the developments of biology and geology; and Anthropology—the 'entire science of man'—was, at the outset, formulated in the closest relation to these physical sciences: in books such as T. H. Huxley's *Man's Place in Nature*
† *Primitive Culture*, Vol. I, p. 1.

philosophical arguments, and simply suggested that it was worth while to pursue scientific methods to such a degree of accuracy as proved possible.

'None will deny', he wrote, 'that, as each man knows by the evidence of his own consciousness, definite and natural cause does, to a great extent, determine human action. Then, keeping aside from considerations of extra-natural interference and causeless spontaneity, let us take this admitted existence of natural cause and effect as our standing-ground, and travel on it so far as it will bear us. It is on this same basis that physical science pursues, with ever-increasing success, its quest of laws and nature. Nor need this restriction hamper the scientific study of human life, in which the *real* difficulties are the practical ones of enormous complexity of evidence, and imperfection of methods of observation.'*

Tylor accepted the perspective of evolution as portrayed by geology and biology and considered the development of man—his culture and his society—within this context. Having discussed the physical attributes of the various 'races' of mankind, and their 'families' of languages, he insisted that these were already laid down before the existence of the 'cultures' within which they were recorded.

'The historic ages are to be looked on as but the modern period of man's life on earth. Behind them lies the prehistoric period, when the chief work was done of forming and spreading over the world the races of mankind. . . .' Also, '. . . the main work of language-making was done in the ages before history'.†

He then went on to clarify how man's *culture* itself—his knowledge, arts, institutions—could accurately be studied, and concluded that stages of cultural development could be clearly distinguished, and that knowledge about these could be testably established whilst avoiding any questionable assumptions or imputations about 'race', or about psychological matters which were difficult to measure. It is worth our while to note that this was quite distinctly a theory of social *development*, as well as of *evolution*.

'On the whole it appears that wherever there are found elaborate arts, abstruse knowledge, complex institutions, these are results of gradual development from an earlier, simpler, and ruder state of life. No stage of civilization comes into existence spontaneously, but grows or is developed out of the stage before it. This is the great principle which every scholar must lay firm hold of, if he intends to understand either the world he lives in or the history of the past.'‡

The cultural stages of development which he distinguished were as follows:

* *Primitive Culture*, Vol. I, p. 3.
† *Anthropology*. Thinker's Library Edn. 1930, p. 3.   ‡ *Ibid.*, p. 15.

'Without attempting here to draw a picture of life as it may have been among men at their first appearance on the earth, it is important to go back as far as such evidence of the progress of civilization may fairly lead us. In judging how mankind may have once lived, it is also a great help to observe how they are actually found living. Human life may be roughly classed into three great stages, Savage, Barbaric, Civilized, which may be defined as follows.

The lowest or *savage* state is that in which man subsists on wild plants and animals, neither tilling the soil nor domesticating creatures for his food. Savages may dwell in tropical forests where the abundant fruit and game may allow clans to live in one spot and find a living all the year round, where in barer and colder regions they have to lead a wandering life in quest of the wild food which they soon exhaust in any place. In making their rude implements, the materials used by savages are what they find ready to hand, such as wood, stone, and bone, but they cannot extract metal from the ore, and therefore belong to the Stone Age.

Men may be considered to have risen into the next or *barbaric* state when they take to agriculture. With the certain supply of food which can be stored till next harvest, settled village and town life is established, with immense results in the improvement of arts, knowledge, manners and government. Pastoral tribes are to be reckoned in the barbaric stage, for though their life of shifting camp from pasture to pasture may prevent settled habitation and agriculture, they have from their herds a constant supply of milk and meat. Some barbaric nations have not come beyond using stone implements, but most have risen into the Metal Age.

Lastly, *civilized* life may be taken as beginning with the art of writing, which, by recording history, law, knowledge, and religion for the service of ages to come, binds together the past and the future in an unbroken chain of intellectual and moral progress. This classification of three great stages of culture is practically convenient, and has the advantage of not describing imaginary states of society, but such as are actually known to exist. So far as the evidence goes, it seems that civilization has actually grown up in the world through these three stages, so that to look at a savage of the Brazilian forests, a barbarous New Zealander or Dahoman, and a civilized European, may be the student's best guide to understanding the progress of civilization, only he must be cautioned that the comparison is but a guide, not a full explanation.

In this way it is reasonably inferred that even in countries now civilized, savage and low barbaric tribes must have once lived. Fortunately it is not left altogether to the imagination to picture the lives of these rude and ancient men, for many relics of them are found which may be seen and handled in museums.'*

It is one very interesting aspect of Tylor's discussion of the 'evidence' for elements of culture which can be placed within the scheme, that, rather like Spencer, he *defended* the evidence of

* *Anthropology*, pp. 18–19.

'travellers' reports' or 'travellers' tales'. Considering criticisms of the reliability of such testimony, he wrote:

'It is a matter worthy of consideration, that the accounts of similar phenomena of culture, recurring in different parts of the world, actually supply incidental proof of their own authenticity. . . . This question is, indeed, one which every ethnographer ought to keep clearly and constantly before his mind. Of course he is bound to use his best judgment as to the trustworthiness of all authors he quotes, and if possible to obtain several accounts to certify each point in each locality. But it is over and above these measures of precaution, that the test of recurrence comes in. If two independent visitors to different countries, say a mediaeval Mohammedan in Tartary and a modern Englishman in Dahome, or a Jesuit missionary in Brazil and a Wesleyan in the Fiji Islands, agree in describing some analogous art or rite of myth among the people they have visited, it becomes difficult or impossible to set down such correspondence to accident or wilful fraud. A story by a bushranger in Australia may, perhaps, be objected to as a mistake or an invention, but did a Methodist minister in Guinea conspire with him to cheat the public by telling the same story there? . . . And the more odd the statement, the less likely that several people in several places should have made it wrongly.'*

Indeed, Tylor argued that the anthropologist is often in a position of being able to judge the accuracy of the reporter!

'The most important facts of ethnography are vouched for in this way. Experience leads the student after a while to expect and find that the phenomena of culture, as resulting from widely-acting similar causes, should recur again and again in the world. He even mistrusts isolated statements to which he knows of no parallel elsewhere, and waits for their genuineness to be shown by corresponding accounts from the other side of the earth, or the other end of history. So strong, indeed, is this means of authentication, that the ethnographer in his library may sometimes presume to decide, not only whether a particular explorer is a shrewd and honest observer, but also whether what he reports is conformable to the general rules of civilization.'†

Like all other evolutionary theorists, Tylor was most careful to insist that his picture of social-cultural development was *not* one of necessary or uninterrupted 'progress', nor one which denied the occurrence of 'arrest' or 'degeneration'. He argued only that such a pattern of cultural development was distinguishable. Here it is sufficient to note only one or two aspects of his treatment. One point of interest was his insistence that the 'mechanisms' of *cultural* development were *more easily distinguishable* than those in other phenomena and other sciences.

'The student of the habits of mankind has a great advantage over the

* *Primitive Culture*, Vol. I, pp. 9–10.　　　† *Ibid.*, p. 10.

student of the species of plants and animals. Among naturalists it is an open question whether a theory of development from species to species is a record of transitions which actually took place, or a mere ideal scheme serviceable in the classification of species whose origin was really independent. But among ethnographers there is no such question as to the possibility of species of implements or habits or beliefs being developed one out of another, for development in culture is recognized by our most familiar knowledge. Mechanical invention supplies apt examples of the kind of development which affects civilization at large. In the history of fire-arms, the clumsy wheel-lock, in which a notched steel wheel revolves by means of a spring against a piece of pyrites till a spark caught the priming, led to the invention of the more serviceable flint-lock, of which a few still hang in the kitchens of our farm-houses, for the boys to shoot small birds with at Christmas; the flint-lock in time passed by modification into the percussion-lock, which is just now changing its old-fashioned arrangement to be adapted from muzzle-loading to breech-loading.'*

A second point of interest was his demonstration that the sequences of cultural development in any particular society were actually in evidence in the form of *survivals* from earlier stages. These could be elements of doctrine and ritual in a religion, elements of language, but a very graphic example was his picture of actual archaeological evidence in a modern city like London.

'The vast lapse of time through which the history of London has represented the history of human civilization, is to my mind one of the most suggestive facts disclosed by archaeology. There the antiquary, excavating but a few yards deep, may descend from the debris representing our modern life, to relics of the art and science of the Middle Ages, to signs of Norman, Saxon, Romano-British times, to traces of the higher Stone-Age. And on his way from Temple Bar to the Great Northern Station he passes near the spot where a drift implement of black flint was found with the skeleton of an elephant by Mr Conyers, about a century and a half ago, the relics side by side of the London mammoth and the London savage.'†

Having discussed all the difficulties of theories of 'progress' and 'degeneration' which involved imponderables of various kinds, Tylor adopted the simple criterion of development in the 'material arts' as a cautious ground of measurement.

'It is an excellent guide and safeguard to keep before our minds the theory of development in the material arts. Throughout all the manifestations of the human intellect, facts will be found to fall into their places on the same general lines of evolution. The notion of the intellectual state of savages as resulting from decay of previous high knowledge, seems to have as little evidence in its favour as that stone celts are the degenerate successors of Sheffield axes, or earthen grave-mounds degraded copies of Egyptian pyramids. The study of savage and civilized life alike avail us to trace in the

* *Primitive Culture*, pp. 14–15.   † *Ibid.*, p. 59.

early history of the human intellect, not gifts of transcendental wisdom, but rude shrewd sense taking up the facts of common life and shaping from them schemes of primitive philosophy. It will be seen again and again, by examining such topics as language, mythology, custom, religion, that savage opinion is in a more or less rudimentary state, while the civilized mind still bears vestiges, neither few nor slight, of a past condition from which savages represent the least, and civilized men the greatest advance. Throughout the whole vast range of the history of human thought and habit, while civilization has to contend not only with survival from lower levels, but also with degeneration within its own borders, it yet proves capable of overcoming both and taking its own course. History within its proper field, and ethnography over a wider range, combine to show that the institutions which can best hold their own in the world gradually supersede the less fit ones, and that this incessant conflict determines the general resultant course of culture.'*

It is also important, finally, to see that Tylor—having elaborated his theory of cultural development and evolution in all the major aspects of social life (the family, religion, government, language, and all the social arts)—also upheld the science of anthropology as a subject which had practical application and great educational significance. Indeed, it was a subject to uphold, serve, and further human progress!

'It is our happiness to live in one of those eventful periods of intellectual and moral history, when the oft-closed gates of discovery and reform stand open at their widest. How long these good days may last, we cannot tell. It may be that the increasing power and range of the scientific method, with its stringency of argument and constant check of fact, may start the world on a more steady and continuous course of progress than it has moved on heretofore. But if history is to repeat itself according to precedent, we must look forward to stiffer duller ages of traditionalists and commentators, when the great thinkers of our time will be appealed to as authorities by men who slavishly accept their tenets, yet cannot or dare not follow their methods through better evidence to higher ends. In either case, it is for those among us whose minds are set on the advancement of civilization, to make the most of present opportunities, that even when in future years progress is arrested, it may be arrested at the higher level. To the promoters of what is sound and reformers of what is faulty in modern culture, ethnography has double help to give. To impress men's minds with a doctrine of development, will lead them in all honour to their ancestors to continue the progressive work of past ages, to continue it the more vigorously because light has increased in the world, and where barbaric hordes groped blindly, cultured men can often move onward with clear view. It is a harsher, and at times even painful, office of ethnography to expose the remains of crude old culture which have passed into harmful superstition, and to mark these out for destruction. Yet this work, if less genial is not less urgently

* *Primitive Culture*, p. 68.

needful for the good of mankind. Thus, active at once in aiding progress and in removing hindrance, the science of culture is essentially a reformer's science.'*

Clearly, nineteenth century Anthropology was as much committed to the service of certain values in society as was Sociology!

We may briefly note the similarity of Frazer's position—especially so that, when, later, we come to consider the twentieth century developments of *Social* Anthropology, we shall be able to see clearly the position from which, critically, they took their departure.

When setting out the problem he wished to study—at the beginning of *The Golden Bough*—Frazer made his theoretical position very clear. Having described the priesthood in the sanctuary of Diana at Nemi, Frazer wrote:

'The strange rule of this priesthood has no parallel in classical antiquity, and cannot be explained from it. To find an explanation we must go farther afield. No one will probably deny that such a custom savours of a barbarous age, and, surviving into imperial times, stands out in striking isolation from the polished Italian society of the day, like a primaeval rock rising from a smooth-shaven lawn. It is the very rudeness and barbarity of the custom which allow us a hope of explaining it. For recent researches into the early history of man have revealed the essential similarity with which, under many superficial differences, the human mind has elaborated its first crude philosophy of life. Accordingly, if we can show that a barbarous custom, like that of the priesthood of Nemi, has existed elsewhere; if we can detect the motives which led to its institution; if we can prove that these motives have operated widely, perhaps universally, in human society, producing in varied circumstances a variety of institutions specifically different but generically alike; if we can show, lastly, that these very motives, with some of the derivative institutions, were actually at work in classical antiquity; then we may fairly infer that at a remoter age the same motives gave birth to the priesthood of Nemi. Such an inference, in default of direct evidence as to how the priesthood did actually arise, *can never amount to demonstration*. But it will be *more or less probable* according to the degree of completeness with which it fulfils the conditions I have indicated. The object of this book is, by meeting these conditions, to offer a fairly probable explanation of the priesthood of Nemi.'†

Here, we can see clearly the 'explanation' in the form of the tracing of 'survivals', and also, in the last few sentences, the modesty of the claims made. There was no question here of *demonstration*; only 'more or less probability'. Frazer especially put forward the theory that 'magic' had everywhere preceded 'religion', and that such a *stage* in the intellectual development of human culture was as definite as the 'age of stone' in material culture. Indeed, his entire

---

* *Primitive Culture*, Vol. II, p. 452.   † *The Golden Bough*, p. 2.

position is of extreme interest in being almost (though not quite) a reiteration of Comte's 'Law of the Three Stages'. Comte's 'Theological, Metaphysical, and Positive' stages, are replaced by 'Magic, Religion, and Science'.

'If we consider, on the one hand, the essential similarity of man's chief wants everywhere and at all times, and on the other hand, the wide difference between the means he has adopted to satisfy them in different ages, we shall perhaps be disposed to conclude that the movement of the higher thought, so far as we can trace it, has on the whole been from magic through religion to science. In magic man depends on his own strength to meet the difficulties and dangers that beset him on every side. He believes in a certain established order of nature on which he can surely count, and which he can manipulate for his own ends. When he discovers his mistake, when he recognizes sadly that both the order of nature which he had assumed and the control which he had believed himself to exercise over it were purely imaginary, he ceases to rely on his own intelligence and his own unaided efforts, and throws himself humbly on the mercy of certain great invisible beings behind the veil of nature, to whom he now ascribes all those far-reaching powers which he once arrogated to himself. Thus in the acuter minds magic is gradually superseded by religion, which explains the succession of natural phenomena as regulated by the will, the passion, or the caprice of spiritual beings like man in kind, though vastly superior to him in power.

'But as time goes on this explanation in its turn proves to be unsatisfactory. For it assumes that the succession of natural events is not determined by immutable laws, but is to some extent variable and irregular, and this assumption is not borne out by closer observation. On the contrary, the more we scrutinize that succession the more we are struck by the rigid uniformity, the punctual precision with which, wherever we can follow them, the operations of nature are carried on. Every great advance in knowledge has extended the sphere of order and correspondingly restricted the sphere of apparent disorder in the world, till now we are ready to anticipate that even in regions where chance and confusion appear still to reign, a fuller knowledge would everywhere reduce the seeming chaos to cosmos. Thus the keener minds, still pressing forward to a deeper solution of the mysteries of the universe, come to reject the religious theory of nature as inadequate, and to revert in a measure to the older standpoint of magic by postulating explicitly, what in magic had only been implicitly assumed, to wit, an inflexible regularity in the order of natural events, which, if carefully observed, enables us to foresee their course with certainty and to act accordingly. In short, religion, regarded as an explanation of nature, is displaced by science.'*

Frazer came very near to Comte, too, in thinking that science was closely bound up with man's material and moral progress; and certainly in thinking that scientific knowledge was never 'final'. But

* *The Golden Bough*, p. 711.

there was a rather larger, more romantic air about Frazer that took him—for better, for worse—a good deal further than this. At the end of *The Golden Bough*, he wrote:

'It is probably not too much to say that the hope of progress—moral and intellectual as well as material—in the future is bound up with the fortunes of science, and that every obstacle placed in the way of scientific discovery is a wrong to humanity.

'Yet the history of thought should warn us against concluding that because the scientific theory of the world is the best that has yet been formulated, it is necessarily complete and final. We must remember that at bottom the generalizations of science, or, in common parlance, the laws of nature are merely hypotheses devised to explain that ever-shifting phantasmagoria of thought which we dignify with the high-sounding names of the world and the universe. In the last analysis magic, religion, and science are nothing but theories of thought; and as science has supplanted its predecessors, so it may herafter be itself superseded by some more perfect hypothesis, perhaps by some totally different way of looking at the phenomena—of registering the shadows on the screen—of which we in this generation can form no idea. The advance of knowledge is an infinite progression towards a goal that for ever recedes.'*

Nineteenth century Anthropology, then, was as committed to an 'evolutionary' and 'developmental' perspective as was sociology, and, without being at all adversely critical, here, it does seem fair to say that Spencer's analysis of social systems had been worked out with a far greater degree of rigour than had these categories of cultural stages. However, the evolutionary perspective was common to both, and firmly accepted.

---

* *The Golden Bough*, p. 712.

Bibliography

For reference and further reading. Many of these books have many editions, but these are the ones chiefly used and referred to in the text.

(1) BEGINNINGS: Books referred to on Early Social Theories, including those just preceding the foundation of sociology—e.g. by Montesquieu, Ferguson, Adam Smith, etc.

ALLAN, D. J. (1952), *The Philosophy of Aristotle*, Home University Library (O.U.P.).

ARISTOTLE, *The Ethics*, Everyman's Edition.

ARISTOTLE, *The Politics*, Everyman's Edition. (An edition of 1853: London, Henry G. Bohn, introduced by Dr Gillies, also contains Aristotle's *Economics*.)

AURELIUS, MARCUS (1906), *Meditations* (An Example of the Stoic philosophy), Everyman's Edition.

BEVERIDGE, W. I. B. (1961), *The Art of Scientific Investigation*, Mercury Books.

BREASTED, J. H. (1912), *Development of Religious Thought in Ancient Egypt*, Charles Scribner's Sons, N.Y.

BURKE, EDMUND (1923), *Reflections on the French Revolution*, Methuen.

BURY, J. B. (1900), *A History of Greece* (contains an excellent account of the Greek City States: their institutions, religion, thought, and the making of their political constitutions), Macmillan.

CONDORCET (1955), *Sketch for a Historical Picture of the Progress of the Human Mind*. (Tr. J. Barraclough, introduced by Stuart Hampshire), London.

EDWARDS, C. (1934), *The World's Earliest Laws* (for some details of Babylonian institutions and thought), Watts.

L'ESTRANGE, ROGER (1705), *Seneca's Morals: Discourses*. (An example of the Stoic philosophy.) London.

EPICTETUS (1926), *The Encheiridion and Discourses* (Tr. W. A. Oldfather. An example of the Stoic philosophy), Loeb Library.

FERGUSON, ADAM (1814), *An Essay on the History of Civil Society* (7th Edition), Edinburgh.

FITZGERALD, W. B. (1903), *The Roots of Methodism*, London, Charles Kelly.

FLINDERS PETRIE, W. M. (1924), *Social Life in Ancient Egypt*, Constable.

FRANKFORT, FRANKFORT, WILSON, AND JACOBSON (1949), *Before Philosophy*, Penguin Books.

FUSTEL DE COULANGES, *The Ancient City*, Doubleday.

GRAVES, ROBERT (Introduction by) (1959), *Larousse Encyclopaedia of Mythology*, Paul Hamlyn.

GUIZOT, M. F. (1848), *General History of Civilization in Europe*, Edinburgh, W. & R. Chambers.

HEGEL, G. W. F. (1872), *Lectures on the Philosophy of History*, (Tr. J. Sibree), London.

HOBBES, THOMAS, *Leviathan*, Everyman's Edition.

HUME, DAVID, *A Treatise on Human Nature*, (2 Vols. The discussion of 'causality' is in Vol. 1), Everyman's Edition.

JONES, W. J. (1947), *Masters of Political Thought*. (Vol. 2. Ch. 6 on Montesquieu, but useful also on Machiavelli, Hobbes, and Burke.) Harrap.

JOWETT, B. (1902), *Select Passages from the Introductions to Plato*. (A useful introduction to Jowett's translations, but also see Plato below.) John Murray.

KAMES, LORD (1813), *Sketches of the History of Man*, Edition in 3 Vols: Edinburgh. (First published, 1788.)

KANT, IMMANUEL, *A Critique of Pure Reason*. (For the analysis of 'causality'. Introduction by A. D. Lindsay.) Everyman's Edition.

KANT, IMMANUEL, *The Idea of a Universal History from a Cosmopolitan Point of View*, (Tr. by Hastie).

KITTO, H. D. F., *The Greeks*, Penguin Books.

LOWES DICKINSON, G. (1896), *The Greek View of Life*, Methuen (21st Edition).

LUCRETIUS, *The Nature of the Universe*, Penguin Classics.

MACHIAVELLI (1935), *The Prince*. (Tr. E. R. P. Vincent), World's Classics.

MACHIAVELLI [1882], *Discourses on the First Ten Books of Titus Livius*, (Tr. C. E. Detmold), London.

MONTESQUIEU (1892), *The Spirit of Laws*. (Tr. Thomas Nugent. Ed. J. V. Prichard. 2 vols), London, George Bell & Sons.

MONTESQUIEU (1961), *The Persian Letters*. (Tr. and introduced by J. Robert Loy), Meridian Books, N.Y.

MOORE, G. F. (1914), *History of Religion* (2 vols), Edinburgh, T. & T. Clark.

MOWAT, FARLEY (1952), *The People of the Deer*, Michael Joseph.

MURRAY, GILBERT (1935), *Five Stages of Greek Religion*, Watts.

NOSS, JOHN B. (1956), *Man's Religions*. (An excellent account of religious 'theories' within their social and environmental contexts.) Macmillan, N.Y.

OAKESHOTT, MICHAEL (1940), *Social and Political Doctrines of Contemporary Europe*. (For some contemporary 'Hegelian-like' theories in practical politics.) London, Basic Books.

PAINE, TOM, *The Rights of Man* and *The Age of Reason*. There are, of course, many editions of these books, but a very useful one was published by Watts in 1915—which contained both, and also a selection from Paine's other political writings, addresses, and manifestos on both the American and the French crises. This edition has a biographical introduction by J. M. Robertson.

PLATO, *The Republic*, Everyman's Edition.

PLATO, *The Laws*. (*See* Jowett below.)

PLATO, *The Works of Plato*. (Tr. and introduced by Benjamin Jowett). A very useful one volume edition was published by the Tudor Publishing Co., N.Y. Full version: 4 vols, Oxford.

PLATO, *See also* Socrates below.

ROUSSEAU, JEAN-JACQUES, *The Social Contract*, Everyman's Edition.

SMITH, ADAM, *The Theory of Moral Sentiments*. (1759). The 2nd edition of 1761 also contains a 'Dissertation on the Origin of Languages'.

SMITH, ADAM, *The Wealth of Nations*, (2 vols), Everyman's Edition.

SOCRATES (1910), *Socratic Discourses by Plato and Xenophon*. (Introduced by A. D. Lindsay.) Gives a good picture of Socrates and his teaching. Everyman's Edition.

SPENCE, LEWIS (1944), *The Outlines of Mythology*, Watts. (*See also:* Myth and Ritual in Dance, Game and Rhyme. Watts, 1947.)

THUCYDIDES (1954), *The Peloponnesian War*. (For Pericles' Funeral Speech: See Book Two, Ch. IV. p. 115. Tr. Rex Warner.) Penguin Classics.

VICO, G. B., *The New Science*, Tr. Bergin and Fisch, Cornell U.P.

WALSH, W. H. (1951), *An Introduction to Philosophy of History*. (For Kant and Hegel.) Hutchinson's Home University.

WALSH, W. H. (1963), 'Historical Causation' (An article), Aristotelian Society, XII. (These, of course, are not *only* concerned with early social theories, but also with contemporary questions of the Philosophy of History.)

WARDE FOWLER, W. (1910), *The City State of the Greeks and Romans*, Macmillan.

WHITEHEAD, A. N. (1911), *An Introduction to Mathematics*, Home University Library, (O.U.P.).

WHITEHEAD, A. N. (1929), *Process and Reality: An Essay in Cosmology*, Cambridge University Press.

XENOPHON, *See* Socrates above.

ZIMMERN, A. E. (1915) *The Greek Commonwealth*, Oxford.

(2) FOUNDATIONS: Books referred to on the making of sociology during the nineteenth century, from Comte's initial statement onwards.

ARON, RAYMOND (1965), *Main Currents in Sociological Thought* (Vol. 1, on Montesquieu, Comte, Marx and Tocqueville), Weidenfeld and Nicolson.

BAGEHOT, WALTER, *Physics and Politics*, London, Kegan Paul.

BARNES, H. E. (1948), *An Introduction to the History of Sociology*, University of Chicago Press.

BECKER, ERNEST (1968), *The Structure of Evil*. (An excellent book tracing the making of sociology from the Enlightenment, and making a plea for this perspective.) George Braziller, N.Y.

BÖHM-BAWERK, E.v. (1898), *Karl Marx and the Close of His System* (Tr. Alice MacDonald), London, Fisher Unwin.

BOTTOMORE, T. B. (1962), *Sociology*, Allen & Unwin.

BRIDGES, J. H. (1866), *The Unity of Comte's Life and Doctrine*, London.

BRIDGES, J. H. (1915), *Illustrations of Positivism*, Watts, 2nd edition.

BUCKLE, H. T. (1904), *Introduction to the History of Civilization in England* (Ed. and introduced by J. M. Robertson), (Originally published in 2 vols 1857–61), London, Routledge.

CARR, E. H. (1964), *What is History?* (G. M. Trevelyan Lectures, 1961), Penguin Books.

CHARDIN, TEILHARD DE (1959), *The Phenomenon of Man*, London, Collins.

COHEN, PERCY S. (1968), *Modern Social Theory*, Heinemann.

COLLINGWOOD, R. G. (1961), *The Idea of History*, Oxford University Press.

COMTE, AUGUSTE (1830–42), *Cours de Philosophie Positive*, tomes I–VI Paris.

COMTE, AUGUSTE (1908), *A General View of Positivism* (Tr. J. H. Bridges), Routledge.

COMTE, AUGUSTE (1858), *The Catechism of Positive Religion* (Tr. Richard Congreve), London.

COMTE, AUGUSTE (1875–77), *System of Positive Polity* (4 vols), (Tr. Bridges, Beesly, Congreve, Harrison), Longmans Green.

COMTE, AUGUSTE (1903), *A Discourse on the Positive Spirit* (Tr. E. S. Beesly), Wm. Reeves.

DUNCAN, D., (1908), *Life and Letters of Herbert Spencer*, Methuen. (with others), *Descriptive Sociology* (8 vols: compiled and abstracted from the comparative material collected for, and by, Spencer), Williams & Norgate.

EDINBURGH REVIEW (1868), 'The Positive Philosophy of M. Auguste Comte', (Vol. CXXVII, No. CCLX, pp. 303–57).

ELIOT, GEORGE (1926), The Letters of George Eliot (with interesting comments on Spencer. Introduced by R. Brimley Johnson), The Bodley Head.

ENGELS, FREDERICK (1892), *The Condition of the Working Class in England in 1844*, Allen & Unwin.

ENGELS, FREDERICK (1902), *The Origin of the Family, Private Property, and the State*, Chicago, C. M. Kerr.

ENGELS, FREDERICK (1894), *Anti-Dühring (Herr Eugen Dühring's Revolution in Science*. Tr. Emile Burns), Martin Lawrence.

ENGELS, FREDERICK, (1892), *Socialism Utopian and Scientific* (Ed. E. Aveling), London.

ENGELS, FREDERICK, *See also:* Marx, Selected Works below.

ESCOTT, T. H. S. (1907), *Society in the Country House* (For comments on Spencer), London, Fisher Unwin.

FISKE, JOHN (1874), *Outlines of Cosmic Philosophy*, Macmillan.

FLETCHER, RONALD (1966), *Auguste Comte and the Making of Sociology* (7th Comte Memorial Lecture), Athlone Press.

FRAZER, JAMES GEORGE (1947), *The Golden Bough* (1 Volume, Abridged Edition), Macmillan.

GIDDINGS, FRANKLIN H. (1898), *The Elements of Sociology*, Columbia University Press, Macmillan, N.Y.

GIDDINGS, FRANKLIN H. (1896), *The Principles of Sociology*, Columbia University Press, Macmillan, N.Y.

GIDDINGS, FRANKLIN H. (1897), *The Theory of Socialization*, Columbia University Press, Macmillan, N.Y.

GINSBERG, MORRIS (1934), *Sociology*, Home University Library, (O.U.P.)

GINSBERG, MORRIS (1962), *On the Diversity of Morals*, Mercury Books.

GINSBERG, MORRIS (1961), *Evolution and Progress*, Mercury Books.

GINSBERG, MORRIS (1947), *Reason and Unreason in Society*, Longmans Green.

GOETHE (1949), *Faust* (Tr. Philip Wayne), Penguin Classics.

GUMPLOWICZ, LUDWIG (1963), *Outlines of Sociology* (Ed. I. L. Horowitz), (First published 1885, in English 1899.) Paine-Whitman, N.Y.

HADDON, A. C. (1934), *History of Anthropology*, Watts.

HARRISON, FREDERICK (Ed.) (1892), *The New Calendar of Great Men*, (for details of Comte's 'Positive Religion'), Macmillan.

HERBERTSON, DOROTHY (1920–21), 'Le Play and Social Science', (*Sociogical Review*, Vol. XII and XIII).

HERBERTSON, DOROTHY (1946), 'The Life of Frédéric Le Play', (*Sociological Review*, Vol. XXXVIII).

HOYLE, FRED (1956), *The Time Scale of the Universe* (47th Conway Memorial Lecture).

HUXLEY, T. H. (1906), *Man's Place in Nature* (and other Anthropological Essays), Everyman's edition (and Macmillian, 1897).

HUXLEY, T. H. (1895), *Evolution and Ethics* (and other Essays), Macmillan.

HUXLEY, T. H., *Scientific Aspects of Positivism*, Lay Sermons, Macmillan.

JORDAN, Z. A. (1967), *The Evolution of Dialectical Materialism* (A Philosophical and Sociological Analysis), London.

685

LANCASTER, LANE W. (1959), *Masters of Political Thought* (Vol. III. On Comte and other 19th Century thinkers), Harrap.

LENIN, See *Karl Marx: Selected Works* below.

LEWES, GEORGE HENRY (1867), *The History of Philosophy from Thales to Comte* (3rd Edition, Vol. II), London.

LITTRÉ, E. (1863), *Auguste Comte et la Philosophie Positive*, Paris.

MACRAE, DONALD G. (1969), *Spencer; The Man Versus the State* (contains an excellent introductory essay on Spencer), Penguin Classics.

MAINE, HENRY SUMNER (1905), *Ancient Law*, Routledge (New University Library Edition).

MAINE, HENRY SUMNER (1875), *Lectures on the Early History of Institutions* (this takes further the ideas in *Ancient Law*), John Murray.

MALINOWSKI, BRONISLAW (1944), *A Scientific Theory of Culture* (For the purpose of comparing Sumner, etc., on the conception of 'institutions'), University of North Carolina Press.

MARTINEAU, HARRIET (1853), *The Positive Philosophy of Auguste Comte* (2 vols) Chapman.

MARVIN, F. S. (1936), *Comte—The Founder of Sociology*, Chapman & Hall.

MARX, KARL (1961), *Economic and Philosophical Manuscripts of 1844*, Lawrence & Wishart.

MARX, KARL (1899), *Value, Price and Profit*, Allen & Unwin.

MARX, KARL (1918), *Capital*, London, Wm. Glaisher. Also Everyman's Edition.

MARX, KARL, *Karl Marx: Selected Works*, Lawrence & Wishart.
For: *The Manifesto of the Communist Party*, *The Eighteenth Brumaire of Louis Bonaparte*, *The Three Sources and Three Component Parts of Marxism* (*Lenin*), *Ludwig Feuerbach and the Outcome of Classical German Philosophy* (*Engels*), Theses on *Feuerbach*, Preface to: *A Contribution to the Critique of Political Economy*, and many other papers, letters, and addresses referred to in the text.

MEDAWAR, P. B. (1967), *The Art of the Soluble*, Methuen.

MERTON, R. K. (1957), *Social Theory and Social Structure*, Free Press.

MILL, JOHN STUART (1884), *A System of Logic Ratiocinative and Inductive* (Chiefly Book VI), People's Edition.

MILL, JOHN STUART (1882), *Auguste Comte and Positivism*, English and Foreign Philosophical Library, Vol. XVI.

MORLEY, JOHN (1888), 'Auguste Comte' (*Miscellanies*, Vol. III, Ch. X), Macmillan.

MURRAY, GILBERT (1950), *Stoic, Christian and Humanist* (Ch. IV. 'What is Permanent in Positivism'), Watts.

NISBET, ROBERT (1966), *The Sociological Tradition*, Basic Books. Heinemann, 1967.

686

PARSONS, TALCOTT (1937), *The Structure of Social Action*, McGraw Hill. Free Press (paper) 1968.

LE PLAY, FRÉDÉRIC (1855), *Les Ouvriers Européens*, tomes I–VI, Paris.

LE PLAY, FRÉDÉRIC (1864), *La réforme sociale en France*, Paris.

POPPER, KARL R. (1945), *The Open Society and its Enemies* (2 vols), Routledge & Kegan Paul.

POPPER, KARL R. (1957), *The Poverty of Historicism*, Routledge & Kegan Paul.

POPPER, KARL R. (1959), *The Logic of Scientific Discovery*, Hutchinson.

POPPER, KARL R. (1963), *Conjectures and Refutations*, Routledge & Kegan Paul.

RADCLIFFE-BROWN, A. R. (1952), *Structure and Function in Primitive Society*, Cohen & West.

RAISON, T. (Ed.) (1969), 'The Founding Fathers of Social Science' (articles commissioned for *New Society*), Pelican Books.

REX, JOHN (1961), *Key Problems of Sociological Theory*, Routledge and Kegan Paul.

Short History of the Communist Party of the Soviet Union (*Bolsheviks*) (1939), (Part 2. Ch. 4 on 'Dialectical Materialism and Historical Materialism), Cobbett Publishing Co.

SIDGWICK, HENRY (1903), *The Growth of the European Polity*, London, Macmillan.

SIDGWICK, HENRY (1902), *Philosophy: Its Scope and Relations* (especially Ch's VI–XII on History and Sociology), London, Macmillan.

SIMPSON, GEORGE (1955), *Man in Society* (a useful introductory book), Doubleday, N.Y.

SOMBART, WERNER (1898), *Socialism and the Social Movement in the 19th Century*, London, Putnam's Sons.

SOROKIN, P. (1928), *Contemporary Social Theories*. (Ch. 11. 'Frédéric Le Play's School'), Harper, N.Y.

SPENCER, HERBERT (1851), *Social Statics*, Chapman,

SPENCER, HERBERT (1900), *First Principles* (6th Edition), Williams & Norgate. Also Watts, 1937.

SPENCER, HERBERT (1893), *Principles of Sociology* (3 vols, 3rd Edition), Williams & Norgate.

SPENCER, HERBERT (1929), *Education—Intellectual, Moral and Physical*, Watts.

SPENCER, HERBERT (1885), *The Man Versus the State*, Williams & Norgate.

SPENCER, HERBERT (1902), *Facts and Comments*, Williams & Norgate.

SPENCER, HERBERT, (1894), *The Study of Sociology*, Williams & Norgate, (New Library Edition).

SPENCER, HERBERT, *Principles of Ethics* (2 vols), Williams & Norgate.

STALIN, J. See *Karl Marx: Selected Works*, above, and *Short History of the CPSU*.

STYLE, JANE M. (1928), *Auguste Comte*, London, Kegan Paul.

SUMNER, WILLIAM GRAHAM, (1907), *Folkways*, Dover Edition 1959, Mentor Books, 1960.

SWINNY, S. H. (1921), 'The Sociological Schools of Comte and Le Play', *Sociological Review*, Vol. XIII, 1921.

TIMASHEFF, N. S. (1955), *Sociological Theory; Its Nature and Growth*, Doubleday.

DE TOCQUEVILLE, ALEXIS (1954), *Democracy in America*, Vintage Books, N.Y.

TÖNNIES, FERDINAND (1955), *Gemeinschaft und Gesellschaft* (Tr. as 'Community and Association', by C. S. Loomis), Routledge & Kegan Paul.

TYLOR, E. B. (1891), *Primitive Culture* (2 vols), John Murray.

TYLOR, E. B. (1930), *Anthropology* (2 vols), Watts.

WARD, LESTER F. (1902), *Dynamic Sociology* (2 vols), Appleton, N.Y. (2nd Edition).

WARD, LESTER F. (1907), *Pure Sociology*, Macmillan, N.Y. (2nd Edition).

WEBB, BEATRICE, *My Apprenticeship* (for comments on Spencer), (2nd Edition), Longmans Green.

WHITEHEAD, A. N. (1948), *Adventure of Ideas* (Ch's III and VIII), Penguin Books.

WHITTAKER, F. (1908), *Comte and Mill*, Constable.

WRIGHT MILLS, C. (1959), *The Sociological Imagination*, Oxford University Press, N.Y.

Subject Index

Author Index